D1497859

PUBLIC
FINANCE

EARL R. ROLPH

PROFESSOR OF ECONOMICS
UNIVERSITY OF CALIFORNIA, BERKELEY

GEORGE F. BREAK

ASSOCIATE PROFESSOR OF ECONOMICS
UNIVERSITY OF CALIFORNIA, BERKELEY

THE RONALD PRESS COMPANY • NEW YORK

To

Helen and *Peggy*

Preface

This book is an attempt to give a logical and coherent exposition of public finance, setting out the theoretical and technical issues involved and indicating what, in our judgment, are the topics especially worthy of serious attention. The approach is at once empirical and analytical; we follow the tradition of trying to explain the evidence—an approach which requires the selection of the evidence to be explained. In the theoretical analysis, we have tried to demonstrate how economic intelligence can be made to shed light on an eminently practical subject.

The work draws mainly on American experience in fiscal affairs, but wherever feasible we have taken advantage of the accumulating evidence about the public finances of other countries, both advanced and less advanced. We have tried to keep in mind the crucial importance of public finance in the underdeveloped countries with their desperate need for effective economic programs and for methods to finance them; partly for this reason a systematic discussion of the spendings tax has been included.

Because many of the topics in public finance are controversial, an account suitable for the student must do justice to various points of view so that he may understand what the issues are. However, we have tried to avoid giving the impression that one idea is just as good as another or that an interminable vacillation is the mark of the sophisticated intellect. Often we have indicated which views we favor; those who want criticisms of these opinions will find in the references and suggested readings an abundance of ammunition.

In the organization of the book, we have tried to make the relationship of government expenditure to government revenues and debt more meaningful by combining our general treatment of expenditures with the descriptive-historical material on revenue and debt. The analytical issues involving government expenditures are discussed under various headings, sometimes separately and sometimes combined with revenues. Current social security programs, a large factor in the expenditures of many governments, are treated in one chapter and the vexing problems arising out of the rapidly expanding metropolitan regions in the United States in another. Fiscal theory and policy have been developed by applying several monetary theories, in the hope of thereby avoiding a superficial treatment of that important subject and of stimulating the student to a further study of monetary theory and experience.

Our main debt in the preparation of this book is to the many students, both graduate and undergraduate, who have been taught many of the ideas it contains and who, in turn, have taught the authors by raising the difficult point and suggesting alternative views. Our wives have served with diligence and tact as editors and critics, eliminating much unnecessary verbiage and many errors—a great service for which we are grateful. As for any remaining errors, the responsibility for discovering them rests upon that invaluable ally, the careful and critical reader, to whom our debt will no doubt be substantial.

EARL R. ROLPH
GEORGE F. BREAK

Berkeley, California
February, 1961

Contents

PUBLIC
FINANCE

Part I

THE FISCAL SETTING

Introduction

Of the many factors affecting government activities, one of the least obvious to the casual observer is economic theory. Yet on numerous occasions in the past the economic beliefs of policy makers and of those on whom they rely for advice have had a crucial impact on fiscal affairs, as Chapter 1 emphasizes. Economic analysis is also an integral part of the subject matter of Public Finance. This point, together with other distinctive aspects of the field, is discussed in connection with the formal definition of Public Finance given in the first chapter.

In recent decades governments have developed new and complex taxes, and going far beyond traditional concerns with defense and the maintenance of law and order, they have concerned themselves with such diverse activities as urban renewal, basic research in nuclear physics and in medicine, and the conservation of natural resources. The resulting fiscal trends in this country are summarized quantitatively in Chapter 2. Attention is then turned to the economic effects of governmental fiscal operations, a subject which Chapter 3 treats in broad perspective without the refinements and details to be added in later chapters.

The essential role of fiscal analysis is to provide a rational basis for practical policy making. Also indispensable for this purpose are sound budgeting procedures and reliable statistical information. The development and use of both of these aids to good decision-making are discussed in Chapter 4. Finally, in Chapter 5 attention is turned to the difficult and controversial issues involved in the achievement of the major goals of government operation—a proper balance between private and public use of resources, a satisfactory allocation of government expenditures to different programs, and an equitable distribution of taxes and of government transfer payments.

1

What Is Public Finance?

The study of Public Finance is a study of economics from the point of view of government. It is first and foremost a study of economics. Anyone who succeeds in becoming moderately expert in Public Finance automatically becomes at least moderately expert in economics. The reverse proposition need not hold. Knowledge of economics in many of its areas may result in less than modest competence in fiscal affairs. Specialization in the study of economics, just as specialization in physics or mathematics, is the necessary outcome of the growth of knowledge and techniques. In this book we study economics from the special point of view of government fiscal policies. The ultimate purpose is to provide a background adequate to permit informed and rational judgments about the effects of government financial policies.

It is tempting to think of Public Finance as a box of knowledge to be set alongside other boxes called "International Economics," "Money and Banking," "Labor Relations," "Business Price Policies," "Business Finance," and so on, that together make up a big box to be called "Economics," but this approach would be wrong. In Public Finance all of economics is studied, but from a certain point of view. The point of view is the influence of certain types of government policies upon the economic affairs of people. For example, let us suppose a state government adopts the policy of taxing the sale of beer. Almost everyone thinks he knows that such a policy will make beer drinking more expensive. The price of beer would rise, some claim, by an amount exactly equal to the tax. Such knowledge, or supposed knowledge, classifies as knowledge about Public Finance. Just what does this mean? It means that people know or think they know something about the factors that determine the price of beer. Unless such knowledge may be assumed, there is no basis for the belief that a tax upon those who produce or sell beer will increase the price of beer. Such knowledge is a part of the subject in economics usually called "Price Theory"; it is not knowledge to be classified under "Public Finance" in any special sense. Statements about the effects of a tax upon the sale of beer are statements about economics from the point of view of the influence of a government policy—the policy of taxing beer.

The point may be illustrated by a much more complicated problem. Consider the case of a country experiencing hyperinflation. Expenditures for goods and services are rising rapidly and so are prices. The statesmen of the country are much disturbed. They want the inflation stopped, and look for suggestions as to how to stop it. They will need to call upon economists for help; to call in experts in public health, in social psychology, or even in political science will not do. If economists are called upon, their first task will be to discover the relevant facts, not just any facts. They need to know those facts that reflect the causes of the inflation. They quickly learn that the government's budget is greatly underbalanced. Government expenditures are much in excess of its tax collections. They also learn that the government deficit is being covered by the issuance of government debt acquired by the central bank of the country. The facts as interpreted, in other words, are that the government, with an assist from its central bank, is pouring money into the economy. The economists, if they happen to believe that large increases in the quantity of money induce people to spend more money and thereby push up prices, can suggest a remedy. The government must stop increasing the quantity of money in private hands. To accomplish this objective, tax yields must be increased or government expenditures reduced or both, so as to make the budget almost balanced, or even better, overbalanced. Furthermore, the economists may suggest what taxes are to be increased or what public expenditures are to be reduced, or both.

At this stage, the main work of economists has been completed. If, because of political objections to high taxation or to more austere public expenditure programs, the government officials choose to ignore the advice, the people must tolerate an environment in which prices keep rising rapidly. A choice has been made, and in fact there are many governments in the world today that choose rapid inflation rather than heavy taxation and smaller government expenditures.

In this illustration, an "expert" on public finance must also be an expert on monetary affairs. To know what tax measures to suggest, he must be acquainted with the effects of feasible tax measures, the administrative problems each is likely to cause, and so on. Needless to say, rarely does one person know enough to give good advice on all these matters.

Influence of Economic Theories upon Economic Policies

In the illustration just discussed, economic theories may turn out to influence economic events. If the officials of the country follow the economic advice suggested, and the chances are small that they would do so in detail, economic ideas about the causes and remedies of an inflation become important in determining subsequent economic conditions. In this role the fiscal expert finds himself in the same position as a doctor. The patient complains of an ailment and wants it cured. The doctor's task calls for diagnosing the precise character of the ailment and for prescribing remedies. He is successful to the extent that he can discover the relevant facts—namely the facts about the patient's illness—and to the extent that he knows of methods to cure the ailment. If the patient is willing to cooperate, the doctor has an important influence upon the patient's subsequent life. The theories he holds affect the behavior of the patient. Similarly, economic advice, when it is accepted by governments, influences government policies and thereby influences the economic affairs of people.

The analogy may be pushed further. A doctor cannot be expected to work miracles. He cannot, fortunately, prolong the life of a patient indefinitely. This limitation upon him is imposed by conditions that he cannot control, by what are called the "laws of nature." A remedy that is inconsistent with the laws of nature is what we ordinarily mean by a miracle. In economics, the equivalent to the laws of nature is the behavior patterns of people in relation to objective facts. For example, a functional relation can be shown to exist between the size of a government deficit and the rate of people's money expenditures upon goods and services. The term "functional" is intended to suggest that the greater is the government deficit, the greater on that account are private expenditures. Many functional relations are believed to exist in economics, and a great deal of the subject is an attempt to discover their precise nature. These relations in economics are unlike natural laws in that they need not be invariant. In similar objective circumstances sometimes groups behave one way and sometimes another. A government deficit of given size accompanied by central bank financing of the deficit may be accompanied by a large inflation in a South American country and little or no inflation in the United States. This lack of an invariant association may simply reflect the fact that factors influencing people's expenditures may differ in different situations. To use an analogy from medicine again, a virus that proves to be deadly to one person may occasion no difficulty for another because in the second case the person has been immunized. But this is a trivial observation. Even relations called "natural laws" hold only for specified conditions. Economic functional relations differ from natural laws because human beings, having been endowed with intelligence, have the freedom to react differently to similar environmental situations. Talk about lung cancer may influence people's demand for cigarettes. Experience with inflation at one time may influence people to react more violently to inflationary circumstances at another time.

Financial policies of governments do not fall in the category of functional relations. Rather, intelligence exhibited by those who control policy determines government activities, and the economic theories held by such officials influence economic events through their effects upon private behavior. Administrators in government are seldom prepared to admit that they entertain economic theories and that their decisions are influenced by such theories. During the past thirty years or so there have been changes in this attitude in Western countries. Practical men are now more inclined to recognize their own limitations in formulating economic theories and more inclined to allow themselves to be influenced by expert advice. Perhaps the most important development leading to this change of attitude was the experience of the Great Depression. Almost anyone could see that the hardships people experienced during that period were unnecessary. The remedies proposed by practical people did not work. The dominating point of view in financial matters generally, and in public finance particularly, was the doctrine of financial traditionalism. The doctrine has many facets, but in the main it taught that individuals and governments who rigorously practiced the financial virtues prospered, whereas those who sinned against them were asking for trouble. The main financial virtue was prudence. A person who worked hard, was thrifty, avoided becoming indebted, and invested carefully would succeed. Applied to government, the same doctrine called for keeping government expenditures low and within the government's revenue, for maintaining the gold standard, and for avoiding an increase in government debt.

The remedies of financial traditionalism failed during the Great Depression, and failed in a way that discredited the doctrine with large groups of people in the United States and in many other countries. Many practical people learned that a close adherence to the financial virtues was not an effective way to get out of a depression;

they became more willing to listen to different voices. The idea of using government finance as a compensatory device to keep business conditions on a more or less even keel has become thoroughly respectable. Financial traditionalism retains many supporters, but it is now on the defensive.

A special obligation rests upon those who undertake to study public finance to explore with utmost care the consequences of alternative financial policies. Inept theorizing is now more likely to result in unfortunate financial policies than was the case a few decades ago, when the best of the economic voices were voices crying in the wilderness. It was careless economic thinking that led many economists to predict unequivocally that the United States would suffer a major depression after the close of World War II unless highly stimulating financial policies were adopted by the government. In this particular instance a point of view called "neo-Keynesianism" dominated the thinking of economists and influenced government policy in an unfortunate way. A lesson of this experience should be that government financial policies need to be adaptable to any economic development. The crucial mistake was to assume that the only possible development could be a depression.

This mistake was nothing like as serious as the fiscal policies of many governments during the Great Depression. The world might, for example, have been spared the miseries of World War II if the Social Democratic government of the Weimar Republic in Germany had applied elementary economic intelligence to the affairs of that country during the earlier stages of the Great Depression. Without dwelling upon the details of that hapless episode, at that time German industry was operating well below capacity, the number of people unemployed was large, and the number partially unemployed even larger. Economic distress was general and severe. The critical matter, critical in the eyes of the German officials, was the pressure on the Mark—the German monetary unit. Foreigners, and Germans as well, wished to convert marks into pounds, dollars, francs, and other monies. The normal way of accomplishing such conversion calls for the central bank to stand ready to sell pounds, dollars, francs, etc. If it has insufficient amounts of these foreign monies to supply the demand at the official exchange rate, it may sell gold to foreign central banks and obtain foreign money in exchange. The German central bank did not, however, own sufficient foreign money and gold to meet the demands. The choices open were (1) to let the exchange rate—the price of foreign money in terms of marks—fall, (2) to institute controls to prevent Germans from trying to buy foreign money and to restrict the amount foreigners were trying to convert, or (3) to attempt to reduce the demand for foreign money and to increase the supply of it by internal deflation. Option (1), also called devaluation, was objected to as "unthinkable"; option (2) was employed as a stop-gap, and option (3) was chosen to correct the underlying trouble.

Option (3) called for reducing the amount of money being spent within Germany. The value of imports would fall as people spent less money, and with lowered costs in the export industries, exports would rise. In this way the drain upon the meager supplies of foreign exchange would be reduced, or so it was hoped. To force the deflation, that is, the reduction of expenditures of all groups, the government reduced its own expenditures, cut the payments made to the unemployed and the relief assistance to others in dire economic straits, substantially increased tax rates, and by regulation of banks made borrowing very difficult and for many people impossible. These measures pushed the German economy further into a deflationary spiral, forced yet more people out of work, and spread destitution to the middle classes. The German people were hungry and desperate. In a society in which democratic traditions were only skin-deep, the stage was set for a demagogue; Hitler rose to power. German militarism revived, and World War II was its product.

The terrible mistake made by the German officials was to adopt deflationary measures, a policy which could lead only to economic disaster. They should have adopted stimulating policies; taxes should have been reduced, relief payments increased, government expenditures increased, and the banks should have been both encouraged and assisted to make borrowing easy. Why then did intelligent and well-meaning people make such a serious blunder?

Their initial mistake was that of elevating the price of foreign money—the exchange rate—to a major goal of economic policy. Now there is no merit in worshipping a price, not even the exchange rate. A price is a device, a useful device; it is a means, not an end. Given the circumstances, the exchange rate could have been permitted to find its own level. The initial mistake led to a second, the deflationary policy. Fuzzy thinking plus emotional attachment to means resulted in policies that were made to order for a Hitler.

It would be comfortable to believe that the dissemination of economic knowledge assures that such unfortunate financial policies would never again be adopted by the more important countries of the world. Whether or not such a comforting belief is justified depends upon how carefully economic theories are developed and how successfully this knowledge is communicated to the public. If we judge by the experience of countries even for the period since the close of

World War II, there is little basis for complacency. Disorderly finance continues in many countries. However, the problem in recent years has become more of controlling inflations than of recovering from depressed business conditions and large-scale unemployment.

A Formal Definition of Public Finance

It may give some order to our thinking to suggest a definition of the subject of public finance. It may be defined as *the discovery and the appraisal of the effects of government financial policies.* To give meaning and content to this definition, each of the crucial concepts employed in it may be further elucidated.

We may start with the concept of government. Long and usually very dull books have been written about the definition of government. Commonly the topic is discussed as the definition of the state. The distinction between government and the state is mainly a matter of usage. In parliamentary systems such as that found in the United Kingdom, the term "government" is used to designate the party in power in contrast to the term "state," used to designate the whole apparatus of power. In this usage governments come and go, but the state remains. In the United States, the "administration" is the term used to describe the group in power, and "government" is used to include the whole official organization. Whether the terms used are "government" or "state," a characteristic of such organizations is power—the power to make the members of the jurisdiction conform to the organization's decisions. A government or state is an organization based upon force in the sense that in any final test the will of the organization, however determined, prevails over the will of particular members or other organizations. If members of the jurisdiction can successfully flout the organization, to that extent the organization is not a state.

Government is a matter of degree. In Abilene, Kansas, during the period following the Civil War when it was a main terminal of the Texas cattle drives, the degree of government was small. Until a local group succeeded in finding effective policemen, the rowdies made their own laws, and the fellow with the quickest draw and the best aim made the law in his immediate environment. This experiment with anarchy, duplicated in various frontier areas in the United States during the nineteenth century, was a failure as a system. Group law, enforced by officially selected people, supplanted the multiplicity of individual lawmakers who attempted to enforce their will with six-shooters.

Different levels of government are to be distinguished by their degree and kinds of power. The central government of a country is the ultimate governing organization within the country because it can enforce its decisions upon subsidiary government units. Absence or loss of such power may result in the breakup of a country with or without civil war in the process. Local governments in the United States, such as states, counties, municipalities, and districts, retain certain types of power appropriate to carrying out their objectives. The power permitted subsidiary governing organizations differs widely from country to country. In general, federal systems, such as the United States system, allow local governments more power than do centralized systems such as that found in France. The history of federal types of political organization has been one of more and more transfer of responsibility to the central government. This transfer reflects the growth of the interdependence of people and thus the need for measures applicable to the entire group.

There are some agencies that are difficult to classify. Should a toll-road authority be looked upon as a government agency? Are the Federal Reserve banks government agencies? How should organizations such as the New York Port Authority be classified? Should General Motors be considered a government agency all of the time, only when a Republican administration is in command, or none of the time? To answer such questions we need tests as to what constitutes a government agency. Ordinarily one of two tests may be employed: government ownership or government control.

The test of ownership means that an organization is identified as a government agency when it is owned by some independently defined government agency. According to this test, which may also be called the nationalization test, the Bank of England became a government agency when its securities were bought by the British Exchequer. Similarly, the Federal Reserve banks are not government agencies because they are owned by the member banks. Just what should be done about "authorities," such as the New York Port Authority, of which there are many in the United States, is not clear. There is no other agency that owns these corporations. Their officials sometimes claim to be government agencies when, for example, questions of taxing them arise, and sometimes claim to be private when questions of examining their records arise.

The control test means that the organization in question is a government agency if it is under the thumb of some official or group of officials who are part of the regular government. By this test the Federal Reserve banks are government agencies because their operations are subject to the control of the Board of Governors of the

Federal Reserve System. Board members are appointed by the President and are responsible to the Congress, if not to the Administration, in the exercise of their power. Likewise, by this test, the several federal corporations are government agencies, because the persons in charge of them are responsible either to the Congress or to the President or to both.

The control test appears to be the more significant one. It goes directly to the issue of who has the power. However, the control test is subject to an awkward difficulty. Control is always a matter of degree. One might claim that all organizations in a country are government agencies because they are controlled by the laws of the land. Furthermore, the control exercised by government officials over organizations that we ordinarily think of as private may be exercised in great detail. Commercial banks and railroads, for example, are closely regulated in the United States. It is not easy to say when government control over an organization becomes sufficiently minute to classify it as a government agency. However, if the employees act as government employees do, if decisions are strongly influenced by political considerations, and if the control group can only be ousted by a political process, the agency may be regarded as a part of the government. We must be prepared to admit that an unambiguous distinction between private and public agencies is not always possible.

In the suggested formal definition of public finance—*the discovery and appraisal of the effects of government financial policies*—the concept of financial policies gives less definitional troubles than that of government. Granted that we know, or think we know, what government includes, "financial policies" are those government operations having to do with money. Since almost anything governments do involves money, have we ruled out any policies by this definition?

What is ruled out is the study of the effects of policies in all their ramifications. A government regulates certain types of business practices and in the course of so doing hires employees and office space and uses supplies. To students of public finance, the regulations administered are of no direct interest, however important they may be in other connections. A policy of hiring people and equipment to accomplish certain results constitutes a financial policy in the sense that money comes into the picture. If the people and equipment were hired for some other purpose, say to regulate labor unions, the change would not matter in a study of financial policies. What matters from the point of view of public finance students are the effects of these policies on the prices of the services of employees of this kind, the loss of manpower for private purposes because it is being used for public purposes, the changes in money incomes, and similar considerations. Students of public finance do not pretend to ascertain the effects of all government policies; they restrict themselves to the implications of the financial aspects of government decisions. Traditionally the general categories describing government financial policies are government expenditures, revenues, and debt operations.

The concept of "effects" in our formal definition of public finance gives rise to especially troublesome issues. Speaking loosely, we know that government financial policies do matter in some way or other. If this were not so, there would be nothing to study. "Effects" may be taken to refer to those economic changes brought about by government policies. The relevant causes are the financial policies of government; the effects are the differences that these policies make in economic affairs. The illustrations already used give some indication of what effects government policies may have. They may aggravate a depression, begin and perpetuate an inflation, or provide greater economic stability. Particular tax policies may increase the price of beer or cut down the quantity of imports. Subsidies may reduce the price of wool and increase the income of farmers. The whole of the economic society in which we find ourselves is made different every day and in innumerable ways because of government financial policies.

Why should there be any particular concern about the effects of government financial policies as opposed to those of some large corporation such as the United States Steel Corporation? There are, of course, interesting aspects in the study of the effects of private financial policies. Special reasons exist, however, for paying close attention to the effects of government policies.

The first is a pragmatic one. In democratic societies, at least, people are concerned about what their government does or does not do. As citizens they are in a position to influence the policies actually adopted. They may oppose or favor certain government operations because they dislike or favor what they believe to be the effects. In some cases the reason may be nothing more elevating than personal advantage. A person may oppose some tax because he thinks that such a tax would be paid partly by him. Or the reason may be highly idealistic. Wealthy people can be found supporting progressive income taxation because they believe such a tax makes for a better type of society even though they personally are required to pay heavier taxes under such a system.

The second reason is a scientific one, if one may use that much abused term. Government policies differ from their private counterparts in that a sovereign government possesses power in this area not matched by that of any private person or organization. Charles O. Hardy once observed that operations by a government central bank could be nullified by a wealthy man who set his mind to do so.[1] If the central bank tried to adopt an expansionary monetary policy by buying government securities on the open market, the wealthy man could counteract the operation by offering an equal amount of government securities for sale. In the opposite case he would buy government securities when the central bank started to sell them. The government's monetary policies would thereby be nullified and defeated. The illustration is farfetched. No private individual or organization is sufficiently wealthy to compete effectively with a central bank. No private organization has the power to create unlimited sums of money as does a central bank. Governments in modern societies can and do say what is money, and they control the means for creating money. In dealing with its own citizens, and this is an important qualification, a central government need never run out of cash even in the extreme case when it might not tax at all. It has not always been considered good taste to stress the fact that governments can create unlimited sums of money, but good taste or not, it is a fact of crucial importance. Any financial limitations of a central government are self-imposed. In times of crisis, such restraints on the uses of financial power disappear. None of the belligerents in World War II allowed a little question of money to come between them and the supplies and manpower they wanted. Because of this great power, the financial policies of government take on a special importance.

We come finally to the appraisal aspects mentioned in our formal definition. How shall an honest man make up his mind whether he should favor or oppose particular types of government policy? Economic purists maintain that appraisal questions do not enter into the study of economics. They like to emphasize that propositions containing the word "ought" are not economic statements. In a sense these purists are correct. No amount of knowledge about economics is sufficient to determine how progressive an income tax should be, or indeed whether it should be progressive at all. Ethical issues are raised in such a question, and ethics is usually considered to be a branch of philosophy. Yet a student should not have to take a course in ethics to make up his mind about the desirability of a progressive tax on income. Such issues may not even be discussed in courses in ethics. Purity can be a bit frustrating. As a citizen and voter one needs to make up his mind.

Any objective discipline, economics included, presupposes certain ethical propositions. For example, the study of a subject assumes that more knowledge about it is better than less. An intellectual approach

[1] Charles O. Hardy, *Credit Policies of the Federal Reserve System* (Washington, D.C.: The Brookings Institution, 1932), p. 31.

to a topic requires a willingness to allow one's views to be influenced by reason and evidence. Otherwise it is impossible to learn. The violation of this ethical principle is only too easy. A progressive income tax, for example, may be regarded as a bad type of tax merely because some radio commentator pronounced it to be bad. Likewise people may denounce government expenditures as being too large without being prepared to say which expenditures are too large or how they might be reduced.

The ethical principle that more knowledge is better than less suggests three sins to avoid in thinking about and discussing government fiscal policies.

The first sin is muddleheadedness. Its characteristic is inconsistency. For example, a senator may vote to cut the size of the armed forces, while at the same time urging aggressive policies toward foreign countries which might lead to war. A large number of slick-paper releases will be found advocating lower taxation and reduced public debt without any mention of government expenditures. Avoidance of the sin of muddleheadedness would of itself greatly elevate the tone of public discussion of government finance.

The second sin is pigheadedness. This sin is the obstinate refusal to look at any evidence or to listen to any arguments which conflict with a preconceived opinion. Some people have so indoctrinated themselves with what they believe to be correct views on government finance that they are unable to think further upon the subject. Such people cannot learn the effects of government financial operations, let alone intelligently appraise them.

The third sin is the uncritical identification of one's personal financial interests with the national welfare. For example, a businessman may condemn high taxes as harmful to the country for many and sundry reasons, when it is only too evident that what he really means is that the taxes are harmful to his financial interests. The sin in question is not simply the identification of personal interest with the national interest because in particular cases they may very well be identical. The sin lies in the lack of critical examination of personal interests.

Beyond the observance of the rules of impartial inquiry, there are many other value judgments that have some special reason to command general respect. These value judgments are not peculiar to public finance. Ideals of fairness, for example, enter into the appraisal of government rules of various kinds, including the rules about taxes. The rigorous application even of this commonly endorsed value judgment to taxation would force us to condemn the tax system used by any government in the world today.

Without supposing that ethical judgments are merely matters of taste, like tastes for beer or opera, we shall in this book avoid attempting to impose our own ideals upon the reader without giving some notice. When appraisal questions are under discussion, we shall try to remind the reader that value judgments are being employed. Reasonable people may differ in their appraisals of government operations. The one value judgment that we shall insist upon is that careful and rigorous examination of government fiscal actions is a necessary prelude to intelligent appraisal.

2

Government Finance in Recent Decades

Governmental activity in the United States in the present century has in some ways resembled Jack's famous beanstalk. Even in an era accustomed to superlatives and to gigantic increases in population, prices, and productivity (all of which play their part in pushing up government expenditures), the rise in government operations is a spectacular one. From a modest $1.5 billion in 1900, government expenditures climbed to $100 billion in the 1950's—an increase of nearly seventyfold—far outstripping other parts even of this fast-growing economy. Whereas in 1902 government expenditures constituted only 7 per cent of the U. S. gross national product, by 1952 their share was 27 per cent. Over the same period per capita government expenditures increased ninefold,[1] and the role of government as employer became a far more significant one (only 4 per cent of the nation's labor force was in government employment in 1900; 15 per cent in 1952[2]).

[1] Measured in constant 1926 prices, this rise for all levels of government was from $33 in 1902 to $338 in 1952. The federal share of this rise was from $11 to $244 (M. Slade Kendrick, *A Century and a Half of Federal Expenditures,* Occasional Paper 48 [New York: National Bureau of Economic Research, 1955], pp. 86-87), while state and local expenditures increased much less markedly, from $22 to $94 (L. Laszlo Ecker-Racz, "A Foreign Scholar Ponders the 1957 Census of Governments," *National Tax Journal,* XII [June, 1959], p. 102).

[2] Solomon Fabricant, *The Trend of Government Activity in the United States Since 1900,* (New York: National Bureau of Economic Research, 1952), p. 14, and the Tax Foundation, *Facts and Figures on Government Finance,* 10th ed., 1958-59, pp. 33, 42.

The changes which make up this dramatic increase in the importance of American government, however, have not affected all governmental activities equally. In this chapter we shall see what they have meant in terms of both volume and kinds of government expenditures, revenues, and public debt, and we shall also look at what effects these shifts have had on the relative importance of the federal, state, and local governments.

Government Expenditures and Gross National Product

At the end of the prosperous decade of the 1920's government expenditures, at 10 per cent of gross national product (GNP), were only moderately higher than they had been at the opening of the century (See Table 2–1). The Great Depression soon changed this picture, however, and by 1934 expenditures had climbed to 20 per cent of GNP, with most of the increase occurring at the federal level. Then

TABLE 2–1

GOVERNMENT EXPENDITURES AND GROSS NATIONAL PRODUCT
SELECTED YEARS, 1902-1958

| Year | Government Expenditures[1] as a Percentage of Gross National Product | | |
	Total	Federal[2]	State and Local[3]
1902	7	2	5
1929	10	3	7
1934	20	10	10
1939	19	10	9
1943-44	49	45	4
1947	19	13	5
1950	21	14	7
1953	28	21	7
1955	25	17	8
1956	25	17	8
1957	26	18	8
1958	28	20	9

[1] Except for 1902 these are as reported in the national income accounts. For a discussion of alternative measures of government expenditures see Chapter 4 below. 1902 expenditures are taken from R. A. Musgrave and J. M. Culbertson, "The Growth of Public Expenditures in the United States, 1890-1948," *National Tax Journal,* VI (June, 1953), 111-13, and although not strictly comparable with the other years, are sufficiently so to reveal the main trends.
[2] Includes grants-in-aid to state and local governments.
[3] Federal grants-in-aid have been subtracted to avoid duplication.

Sources: For 1902, Musgrave and Culbertson, *op. cit.;* for 1929-57, Tax Foundation, *Facts and Figures on Government Finance,* 10th ed. 1958-59, p. 26; for 1958, Department of Commerce, *Survey of Current Business* (July, 1959), pp. 7, 21.

after seven years of relative stability, World War II brought government operations to a high peak of 49 per cent of GNP in both 1943 and 1944. Although the postwar years were highly prosperous, the relationships prevailing in the 1920's were not restored. Instead, government expenditures, after remaining close to 20 per cent of GNP in the late 1940's, increased under the impact of the Korean War to 28 per cent by 1953, and remained on a high peacetime plateau of 25-28 per cent during the last half of the fifties.

Relative Importance of Federal, State, and Local Expenditures

From a subordinate role, accounting for only 25-30 per cent of total government spending in the early years of the present century, federal expenditures expanded rapidly during the 1930's, attained overwhelming predominance during World War II, and, apart from the effects of the Korean War, remained close to 65 per cent of all government expenditures during the 1950's (Table 2–2). While state expenditures have maintained a relatively stable position (18 per cent

TABLE 2–2

RELATIVE IMPORTANCE OF FEDERAL, STATE, AND LOCAL EXPENDITURES
SELECTED YEARS, 1902-1958

Fiscal Year	Percentage of Total Government Expenditures[1]		
	Federal[2]	State	Local Governments
1902	30	11	58
1913	24	13	63
1927	27	18	55
1936	50	20	30
1944	91	4	5
1950	63	18	19
1953	72	13	15
1955	66	16	18
1956	65	16	19
1957	65	16	19
1958	64	17	19

[1] As in Table 2–1 intergovernmental grants-in-aid are counted as expenditures by the granting government and, to avoid duplication, are subtracted from the gross expenditures of the recipient governments.
[2] Federal expenditures are measured in three different ways: 1902-1927 percentages are based on net budget expenditures, 1936-1950 percentages on cash payments to the public, and 1953-1958 percentages on expenditures as measured by the Bureau of the Census. For a discussion of these three measures see Chapter 4.

Sources: For 1902-1957, *Facts and Figures on Government Finance*, 10th ed. p. 19; for 1958, U. S. Department of Commerce, Bureau of the Census, *Governmental Finances in 1958*, p. 16.

of total government expenditures in 1927, for example, and 17 per cent in 1958), local spending has declined markedly from nearly 60 per cent of total expenditures in 1902 to less than 20 per cent in 1958. Since the intergovernmental finance picture is complicated, however, by extensive grants-in-aid (from federal to state, state to local, etc.), it must be explained that the above percentages are based on computations which count these grants as expenditures by the granting government and deduct them from the expenditures of the receiving government. If the alternative procedure were followed, and these expenditures were attributed to the governmental level actually dispensing the funds rather than to the one at which they originate, the figures would be somewhat less for federal and state governments and more for local. In 1958, for example, expenditures on this alternative basis would be 60 per cent federal, 15 per cent state, and 25 per cent local, as compared with the 64-17-19 per cent breakdown shown in Table 2–2.

Structure of Federal Spending Since World War II

That expenditures for national security have been of primary importance at the federal level since the end of World War II is immediately apparent in Table 2–3. The major security programs themselves

TABLE 2–3

STRUCTURE OF FEDERAL CASH PAYMENTS TO THE PUBLIC, 1948, 1953, AND 1959

(billions of dollars)

	FISCAL YEAR					
	1948		1953		1959	
Category	Amount	%	Amount	%	Amount	%
1. Major national security	$13.0	37	$50.5	65	$46.6	48
2. International affairs	5.5	15	2.2	3	2.4	2
3. Veterans' benefits	6.9	19	4.9	6	5.8	6
4. Interest	3.9	11	4.7	6	5.4	6
5. Labor and welfare	3.1	9	6.9	9	18.6	19
6. Agriculture	0.5	1	2.9	4	5.5	6
7. Natural resources	0.8	2	1.5	2	2.0	3
8. Commerce and housing	0.5	1	2.3	3	6.9	7
9. General government	1.4	4	1.4	2	1.9	2
Totals	35.6	100	77.3	100	96.2	100

Source: *The Budget of the United States Government for the Fiscal Year Ending June 30, 1961* (Washington, D.C.: Government Printing Office, 1960), p. 897.

accounted for nearly 50 per cent of federal cash payments[3] in fiscal 1959, and in addition, the major part of the next three categories of spending—i.e., international affairs, veterans' benefits, and interest on federal debt—is closely connected with the same general purpose. Both military and economic grants and loans to foreign countries help to bolster our own security; veterans' benefits are directly attributable to past wars; and a large part of the public debt on which interest was paid in fiscal 1959 was incurred during World War II and the Korean War.

The federal government makes civilian expenditures for a wide variety of purposes, as may readily be seen by reading one of the recent budget messages of the President. Predominant in this area throughout the postwar period have been the social security programs, which in 1959 accounted for three-quarters of federal cash payments in the labor and welfare category. Next in importance in 1959 were the price-support and other agricultural aid programs and expenditures for the promotion of transportation (mainly highways) and housing (categories 6 and 8 in Table 2–3). Both of these categories have increased significantly in relative importance since 1948.

The long-run growth pattern of federal per capita expenditures, measured in constant dollars, shows several notable features. From 1795 to 1929 civilian expenditures increased steadily at an average annual rate of 15 per cent; during the first half of the Great Depression they shot up by nearly 500 per cent in four years; and then for the first time in history they remained relatively stable for nearly two decades from 1934 to 1952. War-connected expenditures, on the other hand, have roughly followed an ascending stair-step pattern, the interwar periods remaining relatively stable, but each major war pushing the level to a new high.[4]

Structure of State and Local Government Expenditures

In 1958 provision for education, highways, public welfare, and health and hospitals took two-thirds of local government expenditures and over three-quarters of state expenditures (Table 2–4). Among these major programs highways ranked first at the state level and

---

[3] Cash payments to the public are used in this section because, for reasons given below in chap. 4, they are a more comprehensive and meaningful measure of federal spending than net budget expenditures. The two series show important differences in structure. In 1959, for example, the major national security programs took 58 per cent of budget expenditures as compared with 48 per cent of cash payments, and the labor and welfare category was only 5 per cent of budget expenditures but 19 per cent of cash payments.

[4] Kendrick, *op. cit.*, p. 39.

TABLE 2–4

STRUCTURE OF STATE AND LOCAL GOVERNMENT EXPENDITURES IN 1958

(billions of dollars)

Program	State[1]		Local		State and Local	
	Amount	%	Amount	%	Amount	%
Education	$ 2.9	18	$13.0	45	$15.9	35
Highways	5.5	35	3.1	10	8.6	19
Public welfare	1.9	12	1.9	6	3.7	8
Health and hospitals	1.8	12	1.7	6	3.6	8
Public safety	0.7	4	2.3	8	2.9	6
General government	0.6	4	1.3	4	1.8	4
Others	2.3	13	6.0	21	8.3	19
Totals	15.6	100	29.3	100	44.9	100

[1] Figures include only direct state expenditures and exclude grants-in-aid made to local governments.

Sources: U.S. Department of Commerce, Bureau of the Census, *Governmental Finances in 1958*, p. 17; *Compendium of State Goverment Finances in 1958*, p. 8.

education at the local level; but for both levels combined educational expenditures of $16 billion were nearly twice the amount devoted to highways. Public welfare programs (such as general relief, aid to dependent children, to the aged, and to the handicapped), which were of minor importance before the Great Depression, have since the mid-thirties accounted for approximately 10 per cent of state and local spending. During the last two decades the general structure of state and local expenditures has remained remarkably stable.[5]

Structure of Government Expenditures as a Whole

Only a nostalgic memory, it would appear, are the days when a textbook author could state complacently, "One of the most creditable facts about the United States is that it is the only nation that uses more money on education than on war or preparations for war."[6]

When the expenditures of all three levels of government are brought together, as is done in Table 2–5, national defense remains by far the most important single category (40 per cent of total spending), with education and social security, which are tied for second place, less

[5] For a detailed discussion of the changes during the first half of the present century in the functional structure of government activity see Fabricant, *op. cit.*, chap. iv.

[6] Edward S. Ellis, *The Youth's History of the United States*, Vol. IV (New York: Cassell and Co., Ltd., 1887), p. 338.

than one-third as important. On the next lower level, each accounting
for about 5 per cent of total expenditures, are veterans' benefits, expenses of general government administration, interest on the public
debt, highway expenditures, and the public health and sanitation programs. Finally, at the bottom are the programs for agriculture, civilian
safety, international affairs, commerce and housing, and natural resources, ranging in importance from 1 to 3 per cent of total governmental expenditures.

TABLE 2–5

FEDERAL, STATE, AND LOCAL GOVERNMENT EXPENDITURES
(NATIONAL INCOME VERSION) BY FUNCTION, 1957

Function	Amount (billions)	Percentage of Total
National defense	$ 45.5	40
Education	13.7	12
Social security	13.7	12
Highways	7.0	6
General government	6.3	6
Interest	6.2	5
Veterans' benefits	5.3	5
Public health and sanitation	4.9	4
Agriculture	3.0	3
Civilian safety	2.8	2
International affairs	2.1	2
Commerce and housing	1.8	2
Natural resources	1.4	1
Totals	114.5	100

Source: Department of Commerce, *U. S. Income and Output*, p. 177. For the definition of the national income version of government expenditures see
Chapter 4.

The importance of national defense in the postwar fiscal picture
raises the question of whether civilian governmental activities have
been held down as a result. In 1957, for example, the ratio of nondefense government output to nondefense GNP was only 10 per cent
as compared with 12 per cent in 1939 and 7.5 per cent in 1929. In
spite of a 50 per cent increase in real civilian output per capita between 1939 and 1957, nondefense government output per capita,
when converted to 1957 dollars, was the same in both years.[7] It is
highly likely that if world tensions had been substantially less than
they actually were, more civilian government services of various kinds
would have been made available.

[7] Francis M. Bator, *The Question of Government Spending* (New York: Harper
& Bros., 1960), pp. 21-22.

Federal Budget Receipts

During the nineteenth century the federal government was frequently criticized for obtaining most of its revenue from highly regressive customs and excise taxes and for collecting, on occasion, more taxes than it knew how to spend.[8] No complaints of this sort have been heard in recent years. Although customs and excises brought in 91 per cent of budget receipts during the first decade of this century, the passage of the Sixteenth Amendment in 1913[9] opened the door for individual and corporate income taxes, and by the 1920's these taxes made up more than half of total federal revenues (Table 2–6). It is interesting to note that this position of primary importance was largely attributable to the inclusion in the federal tax base of capital gains and losses, a type of income that goes untaxed in many countries. During the stock market boom of 1926-29 capital gains taxes constituted no less than 40 per cent of the total yield of the individual income tax.

After a fall in relative importance during the depression of the 1930's, income taxes rebounded to even greater heights, bringing in 69 per cent of receipts during the 1940's and 71 per cent in fiscal 1959. Customs and excise taxes, in the meantime, had fallen by the end of the 1950's into equality, at 12 per cent of total receipts, with the employment (payroll) taxes collected under the various social security acts. Although the list of products subject to federal excises is a long one, alcoholic beverages produce nearly one-third of the total excise tax yield, and tobacco and gasoline each bring in close to a fifth of the revenue. "Miscellaneous receipts" are made up primarily of earnings on federal investments in government-sponsored enterprises, of interest and principal repayments on federal loans, and of revenues from the sale of products and property, but they include also minor amounts of fees and fines, rents and royalties, and even

[8] Cf. Randolph E. Paul, *Taxation in the United States* (Boston: Little, Brown & Co., 1954), pp. 27-31.

[9] The Sixteenth Amendment, ratified on February 25, 1913, reads as follows: "The Congress shall have power to lay and collect taxes on incomes, from whatever source derived, without apportionment among the several States, and without regard to any census or enumeration." Prior to its adoption, the wording of Article I, Section 2 of the Constitution—"Representatives and direct taxes shall be apportioned among the several States which may be included within this Union, according to their respective numbers . . . The actual enumeration shall be made within three years after the first meeting of the Congress of the United States, and within every subsequent term of ten years . . ."—together with the ruling of the Supreme Court that income taxes are direct taxes in *Pollock* v. *Farmers Loan and Trust Co.,* 157 U. S. (1895) 429, 158 U. S. (1895) 601 denied to the federal government the right to raise any revenue from income taxes as such.

TABLE 2–6

STRUCTURE OF FEDERAL BUDGET RECEIPTS DURING THE TWENTIETH CENTURY

(percentage distributions)

Type of Receipt	1901-10	1921-30	1931-40	1941-50	1959
Individual income tax	—	52**	18	40	48
Corporate income and excess profits taxes	*		21	29	23
Estate and gift taxes	*	2	6	2	2
Total taxes on income and wealth	1	54	45	71	73
Alcohol excises	33	1	9	5	4
Tobacco excises	9	8	12	3	2
Other excises	1	9	14	7	5
Customs duties	48	13	8	1	1
Total customs and excise taxes	91	31	44	17	12
Employment taxes	—	—	6	5	12
Miscellaneous receipts	8	14	5	7	4

* Less than ½%
** Separate data for individual and corporate taxes not available.

Sources: Decade figures are from *Facts and Figures on Government Finance*, 1954-
      55, Table 89; fiscal 1959 figures are from the 1961 *United States Budget*,
      pp. 904-6.

outright gifts and contributions. Some of these gifts are earmarked
for specific projects in which the donor is interested; others arrive
unannounced and unidentified and are known simply as the "conscience fund" ($0.4 million in fiscal 1959).

State and Local Revenues

While income taxes are by far the most important source of federal
revenue, sales taxes predominate at the state level and property taxes
at the local level. In 1958 general sales taxes brought in 24 per cent
of state tax collections; and selective sales taxes, among which those
on motor fuels were the most important, added another 35 per cent
(Table 2–7). State individual and corporate income taxes together
were 17 per cent of all tax receipts, a relative level that was exceeded
only during the war years of 1944, 1945, and 1952. In contrast,
local income taxes in 1958 were only 1 per cent, and sales taxes only
7 per cent, of total tax collections of counties, cities, school districts,
and other local governments, while levies on property brought in 87
per cent of tax revenues (Table 2–7).

TABLE 2–7

STATE AND LOCAL TAX COLLECTIONS IN 1958, BY TYPE OF TAX AND
LEVEL OF GOVERNMENT

(billions of dollars)

Type of Tax	State			Local		State and Local
	Amount	%	Number of States Using Tax	Amount	%	%
General sales and gross receipts	$ 3.6	24	34	$ 0.7	5	14
Selective sales	5.3	35	50	0.4	2	19
Tax on sales of motor fuels*	2.9	20	50	0.0	0	10
Individual income	1.6	10	33	0.2	1	6
Corporate income	1.0	7	36	—	—	3
Motor vehicle and operators' licenses	1.4	9	49	0.1	1	5
Property	0.5	4	46	13.5	87	46
Death and gift	0.4	2	49	0.0	0	1
Other	1.2	8	—	0.6	4	6
Totals	15.0	100	50	15.5	100	100

* Included in selective sales category.

Source: Bureau of the Census, *Governmental Finances in 1958,* p. 15.

Both state and local tax structures have become more diversified during the present century. In 1902 no use was made of either sales or income taxes, property taxes in that year constituting 89 per cent of local, and 53 per cent of state, tax receipts. Income taxes became important at the state level in the 1920's, and sales taxes expanded rapidly during the next decade. Thereafter the most notable change was the introduction of local income taxes in five states and in the District of Columbia. Throughout the period property taxes have tended to decline in relative importance while both sales and income taxes have expanded their roles.

Although taxes are the most important source of funds, bringing in 57 per cent of state and 50 per cent of local revenues in 1958, substantial amounts are also received both from the operation of public enterprises such as utilities, liquor stores, and insurance and retirement trust funds, and from intergovernmental grants of various kinds. In 1958 state governments obtained one-sixth of their revenues from public enterprises and nearly one-fifth from intergovernmental grants, whereas local governments relied more heavily on grants (26 per cent) and less on enterprise receipts (12 per cent). At the beginning of the twentieth century both sources of revenue were much less important, grants providing only 5 per cent of state and local receipts, while public enterprise revenues brought in 7 per cent of state and only 1 per cent of local revenues.

Structure of Government Receipts

When the revenues of all three levels of government are combined, personal income taxes maintain a commanding lead of over 30 per cent of total receipts; corporate profits and sales taxes come second and third, each accounting for about one-fifth of total revenue; and property taxes and social security contributions, with one-eighth of the total each, round out the top group (Table 2–8). No other revenue source brought in as much as 5 per cent of the total in 1957. Federal grants-in-aid, which are not shown in the table, were $4.1 billion in 1957, or nearly 4 per cent of total governmental revenues.

TABLE 2–8

FEDERAL, STATE, AND LOCAL GOVERNMENT REVENUES
(NATIONAL INCOME VERSION) BY TYPE, 1957

Type of Revenue	Amount (billions)	Percentage of Total
Personal income tax	$ 37.7	32
Corporate profits tax	21.6	19
Sales taxes	19.9	17
Contributions for social insurance	14.2	12
Property taxes	12.5	11
Death and gift taxes	1.8	2
Miscellaneous taxes	4.6	4
Nontax revenues	3.9	3
Total	116.2	100

Source: Department of Commerce, *U. S. Income and Output,* pp. 164-65.

In its heavy reliance on income taxes, rather than on customs, excise, and other types of sales taxes, the United States revenue system differs from those of most other countries. Only Australia, Canada, Japan, the Netherlands, Sweden, Switzerland, the Union of South Africa, and the United Kingdom typically collect more in taxes on income and wealth than in taxes on the sale of goods and services.[10] Most other countries rely heavily, and some almost exclusively, on sales taxes of one kind or another. The U.S.S.R. derives one-half or more of its revenues from a turnover tax levied each time that goods

[10] United Nations, *Statistical Yearbook, 1958,* Table 171.

and services are sold; Finland uses a manufacturers sales tax, New Zealand a wholesale sales tax, Norway a retail sales tax, and France an unusual levy which has evoked considerable interest in recent years and which is imposed on the value added by manufacturing enterprises in the course of their business operations.[11] A number of countries—Ecuador, Ghana, and Malaya are examples—make extensive use of both export and import duties, and Italy has lucrative fiscal monopolies over tobacco and salt. Scandinavian tax systems are distinguished by the widespread use of local income taxes and a progressive tax on personal net worth. Both income and net worth provide widely accepted measures of an individual's ability to pay taxes, and personal consumption has been strongly advocated as still another measure.[12] Only recently, however, has a progressive tax on consumption expenditures been enacted, in India and Ceylon, and in each case generous exemption allowances restrict the levy to relatively few people.

Government Debt

Whenever receipts fall short of expenditures, governments must finance their excess spending by reducing the level of their cash balances, by borrowing from the public, or, in the case of national governments endowed with the necessary powers, by the creation of money. In this country the rapid growth of government debt during both the 1930's and World War II has given rise to much discussion and to considerable concern about the fiscal and economic effects of these developments.[13] In this section we shall consider the magnitudes involved and their relation to other important economic variables.

The most widely publicized figures on federal debt, by including obligations of the Treasury to other parts of the federal government, overstate significantly the true amount of debt in existence. In mid-1959, for example, the gross federal debt was $285 billion, but since $55 billion of this was owed to United States Government agencies and trust funds and another $26 billion to the Federal Reserve System, the net debt (i.e., the amount owed either to private investors or to state and local governments) was only $204 billion. Nevertheless, it is clear that a tremendous growth has occurred in recent decades in federal obligations to outside investors. Between 1930 and 1940 the net debt increased from $14 to $41 billion, and then during World War II it spurted to the unprecedented level of $227 billion, or over

[11] These different types of sales taxes are discussed in chaps. 13 and 14.
[12] See chaps. 8 and 9.
[13] See chaps. 22 and 23.

100 per cent of the country's gross national product (Table 2–9). Since the end of 1945 the amount of federal debt has remained close to $200 billion, but the postwar increase in both output and prices has steadily reduced the debt/GNP ratio to 75 per cent in 1948, 50 per cent in 1955, and 43 per cent in 1959.

TABLE 2–9

AMOUNTS OF GROSS AND NET FEDERAL DEBT AND THE RATIO OF NET DEBT TO
GROSS NATIONAL PRODUCT, SELECTED YEARS, 1920-1959

(amounts in billions)

Year*	Amount of Gross Debt	Amount of Net Debt	Ratio of Net Debt to GNP (%)
1920	$ 23.8	$ 23.2	27
1930	15.8	14.0	15
1940	50.6	40.8	40
1945	278.7	227.4	106
1948	252.4	195.2	75
1950	257.4	201.3	71
1955	274.4	200.3	50
1957	270.6	192.0	43
1959	284.8	204.2	43

* As of the end of December for the first four years given; otherwise as of the end of June.

Sources: Department of Commerce and Treasury Department.

While the amount of federal debt increased only slightly between the end of 1947 and the end of 1959, gross state and local debt almost quadrupled during this period, rising from $14 to $56 billion (Table 2–10). The postwar increase in private debt, however, has been much greater, and the ratio of public to total debt has consequently fallen from 54 per cent in 1947 to 34 per cent in 1959 (column 5, Table 2–10). It is interesting to note that the ratio of total debt to GNP has remained relatively stable, falling from 168 per cent at the end of 1947 to 152 per cent at the end of 1952 and then rising again to 168 per cent at the end of 1958 (column 6, Table 2–10). Finally, the gross state and local debt figures given in Table 2–10 should be compared with state and local holdings of the debts of others. The recent growth of employee-retirement and unemployment compensation trust funds has made both state and local governments important holders of financial assets. At the end of 1957, for example, local governments held $11 billion in the form of securities, and state governments held more in securities ($18 billion) than they owed to outside interests. This surprising position of state governments as net creditors rather

TABLE 2–10

NET PUBLIC AND PRIVATE DEBT OUTSTANDING, 1947-1959

(billions of dollars)

End of Year	Federal Government and Federal Agency Debt (1)	State and Local Government Debt (2)	Private Debt (3)	Total Public and Private Debt (4)	Ratio of Public to Total Debt (%) (5)	Ratio of Total Debt to GNP (%) (6)
1947	$200.7	$14.4	$179.7	$394.8	54	168
1948	193.2	16.2	200.9	410.3	51	158
1949	199.7	18.1	211.7	429.5	51	166
1950	197.9	20.7	250.9	469.5	47	165
1951	194.7	23.3	282.2	500.2	44	152
1952	198.2	25.8	306.5	530.5	42	153
1953	202.2	28.6	329.7	560.5	41	153
1954	205.3	33.4	348.2	586.9	41	162
1955	206.7	38.4	402.3	647.4	38	163
1956	200.5	42.7	439.1	682.3	36	163
1957	200.2	46.7	464.9	711.8	35	161
1958	206.4	50.9	486.6	743.9	35	168
1959p	216.4	55.6	529.0	801.0	34	167

p—preliminary

Source: Economic Reports of the President.

than debtors has been characteristic of the 1950's.[14] The fact that a large proportion of state-held financial investments are earmarked for specific purposes, however, prevents any widespread consolidation of obligations and a consequent reduction of state gross indebtedness.[15]

Factors Accounting for the Growth in Government Activity

The remarkable growth in government activity described in this chapter has resulted from a complex set of economic and social forces. Population growth has, of course, raised the demand for government services, and general price increases have pushed up government costs and revenues. Per capita government expenditures, measured in constant dollars, have, however, shown a sustained and rapid growth which must be attributed to other factors.

The important role played by wars and by international insecurity has already been noted. The great building booms just prior to World

[14] See chap. 22.
[15] Government debt is discussed further in chaps. 23 and 24.

War I, in the 1920's, and again in the 1950's all increased the need for streets, sewers, water facilities, and other municipal services. The invention and improvement of the automobile greatly stimulated the development of highways and, by accelerating the movement of population from the central city to the suburbs, contributed to the building booms just mentioned. As the world has become more complex the need for education has expanded, under the stimulus of rising living standards and the corresponding demands for mass education, plus an increasingly specialized technology requiring even more skilled manpower. Greater utilization of scarce natural resources has made for growing interest in the conservation activities of governments. By its painful lessons the Great Depression stimulated public provision of retirement, disability, and unemployment benefits and thereby quickened the growth of public welfare and social security programs. Finally, the development of concentrated economic power, in the form of huge corporations and wealthy labor unions, has given rise to intricate programs of public control that would have been unthinkable a hundred years ago.

These and many other forces have all contributed to the growth of modern governments. What the future may hold in this respect depends to a large extent on the prospects for some easing of international tensions. Widespread disarmament would permit either an expansion of the private sector of the economy or an increase in the flow of those public services the level of which is currently held down by the massive national security programs. Quite apart from defense requirements, it may well be that government services are mainly a luxury good, the demand for which increases more than in proportion to income. If this is the case, we may, as countries become wealthier, expect a continued increase in civilian governmental expenditures.

3

Effects of Governmental Fiscal Operations

In the last chapter the main features of governmental expenditures, revenues, and debt operations in this country during recent years were described. Each of these fiscal activities has important economic effects, the general nature of which will be discussed in this chapter. We are, so to speak, about to view the outstanding features of the fiscal landscape from a rather high-flying airplane. As a result of this survey it is hoped that when landings are made in later chapters the more detailed governmental effects thus seen will be more meaningful to the reader.

Economic Effects of Taxes

A tax is a compulsory transfer of money (or occasionally of goods and services) from private individuals and groups to the government, in return for which the taxpayer receives nothing of material value. The payment of a price implies that commodities are thereby acquired; the payment of a tax implies only that a liability to the government is canceled. The benefits of national defense expenditures, for example, accrue to specific individuals in this country regardless of the amount of taxes they pay to the federal government; the services of a municipal transit system, on the other hand, are ordinarily provided to riders only at a price—that is, in return for explicit money payments. A stamp placed upon a letter is not a tax because in return the government provides the service of carrying the letter to its destination, but a stamp placed on a personal check (as is required in England, for example) is a tax because the use of that stamp does not entitle the buyer to any valuable government service.

From the point of view of society as a whole, taxes may be regarded as monetary payments made in order to acquire government output. What is true for the group, however, is not in this case true for the individual member of the group, a distinction which has given rise to much confusion in public finance literature. Tax-financed government services, in other words, are not allocated to specific individuals on the basis of the amount of taxes they have to pay. Furthermore, the view that society buys government output by paying taxes must be qualified by noting that taxes need not be used for this purpose. Governments can be, and are, endowed with the power of money creation, and they may therefore finance expenditures with new money rather than with additional taxes.[1]

EFFECTS ON PRIVATE DISPOSABLE INCOME. Since it is a compulsory monetary transfer to the government, a tax lowers both the cash balance of the taxpayer and his disposable money income and increases the cash balance and income of the government.[2] It is not always an easy matter, however, to tell who the payer of a given tax actually is. In the case of a sales tax, for example, it may be the consumer, or the storekeeper, or even workers in totally different industries. Similarly, a corporation income tax may burden stockholders or consumers or even holders of government bonds. The somewhat devious routes by which such results may come about will be considered in later chapters. At the moment we are interested only in the general fact that taxes do reduce the money incomes of some people and that this effect sets in motion a whole series of important further developments.

Since taxes seldom reduce all individual incomes equally, they ordinarily make some change in the degree of inequality prevailing in the distribution of personal disposable income. A tax which takes an increasing proportion of income as income rises will lower the degree of inequality and is called a *progressive* tax. A *regressive* tax, on the other hand, takes proportionately more money from the poor than

---

[1] They may also finance expenditures by borrowing money, but a government's ability to sell debt rests essentially on its future tax-collecting powers.

[2] A few minor exceptions to this statement have existed from time to time in the form of taxes which yield no revenue to the government. A customs duty levied at sufficiently high rates may keep the products in question out of the country altogether, and an internal excise, such as the levies that different states have imposed on colored margarine, may make it unprofitable to produce the taxed item at all.

from the rich and consequently increases income inequality. In the neutral position between these two categories is a *proportional* tax, which assesses all incomes at the same rate.

These distinctions are illustrated in Table 3–1 for a very simple income distribution, half of which, before taxes, goes to the top 25 per cent of the income receivers and half of which goes to the remaining 75 per cent. Total income, in other words, is $100 billion, and if

TABLE 3–1

EFFECTS OF PROPORTIONAL, PROGRESSIVE, AND REGRESSIVE TAXES ON A
HYPOTHETICAL INCOME DISTRIBUTION

(billions of dollars)

Income Group	Pretax Income Distribution		Posttax Income Distributions					
			Proportional Tax		Progressive Tax		Regressive Tax	
	Amount of Income (1)	% of Income (2)	Amount of Income (3)	% of Income (4)	Amount of Income (5)	% of Income (6)	Amount of Income (7)	% of Income (8)
Top 25%	$ 50	50	$40	50	$35	44	$45	56
Bottom 75%	$ 50	50	$40	50	$45	56	$35	44
Totals	$100	100	$80	100	$80	100	$80	100

all income receivers are arrayed in order from smallest to largest income, the top fourth of these receivers has $50 billion and the bottom three-fourths divide among themselves the remaining $50 billion. A proportional tax of 20 per cent on all incomes will reduce the disposable incomes of these two groups to $40 billion each (column 3) but leave the degree of income inequality unchanged (column 4). A progressive tax of 30 per cent on the top fourth of the income receivers and only 10 per cent on all the others, however, will leave the top group with only 44 per cent of the total disposable income and give the bottom three-fourths 56 per cent (column 6). Conversely, a regressive tax of 10 per cent on the top group and 30 per cent on the bottom one will increase the income share of the wealthiest fourth to 56 per cent and reduce the share of the rest to 44 per cent (column 8).

EFFECTS ON PRIVATE SPENDING, PRICES, AND OUTPUT. Regardless of the effects of taxation on income inequality, some fall in the level of private spending may be expected as a result of the reductions in money incomes and cash balances brought about by taxes. The specific form which these decreases in spending will take cannot, in the present state of economic knowledge, be predicted with a high degree of accuracy. Faced with higher tax bills, one taxpayer may give up the idea of purchasing a new pocket-size radio; another may buy less perfume for his wife; another, with unusual strength of mind, may buy fewer candy bars for his children; and still another may fail to purchase a new delivery truck for his business or to construct an addition to his plant. Both private consumption and private investment expenditures, in other words, will respond to higher taxation either by rising less rapidly than they otherwise would have risen or by actually declining in amount.

Under inflationary conditions the primary effect of the tax-induced reduction in private spending will be to slow down, or perhaps even to eliminate, the general rise in prices. In the absence of widespread inflationary pressures, however, higher taxes will tend to bring about an actual decline in the price level. Under favorable conditions this price decline will not have adverse effects on the level of national output. Under other circumstances—if, for example, falling prices induce further cuts in private spending, or if a significant number of prices and wage rates do not adjust downward readily when the level of demand falls off—higher taxes will tend to lower output and raise unemployment and may even initiate a cumulative downward spiral in productive activity. Needless to say, few modern governments would welcome developments such as these as a result of their own tax policies.

Properly used, then, taxation will make prices lower than they otherwise would have been without depressing the level of output in the process. Such a result is more likely if governments use taxes to slow up or eliminate an increase in the price level than if they attempt to bring about an actual decline in prices. Taxation, in short, is primarily an anti-inflationary device. It is also, of course, a revenue-raising device, as are debt issue and money creation. All three are equally able to provide a government with a given amount of money,[3] but they are not equally capable of offsetting inflationary pressures. In this respect taxation stands by itself. Although government borrowing, as we shall see, does have some anti-inflationary effects, these are likely to be considerably less than those of an equal amount of taxation; and money creation, of course, has no anti-inflationary effects at all.

---

[3] State and local governments in this country, of course, do not possess the power of money creation.

EFFECTS ON THE COMPOSITION OF OUTPUT AND ON RELATIVE PRICES. In addition to their deflationary impact on the general price level, higher taxes are likely to induce a contraction of output in certain industries and an expansion in others, thereby making some prices and wage rates higher, and some lower, than they otherwise would have been. An excise tax on automobiles, for example, will reduce the output of new cars and raise their price to the consumer; and as a result a wide range of supplying industries, such as steel, rubber, and plastics, will find their sales falling. Resources of various kinds, including labor, will be released from employment in all of these areas and shifted to the making of different products, which will then be available in larger quantities and at lower prices than they would have been if the automobile excise had not been imposed. After all adjustments to the tax have worked themselves out, both the composition of final output and the relative price and wage rate structure will be materially altered.

People will be affected by changes of this sort both as consumers and as producers. Take, for simplicity, a tax on wine, which shifts resources into the production of cotton. Gourmets are likely to be rather annoyed by this turn of events, since wine sellers will be careful to emphasize the reason for the higher prices at which that beverage is available. Purchasers of cotton shirts, dresses, and sheets, on the other hand, are likely to be pleased about the lower prices at which these textile products will be offered in the stores. It is most unlikely, however, that they will attribute the price reductions to a tax levied on an entirely different product. The consumer burdens of the tax, in other words, will be well publicized, but its benefits will be largely, if not completely, ignored. Still other consumers will be able to view the tax quite dispassionately, being purchasers in significant amounts of neither cotton goods nor wine.

The effects of the wine tax on producers are no less important than those on consumers. Workers such as highly skilled wine tasters, whose special talents are valuable only to the taxed industry, will find the demand for their services falling, and their earnings will be reduced regardless of whether they remain employed at wineries or move to other jobs. Even less specialized workers, with employment opportunities in many industries, are likely to experience some reduction in their earning powers because of the tax-induced contraction in wine production that forces more people onto the labor market in search of work. Nor will workers be the only ones to suffer losses of income. Land that is particularly adapted to the growing of wine grapes will earn less for its owners than it did before the wine tax was imposed, and because of these income cuts some farmers will find it profitable to shift land and other resources into cotton production. In general a sales tax will reduce the money incomes of people owning resources either in the taxed area or in other competing industries. Finally, it should be noted that although the effects of the tax on consumers are both beneficial and burdensome, those on producers are detrimental only, involving as they do a reduction in producer money incomes.

By reducing private incomes, any tax sets in motion a complex set of secondary economic effects. Since different people have different tastes, the effects of taxation on the pattern of consumer buying will depend upon whose disposable income is reduced. If a tax imposing a money burden on individual X is chosen, he may react by going less frequently to restaurants and the theater; if Y's disposable income is reduced instead, he may spend less on cigarettes and clothes; and so on. The specific nature of these tax-induced cuts in consumer purchases will be of interest to many people who bear no part of the direct money burden of the tax. Producers and sellers of items on which taxpayers decide to economize will suffer an impairment of their income prospects, but nontaxed consumers will gain if the fall in demand leads to lower product prices. In general a resource owner is hurt either by a tax on other resources that compete with his in production or by a tax on his customers, whereas a consumer stands to gain from a tax on other consumers who buy the same goods and services as he does.

EFFECTS ON INCENTIVES TO WORK AND TO INVEST. Taxation typically affects a person's willingness to work in two different and offsetting ways, one simple and straightforward and the other more subtle and consequently less apparent to taxpayers. In the first place, many taxes impair the desire to work either by reducing the net wage rate in money terms—i.e., the amount of disposable income resulting from a given amount of work—or by lowering, through higher prices, the real value of the money earned by the worker. As effective rewards for labor fall in either of these two ways, the cost to the worker of taking an extra hour of leisure time is reduced, and this change will create in many people's minds a desire for more leisure.

This desire for more leisure may, however, be more than offset by the second effect of taxation on work incentives. Since leisure is an item which is typically consumed in greater quantities at higher levels of income and which will be sacrificed to a greater or lesser extent as incomes fall, any tax must reduce the desire for leisure by lowering the worker's disposable income. This "income effect," as economists call it, will be most obvious to families in the lower income ranges who were consuming all of their disposable income before the new tax was imposed and to families at higher income levels who have committed themselves, by means of home mortgages, insurance contracts, or consumer credit agreements, to a high and inflexible level of consumption and investment expenditures. Such people may be virtually forced by a tax to work harder in an attempt to maintain their pretax spending levels. Other workers may observe only the fact that the tax has reduced their earning powers and consequently may feel that it has only a disincentive effect upon them. As they continue to live at a lower level of disposable income, however, their desires for additional material goods may gradually become more pressing, and the attractions of work will thereupon rise. The income effect of taxation on work incentives, in other words, frequently operates rather slowly and in ways not readily perceived by the worker.

Taxation, then, exerts both an incentive and a disincentive influence on the supply of labor services, and the net result can be determined only by careful empirical studies of how different people do in fact react to higher taxes of various kinds. At this stage we may simply note that, because of the nature of their jobs, many people are not free to change the amount of work they do, and moderately higher or lower taxes will consequently not affect their working habits. Taxation can, however, induce married women and people not in the normal working ages to enter or leave the labor force; it can persuade older workers to postpone or speed up their retirements; and it can lead the self-employed to increase or decrease the length of their vacations.

Incentives to invest, and hence to risk the loss of income if the project in question turns out badly, are affected by taxation in much the same way as are incentives to work. On the one hand, by reducing disposable income any tax will increase the pressure on investors to take more risks in order to earn more income (since, on the average, the riskiest assets carry the highest rates of return), and on the other, any tax which reduces the amount of (after-tax) income earned by risking a dollar will on that account discourage investment. The effects of most taxes on investment incentives, therefore, cannot be determined theoretically but may be brought to light by empirical analyses of investor behavior.

This completes our survey of the main economic effects of taxation. We have seen that each tax must reduce private money incomes by the amount of its yield to the government and that this in turn will influence the degree of income inequality that exists in the society. The level of private spending will fall to some extent, a development which will offset any inflationary tendencies that may exist in the country. Individual incentives to work and to invest may be either strengthened or weakened. Finally, both the composition of private output and the kinds of work done by various people are likely to be altered. Such tax-induced reallocations of productive activity will fit well with some people's tastes but badly with those of others, and hence we may speak not only of tax burdens—which form a popular topic of conversation in most modern societies—but of tax benefits as well.

Economic Effects of Government Expenditures

For purposes of economic analysis government expenditures may be divided into four main categories: (1) purchases of goods and services, (2) transfer payments, (3) purchases of land and other existing assets, and (4) loans. The relative importance of these types of expenditures in fiscal 1956 is shown in Table 3–2. It will be noted that purchases of goods and services, at $76 billion, were three times as important as transfer payments, that federal loan disbursements of $5 billion exceeded loan repayments to the federal government by only $1 billion, and that purchases of land and existing assets of $1 billion were all concentrated at the state and local level. Finally, it should be mentioned that the federal government not only makes direct loans in its own funds to various borrowers but also insures private lenders against loss on some of their own loans. As we shall see below, these loan insurance programs, which involve the expenditure of federal money only to the extent that private borrowers default on insured loans, may have economic effects very similar to those of direct government loans. Since the mid-1930's federal loan insurance has grown rapidly in importance, and it will be noted in Table 3–2 that in 1956 new authorizations of insured loans were nearly $16 billion as compared with only $2.5 billion for direct federal loans. Federal loan insurance, in short, has become sufficiently important that consideration of its economic effects must be included in any analysis of government expenditure programs.

Modern nations differ widely in the extent to which they make use of government transfer payments and government output. In 1952-53, for example, transfer payments were only 5 per cent of GNP in the United States, as compared with 11½ per cent in West Germany, 13 per cent in the United Kingdom, and 14 per cent in Belgium. Government purchases of goods and services, in contrast, were a higher proportion of GNP in both the United States and the United Kingdom (23 per cent in 1953) than in either Belgium (17 per cent) or West

TABLE 3–2

ECONOMIC CLASSIFICATION OF GOVERNMENT EXPENDITURES IN FISCAL 1956

(billions of dollars)

	Federal	State and Local	Total
I. *Expenditure Programs:*			
1. Purchases of goods and services	45.1	31.4	76.5
2. Transfer payments[1]	21.4	4.0	25.4
3. Purchases of land and existing assets	0.0	1.2	1.2
4. Direct loans:			
New authorizations	2.5	n.a.	n.a.
Gross disbursements	5.1	n.a.	n.a.
Net disbursements	0.9[2]	1.3[3]	2.2
II. *Related Programs:*			
5. Federally-insured private loans:			
New authorizations	15.9		
Increase in amount of loans outstanding	5.7		

n.a.—not available.

[1] Includes net interest paid and federal subsidies (less surplus of federal government enterprises).

[2] Gross disbursements minus principal repayments.

[3] Average amount of increase in state and local holdings of corporate bonds and mortgages during calendar 1955 and 1956. See *Federal Reserve Bulletin* (Aug., 1959), p. 1059.

Sources: *United States Budget for 1958,* Special Analysis F, pp. 1104-6; Department of Commerce, *U. S. Income and Output,* pp. 169, 179.

Germany (19 per cent). It is significant that the U.S. position in this last foursome is exactly reversed if national defense activities are eliminated from the picture. Government nondefense output, that is, was only 10 per cent of GNP in this country in 1953, as compared with 11 per cent in Belgium, 13 per cent in the United Kingdom, and 14 per cent in West Germany.[4]

PURCHASES OF GOODS AND SERVICES. By buying output from private businesses and hiring workers governments provide a wide variety of services, usually without explicit charge, to the rest of society. The specific nature of these activities, which include such important items as highways, missiles, education, and police protection, has already been indicated in the preceding chapter. Here we

[4] Francis M. Bator, *The Question of Government Spending* (New York: Harper & Bros., 1960), p. 157.

are concerned with two characteristics which all such programs have in common: the fact that they involve government use of real resources, on the one hand, and, on the other, the fact that the resulting services are provided to the public either completely free of charge or at only nominal prices.

Government employment of real resources, such as land, labor, buildings, and machines, means that none of these items can be used to produce output in the private sector of the economy. The benefits of increased governmental services, in other words, can ordinarily be obtained only at the cost of having fewer private goods and services. The most dramatic illustration of this proposition occurs in wartime when manpower and other resources must be shifted in vast numbers to the armed services and the war industries. Civilian production will decline, guns having replaced butter, as the phrase goes; and this cut in private output is an important part of the economic burden of war. Similarly, the economic burden of international distrust and tension consists of the material goods and services given up by all countries who spend money on national defense.

It is frequently argued that an important exception to the proposition that government resource-using programs reduce the amount of private output occurs in a severe depression, since at that time a government may use for its own purposes resources which otherwise would have remained unemployed. The conclusion that additional government output under these conditions is economically costless, however, rests on the assumption that the government could not have expanded private output by alternative fiscal and monetary policies. For if this could have been done, the new government output has in effect been chosen in preference to, and at the expense of, additional private output. Only if the private use of unemployed resources cannot be induced by any reasonable means, can we say that governmental use of them is economically costless.

For the most part, then, all government purchases of goods and services involve a sacrifice of private output. From an economic point of view such government programs are desirable only if their benefits to society exceed the value of the resulting loss of private goods and services. Ideally, in other words, the value of each new governmental resource-using program should be balanced against the alternative uses to which those resources could be put. If one government program is superior to another in this respect, the latter should be rejected, and even the first should be discarded if private use of the same resources would yield still greater benefits.

Unfortunately, it is frequently very difficult to evaluate government projects on this basis. In the private sector an efficient test of worthiness is provided by the pricing system, since a new product which cannot be sold at a price sufficient to cover its cost of production either will not be produced at all or will soon be discontinued or changed into a more profitable form. For one reason or another, however, much government output is not sold to beneficiaries at a price, and hence its desirability cannot be put to a test in the market place. Some public services—the national defense programs provide a good example—are of such a character that they cannot be sold in varying amounts to different consumers. Highway services, on the other hand, could all be sold at a price, but in practice this is done only when, as in the case of limited-access freeways, the collection of fees is not excessively costly. Still other services are provided at nominal prices either because their benefits are disseminated well beyond the immediate recipients or because it is felt that those recipients should, as a matter of public policy, be encouraged to consume more of the services than they would at a higher price. Some examples of this, such as state universities, are obvious enough; others, such as the transportation of newspapers and magazines at less than cost, are less well known. In any case, the important thing about all these kinds of government output is that the conventional, market test of economic worthiness is either not feasible or not desirable.

Instead of the market test we have the political test of vote-getting power. Instead of a clearly defined set of prices at which different goods and services may be acquired, individuals have, for one thing, a general knowledge of the tax system to aid them in evaluating different kinds of government output. School construction financed by a special bond issue which must be approved by the voters is an example of a public good whose desirability may be determined by parents and other taxpayers in much the same way as they decide to buy or not to buy any consumer product. In each case the cost of having the additional services should be apparent. Most governmental output programs, however, are not tied to specific taxes, and citizens must therefore evaluate them by estimating the extent to which their own taxes are likely to be higher as a result. Under such circumstances some people will favor projects which they would not support on the open market because they feel that their own taxes are not likely to rise, while others may oppose government spending of considerable value to themselves because they fear that their taxes will increase more than in proportion to their potential benefits.

The tax test, then, is not ordinarily a very precise method of choosing different amounts and types of governmental services. For some projects, however, a direct comparison of economic benefits and costs is feasible. The estimated accomplishments and costs of public water resources developments, for example, may be compared with the benefits and costs of one or more private plans designed to achieve the same general purposes, and the best of these projects may then be evaluated in relation to the alternative products that could be obtained if no water development were undertaken at all. Unfortunately, the difficulties encountered in such procedures are frequently formidable, and much remains to be accomplished in this area.[5]

Provision of government output to the private sector free of charge not only complicates the whole process of choice and evaluation but also gives rise to an inflation problem. When a private business expands, its additional payments to the rest of the economy for resources are matched by additional payments from the rest of the economy for the increased output of the business. Private incomes rise, but output increases at the same time so that increased spending need not drive up prices. A new government program, however, increases private incomes and spending without providing additional output at prices which will absorb that additional spending. Prices still need not rise under these circumstances if there is sufficient slack in the economic system. Higher private spending may merely give rise to increased private output at constant prices if a considerable amount of unemployment exists or if, at full employment, productivity is increasing fast enough so that the flow of additional goods matches the rise in money spending. In the absence of these conditions, however, additional government spending may be expected to exert an upward pressure on the price level. Either additional taxes or the sale of public debt to private investors will be needed to counteract these tendencies.

TRANSFER PAYMENTS. Government expenditures, such as unemployment assistance grants, social security payments to the aged, or producer subsidies, increase the disposable incomes of the recipients but bring no valuable services or products to the government in return. These unilateral transfers are in essence negative taxes, and their effects, therefore, are exactly the opposite of those already discussed above.

Consider, by way of illustration, a baby bonus like that paid by the government of Great Britain or of Canada each month to parents for their dependent children. These money grants, which increase as the number of children increases, raise the disposable incomes of

[5] See, for example, J. V. Krutilla and Otto Eckstein, *Multiple Purpose River Development: Studies in Applied Economic Analysis* (Baltimore: Johns Hopkins Press, 1958), and R. N. McKean, *Efficiency in Government Through Systems Analysis with Emphasis on Water Resources Development* (New York: John Wiley & Sons, 1958).

the recipients and alter the income distribution in favor of large families. The level of consumer expenditures is presumably raised by these transfers, but the additional purchases need not be for the immediate benefit of the children involved. While some families may spend their bonuses on toys and children's clothing, others may put it aside to finance a university education, and still others may simply spend it on themselves. Since wage rates are not affected by the bonuses although disposable incomes are increased, incentives to produce (though not incentives to reproduce) will be weakened so that the husband may have to work less hard in order to support his family or the wife may be relieved of the necessity of entering the labor force. On the other hand, the bonuses can make an important contribution to working abilities by raising the living standards of families who would otherwise be unable to afford sufficient food or decent housing.

Transfer payments ordinarily increase the demand for output less than does an equal amount of government purchases of services and newly produced goods. The latter not only increase national output immediately by the full amount of the money spent, but by raising disposable private incomes they generate in addition a secondary flow of increased consumer spending that continues for some time. Transfer payments can be equally expansionary if the recipients spend the full amount on new output. Since, under most circumstances, a part of the transfers will be saved by the recipients, the immediate increase in spending will be less than the amount of the transfers, and this smaller increase will in turn induce a smaller secondary flow of consumption expenditures.[6]

PURCHASES OF LAND AND EXISTING ASSETS. When a government embarks upon a new resource-using project, it need not, of course, buy for the purpose only newly produced goods. Land will frequently be required, and the purchase of used assets of various kinds may be advisable for economy reasons, especially if the Administration or Congress is intent on holding down the level of government expenditures. While the buying of land and other existing assets does not bring about an increase in national output, the purchases do raise private incomes by bidding up the prices of the assets in question. Some increase in private spending, therefore, is likely to result from this third type of government expenditure, but the amount of the increase is more difficult to predict than in either of the first two cases. Not only is the amount of the increase in private incomes not necessarily equal to the volume of government expenditures (as it was

[6] For a fuller discussion of these matters see chap. 20 below.

in the first two cases) but some of it will take the form of accrued capital gains—for example, increases in the value of land occupied by home owners—which may have no effect on the spending of some families but a large effect on others.

DIRECT PUBLIC LOANS AND GUARANTIED PRIVATE LOANS. Although direct government loans neither increase the demand for new output nor generate additional private incomes, they will normally induce the borrower to do both. At least part of the loan proceeds, in other words, is likely to be used to purchase new goods and services that otherwise would not have been bought; these transactions will create additional private incomes; and these additional incomes will initiate a secondary flow of increased spending. Nor need the primary increase in spending be restricted to the recipients of government loans. By competing with private lenders, government credit agencies may bring about a liberalization of private loan terms that will increase the demand both for credit and for new output on the part of all borrowers.

In their immediate effects direct government loans are very similar to transfer payments. Unlike transfers, however, loans must be repaid and consequently should not have as expansionary effects as outright gifts and grants. If principal repayments contract private consumption and investment to exactly the same extent as loan disbursements increase them, a loan program, over its entire lifetime, will have no effect on the total level of spending. It will, however, change the timing of private expenditures, increasing them during the early years of the loan program when credit disbursements exceed principal repayments and reducing them in later years when the reverse relationship prevails. If these are in fact the economic effects of government loans, the standard procedure adopted in the federal budget of showing only the net credit flow (i.e., disbursements minus repayments) correctly measures those effects. It may well be, however, that principal repayments do not depress private spending by as much as new loans increase it. If this is the case, disbursements and repayments should not be simply offset but should be shown separately in the government budget.

Governmental guaranties of private lenders against loss on defaulted loans may have the same economic effects as direct government loans. As a result of the shift of credit risks to the government, private lenders may not only offer loans to borrowers who otherwise would not have been able to qualify for credit but may also liberalize the terms—i.e. interest rates, terms to maturity, and down-payment requirements—on which they extend loans to anyone. In these ways a loan guaranty program can increase the flow of private credit and stimulate the demand for such things as business plant and equipment and new homes. In spite of these important effects, however, government loan guaranties will normally involve the expenditure of only very small amounts of public money. Administrative expenses will be incurred, and to the extent that borrowers default on their guarantied loans the government will have to make payments to private lenders. Unless the program is singularly unsuccessful, these payments will be only a small fraction of the total volume of loans disbursed and hence are not likely to measure the economic impact of the guaranties accurately. Regular budgetary statistics, therefore, should be adjusted to reflect the changing importance of federal loan insurance and loan guaranty programs.

Economic Effects of Government Debt Operations

The sale of government debt to private groups, like the imposition of new taxes, is a fiscal policy designed to lower the level of private spending on goods and services. Unlike taxation, which, as we have seen, discourages spending on the part of the taxpayer by lowering his disposable income, debt issue leaves money incomes unimpaired and relies for its effects on a more complicated line of developments. To some extent the appearance of a new government bond issue at attractive interest rates may simply induce private individuals to buy bonds rather than automobiles or new plant and equipment for their businesses. Since bonds are not close substitutes for either consumer goods or business capital assets, spending shifts of this sort are not likely to be widespread.

In order to sell its new securities, however, the government will have to offer them at sufficiently attractive interest rates. The increased supply of financial assets in the economy will, in other words, tend to raise interest rates, and the increased cost of borrowing is likely to discourage some private individuals from carrying out spending plans, such as the purchase of new houses. Other borrowers may be unable to obtain funds on any terms because lenders have been attracted instead to the new government bonds. Nor is this the full extent of the effects. The upward pressure on interest rates will depress the prices of all fixed-income securities (a bond yielding $4 a year being worth $100 at 4 per cent but only $80 at 5 per cent, for example), and these capital losses are likely to discourage consumption on the part of security holders. Common stock prices may also fall as investors shift into government bonds, and it is well known that a bearish stock market discourages spending, particularly on luxury goods.

The deflationary powers of debt issues, therefore, depend upon the extent to which private spending is sensitive both to capital losses on existing financial securities and to the more stringent terms on which new capital funds will be offered as a result of the increase in the public debt. Different types of spending evidently react differently to higher interest rates and tighter money conditions. While residential construction, state and local government construction expenditures, and capital outlays by small businesses are all likely to decline significantly, plant and equipment expenditures by larger businesses, credit-financed purchases of consumer durables, and inventory investment are likely to contract only slightly, if at all.[7] As an anti-inflationary fiscal policy, therefore, debt issue is far from general in its effects, and most economists regard it as considerably less effective than an equal volume of additional taxes. By taking money away from people taxes are able to have a powerful influence on private spending. Debt sales, on the other hand, not only raise prospective investor incomes but also provide investors with assets which continually become more liquid and hence more readily usable to finance the purchase of either consumer goods or business capital assets. It seems reasonable, therefore, to regard debt issue as generally less anti-inflationary than taxation.

The effects of the purchase by the government of its own debt from private holders (i.e., debt retirement) need not detain us at this point. The influence on private spending is precisely the opposite of that of debt issue, and the reader is encouraged to work out for himself the nature of the various avenues by which debt retirement tends to stimulate expenditures on consumption and investment goods.

Some effect on private spending may also be exerted by changing the maturity composition of a given amount of outstanding government debt. Suppose, for example, that the average maturity of the debt is lengthened by converting short-term issues into long-term securities. Such a policy reduces the amount of highly liquid assets in existence in the economy and may therefore induce people to try to build up their money balances in order to restore their former degree of liquidity. If the monetary authorities do not increase the total supply of money, people can be successful in their search for liquidity only by spending less money (i.e., by holding their money balances for longer periods than previously). An increase in the relative pro-

---

[7] U. S. Congress, Joint Economic Committee, *Staff Report on Employment, Growth, and Price Levels* (Washington, D.C.: Government Printing Office, 1959), pp. 362-94.

portion of long-term issues in the total outstanding public debt, therefore, is an anti-inflationary debt-management policy.

Summary and Conclusions

In this chapter the economic effects of the three major kinds of fiscal policy have been discussed briefly. Once the separate influences of taxes, expenditures, and debt operations are known, they may be combined in order to deal with composite government activities of various kinds. In practice, of course, it is extremely difficult to establish the separate effects with any degree of precision. In the absence of such quantitative information economists have built up a set of rough rules of thumb which serve as first approximations to the answers sought. Indispensable as these approximations are, they must be used with full appreciation of their limitations. It is generally held, for example, that a budget surplus used to retire part of the public debt has an anti-inflationary impact on the economy. Since debt retirement by itself has an expansionary effect, it is clear that the conclusion in question rests on the assumption that a tax surplus will reduce private demands by more than an equal amount of debt retirement will increase them. This relationship may well prevail under most circumstances, but there may also be conditions under which exactly the reverse is true.

Nor can it be taken for granted that all government purchases of goods and services have equal expansionary effects and that all taxes have equal contractionary effects. Wide individual differences may exist so that equal changes in expenditures and taxes cannot be counted upon to have offsetting influences on the private sector of the economy. Indeed, given the great increase in importance of federal loan guaranty programs in recent years, the economic effects of the federal government may change significantly even though both expenditures and tax revenues are perfectly constant and debt operations completely absent.

4

Government Budgeting

Modern governmental budgets, whose scope extends all the way from such global questions as whether missiles should replace manned aircraft for defense purposes to such minor matters as the proper purchase price for the paper clips used by a given agency, grew out of the spread of representative government and the rapid increase in the economic importance of governmental activities. Containing a systematic and comprehensive listing of government expenditures and revenues, the budget document is designed to assist the executive and the legislature both in determining the best set of programs to be adopted and in achieving the optimum level of efficiency in governmental operations. In the process, the budget also provides a wealth of quantitative information that is of interest to the general public.

In this chapter, after a brief review of the development of government budgeting in this country and a description of the budget process at the federal level, the ways in which budget procedures may improve the choice of specific expenditure and revenue programs will be discussed. The contributions which careful budgeting can make to the goal of operating given programs at minimum costs will then be assessed. In both of these important areas, it should be stressed that although good procedures can clarify the issues involved, they cannot by themselves ensure wise and responsible government actions. Only intelligent behavior on the part of a large number of individuals can do this, but well-planned budgets provide an important foundation for such behavior. Finally, the economic usefulness of budgetary data on federal expenditures and receipts will be discussed in the last section, together with the interrelationships between these statistics and similar series prepared by the Bureau of the Census and the Department of Commerce.

Development of Budgeting in the United States

Government budgets appeared relatively late in the United States, almost a century after their development in western Europe, and contrary to their history in most other countries they were established here first at the local level, then in a number of state governments, and only thereafter at the national level.[1] The lag in federal budgeting is attributable partly to the minor economic role played by the national government up to World War I and partly to the large surpluses generated by the tariff during the last part of the nineteenth century. Needless to say, a government whose main fiscal problem was to find ways of spending its excess revenues felt little need for detailed budgetary controls.

Municipal budgeting developed rapidly in the United States during the first part of the present century, and by the mid-1920's most major cities had reformed their financial practices through the establishment of budget systems. These changes were greatly stimulated by conservative businessmen who, concerned about the increase in local tax burdens, saw in budgeting a means of reducing government expenditures. The movement also gained support from various groups of reformers who were alarmed by the widespread existence of graft and corruption and wanted to transform municipal governments into effective instruments for the improvement of social welfare. When a political innovation can command the support of people with such widely different viewpoints and aims, it is likely to be adopted relatively quickly, and this indeed turned out to be the case with municipal budgeting.

Essentially the same forces supported subsequent budget movements at the state and federal levels. A major step was taken in 1910 when President Taft appointed the Commission on Economy and Efficiency, which during the next two years made the first detailed study of the nature of federal expenditures and of the federal organizational structure. The work of the commission greatly stimulated interest in budgeting at all levels of government, and a federal budget system was finally established by the Budget and Accounting Act of 1921. Since that time numerous improvements have been made in the budget document, so that anyone interested in tracing a given federal activity over a number of years must be prepared for changes

[1] For further details see Jesse Burkhead, *Government Budgeting* (New York: John Wiley & Sons, 1956), pp. 2-30.

in both format and scope that make long-period comparisons difficult, and occasionally impossible. The nature and sources of these improvements cannot be specified here, but mention may be made of the Commission on Organization of the Executive Branch of the Government (Hoover Commission), which in the late 1940's made a comprehensive study of the federal budget process and recommended extensive reforms in it. As in the case of the 1910 commission, legislative enactment of the Hoover recommendations has been both slow and incomplete. The influence of the commission, however, has by no means disappeared, and future years may well see more of its reforms put into operation.

The Federal Budget Process

Government budgeting begins in the executive branch with the preparation of new expenditure, tax, and debt programs and the estimation (consistent with economic forecasts) of expected government expenditures and revenues for the coming fiscal year. The process continues in the legislature with the enactment of laws authorizing new programs and the appropriation of money for those and already existing programs; it then returns to the executive for execution, and ends with an audit of completed transactions to determine whether or not legislative intentions have been carried out. The details of these four phases naturally vary from one government to another. The federal budget process, however, is sufficiently important and sufficiently similar to those of other governmental levels to warrant detailed discussion and evaluation.

Federal budgeting is a continuous activity. Indeed, since it takes approximately twenty-seven months from the initial planning to the final execution of the budget, different phases of the process are typically going on concurrently. Preparation and congressional enactment alone ordinarily take more than a year, and this slowness of pace frequently means that budgeting is unresponsive to changing economic conditions and program requirements.

PHASE I—EXECUTIVE PREPARATION AND SUBMISSION. The federal budget process begins fourteen months or more before the start of the fiscal year to which the document is to apply. At that time all federal agencies prepare preliminary estimates of their expected (or hoped for) expenditures. These estimates pass through higher organizational units to the Bureau of the Budget, which, armed with revenue estimates prepared by the Treasury Department and with economic forecasts made by the Council of Economic Advisers, the Federal Reserve System, and other federal departments, begins in early summer to set tentative expenditure ceilings in line with presidential program objectives. These broad policy decisions are then transmitted back to the departments and agencies, where final expenditure estimates are prepared during the rest of the summer. In spite of modern air conditioning this may be hot work, especially if relatively stringent ceilings have been imposed from the top. The estimates which emerge need not conform with presidential targets, but all excess requests must be justified before specialized examiners in the Bureau of the Budget during hearings at which detailed reviews of all final agency estimates are made. On the basis of these hearings, which take place from September to December, the budget examiners prepare recommendations for the Director of the Bureau of the Budget. The first phase then ends with a final review by the Director and the President, the preparation of the latter's budget message, and the transmission of the finished document to the Congress, usually during the third week of January.

PHASE II—LEGISLATIVE REVIEW AND AUTHORIZATION. Budget day in the United States Congress lacks most of the drama associated with that occasion in Great Britain or in other countries with a parliamentary system of government. A carefully guarded secret until the presentation of the budget, proposed changes in British tax and expenditure programs elicit great public interest on Budget Day because they will almost certainly be enacted without alteration by the parliament.[2] In the United States, on the other hand, Congress is likely to make extensive changes in the President's budget recommendations.

Legislative review begins in hearings held before various subcommittees of the House Committee on Appropriations, at which the executive agencies and departments defend and discuss their expenditure requests. These hearings are frequently lengthy, and full opportunity is given subcommittee members to praise or criticize agency programs. As finally printed the record contains much valuable information about federal activities, but it is no small research project to separate it from the great mass of unimportant detail that is always present. Non-subcommittee members, therefore, have only limited opportunities to understand the programs being dealt with.

After their hearings the subcommittees recommend appropriations for purposes already authorized by legislation, and these proposals, in the form of individual bills, are considered by the full House Appropriations Committee, which seldom makes any modifications. Nor is the final debate on the floor of the House likely to be extensive;

---

[2] On rare occasions the budget proposals, together with the government in power, will be defeated, and a new election must then be called.

appropriation bills are typically passed unchanged and sent to the Senate for further review. Senate procedures are the same as those followed by the House, but attention tends to be centered on the differences between the appropriations requested by the President and the actions taken by the House. In recent years the typical pattern has been a substantial cut in appropriations by the House, a restoration of most or all of these cuts by the Senate, and a final compromise worked out in a joint conference committee and passed by both houses.

The appropriation bill then goes to the President, who may veto it *in toto* but not in part, sign it without comment, or combine his signature with a message pointing out what he considers to be the deficiencies in the legislation. Lack of an item veto means that presidents are frequently forced to accept programs of which they disapprove in order to provide for other programs which they accept, so appropriations measures are rarely vetoed.

It will be noted that congressional review of budget expenditures takes place mainly in the appropriations subcommittees. Individual congressmen may attempt to evaluate specific programs insofar as their staffs are able to assemble the necessary information in the time available, but consideration above the subcommittee level is ordinarily perfunctory. Appropriation bills, furthermore, are taken up separately, and there is no machinery for a careful weighing of one expenditure program against another or a balancing of all expenditures against total revenues.

The President's budget is primarily concerned with appropriations and expenditures, and little attention is given to either tax or debt policy. In a 1960 budget message of seventy-four pages, for example, analysis of budget receipts took only three pages, and proposed changes in the management of the public debt took only one page. Most of the staff work on the Administration's tax program is done in the Treasury Department, and it is the Secretary of the Treasury, rather than the President, who transmits these proposals to the Congress and defends them there.

Since the House of Representatives has the exclusive power to originate tax legislation, the first formal step in the tax-making process is the decision of the Committee on Ways and Means to take up such legislation and (ordinarily) to hold public hearings on it. The initiative, of course, may come from elsewhere, perhaps from the President or from a group of other congressmen, but consideration by the Ways and Means Committee is indispensable. At the hearings witnesses who generally represent organized economic groups, present their views on the proposed legislation and on tax burdens in general. With few exceptions each group advocates a reduction in its own taxes, and if all taxpayers were equally well represented, the arguments might simply offset each other in the aggregate. In practice, however, some witnesses make better cases than others, and some groups in the country are not represented at all, except insofar as the Treasury Department considers their interests in its own testimony. As a result some observers have felt that the general public interest has not been adequately represented in the tax-making process.[3] In recent years, however, both the Joint Economic Committee and the House Ways and Means Committee have sponsored detailed and comprehensive analyses of the federal tax structure from all points of view, the Ways and Means Committee's 1959 *Compendium of Papers on Broadening the Tax Base* being a three-volume work of almost 2,400 pages.[4] Both the papers themselves and the hearings conducted on them considerably broaden the range of information and viewpoints available to congressmen.

When the Ways and Means Committee decides on the specific terms of its tax bill, it issues a report which, by describing the law in relatively simple language and giving the committee's reasons for recommending it, becomes an important public document. On its way to passage, a tax bill faces hurdles similar to those confronting any new law—passage by the House, consideration and approval (with or without amendments) by the Senate Committee on Finance, passage by the Senate, revision where necessary in a joint House-Senate conference committee, passage in revised form by both houses, and finally acceptance by the President.

PHASE III—EXECUTION. With a few major exceptions, such as foreign aid, spending authority is given directly to the relevant agencies and departments rather than to the President or the Bureau of the Budget. The Bureau, however, exercises administrative control by apportioning authorizations to the operating agencies, frequently on a quarterly basis. This procedure is designed to guard against the danger of an agency's spending all of its funds early in the fiscal year and then having to plead for deficiency or supplemental appropriations to keep its programs alive. In addition, the Budget Bureau may, in line with the President's wishes, attempt to curtail expenditures by holding up apportionments.

[3] See, for example, Roy Blough, *The Federal Taxing Process* (New York: Prentice-Hall, Inc., 1952), p. 41.

[4] U. S. Congress, Committee on Ways and Means, *Tax Revision Compendium: Compendium of Papers on Broadening the Tax Base* (Washington, D.C.: Government Printing Office, 1959). See also the Joint Economic Committee's *Federal Tax Policy for Economic Growth and Stability* (Washington, D.C.: Government Printing Office, 1956).

Having received their budget authorizations, government agencies may place orders for goods and services and thereby commit themselves to spend money. These commitments are known as *obligations* and constitute, as we shall see in the last section of this chapter, an important source of economic information. Finally, as creditors present their bills, administrative officers certify the transaction, and disbursing officers issue payment checks. Since checks are not always cashed immediately, measurements of federal expenditures will differ somewhat, depending upon whether they are based on "checks issued" or "checks cashed."[5]

PHASE IV—AUDIT. Each agency or department to which appropriations are made is itself responsible for complying with the law. Through the Comptroller General, who heads the General Accounting Office, however, Congress has an independent check of its own. The GAO carries out audits both to forestall illegal and irregular transactions and to determine whether funds were spent in accordance with legislative intentions. An annual report on these activities, together with the results of special investigations made by the GAO from time to time into financial affairs and administration, is submitted to the House and Senate committees on government operations for their information and consideration.

Problems of Effective Programming

Rational decisions concerning the proper amount and kinds of government expenditures, taxes, and debt operations must rest, as noted in the preceding chapter, on detailed comparisons of the benefits of one program with those of another, on similar comparisons of program costs, and on the assessment of the economic effects of different aggregate levels of expenditures, taxes, and the public debt. As we have seen, the federal budget process does little to facilitate evaluations of this sort. In this section we shall consider possible solutions to this problem.

THE LEGISLATIVE BUDGET OF 1946-1948. In the Legislative Reorganization Act of 1946 Congress created a Joint Committee on the Legislative Budget which was to meet early in each session and, after considering the President's budget, was to set ceilings on both appropriations and expenditures. When adopted by both houses, these ceilings were to be binding on the actions of the appropriations

---

[5] In 1954 the reporting of all budget expenditures was put on a "checks issued" basis. See Sidney G. Tickton, *The Budget in Transition,* Planning Pamphlet No. 89 (Washington, D.C.: National Planning Association, 1955), pp. 26-28.

committees for the remainder of the session. It was hoped that this procedure would keep federal expenditures within strict bounds, but in 1947 agreement could not be reached on the appropriate ceiling, and although a 1948 ceiling was set, it was not observed in subsequent legislation. After this discouraging experience the legislative budget was not used in the 1949 session, and it has not been revived since.

The principal difficulty with the legislative budget was that by starting with an appropriation total and ending with the detailed consideration of specific programs it reversed the logical budget procedure of building totals from their component parts. On the other hand, a legislative budget that was derived in the proper way would duplicate much of the work of the executive branch, and hence might well increase, rather than reduce, government expenditures. One aspect of the 1946-48 experiment—namely a full-scale congressional debate on the budget as a whole—is widely regarded, however, as a desirable feature of the federal budget process.

THE JOINT BUDGET POLICY CONFERENCE. The Committee for Economic Development (CED) has recommended the formation of a small Joint Budget Policy Conference made up of congressional leaders and representatives of the appropriations and revenue committees of both houses.[6] This body would meet several times during each session to consider the relationships between projected federal expenditures and taxes and to discuss the effects of these on economic stability and growth. Although reports might be issued from time to time for congressional consideration, the Conference would be expected to exert most of its influence informally, through its members in the appropriations and revenue committees, as well as elsewhere in Congress. By these means the CED hopes that greater congressional attention would be focused upon current fiscal policy and the long-run effects of the budget.

It will be noted that, unlike the Committee on the Legislative Budget, the Joint Budget Policy Conference would issue no appropriations ceilings to bind subsequent congressional action, its role being entirely advisory. The functions proposed for the Conference are closely related to the activities of the Joint Economic Committee, which considers the President's annual Economic Report and studies various means of achieving an optimal amount of economic stability and growth, and some observers have recommended the consolidation of the two bodies. Joint Economic Committee members, however, are not necessarily strategically located throughout Congress, and it

[6] Committee for Economic Development, *Control of Federal Government Expenditures* (Jan., 1955).

seems essential to set up some means whereby congressional leaders and the chairmen of the four finance committees can review the budget as a whole.

THE OMNIBUS APPROPRIATIONS BILL. If appropriations for different programs are to be balanced against one another and considered in relation to total tax burdens, a single consolidated appropriations bill is a natural suggestion. One was tried by the House in 1950, but because of delays—the bill was not signed by the President until two months after the beginning of the 1951 fiscal year—the practice was abandoned the next year and has not been reinstated. Critics of the device argue that it gives too little time for consideration of appropriations on the floor of the House and in the Senate and thereby encourages flat, across-the-board percentage cuts which ignore the relative importance of different programs. In addition, the executive veto power is weakened because a President is likely to be reluctant to delay the appropriation of funds for all agencies by rejecting a single bill arriving late in the session. An omnibus bill, therefore, would invite legislative riders and "pork-barrel" amendments. This difficulty could, of course, be removed by granting the President an item veto, a budget reform which has long been advocated.[7]

In evaluating the omnibus appropriations bill one should remember that it has only been tried once and then in a year dominated by the outbreak of the Korean War. It may be that excessive delays are inherent in the method, but this can only be determined on the basis of further experimentation. A gradual moving of separate appropriations bills closer and closer together in time, as suggested by the CED, appears to be a promising procedure.

CAPITAL BUDGETS. A dual budget system which treats current and capital outlays differently is used in a number of countries, such as Sweden, Ecuador, and the Union of South Africa, and has frequently been advocated as a means of improving government programming in this country. In general the procedure would be to set up a capital budget to cover physical and financial assets expected to yield the government a return in future years and to place all other expenditures in a separate current or operating budget. A system of depreciation accounting could then be initiated, so that the value of all government owned capital assets would be written down as they wore out, and these depreciation allowances would be incorporated each year in the operating budget as expenditures. The current budget, therefore, would spread the cost of a durable asset, such as a public dam, evenly over the different years of its useful life rather

[7] Discussed more fully at a later point in this section.

than recording these costs, as is done in a unitary budget, all in the period of construction.

The first difficulty with capital budgeting lies in the distinction between capital and current items. Although some expenditures can readily be classified on this basis—a new highway, for example, will provide services for many years to come, whereas a secretary's salary buys services in the current year only—other expenditures cannot. A government scientist may provide services which will benefit the country over a long period of time, and education expenditures may increase future levels of national income even more than outlays for buildings or dams. The singling out of capital expenditures, therefore, is necessarily an arbitrary process, and this difficulty reduces the usefulness of capital budgets.

Were this the only problem, a federal capital budget might still be widely accepted as a desirable reform because of the increased information it would make available as to government capital formation and net wealth. The establishment of a separate capital budget, however, would carry a strong presumption that capital outlays should be financed by borrowing, as distinct from current expenditures, which would be financed by taxation; and if fiscal policy did become rigidified in this way, its ability to stabilize prices and employment and to contribute to economic growth would be materially reduced. Capital budgeting has its greatest attractions during a depression, when the need for expansionary fiscal policies may be stalemated by public dislike of the deficits that would result from such policies under a unitary budget system. With a capital budget, expenditures on durable assets could be expanded without unbalancing the current operating budget.[8] It might well be, however, that the economy would be in greater need either of private goods and services or of noncapital public expenditures. Unless the general public simply cannot be educated to accept government deficits during periods of high-level unemployment, and there is little evidence that this is the case, anti-depression fiscal policies should be selected not only for their effects on employment but also with an eye to the kinds of increased output best suited to the needs of the time.

Since borrowing is ordinarily less deflationary than taxation, capital budgeting, if rigidly adhered to, would increase the inflationary pressures that develop during rapid economic expansions. At such times it may be desirable not only to finance all capital expenditures by taxation but even to make total tax revenues greater than government expenditures of all kinds. The latent inflationary bias of capital

---

[8] In later years, of course, the operating budget would have to absorb annual depreciation charges on the newly acquired capital assets.

budgets is particularly dangerous for underdeveloped countries since, given their limited private financial markets, new government securities must in large part be sold to a banking system empowered to create the money necessary to buy them. Since many poor countries already exhibit a chronic tendency toward inflation, their need is for more taxation and less borrowing, rather than the reverse.

Capital budgets, then, are subject to a number of important drawbacks. Fortunately, at the federal level, where these defects are the most serious, a unitary budget system can provide the same advantages as capital budgeting—namely, the supplying of quantitative information about government gross and net capital formation in order to facilitate internal management and control and to permit more realistic public evaluations of government operations. A major step in achieving these aims was taken in 1946 when a special analysis called "Federal Activities in Public Works and Other Construction" was included in the budget document for the first time. Depreciation estimates are not available for durable government assets, and hence net capital formation cannot be computed for the federal government, but the special budget analyses do show that gross expenditures for public works during the 1950's rose from a low of $2.2 billion at the beginning to a high of $6.7 billion at the end. Finally, it may be noted that business-style budgets, showing asset acquisitions and annual depreciation charges, are used for most federal enterprise operations.

Since state and local governments have fewer responsibilities for the stabilization of economic activity, the drawbacks of capital budgeting are less serious for them than for the federal government. At the same time, some of the advantages of capital budgets are frequently more important, particularly to the smaller governmental units. In the first place, the irregular timing of capital expenditures is more likely to destabilize a small than a large budget, and capital budgeting can eliminate the sudden changes in tax laws which an annually balanced unitary budget would require in the presence of widely fluctuating total expenditures. Not only are frequent changes in the tax structure troublesome to the legislature, but they also make long-range business planning more difficult and consequently may reduce the level of private capital formation. Secondly, state and local credit ratings need very careful handling, and a capital budget, insofar as it stimulates orderly financial planning and resource development, will make an important contribution to this end. As a result a considerable number of cities have adopted capital budgeting, and New York State has a Capital Construction Fund that is used to facilitate the budgetary appraisal of all new construction projects.

PUBLIC ENTERPRISES AND SPECIAL FUNDS. The extent to which the activities of public enterprises are controlled by regular budgetary procedures is subject to wide variation. Since these governmental undertakings obtain revenues of their own from the sale of goods and services, they may at the one extreme be fiscally and administratively independent of both the executive and legislative branches of the government. Programming decisions in such cases are made by a separate group of public officials. Many public authorities operating in this country under state law fall in this category. Federal corporations, on the other hand, must prepare and submit for review to the Bureau of the Budget, the President, and the Congress detailed budget accounts similar to the income and expense statements and balance sheets used by private business. In addition, the Comptroller General conducts a commercial-style audit and reports any irregularities to Congress. Although clearly greater than that accorded independent public authorities, budgetary control of federal corporations is not so restrictive as it is for other government programs, since federal enterprises may use their own revenues to finance further operations. To this extent they are free of control by congressional appropriations committees.

The degree to which government enterprises should be subject to centralized control is the same difficult question which faces the management of any large-scale undertaking, public or private. On the one hand, a high degree of centralization can produce consistency in policies and operations so that during an inflation, for example, some government programs are not expanding while others are being contracted in order to lessen upward pressures on prices. On the other hand, efficient management of public corporations, like that of the separate divisions of a large private business, may require decentralization and freedom from bureaucratic restrictions imposed from the top. It is interesting to note in this connection that in Great Britain, in spite of its tradition of strong Cabinet leadership and centralized executive control, public corporations are typically more independent than they are in this country.[9]

Government agencies which cannot sell their services at a price, and hence cannot function as public enterprises, can still be more or less removed from regular budgetary reviews. Ordinarily this is done by setting up a special fund and earmarking specific revenues to finance it. The purpose may be to approximate the operations of a public enterprise by taxing the people who benefit from the program in question, or it may simply be to remove the program from the

[9] Burkhead, *op. cit.,* pp. 405-11.

political uncertainties of regular budgetary review. The earmarking of gasoline taxes for highway construction illustrates both of these purposes, although as we shall see later, there is doubt about how well gasoline taxes allocate highway costs according to benefits received.[10] Special funds may also be useful in underdeveloped countries where people are reluctant to pay taxes because they fail to perceive the benefits to be received. Since the need for additional taxation to prevent inflation is likely to be difficult to sell, the government may be able to get support for its proposed new taxes by tying them to the financing of public projects which the people either already want or will want when the benefits are explained to them.

The difficulties with special funds are twofold: being free of regular budgetary review, their operations may be continued long after public tastes have shifted away from their services to other public or private goods; and being assured of ample revenues, their management may become lax and inefficient. In essence, a special fund represents a long-term commitment to a particular program, the value of which in relation to alternative public or private expenditures will be reviewed only at very irregular intervals. A government which makes extensive use of earmarked revenues may consequently find its freedom of action severely restricted, and may be forced under conditions of financial stringency to cut back programs of greater public importance than some of those protected by special funds.[11]

THE ITEM VETO. Presidential power to accept some items in an appropriations bill but to veto others has long been advocated as a means of improving federal programming. Too frequently, it is argued, has Congress attached to appropriations bills provisions known to be objectionable to the President in the hope that he would refuse to veto the entire bill in order to kill one small part of it. By strengthening the power of the executive, however, an item veto would not necessarily improve the process by which federal programs are selected and rejected. At certain times the legislature may be more responsive to public desires, while at other times, the executive may be. Abuses are possible on both sides: the President might use the item veto as a weapon against individual congressmen, whereas legislators might put forward appropriation items favorable to their constituents solely to force the President, to his own political disadvantage, to veto them. The case for an item veto, then, is by no means a simple

[10] Chap. 13.

[11] The earmarking of the pari-mutuel tax revenues in California provides an interesting example. Sole beneficiary of a 4 per cent levy on betting pools is the State Fair and Exposition Fund, which basks in increasing affluence as a result.

one, and its adoption at the federal level is likely to remain a controversial issue.

LENGTH OF THE PROGRAMMING HORIZON. Congressmen and others frequently complain about the difficulties involved in making rapid reductions in the level of federal spending. Large-scale programs cannot be authorized and put into operation overnight. Often many months or even years are spent in drawing up plans and making preparations before a project really gets underway. Hence at any given moment in time there are many appropriations which will not be spent until the following fiscal year, though they have already been authorized. Still other expenditures are part of continuing programs and cannot be cut back by Congress without basic legislative revisions. Curtailing expenditures, therefore, tends to be a slow process.

Given the problem of significant time lags between the passage of the bill authorizing a program and the spending of the money, effective programming must take carefully into account the long-range involvements and the relationship between the expected outlays in future years and the likely fiscal requirements of those years. Particularly in such programs as national defense and public works, attention should be directed to the entire spending stream, regardless of how remote some of the expenditures in question may be.[12]

SUMMARY. In spite of the assistance which decision-makers can draw from modern techniques of statistical and economic analysis, government budgeting remains an art resembling that of a juggler or a tightrope walker. General appropriations by the legislature may leave the executive too much freedom to depart from the original intention of the law; specific and detailed appropriations, on the other hand, may defeat the purposes of a program by so restricting its execution that necessary adaptations to changing circumstances cannot be made. If requests for deficiency appropriations are granted rarely or are forbidden outright, administrators may react by padding their original requests for funds or by sacrificing valuable services which could have been provided at little additional cost; if deficiency appropriations are granted readily, however, faulty planning, management, and cost control may develop in many executive agencies. The budget document itself should contain neither so much information that programmers become bogged down in insignificant detail nor so little that rational decisions concerning the desirability of different programs cannot be made.

[12] Cf. Burkhead, *op. cit.,* pp. 316-21, and Roland N. McKean, *Efficiency in Government Through Systems Analysis* (New York: John Wiley & Sons, 1958), chap. xiii.

Still other difficulties in the way of effective governmental programming have been mentioned above. Although procedural changes of the sort considered can serve a useful purpose, little can be accomplished if government personnel are not of high quality. Higher salaries for legislators and civil servants may not only result in a better choice of government programs, but paradoxically enough, may even reduce government expenditures in the long run by increasing the efficiency of its operations.

Efficiency of Operation

Spectacular instances of government waste are uncovered at more or less regular intervals, both by those who are attempting to improve governmental efficiency and by those who like to raise the blood pressure of long-suffering taxpayers in the hope that they will rebel and force a significant curtailment of public activities. The Navy, for example, has been known to pay $2 for a 1-cent gasket, thereby providing its supplier with a 20,000 per cent gross profit,[13] and in 1960 military hospitals were so numerous that their beds were less than 40 per cent occupied. An Air Force base of 400 men in Germany once dispatched an order for 300 footlockers, which grew in transit to 30,000, and this number was shipped from Texas and Tennessee without any questions as to the need for such a quantity and in spite of the fact that thousands of footlockers were already available at an Army supply depot elsewhere in Germany.[14] It is no wonder that many people have come to regard the government as a model of bureaucratic inefficiency and to despair of ever seeing anything done about it.

Yet exactly the same problems afflict many large-scale private businesses, as any efficiency expert will testify, and solutions to them can be and are found in most instances. Even granted that the government is in some respects a different kind of enterprise, it would be surprising if similar improvements could not be made in its operations. In this section we shall consider the contributions which budgeting procedures can make in this area.

PERFORMANCE BUDGETS. Since optimal efficiency requires that a given amount of output be produced by using the smallest possible volume of resources (or, alternatively, that a given supply of resources be organized so as to yield the largest possible amount of output), quantitative measures of the relationships prevailing between inputs

[13] Paul H. Douglas, *Economy in the National Government* (Chicago: Univ. of Chicago Press, 1952), p. 172.
[14] *Wall Street Journal,* May 2, 1960, pp. 1, 12.

and outputs in different governmental programs are indispensable. The process by which such measures are derived, known as performance budgeting, is seldom free from formidable difficulties, and its use in this country is still in a rudimentary stage.

One difficulty is that many government services are intangible in form and hence virtually impossible to measure objectively. Consider, for example, the benefits received from the federal diplomatic corps or from state and local schools and universities. In the first case there might even be disagreement as to whether any benefit at all was received, and in the second the amount of education clearly varies not only with the average number of years spent in school but also with the quality of the services received. An increase in the educational output-to-input ratio (i.e., in the number of students per teacher), therefore, may represent a decrease, rather than an increase, in the efficiency of the public schools.

Even when the flow of physical services is more readily identified, the fact that they are not sold at a price to the public may make valuation a highly arbitrary procedure. What, for instance, is the value of the services rendered by the nation's highways and streets? In other cases, however, comparable prices are available in the private sector of the economy. Take expenditures for forest-fire control by the federal Forest Service, one of the benefits of which is the saving of timber which could be sold on the lumber market. Prices for the different types and grades of trees can be obtained, and provided the federal sales would not be large enough in relation to total timber sales in any period of time to influence market prices materially, those prices can be used for valuation purposes. The amount of timber saved by the Forest Service must still, of course, be measured by estimating the losses that would be suffered in the absence of fire control expenditures and subtracting the average losses that occur under the existing program. Needless to say, errors are possible in such procedures because of the use of hypothetical figures.[15]

As a result of these and other problems, the development of performance budgets has been a slow and painful process. Valuable results have already been obtained, however, and further substantial gains are highly likely. Measurements of the volume of forms processed or letters written per employee can readily be made and will help administrators evaluate the performance of their own agencies. Even when hypothetical estimates are required, a presentation of reasonable alternatives will frequently make possible a better evaluation than one based on no quantitative measures at all.

15 For a detailed analysis of this kind of problem see McKean, *op. cit.,* chap. xiii.

In addition to their value to the administrator, performance budgets can aid legislators and top-level officials in the executive branch in their review of government programs. In the first place, input-output measures provide a basis for rewarding administrators with a high efficiency rating and for putting pressure on those whose agencies have become lax and wasteful. Incentives of this sort must be provided if government economy is to be achieved. In their absence, the prestige and salary of the administrator are likely to increase with the size of his establishment rather than with the efficiency attained in its operations, and there is a natural human tendency to avoid whenever possible the painful task of reorganizing well-established work habits and firing unproductive employees. A second use of performance budgets is to provide the quantitative basis for decisions to expand some programs and to contract others. For this purpose measures are needed of comparable gains and losses at the margin—that is, of the benefits to be received by expanding expenditures on program X by $1 million and of the losses to be suffered by reducing expenditures on program Y by a similar amount.

SUMMARY. Since performance budgeting is designed to increase efficiency in government, it may have very important economic results. With its help we can have either more government output at a given cost or a given output at a lower cost, and hence more private goods without the sacrifice of any public ones. In either case national output is increased and economic welfare improved. In the attainment of these gains, however, two relatively minor problems may arise. The first has to do with the effects of increased efficiency on government employment. In contrast to gradual improvements in efficiency, which can usually be handled by hiring fewer new employees each year, sudden economy drives mean the discharge, sometimes in large numbers, of workers who must then seek alternative employment for their talents. The economic gains of the efficiency drive, in the latter situation, will depend on the rapidity with which these people can be put back to work. The second problem has to do with people who are inherently inefficient workers. When all avenues for their personal improvement have been exhausted, no more can be accomplished. The discharge of such people from government service will, of course, increase government efficiency, but re-employment of them in the private sector will make for greater waste there. Such shifts, therefore, have nothing to recommend them, and indeed it may be preferable to have inefficient workers steadily employed in public service than continuously shifting from one private job to another with all of the psychological and economic losses which such a procedure inevitably involves. This is not to suggest that the government should employ every substandard worker but simply that the solution is to be found not in leaving such people to shift about but in attempts to improve their working efficiencies.

Provision of Quantitative Information

In addition to its primary functions of improving programming and raising the level of operating efficiency, government budgeting generates an extensive flow of quantitative information that is of interest to layman and expert alike. Although the nature of the available statistics has already been indicated in Chapter 2, nothing has been said concerning the interrelationships among the different series.

ADMINISTRATIVE AND CASH BUDGETS. The regular, or administrative, federal budget, which in the past has received the lion's share of public attention, covers only part of the government's total activities. Omitted from it are such important programs as federal old-age and survivors insurance, unemployment insurance, and the construction of the 41,000-mile National System of Interstate and Defense Highways. Although appropriate for administrative purposes, since the activities in question are organized as trust funds with their own revenues and management, this procedure makes budget receipts and expenditures seriously incomplete as measures of the fiscal activities of the federal government.

To repair this deficiency, the consolidated cash budget, showing total federal receipts from and payments to the public, was developed. In addition to including all trust fund activities, the cash budget excludes various intragovernmental transactions. Payments by the Treasury of interest on federal securities held by the social security trust funds, for example, increases both budget expenditures and trust fund receipts, but since the transaction is from one federal agency to another, it should not be included in consolidated measures of federal receipts and expenditures. Finally, a limited number of budget expenditures that are reported on an accrual basis must be shifted to a cash basis before being included in total federal payments to the public. In the regular budget, for example, interest on savings bonds is counted as an expenditure as it accrues to the credit of individual bondholders. This interest, on the other hand, does not become a cash payment by the government until the bondholders decide to cash in their holdings, and at that time the total interest paid is included in the cash budget. By thus aggregating all federal payments and receipts, the consolidated cash budget provides the basic framework for monetary and economic analysis.

The extent of the difference between the two federal budgets may be seen by noting that in fiscal 1959, when budget receipts were only $68 billion, total cash receipts were nearly $82 billion, and in that same year cash payments were $95 billion as compared with budget expenditures of $81 billion. Not only have cash payments and receipts been larger, but the relationship between them has been radically different from that between budget receipts and expenditures. Since in the postwar period federal trust funds have typically received more funds than they have spent, the consolidated cash budget showed a surplus of nearly $6 billion between mid-1946 and mid-1959, whereas the administrative budget indicated a deficit of nearly $25 billion (Table 4–1). Among the individually notable years of this

TABLE 4–1

FEDERAL BUDGET AND CASH SURPLUSES AND DEFICITS,
BY FISCAL YEAR, 1947-1959

(billions of dollars)

Fiscal Year	Budget Surplus or Deficit (—)	Consolidated Cash Surplus or Deficit (—)
1947	0.8	6.6
1948	8.4	8.9
1949	—1.8	1.0
1950	—3.1	—2.2
1951	3.5	7.6
1952	—4.0	0.1
1953	—9.4	—5.3
1954	—3.1	—0.2
1955	—4.2	—2.7
1956	1.6	4.5
1957	1.6	2.1
1958	—2.8	—1.5
1959	—12.4	—13.1
Totals	—24.9	5.8

Source: United States Budgets

period were 1949 and 1952, when substantial budget deficits were matched by cash surpluses, and 1959, the first year in which the cash deficit exceeded the deficit shown in the administrative budget. It is clear, therefore, that one's impression of the postwar monetary and economic effects of federal receipts and expenditures would be seriously distorted if he looked only at the administrative budget.

RELATION OF CASH SURPLUSES AND DEFICITS TO FEDERAL DEBT OPERATIONS. Federal cash surpluses may be used either to retire part of the public debt or to increase Treasury money balances. In fiscal 1951, for example, $1.8 billion of the $7.6 billion surplus was added to federal cash holdings, and the rest ($5.8 billion) went to retire outstanding federal securities. Alternatively, as occurred in 1957, a cash surplus ($2.1 billion) and a decline in Treasury balances ($1 billion) may be combined in order to retire a larger amount of public debt ($3.1 billion).

Similar relationships prevail between cash deficits and federal debt operations. In 1953 a deficit of $5 billion was financed about equally by debt sales and a reduction in Treasury cash balances, and in 1950 Treasury balances were increased by $2 billion in spite of a deficit of $2.2 billion by means of total debt sales of $4.2 billion.

The basic equation with which we are dealing here may be stated as follows:

Federal cash surplus or deficit (—)	PLUS	Net cash borrowing or repayment (—)	EQUALS	Increase or decrease (—) in Treasury cash balances

Since cash borrowing from, or repayment to, the Federal Reserve banks has economic effects that are different from those of debt operations involving private individuals or groups,[16] this equation must be expanded for purposes of economic analysis to separate these two types of debt operations.

SPECIAL BUDGETARY ANALYSES. In addition to the consolidated cash budget, the federal budget document contains a number of very useful special analyses. We have already noted the annual summary of federal activities in public works and other types of construction, and along with it in recent years have been included analyses of federal research and development programs, operations in foreign currencies, federal credit programs, and federal aid to state and local governments. Each of these provides an important source of information for anyone interested in the areas covered.

NATIONAL INCOME AND CENSUS MEASURES OF GOVERNMENT OPERATIONS. Government budgets are not the only source of quantitative information concerning federal, state, and local expenditures and revenues. Both the national income accounts, prepared by the Office of Business Economics in the Department of Commerce, and a number of annual publications of the Bureau of the Census[17] contain governmental statistics which are at least as useful as those contained

16 See the discussion in chap. 22 below.
17 See below, p. 102.

in budget documents. In this section the principal differences among the series in question will be summarized.

The national income version of federal receipts and expenditures differs from total federal cash receipts and payments (as shown in the consolidated cash budget) in six main ways:

1. National income measures are for calendar, rather than fiscal, years.
2. The District of Columbia is included with state and local governments in the national income accounts.
3. Contributions to the veterans' life insurance funds and to federal employee retirement funds, which are omitted as intragovernmental transactions from the consolidated cash budget, are included in national income measures of both federal receipts and expenditures.
4. Federal receipts and payments of interest are shown partly on a gross basis in the cash budget (i.e., receipts are included on the revenue side and payments on the expenditure side) but always on a net basis (i.e., only the difference between receipts and payments is given) in the national income accounts.
5. Federal transactions are converted for national income purposes from a cash to an accrual basis. Measures of corporate income taxes, for example, apply to the period over which the liability of the corporation increases, and not, as in the cash budget, to the period in which the money is actually transferred to the Treasury.
6. Federal purchases of land and existing assets, as well as loans to private groups, are excluded from the national income version of federal expenditures; similarly, sales of property and principal repayments on loans are both excluded from federal receipts in the national income accounts.[18]

Like the federal cash budget, Census publications show government expenditures and revenues for fiscal years, mostly on a cash basis, and with intragovernmental transfers excluded. Unlike the cash budget and the national income accounts, which show government enterprises on a net basis (i.e., with receipts cancelled against expenditures), Census measures treat public utilities and state-owned liquor stores on a gross basis. Finally, it may be noted that transactions of the joint federal-state unemployment insurance funds are included by the Census Bureau with other state government measures, but are placed in the federal sector by both the cash budget and the national income accounts.[19]

[18] For a detailed analysis of these six differences see Marilyn Young, "The Government Sector: a Reconciliation of Alternative Budget Concepts," in *Problems in the International Comparison of Economic Accounts* ("National Bureau of Economic Research Studies in Income and Wealth," Vol. XX [Princeton: Princeton Univ. Press, 1957]), pp. 135-216.

[19] For a convenient summary of the importance of the differences discussed in this section see U. S. Department of Commerce, *U. S. Income and Output* (Washington, D.C.: Government Printing Office, 1958), pp. 178-79.

USE OF GOVERNMENT STATISTICS FOR ECONOMIC ANALYSIS. There can be no doubt that students of public finance in this country are provided with a wide variety of statistical information upon which to base their economic analyses. Such studies, however, require numerous refinements of the available data, and although the detailed nature of these adjustments can only be taken up in later chapters, their general characteristics may be summarized at this point.

1. *Differential Effects on Output, Employment, and Prices.* Although as a first approximation, taxes and expenditures are widely assumed to have exactly opposing economic effects, so that a government surplus is regarded as having a deflationary, and a deficit an expansionary or inflationary, effect on the economic system, there is no justification for stopping the analysis at this point. Not only may different taxes induce widely differing reductions in the level of private spending, but some expenditure programs may expand private employment much more rapidly and extensively than others.[20] Moreover, the economic significance of a given budget deficit is one thing if it is financed by money creation and quite another if it is matched by the sale of an equal amount of long-term debt to private investors. Similarly, the economic effects of government surpluses will differ, depending upon whether the excess cash is added to Treasury balances or returned to the private sector through debt retirement. In view of all these possibilities, the need for extensive refinement of aggregate government statistics is eminently clear.

2. *Timing of Governmental Economic Effects.* The federal spending process, as we have seen, begins with the granting to the executive branch of new obligational authority, which is the total of appropriations and other financial authorizations made available by the Congress for a given period of time. Even at this early stage effects will occur in the private sector of the economy if business firms alter their behavior in anticipation of future government expenditures. The first direct impact on private business, however, occurs only sometime later, when the different federal agencies incur obligations by placing orders for goods and services and entering into binding contracts. Production for government order then gets under way, and although progress payments are sometimes made on large orders, most federal expenditures occur only when the items ordered have been delivered, inspected, and approved.

Many of the effects of governmental spending programs, therefore, occur prior to the actual making of expenditures, and in the case of

[20] Cf. Alan M. Strout, "Primary Employment Effects of Alternative Spending Programs," *Review of Economics and Statistics*, XL (Nov., 1958), 319-28.

items with a long production process, these differences in timing may be substantial.[21] Measures of federal expenditures, consequently, should be supplemented with measures of new obligational authority and of net obligations incurred until such time as a single spending series, closely correlated in its timing with the economic effects of federal programs, is derived. In Table 4–2, for example, it will be noted that although new obligational authority, net obligations incurred, and budget expenditures all increased by $11 billion from fiscal 1957 to 1959, the first two series rose in the first half of that period by $6.1 and $4.9 billion respectively, while budget expenditures were increasing by only $2.5 billion.

TABLE 4–2

NEW OBLIGATIONAL AUTHORITY, NET OBLIGATIONS INCURRED, AND BUDGET EXPENDITURES FOR THE FEDERAL GOVERNMENT, 1957-1959

(billions of dollars)

Fiscal Year	New Obligational Authority	Net Obligations Incurred	Budget Expenditures
1957	70.2	69.0	69.4
1958	76.3	73.9	71.9
1959	81.4	80.6	80.7

Source: United States Budgets.

Nor are timing problems confined only to spending programs. Many tax changes may begin to exert their influence as soon as the necessary legislation has been passed (or even earlier during hearings held by the legislative tax committees), while the effects on government tax collections will be delayed for weeks, or even many months. For the same reasons, it is unlikely that the pronounced seasonal pattern in federal tax receipts (high in the first two quarters of the calendar year and low in the other two) is matched by a similar seasonal pattern in economic tax effects.

3. *Extra-Budgetary Effects.* Finally, it should be noted that such extra-budgetary activities as federal loan guaranties and insurance, which have been widely used in the various housing programs, can have economic effects far in excess of their nominal impact on budget and cash expenditures. On the other hand, it is doubtful that these effects are as great as the total volume of insured (or guaranteed) loans authorized or disbursed. Statistics given in the special budgetary

---

[21] See Murray L. Weidenbaum, "The Timing of the Economic Impact of Government Spending," *National Tax Journal,* XII (March, 1959), 79-85.

analysis of federal credit programs, therefore, should be deflated to varying degrees for purposes of economic analysis.[22]

Government loan insurance is not the only program whose economic effects are likely to exceed its budgetary impact by a substantial margin. Consider in this light a high protective tariff which brings in little revenue, or a vigorously enforced antitrust program. In these cases, however, the problems of quantitative measurement are even more formidable than they are for loan guaranties and insurance.

---

[22] George F. Break, *The Economic Impact of Federal Loan Insurance* (Washington, D.C.: National Planning Association, 1961).

5

The Scope and Limitations of Government Programs

The student of public finance would like to be able to say exactly what functions a government should perform and on what scale. Deviations of actual government functions from the prescribed norm could then be criticized. Careful study by citizens of the subject would permit them, when they vote on public issues or select candidates for public office, to know what issues to approve, what to reject, and what platforms of parties or candidates accord with the proper principles.

One must immediately deny that there exists or promises to exist any principle or set of principles that would provide such a definite pattern for government behavior. The topic is too complicated and nebulous for simple solutions. Yet it does not follow that there is nothing to be said. A government has grave limitations, for example, as an agency to bring up children. Even inept parents do better than orphan asylums. On the other hand, no one except an extreme anarchist would hold that government has no functions at all, at least no proper functions, and hence should be abolished as a nuisance. Suggesting these extremes does not demonstrate that there is some one combination of government that is the best possible; it does suggest that, if one is prepared to think hard enough and long enough, one may be able to suggest some combinations of programs that are better than others.

The scope and limitations of government action immediately involve questions of the "ought" kind, and as mentioned in Chapter 1, there are purists who insist that mere economists have no business discussing ethical topics.

Apart from questions of purity, there is the more fundamental objection that ethical issues are matters of taste, and that there is really nothing to discuss. A statement of an ethical type, such as "a man should not punch a lady in the nose," really means that the speaker disapproves of such an action. If, then, a man does punch a lady in the nose, he merely shows that his tastes differ from those of the speaker, and also of the lady. If this view is adopted, ideals go out the window and pure cynicism remains.

The taste approach to ethical issues gains support from the doctrine that only statements of "operational" significance have meaning. Accordingly, a statement is meaningful only if it can at least in principle be refuted. Thus the factual statement, "the grass is green," is supposedly meaningful because the grass instead of being green might be yellow. The esthetic statement, "the sunset is beautiful," may be claimed not to be meaningful as it stands. One should say, "I am enjoying the sunset," to make clear that one is merely verbalizing his own experience. Yet there is no way to establish that the statement "the grass is green" is any more objective or "operational" or factual than the statement "the sunset is beautful." Both are statements about a person's experience. Another observer may state that the same grass is yellow or that the sunset is hideous; no definite test exists to reconcile the apparent differences. Philosophers have reflected upon issues of this type for many, many years and, insofar as there is agreement, it is that the position of complete skepticism is the only irrefutable one.

Ethical propositions are inescapable, including even the statement that economists should not become entangled in ethical issues. That being the case, one might as well accept this fact and attack the issues as best he can.

The Good Society

The government of a given society consists of organizations engaged in various activities. Like all human institutions, their excuse for existence must be that their presence makes the society better in some way than it would otherwise be. Government programs should presumably aim at promoting the good society. If the characteristics of such a society can be determined, we are on the way to learning what is the proper scope of government activities.

Visions of the good society have been many and various. In general, however, they ordinarily fall into one of two types: an unchang-

ing pattern of social behavior and organization—the static ideal—
or some type of progressive improvement with or without a certain
ultimate end in view. Conceptions of static perfection in society
have often characterized religious movements. The hope or belief
rests upon the idea that there is some best form of society and this
form, once realized, is to be endlessly repeated. The progressive
approach aims at improvements here and now in actual social affairs.
No idyllic state, no paradise on earth, may ever be expected. Social
problems will always be encountered but in different forms as society
changes. Juvenile delinquency, for example, has not been a problem
of any importance in China. As the Chinese people industrialize and
concentrate themselves more and more in cities, their economic position will, in all likelihood, improve, but the weakening of family ties
arising from urbanized living will create social difficulties not encountered in simpler forms of social organization. The conception of
an improving society, as opposed to one of a static perfection, takes
as a premise the actual and rather sordid world of fact and concentrates on what may be done to make that world a better one.

Both the conceptions of a static perfection and of an improving
society require the identification of good and bad social arrangements.
Improvement, for example, implies change but not just any kind of
change; the change must be, in some sense, an addition of what is
regarded as good or a subtraction of what is regarded as evil. The
vision of a static perfection defined as a state in which nine-tenths
of the human race are slaves of the other one-tenth has a limited
appeal; those selected to be slaves are not likely to take kindly to the
arrangement. Some way of detecting the good and the bad is clearly
necessary.

Fundamental philosophical issues are at stake and only some
aspects of the question can be pursued here. In economic thinking,
the emphasis has been placed upon achieving a goal or goals, subject
to the limitations imposed by existing resources. At the hands of
many nineteenth-century thinkers, the goal was defined as the greatest
happiness. Happiness in turn was defined as satisfaction or the fulfillment of one's desires. A thirsty man presented with a glass of beer
became on that account a happier man. This point of view, usually
labelled Utilitarianism, has been highly influential both within and
without economics. It has a kind of no-nonsense tone. A person can
be more or less happy. Total happiness of a group of people may be
found by a process of simple addition. Improvement then refers to
those changes that increase total happiness. Likewise, measures that
may be taken by government are to be judged good or bad with reference to their net effect upon total happiness.

In economic thinking, the maximum happiness principle in recent decades has been on the defensive (for reasons to be pursued presently) and, in its place, various welfare views have been advocated which attempt to avoid reliance upon the summing up of the satisfactions of different people. By procedures that are rarely simple, a social goal is defined in a manner designed to avoid having to weigh and add the satisfactions of different people. One of the less complex, for example, is the compensation principle. If some measure, such as some type of government expenditure, would improve the position of some people and worsen the position of others, when improve or worsen is defined by each person for himself, the measure is defined as a social improvement provided that those who gain could fully compensate those who lose and have some gain left over. In this approach, each person remains the judge of what is good or bad for him. Like the greatest happiness principle, the definition of what is socially good or bad elevates prudence into an ultimate rule. A prudent person takes account of his needs and interests to avoid actions which he may later regret. Approaches of this and of similar types have a certain usefulness in crystallizing some types of questions. Yet it is doubtful that any society could successfully function if prudential behavior were generally accepted as the ultimate principle for social conduct.

What then are the characteristics of the good society? Appeal must be made finally to intuition—to social relations that strike one as good relations *per se.* Anything resembling rigorous proof is out of the question. The appeal is to ideals. Why or how human beings discovered ideals is one of the great mysteries and yet, as a force for determining behavior, ideals have no serious rivals when large questions are to be solved.

The following characteristics are suggested as those defining the good society and hence as goals worth striving for in actual societies: harmony in relations among individuals and groups, civil and personal liberties or freedoms, a certain minimum of economic affluence for all people in the society, fairness in treatment, opportunities that challenge individual talents, and an attractive physical environment. The order of listing is not intended to convey any suggestion of the relative importance, nor is the list to be considered as necessarily exhaustive.

HARMONY, applied to social affairs, calls for a pervading sensitivity and concern with the feelings and interests of others and for a pattern of behavior that makes each person feel comfortable. Lack of harmony reveals itself in violent acts, in the use of deceit and fraud to gain objectives, and by appeals to prejudice or even hate. A friendly concern for other people, respect for their opinions, a willingness to tolerate tastes differing from one's own make for greater social harmony. In contemporary societies, the British society displays, perhaps, a greater harmony than does that found in the United States.

Of great importance in this era of human history is harmony in the relations among countries. Since the rise of national states to dominance, warfare has been the ultimate means used by one country to impose its will upon others. International anarchy as a political system cannot claim to have been a great success during the past four centuries. A revision of that system has now become a necessary condition for survival of civilized societies. It goes almost without saying that of all immediate goals, the goal of friendly relations among countries takes precedence over goals of immediate domestic concern.

FREEDOM. Freedom is a concept that defies precise definition. Yet of all ideals it has been one of the most influential. Without some freedom, human society would differ insignificantly from that of an ant colony. Without freedom there is no economics as ordinarily understood; some options or alternative modes of behavior must be possible, some choice available. Yet freedom in the sense of being able to do anything at all one pleases is an illusion. We are bound and restricted by physical laws. In dealing with other people, we are bound by manners, customs, and law. Of these, manners and customs are much more influential in everyday life than are laws.

Freedoms or liberties may be looked upon as options subject to restrictions, as doing this instead of that, as making one statement instead of another, as writing one view instead of another. Pure uninhibited behavior cannot be tolerated in actual societies; persons who attempt to do so are likely to find themselves in institutions. Yet, given these restrictions, it remains true that societies may and do exhibit vast differences in liberty. Soviet society permits much smaller degrees of freedom in speech and communication generally than does Indian society. The goal of freedom means that people shall be entitled to communicate with one another, to speak and write without fear of punishment for having done so, always within a framework of self-constraint necessary for effective communication. It also means ability to select occupations, organize a business, marry some one of his own choice. Government interference with options of this nature may on occasion be justified, but the burden of proof must be clear and definite that such interference is justified. Governments have positive obligations as well to protect individuals in these rights not merely from their possible violation by some overzealous public official, but also by those in control of private organizations in a position to punish offending individuals.

ECONOMIC AFFLUENCE. Another characteristic of the good society is a minimum of grinding poverty or, ideally, none at all. Just where the line defining poverty is to be drawn must be somewhat arbitrary because economic affluence is a matter of degree. Yet wherever the line is drawn, there are sizable groups in the United States that will fall below it on almost anyone's definition. In addition to the negative effects of a large number of poor people upon the operation of the political system and the costs they impose as a result of crime and spoiling of cities by perpetuating slums, poverty is objectionable *per se*. People in such circumstances experience hardships that preclude the development of their talents. Their lives and the lives of their children are blighted by the handicap of inadequate financial means. The persistence of large-scale poverty in a country such as the United States stands out as a major weakness of the social system. Unlike the circumstances in a large section of the world, poverty in this country does not need to be tolerated because of inability to produce sufficient goods and services to prevent it.

FAIRNESS. Another feature of the good society is fairness or equity in personal relations and in group relations. Any kind of social class system, for example, which places some people below other people, even if those so degraded do not especially mind, is objectionable. Social classes in the sense of groups ranked by some inferior-superior test violate the basic ethical notion that a human being is precious merely by being human. Without this ethical doctrine, a large part of civilized behavior would have no basis. In the United States and indeed in all democratic countries, the ideal of the preciousness of human personality must be taken as a fundamental ethical postulate. It follows that, ideally, a good society is a socially classless society.

ADVENTURE. The society in which a person finds himself should also provide a challenge. Without the opportunity for adventure, there is little zest for living and boredom takes over. Visions of the good society as set forth by many religious sects are commonly deficient because of the omission of challenging features. The aim is a static perfection. The ideals announced have little appeal to the young; a rest home scarcely provides the best setting for an interesting life even if the food is good and the attendants kind and considerate. The period of the Renaissance, for example, was an adventurous period; such periods stimulate talented people to great achievements. By contrast, the present century has been comparatively dull. The large challenges of recent times have mainly been occasioned by breakdowns of peaceful international relations and by the fear of war. Challenges arising from freshness of thought, from great ideas, or from great new art forms have been infrequent in human history. There is a special staleness about contemporary living, a preoccupation with personal aims and small achievements.

ESTHETICS. A further feature of a good society is a pleasant, attractive physical environment. Esthetic considerations somehow became dulled during the nineteenth century, in large part because of the obsession with material progress. Although greater significance is now attached to esthetics, ugliness abounds both in cities and in the countryside. Governments in the United States have exhibited rather less sensitivity to such matters than have governments in Western Europe, as illustrated by the comparative architectural features of public buildings. Esthetic sensitivity appears to be increasing both in private and in public affairs. Opposition to garish signboards, elevated freeways, and boxlike public structures based on strictly esthetic grounds sometimes gets a hearing and occasionally becomes effective. Business firms in recent decades take pains to make their structures attractive and to provide working environments pleasing to employees.

Means of Achieving the Good Society

The social goals of harmony, freedom, general affluence (at least in the minimum sense of the absence of dire poverty of any group), a prevailing concern for fair treatment of individuals by others and by organizations, adventure, and a pleasant and attractive physical environment—these at least we suggest are ingredients of the good society. If effective measures can be found which forward these goals, those measures are thereby good ones. Likewise good government means the kind of government that successfully selects measures that do help to accomplish these goals.

The means themselves, however, are inseparably tied to the goals. Even if a society should select some person having the characteristics of one of Plato's philosopher-kings with complete power to impose his will upon the group, such political means are objectionable even though the man may have the wisdom of a Solomon. It is easy to believe that the ideal political system is one-man rule if the ruler is all-wise and kindly. Apart from the difficulty of elevating such a person to a position of untrammelled power, assuming such a person could be found, or the likelihood of his remaining wise and kindly with such power, such a political system violates the ethical principles inherent in a democratic society. The decision-making process becomes a goal in itself. Ideally the group through a meeting of minds is to reach a decision. The appeal is to reason and to ideals. If the decision turns out to be a mistake, it remains better to have made the decision by a democratic process than to have avoided the mistake by some alternative process. The weaknesses of actual group decision-making are many and varied in detail, but their crucial weaknesses arise from their undemocratic aspects.

One danger in any society dedicated to the democratic virtues is the presence of any large influential group that denies these virtues. In British society, for example, there are groups who classify themselves as the elite, and these people are to be found in both of the two main political parties, who are prepared to impose their will upon others. They know what is best for the British "working classes" even though they have carefully avoided living as working people live. This attitude has not, however, prevented a democratic form of political system.

In the United States, there are groups with a nihilistic philosophy, who find a conspiracy under every bush, who appeal to hate and prejudice, and who proclaim themselves to be the true patriots. Their positive proposals are clothed in ambiguity and their political emphasis is the powerful leader. In terms of effective political power, they have been more successful than their opposite numbers, the political radicals, who advocate specific and vast changes in economic and social organization to be accompanied, also, by the elimination of democratic procedures. They too appeal to hate and prejudice, using differing words and phrases and addressing themselves to somewhat different groups. Political movements of either type are inherently divisive.

When people of a society group themselves on the basis of their common hates or fears of other groups, a setting is made to order for trouble. Such was the case in the United States in the 1850's and in France in the 1930's. In France the resulting general demoralization permitted German military power to conquer the country with comparative ease. Any political means advocated, therefore, however noble the goals may appear to be, should be consistent with democratic ethics and procedures. This condition places rather important limitations on the social reformer. A clear and definite evil found in a society is not to be eliminated by some short-cut device which circumvents democratic procedures. There are ends associated with the means, and these have some importance.

Special Role of Government

In primitive societies, an identifiable government does not exist. The tribe as a unit has some kind of leadership, and the rules of behavior are the customs of the tribe. Such societies are collective with a vengeance, and the toleration of individual idiosyncrasies is small or zero. Government emerges as a recognizable organization only at fairly high levels of civilization. At such levels, analysis of what governments do and what they should do begins to influence public programs. The erosion of tyrannical governments in Western Europe began when people started to think about government. The ideas that arose in the long struggle against political tyranny are still important; they continue to profoundly influence what governments do.

Out of the process of analyzing the role of government, a great variety of political philosophies has emerged. It is not our task to review these ideas here.[1] Our concern is restricted to the role of government in connection with economic affairs. However, even this restriction is not very restrictive, because governments are in fact heavily committed to activities with economic consequences.

Government activities may be classified into those involving (1) the promotion of what here will be called public ends or objectives; (2) enterprise-like activities providing goods and services for private use; and (3) transfers both to and from government. The defense establishment illustrates the first category, a local municipal water works illustrates the second, and the social security program and all taxes illustrate the third.

ACTIVITIES DIRECTED TO PUBLIC ENDS. These activities are defined by the condition that the "product" cannot even in principle be assigned to particular members of the society. A military establishment provides protection to all members of the society, regardless of the likes or dislikes of a person for the service. Some students have described this case as a commodity whose total quantity automatically accrues to each individual. The rationale of this point of view will be examined presently. Public functions of this sort include education, regulation of business, control of the monetary system, relations with other countries, the whole gamut of policing, court facilities, prisons and corrective institutions, public health services, provision of information, legislatures, voting facilities, public housekeeping, control of pollution of various kinds, mental institutions, and many others.

[1] See George H. Sabine, *A History of Political Theory* (2d ed.; New York: Holt, Rinehart & Winston, 1950).

The selection of the particular type of activities falling into this class and their scale depends in fact upon the actual political setting of the government in question. In a democratic society, the actual facts are determined more or less on a pragmatic basis. If there exists a strong belief, for example, that there should be public schools, and if the group having this belief is politically potent, then there will be public schools.

Principle in the abstract does matter in determining the actual menu of government services found. Even those intent on using government to protect their personal financial position appeal to the public interest as justification. As long as people are permitted to organize themselves into groups, and in this country there appear to be almost as many organizations as there are people, political influence will be used to get a government unit to carry out the program being advocated. Against a more or less common background of ideals, political parties compete for power by a variety of means; they must somehow successfully appeal to groups with different views. Appeals to principle are thus commonly made in vague terms, permitting a variety of interpretations.

As long as the issues in political life are numerous small ones, one group acts as a check on another, more or less assuring that the use of government power for personal or business advantage will not completely sabotage other objectives. When large issues do arise, appeal to principle becomes unavoidable as well as, in one sense, dangerous. The appeal is unavoidable because no solution can emerge out of mere competition among economic or regional pressure groups, as was illustrated for example by the question of what policy was to be adopted in the late 1930's toward the rise of German military power. Appeals to principle are often dangerous because people's deep emotions are aroused. Whether the walnut growers are given protection from foreign competition is not the kind of question capable of arousing strong passions in a large segment of the population. Whether Formosa should or should not be protected from the government of mainland China can be decided only by appeal to principle. Differences in views on such a question lead to strong positions and strong feelings.

The pressures to use government for personal or business advantage result in inconsistent policies and in inefficient government organization. The objective of many pressure groups becomes that of the establishment of an agency or group within government to look after their interests. Conflicting groups outside government then have their counterparts within government. Everyone might be better off if none were so represented. Government would then have fewer functions and less expense. If all such functions were deleted from the federal government and from the state governments, non-military and non-transfer government expenditures would fall substantially and the government organization could be much simplified.

The large issues, however, give rise to especially expensive government programs, illustrated by the military services. Inept handling of international relations, apart from other considerations, becomes expensive merely in dollars and cents.

Public Welfare Approach. The selection and scope of government programs may be appraised and hence approved or disapproved initially by reference to ideals, by whether they promote the good society by the means used, by whether they are appropriate to achieve the goals, and by the costs involved. The issues are often difficult, if merely because of the lack of relevant information. In some cases, such as military affairs, their scale and complexity make it almost impossible for a layman to reach an informed judgment. In this as well as in many other cases, the layman has no choice but to rely upon experts. As social life becomes more complicated, more and more reliance must be placed upon authoritative opinion. Unfortunately, those in a position to be authorities may, and often do, have a special axe to grind, because they may be members of the government agencies performing the function, and outsiders may be unable to obtain the relevant information. The growth and development of genuine professional standards on the part of experts both within and without government provides one means of permitting laymen to appraise government programs on an intelligent basis. Inefficiencies of court procedures may be exposed by bar associations. The qualifications, or lack thereof, of members of the Board of Governors of the Federal Reserve System may be pointed out by economists. Selection of a spokesman for the gas industry to a governmental body charged with the regulation of the gas industry may be criticized by anyone.

Application of the tests of the appropriateness of the goals, the appropriateness of the means, and of the costs involved may or may not lead to the conclusion that government operations in the United States are, on the whole, too niggardly, as Professor Galbraith has argued, or much too large, as most spokesmen for taxpayers' associations argue. Consider for example the defense establishment. The presumed long-range goal is a peaceful world—surely a worthwhile ideal. The means being employed consist of maintaining an arsenal of destructive weapons. Such means can at best be a deterrent. If no one makes a miscalculation, life goes on as an armed truce. With the goal of a genuinely peaceful world, are there other and more appropriate means? Measures designed to reduce world tensions, policies relying upon the undeniably overwhelming desire of peoples for peaceful international relations, fewer, or better yet, no truculent speeches by political leaders, economic measures designed to cultivate good will and higher living levels in developing countries—these and others may be more efficient means to achieve the goal.

On a different plane, the facts have long been established to demonstrate that preventive medicine is more effective than the treatment of patients after they become ill. Preventive medicine, however, must be undertaken by government if it is to be undertaken on a large scale. There is the further aspect that the results of successful preventive measures cannot be readily seen; the people who would have become ill without it do not know that they have been helped. If the electorate is ignorant of the large results to be achieved by proper preventive measures and refuses to support such a public operation on the required scale, there are greater costs in the form of the care of illness and loss of working time. Given the goal of a smaller incidence of illness, public means are more efficient than the alternative private means.

Education, a field in which there is a large measure of agreement about the importance of the goals, suffers from a variety of ills, including in many states a rigid educational bureaucracy and in many, inadequate financial support. The financial difficulty of schools has been aggravated by partial reliance upon an unpopular tax—the property tax. Also, the increasing criticism of the professional educator leads some groups to give voice to protests by voting against bond issues or increases in local tax rates. Unless new and effective measures can be devised, educational service in the United States may seriously deteriorate. Already a strong movement exists to provide large-scale federal financial assistance for this function. If government fails in this function, private schooling may be expected to increase with rather unpleasant by-products already to be observed in large metropolitan regions, where many central city schools have become in effect segregated institutions for the instruction of the children of poor parents.

The public welfare approach provides, as these examples suggest, no simple touchstone for the scope and restriction of government activities. Positively the approach means the application of intelligence to the selection of government programs and to the determination of their scale. Negatively it repudiates any doctrinaire position, such as that government is too big, or that doing nothing is better than doing something, or the reverse.

The Voluntary-Exchange Theory of Government Programs. The distinguishing feature of this approach is its insistence that the type of government program and its size should in principle be determined in a manner analogous to the workings of the market system in the private sphere. The size of the educational program of a community should be governed by the same principles as those used in determining the amount of ice cream to be produced and sold.

If the government program in question is, say, providing water to the people of a region, the amount of water to be supplied should be the amount which makes the value of a gallon of water equal to the costs to government of delivering a gallon. If it costs one mill to deliver a gallon of water to a customer, the amount supplied should be determined by the amount demanded at that price. A price should be charged both to determine the size of the operation and to assess the costs against the users. Those who benefit are to pay. The amount each is to pay shall be in proportion to the amount of the commodity he obtains.

If all government services were similar to water service, all should be determined on the same principle. In applying this principle, the benefits of the defense establishment or of a local police force are to be assigned *in toto* to each person. For example, there are a number of policemen in a city. Their presence provides the service of protection. Each resident gets all of this protection. Some students call this service a "public good," meaning by this expression a good provided by government that is available to each person in its total amount (hence each gets an equal amount). The rain falls upon the just and upon the unjust; police service does likewise.

Since police service is available to all in equal amounts, price cannot be used to ration the service. Indeed, there is no rationing to be accomplished. The problems to be solved are two: (1) how large should the police force be, and (2) what people are to pay what sums to finance the police force? The answers to these two questions should, according to the voluntary-exchange approach, be provided by reference to the benefits received.

The point of view may be illustrated graphically. In Figure 5–1, let the horizontal axis measure units of police service, which may be thought of in terms of hours of police service. Along the vertical axis, we measure the money value per unit of service. Let us now divide the community into two groups and select a person who is representative of the tastes of each group. Then the line D_b is the "demand schedule" of a person representing one group. This schedule is constructed in the following fashion. Let there be some number of units of police service, say, the quantity *OR*. Since each and every person gets all of this service, we ask the person what he would be willing to pay per unit if the quantity of police service were a little smaller or a little larger. His answer is shown by the vertical *SR*. He is willing, say, to pay one cent for another hour of police service. It is possible, to be sure, that he might value an added hour at zero. If his business is robbery, he may place a negative figure on another hour, or even one hour, of police service. However that may be, we pose the same question for various quantities for the purpose of arriving at a person's marginal valuation of the service.

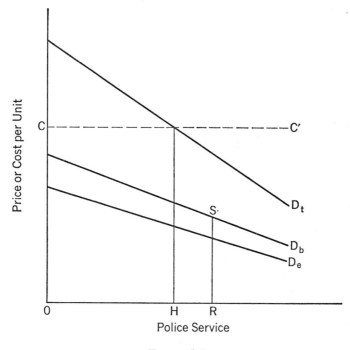

FIGURE 5–1

The same procedure may be used to construct the schedule D_e for a person whose tastes are typical of the second group. Thus various demand schedules are found. These schedules are then to be added, but instead of adding the quantities at each "price," we add the prices for each quantity. If there are ten policeman working eight hours per day, there are 80 hours of service, and each person in the community obtains all 80 hours of police service per day. He does not share the service with others. Each gets all of it. Hence for any given quantity of police service, we wish to find out how much the people in that community are willing to pay. The result is found by adding prices for each quantity, giving the global demand schedule, labelled D_t.

The cost of police service is shown by the dotted line CC'. According to the voluntary-exchange theory, the quantity of service should be the amount given by the common point of D_t and CC', or the quantity OH. This amount is the theoretically "correct" amount of police service to provide in that community. Hence the answer to one of our questions is provided.

The financing of this quantity of police service may also be discovered. Each person is to pay his marginal valuation of the service multiplied by the total amount of the service. Thus if there are delinquents in the community who find policemen a nuisance, they should not be asked to pay. Rather, they should "pay" a negative price, or, in other words, be paid for having to put up with policemen, because their marginal valuation of police activity is negative.

The only departure from the normal market principle requiring each person to pay for what he gets comes about because a person will obtain services whether he pays for them or not. Therefore, given this fact, the problem becomes that of finding how much each person values the service. The person is to be his own judge, at least in principle, about how valuable these services are. If he likes them very much, he pays more than does a person to whom the services are of little or no importance.

There is a technical difficulty, a rather formidable one, in ascertaining how much each person values any given type of government service. If one were to conduct a census and request the census-taker to ask each person how much each kind of government program is worth to him, there would be some who might misrepresent the truth. They might say that the service is worth nothing to them when in fact they like it very much. There would also be many who would be completely at a loss to ascertain the worth of a program on this basis. The proponents of the voluntary-exchange theory of government programs have not as yet been able to suggest any solution of this difficulty consistent with the underlying principle.[2]

Advocates of the voluntary-exchange approach have suggested various voting techniques to provide a closer approximation to the

[2] Knut Wicksell advocated that legislative decisions on the size of programs and their financing be reached by unanimous consent. Such a principle has been applied in some circumstances, such as some decisions of business corporations where a single stockholder can block certain types of action. Unanimous consent is not merely unworkable; it is contrary to the rule that the tastes of all persons should determine the characteristics of government programs. One person could veto any government program. It is rather surprising that Wicksell should have recommended such a curious solution to an important problem.

desired result than that believed likely to emerge under present practices. Proportional representation of political interests has been advocated because minority groups would be given more effective power in a legislature, and hence a closer approximation to the ideal of mirroring individual tastes in a government tax-expenditure program could be expected than under present procedures. Conceivably a system of buying and selling votes might be introduced. There is no sanctity in the rule of one-person, one-vote in this approach. A wealthy person should in principle have more voting power than a poor one, for the same reason that a wealthy man can outvote a poor one in the markets for goods and services. These rather strange results, strange when viewed against the democratic traditions as to how government decisions should be reached, follow from the initial premise of the doctrine. Once the analogy of the market place is accepted, it follows easily enough that the wealthier one is, the more voice he should have in decisions about government activities.

The Achilles heel of this approach is the premise that government programs and taxes should be decided upon in a manner analogous to the way that the quantity and price of vanilla ice cream are determined in a price system. The "should" in the above statement is crucial. Is there any compulsion in this ethical postulate? Why, for example, should a person who believes in good public schools be required in principle to pay more in taxes to support public schools than a bigoted person who believes that others should be kept in the same state of ignorance as himself? The approach can be criticized as an indirect (and certainly unintentional) attack upon democratic ideals.[3]

SCOPE OF GOVERNMENT ENTERPRISE ACTIVITIES. Much of the discussion of political affairs concerns the scope of government enterprise activities as already defined. The debate between the socialists and the capitalists has in the main been concerned with this issue. Socialists believe that some large, but usually undefined, portion of all business activities should be operated by government. Their opposite numbers argue for little or none.

Socialism has been one of the most important and most influential reform movements the world has ever seen. At least since the publication of Karl Marx's works, the ideal of government ownership and operation of industry has offered a vision with sufficient power to attract the devoted following of millions of people. European countries have witnessed strong socialistic political movements for decades. The heyday of the movement in the United States came just before the

---

[3] See Richard A. Musgrave, *The Theory of Public Finance* (New York: McGraw-Hill Book Co., 1959), chap. iv.

First World War, but this country is one of the few industrial countries in which socialism as a political movement has been persistently weak.

Socialism of some varieties encompasses more than a program of economic reform. It includes political change as well, and in this connection, the differences among socialists are large. At one extreme are those believing in some variety of dictatorship, with force to be used if necessary, to install and maintain the socialist regime. Democratic socialist movements, such as are found in Fabian socialism in Great Britain and the various cooperative types of socialism in the Scandinavian countries, differ from the totalitarian variety as does night from day. The socialist label conceals large differences in political and economic views.

Socialism defined as government operation of business may be restricted by its advocates to the so-called natural monopolies; or it may include practically all enterprise requiring more than one employee, as is the approximate case in Russia. According to the first definition, Great Britain has a socialistic system. Some transportation and virtually all communication facilities are government owned and operated. Measured in terms of the value of what is produced, however, private enterprise in that country dominates and is much more important than public enterprise.

Whether some industry should or should not be under government control or private control may be determined by invoking the socialist doctrine that government enterprise is *per se* superior to private or the conservative doctrine that private enterprise is *per se* superior to public. These approaches lead to fixed positions, leaving no method of determining which may be the better arrangement in any actual case.

There are other ways of trying to solve the question. Government enterprise is commonly believed, regardless of political philosophy, to be better than private in some fields. Any attempt to place the water works of many cities in the hands of private companies would be strongly opposed, even by those who in principle dislike public enterprise. Likewise, the operation of night clubs by a government agency would not be likely to get much support even from the most avid socialist. These considerations suggest the desirability of judging each case on its individual merits rather than appealing to an all-or-none doctrine. If railroads can be shown to be managed more efficiently and to give better service under public auspices, let the government run them. The government may operate some rail lines and private groups others within the same country. The test being employed, the comparative efficiency one, was advocated by Adam Smith.[4]

[4] This test is discussed more fully in chap. 16.

TRANSFER FUNCTIONS OF GOVERNMENT. In addition to government activities devoted to satisfying public ends and those devoted to satisfying private ends, governments make transfer payments to the public and governments receive transfer payments, mainly in the form of taxes, from the public. Transfer payments whether paid by or paid to government may be further classified as contractual, gratuitous, and compulsory. In the case of payments involving governments, interest on an outstanding debt illustrates a contractual transfer, payment for relief purposes illustrates a gratuitous transfer, and a tax illustrates a compulsory transfer.

The central question to be discussed concerns the proper scope and limitations of gratuitous transfers made by governments and compulsory transfers made to governments. Contractual transfers may be left to one side, except we may observe that once a government makes a contract, it has an obligation to carry out its side of the bargain. There are qualifications, to be sure. A government may somehow so entangle itself in various contractual obligations as to impair its effective functioning and might have to revise contracts. But with regard to compulsory and gratuitous transfers (taxes and what have been called negative taxes), what principles should be applied to determine their characteristics?

In public finance literature, this question has usually been discussed under the heading of "Canons of Taxation." As long as negative taxes are understood to be included, our topic may also be thus described.

To discover the canons applicable to taxes in our larger sense, one may adopt any of several approaches. The standard approach has been to lay down a set of rules for government conduct in this field. A tax or tax structure that violates one or more of these rules is thereby censured. Such an approach was adopted, for example, by Adam Smith.[5]

The procedure leads to difficulties whenever a tax in order to satisfy one rule must break another. The equivalent in personal behavior is the conflict that arises between telling the truth and hurting a person's feelings by so doing. People usually solve this dilemma by taking liberties with the truth, regarding the other person's feelings as more important. There is yet another difficulty. Whatever the canons laid down for government conduct in this field, even if they are never conflicting, actual tax programs of governments liberally violate the canons. The divergence between practice and what practice ought to be becomes so large that the canons may seem to be merely irrelevant. If, for example, the rule is adopted that tax laws ought to be fair in the sense of treating people in similar circumstances in a similar

[5] *Wealth of Nations,* Book V, chap. ii, part 2.

manner, the tax structure in every country immediately becomes an object of censure. But after thus criticizing the tax structure found in a country, what has been accomplished? Here, as in other questions of public policy, the issues that matter are what to do and what not to do. The choice in fact is not between some ideal tax structure and the one actually in use. The options confronting members of the House Ways and Means Committee or the officials of New York City relate to changes, usually small changes, in the taxes already in effect. However, canons remain important. Some changes are better or worse than others. Hence, touchstones must be employed to give meaning to "better" or "worse" in this context.

The Benefit Rule. The benefit rule demands in principle that the amount of taxes paid by each person in a society be equal to the value of the services provided by government activity. To apply the rule, some tests must be found to value and allocate the benefits of government. If it is impossible to find such tests, the benefit principle may stand as a principle but fail for lack of applicability. Enthusiasts for the benefit principle, such as those advocating the voluntary-exchange principle of public finance, endeavor to assign benefits of government to individuals. Insofar as the benefits cannot be assigned, supporters of the benefit principle must to that extent abandon it and find some other.

To understand the implications of the benefit principle, let us consider first the case of negative taxes. A widow with three children is paid $150 per month under a social security program. In this event, she and her children clearly are benefited by the amount paid to her. According to the benefit principle, the tax imposed upon her should be equal to the value of the benefits received or, in this case, $150 per month. But if such a tax were imposed, the result would be a zero net benefit. In other words, the benefit principle would call for not paying her the money in the first place. Others may benefit, such as close relatives, because otherwise they would feel obligated to keep the family from destitution. In this event, the benefit principle calls for their contributing in tax to the extent of the value of the benefits they receive. If somehow the value of the benefits in question can be established at $50 per month, they should be taxed by that amount, and the widow provided with a net sum of $50. The same effect could be accomplished without any government intervention at all.

We turn now to government programs designed to promote public ends, such as, say, police services. According to the benefit principle, the value of these services must first be allocated to particular persons. One may hold that an allocation is impossible. However to study the implications of the benefit principle, let us ignore this difficulty. Each family in a given community gets benefits in the form of police services worth, let us assume, $10 per year. According to the principle, each family should then be taxed $10 per year. In this way, the net gain to them measured in money terms is zero. The government has provided them with services worth a given sum, and the government gets back its "gift" by an equal tax.

What principle lies behind the benefit rule? The principle is simple: the status quo with respect to income distribution is not to be disturbed. Government services are income in kind, similar to the income one obtains by being paid in goods instead of money. If the benefit principle could be precisely applied, the result would be the same as if all government services were priced and sold to people on a cost basis. If for various technical reasons pricing devices cannot be applied, the government is requested to adopt the substitute of charging a tax equal to the value of benefits obtained.

Apart from the question of whether government services of all types can be regarded as assignable to individuals, the benefit principle implies, as we have seen, a definite value judgment: the distribution of income should not be disturbed by government. In turn, how may this value judgment be supported?

Perhaps the most common justification is what Henry Simons called "productivity ethics."[6] If A earns twice as much as B, A is entitled to keep twice as much as B because A has been twice as productive as B. Productivity ethics would call for government interference in cases where people obtain income without having produced the value equivalent. Karl Marx used productivity ethics when he passed from the proposition that labor produces all value to the proposition that laborers are entitled to all the product; to the extent that capitalists receive income, they are then "exploiting" labor. Likewise, followers of Henry George, holding that landowners should be taxed an amount equal to the net rental of land, proceed from the proposition that landowners as such do not produce anything to the proposition that they are therefore not entitled to retain the income from land. Those accepting productivity ethics may argue with one another at length about who or what produces how much, and indeed the debates on this topic have been long and frequent,[7] but the proponents are in agreement about the underlying ethical principle.

[6] See his work, *Personal Income Taxation* (Chicago: Univ. of Chicago Press, 1938), pp. 12 ff.
[7] The Austrian economist Boehm-Bawerk devoted much attention to the question of whether "capital" is productive, demonstrating to his own satisfaction that it is, thereby justifying its yield to owners of capital.

Proposals to tax earned income, meaning income derived from work, at a lower rate than other income often rest upon an appeal to productivity ethics. This point of view justifies the value judgment that the distribution of income is not to be disturbed, provided that the actual incomes obtained by people are treated as being, in some sense, produced by them. The one exception commonly endorsed by adherents to this view is death taxation, because on a productivity test there is a difficulty in understanding how a son who inherits wealth from his parents produced it.

Those who adhere to the productivity theory of ethics are not logically compelled to endorse the general application of the benefit principle. The latter requires that government programs be looked upon as providing services in kind assignable to the particular persons. If this view is rejected as impossible or meaningless, the general application of the benefit principle must also be rejected. As already pointed out, productivity ethics may lead to proposals for heavy taxation upon those gains which are deemed not to have been the results of productive activity. Heavy taxation of speculative gains may, therefore, be justified on the grounds that those who receive the gains do not produce them. A similar justification may be found for heavy taxation of gambling gains. This ethical position in some hands has led to highly radical proposals. If, for example, one holds that owners of wealth are not productive, a case can be made for government confiscation of private wealth altogether.

Ability-to-Pay Principle. The ability-to-pay principle, like the benefit principle, was originally developed to provide canons for positive taxation. Its implications for large-scale negative taxation have been explored only occasionally.

The ability-to-pay principle taken literally means that there exists some measure of "ability" and that the amount of tax, in the case of ordinary taxes, should be systematically related to this index. Actually, proponents of the idea have had even more specific requirements in mind. As ordinarily expounded, people with greater "ability" are not only to pay absolutely more than those with less ability, they are to pay relatively more as well. On this interpretation, the doctrine becomes a plea for systematic progressive taxation. Thus if income is taken as the measure of ability to pay, taxes, both positive and negative, should be designed so as to lessen the inequality of income. The ethical principle lying behind the words "ability to pay" is the philosophy of egalitarianism or equalitarianism, a subject to which we may now turn.

Equalitarian ideal. The idea that people are in some sense equal has been one of the more important ideals leading to a democratic political climate. The passion for political equality has deep roots in the United States. Some observers have suggested that of all ideals, that of equality has been the dominant one in the history of this country. The striving for political equality, a movement that continues with, if anything, increasing vigor, can readily be extended to economic affairs. If it is right and proper that each person be permitted one vote in political affairs, why is it not equally right and proper that each person be permitted equal votes (i.e., dollars) in the market place?

In economic thinking, the utilitarian ethical philosophy led to a strong presumption in favor of less inequality of economic power and, in some cases, to literal equality. Among its economic advocates were such thinkers as Mill, Jevons, Wicksteed, Edgeworth, Marshall, Pigou, and many of the British socialists. Bentham, the political philosopher and legal reformer, was perhaps the dominant figure in setting forth the case for economic equality. In the American tradition, there were few important economists before the twentieth century; the sentiment for equality was voiced mainly by political figures and thinkers.

Utilitarian philosophy justifies economic equality by the argument that the marginal utility obtained by any person from income diminishes as income increases. Hence the utility of a dollar to a person with a large income is smaller than the utility of a dollar to a person with a small income. Equalization would increase the sum of the utility of two people who initially had unequal income, because the utility taken away from the more affluent person would be less than the utility gained by the less affluent one. In principle, this approach leads to the conclusion that literal equality maximizes total happiness.

As a logical argument, the conclusion does not follow merely from the assumption or assertion that income is subject to diminishing marginal utility. It must also be assumed that each person has the same capacity for happiness. In turn, the happiness of different people must be compared and in principle be subject to the ordinary rules of arithmetic.

Let us examine these in reverse order. The happiness of person A and the happiness of person B must somehow be measured and compared, so that it is meaningful to say, for example, that if the happiness of A is made larger and that of B is made smaller, the total happiness of the two is changed by some measurable amount. The position is now on the defensive; the main difficulty is in meaning. If we pour one gallon of water and two gallons of water into a bucket, there is an object than can be said to be a measurable quantity of water. What object corresponds to the happiness of one person plus the happiness of another person?

If somehow this difficulty can be surmounted, what of the assumption that each person has the same capacity for happiness? Insofar as one can detect degrees of happiness or the reverse in people, an observer would hardly be likely to conclude that people have equal capacities in this regard. On the face of it, such a finding would be highly improbable. People differ in their capacities in many regards; it would appear peculiar that they should have exactly the same capacity for enjoying life. Once the proposition that people have different capacities for happiness is accepted, the conclusion that equality of income is better than inequality does not follow from utilitarian ethics. In fact, the same ethical doctrine could be employed to justify vast inequalities on the grounds that those with high incomes happen to have greater capacities for enjoyment than those with low.

Nevertheless the utilitarian philosophers, including many eminent economists, did give support to the equalitarian ideal. In many cases, their hesitations about government measures directed to achieving this ideal stemmed from such matters as possible adverse effects upon people's inclination to work, save, and invest. The same doubts still influence advocacy of egalitarian measures.

The advocacy of economic equality and hence of government interference to reduce inequality may appeal directly to the value judgment that a state of equality is a better state than that of inequality. Some philosophical positions may or may not be used to support this view. Actually thinkers who have been identified with the egalitarian ideal rarely are prepared to advocate literal equality in economic power. They wish to see less inequality and leave unanswered what degree of inequality is to be judged acceptable. No such compromise is ordinarily visualized by reformers advocating political equality. They would not ordinarily be content, for example, with a rule that gave some people one vote, some five votes, and some one-half vote. Literal equality in voting power is held to be the only right and proper one.

Yet another approach to the proper role of government in changing the distribution of economic power champions measures that successfully reduce inequality, not because of the value judgment that less inequality is better than more, but because of the alleged effects of various states of inequality. This approach calls first for a study of the effects in question and only then for the application of value judgments. The ramifications of this approach are many and various.

Consider a society in which the pattern of income distribution consists of the upper ten per cent receiving fifty per cent of total income, while the remaining ninety per cent receive fifty per cent of total income. A certain government tax-transfer measure under consideration could reduce the share of income of the upper tenth from fifty to thirty per cent and increase that of the remainder from fifty to seventy per cent. Research establishes that, as a result of the improvement in the level of living of the low-income group, their improved health, stamina, and working capacity increases the total output by such a large amount that the upper one-tenth finds that its absolute level of living has not fallen at all. Its smaller share of income is fully compensated by the increase in total output. In this case, the reduction in inequality becomes a means to accomplish an improvement in the productive capacity of the society. A direct value judgment about income distribution need not be made.

If, however, the same redistribution is accomplished and, among other developments, productive capacity remains unchanged, the ethical issue cannot be so easily avoided. Those who advocate progressive taxation on the grounds that the consequences of lessened inequality improve the society on balance will have difficulties whenever the consequences cannot be clearly shown to be improvements. Indeed they may logically be forced to advocate government measures which increase inequalities, as do those people, for example, in the United States who would prefer to see federal income taxes abolished or the rates substantially reduced, with the revenue lost to be restored by some presumed distributionally neutral or regressive tax structure. The debate involves both the effects of measures designed to alter inequality and the merits and demerits of these effects. If, however, the distribution of income is looked upon merely as a means and not as a goal, the ethical position is automatically taken that income distribution *per se* does not matter. This position, it should be noted, is a definite ethical point of view. There is no logical way to avoid the distribution question in appraising tax formulas.

Other Canons for Tax-Transfer Measures. In addition to the fundamental question of how much each person is to be burdened or benefited by taxes and transfer measures, there are many other considerations involved. For every effect of a tax or transfer measure, there are many possible value judgments that may be applied. Only some of the more important ones need be mentioned here. These are the canons of fairness, efficiency, allocation, and stabilization.

Fairness. One general rule for the conduct of government toward individuals calls for fair treatment of each person; this applies with equal force to tax laws or transfer laws. The opposite of fairness is discrimination. To hold that a particular government action is unfair is to condemn it; to define unfairness involves difficult and subtle problems.

In tax and transfer programs, the general definition that has often been used is the one of similar treatment of people who are similarly situated in all relevant respects. A tax measure that called for a tax payment by people with red hair would be deemed unfair because color of hair is an irrelevant difference among people. On the other hand, a transfer program that provides payments to veterans but not to others may be regarded as fair; the difference between veterans and non-veterans is deemed to be a relevant difference among people. Many business groups favor taxing cooperatives more severely under the federal income tax on the grounds that cooperatives are at present given an unfair advantage. In this case the position is taken that the difference between one form of business organization and another is not a difference sufficient to justify the differences in tax treatment which in fact exist.

All tax-transfer programs found in any country are unfair in the sense that people with the same income are in fact called upon to pay different amounts of tax. Fair treatment in this sense could not as a practical matter be achieved by a tax structure consisting of a variety of taxes—the typical pattern. If fairness is to be obtained even approximately in this sense, the tax structure of a country would need to be a monolithic one, such as a single tax upon income or a single tax upon net worth. Transfer payments, too, would need to be determined by an index of "ability" such as size of income. Even then, these measures would have to be drawn in a highly rigorous and comprehensive fashion. In a federal system of government, a single tax-transfer measure of this kind would require the federal government to provide all funds to be spent at state and local levels. Local autonomy in taxation would have to be abandoned because it violates the condition of equal treatment of people with equal incomes.

Efficiency. There are always some costs of administering tax and transfer programs. An efficiency test calls for minimizing these costs. The costs should include not only those of the government itself, but of the taxpayers and others who may be involved. A collection-at-the-source type of income tax imposes costs upon employers. These are costs to society, and weight should be given to them. Income taxes entail costs to the taxpayers, in the form of bookkeeping and time in making out tax returns. By simplifying the law and the regulations, these costs could be reduced.

Larger questions of efficiency arise. Tax measure A that yields $10 billion per year may be deemed to be more efficient than tax measure B that yields the same sum, because the negative effect of tax A upon private expenditures is greater than that of tax B. Efficiency in this context refers to the comparative differences in the potency of dollars to achieve a given goal—namely, the reduction of private expenditures. If a tax revenue of $10 billion by tax measure C does the same work as a revenue of $12 billion by tax measure D, then C is more efficient than D. Whether taxes differ in fact in this way involves complicated issues that will not be pursued here.

Allocation. This test refers to the changes in the product composition—the menu—of an economy resulting from alternative tax measures. Taxes on some commodities and not on others change their prices and the relative quantities produced. The new composition may be better or worse than the old. Tests are needed to make such a judgment. This question need not be pursued here; it is discussed in Chapter 3 and in more detail in Chapters 13 and 14.

Stabilization. One type of tax-transfer measure may be preferred to another because one keeps the economy on a more even keel than does the other. Stabilization itself is a means to yet other goals, such as full employment, price-level stability, and general economic efficiency. Various tax-transfer measures may be ranked by effectiveness in promoting stability. For example, poll taxes rank well below income taxes in this regard. This topic is discussed in Chapter 21.

Over-all Appraisal of Tax-Transfer Measures. When government measures are appraised by the use of more than one canon, they will ordinarily receive different ratings according to each particular canon. Some taxes will get high marks on some grounds and low marks on others. If any tax has been appraised on all the grounds suggested, and this process is of course no simple task, how then is it to be rated in general?

At this point, if not earlier, wide differences in views develop even among students of government finance. To resolve such differences, if they are to be resolved, appeal must be made to some principle to rate the relative importance of different canons. For example, an income tax is a much more expensive tax to administer, from the standpoint of both government and taxpayers, than is a tax upon cigarettes. Few, if any, students of taxation would allow this consideration to influence their appraisal of the two tax devices. On the other hand, people who believe that a highly progressive tax induces people to work less and who disapprove of such effects may argue for a less progressive rate schedule. They may or may not care about the differences in income distribution implied.

Reconciliation of differences in views about the weight to be given to various canons, all of which are acceptable, involves a retreat to yet more fundamental ethical ideas. Would a tax proposal calling for the substitution of a net worth tax in place of a system of high-yielding import duties be an improvement for the people of Venezuela? As a preliminary to answering such a question, the comparative effects of each tax device must be studied and exposed. Having accomplished this much, one finds that import duties are less costly to administer than a net worth tax and do nothing significant to change the pattern of income distribution, whereas a net worth tax would have large effects in this regard. Then the question to be decided is whether the extra costs are worth the gain—the reduction in income inequality. If the stability of the society requires a substantial reduction in income inequality, the question becomes relatively easy to answer. But rarely is the issue so clear-cut. In principle, appeal is then made to what are deemed to be the characteristics of the good society, or rather, the improving society. Differences of opinion may yet remain. Reasonable people may differ in their views and do so reasonably.

Part I

SUGGESTED READINGS

General:

Bator, Francis M. *The Question of Government Spending.* New York: Harper & Bros., 1960.
   Part I gives a concise quantitative analysis of government expenditures—federal, state, and local—from 1929 to 1957, and Part II contains a discussion, designed primarily for the layman, of the basic issues in the allocation of resources between government and private use.
Colm, Gerhard. *Essays in Public Finance and Fiscal Policy.* New York: Oxford Univ. Press, 1955.
   See especially the essay entitled "Why Public Finance?" and Part IV on Government Budgets and National Income.
Musgrave, Richard A., and Alan T. Peacock (eds.). *Classics in the Theory of Public Finance.* New York: The Macmillan Co., 1958.
   Contains selected writings, translated into English, from the 1880-1930 Continental European debate on the optimum distribution of resources between the government and the private sector and on the ideal means of taxing individuals. The editors' introduction summarizes the evolution of the basic ideas.
Musgrave, Richard A. *The Theory of Public Finance.* New York: McGraw-Hill Book Co., 1959.
   Sets forth and defends the voluntary-exchange approach to government expenditures (see chaps. i and iv).
Rolph, Earl R. *The Theory of Fiscal Economics.* Berkeley: Univ. of California Press, 1954.

See especially the first five chapters for further discussion of fiscal problems in general.

U. S. Congress, Joint Economic Committee. *Federal Expenditure Policy for Economic Growth and Stability.* Washington: Government Printing Office, 1957. Papers submitted by panelists appearing before the Subcommittee on Fiscal Policy.
See especially the parts on Historical Magnitudes, Considerations in Determining Government Functions, Economy and Efficiency in Government Expenditures, Federal Expenditures and Economic Growth, and Procedures for Determining Federal Spending Programs. In addition there are separate sections on each of the major kinds of federal spending.

Historical:

Abramovitz, Moses, and Vera Eliasberg. *The Growth of Public Employment in Great Britain.* ("A National Bureau of Economic Research Study.") Princeton: Princeton Univ. Press, 1957.
A statistical study of government employment trends in Great Britain, 1890-1950, and a comparison of government employment in Great Britain and the United States, 1900-1950.

Ecker-Racz, L. Laszlo. "A Foreign Scholar Ponders the 1957 Census of Governments," *National Tax Journal,* XII (June, 1959).
A quantitative analysis of government finances in 1957 with comparisons back to 1902.

Fabricant, Solomon. *The Trend of Government Activity in the United States Since 1900.* New York: National Bureau of Economic Research, 1952.
A comprehensive statistical study for all levels of government from 1900 to 1950.

Kendrick, M. Slade. *A Century and a Half of Federal Expenditures.* Occasional Paper 48. New York: National Bureau of Economic Research, 1955.
A quantitative analysis of federal expenditures, including a comparison of war-connected and civil expenditures, from 1794 to 1952.

Paul, Randolph E. *Taxation in the United States.* Boston: Little, Brown & Co., 1954.
A detailed history of federal taxation.

Budgeting:

Blough, Roy. *The Federal Taxing Process.* New York: Prentice-Hall, Inc., 1952.
An informative treatment of the way in which revenue laws are developed and passed and of the conflicting issues, opinions, and group interests underlying this procedure.

Burkhead, Jesse. *Government Budgeting.* New York: John Wiley & Sons, 1956.
A comprehensive economic analysis emphasizing organizational and administrative procedures.

Committee for Economic Development. *Control of Federal Government Expenditures.* New York, 1955.
Suggestions for the improvement of the federal budget process by the CED's Research and Policy Committee.

Douglas, Paul H. *Economy in the National Government.* Chicago: Univ. of Chicago Press, 1952.
A discussion of federal efficiency which combines economic, political and practical considerations.

Goode, Richard, and Eugene A. Birnbaum. "Government Capital Budgets," *Staff Papers of the International Monetary Fund* (Feb., 1956), pp. 23-46.
A concise analysis of the economic implications of the use of separate capital and current budgets by different types of governments.

McKean, R. N. *Efficiency in Government through Systems Analysis with Emphasis on Water Resources Development.* New York: John Wiley & Sons, 1958.
See the analysis of performance budgeting in chap. xiii.

SMITHIES, ARTHUR. *The Budgetary Process in the United States.* New York: Mc-Graw-Hill Book Co., 1955.

A Committee for Economic Development research study of past federal budgetary procedures and of methods of improving them.

TICKTON, SIDNEY G. *The Budget in Transition.* Planning Pamphlet No. 89. Washington, D.C.: National Planning Association, 1955.

Discusses the nature and significance of changes in the treatment, form, and method of reporting Budget statistics made during the fiscal years 1951-1956.

Ethical and Philosophical:

KNIGHT, FRANK H. "Professor R. B. Perry on Value," *Journal of Political Economy,* LXIII (April, 1955), pp. 162-73.

A criticism from an economic point of view of an important contributor to the philosophical theory of value.

LAMPMAN, ROBERT J. "Recent Thought on Egalitarianism," *Quarterly Journal of Economics,* LXXI (May, 1957), pp. 234-66.

Assesses developments in egalitarian thinking, pro and con.

SABINE, GEORGE H. *A History of Political Theory,* 2d ed. New York: Holt, Rinehart & Winston, 1950.

A comprehensive, scholarly study of political ideas, including ethical ideas, as applied to political affairs.

SMITH, ADAM. *The Wealth of Nations.* New York: The Modern Library, 1931.

The famous four canons of taxation are in Book V, chap. ii, part 2.

WHITEHEAD, ALFRED NORTH. *Adventures of Ideas.* New York: The Macmillan Co., 1952.

A philosophical analysis of ethical and sociological topics.

WICKSELL, KNUT. "A New Principle of Just Taxation," reprinted in *Classics in the Theory of Public Finance,* ed. Richard A. Musgrave and Alan T. Peacock. New York: The Macmillan Co., 1958.

The original exposition of the voluntary-exchange theory of public finance.

Current Statistical Sources:

TAX FOUNDATION. *Facts and Figures on Government Finance,* 10th ed., 1958-1959. New York: Tax Foundation, 1958.

A very useful statistical summary covering all three levels of government.

UNITED NATIONS. *Statistical Yearbook.*

Gives budgetary data (in broad categories only) for a large number of countries.

The Budget of the United States Government.

Detailed statistics are included in the statements of separate departments and agencies, in summary tables, and in a number of special analyses at the end. Students wishing more general summaries of the content of the budget are referred to the following:

　　Budget Message of the President, included each year in *The Budget of the United States Government;*

　　The Federal Budget in Brief, an annual summary of the federal budget published by the Bureau of the Budget.

U.S. BUREAU OF THE BUDGET. *Federal Budget Midyear Review.*

Published annually, usually in the early fall, giving revised estimates of federal revenues and expenditures for the fiscal year then about one-quarter under way.

Economic Report of the President, transmitted to the Congress in January.

U.S. DEPARTMENT OF COMMERCE. *Survey of Current Business.*

See especially the issue for July.

U.S. DEPARTMENT OF COMMERCE, BUREAU OF THE CENSUS. *Compendium of City Government Finances; Compendium of State Government Finances;* and *Summary of Governmental Finances.*

Each published annually.

U.S. SECRETARY OF THE TREASURY. *Annual Report.*

U.S. TREASURY DEPARTMENT. *Treasury Bulletin* and *Statistics of Income.*

Bulletin published monthly, *Statistics of Income* annually.

Part II

TAXATION

Introduction

In the chapters of Part II, various types of taxes used by governments are discussed. In addition to setting forth the characteristics and effects of these various tax devices, the discussion emphasizes certain basic principles of analysis. If these are mastered, one may investigate any tax to discover what effects it may be expected to have, to learn what information one should have to determine the importance of these effects, and in the light of canons of taxation, to appraise the tax as a feature of a revenue system.

Of the various taxes found in any actual revenue system, their joint effects must be brought together in answering such questions as whether high-income groups are taxed more or less heavily than are low-income groups, or whether particular industries are subject to higher taxation than are others, and so on. Questions of this type cannot be answered simply by examining the effects of one tax and leaving others out of account. To find out whether the petroleum industry is over- or under-taxed in relation to others, for example, the special depletion allowances granted the petroleum industry under the corporate and individual federal income taxes must be considered along with any special local taxes, such as those on motor vehicle fuels, the severance taxes imposed by some states, and possibly property taxes, if they are different from those imposed upon other industries. The effects of all such taxes must be combined before a final, even a tentatively final, answer may be obtained, and as the reader will see later, the process has complexities of a high order.

Even experts in public finance come up with different answers to questions of the shifting of particular taxes. When the experts differ, what then shall those who can make no such claim believe? Where topics are controversial, and many in the field of taxation are of this character, the reasons for differences may in many cases be pinpointed and a judgment made as to the pertinence of the particular reasons. Going beyond this, careful study of a subject should permit an independence of thought, an ability to investigate a topic and reach a sensible conclusion, including the conclusion that the necessary evidence to permit a positive conclusion is as yet unavailable. Independence of thought carries with it an ability to select among points of view, including one perhaps never before suggested. The following discussion attempts to provide a background of ideas out of which independent thinking about taxation may be developed.

6

Personal Income Taxation: Structure of the Tax

The development of income taxes may be viewed as a response to increasingly insistent and articulate demand for a more equitable apportionment of tax burdens. These taxes are the outstanding contribution of popular government and liberal political philosophy to modern fiscal practice . . . Income taxation is broadly an instrument of economic control, a means of mitigating economic inequality.

Henry C. Simons,
Personal Income Taxation,
p. 41.

The personal income tax is in many ways the most impressive development of modern fiscal theory. As simple and majestic in its basic conception as a medieval cathedral, it has a wide appeal to many people as an equitable and rational base for taxation. Its simplicity, however, is a surface phenomenon only. Like the cathedral, the concept of income becomes increasingly complex and mysterious as one studies it more closely. To the interested person its intellectual fascination is virtually endless—the problems involved in defining an objective and equitable tax base are not only, as we shall see in this chapter, extremely difficult but they are also continually changing in form as the economic environment itself changes and develops. The growth of the modern corporation, to cite only one example, has greatly complicated the task of taxing people according to their individual abilities to pay.

The political problems involved in administering a progressive income tax that brings in nearly 50 per cent of all federal tax revenues are equally challenging. As only a short glance at the hearings conducted before the House Committee on Ways and Means or the Senate Finance Committee will indicate, Congress is continually bombarded with requests and pleas for special concessions of one kind or another. To the extent that these pressures are successful, the size of the tax base is whittled away, and the law itself becomes so complicated that only the expert can hope to understand it. Both of these developments raise serious questions about the future usefulness of a tax which relies heavily on wide popular support for its successful operation. It will not be possible to examine all of the baroque embellishments with which the original form of the income tax has become overlaid, but the main features of the important ones will be discussed below. The chapter begins with a brief description of the federal personal income tax law as it existed in 1960 and then proceeds to a more detailed treatment of the main problems involved in setting up and administering an equitable tax.

Federal Personal Income Tax

TAX BASE. The derivation of the tax base begins with *gross income,* a concept which includes such well-known income items as wages and salaries, interest, dividends, business profits, rents, royalties, pensions and annuities. Excluded from gross income, however, are all government payments and benefits to veterans, federal and state social security benefits received by individuals, gifts and inheritances, interest on state and local government debt, and life insurance proceeds paid on the death of the insured. Capital gains and losses, as well as various types of income received in kind rather than in monetary form, are given special treatment, to be discussed below.

From gross income the taxpayer may deduct all out-of-town travel expenses—i.e., all expenditures for transportation, meals, lodging, tips, and baggage charges if he has been away from home at least one night—as well as any local transportation expenses which he is required to pay in connection with his job.[1] The result of these deductions is *adjusted gross income,* an aggregate which plays an important role in the subsequent definition of the tax base. It should be stressed that while the adjusted gross income of a business or professional man is his gross receipts less all ordinary and necessary expenses under-

---

[1] Any payment which his employer gives him to cover these expenses is part of the employee's gross income. Commuting expenses between home and work are not deductible for tax purposes.

taken in order to earn that income, wage earners can deduct similar expenses only at a later point.

The third step in the computation of the tax base is to subtract various personal deductions from adjusted gross income in order to obtain the taxpayer's *net income*. There are seven main kinds of personal deductions:

1. Contributions to charitable, religious, or educational organizations are deductible up to a maximum of 20 per cent of adjusted gross income, and an additional 10 per cent is allowed if the recipients fall in the narrower category given special preference under the law (e.g., churchs, tax-exempt educational institutions, or hospitals).

2. Medical and dental expenses may be deducted to the extent that they exceed 3 per cent of adjusted gross income, but maximum limits are placed on the deduction according to the family status of the taxpayer. The allowance, in short, is for extraordinary medical and dental expenses, provided they are not too extraordinary.

3. A working wife may deduct the expenses of child care up to a maximum of $600. A family with an adjusted gross income of over $4,500, however, must reduce this deduction by the amount of income that they receive in excess of $4,500. If they reach an adjusted gross income of $5,100, therefore, they cease to receive any tax allowance for child care expenses.

4. Interest on personal debt incurred to purchase homes or consumer durables is deductible for tax purposes.

5. Similarly deductible are state income taxes, real and personal property taxes, and state sales and gasoline taxes. Other taxes, of which federal excises and social security payroll taxes are the most important examples, may not be deducted.

6. Losses resulting from the destruction of personal property by natural forces such as fire or storm or by automobile accidents are deductible, as well as losses suffered as a result of theft.

7. Finally, wage and salary earners may deduct all ordinary and necessary employee business expenses, as well as any expenditures required for the production or collection of income. Note that self-employed people will already have deducted this type of expenditure in the computation of their adjusted gross incomes.

The taxpayer may either deduct the total of whatever expenditures he has incurred in any of the above categories or he may take a standard deduction of 10 per cent of his adjusted gross income up to a maximum allowance of $1,000. The latter procedure is, of course, considerably simpler than the detailed itemization of specific personal deductions, and for many taxpayers it may also be an advantageous alternative. Approximately three-quarters of all taxpayers use the standard deduction.

Taxable income, which forms the base to which the tax rates given in the next section are applied, is obtained by subtracting personal exemptions from net income. The taxpayer is allowed one exemption of $600 for himself, one for his wife, and one for each of his dependent children. Additional $600 exemptions are allowed if the taxpayer is supporting a relative who receives less than $600 gross income or if either the taxpayer or his wife is blind. Finally, any person who reaches the age of 65 may count on a birthday gift from the Secretary of the Treasury in the form of an additional $600 exemption. The value of this gift may, under 1960 tax rates which went as high as 91 per cent, vary anywhere from $546 to zero, depending on the amount of taxable income the taxpayer has.

In summary, then, the tax base is derived from gross income in three steps:

1. gross income — travel and other business deductions = adjusted gross income,
2. adjusted gross income — personal deductions = net income, and
3. net income — personal exemptions = taxable income.

RATE STRUCTURE. Tax rates under the federal personal income tax ranged in 1960 from 20 to 91 per cent, as shown in Table 6–1. Each rate applies only to the range of income shown opposite it in the first column of the table. A single person with a taxable income of $5,000, for example, would pay tax at 20 per cent of his first $2,000, 22 per cent of the next $2,000, and 26 per cent of the last $1,000 for a total tax of $1,100. The average rate of tax ($1,100/$5,000) is 22 per cent, but at the margin—i.e., on any additional dollars that he may receive—the person pays tax at the rate of 26 per cent. The table, then, shows only marginal rates of tax. Average rates also rise as taxable income increases but less rapidly than the marginal rates. At a taxable income of $10,000, for example, the marginal rate is 38 per cent and the average rate 26 per cent, and at $50,000 the two rates are 75 per cent and 54 per cent respectively.[2] Another important feature of this type of progressive rate structure is that in no case will an additional dollar of taxable income result in a tax increase as large as a dollar. In other words, as an English taxpayer said to one of the authors in explaining why income taxation did not induce him to work any less than he otherwise would: "Something always sticks no matter how high the tax rate."

---

[2] The federal law also provides that the average rate of tax may not exceed 87 per cent. For a single person this point is reached at a taxable income of $629,500; beyond that level his marginal tax rate falls from 91 to 87 per cent and is thereafter equal to the average rate.

TABLE 6–1

<small>TAX RATES FOR SINGLE TAXPAYERS UNDER THE FEDERAL PERSONAL INCOME TAX, 1960</small>

Taxable Income	Marginal Tax Rate
$ 0 – $ 2,000	20%
2,001 – 4,000	22
4,001 – 6,000	26
6,001 – 8,000	30
8,001 – 10,000	34
10,001 – 12,000	38
12,001 – 14,000	43
14,001 – 16,000	47
16,001 – 18,000	50
18,001 – 20,000	53
20,001 – 22,000	56
22,001 – 26,000	59
26,001 – 32,000	62
32,001 – 38,000	65
38,001 – 44,000	69
44,001 – 50,000	72
50,001 – 60,000	75
60,001 – 70,000	78
70,001 – 80,000	81
80,001 – 90,000	84
90,001 – 100,000	87
100,001 – 150,000	89
150,001 – 200,000	90
200,001 and over	91

Under federal tax law a married couple, by filing a joint return, may split their total income into two equal parts, compute the tax due on one of these parts and then double it to determine their total tax liability. In effect, this provision simply doubles the size of each of the tax brackets shown in Table 6–1. The single person whose tax was computed in the preceding paragraph could, through marriage, reduce his tax liability from $1,100 to $1,020 (20 per cent of the first $4,000 of his taxable income plus 22 per cent of the last $1,000) even if the law allowed him no additional exemption. Private dowries may have gone out of fashion some years ago, but since 1948 the Secretary of the Treasury has, in some cases at least, been extremely generous in this regard. In our example the husband saves $80 a year on his tax bill as long as he continues to have a taxable income of $5,000. If his taxable income should rise to $50,000, he would save $6,500 a year and at $500,000 annual taxable income the wife's signature on the joint tax return would be worth over $25,000. The pauper and the millionaire, however, are provided with no tax dowry at all. Income splitting for tax purposes confers no advantage on anyone receiving a taxable income of $2,000 or less or on the person whose taxable income exceeds $1,259,000.

The tax gain to the bridegroom from income splitting becomes, of course, a tax loss to the widower. If he has dependent children, the bereaved husband may well feel that the financial burden involved in looking after both himself and them without the help of his wife is quite enough to bear without having the Secretary of the Treasury suddenly demanding increased tax payments. To ease his discontent somewhat the law has, since 1954, allowed income splitting to be continued for two years after the wife's death under these circumstances, and, after that period, the widower may still qualify as a "head of a household" entitled to receive one-half of the tax advantages which income splitting would give him.[3] The "head of the household" regulations, which were added by the Revenue Act of 1951, are not only complex but are also open to question on grounds of equity and logic. Why, for example, should the tax advantage be only one-half of that arising from income splitting; why should it be restricted to the person with dependents living in the same household, especially since those living elsewhere may well involve a greater financial burden; and, finally, why should the parent of a grown and self-supporting child receive a tax benefit simply because the two decide to live together?

In any case, whatever the inequities arising from the tax treatment of family income in this country, they are probably less annoying than the problem facing a married couple in England, where the wife's income must be added to the husband's for tax purposes with the result that a married couple pays more taxes than two single people earning the same income.[4] Taxwise, as critics are fond of pointing out with raised eyebrows, it pays a young British couple to dispense with the benefit of clergy. Indeed, one pair of talented parents did write to the editor of a leading English newspaper pointing out that they had not married because of the tax penalty on such an arrangement when both earned substantial salaries. They had computed the tax savings they were reaping to the last shilling, were investing these to provide for the education of their children, and intended to marry only when the children were over 21 years of age.

CURRENT COLLECTION. Since the early part of World War II, taxpayers have paid their income taxes more or less concurrently with

[3] Lest the reader carry away the impression that the tax law is particularly partial to widowers, we hasten to point out that similar tax privileges are also granted to widows.

[4] To illustrate the effect of this treatment of family income under 1960 tax rates in this country, a married couple, each of whom had a taxable income of $5,000, would pay a total tax of $2,640 whereas by not marrying they would reduce their joint tax bill to 2 $\times$ $1,100 = $2,200.

the receipt of the income on which these taxes were due. For wage and salary earners the employer withholds a part of the weekly or monthly earnings and send it directly to the Treasury. The portion withheld varies inversely with the number of personal exemptions to which the taxpayer is entitled, but is computed at the same standard rate for everyone (18 per cent in 1960) so that those with large salaries ordinarily find that their income taxes are underwithheld. These people, together with anyone who receives over $200 of non-wage income (such as dividends, business profits, interest, or rents), are required to file each April 15 a declaration of the estimated amount of tax they will have to pay that year, over and above any amounts which will be withheld at the source, and to pay that amount in four equal instalments during the remainder of the year. Taxpayers with less than $40 of estimated tax, however, need not file a declaration.

This current collection system has three important advantages. In the first place, the budgeting problems of the individual taxpayer are considerably simplified. No longer is it necessary for him to pay his taxes all in one lump sum in the spring of the year, perhaps discovering at that time that he has already spent most of the money owed to the government. Indeed, many taxpayers now prefer to understate the number of their personal exemptions for withholding purposes so that the deductions made more nearly match their actual taxes due. Secondly, current collection increases the sensitivity of the personal income tax both to economic changes that affect the aggregate level of personal incomes and to changes in the tax law itself. This increases the usefulness of the tax as a fiscal tool designed to help stabilize employment and price levels. Finally, withholding of taxes at the source increases materially the yield of the tax by reducing the extent to which taxable income is underreported or not reported at all. Holland and Kahn, for example, estimated that in 1952, 95 per cent of the wages and salaries that should have shown up on individual tax returns actually did show up, whereas for types of income on which taxes were not withheld at the source the corresponding figures were 87 per cent for dividends, 39 per cent for interest, and 70 per cent for entrepreneurial income (i.e., income of sole proprietors and partners).[5] The surprisingly low figure for interest may be explained by the fact that a large part of personal interest is received in small

[5] Daniel M. Holland and C. Harry Kahn, "Comparison of Personal and Taxable Income," in *Federal Tax Policy for Economic Growth and Stability*, pp. 313-38. Estimates by the same authors for 1957 raised the percentage of interest reported to the 42-63 per cent range but made little change in the figures for dividends and entrepreneurial income. See *Tax Revision Compendium*, Vol. II, pp. 1397-1459. Both of these extremely useful government publications are annotated below in Suggested Readings for Part II, pp. 348-49.

amounts from a large variety of different sources, and much of it flows to people in the lower income groups who, in many cases, keep inadequate records.

ADMINISTRATION. Expenses of the Internal Revenue Service have consistently been less than ½ per cent of total revenues. One of the most important duties of the service is to keep down the amount of income tax evasion. Underestimation of tax liabilities is not only costly to the government (and indirectly to other taxpayers), but if it becomes widespread enough, there is the danger that it will undermine taxpayer morale to the extent that income taxation can no longer play an important role in the fiscal system. Available evidence indicates that while the amount of evasion is small relative to total income-tax yields, its distribution is highly concentrated in certain areas so that important inequities do exist. Fortunately, it also appears that the allocation of additional funds to tax administration, together with the improvement of existing techniques, would reduce evasion everywhere to reasonable dimensions.[6]

Information about the underreporting of taxable income is obtained in a variety of ways. All tax returns reporting high incomes and a selection of those with smaller incomes are examined carefully each year, particular attention being paid to those which, on the basis of past experience, are most likely to contain errors. Information returns are required from corporations which pay out dividends and from anyone who pays out $600 or more in the form of wages and salaries, interest, fees, or other types of income. The recipients' tax returns are then checked to determine whether or not they reported the income shown on the information returns. Bureau agents pay close attention to newspaper stories, court proceedings, or business transactions where large sums of money are involved. A thief who enters a house and absconds with a large amount of cash may get the owner of the house into trouble for tax evasion; property settlements in divorce cases may be quite incompatible with the incomes the husbands have been showing on their tax returns in past years; big spenders may give themselves away by living well beyond their reported means. Anonymous informers frequently supply valuable tips either because they are interested in the rewards to be obtained thereby or simply because they are annoyed with the supposed tax cheater for some reason or another. Unusual currency transactions may be reported by banks, brokers, and other financial institutions. The would-be tax evader is well advised to live a spartan and inconspicuous life; otherwise the

[6] Harold M. Groves, "Income-Tax Administration," *National Tax Journal,* XII (March, 1959), 37-53.

enjoyment of his ill-gotten gains may be short-lived. Penalties for willful tax evasion include a 6 per cent annual interest charge on all unpaid tax liabilities and a fine of $10,000 or a five-year prison term or both on each felony charge.

The Bureau of Internal Revenue's Audit Control Program has turned up some interesting information with regard to tax evasion in 1948.[7] Twenty-six per cent of all the returns filed for that year had tax errors of $2 or more and underestimates outran overestimates by nine to one. As might be expected, tax errors occurred much more frequently among high income taxpayers than among those with small incomes. The total tax change disclosed by the audit was approximately 20 per cent of the tax liability reported on all returns containing a tax error. By far the most frequent and important error occurred in the reporting of adjusted gross income; next came misrepresentation of personal deductions or exemptions. Errors in the latter occurred almost exclusively among low-income taxpayers and particularly among those who listed an exemption for relatives other than children. One out of every three returns listing itemized deductions contained an error but only one in every 250 returns which used the standard deduction contained a mistake. The standard deduction, in short, has made an important contribution to the administration of the personal income tax. The increased tax yield per man-year of effort devoted to the examination of tax returns selected at random was placed between $9,000 and $18,000 for the low-income returns and rose to $197,000 for those in the highest income brackets. If all leads obtained from the selected returns were followed up (i.e., to returns for the same taxpayer in other years or returns filed by related taxpayers) the yields would increase by almost 50 per cent in the lower income groups and by over 100 per cent at the very top.

Concept of Income

A person's income is simply his total gain measured in money terms over a given period of time. To obtain it we ordinarily start with his gross receipts and subtract all expenditures which were required to obtain those gross receipts. A doctor's income, for example, is the difference between the total fees received from his patients and the costs of operating his office and of making his professional calls. One

[7] The study was based on a sample of 160,000 tax returns selected from the 52,000,000 returns filed for the 1948 income year. The data given in the text are taken from Marius Farioletti, "Some Results from the First Year's Audit Control Program of the Bureau of Internal Revenue," *National Tax Journal,* V (March, 1952), 65-78. See also Harold M. Groves, "Empirical Studies of Income-Tax Compliance," *National Tax Journal,* XI (Dec., 1958), 291-301.

of the most important of the deductible expenses is an allowance for capital maintenance. An investor who buys 10 shares of stock for $300, receives dividends of $20, and subsequently sells the stock for $290, has a net gain of only $10 from the transaction, half of the dividends received being required to offset the loss of capital value. In other words, his gross receipts are $290 + $20 = $310, his allowance for capital maintenance is the original cost of the shares ($300), and hence his income is simply the difference between the two.

In principle, it is an easy matter to set forth the main bases on which an equitable and practicable income tax should rest. There are three of them:

1. All gains, in the eyes of the Internal Revenue Service, are created equal and are part of the tax base. This rule follows directly from the equity principle, discussed in Chapter 5, that similarly situated taxpayers should be treated similarly. Two taxpayers who have the same total gain, and who are alike in other important respects such as family status, should pay the same income taxes.

2. Taxable income must be measurable, both quantitatively and objectively, by methods which are simple enough to be understood by the average taxpayer. The exercise of subjective judgment in the computation of income should be kept to an absolute minimum and, if possible, eliminated completely. Ideally, if several different people were given the same basic information, each would arrive at exactly the same final income figure.

3. Each taxpayer is allowed full capital maintenance and, in addition, may deduct any expenses which are necessary to the production of income. Other expenditures should not be deductible unless such a policy serves a well-defined and widely accepted public purpose. Losses of all kinds, however, should be deductible from gains in the computation of net taxable income.

Straightforward as these three principles may appear, their application to specific situations is frequently a complex procedure. How complex it may be we shall see in the remainder of this chapter. Before embarking on that discussion, however, the reader is invited to review the previous description of the federal personal income tax and to decide for himself how each of its specific features conforms to the three basic principles given above.

Wages Received in Kind

An important, and probably increasing, portion of employee compensation is received not in the form of money but rather in the shape of desirable goods and services. Meals, lodging, medical or recreational services are all examples if they are provided by the employer either free or at only a nominal charge. At first glance it might appear that the difference between the full market value of the goods received and whatever nominal sum the employee has to pay in order to obtain them should be included in his taxable income. Such a procedure, however, ignores the fact that in many cases the employee may have only limited freedom of choice as to whether or not he accepts the goods or services. The worker, for example, may be expected to participate in certain organized recreational activities which, as far as his own tastes are concerned, are far from being worth what the employer has to pay to provide them. Lodging may be provided only on a short-term basis so that the employee has to maintain a separate establishment of his own; such an arrangement, apart from a less rapid depreciation of his own home, adds nothing to his total income. Free housing for the whole family, however, can be a very important part of his salary.

In essence, then, it is a matter of determining the extent to which the receipt of compensation in kind relieves the taxpayer of an expenditure that he otherwise would have had, or wished, to make. Let us see how this rule could be applied to some of the most important types of nonmonetary compensation:

1. Employee discounts on products bought within the firm. Since the taxpayer has complete freedom to take these items or leave them, his income should include the difference between full market value and whatever he had to pay to obtain them.

2. Meals provided free of charge. In each case the employee is relieved of some expenditure which he otherwise would have had to make, but the meals may not always be worth full market value to him. Inclusion in his income at some lower value, perhaps at the average amount which people in his general income group spend for the meal in question, is appropriate.

3. Meals eaten while away from home on business. Full deductibility is inappropriate because the taxpayer does save on his food bills at home; zero deductibility, on the other hand, involves the unwarranted assumption that he would have spent the same amount of money on food if his job had not involved travel. Again an intermediate figure, related to the extra cost of restaurant meals, is the proper solution.

4. If the employee has to maintain a full-time establishment of his own, whatever additional lodging he receives free is not income in kind, and whatever he has to pay for while on business trips qualifies as fully deductible. To the extent that the lodging takes the place of other accommodation, however, it should be included in taxable income. In such cases the employee might well be allowed to choose the lower of (a) the full market value of the housing services received or (b) the average amount spent on such services by people in his same general income class.

Federal law is typically overly generous as far as compensation in kind is concerned. Many fringe benefits, such as employee discounts or free medical and recreational facilities, are not taxable at all. Free meals and lodging need not be included in taxable income if they are provided for the convenience of the employer, a test which is far from being free from ambiguity. In practice, these items are exempt if they are provided at the employee's place of work, but they become taxable if he has the option of taking them in the form of cash.

Income in Kind from Owner-Occupied Homes

One of the less obvious forms of nonmonetary income is that received by every person who lives in his own home. In England, where such income is included in the tax base, many people find it difficult to understand why they should be assessed in this way. In the United States, although this kind of income amounted to $6.4 billion in 1957, it has so far escaped taxation. Yet it must be clear that if landlords can make a living from the renting of housing services to others, the home owner must receive some net income when he rents his own home to himself.

Consider, by way of example, an individual who initially has $30,000 invested in stocks and bonds and uses the $1,200 annual income from these to rent a $10,000 house. We need not be concerned with whatever other income he has, although presumably he has some. He includes, of course, the $1,200 in his total taxable income. Suppose, now, that he decides to buy the house he is living in by selling $5,000 worth of his investments and taking a $5,000 mortgage on which he pays $200 interest each year. In addition, he pays, as a home owner, property taxes of $300, maintenance and insurance expenses of $200, and allows for depreciation on the house $300 each year. These expenses of home ownership total $1,000, which is the exact amount of income that he now receives from his investments. As far as housing services are concerned, he is in the same position as he was as a renter. In computing his taxable income, however, he may start with the $1,000 income from his investments and deduct the interest paid on his mortgage and his property taxes. His shift to home ownership, therefore, has reduced his taxable income from $1,200 to $500.

Home owners, then, are granted a substantial subsidy under the current federal tax law. In support of this treatment one might argue cogently the various advantages to be gained from encouraging people to own their own homes. Use of the income tax for this purpose, however, is a very inefficient approach to the problem. The largest subsidies are given in the upper income groups where they are least needed, and many people who need financial assistance in acquiring a home are given none because they are not subject to income taxation. Furthermore, the subsidy is a hidden one that is difficult to appraise because the total amount of money involved is unknown. The equity of the personal income tax would be considerably improved if each home owner were required to include in his taxable income an imputed net rental calculated as the difference between the gross rental value of the premises occupied and all expenses of ownership such as depreciation, maintenance, insurance, and property taxes. The encouragement of home ownership could then be pursued on a more direct and efficient basis.

Houses, of course, are not the only item yielding a return in kind to the owner-user. All consumer durables fall into this category and should, strictly speaking, be treated in exactly the same way as owner-occupied homes. The amounts of income involved, however, are considerably smaller. Only empirical studies can indicate whether the equity gains from the inclusion of such items in the tax base would exceed the administrative costs of doing so.

Self-Service and the Services of Housewives

Most people receive some nontaxable income in kind by consuming their own services. Taxwise it pays a person to do his own gardening, paint his own house, or build his own kitchen cabinets rather than to earn additional money, on which he must pay taxes, in order to pay a professional worker to do the same job. The great popularity of "do-it-yourself" kits in a period of high income tax rates is probably no accident. It is interesting to note that in a highly specialized, monetary economic system the tax laws tend to encourage a movement toward old-style self-sufficient households. The extent of the movement, of course, is considerably limited by the inability of many people to master more than one or two additional skills. The jack-of-all-trades is the man-of-few-taxes in the modern world. Furthermore, there is probably little that can be done about discriminations of this sort because objective calculation of the amounts of income involved would be extremely difficult, if not impossible. We shall have to console ourselves with the comforting thought that services rendered by the taxpayer to himself are more or less evenly distributed within any given income group. Those who feel that income tax rates should not be less progressive than they now are will be further reassured by the fact that self-services tend to be more heavily concentrated in the lower income groups. To include their value in the tax base without also adding the value of the pleasures of leisure time, which are enjoyed more than proportionately by the wealthier groups, would represent a significant decrease in the progressivity of the tax rate structure.

Although the services rendered by housewives to their families constitute the largest industry in the United States, national income estimators have so far avoided quantitative measurement of their importance (perhaps, being men, they dare not try). Current exclusion of these services from the tax base gives rise to significant discriminations between single persons and married couples and between families where the wife has an outside job and families where she does not. It may not be true that two can live as cheaply as one, but two can certainly live more cheaply together than apart, as long as one of them is a reasonably eager and efficient housewife. Similarly, the family with a working wife is involved in consumption expenditures which it otherwise would not have to make. These range all the way from the cost of hiring a housekeeper or baby sitter, to the less obvious costs arising from the need to eat more meals in restaurants or from reduced opportunities to look for price discounts and other bargains. In principle, the tax law should permit working wives and single persons to deduct whatever additional costs of this sort they have to meet as compared to married couples where the wife is free to devote most or all of her time to housewifely activities. The 1954 code's allowance to working wives for certain expenses of child care represents a step in this general direction. The difficulty, of course, lies in segregating within the deductible category only those expenses which the single person would not make if he were married or the working wife would not have to pay if she were a housewife.[8] A solution that would be considerably simpler to administer would involve setting the total personal exemption for a married couple at less than twice the exemption allowed a single person, and increasing it in amount as the wife does more and more outside work until, for all wives with full-time outside employment, it reaches a figure equal to twice the single person's exemption.

Interest on Government Debt

All interest paid on state and local government debt has been exempt from income taxation since the federal income tax was first levied in 1913. This statutory exclusion is directly traceable to the

[8] The $5,100 adjusted gross income ceiling beyond which no child care expenditures are deductible represents a rough solution to this problem if families above that income level typically pay others to look after their young children even when the wife is not gainfully employed.

doctrine of intergovernmental tax immunity first propounded by the United States Supreme Court in *McCulloch* v. *Maryland*[9] and later extended to exempt from federal income taxation both the salaries received by state and local government employees and any interest paid on state and municipal bonds.[10] Since the beginning of the present century, at which time the immunity doctrine had its greatest scope, the Supreme Court has successively circumscribed it more and more. Taxes on capital gains realized from the sale of tax-exempt government bonds were held taxable in 1931, and later in that decade each level of government was granted the right to levy an income tax on the salaries of employees of the other level of government.[11] In view of these developments and particularly the lines of reasoning used by the Court in upholding the taxation of governmental salaries, there is a strong probability that the Court would remove the immunity granted to interest on government bonds if the issue were now presented to it.[12]

The interest exemption conflicts, of course, with the equity requirement that similarly situated taxpayers be treated similarly. Its importance is indicated by the fact that in 1957 individuals received nearly $600 million of tax-exempt interest and that in 1958 corporations received $660 million.[13] In effect, state and local bonds are sold to different people on widely differing terms. To a person with a taxable income of $10,000, for example, a 2½ per cent tax-exempt bond is equivalent to a 4 per cent taxable security since taxable interest would, at 1960 tax rates, be subject to a marginal tax rate of 38 per cent.[14] To a taxpayer with $100,000 taxable income, on the other hand, the equivalent taxable rate is 22.7 per cent and it rises as high as 28 per cent for someone subject to a marginal tax rate of 91 per cent. High-income investors are consequently attracted away from invest-

[9] The Court's decision [4 Wheaton 316 (1819)] held unconstitutional a heavy discriminatory tax levied by the State of Maryland on any out-of-state bank which issued bank notes within the state.

[10] See *Collector* v. *Day,* 11 Wall. 113 (1870) and *Pollock* v. *Farmers' Loan and Trust Co.,* 157 U.S. 429; 158 U.S. 601 (1895). Any government, of course, has the constitutional right to tax interest on its own debt, and this the federal government has done since 1941.

[11] The capital gains tax case was *Willcuts* v. *Bunn,* 282 U.S. 216 (1931); this was followed by *Helvering* v. *Gerhardt,* 304 U.S. 405 (1938), upholding a federal income tax on the salary of a municipal employee, and *Graves* v. *O'Keefe,* 306 U.S. 466 (1939), which held constitutional a New York State income tax levied on a federal employee and expressly overruled *Collector* v. *Day.*

[12] Cf. B. U. Ratchford, "Intergovernmental Tax Immunities in the United States," *National Tax Journal,* VI (Dec., 1953), 305-332.

[13] *Tax Revision Compendium,* Vol. I, pp. 263, 289.

[14] Table 6–1. A 4 per cent return before taxes becomes $4 - .38 \times 4 = 2.48$ per cent after taxes if the tax rate is 38 per cent.

ments in private undertakings and this is particularly damaging to the investment market because many of the opportunities passed by involve relatively high risks which wealthy individuals, because of their ability to diversify their holdings, are peculiarly suited to undertake. At the same time, the progressivity of the federal income tax is reduced because tax-exempt securities are highly concentrated in the hands of high-income groups. In 1940, for example, individuals receiving net incomes over $25,000 a year, who constituted only 6.5 per cent of all those reporting net incomes of $5,000 and over, received over 65 per cent of the wholly tax-exempt interest reported by that group. By contrast, the same people received only 30 per cent of the adjusted gross income, 26 per cent of the taxable interest, and 53 per cent of the dividends reported by the entire group.[15]

The result of this tax treatment is a federal subsidy to state and local governments equal to the difference between the interest rates at which they are now able to borrow and the higher rates which they would have to pay if all interest payments were fully taxable. In recent years this rate differential has hovered between 0.4 per cent and 1 per cent. This subsidy has two peculiar features. In the first place, it costs the federal government a good deal more money than the state and local governments receive. With progressive tax rates a government can expect to sell tax-exempt bonds at a price sufficiently high (interest rate sufficiently low) to reflect the full value of the tax exemption only if the bonds are sold exclusively to persons otherwise subject to the maximum marginal tax rate. Since tax-exempts are much more widely distributed than that in this country, the interest-rate gain to the state and local governments is significantly less than the revenue loss to the federal treasury.[16] Secondly, the subsidy is not closely related to need since there is, if anything, a positive correlation between per capita state debt and per capita state income payments (which may be taken to vary inversely with the state's need for a subsidy). In addition the subsidy, like any other generated through the structure of the personal income tax, is a hidden one and the desirability of encouraging state and local government investment relative to private investment by this means is consequently difficult to appraise.

[15] George E. Lent, *The Ownership of Tax-Exempt Securities, 1913-1953,* Occasional Paper 47 (New York: National Bureau of Economic Research, 1955), pp. 98-99.

[16] A recent study estimates that although in 1947 the exemption reduced state and local borrowing costs by approximately 70 cents of each dollar of revenue lost by the federal government, this reduction had fallen to less than 20 cents per dollar by 1956. See Roland I. Robinson, "Factors Accounting for the Sharply Increased Cost of State and Local Government Borrowing," *Journal of Finance,* XII (May, 1957), 131-32.

Removal of government bond interest from the tax-exempt category has so far been successfully opposed by state and local governments who stand to lose the most from such a change in tax policy.[17] Presumably they distrust the willingness of the federal government to make up at least some of this loss by means of direct subsidies. To the extent that they are right we have yet another argument against the present tax exemption—namely, that the subsidy is larger than it should be (i.e., larger than would be voted by a democratic legislature having all the relevant facts). A subsidy, it would seem, is a delicate flower that is likely to shrivel and shrink if exposed fully to the light.

The taxation of interest on all future issues of government debt would involve no difficult administrative problems. Such a policy would, of course, mean that the phenomenon of tax-exempt interest would be eliminated gradually as all outstanding issues reached maturity and were retired. A more drastic solution, whereby all government debt interest currently paid was made taxable immediately, would precipitate widespread capital losses on outstanding debt issues. Since the lowering of tax bills is only one of several reasons people may wish to hold state and local government securities, these capital losses would be difficult to justify on an equity basis. They could be offset by having the federal government pay to all holders of exempt securities the sums so lost, but this would involve some administrative problems. In any case, whatever the prospects for future elimination of tax-exempt interest on government debt, the arguments developed above apply equally well to the suggestion, which appears from time to time in Congress (especially when interest rates are rising), that the federal government save itself some interest expense by issuing tax-exempt securities. Even on straight economy grounds this policy is undesirable since interest expense would be saved only by the sacrifice of a greater amount of tax revenue. General tax rates might well have to be raised as a result.

Annuities, Social Security, Pensions, and Life Insurance

Each of these items involves complex problems in tax equity and administration. Ordinarily, a person buys an annuity out of taxed income, and he should be allowed, therefore, to deduct the total of these expenditures from his subsequent receipts as an allowance for capital maintenance. Since the 1954 tax code went into effect the

---

17 Their loss would come from the increase in their costs of borrowing that would accompany the policy. Offseting this loss to some extent would be the ability of the state governments with personal income taxes to tax interest on federal government debt.

recipient of a life annuity has been allowed a deduction as follows: he can divide his total cost by the number of years of life expectancy which he has (according to recognized mortality tables) at the time he starts to receive benefits from the annuity and can deduct this amount from his annual gross receipts from the annuity in determining his taxable income. These deductions may be taken each year as long as the annuitant lives. Those who die relatively soon, therefore, will be denied full capital maintenance; more vigorous (or tenacious) taxpayers are granted larger deductions than they are entitled to. In effect, the federal government is making them a gift of what it gains from the group that fails to live up to its life expectancy. If the mortality tables used are accurate, annuitants will, on the average, be allowed exact capital maintenance.[18]

In contrast to this treatment, persons under social security are taxed on their contributions to the Old Age and Survivors Insurance Fund, but all benefit payments are tax-free when received. Since benefit payments typically exceed the person's own contributions by considerable amounts, persons under social security are more favorably treated than those who provide for their own retirement through annuities or other types of investment. This discrimination, needless to say, has been the cause of considerable discontent among retired taxpayers. The simplest and most equitable way out of the difficulty would have been to make social security benefits taxable to the extent that they exceed the recipient's own contributions to the fund. Politically, however, this solution lacked glamour. Instead, Congress added in the 1954 code a marvelously complicated device known as the retirement income credit. This is a tax credit at the first bracket rate of 20 per cent allowed on the first $1,200 of so-called "retirement income," so that a taxpayer over 64 years of age may, at a maximum, be able to deduct $240 from whatever other federal income taxes he may be subject to. Retirement income includes all pensions, annuities, interest, rents, or dividends received but must be reduced by the amount of any tax-exempt pension or annuity received (like social security benefits) and, for persons under 72 years of age, by any amount of earned income in excess of $1,200 received during the year. Unless the maximum credit base of $1,200 of retirement income is increased in the future, the growth in social security benefit payments will gradually eliminate this special provision from the tax laws.

[18] If the annuity is not for life but for a fixed number of years, the annual allowance for capital maintenance is simply the total cost of the annuity divided by the number of years over which benefit payments are to be made. In this case, full capital maintenance is granted to any person who lives long enough to receive all benefit payments to which he is entitled under the annuity contract.

Private pension plans are treated in various ways, but a plan which meets the requirements of the Treasury as to its permanence, the number of employees covered, and its nondiscriminatory nature, receives several tax advantages. Employee contributions to the plan are tax-exempt as is any income earned by the pension trust through investment of the funds which it has at its disposal. If the employee receives benefit payments over a number of years, these are treated as an ordinary annuity with the employee's cost being the sum of his previous contributions into the fund. If, on the other hand, all the benefits are taken in a lump sum on retirement, the excess over total previous contribution is taxed at the lower rates applying to a long-term capital gain.[19]

The tax benefits arising from a fully qualified pension plan, then, may include: (1) employee contributions into the plan (which, though they are a type of saving, are not subject to income tax as are other types of savings); (2) income earned on the funds invested (completely tax-exempt); (3) a deduction for capital maintenance permitted recipients of benefits (even though they are entitled to none since their contributions were not taxable in the first place); and (4) favorable capital gains treatment accorded benefit payments taken in a lump sum.

Life insurance typically provides both protection for the family against the risk of premature death of the insured person and a form of investment on which interest accumulates and is paid out when the policy matures. Under present law this interest is not taxable and thus provides another source of tax-free income for the wealthy. The simplest solution to the problem would be to make it taxable, either to the insured or his estate, when the policy is terminated.

Capital Gains and Losses

One of the more curious inconsistencies in American tax law is the treatment accorded capital gains and losses. British law, to be sure, is even more paradoxical on this score. In the United States a man can make a million dollars in the stock market and be taxed on his gains at a maximum rate of 25 per cent; an Englishman with similar good fortune in his speculations would pay no income tax at all on this gain. In either country, however, equally large incomes from salaries or dividends or rents are assessed at rates approaching, and even exceeding, 90 per cent.

Capital gains occur whenever a capital asset increases in money value so that the owner could sell it for more than he paid for it.

[19] See below, p. 124.

Strictly speaking, the owner has income to the extent of the gain even though he continues to hold the asset. Taxation of capital gains as they accrue, however, would require annual valuations of all capital assets, an administrative problem likely to appall the most conscientious tax official. In practice, then, capital gains must be made taxable, and capital losses deductible, only when the assets in question are sold or exchanged. The great majority of capital gains in this country (perhaps as high as 80 per cent) are realized on the sale of stocks and bonds.

CURRENT TAX TREATMENT. If capital gains are realized on an asset that has been held for six months or less, they are fully taxable on the same basis as any other kind of income. If, however, the asset has been held more than six months, the capital gain on it qualifies as a long-term gain and the taxpayer may choose from two alternative treatments the one which yields the smaller tax. On the one hand, he may add 50 per cent of his long-term gain to his other income and compute his taxes in the ordinary way; on the other, he may segregate his long-term gains and pay a flat-rate tax of 25 per cent on the full amount of these gains. At 1960 tax rates it paid a single taxpayer to begin segregating his long-term gains as soon as his taxable income reached $18,000 (for a married couple the corresponding figure on a joint return was $36,000). At the worst, then, long-term capital gains are taxed only half as heavily as other types of income. For people in the top tax bracket, on the other hand, an additional $100 of salary would yield only $9 net of taxes, but an additional long-term capital gain of $100 would bring in $75.

Capital losses, regardless of how long the asset has been held, may be deducted in full from capital gains, and if there is still a net loss it may be subtracted from other income up to a maximum of $1,000.[20] Any loss that remains unabsorbed by this procedure may be carried forward for the next five years and offset in each year against any realized capital gains plus a maximum of $1,000 of other income. Restricted deductibility against other income is attributable to the fear that if capital losses were fully deductible, taxpayers could lower their taxes unduly by realizing all of these losses but few of their gains. It might appear that this procedure would simply pile up

[20] It might at first glance seem unfair that long-term capital gains are taxable at only 50 per cent of their full value while long-term capital losses are deductible in full. Such a conclusion, however, assumes that the same people suffer the losses as receive the gains, and this is typically not the case. It would be small consolation to the person who, after perhaps a lifetime of maneuvering in the stock market, has come up with a $100,000 capital loss to be told that he can deduct only half of it for tax purposes because someone else has been taxed only one-half on his $100,000 capital gain.

capital gains for future taxation, but the current treatment accorded property passed to others at the death of the owner eliminates this danger. Although the property is valued as part of the total estate, no income tax is assessed on any gain that may have accrued during the lifetime of the decedent. The heirs, furthermore, compute their own capital gains and losses with reference to the market value of the property at the time they receive it. In this way a person with substantial capital gains may remove them completely from income taxation by retaining the property until his death.

THE CASE FOR SPECIAL TAX TREATMENT. It is clear, then, that capital gains and losses are taxed a good deal more leniently than are other kinds of income. Are there any logical considerations that would support such favorable treatment? In the first place, capital gains and losses are a type of income which typically accrues rather irregularly from year to year, and taxation of them on a realization basis tends to accentuate that irregularity. Under a proportional rate structure this fact would not give rise to any tax problems, but with progressive tax rates a fluctuating income is taxed more heavily than a stable income of equal amount. A single person with an annual taxable income of $5,000, for example, would pay $1,100 in taxes each year, whereas a person with $1,000 in one year and $9,000 in the other would have a two-year tax bill of $2,500 ($200 + $2,300).[21] The solution to this discrimination is to allow the second taxpayer to average his total income equally over the two years so that he would pay the same taxes as the first man, and several averaging schemes are described at the end of this chapter. The current treatment of capital gains and losses, however, is not even a very approximate approach to such a solution. In the first place, capital gains and losses are not the only kind of income that fluctuates widely. Secondly, the six-months distinction between short-term and long-term gains makes no sense as an averaging device, and even a more complex arrangement whereby the effective rates on capital gains were lowered in a number of steps as the holding period of the asset increased could only provide a crude offset for the higher taxes imposed on fluctuating incomes.[22]

A second frequently cited reason for special tax treatment of capital gains and losses is the inequity involved in taxing a money gain which, because of generally rising prices, does not represent an in-

---

[21] An annual progressive income tax also discriminates against losses which occur irregularly over time.

[22] Such an arrangement existed in this country from 1934 to 1938. See Anita Wells, "Legislative History of the Treatment of Capital Gains Under the Federal Income Tax, 1913-1948," *National Tax Journal,* II (March, 1949), 12-32.

crease in purchasing power over goods and services. In the postwar period many people found themselves selling homes at higher prices than they had paid for them before the war and being required to pay a tax on their capital gain even though they needed to invest the whole proceeds of the sale in order to obtain another home of comparable quality. An adjustment for this sort of difficulty was made in the Revenue Act of 1951, whereby gain on the sale of the taxpayer's residence was to be recognized only to the extent that the selling price of the old house exceeded the cost of the new, provided the new house was acquired within one year of the sale.

This, of course, represents only a small step away from straight money income toward taxation based upon what economists call real income—i.e., money gains computed in dollars of constant general purchasing power. Any attempt to take the remaining steps would be fraught with enormous administrative complexities. It would be difficult enough to guide taxpayers through the various adjustments that would have to be made in money values by means of approved price index numbers and to explain to them why, when prices in general were falling, they had a taxable capital gain even though they sold their capital assets for no more money than they paid for them. Even more troublesome would be the problem of constructing acceptable price adjustors. A single index number would be open to the criticism that, by reflecting only the average change in prices, it failed to adjust accurately for the actual price changes faced by large groups of people who, because of their consumption habits, were not average taxpayers. Construction of more than one index, however, would skyrocket the costs of tax administration. Furthermore, there is as yet no adequate solution to the problem of measuring price change for goods that undergo significant alterations in quality. Over the past 20 years, for example, the average retail prices of automobile tires have about doubled, but rubber company officials estimate that the cost per 1,000 miles has held steady at about $3 because of improved durability. In this case nominal prices would be completely unacceptable as a basis for measuring changes in the cost of living. In an economy characterized by rapid technological growth extensive (and expensive) studies of quality change would be continually necessary in order to provide even an approximately accurate price index number. Furthermore, in many cases it may be virtually impossible to derive any quantitative measure of quality change. To what extent, for example, are longer and lower cars better than preceding models or how much is a more comfortable ride worth? The more one reflects on these problems the stronger his advocacy of the maintenance of stable price levels by monetary and fiscal policy is likely to become. Given such stability, however achieved, our second argument in favor of special treatment for capital gains and losses evaporates completely.

Other arguments that have been advanced in favor of special tax treatment for capital gains and losses are considerably less fundamental than the first two. It has been contended, for example, that full taxation would unduly restrict the transfer of capital assets and accentuate price fluctuations on the stock market because people would be reluctant to sell assets on which capital gains had accrued but eager to sell those entitling them to capital loss deductions. Empirical evidence indicates, however, that realized capital gains and losses have been markedly inflexible to changes in their tax treatment and have changed closely in line with stock prices. In addition, the taxation of gains and losses whenever property is transferred either by gift or at the death of the owner would not only remove a glaring inequity from the current tax law but also tend to stimulate asset transfers. The argument that taxation of capital gains and losses discourages risk-taking to an undesirable extent overlooks the fact that profits, dividends, and rents are also rewards for risk-taking and fails to give adequate consideration to other tax changes, such as more generous loss offsets, which would also stimulate risk-taking and do so without introducing inequities into the tax law.[23] Some experts have shied away from increased taxation of both capital gains and losses for fear that little if any additional revenue would be obtained thereby. In a progressive economy, however, gains may be expected to exceed losses over the long period, and taxation on a realization basis need not allow gains to escape taxation as long as transfers by gift and at death are made taxable.[24] Even with this escape valve in full operation, net capital gains in the United States exceeded net taxable losses by about $16 billion over the thirty-year period from 1917 to 1946, and during the late 1920's the tax on capital gains contributed almost one-half of total federal tax revenues.[25] Furthermore, since capital gains and losses are very unevenly distributed both within any given income group and from one income level to another,[26] interpersonal equity would be considerably im-

---

[23] The effects of income taxation on risk-taking are discussed below in chap. 7.

[24] On the basis of data for the period prior to 1950 Wilbur A. Steger has estimated that the constructive realization for tax purposes of capital gains at the death of the taxpayer would increase federal revenues by approximately $1.2 billion annually. See "The Taxation of Unrealized Capital Gains and Losses: a Statistical Study," *National Tax Journal*, X (Sept., 1957), 266-81.

[25] Lawrence H. Seltzer, *The Nature and Tax Treatment of Capital Gains and Losses* (New York: National Bureau of Economic Research, 1951), pp. 112, 528.

[26] *Ibid.*, pp. 115-31.

proved by full taxation of this type of income even if no additional revenue at all were raised.

The effects of the current tax treatment of capital gains and losses on the progressivity of the personal income tax are indeed impressive. Although in 1956 the average tax rate, as shown in *Statistics of Income,* rose steadily to a level of 52 per cent on individuals reporting adjusted gross incomes of $1 million and over, the actual rate on income inclusive of all net capital gains and losses rose only to 36-37 per cent. These top effective rates, furthermore, applied to all individuals with adjusted gross incomes of $100,000 and above.[27] One effect of the special treatment of long-term capital gains, apparently, is to convert the federal income tax from a progressive to a proportional levy, on the average, at the highest income levels.

THE CASE AGAINST SPECIAL TAX TREATMENT. For the most part this case has already been made. As we have seen, full tax treatment for capital gains and losses would materially improve the equity of the federal income tax. In addition, the inducement which taxpayers now have to convert ordinary income into capital gains form by increasingly complex devices would be completely removed. Tax avoidance of this sort may range all the way from a simple conversion of dividends into capital gains by having a corporation retain its earnings rather than distribute them, to the creation of a relatively sophisticated collapsible corporation set up to produce, say, a motion picture with the writers, producers, and actors all stockholders; the company is then liquidated at the appropriate moment so that the earnings from the picture qualify as long-term capital gains rather than fully taxable profits, wages, and salaries.[28] With capital gains and losses taxed in the same way as other income there would be no need for the complex provisions of the present law that are designed to distinguish between the two types of income.

SUMMARY. On grounds of simplicity, administrative economy, and interpersonal equity, then, capital gains and losses should be treated in the same way as other types of income. This would require the inclusion of all capital gains and losses in taxable income at 100 per cent of their value, the adoption of income averaging—at least for capital gains and losses and preferably for all kinds of income—and the elimination of the death and gift loopholes by recognizing a taxable realization whenever property is given away or becomes part of

---

[27] See George F. Break, "Income Tax Rates and Incentives to Work and to Invest," *Tax Revision Compendium,* Vol. III, p. 2254.

[28] For further illustrations see Seltzer, *op. cit.,* chap. ix.

an estate. No additional administrative problems would be involved in the latter change since property already has to be valued for the federal gift and estate taxes and for state inheritance taxes.[29] Capital losses should be deductible in full from other kinds of income and generous carry-over provisions should provide for the taxpayer who has a run of bad luck.

Gifts and Inheritances

In principle, gifts and inheritances result in gains to the recipient and should be included in his total taxable income. Since these transfers typically occur with great irregularity, some averaging arrangement would be necessary to ensure that they were not more heavily taxed than other, more regularly recurring, income items. Inclusion of the average annual value of all gifts and bequests in the income of the recipient for tax purposes would make the after-tax value of such windfalls vary inversely with the income position of the person receiving them—a result which would appear equitable to most people. Under current federal law, however, an estate of given size is subjected to exactly the same tax regardless of whether it is being transferred to a pauper or to a millionaire.

The inclusion of gifts and inheritances in the income of the recipient would not imply that they should be made deductible from the income of the donor. Being voluntarily made, gifts must give the donor at least as much pleasure as any alternative use of his money, and hence they need not be treated differently from either consumption or saving. Moreover, deductibility of gifts under the income tax would risk a decline in the tax base as a result of increased evasion. One might, in other words, obtain quite a different picture of the generosity of the American people from the tax returns of the donors than he would from the returns of the recipients. The administrative

[29] It is frequently argued that such a reform would represent double taxation and hence be inequitable. Double taxation, however, is not inequitable so long as everyone is double taxed to the same extent. (Indeed, we are all multitaxed in the modern world.) The substantive issue is whether death taxation can offset whatever favorable treatment is given to capital gains and losses under the income tax. At present a person with accrued capital gains is able to accumulate a larger estate than someone with an equal income who has had to save out of taxed income. This discrimination, however, is only partly removed by the estate tax, since the first person is still able to pass on a larger sum to his heirs. Only death taxes at a 100 per cent rate could equalize the bequeathing powers of the two persons (by reducing each of them to zero), and even then the person with accrued capital gains would have important advantages of power and flexibility during his own lifetime. It would, of course, be necessary to make deductible from the gross value of the estate for death tax purposes whatever income taxes were levied on the capital gains accrued on the assets that made up the estate.

problems of preventing such a shrinkage of the tax base might well be formidable.

Deductions

BUSINESS EXPENSES. Every taxpayer is allowed to deduct all or-dinary and necessary expenses undertaken in order to earn income; personal or consumption expenses, on the other hand, are not de-ductible because they are undertaken purely for the pleasure of the consumer. They are, in short, an important part of his total gain (income). The difficulty, of course, is that many expenditures are mixed in nature—although made in order to earn income, they also contribute directly to the taxpayer's total consumption. A business executive may be required by his firm to belong to a golf club because of the valuable contacts with customers that can be made there; if he is also an avid golfer, it is clear that his employer is providing him with something which he otherwise would have purchased for him-self. Complete deductibility of the golf dues understates his true income; no deductibility at all may, however, be unduly harsh if he would, on his own initiative, have joined a less expensive club.

Illustrations of mixed personal-business expenses are not difficult to find. The dentist who reads his office subscription to *Life* and *Time,* the doctor who goes to a medical convention partly to learn something about new drugs and partly to relax in the sun by the swimming pool, and the professional photographer who uses his equipment on a vacation trip are all enjoying consumption gains for which the United States Treasury helps pay. A 1957 estimate placed expense-account spending in this country at $5 billion a year, with 80 per cent of the people eating in high-priced restaurants and 30-40 per cent of those buying tickets to New York theaters charging the costs to business expenses.[30] In one European corporation with a high taxable income it is said to be a custom of the president to pro-pose the first toast at the annual executives' dinner, "To the Chan-cellor of the Exchequer, who is paying for most of what we are enjoying tonight." In England a strong postwar urge to return to the land is said to have developed; wealthy taxpayers have discovered that a farm, even if run at a loss, does provide such things as horses to ride on week ends, a domain within which to hike and hunt, and quite possibly a stream containing a few trout. The loss, furthermore, is deductible from other income, with the result that the government may in the end pay as much as 92.5 per cent of it.

[30] *U. S. News and World Report,* Aug. 16, 1957, p. 83.

It is undoubtedly true that in all of these cases, as Simons has said, "a thoroughly precise and objective distinction is inconceivable."[31] Only a person with unusually sound judgment and a strong conscience could be expected to make a realistic separation of the two elements, especially when considerable tax gains result from augmenting the business expense category. There is a widespread belief among both taxpayers and tax experts that unjustifiable deductions of this sort constitute a major loophole in the present federal income tax. Some tightening up is undoubtedly possible, but it is not likely that any very satisfactory solution could be reached. Complexities of this sort materially strengthen the case for lowering tax rates in the upper ranges.

DEPRECIATION. Most assets used in trade or business lose their value gradually as a result of wear and tear and exposure to the elements. In addition to these more or less foreseeable developments new inventions may make an item obsolete virtually overnight, with the result that its value falls sharply. Depreciation deductions are designed to allow for all such reductions in value and to spread them over the useful life of each asset in some reasonable fashion.

Until the Revenue Code of 1954, federal tax law was based almost exclusively on straight-line depreciation whereby annual depreciation changes were computed by taking the original cost of the asset (minus salvage value if any) and dividing this figure by the asset's expected number of years of life. In this way the same amount of depreciation was deducted each year. There is considerable evidence, however, that many assets lose value more rapidly in the early years of life. The margin from which capital maintenance deductions must be made, being the difference between gross receipts from the sale of the asset's services and maintenance and operating expenses, may be expected to shrink as the asset becomes older. For one thing, maintenance expenses typically increase over time; for another, the flow of services from the asset may either decrease in volume as it becomes older or they may be worth less in money terms as better assets are invented. Shrinking gross margins for any of these reasons support a depreciation pattern which allows greater deductions in the early years than does the straight-line rule, and the Revenue Code of 1954 allowed the taxpayer the choice of two such accelerated depreciation patterns.[32]

[31] Henry C. Simons, *Personal Income Taxation* (Chicago: Univ. of Chicago Press, 1938), p. 54.
[32] For a detailed analysis of the two methods, see E. Cary Brown, "The New Depreciation Policy under the Income Tax: an Economic Analysis," *National Tax Journal,* VIII (March, 1955), 81-98.

As far as any one asset is concerned, accelerated original-cost depreciation simply means greater deductions during the early years and correspondingly smaller ones later. The total deduction is still confined to the original money cost of the depreciable asset. The business unit as a whole, however, will benefit from accelerated depreciation as long as it either grows in size or remains stable. Only when the firm begins to decline will accelerated depreciation deductions begin to fall short of those permitted under a straight-line pattern.[33]

The more accelerated the depreciation pattern used by the taxpayer the more likely is the depreciated value of an asset to fall short of the value for which the firm could sell it on the open market.[34] A sale of the asset under such conditions would result in a capital gain equal to the sale price minus the depreciated value, but capital gains, as we have seen, are taxed considerably more leniently than other types of income. Here, then, is another device for tax avoidance. The acceleration of depreciation increases deductions during the time the asset is owned but at the cost of increasing the gain realized when the asset is sold. Under a proportional income tax applied equally to all gains the tax value of the increased deductions would precisely equal the tax due on the final capital gain. Even so, the taxpayer would benefit by the postponement of his tax bills. Under current tax law there is the further gain made by reducing ordinary income, subject to tax rates as high as 91 per cent for individuals or 52 per cent for corporations, in one year and increasing capital gains, taxed at a top rate of 25 per cent, in another.

As a result of rising price levels in recent years many firms have found that the replacement of worn-out equipment involves the expenditure of considerably greater sums of money than were originally spent for the discarded assets. Under these conditions, original cost

---

[33] The more accelerated of the two depreciation patterns permitted by the 1954 code is the so-called sum-of-the-years-digits (SYD) method. Each year the ratio between the number of years remaining in the useful life of the asset and the sum of all of the digits used in counting up to that total useful life is multiplied by the original cost of the asset to determine the depreciation charge. For a 10-year asset the depreciation deduction for the second year of its life is, therefore, $9/(1 +2+3+4+5+6+7+8+9+10) = 9/55$ths of the original cost. A firm spending a constant amount of money on 10-year assets each year would find the use of SYD depreciation more advantageous than straight-line depreciation for the first 10 years (in the fifth year, for example, SYD depreciation would be approximately 20 per cent greater), and after that time the two depreciation patterns would yield exactly the same annual deduction. For a firm growing at a constant annual rate of 5 per cent, however, SYD depreciation would always be at least 10 per cent greater than straight-line depreciation, and in the early years the excess would be as great as 80 per cent.

[34] Depreciated value at any given date equals the original cost of the asset minus all depreciation deductions taken up to that date.

depreciation appears altogether inadequate, and many experts have proposed that business firms be allowed to base their depreciation charges on replacement, rather than original, cost. Such a change would, of course, represent a shift from money income to real income for tax purposes, but there is no reason why owners of depreciable assets should be granted the resulting tax benefits and not owners of other types of property. We have already noted the difficulties involved in any adoption of real income for tax purposes. These are augmented in the present instance by the impressive productivity gains that have recently been scored in many types of capital equipment. Writing in the *American Machinist* in 1949, E. J. Tangerman concluded that "both tools and machines have been tremendously improved—so much so that even the rather sharp price increases of the last three or four years are more than balanced," and Burck and Parker noted that the Prudential Life Insurance Company expected to save up to $500,000 a year as a result of substituting one IBM processing machine for sixty to seventy-five oldstyle machines and most of their operators.[35] Under these conditions, nominal prices seriously overstate the amount of inflation that has taken place, and a shift to replacement cost depreciation would not necessarily grant taxpayers larger money deductions for tax purposes than they now receive under original cost depreciation. In any case, the determination of the proper allowance would be exceedingly complex.

DEPLETION. The owner of a wasting natural resource such as an oil well or a copper mine is, like any other businessman, entitled to deduct from his gross receipts whatever expenditures he has had to make in order to acquire the assets and bring them into production. Some of these costs may be deducted immediately as ordinary expenses, and the others may be capitalized and deducted gradually over the productive life of the mine or oil field as a depletion allowance. During the early years of the federal income tax depletion was granted on an original cost basis so that the treatment of wasting assets was parallel to that accorded depreciable property. More recently, however, Congress has become considerably more generous to the owners of natural resources. The history of these developments provides an interesting illustration of how a relatively innocent-looking, minor tax advantage can mushroom into a substantial subsidy.[36]

---

[35] E. J. Tangerman, "Do Machine Tools Cost Too Much?" *American Machinist*, Sept. 8, 1949, p. 90, and Gilbert Burck and Sanford S. Parker, "The Mighty Multiplier," *Fortune*, Oct., 1954, p. 228.

[36] Cf. William F. Hellmuth, Jr., "Erosion of the Federal Corporation Income Tax Base," *Federal Tax Policy for Economic Growth and Stability*, pp. 899-903.

The first income tax acts, although based primarily upon original cost depletion, made an exception for property that was already in existence in 1913 when income taxes were first levied by the federal government. Depletion for such properties could be based on their market value in 1913. Since the market value of successful mineral finds is typically considerably greater than the costs involved in developing them (in one case the costs were $250,000 and the market value of the discovered resource was $39 million), the differential tax treatment accorded properties discovered before and after 1913 received heavy criticism, especially as tax rates rose during World War I and the need to stimulate the discovery of minerals because of the war was stressed. In 1918, therefore, the law was changed to allow depletion to be based on the fair market value of the property at the date of discovery. In this way the capital gain resulting from the discovery of the mineral (i.e., the difference between the market value of the property at the date of discovery and the owner's costs) was made completely tax-exempt to anyone who continued to operate the property long enough to make full use of his depletion allowance.

The administrative problems involved in determining discovery values, however, were soon found to be formidable. Percentage depletion, whereby the mine owner could deduct each year a certain percentage of his gross receipts from the sale of output at the mine or wellhead, was accordingly substituted for discovery depletion for oil and gas wells in 1926 and for other minerals in 1932. The percentages, which ranged from 27½ per cent for oil and gas to 5 per cent for coal, were set so as to allow approximately the same deductions as if discovery depletion had been continued.[37] It is clear, however, that percentage depletion is limited only by the gross receipts which may be obtained from exploiting the mineral deposit; unlike discovery depletion the total amount allowed on existing mineral enterprises will rise as technological developments bring submarginal deposits into production or as prices in general increase. Since 1932 the advantages of percentage depletion have been granted to still more minerals, including some of the less obvious ones such as sand, gravel, and oyster shells.

Both discovery and percentage depletion permit the double deduction of exploration and development costs. Since these expenditures create assets whose economic usefulness will extend over many years, the appropriate treatment would be to deduct them gradually, in the form of depletion expenses, over the life of the mine or oil

[37] Cost depletion could still be used by the taxpayer if it was to his advantage to do so. In addition, percentage depletion could not exceed 50 per cent of the net income from the property in question.

field. If they were completely deducted in the year in which the money was spent, there would be no need for any depletion allowances at all. It is sufficient, in other words, that the costs of earning income be deducted once from gross receipts. This requirement is met if original-cost depletion is used, since under it the immediate deduction of development costs automatically reduces the mine-owner's depletion allowance by an equal amount. No such reduction, however, takes place under either discovery or percentage depletion.[38] Since current law is very generous in allowing exploration and development costs to be deducted when made, percentage depletion allowances to a large extent represent extra deductions which are not required by the definition of income. Pechman and Hellmuth have estimated that in 1957 these subsidies reduced the personal income tax base by $400 million and the corporate income tax base by $4 billion.[39]

It is clear, then, that substantial tax favors have been conferred on the owners of oil and mineral deposits. The effects which this tax treatment has on the economic system, and the arguments both for and against it, will be considered in the following chapter.

TAXES. With the single exception of state and local income taxes, there is no logical justification for the deduction of personal or consumption taxes in the computation of taxable income.[40] In the first place, it is extremely difficult, as we shall see later,[41] to determine the exact extent to which the consumer really pays sales, gasoline, and other consumption taxes. Some theorists, indeed, deny that these taxes are paid by the consumer at all. Secondly, measurement difficulties are such that current tax law draws a number of arbitrary distinctions. Sales taxes, for example, are deductible if the law says they are levied upon the buyer (regardless of what the economic facts are) or if they are imposed upon the retailer and he in turn states them separately from the rest of the price charged to the consumer. Excises levied on manufacturers, however, are not deductible even though they affect retail prices in much the same way as sales taxes. Thirdly, it is extremely difficult for the Treasury to check the

[38] In the example cited above in the text, original-cost depletion would be $250,000 if no costs were deducted in the year in which they were incurred, and zero if all costs were deducted immediately. Discovery depletion, however, would be $39,000,000 in either case and percentage depletion might turn out to be even greater before the mine generated its final dollar of gross receipts.

[39] See the papers by Joseph A. Pechman and William F. Hellmuth, Jr., in *Tax Revision Compendium*, Vol. I, pp. 251-316.

[40] Business taxes, of course, are a legitimate cost of producing income and as such are properly deductible.

[41] Chaps. 13, 14.

amounts claimed by taxpayers as deductible taxes. Finally, we have already noted the fact that deduction of property taxes by home owners tends to increase the discrimination against renters under the personal income tax.

There would be no exceptions to the nondeductiblity rule for non-business taxes in a country where only one level of government imposed an income tax. Where several levels do this, as is currently true in the United States, income taxes could conceivably add up to more than the person's total income unless some integrating provision is adopted. Deduction of state and local taxes in the computation of taxable income for federal purposes not only eliminates completely any danger that taxation will take all of a person's income but also encourages state and local governments to substitute income taxes for other taxes less closely related to the ability of the taxpayer to pay. The further step of making the federal income tax deductible under state income tax law is completely unnecessary as far as the danger of confiscation is concerned, makes the progressivity of the total income tax structure much less than it appears to be, and, as compared to deductibility at the federal level only, seriously reduces the amounts of income taxes collected by the states from high-income taxpayers.[42] In addition, double deductibility would, in many cases, require the solution of simultaneous equations (or the use of complex tables approximating thereto), neither tax being computable until the other tax was known in amount.

CHARITABLE CONTRIBUTIONS. Deductions of this sort go back to the Revenue Act of 1917. Although they are not logically required under an income tax, most people would undoubtedly support them as a desirable part of public policy. The recipients of the tax-encouraged contributions provide valuable services to the community, and in many cases these are services which the government would otherwise have to provide itself. Its net loss, in such cases, is likely to be very small indeed. The tax incentive to make charitable contributions, of course, varies directly with the total income of the taxpayer. In the 91 per cent bracket, for example, the individual has in effect only to put up nine cents of every dollar contributed, the

---

[42] In 1960 the federal income tax for a single person with a taxable income of $200,000 was $156,820. The imposition of a proportional state income tax of 10 per cent on the same tax base would have increased his total tax liability by $20,000 if neither tax law permitted deduction of taxes paid under the other. Federal deductibility of state income taxes would reduce the individual's federal liability by .9 × $20,000 = $18,000 and make his total tax bill of $158,820 only $2,000 more than if the state had not levied an income tax in the first place. Double deductibility would make the federal tax $152,550, the state tax only $4,745, and the total tax $157,295, only $475 more than without the state tax.

federal government making the remainder of the payment to the institution of his choice. Indeed, since capital assets given to charitable organizations may be deducted at current market value and any accrued capital gains are not taxable to the contributor, he may well find it more profitable to give the asset away than to sell it and keep the proceeds for himself.[43]

MEDICAL EXPENSES. A deduction for medical and dental expenditures was initiated by the Revenue Act of 1942. At the outset both floor and ceiling restrictions were imposed and, although liberalized considerably by the Revenue Code of 1954, these have been retained up to the present time. A strong case can be made for some floor below which medical expenses are not deductible. At present the floor is set between 3 and 4 per cent of adjusted gross income.[44] Each family is subject to a number of ordinary, run-of-the-mill medical and dental expenses that impose no undue amount of hardship on its financial position. Extraordinary medical expenditures, however, may impose great financial burdens, and their incidence is both unexpected and involuntary. In this sense they are akin to casualty losses that reduce the total gain of the taxpayer. Present federal law appears, if anything, to be overly generous in its distinction between ordinary and extraordinary medical expenses. A 1954 study, for example, showed that for all families with incomes under $10,000 the median per cent of income spent on medical and dental care was 4.1.[45] By the current legal test, then, virtually one-half of all such families have extraordinary medical expenses. In addition, taxpayers 65 years of age and over are allowed to deduct their medical and dental expenditures in full.

The ceiling on deductible medical expenses ($2,500 for each exemption with limits of $5,000 for single persons and $10,000 for married couples filing joint returns) is less easy to justify. One difficulty is the familiar one of distinguishing between medical expenses and

[43] Consider a person in the 91 per cent tax bracket with a capital asset which he bought for $1,000 and which is now worth $9,000. If he sells this asset, he will pay a capital gains tax of $2,000 and will therefore have net proceeds of $7,000. If, on the other hand, he gives it away to a charitable organization, he is allowed to deduct $9,000 from his adjusted gross income at a tax saving to him of $8,190 (= .91 × $9,000). By giving the asset away he receives $1,190 more than if he had simply sold it for his own benefit.

[44] Medical expenses other than those incurred for the purchase of drugs and medicines may be deducted to the extent that they exceed 3 per cent of adjusted gross income; expenditures on drugs and medicines are deductible to the extent that they exceed 1 per cent of adjusted gross income. For those who spend as much as 1 per cent of adjusted gross income for medicines the total floor is 4 per cent; for others it is between 3 and 4 per cent.

[45] Health Information Center, *National Family Survey of Medical Costs and Voluntary Health Insurance* (New York, 1954).

personal consumption expenditures. The classic case cited is the wealthy businessman whose doctor prescribes a winter sojourn in Florida or Southern California. The 1954 code, however, tightened up this loophole considerably by limiting permitted deductions to those for transportation alone (excluding expenditures on meals and lodging incurred during health-giving rests). Retention of the present ceiling may well keep other questionable expenses from the deductible category. Some taxpayers, however, will be refused tax relief for altogether legitimate expenses, and this will happen precisely when these are imposing the greatest possible financial burden.

Personal Exemptions and the Size of the Taxpaying Unit

Personal exemptions may be thought of as serving three basic purposes:

1. To exempt from taxation the minimum amount of money needed for consumption if the taxpayer is to be a healthy and productive member of society
2. To make the effective tax rate smoothly progressive for all taxpayers with incomes above the exemption levels
3. To differentiate between taxpayers with equal incomes but different numbers of dependents

Let us consider how each of these goals is served under current tax law.

The exemption of a minimum subsistence level of living is the most commonly mentioned justification for personal exemptions under an income tax. No one, it is argued, should be forced by income taxation to cut his consumption expenditures to the point where either his health or his productive efficiency suffers. This position may be advanced on purely humanitarian grounds, to the effect that a person who is barely able to support himself and his family has no ability to pay taxes. For the more hardheaded, who may be inclined to feel that taxpayers will be more realistic voters than nontaxpayers (especially when it comes to supporting expensive governmental programs), the exemption may be justified on grounds of economic efficiency. Taxation of those at or below minimum subsistence levels will either reduce their productivity so that society loses the output they otherwise could have produced (and government tax collections suffer as a result), or government and private welfare agencies will be forced to increase their benefit payments to the unfortunate taxpayers. In either case, the attempt to tax the lowest income groups is not likely to add substantially to the net financial position of the Treasury.

It is by no means easy to define the content of a minimum subsistence budget. Should we, for example, include only the types of food capable of providing the needed calories, vitamins, and other values at the lowest prices without regard for variety in the diet or for the fact that people in this country, even at the lowest income levels, (typically) do not buy such foods in large quantities? Most minimum budgets contain many consumption items which, in principle, could be dispensed with without harm to health or working efficiency but which may effectively be required by the social and cultural environment in which the family is living. Opinions differ considerably as to what these minimum cultural requirements are but there would undoubtedly be wide agreement that present exemption allowances are too low for single individuals and small families, become more realistic as the size of the family increases, and may well be overgenerous for large families.[46]

The main difficulty involved in raising personal exemptions to a level more in line with minimum subsistence budgets is the huge loss in tax revenue that would result from such a change. Increased personal exemptions, of course, lower taxes for all taxpayers and reduce them most for those in the highest income groups. Pechman estimated that at 1957 tax rates and income levels an increase in personal exemptions from $600 to $700 would reduce tax receipts by $2.8 billion, which was 8 per cent of federal personal income tax collections in that year.[47] In order to protect minimum subsistence levels of living, however, personal exemptions need not be granted to the middle and upper income groups. An arrangement by which exemptions would be gradually decreased as the taxpayer's net income increased until they finally disappeared entirely at some middle income level would allow adjustments to be made for increased subsistence costs without sacrificing large amounts of tax revenue.[48]

Any flat-sum exemption allowance granted to all taxpayers will convert a proportional income tax into a progressive one. If income

[46] U. S. Treasury Department, Division of Tax Research, *Individual Income Tax Exemptions* (Washington, D.C., 1947).

[47] *Tax Revision Compendium*, Vol. I, p. 268.

[48] Alternatively, a low personal exemption could be granted to all taxpayers with an additional subsistence allowance that decreased gradually as the taxpayer's net income increased. Gradual reductions of this sort are necessary to avoid the so-called "notch problem" whereby the sudden withdrawal of deductions results in marginal tax rates greater than 100 per cent for a limited range of income. Suppose, for example, that the present $600 personal exemption were granted to all taxpayers with net incomes of $800 or less but refused to all with greater incomes. A taxpayer with an $800 net income would then pay $40 in taxes if the first bracket tax rate were 20 per cent, but if he earned an additional $100, his tax bill would jump to $180, an increase $40 greater than his entire additional earnings.

is taxed at a single rate of 20 per cent, an exemption of $600 will ensure that the effective tax rate (i.e., total taxes paid divided by net income before deduction of the $600 exemption) starts at zero and rises slowly and smoothly to a maximum level just short of 20 per cent. The present federal income tax, then, is progressive in relation to net income even for the relatively large group of taxpayers who are taxed only at the first-bracket rate of 20 per cent.

The question of how the taxpaying abilities of families at the same income level but with different numbers of dependents are related to one another can be given no precise answer. On the one hand, it appears rather harsh to argue that children provide their parents with additional consumption pleasures worth at least as much as their maintenance costs so that no tax allowance for children is justified; on the other hand, it is rather cynical to discount the gratification element completely and arbitrarily allow the same material standard of living to all families at a given income level. Generous fiscal allowances for children, either under the income tax law or by means of direct subsidy payments such as are made in Canada or Great Britain, may also be part of a positive public policy designed to increase the birth rate.

Even though no precise answers are possible, a number of useful generalizations may be obtained from budget studies:

1. The maintenance costs of children, apart from expenses at birth, increase gradually with age.
2. The maintenance cost of any dependent living in the same household is less than that for a single person.
3. The maintenance costs of children increase as the income level of the family rises.

Present federal law conforms only to the last of these three rules. The tax value of the $600 per capita exemption increases steadily as the income of the family rises. A tax credit, such as some states allow for dependents, however, is the same at all income levels. Approximately one-third of the states with income taxes conform to the second rule by setting the personal exemption for a married couple at less than twice that for a single person, and even more states allow less for a child or other dependent than they do for either the taxpayer or his wife. Great Britain took account of the first rule in 1957 by allowing an exemption of $280 for a child under twelve years of age, $350 for a child between twelve and sixteen, and $420 for one seventeen or over.

Income splitting for tax purposes also represents an adjustment for families of different sizes. Its incidence, however, is difficult to justify on rational grounds. In Table 6–2 (in order to isolate the effects of income splitting) the tax burdens of a single person are contrasted with those of a married couple filing a joint return but not taking the additional $600 exemption. It will be noted that at either extreme of the income scale the two tax burdens are equal but that in the range between $10,000 and $100,000 the married couple's tax is only 70-80 per cent of the single person's liability. The logic behind these wide divergencies is difficult to discover. Income splitting results in a substantial reduction in the revenue raised from the personal income tax (an estimated $4 billion in 1957),[49] but its advantages accrue to a relatively small group of high-income taxpayers.

TABLE 6–2

Tax Burdens of Single Persons and Married Couples Filing Joint Returns at Selected Taxable Income Levels, 1960 Tax Rates

Taxable Income	Tax on Single Person	Tax on Married Couple Filing Joint Return	Married Couple's Tax as Percentage of Single Person's Tax
$ 2,000	$ 400	$ 400	100
5,000	1,100	1,020	93
10,000	2,640	2,200	83
25,000	10,150	7,230	71
100,000	67,320	53,640	80
500,000	429,820	404,640	94
5,000,000	4,350,000	4,350,000	100

The Revenue Act of 1948 instituted two new personal exemptions —one for any person who is 65 years of age or over and another for any person who is blind—which do not serve any of the purposes given at the beginning of this section. At the time the special old-age exemption was justified by the argument that elderly people were heavily concentrated in the lower income groups and had been especially hard-hit by the postwar inflation. The first difficulty, however, is already taken care of by the progressive rate structure under the present tax, and if minimum subsistence costs have risen above $600 per person because of postwar inflation, the equitable solution would be to raise them for everyone receiving very low incomes regardless of age. Extraordinary medical and dental expenses, to which elderly people are especially subject, are allowed for by means of the special medical-dental deduction, and, apart from these expenditures, there is evidence that a family headed by someone 65 years of age or over does not typically spend more than other families

[49] *Tax Revision Compendium,* Vol. I, p. 276.

at the same income level.[50] The special exemption for the blind is subject to the criticism that its benefits are inversely related to need, and it raises the equity question of whether other handicapped persons are not equally entitled to tax benefits. An alternative solution would allow all such people to deduct whatever additional costs of earning income they have to incur because of their handicaps.

Allowance for the needs of families of different sizes also raises the question of how the incomes received by different members of the family should be treated for tax purposes. As we have noted earlier in this chapter, the basic taxpaying unit in the United States is either the single person or the married couple (if they wish to file a joint return). Dependent children with incomes of their own are treated as separate taxpayers.[51] Under this arrangement wealthy families may reduce substantially the total amount of taxes paid by the family by transferring income-producing property either directly to the children or to a trust fund set up for their benefit. In either case, income is removed from taxation at the top marginal tax rate applicable to the parents and made subject to bottom tax rates as separate income either to the child or to the trust fund. There is a story of one highly successful business, the income from which would have been taxable at top rates had it been received by one person. Investigating Internal Revenue agents, however, discovered that the owner had taken his wife and each of his six children, some of whom were quite young, into the firm as partners with the result that large tax savings had been realized. The legality of such arrangements rests upon whether or not each partner renders legitimate services to the business, and when the agents asked the wife what her function in the firm was, she replied: "My husband is anxious to expand the firm as rapidly as possible. My function is to provide more partners."

The great majority of families undoubtedly pool their resources for consumption purposes, each person contributing according to his abilities and receiving benefits according to his needs. In all cases

[50] See *The Taxation of Pensions and Annuities,* a report of the Joint Committee on Internal Revenue Taxation on H.R. 2948 of the 79th Congress, 2d Sess., 1946, pp. 14-20, 44-54.

[51] Prior to 1954, parents lost an exemption allowance for any dependent child with a separate income of more than $600. This meant, however, that as soon as a child earned slightly more than $600 in a year the family tax bill increased suddenly by at least $120 (the bottom tax rate of 20 per cent times the lost $600 exemption), and the 1954 code removed the restriction completely. If a child meets the other requirements for a dependent, the parents may now claim an exemption for him on their tax return regardless of how much income the child receives. In effect, families are granted two $600 exemptions for each child earning more than $600 a year, one on the parents' return and one on that of the child.

of this sort the logical unit for taxation purposes is the entire family. A single return, including the incomes of all members of the family and claiming a separate personal exemption for each of them, would be filed each year. Some experts feel that such a system, while desirable insofar as it bars some of the avenues to tax avoidance through income splitting within wealthy families, would not increase the effective allowance for children rapidly enough as family income increased. An alternative solution, similar to that used in France, would eliminate personal exemptions entirely, allocate a needs factor to each member of the family (in France the husband and wife each count as one and each child as one-half), divide the total family income by the sum of these factors, compute a per capita tax on this "per capital income," and multiply this tax by the sum of the needs factors to obtain the total tax for the family. The needs factors for children could be graduated upward with age,[52] and the wife's factor could start at some value less than one if she had no earned income of her own and increase gradually as the amount of time devoted to outside jobs increased until a limit of one was reached for a wife with a full-time income-earning position.

The separate taxation of trust funds is inconsistent with the rationale of the income tax as a levy on persons according to their abilities to pay. In principle, the income received by each trust should be assigned to the proper beneficiary and taxed as part of his total income. In practice, complications would arise where the beneficiaries of the trust were contingent or undetermined. In such cases the gains would have to be aggregated and taxed at some later date when the correct recipient had been ascertained. Because of the lumpiness of such taxable gains, some form of income averaging for tax purposes would be essential.

Income Averaging for Tax Purposes

We have already noted that under a progressive rate structure a fluctuating income is taxed more heavily than a stable one of equal total amount. Similar discriminations would arise even with a proportional tax insofar as taxpayers with losses in some years were not allowed to offset them against income in other years, and to the extent that people with insufficient income to use up their entire

[52] Vickrey has suggested a factor of .3 for a child between one and five years of age, rising by one point for each additional five years until a maximum factor of .6 for children over fifteen is reached. William Vickrey, *Agenda for Progressive Taxation* (New York: The Ronald Press Co., 1947), pp. 295-96.

personal exemption in one year were not able to carry over the unused portion of the exemption to some other tax year.[53]

Only comprehensive income averaging for tax purposes can avoid inequities of this sort. In addition, under the current annual system taxpayers are induced to shift income from one year to another in order to minimize their tax burdens. Attempts to stop such practices have increased considerably the complexity of tax law. An averaging scheme that made the aggregate tax bill independent of the annual income pattern would simplify this aspect of tax administration, although, as we shall see, it is likely to add some complications of its own.

INCOME AVERAGING UNDER PRESENT TAX LAW. Current law allows for fluctuating incomes in three main ways:

1. Business losses may be carried back three years and forward for five years and offset in each year against other income.
2. Capital losses may be carried forward for five years and offset against capital gains plus $1,000 of other income in each year, and long-term capital gains are granted favorable tax treatment which allows very roughly for their irregular character.
3. Under sections 1301 and 1302 of the 1954 Internal Revenue Code, authors, inventors, and others who receive in one year at least 80 per cent of the compensation due them for services rendered over a two-year period or longer may spread their income over the period during which it was earned up to a maximum of three years.

In principle, all losses should be offsettable against income without limitation, but administrative costs make necessary some restriction of this right. The extent to which a one-year carryback and a five-year carryforward would permit the offsetting of business losses has been studied by Morris Beck for a sample of sixty large corporations during the period from 1923 to 1939. For the group as a whole 90 per cent of the losses suffered in the four-year period 1930 through 1933 were offsettable although individual experience within the group varied considerably. Petroleum corporations whose losses over the entire 1923-39 period constituted only 8 per cent of their profits during that period, for example, would under this arrangement have received 100 per cent offset privileges whereas textile firms with losses equal to over 90 per cent of their profits could have offset only

[53] Consider a married couple, entitled to two $600 exemptions, who received exactly $1,200 in net income each year so that they had no taxes to pay. Another couple with net incomes of $600 and $1,800 in alternate years, however, would pay $120 in taxes every two years under a 20 per cent proportional tax unless they were allowed to carry over the unused exemption of $600 to the year in which $1,800 was received.

slightly more than 50 per cent of these losses.[54] On the other hand, the 1930's were a period of large and sustained losses, and since 1954 carryback provisions have been liberalized.[55] Generous allowances for loss offsets, as we shall see in the next chapter, are a very effective way of minimizing the depressing effects of income taxation on incentives to invest.

The extent to which loss offsets should consist of carrybacks or carryforwards depends upon a number of considerations. The existence of both types in the law is supported by the fact that new firms cannot make use of carrybacks whereas an old firm on the verge of liquidation will have little interest in carryforward provisions unless the tax benefits arising from them can be sold to some more successful firm. Carrybacks have distinct advantages as part of a fiscal policy designed to offset fluctuations in private business activity. When a depression threatens and businesses begin to suffer losses, a carryback provides immediate and certain relief so that businesses have additional funds to spend when they are most needed. A carryforward alone, however, would be less certain in its operation—sufficient profits might not be earned in the appropriate years and Congress might decide to behave again as it did in 1932 and 1933 when the two-year carryforward existing before those years was first reduced to one year and then eliminated completely. In addition, a rapid recovery from the recession might mean that carryforwards would provide tax relief during a period of incipient inflation when it was least needed. Carrybacks, on the other hand, tend to favor established firms at the expense of new ones. If the entry of a new firm into the industry precipitates general losses, the established firms obtain immediate tax credit for these whereas the new firm must wait until profitable operations become possible. The extension of loss carrybacks, then, must involve a balancing of these advantages and disadvantages.

AVERAGING PROPOSALS. Apart from the provisions for loss carryovers, current tax law makes little allowance for irregular incomes. Sections 1301 and 1302 are much too restricted in their applications to provide an important amount of relief, and the treatment of long-term capital gains is a very rough offset for the absence of averaging privileges. Let us consider a number of averaging arrangements that

[54] Morris Beck, "Carryover of Business Losses," *National Tax Journal,* VI (March, 1953), 69-85.

[55] In addition, Beck's computations for the entire 1923-39 period understate the effectiveness of the five-year carryforward since the extent to which losses suffered in 1935 and later could be offset against profits in 1940 and later years was necessarily left out of consideration. *Ibid.,* p. 73.

might be adopted, beginning with the most simple and proceeding to those of increasing comprehensiveness.

Offset of Unused Personal Exemptions. Carryover allowances for unused personal exemptions similar to those already in existence for business and capital losses could readily be adopted for the benefit of taxpayers whose taxable incomes become negative in certain years.

Pechman Proposal. Joseph Pechman has proposed the liberalization and extension of Sections 1301-2 of the Internal Revenue Code. Income items such as deferred compensation, accumulated dividends on preferred stock, and capital gains and losses, which are typically received in irregular amounts, would be segregated and used for the computation of a special tax credit. This credit would equal the difference between the taxes actually paid on an annual basis over the past five years and the taxes that would have been paid if the segregated Section 1301-2 income had been received in equal annual installments over the five-year period. Taxes would be computed in the fifth year in the ordinary way on all income received, including Section 1301-2 income, and from this figure the special tax credit would then be subtracted to obtain the taxes due.[56]

The plan would clearly involve some increase in both compliance and administrative costs. Taxpayers with Section 1301-2 income in any one year would have to recompute their taxes for the past four years, and the Internal Revenue Service would have to be prepared to check these calculations. Income averaging, however, appears to carry sufficient tax advantage to warrant some increase in the complexity of the tax law. One of the great virtues of the Pechman proposal is that it could be granted first on a limited basis to the most irregular types of income and then extended more generally if administrative problems proved to be tractable.

Simons Proposal. Generalization of the Pechman plan to cover all types of income would bring us close to Henry Simons' proposal that taxpayers continue on the annual basis as at present but that every fifth year they be allowed to compute their average taxable income over the past five years, find the taxes they would have paid if they had received that amount of income in each year, and then claim a rebate for the amount by which their actual tax bills exceeded this average figure.[57] This proposal would, of course, permit averaging only within each arbitrarily determined averaging period, and, being

[56] Joseph A. Pechman, "A Practical Averaging Proposal," *National Tax Journal,* VII (Sept., 1954), 261-63.
[57] Simons, *op. cit.,* p. 154. Some restriction on the claiming of small rebates would probably be necessary for administrative reasons.

optional, it would make no allowance for the fact that with fluctuating tax rates irregular incomes will occasionally be assessed with lower taxes than stable incomes. Although not a complete solution to the fluctuating-income problem, however, it would represent a significant improvement over current tax law.

Vickrey Proposal. The most comprehensive averaging scheme is William Vickrey's cumulative averaging proposal.[58] Under this plan the taxpayer would, in his first year of entry into the scheme, compute his taxes exactly as he does now. In the second year, however, income averaging for tax purposes would begin and be continued on a cumulative basis in all subsequent years. In the second year the taxpayer would compute his tax as follows:

1. Copy from his first year's tax return the amount of tax paid for that year.
2. Add to that amount an imputed interest credit obtained by multiplying the tax paid by some specified interest rate (say 4 per cent). This step yields the current value of all previously paid taxes.
3. Copy from the first year's return his taxable income and add to it both the imputed interest credit (derived in step 2) and his taxable income for the second year. The result is his cumulated taxable income for the two years.
4. Compute the total tax due on this cumulated income from a special tax table in the manner now employed.
5. The tax due at the end of the second year is then simply the difference between items 4 and 2.

Under cumulative averaging tax adjustments for fluctuating incomes are kept completely up-to-date, and the incorporation in the scheme of the imputed interest credit would mean that taxpayers who were considering the possibility of shifting income to later years would have to reckon with the fact that such shifts would reduce their interest credit for prepaid taxes and thereby offset most, if not all, of the gains to be obtained from the postponement of taxes.[59] To the extent that income shifting in order to minimize tax burdens was

[58] Vickrey, *op. cit.,* pp. 172-95.
[59] Consider a person who postpones payment of $100 in income taxes for exactly one year. His gain from this procedure is the income he can earn by investing the $100 for one year, say $4, minus the tax due at the end of the second year on that $4 increment to his taxable income. If his marginal tax rate is 25 per cent, then, his net gain will be $3. Under cumulative averaging, payment of the $100 tax in the first year yields him an interest credit of $4 for the second year (if the imputed interest rate under the tax law is 4 per cent); this increases his second-year tax liability by $1 (= .25 × $4), but deduction of the full interest credit reduces his taxes due in the second year by $4, for a net gain of $3. In this case the potential gain from tax postponement is exactly offset under cumulative income averaging and the taxpayer would be indifferent as to the year in which the $100 tax bill was paid.

eliminated, the tax law could be enormously simplified. Cumulative averaging itself would not increase the compliance costs of the tax-payer to any significant extent. Special tables would have to be computed by the Treasury, but once this had been done they would be used in the same way as present tables. One difficulty would be that few taxpayers would be able to understand how the tables were set up or why their taxes were what they were. The setting of the rate at which the interest credit was to be imputed would also be an arbitrary procedure. Presumably it should be set at a level of return to which all taxpayers had easy access, such as the rate of long-term government bonds. Taxpayers with higher-yielding investment opportunities at their disposal would still be able to gain from tax postponement, but those gains would be considerably less than are now possible.

Summary and Conclusions

We now have at least a nodding acquaintance with the most important problems involved in defining the base of the federal personal income tax. It is, as we have seen, an enormously complex structure and, furthermore, one whose base has become considerably eroded by the ravages of political pressure. If the entire edifice is not to become so weakened as to threaten the very existence of the most equitable tax yet devised and put into effective operation, this eroding process must be stopped and, if possible, reversed.

At what points could the repair work be concentrated? In the first place, large amounts of income are currently excluded from the tax base. These include benefit payments under the Old Age and Survivors Insurance Fund, the imputed net rental on owner-occupied homes, income in kind paid to employees, the consumption value of home-produced food and business stock-in-trade, interest on state and local debt and on savings invested in life insurance. Highly favorable tax treatment is accorded to long-term capital gains and losses and to income from mining enterprises through percentage depletion. Personal deductions could, in principle, be reduced to an allowance for state and local income taxes paid and for extraordinary medical and dental expenses, and, if this is done, the optional standard deduction could reasonably be reduced to 2 or 3 per cent of adjusted gross income. Mixed expenditures that are partly business expenses and partly personal consumption are typically treated with undue generosity under current law. The special personal exemptions granted to those 65 years of age and over and to the blind could be replaced with a more adequate minimum subsistence allowance for everyone and perhaps by a special deduction for the increased costs of earning income which all handicapped people face. The entire family could be treated as a unit for tax purposes and the income accruing to trusts taxed as part of the income of the beneficiaries. Personal exemptions need not extend into the middle and upper income brackets in order to exempt from taxation a basic subsistence budget, and the other purposes for which they are currently used may be served by other means. Finally, income splitting, which benefits a relatively small number of married couples in the upper-middle and upper income groups, could be eliminated by halving the size of all tax brackets for those who file joint returns, and then the tax burdens of families of different sizes at all income levels could be brought into some consistent relationship with one another.

Most of these changes would result in an increase in the tax base so that tax rates could be lowered without impairing the yield of the personal income tax. Pechman, in a comprehensive study of the extent to which a more broadly based and equitable tax structure could be achieved, estimated conservatively that tax rates could thereby be reduced anywhere from 25 to 33 per cent in all brackets.[60] In the latter case tax rates could range from 13 to 61 per cent rather than from 20 to 91 per cent as they do at present. In the next chapter we shall see that a broadly based income tax with relatively low rates is frequently more desirable as far as its economic effects are concerned than is a high-rate tax imposed on a narrow base.

[60] Joseph A. Pechman, "Erosion of the Individual Income Tax," *National Tax Journal,* X (March, 1957), pp. 1-25, and *Tax Revision Compendium,* Vol. I, pp. 279-80.

7

Economic Effects of the Personal Income Tax

The federal personal income tax has a pervasive influence on the economy of this country. Changes in the tax can alter not only the level of national output, prices, and employment but also the structure of each of those entities. After a discussion of these economic effects, the incidence of the personal income tax is summarized, and the chapter closes with an appraisal of the role of income taxation at the state and local level.

Distribution of Personal Income

The distinguishing feature of any progressive income tax is that it makes the after-tax distribution of income less unequal than the before-tax distribution. The income-equalizing powers of the federal personal income tax in the United States are illustrated in Table 7–1 for the year 1958. Before income taxes, for example, the wealthiest 20 per cent of the nation's families (those receiving incomes of $8,360 or more a year) received 45.5 per cent of the country's total personal income but paid 62 per cent of all income tax liabilities. As a result, this group's share of after-tax income was reduced to 43.7 per cent.

It will be noted that a classification of families by income fifths shows only a limited amount of redistribution as a result of taxation. To a large extent this is attributable to the width of the first tax-rate bracket of the federal individual income tax[1] and the consequent con-

---

[1] The lowest tax rate of 20 per cent applies to the first $2,000 of taxable income for single persons and to the first $4,000 for married couples filing joint returns.

TABLE 7–1

PERCENTAGE DISTRIBUTIONS OF PERSONAL INCOME AND TAX LIABILITIES
IN THE UNITED STATES, 1958

Families	Personal Income Before Taxes	Income Tax Liabilities	Personal Income After Taxes	Lowest Income Before Taxes Within Group
Lowest fifth*	4.7%	1.5%	5.0%	not available
Second fifth	11.1	6.2	11.6	$2,590
Third fifth	16.3	11.3	16.9	4,300
Fourth fifth	22.4	19.0	22.8	5,970
Highest fifth	45.5	62.0	43.7	8,360
Top 5%	20.2	38.3	18.2	14,640

* Income fifths were obtained by ranking families according to family personal income before taxes.

Source: Selma F. Goldsmith, "Size Distribution of Personal Income, 1956-59," *Survey of Current Business,* April, 1960, p. 14.

centration of the effects of progressive tax rates on a small minority of the nation's families. If we confine our attention to the wealthiest 5 per cent of families, Table 7–1 indicates that income taxation in 1958 reduced their income share by two percentage points. These figures, however, must be interpreted with caution. Not only are accurate data more difficult to obtain for the highest income groups, but the distributions in Table 7–1 omit capital gains and losses, which, as we have seen, are mostly received by high-income families.

Incentives to Work

To many people it is virtually axiomatic that high and progressive income taxation impairs incentives to work and interferes seriously with economic progress. This argument is appealing to critics of the personal income tax on two grounds: first, the *prima facie* case for some reduction in work incentives is a strong one—surely most people who have continually to pay over to the Treasury more than half of any additional income they earn must find it less and less attractive to work hard; and second, a tax-induced reduction in the amount of work done is clearly an undesirable tax effect. At this point the critic is likely to rhapsodize on the virtues which "made America great," and to reflect nostalgically on the days when income taxation was an infinitesimal bubble on the steady stream of progress.

Faced with such forensic eloquence the tax student is likely to feel somewhat daunted, particularly since his only rebuttal is to maintain that the matter is not nearly so simple. It is true, of course, that higher income taxes, by reducing the net monetary reward to be earned by an extra hour's work, tend to make the task of performing that additional work less attractive. At the same time, however, the taxpayer's disposable income is lowered, and this increases the pressure on him to earn more money. Indeed, to the extent that a family is committed to a high level of living expenses, either as a result of contractual obligations (such as mortgage payments, life insurance premiums, educational costs for the children, or monthly payments on a new deep freezer or automobile) or because of the more subtle pressures on it from advertizers and the conspicuous consumption of higher-income families, higher income taxes may virtually force the income earner to work harder in order to make ends meet. Work incentives, then, may either be strengthened or weakened, and, in general, theoretical analysis alone cannot prove that either result must necessarily emerge.

This does not mean, however, that theory is completely useless in the present instance. There are some tax changes whose net effect on work incentives can be satisfactorily determined from the depths of a comfortable armchair. For others, empirical studies, designed to determine how people actually do react to taxation as far as the amount of work they do is concerned, are indispensable, but even here theory can guide us to the groups of individuals who are likely to be particularly sensitive to either tax disincentives or tax incentives.

To illustrate the first possibility, consider the effects on the labor supply of a general increase in personal exemptions. Taxpayers find their disposable incomes increased and on this account will typically wish to reduce the amount of work done. Marginal tax rates, however, remain unchanged and no additional incentives are forthcoming from this quarter. This type of tax change exerts its effects in one direction only, and they are to induce taxpayers to take more leisure time.[2]

---

[2] A limited number of people are to a limited extent faced with the more common double incentive-disincentive effect. These are the taxpayers who, when personal exemptions are raised, find themselves with negative taxable incomes and hence no longer subject to income taxation at all. Their disposable incomes are increased (since they did pay taxes under the lower exemption allowances) but, for a limited range of income, their marginal tax rates have been reduced to zero. It is quite possible that some of these people will be induced to work harder as a result of the tax change. Incentive reactions of this sort, however, can only prevail up to the point at which the people in question become subject to income taxation again. Since others in this same group may react in the disincentive direction, it appears unlikely that the behavior of this group as a whole will invalidate the general conclusion reached in the text. Furthermore, as we shall see later, people in the lower income levels seem typically to react to higher effective rates of pay by taking more leisure time; these groups, then, are more likely to add to the general disincentive effect stemming from an increase in personal exemptions.

Conversely, an increase in tax burdens by means of lowered personal exemptions may be expected to have a net incentive effect.

Given the amount of money to be raised, disincentive effects may be minimized by employing taxes with low marginal rates. Having a zero marginal rate, a flat-sum, or poll, tax will only produce incentive reactions, but few people would favor the tax on other grounds. An annual net wealth tax is a much more equitable levy which could raise large sums at relatively low marginal tax rates. Death taxes are also favorable to work incentives, even when employing a steeply progressive rate structure. From the point of view of the accumulator of an estate, the rates may not appear to be high until his working life is near its end, and from the point of view of the heirs, the only possible effect is an incentive one, since the tax reduces their incomes but leaves their wage rates unchanged.

High income tax rates, however, are far from inconspicuous, and although the incentive effects of the taxpayer's loss of disposable income are probably less apparent to most people, a moment's reflection is sufficient to establish their potential importance. What people are likely to be most sensitive to the incentive or disincentive powers of income taxation? In the first place, it is clear that wage and salary earners have only limited opportunities to vary the amount of work they do. Most of them have all-or-nothing commitments to their jobs. Only to the extent that they have opportunities for overtime work or for separate income-earning ventures are they free to respond to tax changes according to their own wishes. Self-employed people, on the other hand, are considerably freer in this regard. People in the lowest income groups are virtually certain to react to an increase in income taxes by working harder because they already are close to a minimum subsistence level of living. Taxpayers in the upper income groups, being relatively free of strong commitments to existing levels of consumption and saving, may be expected to behave in the opposite way. Young married couples who are building up their stock of consumer durables, with or without a high level of mortgage and consumer indebtedness, will be highly susceptible to tax incentives, particularly if they have children to support. Older couples whose children are grown and who have already acquired a reasonably satisfactory inventory of both consumer durables and investment assets are much more likely to contract their labor supplies in the face of rising income taxes. With these possibilities in mind let us look at the state of our factual knowledge.

EMPIRICAL STUDIES OF WORK INCENTIVES. Studies of actual worker behavior in response to changing wage or tax rates may be divided into two main types: those which analyze large masses of quantitative data, on the one hand, and try to sort out by statistical methods the important factors which affect the amount of work that people do; and the more personal surveys which, through interviews of a randomly selected sample of workers, attempt to determine the same thing by asking the people directly. Each approach has its own difficulties. In the first case, the problem is to make as certain as is possible, in the absence of rigidly controlled experiments, that the variation in the labor supply that appears to be associated with changes in wage or tax rates is really attributable to those factors. Sample surveys, on the other hand, rely upon the ability and willingness of the respondent to give full and frank information about his own personal behavior. The interviewer must establish a high degree of rapport and avoid questions which suggest answers that otherwise would not have been given. With careful procedures, however, either approach can yield highly useful factual information.

Labor Force Studies. On the basis of a comprehensive analysis of labor force data for five countries (United States, Great Britain, Canada, New Zealand, and Germany), Clarence D. Long concluded that the labor force in general is highly insensitive to changes in money or real incomes or to fluctuations in income tax rates.[3] This finding is in close agreement with the results of previous studies of the labor force which found the supply of labor to be either unresponsive to changes in real wage rates or inversely related to them. To the extent that the latter result prevails, higher income taxes would bring about an expansion in the total labor supply. In any case, none of these studies raised the possibility of a serious disincentive influence as a result of taxation.[4]

Industrial Workers in England and Wales. In 1952 the Royal Commission on the Taxation of Profits and Income sponsored a sample survey, covering 1,429 randomly selected industrial workers, one main purpose of which was to determine the effects of income taxation on work incentives.[5] Every worker interviewed had some

[3] For the major research findings see Clarence D. Long, *The Labor Force Under Changing Income and Employment* (Princeton Univ. Press, 1958), a National Bureau of Economic Research study. The tax implications, however, were summarized earlier in Long's paper for the Joint Economic Committee entitled "Impact of the Federal Income Tax on Labor Force Participation," and included in *Federal Tax Policy for Economic Growth and Stability,* pp. 153-66. (See annotation below in Suggested Readings for Part II, p. 348.)

[4] For a summary of the findings of these studies see George F. Break, "Income Taxes, Wage Rates, and the Incentive to Supply Labor Services," *National Tax Journal,* VI (Dec., 1953), 350-51.

[5] *Second Report of The Royal Commission on the Taxation of Profits and Income,* Cmd 9105 (London: H.M. Stationery Office, 1954), pp. 91-124.

freedom to vary the amount of work he did in response to tax changes either because he was paid on a piecework basis or because overtime opportunities were available to him. Although 73 per cent of the men interviewed, and 60 per cent of the women, felt that, in general, income taxation tended to impair incentives to work, less than 5 per cent of them said that they themselves had been subject to a tax disincentive. The Royal Commission accordingly concluded that income taxation did not have a significant influence on the amounts of labor supplied by these workers. As a group, to be sure, very few of them knew to any accurate degree how taxation affected their additional earnings, and the majority of them faced a marginal tax rate of 27 per cent or less.[6]

The next two surveys, however, dealt with taxpayers who were much more knowledgeable about their tax burdens and who typically faced very high tax rates.

U. S. Business Executives. Approximately 160 business executives, selected to represent large and small companies in manufacturing, banking and finance, selling and advertising, and the petroleum industry, were interviewed about their reactions to income taxation during the 1946-1950 period. Thomas H. Sanders' conclusion was that the executive's ". . . grumbling at the taxes he pays, and his wry allusions to working most of the time for the government rather than for himself, are only a superficial front on the large fact that his effort is not abated by reason of them; he is still going full blast. So far as any statistical computation has been possible, this fact is attested in a ratio of ten to one as against any other view; and with one small group saying that taxes drive the executive to harder work, and another small group giving examples of some relaxing of effort, these views practically canceled each other out."[7] In addition, Sanders noted that executives probably retire later on balance because of taxation, that their married daughters are under greater pressure to take jobs in order to help build up the economic basis of their homes and families than they would be under lower taxes, and that a considerable number of executives had turned down promotions partly as a result of taxation although few of them were able to say whether or not taxes were the decisive factor.[8] For the most part, Sanders did not attempt to derive a quantitative estimate of the effects of taxation on the supply of executive labor, and he noted that in many cases execu-

---

[6] The Royal Commission estimated that only 3-5 per cent of the whole sample knew very precisely how they were affected by income taxation. *Ibid.,* pp. 116-17.

[7] Thomas H. Sanders, *Effects of Taxation on Executives* (Boston: Harvard Univ. Graduate School of Business Administration, 1951), p. 17.

[8] *Ibid.,* pp. 50, 63, 65.

tives worked under the direct supervision of a superior officer in the corporation so that they had only limited freedom to vary the amount of work they did on a day-to-day basis.

Self-Employed Accountants and Solicitors in England. Our last study is concerned with a group of people who faced equally high tax rates but, being self-employed, were considerably freer to react to these according to their own balancing of the pleasures of leisure time and the material advantages to be obtained from increased earned income net of taxes. For this survey 306 randomly selected accountants and solicitors, all self-employed, were questioned by one of the present authors during the first half of 1956.[9] Each interview was based on a prepared questionnaire that, in order to minimize the risk of suggesting answers, gave respondents a full opportunity to discuss the reasons that led them to do as little or as much work as they did before taxation was explicitly suggested to them as a possible factor. Approximately 12 per cent of the respondents said that they had definitely curtailed their professional efforts because of high tax rates, but another 10 per cent reported an equally definite tax incentive influence. It would appear that the group as a whole, even though 63 per cent of them faced marginal tax rates greater than 50 per cent and almost all of them, because of the nature of their practices, were extremely tax conscious, had not had its incentives to work impaired to any significant extent. Within the group certain subclasses were somewhat more sensitive to tax disincentives. These were people with significant amounts of independent income from property; those who were in business entirely on their own, so that they had maximum freedom to set the amount of work they did according to their own wishes; and those in the upper income groups, particularly the ones who faced marginal tax rates of 70 per cent or more.

SUMMARY AND EVALUATION. The chief characteristic of the empirical evidence that has so far been gathered—and there is an impressive amount of it covering the behavior of the widely different groups of workers—is its remarkable consistency. Nowhere does taxation appear to have a great effect on the amount of effort that people put into their jobs, and when these effects do occur, they appear to be about equally divided between the incentive and disincentive influences. The omnipresent warnings about the impairment of work incentives by penal taxation are apparently much ado about nothing.

---

[9] George F. Break, "Income Taxes and Incentives to Work: An Empirical Study," *American Economic Review*, XLVII (Sept., 1957), 529-49.

Nor is it at all obvious that disincentive tax influences are always undesirable. It may be that many people would be better off if, as a result of high taxation, they were led to take things a little easier. Only in wartime is a maximum productive effort of paramount social importance, and then the appearance of a relatively few tax disincentives which the empirical evidence indicates are likely to occur in peacetime will be further discouraged by the strong patriotic motives which prevail in such times.

Incentives to Enter Specific Occupations

If all types of income were assessed equally, the personal income tax would not be a factor in individuals' decisions to enter certain occupations rather than others. Under present tax law, however, there are a number of ways in which the flow of human talent may be diverted.

1. Occupations in which personal incomes fluctuate from year to year are less attractive from a tax point of view than jobs which yield a stable income. Income averaging for tax purposes could, of course, remove all or most of these differences.

2. Taxation increases the relative attractiveness of occupations which reward the worker with smaller amounts of money (i.e., taxable) income but larger amount of nonmonetary (nontaxable) income. Wage earners may be attracted to employers who provide generous fringe benefits (i.e., consumer goods and services given directly to the employee at nominal cost to him) and away from those who rely more heavily on money wages. To the extent that unions are more successful in obtaining income in kind from employers than are individual employees, labor will be drawn to the more highly unionized occupations.

3. Individual business entrepreneurs or partners are in general able to deduct for tax purposes more mixed consumption-business expenditures than are people on straight salaries.

4. Many government jobs pay lower salaries than private jobs with comparable responsibility but attract people because of the prestige and power that go with the appointment. High income taxation makes these jobs relatively more attractive than they otherwise would be and thereby enables the government to attract candidates despite the offer of lower money wages.

5. Income taxation also favors those occupations in which tax enforcement is particularly difficult. Whenever income is received in the form of small but frequent cash payments which are consequently difficult to trace, the temptation to understate taxable income is especially strong. In England small shopkeepers have acquired a reputation for tax evasion on this

basis, and it is said that the consumer can frequently have his house painted or his car repaired at bargain prices if he deals directly with certain skilled workmen on a cash basis.

Some tax influence on the allocation of labor to specific occupations, then, is a definite possibility. We must note, however, a number of important factors which tend to reduce these tax effects. Young workers may not have very accurate or very complete information about the ways in which taxation affects different types of income, and by the time they have acquired this knowledge it may be too late to make a change that would involve loss of seniority, wastage of specialized talents and experience, and perhaps the sacrifice of established social relations because of a move to another community. Tax-induced redirections of human talent may also be frustrated by restrictions on entry into certain occupations.

To the extent that taxation does increase the flow of talent into certain occupations, however, money incomes there will be lowered, the level of output increased, and the prices at which it is sold to consumers will be reduced. In the occupations which people shun, for tax reasons, the scarcity of labor will cause money incomes to rise, and less output will be sold to the public at higher prices. In this way consumers will find the composition of final output changed and workers in tax-favored jobs will find that some of their tax advantages have been competed away from them by the entry of new workers.

Quality of Labor Services

We have already noted that people in the highest income groups, insofar as they react at all, work less hard when income taxes increase, while people in the lowest income groups work harder when taxes rise and less hard when they fall. Through its effects on work incentives, then, an increase in the progressiveness of the income tax, with no change in its total yield, would bring about some decrease in the total labor supply. Increased taxes on the wealthy and reduced taxes on the poor would in each case induce workers to do less work. At the same time, however, lower tax burdens on the poor may permit a substantial improvement in the quality of the labor services that they are able to render. Their health and working efficiencies may improve as their disposable incomes rise, and they may also be induced to spend more money on education and training, either for themselves or for their children. No nation which aspires to rapid economic growth can afford to neglect the capacities of its workers, and high taxation of the lowest income groups is consequently a dangerous fiscal experiment.

Incentives to Invest in Financial and Real Assets[10]

Because of the highly organized nature of modern financial markets, a person with money to invest is able to choose among a wide variety of earning assets. These investment opportunities differ as to current yields, the prospect for future gains, and the risk of future losses. On the average, a person can obtain a higher yield by purchasing an asset with a greater risk of capital losses. These risks increase as one moves from cash (which, in money terms, has no yield and no risk of capital loss) to short-term bonds, to long-term bonds, to preferred stock, and to common stock, and for any one type of security they vary according to the size of the issuing business, its future profit potentialities, and the extent to which more senior securities have a prior claim to the actual profits earned. Short-term federal government bonds, for example, ordinarily pay a lower rate of return than long-term federal bonds because imminent maturity, at which time the bond is redeemed at par, keeps the prices of the former within narrower limits than long-term prices. A holder of a long-term bond who has to sell before maturity may well find himself having to take substantially less than he originally paid for the bond; had he held short-terms, this eventuality would have been much less likely. Even when the investor has decided to place his funds in common stock his choices may range all the way from a large, well-known company in a stable, basic industry to a small concern in some highly speculative area. A similarly wide choice is faced by any businessman, from the top executive of a giant corporation to a retired person who owns one or two rental properties in a small town. Money may be invested in machines and factories, homes and apartment buildings, land and underwater oil drilling equipment, pickup trucks and jet airliners, or any of the myriad other real assets that promise some monetary gain in the future. Any person with money to invest, then, is continually assessing assets of varying risks and yields in relation to his own desires for income, on the one hand, and security or liquidity on the other. To what extent will income taxation influence his choices? In particular, we wish to determine whether the individual investor will be induced by income taxes to take fewer or to take more risks.

[10] The classic treatment of this topic is Evsey D. Domar and Richard A. Musgrave, "Proportional Income Taxation and Risk-Taking," *Quarterly Journal of Economics,* LVIII (May, 1944), 388-423, reprinted in the American Economic Association's *Readings in the Economics of Taxation* (Homewood, Ill.: Richard D. Irwin, Inc., 1959). For further refinements of the theme see Richard A. Musgrave, *The Theory of Public Finance* (New York: McGraw-Hill Book Co., 1959), chap. xiv.

A General Income Tax with Full Allowance for Losses.
Let us consider first the ideal form of income tax—one which treats
all types of income exactly the same way and allows for the full deductibility of all losses. As in the case of work incentives, we may
distinguish two separate influences: by reducing his disposable income
the tax will increase the investor's need to take risks, and to the extent
that it reduces the amount of additional income to be gained by assuming greater risks the tax will reduce the investor's willingness to take
on those risks.

At first glance it would appear that a proportional income tax
will cut down the gains to be realized by taking on greater risks. If, for
example, short-term government securities yield 2 per cent per annum,
corporate bonds yield 4 per cent, and common stock brings 6 per
cent, a 50 per cent proportional tax will reduce these yields to 1, 2
and 3 per cent, respectively, after taxes. The three rates will remain
in the same proportionate relationship to one another (common stock
still brings in three times the income from short-term governments)
but the absolute differences have been cut in half and it may be these
differences which are important to the investor.

We must not, however, neglect the effect of the tax on the size
of the risks assumed by the investor. If full loss deductions are
allowed, privately assumed risks are reduced in the same proportion
as yields are reduced, and hence the gain per unit of risk assumed
is left completely unaffected by the tax. Investor willingness to assume
risks should not, therefore, be affected one way or the other by the
tax. An example will help clarify this important point. Consider an
investor with an annual taxable income of $10,000 who has $2,000
to invest and is thinking about a venture expected to yield $160 a year
if successful but for which there is some chance of total loss of the
capital invested. With no income tax the annual rate of return per
$100 risked is 8 per cent. Assume now a proportional income tax of
50 per cent. If the $2,000 is held in the form of cash (i.e., no risks
are taken), the taxpayer will have a disposable income of $5,000 and
pay taxes of equal amount. If, on the other hand, the venture is em-
barked upon and turns out to be completely unsuccessful, taxable
income is reduced to $8,000 ($10,000 minus the total capital loss of
$2,000), taxes due are $4,000 and disposable income is also $4,000.
The investor, in short, bears only one-half of the total amount of risk
taken, the government having shifted the other half to its own shoulders by means of the 50 per cent tax with full loss deductions. The
annual reward for undertaking the venture is also split equally between
the taxpayer and the Treasury, and hence for the individual investor
the after-tax rate of return per $100 risked is $80/$1,000 = 8 per

cent, which is exactly the same rate that could be earned without any income tax at all. The attractiveness of risky investments is left completely unaffected by such a tax.

Income taxation, then, does not impair incentives to invest in risky ventures. Indeed, a general income tax, levied at proportional rates and allowing full deductions of losses, will increase risk-taking if it has any effect at all. The rewards to be earned by assuming risks are as high with the tax as they were without it, and investors' needs to earn additional income are increased by the pressure of the tax on their spending powers. The present federal personal income tax, however, has a progressive rate structure and allows only for a partial offset of capital and other losses. Let us see what may be said about the effects of such a tax on incentives to undertake risks.

Consider, first of all, a progressive income tax which allows for full deduction of all losses. In this case it may well be that the gains from risk-taking are taxed at higher rates than the losses will be compensated for if they materialize. If, in our previous example, income above $10,000 is taxed at 50 per cent and all income below that figure is taxed at only 40 per cent, the rate of return after taxes, per $100 risked, will be $80/$1,200 = 6.67 per cent, as compared to 8 per cent without the tax.[11] A progressive income tax, then, both stimulates and impairs incentives to invest in risky assets, the stimulus coming from the tax-produced reduction in spendable income, and the impairment from the lowering of the monetary rewards to be earned by the assumption of greater risks. As in the case of work incentives, theory alone does not provide us with an unequivocal answer. It is worth noting, however, that the present federal tax is proportional above taxable incomes of $200,000 for single persons and $400,000 for married couples filing joint returns, and that comprehensive income averaging would narrow significantly the spread between the rates at which gains were taxed and losses compensated for.

GENERAL INCOME TAX WITH PARTIAL LOSS ALLOWANCES. Failure to allow for the full deduction of all losses is likely to offset the attractions of risk-taking even more than rate progression. Strictly speaking, full tax allowance for losses requires the payment of a rebate (i.e., a negative tax) whenever the taxpayer has a negative taxable income. Suppose that our hypothetical taxpayer with a $10,000 annual taxable income invests $20,000 and loses it all in one year. For that year his taxable income is —$10,000, and under a 50 per

---

[11] As before, the gains from risk-taking are taxed at 50 per cent and reduced to $80 per annum after taxes. The capital loss of $2,000 reduces taxes by only 40 per cent of $2,000 or by $800, and hence the investor bears the risk of losing the remaining $1,200 himself.

cent proportional tax he would be entitled to a rebate of $5,000. This result could be achieved in the present instance by a one-year carry-back for losses. A carryforward, however, would be somewhat less attractive because gains from risk-taking would be taxed immediately but losses suffered would be compensated for only at some later date. Even if complete offset were permitted, the taxpayer might well regard the differences in timing as an important tax discrimination against risk-taking. These feelings would be strengthened if the carryforward period were limited and he were uncertain about his ability to earn sufficient other income to offset his total loss within the permitted period.

The effects of limited loss allowances on the rewards for risk-taking are easily shown with reference to our hypothetical investor. Under a 50 per cent proportional tax which permits deduction of only one-half of all losses suffered, he gains $80 net of tax by investing $2,000 if the venture is successful and is compensated for only .5 $\times$ $1,000 = $500 in the case of failure, so that the annual rate of return per $100 risked is $80/$1,500 = 5.33 per cent. In the extreme case where no losses were deductible for tax purposes, the rate of return would be as low as 4 per cent. A flat-rate 50 per cent tax, then, can set the net reward for risk-bearing anywhere between 8 per cent (which is the rate earned under a tax with full loss offsets or if no tax at all is imposed) and 4 per cent according to the extent to which losses are made deductible, and, as we saw in the preceding section, the conversion of the tax to a progressive rate structure would lower these rates of return somewhat further.

PARTIAL INCOME TAX WITH FULL LOSS ALLOWANCES. A proportional tax of this kind would not affect the investor's choice between a venture yielding taxable income and one bringing in rewards that were tax-exempt. This is so because the rate of return from risk-taking is not changed by the tax. The greater attractiveness of tax-exempt income is exactly offset by the fact that the investor must bear all losses himself. Placement of his funds in a taxable venture lowers his net rewards but also shifts part of his potential losses to the government.

A progressive tax, however, does lower the net reward for risk-bearing and will thereby induce investors to shift funds into tax-exempt or tax-favored investments.

PARTIAL INCOME TAX WITH PARTIAL LOSS ALLOWANCES. The present federal personal income tax falls in this category, and it is readily seen from the preceding discussion that, under it, investment in tax-exempt or tax-favored areas will be stimulated. State and local bonds, mineral enterprises entitled to depletion allowance subsidies, and any venture expected to yield long-term capital gains will be more attractive than they would have been without an income tax or under one which was more general in its coverage of income items and its allowances for losses. As to the effects on risk-taking within the wholly taxable area, these, being a resultant both of reduced disposable incomes, which stimulate risk-bearing, and of lowered net rewards, which have exactly the opposite effect, must remain indeterminate on theoretical grounds alone. We turn, therefore, to empirical studies of the effects of taxation on risk-taking by individuals.

EMPIRICAL STUDIES OF INVESTMENT INCENTIVES. *Butters-Thompson-Bollinger Study of Investments by Individuals.* This study, based upon detailed personal interviews with 746 randomly selected individuals who were active in the investment market, is the most comprehensive one that has yet been made of individual investment behavior.[12] The respondents, who were interviewed during 1949, were well scattered geographically and highly concentrated in the upper income brackets. Although the sample cannot be interpreted as representative of all individual investors, it does cover an important segment of that total population, and the authors supplemented it with data taken from more comprehensive sample and census surveys.

Their findings may be summarized as follows.

1. The ownership of corporate stock is very highly concentrated in the upper income groups. In 1949, for example, the top 1 per cent of all income receivers (spending units receiving $15,000 a year or more) held about 65 per cent of the total marketable stock owned by private investors and the top one-tenth of 1 per cent (receiving $50,000 a year or over) owned about 35 per cent. Changes in the tax treatment of these people, therefore, may be expected to have important effects on the supply of equity capital available to business enterprise.

2. Over two-thirds of the active investors interviewed reported no tax influence on their investment decisions.

3. Among those who were affected by taxation in some way, a shift toward more conservative investments outnumbered a move toward riskier ventures by more than two to one. Unfortunately it is impossible to determine, from the information given, to what extent either of these shifts is due to income taxation as such rather than to the existence of certain tax-

---

[12] J. K. Butters, L. E. Thompson, and L. L. Bollinger, *Effects of Taxation: Investments by Individuals* (Boston: Harvard Univ. Graduate School of Business Administration, 1953).

favored types of investment income. Those taking less risk because of taxation, for example, were attracted by tax-favored state and local bonds and life insurance, and for those who were induced to bear greater risks, the differentially low rate on long-term capital gains was by far the most important feature of the tax law.

4. Tax effects of either kind were strongly related to income. Less than 25 per cent of the respondents receiving less than $5,000 a year were influenced by taxation whereas over 90 per cent of those with annual incomes of $100,000 and over were so affected.

5. Both income and estate and gift taxes induce the placement of property in trusts for the benefit of heirs, and such property is, on the whole, invested more conservatively than property controlled directly by private investors. In this way, taxation has restricted particularly the flow of funds to new or unknown businesses.

Butters-Lintner Study of Growing Enterprises. A detailed case study of five small, independent enterprises, which were unknown and highly speculative at the beginning but which subsequently grew rapidly, has been made by Butters and Lintner.[13] In addition, they interviewed the officers of approximately one hundred companies. Three of their conclusions are highly relevant to the present discussion:

1. Income taxes seldom affect the incentives of promoters of new enterprises. In the early stages of development of a new business, the burdens to be imposed by income taxation are far in the future and impossible to predict to any high degree of accuracy. In addition, the men who found new firms are typically venturesome, confident of their ability to succeed, and intensely interested in an idea which they have a firm determination to develop through their new business. Such people are not easily deterred by moderate, or even high, tax rates.

2. Once a new business has progressed to the point where commercial operations are beginning and the risks of loss are consequently less than they were at the very outset, the relatively low tax rate on long-term capital gains will frequently increase the amount of outside capital available to the firm on attractive terms.

3. By lowering disposable profits, income taxation reduces the ability of any business to expand its operations. This impact is likely to be relatively more severe for small than large businesses because small firms must rely primarily upon retained profits to finance expansion and because their opportunities to offset losses suffered, if the new venture is unsuccessful, are frequently very limited. Limited deductibility of losses will, as we have seen, reduce the incentives both of the owners of small firms to expand and of outside individuals to invest in those businesses.

[13] J. Keith Butters and John Lintner, *Effect of Federal Taxes on Growing Enterprises* (Boston: Harvard Univ. Graduate School of Business Administration, 1945).

Individual Abilities to Spend

The main function of taxation, as we have already noted in Chapter 3, is to restrict private spending by reducing the abilities of people to finance expenditures of various kinds. The important questions here all concern the types of expenditures that will be discouraged by different kinds of taxes. Since spending habits differ from one income group to the next, the impact of an increase in personal income taxes on the structure of private spending may be widely different according to which income levels bear the main burdens of the tax increase.

If it is the wealthy that are mainly affected, spending on Cadillacs and yachts, on swimming pools and Steuben glass, may begin to fall off. Those who are in business on their own or as partners may cut back the rate at which their firms are expanding because of the lack of funds. Others are very likely to reduce their purchases of financial assets of various kinds, thereby making the terms on which businesses may obtain outside capital less favorable and perhaps, as a result, curtailing business expenditures on plant and equipment. The "perhaps" is necessary because economists are by no means agreed as to how much effect a rise in interest rates or a fall in common stock prices, brought about by a tax-reduced flow of funds into financial markets, will have on business spending for capital equipment or additional inventories. At one time it was felt that business investment in such assets was highly responsive to interest rate changes; then a series of empirical studies of business behavior uncovered what appeared to be a wide area of insensitivity to the terms on which outside funds could be obtained. Still more recently, however, the significance of these findings has been seriously questioned,[14] and postwar empirical studies have identified several types of expenditures which appear to be sensitive to changing monetary conditions. These include residential construction, capital outlays by small businesses, construction expenditures by state and local governments, and plant and equipment purchases by manufacturing firms.[15] Business inventories, plant and equipment expenditures of large corporations, and

[14] Cf. William H. White, "Interest Inelasticity of Investment Demand—The Case From Business Attitude Surveys Re-examined," *American Economic Review,* XLVI (Sept., 1956), 565-87.

[15] An excellent summary is given in U. S. Congress, Joint Economic Committee, *Staff Report on Employment, Growth, and Price Levels* (Washington, D.C.: Government Printing Office, 1959), pp. 362-94. See also Franz Gehrels and Suzanne Wiggins, "Interest Rates and Manufacturers' Fixed Investment," *American Economic Review,* XLVII (March, 1957), 79-92.

consumer purchases of durable goods, however, show little sensitivity to monetary changes.

Higher income taxes on the middle or lower income groups, on the other hand, may be expected to reduce consumption relatively more and saving and investment relatively less. The specific items sacrificed will depend upon the tastes of the individual taxpayer, but, in general, the consumer goods and services foregone will be more commonplace than those which the wealthy give up when faced with higher taxes. Similarly, since the lower income groups hold relatively few financial assets, particularly of the riskier kinds, demand for these will be reduced only slightly when taxes rise. Indeed, some families may even be forced to sell some of the bonds they already own in order to maintain consumption levels which they regard as irreducible.

Incidence of the Personal Income Tax

The monetary burdens imposed by a perfectly general tax on the incomes of individuals remain largely on the taxpayers themselves and are only rarely shifted to other receivers. To a large extent this is a result of the very generality of the tax—there is, in effect, no place to hide. There is no incentive to change one's occupation or business because income earned elsewhere is subjected to exactly the same tax burdens; if a business is charging the price for its output which maximizes its profits, the imposition of an income tax leaves profits after tax greater at that price than at any other, and there is no incentive, therefore, for the firm to alter either its output or its selling price. In highly competitive industries individual firms have little or no power to raise prices in response to a tax increase in an attempt to shift part of the monetary burden. Price increases must wait upon an exodus of resources from the industry, and under a general income tax the prospects of profit net of taxes are no better elsewhere. In industries dominated by a few large firms the individual business has greater freedom to set its own selling prices and some scope for tax shifting may exist there. Since it is the corporate, rather than the personal, income tax which ordinarily hits such industries, a discussion of these possibilities is postponed until the following chapter.

There is, however, one way in which the money burdens of a general personal income tax may be shifted to others. Suppose that certain taxpayers react by doing less work. Withdrawal of their services from the market will increase the wage rate paid to all workers of the same type, and let us assume, for the present, that this rate rises just enough to hold the total amount of wages paid to the group constant in money terms. Total taxes paid by these people are, therefore, the same as they would have been had no one withdrawn any labor services. Within the group, however, the withdrawal has reallocated individual tax burdens. Those with a strong liking for leisure have reduced their own liabilities by working less hard and earning less taxable income; all others find their incomes rising as the wage rate goes up and hence pay higher taxes than they otherwise would have paid. In effect, those who withdraw labor services have shifted part of the total money burden of the tax to those who continue to work as hard or harder as tax rates rise.

A further effect of the withdrawal of labor services is a decrease in the output offered for sale in that particular industry and, at given levels of monetary demand, the price at which it is sold will rise. Some writers interpret this change as a shifting of part of the burden of the income tax to consumers. There is no doubt that those consumers who have strong tastes for the products now in shorter supply will experience a real burden as a result of the tax. We must not forget, however, that the tax also gives rise to some important consumer benefits which in this case arise from the fact that the price at which leisure may be acquired (i.e., the wage rate net of taxes) has been reduced. Those who like leisure time will find this change a welcome one. Since the tax gives rise to both real benefits and real burdens, there is no theoretical presumption that the tax must impose a net burden on consumers as a whole. To establish this result one would have to show either that the pretax structure of consumption (including the taking of leisure time) was ideal, or, if not ideal, closer to that millenium than the structure resulting from the imposition of the tax. Theory, however, has not reached the stage at which such demonstrations are feasible.

Let us now drop the assumption that the total wages paid to a group of workers remain constant as some of the workers withdraw labor services and thereby bring about an increase in the wage rate. It may be that the demand for their services is so strong that the wage rate will rise more than proportionately to the decrease in the supply of labor, so that total wages paid actually increase. Before the tax was imposed the group may have received an aggregate income of $100 million; with an income tax of 10 per cent which induces some withdrawal of labor services, total incomes may rise to $110 million before taxes so that, after taxes, incomes fall only to $99 million. A potential tax burden of $10 million has been converted into a net burden of only $1 million. The difference will initially come from the pockets of consumers whose demands for the labor services, or for the products made with the assistance of those services, are strong enough to support the increased wages bill. Having spent more money in this way, however, the consumers will have less to spend on other things. Forced economizing elsewhere will reduce prices and incomes in those areas. Other consumers will benefit from the price declines, but the owners of factors of production employed in the contracting areas will experience monetary burdens. Some of the incidence of the income tax has been shifted onto them.[16]

A general personal income tax, then, will be shifted to others to the extent that some workers withdraw labor services as a result of the tax. Reactions of this sort, however, are relatively unimportant, as we have seen above, and hence little shifting of this kind is likely to take place in practice.

A number of writers cite a tax-induced reduction in the level of business investment in plant and equipment as a second way in which the incidence of an income tax may be shifted to consumers. Reduced capital expenditures, it is pointed out, lower the productivity of the economic system so that, in later years, consumers receive fewer consumer goods and services than they otherwise would have obtained. In this way the income tax imposes future real burdens on consumers. This argument, however, neglects the present benefits which consumers receive because of the reduction in investment. At given levels of national output, less investment means more consumption, and hence by reducing consumption levels in the future the tax raises them in the present. As in the case of the other tax-induced consumer benefit and burden patterns that we have discussed, there is no presumption that the result must be a net burden on consumers as a group.

Although the monetary burden of a general personal income tax remains largely where it is first imposed, the same cannot be said for a partial tax. We have already noted how workers will shift from occupations which are relatively heavily taxed into those which are undertaxed. Wage rates rise in the former areas and fall in the latter, and by this means part of the burden of the tax is shifted from the overtaxed to the undertaxed. Nor is labor the only resource which will react to unequal income tax burdens. Capital will flow into the lightly taxed industries, and land may be converted from one use to another. In all of these ways the inequalities among the individual tax burdens as initially imposed are reduced and even, if resources are mobile enough, virtually eliminated.

---

[16] The remaining case in which a tax-induced withdrawal of labor services leads to a fall in the total wage bill for the group of workers need not be discussed in detail since its developments are precisely the opposite of those just outlined in the text.

Income Taxation at State and Local Levels

In 1958, thirty-three states including Alaska and Hawaii imposed an income tax on individuals, and four additional states had a tax on corporate income only. For five states income taxation provided the main source of revenue, ranging from over 50 per cent of total tax collections in New York and Oregon to 45 per cent in Wisconsin and 39 per cent in Delaware and Alaska.[17] For all fifty states together, however, individual income taxes provided only 10 per cent of total tax collections in 1958, and corporate income taxes added another 7 per cent.

State tax rates typically start at 1-2 per cent, and in only three states do they reach as high as 10-11 per cent. Personal exemptions are frequently larger than those allowed at the federal level, and progression usually stops at or below a taxable income of $10,000. Local income taxes, pioneered by Philadelphia just prior to World War II, were imposed in five states in 1958, the tax typically being levied on wages and salaries without allowances for personal exemptions and at low rates of 1 per cent or less. As a result of these developments individuals in Kentucky and Missouri may have to pay income taxes to three different levels of government.

Extensive use of income taxation by state and local governments poses three main problems:

1. ALLOCATION OF INTERSTATE INCOME. Whenever the residence of the income recipient and the source or sources of his income lie in different taxing jurisdictions, at least two different governments have a claim on his income. Under these circumstances the person with widespread sources of income may well pay higher taxes than the individual who lives and works in the same place. If such discouragements to interstate operations are to be eliminated, some reasonable and uniform method of allocating interstate income to the states having a claim on it will have to be adopted.[18]

In the first place, each state might tax only its own residents, and the tax could then rest on their total incomes regardless of where they arose. This arrangement would have the advantage of taxing each person according to ability to pay, but debtor states with a relatively large number of absentee owners would not be able to levy income taxes on a significant portion of the income arising within their borders.

---

[17] *Facts and Figures on Government Finance,* 10th ed., 1958-1959 (New York: Tax Foundation, 1958), pp. 170-71.
[18] For a fuller discussion of these problems see chap. 18.

The alternative solution of having each state tax only the income originating in it, regardless of the residence of the recipient, would frequently underweigh the claims of the state of residence. In addition, under progressive income taxation, recipients of large amounts of interstate income would pay lower taxes than those obtaining equal incomes entirely within one state. This discrimination would result from the familiar advantages of splitting income into several separate taxable sums and thereby avoiding the higher tax rates.

A third possibility would be for each state to tax its own residents on their total incomes, to assess non-residents on any income arising within the state, and to allow the same kind of credit for taxes paid to other states. Two types of credit could be used. A credit to residents for income taxes paid to the state of origin would give recognition to the claims of debtor states without permitting the avoidance of progressive rates on interstate income as a result of income splitting. A credit to nonresidents for income taxes paid to the state of residence would also preserve the progressive nature of state income taxation but would be relatively unattractive to the large net debtor states.[19]

It is clear that an equitable and reasonable solution is possible only on the basis of interstate cooperation and the compromise of conflicting claims. Although progress has been made along these lines in recent years, much remains to be accomplished.

2. EXCESSIVE ADMINISTRATION AND COMPLIANCE COSTS. Use of the income tax by several levels of government entails the risk that duplication of tax-collecting facilities will increase administrative expenses unnecessarily. In addition, to the extent that the individual tax laws differ from one another, the taxpayer will have to fill out separate forms for each government and the burden on businesses which carry on activities in several states may be great. Surrender of the income tax to the sole use of that level of government which can administer it most efficiently—i.e., the federal government—would, however, seriously weaken the fiscal resources of state and local governments at a time when they are typically hard-pressed for revenue. There are three possible solutions to this problem, two of which have already been given a trial in this country.

---

[19] Even though each state had one of these credits, excess taxation of interstate income would still exist whenever the provisions did not dovetail. Suppose that state A allows a credit to residents for income taxes paid to the state of origin and that state B allows a credit to non-residents for taxes paid to the state of residence, and consider the taxability of X who lives in A and receives all of his income from sources in B as compared to the taxability of Y who lives in B and receives all of his income from A. Unless the state laws specify the action to be taken, X may choose the state to which he will pay the majority of his taxes, whereas Y finds himself double taxed on all of his income.

a) *Shared Taxes.* In the first place, the federal government could be given the sole use of the income tax on the understanding that part of the proceeds would then be shared with the states according to some agreed-upon formula. This formula might simply attempt to return to the states a fixed proportion of the income tax revenue collected within their borders or it might try to adjust the allocation to need by taking into account state per capita incomes or the age distributions of the population or population density or any other relevant factor.

Tax sharing would minimize both administration and compliance costs, but critics have stressed the danger of increased central control because of the federal government's ability to change the allocation formula. In addition, a significant portion of state tax revenues would be beyond the control of state legislatures, and this might interfere with effective government budgeting at the state level. When federal revenues fell, states would have to scramble for new taxes, and when they rose states might increase expenditures which their citizens otherwise would not have supported. In any case, there is the very practical question of whether the federal government could ever induce the states to leave the income tax field on any reasonable terms.

b) *State Tax a Fraction of Federal Income Tax.* In 1949, Alaska adopted the very simple device of setting its income tax at 10 per cent of the individual taxpayer's federal liability.[20] Here, too, administrative and compliance costs are kept to a minimum, and the state has greater fiscal independence than with a shared tax arrangement because of its ability to vary the percentage of the federal tax to be collected.

c) *Use by the State of the Federal Income Tax Base.* A less rigid method of integration is for the state law to adopt the federal definition of taxable income but to leave itself free to set its own personal exemption allowances and tax rates. In practice, some minor differences between the two tax bases, such as the treatment of interest on state and local debt and the deductibility of state income taxes, are likely to be necessary, but these need not increase the compliance costs of the taxpayer materially. Seven states—Arizona, Idaho, Iowa, Kentucky, Montana, Utah, and Vermont—had adopted a plan of this sort by 1955.[21] Administrative costs are likely to be greater here than under either of the preceding plans, but the state does obtain greater control over its own resources, and excessive costs may be minimized

[20] Two states (Utah and New Mexico) experimented briefly with a similar plan on an optional basis but subsequently repealed it. See Robert M. Kamins, "Federally-Based State Income Taxes," *National Tax Journal,* IX (March, 1956), 46-54.

[21] *Ibid.,* pp. 47-48.

if the state takes full advantage of the fact that federal tax returns are open for state inspection and that the changes brought about on individual returns by federal audit are also available for state use. It may also be noted that extensive use of each of these last two plans has been made in Scandinavian countries.[22]

3. TAX-INDUCED REALLOCATION OF RESOURCES. Any proposal that the role played by income taxation in state and local fiscal structures be substantially expanded is likely to invoke the fear of legislators and others that high income taxes tend to drive capital and labor into low-tax areas. There is, however, little evidence that state tax differentials play anything but a very minor role in the location of industry.[23] For one thing business location must be based not upon current tax burdens but upon precarious forecasts of future tax laws, and for another, federal income taxes, by allowing the deduction of state and local income taxes, reduce interstate tax differentials, especially for high-income taxpayers. Since movement from one local community to another is considerably less costly than interstate moves, local income taxation may have to be kept at relatively low levels unless adjacent government units cooperate with one another in maintaining tax rates. Local governments, on the other hand, are much more dependent on state governments than the latter are on the federal government, and tax sharing, consequently, is likely to be less objectionable between state and local levels than between the federal and state governments.

CONCLUSIONS. Extension of the use of income taxation by state and local government units is an important fiscal goal because income taxes are more equitable and more closely adaptable to individual abilities to pay than are the other taxes on which those governments rely for the main part of their revenue. Such a move does involve a number of problems, but these can be handled satisfactorily by the various devices discussed in the present section. Should the people desire it, state and local income taxation can easily be increased substantially in scope and other taxes reduced correspondingly.

[22] Harold M. Groves, "New Sources of Light on Intergovernmental Fiscal Relations," *National Tax Journal,* V (Sept., 1952), 234-38.

[23] See, for example, William Vickrey, *Agenda for Progressive Taxation* (New York: The Ronald Press Co., 1947), pp. 446-48; J. S. Floyd, Jr., *Effects of Taxation on Industrial Location* (Chapel Hill: Univ. of North Carolina Press, 1952); and John D. Garwood, "Taxes and Industrial Location," *National Tax Journal,* V (Dec., 1952), 365-69.

8

Spendings Tax

The individual income tax assesses the liability of a person according to the size of his income. People with larger incomes are deemed to have larger "means," or alternatively larger tax-paying capacity, than people with smaller incomes. Income is, however, only one of several possible indices of taxable capacity. Two others, spendings and net worth, may also be looked upon as providing the government with a measure of individual financial power. Accordingly, governments have sometimes been advised to adopt these measures as substitutes for the personal income tax or, more commonly, as adjuncts to the income tax.

Neither the spendings tax nor the net worth tax has been imposed as such in the United States, although some of our taxes, for example the estate tax, can be construed as a form of net worth taxation. The spendings tax has been adopted by India and Ceylon, and net worth taxation has had a long history in the Scandinavian countries.

The base of the spendings tax is the money value of a person's consumption. Consumption in this context has the same meaning as that already discussed in connection with the income tax;[1] it refers to the living expenses of the taxpayer and his family. Although the term "spendings," or in the British usage, "expenditure," suggests that the tax base is to be the total amount of money spent, the tax, as ordinarily proposed, excludes certain classes of expenditures and includes items that are not expenditures at all. The tax base is intended to approximate as closely as possible the money value of consumption taken by a person during a given period of time, and certain expenditures are

[1] See pp. 113-18 above.

173

deemed to be an approximate measure of the value of consumption. Hence a more accurate label for the tax is the *value of consumption,* or simply *consumption.*

Consumption may be defined directly as the value of final services taken, or it may be defined as a residual. The residual definition is used when it is said that the consumption of a person is equal to his income minus his saving, or in equation form,

$$c = y - s,$$

where c is consumption, y is income, and s is saving, all for the same period and for the same person. This definition holds provided that both income and saving can be defined independently of consumption and that the difference conforms to some intuitive meaning of consumption. Accordingly, a spendings tax has been described as an income tax that exempts saving. This description is accurate on its face, but is perhaps likely to cause confusion. It suggests that the amount of a person's spendings will be less than his income, whereas in fact spendings may exceed income and by large amounts. The prodigal son who inherits a large fortune in oil wells may dissipate his assets in riotous living and be called upon to pay more tax under a spendings tax than under an income tax. A spendings tax penalizes spending on consumption regardless of how a person manages to finance the level of his consumption spending. In principle, income is irrelevant to the amount of tax to be paid.

History of Advocacy of the Spendings Tax

Even though it has never been tried in Western countries, the spendings tax has to its credit the support of several renowned economists. In the literature of English economics, John Stuart Mill appears to have been the first to set forth the scheme clearly. Mill held that an income tax involves double taxation of saving and therefore discriminates against those who save as compared with those who do not. The heart of his argument is as follows:

> For when saved and invested (and all savings, speaking generally, are invested) it [saving] thenceforth pays income tax on the interest or profit which it brings, notwithstanding that it has already been taxed on the principal. Unless, therefore, savings are exempted from income tax, the contributors are twice taxed on what they save, and only once on what they spend . . . To tax the sum invested, and afterwards tax the proceeds of the investment, is to tax the same portion of the contributor's means twice over.[2]

[2] John Stuart Mill, *Principles of Political Economy,* Book V, chap. ii, sec. 4.

He goes on to claim that an income tax disturbs the "natural" competition between saving and consumption by inducing people to save too little. Mill was too concerned with the administrative difficulties he visualized to advocate the substitution of the spendings tax for the low-rate (3 per cent) British income tax of the time, but he had no doubt at all that on theoretical grounds the spendings tax is superior to the income tax. Curiously, it was not until about eighty years later that the administrative difficulty that bothered Mill was solved, as we shall later see.

Alfred Marshall, an eminent Cambridge economist, was also convinced that a spendings tax is superior to an income tax.[3] His remarks were not, however, a significant advance over those set forth by Mill. A. C. Pigou, another Cambridge economist, though holding essentially the same position as Mill, was much concerned about the possible distributional effects of the tax.[4] He feared that the rich would come off too well. As we shall see, this fear is largely baseless.

The real possibility of making a spendings tax practical was one of the many accomplishments of Irving Fisher.[5] Much of his extensive writings throughout a long lifetime were devoted to proving that the fundamental meaning of *income* should be consumption. In a sense, this insistence may be looked upon as purely verbal. Of what concern is it whether we label the concept ordinarily called "consumption" as "income," as Fisher himself did, or stick to ordinary usage? Fisher's point is not purely verbal. He was convinced that what people really want from this world is "consumption" in the usual sense, and therefore that "income," the basic concept of economic thinking, should be identified with consumption. He was, furthermore, thoroughly convinced of the Mill arguments that the taxation of income in the usual sense involves double taxation of saving and that people who save are social benefactors. His campaign for a spendings tax (which of course he called an income tax), like his campaigns for 100 per cent reserve requirements for commercial banks, a stable dollar, prohibition of the drinking of alcoholic beverages, and vegetarianism, was carried on with vigor and enthusiasm. Finally in the dark days of June, 1942, Fisher, then retired from Yale University, appeared be-

[3] Marshall's views appear in *Official Papers of Alfred Marshall* (London: Macmillan & Co., Ltd., 1926), p. 238 and in *Memorials of Alfred Marshall,* ed. A. C. Pigou (London: Macmillan & Co., Ltd., 1925), pp. 350-51.

[4] Pigou provided an interesting analysis of the issue in his work *A Study in Public Finance* (London: Macmillan & Co., Ltd., 1947), pp. 118-33. He found the curious result that the amount of the "double" taxation decreases as the rate of income tax increases.

[5] See *Constructive Income Taxation* (New York: Harper & Bros., 1942). This work contains an excellent bibliography.

fore the Senate Finance Committee to make a plea for a wartime spendings tax. He offered a plan to make a spendings tax workable. The senators listened politely, asked questions, and turned their attention to the more weighty task of listening to the special pleaders. Fisher was regarded as just another impractical reformer.

Imagine their shock when, a few months later, Secretary Morgenthau appeared before them demanding the introduction of a wartime spendings tax. A specific plan was proposed, consisting of a refundable portion to be imposed at a rate of 10 per cent and a second, nonrefundable portion with rates going up to 75 per cent. One newspaper writer reported on the reaction as follows: "Members of the Senate Finance Committee sat straight up in their chairs. Then they gasped. Some laughed."[6]

Like the income tax, the spendings tax as proposed by Fisher would be self-assessed. A person would be asked to report his cash holdings at the beginning of the year. To this amount, he adds all money received from whatever source, including wages and money obtained from the sale of securities or borrowing. The figure so obtained would be the total source of funds to be accounted for during the taxable year. The "accounting-for" process would call for deducting all sums of money paid out during the year *except money spent for consumption,* plus his cash holdings at the end of the year. It follows that the accounting-for process would give as a residual the amount spent for consumption.

Thus to take a simple case, let us suppose a person begins the year with $500 in cash. He receives $4,000 in salary, $100 in dividends, and $1,000 from the sale of shares of stock during the year. Thus the amount to be accounted for is $5,600. During the year he buys $1,500 in bonds, repays a debt of $200, and his bank account at the end of the year is $100. The "funds" unaccounted for are therefore $5,600 minus $1,800 or $3,800. This amount is taken to be his consumption or taxable spendings. Exemptions may of course be provided. Thus if the exemption is $1,000 and the first bracket rate (say the first $1,000) is 5 per cent and the second bracket rate ($2,000 to $4,000) is 10 per cent, he would be called upon to pay $230 in tax.

Actually, of course, the calculation is not this simple; it never is. In the 1942 Treasury proposal, an attempt was made to take into account the differences in the positions of people who rent the houses they live in and those who are owner-occupiers. The latter group was required to exclude from funds accounted for (i.e., to include in spendings) the interest on mortgages and real property taxes. Sena-

[6] *Wall Street Journal* (Pacific Coast Ed.), Sept. 4, 1942, p. 1.

tor LaFollette reportedly objected to the failure to exclude from spendings all rent and medical expenses. The definition of spendings for tax purposes involves issues identical with certain of those found in the definition of income for income tax purposes.[7] Houses, furniture, automobiles, clothing, boats, works of art, golf clubs, when owned by the person who uses them, provide valuable services which are at once both consumption and income. Likewise, the long-suffering housewife provides services in kind to her family as does the not-so-long-suffering "househusband." The problem is to draw lines which simultaneously satisfy the conditions of permitting the taxpayer to set down a firm figure in his tax return and of taxing different people with the same consumption at the same rate. Under the Treasury proposal, consumption-in-kind of previously acquired household possessions was restricted to houses, and then only to the portion of the value of housing services measured by the interest, if any, paid on the mortgage and by real property taxes.

The story of how a spendings tax would have worked in the United States cannot be written. The proposal never got past the committee, a fact scarcely surprising in view of the novelty of the tax and the conservatism of the committee membership. Nor is there firm evidence that the Administration was prepared to fight for the proposal. President Roosevelt, in his talks about economic conditions at the time, gave the impression of being innocent of the Treasury's spendings tax proposal. Nor was there much intelligent comment about it. The *New York Times* pontificated:

> ... it does not seem to the best interests of the nation that we should accept so radical a tax measure. Instead of placing the equivalent of a service or sales tax on essentials of the home, directed at a class already taxed to the uppermost, a general retail sales levy should be spread uniformly over all the buying power of the country.[8]

In the postwar period, two economists, William Vickrey and Nicholas Kaldor, have attempted to keep the issue alive.[9] With the qualification provided in the footnote, these works have attracted little attention outside of academic circles. No important movement to

---

[7] See above, p. 113.

[8] *New York Times,* Sept. 6, 1942, p. 2F.

[9] William Vickrey, *Agenda for Progressive Taxation,* (New York: The Ronald Press Co., 1947), and Nicholas Kaldor, *An Expenditure Tax* (London: George Allen and Unwin, 1955). The *Agenda* analyzes the spendings tax, the income tax, and others, such as succession taxes. Kaldor's work concentrates on the spendings tax and is a plea that it be used instead of the high surtax rates of the British income tax. Kaldor's suggestions have been influential in India and Ceylon. It remains to be seen whether these ideas will have any substantial appeal to the Labour Party in Great Britain. The analysis here owes much to the works of Vickrey and Kaldor.

promote the spendings tax proposal exists in the United States, or for that matter in any Western country.

The Equity Question

Is a spendings tax fair and equitable? One's immediate reaction may be in the negative, because a spendings tax sounds like a sales tax, and sales taxation is commonly believed by many people to be defensible solely on grounds of providing the government with some revenue. But the question cannot be answered so quickly. Spendings may be taken as an index of a person's ability to contribute to government, just as income is commonly so taken. The issue can be brought into focus by a hypothetical example. Imagine three families, A, B, and C, situated as follows:

Family:	A	B	C
Income	$ 10,000	$ 25,000	$ 10,000
Spendings	$ 6,000	$ 6,000	$ 50,000
Net worth	$100,000	$250,000	$100,000

It is assumed that all three families are similar in all other relevant respects. There are no important differences in health, age, or number of dependents; all have access to the same markets for goods and services at the same prices, and all receive the same benefits from government.

If a spendings tax is imposed at progressive rates, that is, if the average rate of tax rises as the size of spendings increases, then families A and B will pay the same tax, whereas family C will pay much more. For example, if the average rate of tax is 10 per cent for spendings of $6,000, A and B will be asked to contribute $600 per period, whereas C may be taxed at an average rate of 25 per cent, depending upon the rate schedules, or $12,500.

Let us compare families A and C. Both have the same income and the same net worth, but C is called upon to pay $12,500 in taxes whereas A pays only $600. C may protest that he is being treated unfairly, pointing out that he has the same income and the same net worth as A; yet he is called upon to pay a substantially larger tax. What have the advocates of a spendings tax to say in answer to C's protests?

One answer, and this is the answer that Fisher might give, is that C as opposed to A enjoys a larger share of the fruits of economic activity. The fact that both have the same income (what Fisher calls "earnings") and the same wealth is immaterial. Kaldor might join in with the view that income measures what a person contributes to others, whereas consumption measures what others contribute to him. Therefore C should not complain. C has chosen for reasons best known to himself to "live off his capital," and having done so he should be prepared to pay the penalty in the form of taxation. If he had chosen to live frugally, his tax need not have been greater than A's, and hence the complaint is without merit.

To this line of reasoning, C may reply in the following vein: "I understand that this is a free country and that a man may spend his money as he sees fit. It so happens that I chose to take my family on an expensive round-the-world trip because my wife and I decided that it would be the best education the children could get. May I point out that henceforward we shall have to be economical because my income will fall, since we no longer have the assets used to finance the trip, and I shall have to work harder to get along. I do not understand why the government should, by its tax policy, penalize me in particular because of my decision; or am I wrong in assuming that this is a free country?"

If we let A in on the debate, he, having studied the writings of Mill and Pigou, might argue: "The spendings tax is superior to an income tax because a person does not get taxed doubly, once on the amount he saves and indefinitely on the income from the assets he acquires. A spendings tax avoids this unfairness because saving is excluded from the tax base."

Does A or C have the better case? Fairness, one could point out to our contestants, concerns the treatment of people, not the treatment of income or saving or consumption. If income were the tax base, each would pay the same tax. It is not sufficient to argue that a spendings tax is more fair than an income tax because a spendings tax exempts saving.

The double taxation argument is not a strong one. Under an income tax, a person is taxed an amount that depends on the size of his income; he is not taxed separately on the amount he saves and the amount he consumes. It is precisely an advantage of an income tax as opposed to a spendings tax that a person is free to decide on how to take his income without thereby altering his tax liability. A person is taxed once under an income tax. If he does save and the assets acquired do yield an income, he will in the future be taxed on his total income, including this portion. Mill, Marshall, Pigou, and Fisher confused the issue. They assumed that one can tell from the character of the tax base the source of the funds used to pay the tax. Such a view is like arguing that if there were a tax based on the size of waistlines, the government would collect the tax in pounds of flesh. One cannot logically conclude that either an income tax or a spendings tax comes "out of consumption" or "out of saving" merely from the definition of the tax. That question remains an open one.

Returning to the debate, C, having worked himself up a bit, now points to B. "How can any reasonable person maintain that I have greater taxable capacity than B? Look at B; his income is much larger than mine and so is his wealth. If the term ability-to-pay means anything, it means that B has more ability to contribute to the government than I do. Otherwise the discussion must cease for lack of any test of what fairness means as applied to taxation."

But the advocates of spendings taxation, although perhaps taken aback by the vigor of C's onslaught, may claim in defense of the spendings tax that C fails to take account of the socially beneficial effects of A's and B's frugality. The assets they are accumulating can be used to finance directly or indirectly new real investment, whereas C in marked contrast has dissipated the resources of society in luxurious living. Surely what both underdeveloped and developed countries of the world need is large amounts of investment. Otherwise standards of living cannot rise, or at least not rise as fast. After studying this line of argument, C may counter that investment may be a fine thing, but then so is consumption, and go on to insist that the point has nothing to do with the question of fairness, which concerns relations among people.

We leave the question of fairness here, except to emphasize that the spendings tax has been compared with an income tax. If the comparison had been made with some other forms of taxation, such as import duties, sales taxes, or real property taxes, the case for a spendings tax would look much better.

Effects on Saving

Those who have approached the spendings tax from the point of view of an income tax that exempts saving have often emphasized that a shift to a spendings tax would augment saving and indirectly increase the rate of investment. Without passing on the question of whether or not a tax system that stimulates saving is superior to one that does not, we may examine first the comparative effects of a spendings tax and an income tax on the amount saved.

The commonsense approach to this topic begins by asking whether the tax will induce people to save more or less. Because a spendings tax leaves saving out of the tax base, it seems only reasonable to conclude that a person will save more than he would if confronted by an income tax of the same amount. Therefore, one may try to add the extra saving of each family to obtain the total or aggregate extra saving. Thus, if people save $20 billion per year under an income tax, the conclusion may be reached that saving under a spendings tax will rise to (say) $30 or $40 billion per year.

This commonsense approach does not, however, stand up under close scrutiny. It is not true that each person can decide to save so many dollars per period, and hence aggregate saving is not a simple addition of the amount each person decides to save. What has been hidden from sight by this reasoning is the necessary relation between the amount invested and the amount saved. For a person to save $100 this month, he must consume $100 less than his income. With an income of $500, his consumption is $400. If we think of him as deciding to save $150 instead, we assume his consumption will be $350 instead of $400. But if in fact his consumption is $350 this month, people who produce the commodities he buys will obtain $350 rather than $400 and hence these people will have different incomes. Their saving will be affected because their incomes are affected.

To understand the effects of any tax upon saving, one should look at the facts from the side of expenditures rather than from the side of personal income. The amount of saving actually forthcoming during any period of time will be equal, and necessarily so, to the amount of investment forthcoming during the same period of time.[10] This result holds from the definition of terms.

Applied to the topic at hand, given the amount of investment and government expenditures, a shift from an income tax to a spendings tax of equal yield leaves the amount of private saving, that is, the saving of all groups except the government, unaffected. Investment equals total saving by definition because investment is defined as the money value of new physical resources produced and hence (ignoring government) as that part of national product not already counted as consumption. Saving is the difference between national income (which equals national product) and consumption. Hence investment and saving are equal to the differences between the same two quantities, national income and consumption.

Private saving is then the difference between total saving and government saving. As long as government expenditures and government revenue are kept unchanged, private saving cannot change. A shift

[10] "Necessarily" in a closed economic system, meaning one without economic relations with other economies. Investment carried on in one region, say the United States, need not equal the saving of people living in the United States if, for example, any income generated within the United States is obtained by people living abroad. The equality between the payment of money and the receipt of money holds for a closed system.

from one tax to another, then, as long as yields are kept constant, must leave private saving at exactly the same figure.[11]

It is not therefore instructive to investigate the effects of a spendings tax as compared with an income tax by asking how the two taxes affect the amount of saving.[12] That problem is solved at the definitional level. Rather we should ask: What is the effect of a spendings tax as compared to an income tax on the amount spent for consumption?[13] The further question, then, is: What is the effect of a spendings tax as compared to an income tax on the amount spent for investment? If these two questions are answered, the effects of a spendings tax on savings are determined as well, and we shall then be in a position to judge whether the altered pattern of consumption-investment expenditures is to be preferred or not.

[11] In symbols:
$$C + I + G = Y, \quad (1)$$
where Y is national product, C is consumption, I is investment, and G is government expenditures upon goods and services.
$$Y = (Y - T) + T, \quad (2)$$
where T is the net tax yield.
Hence,
$$C + I + G = (Y - T) + T. \quad (3)$$
$$S_g = T - G, \quad (4)$$
by the definition of government saving, S_g, and
$$S_p = (Y - T) - C, \quad (5)$$
by the definition of private saving, S_p.
Hence,
$$S_g + S_p = (Y - T) - C + (T - G), \quad (6)$$
or total saving,
$$S_t = Y - (C + G) \quad (7)$$
and
$$I = Y - (C + G). \quad (8)$$
Hence,
$$I = S_t. \quad (9)$$
Further, by holding net revenue constant (T), a substitution of any tax for another, with given investment and government expenditures, leaves private saving unaffected, or
$$S_p = S_t - S_g. \quad (10)$$

[12] Much of the discussion of this topic has been muddied by inattention to definitional relations. Thus Vickrey states: "In general, it appears clear that the spendings tax tends to produce a larger volume of individual saving than an income tax, given the same general progressivity of the burden." Vickrey, *op. cit.*, p. 335. Kaldor makes similar remarks. See *An Expenditure Tax*, chap. ii.

[13] Note that the statement "a person saves more" is not equivalent to the statement "a person consumes less."

Effects on Consumption

We assume a spendings tax of equal yield is to be substituted for an income tax. The new structure of taxation may differ from the old because some people are taxed more or less heavily than under the income tax. Let us put aside this distributional aspect for the moment to permit concentration on the effects of the difference in the form of the taxes in question.

Under a spendings tax, a taxpayer is told in effect that for each dollar spent on consumption he must pay some x per cent of a dollar in tax. Let us suppose that the spendings tax rate is 100 per cent, and that this tax is imposed instead of an income tax of 50 per cent. (The relation between the rates of the two taxes will be discussed presently.) If a taxpayer spends the same amount on consumption under the spendings tax as he does under the income tax, his tax liability is to be the same. Under the spendings tax, the person in question finds that it costs him twice as many dollars to acquire the same amount of consumption items; for every dollar he pays in the market, the government tells him to contribute a dollar in taxes. Now it would seem that he would have to curtail his expenditures; but this is not so, because he has the income tax money the government no longer collects. He finds, however, that if he spends more money on such items as government bonds, corporate stocks, and insurance, or merely holds more cash on the average, he can reduce his tax liability. One set of costs, the costs of consumption, has doubled for him whereas another set of costs, the costs of acquiring assets, has remained unchanged. It seems reasonably obvious what he will do. Either he will spend the same dollar amount for consumption items exclusive of tax, *or he will spend less.* In general, the holding of assets competes with consumption for the dollars of a person. A spendings tax shifts the balance in the direction of assets, since their purchase entails no tax liability.

Furthermore, there is an added incentive to hold a larger amount of wealth, particularly a larger amount of cash. People hold money for various reasons. One important reason is to finance expenses that cannot be predicted in detail. Such expenses will now cost him twice the number of dollars, so that he will need to hold twice as many dollars to meet the same contingencies. As an additional factor, if he loses his job, the income tax stops so that he has at least the comfort that the government no longer insists upon a contribution. But under a spendings tax, this comfort is denied him. As long as he and his family continue to buy goods and services, he is subject to taxation. Thus if he finds himself in an occupation that entails the risk of being put on short-time or shunted into unemployment, he will need to be more careful about his consumption expenditures while he is employed so as to have a larger stock of assets to draw upon in bad times. We may conclude then that, as compared to an income tax, a spendings tax will induce people to spend less on consumption and also to reshift their holdings toward more conservative assets, such as money and savings accounts.

The distributional aspects of a spendings tax may also affect consumption expenditures. But there is the difficulty that the distributional effects cannot be ascertained merely by specifying a shift from an income tax to a spendings tax. It would be impossible to design a spendings tax in such a manner that each person is called upon to pay the same sum as he would under an income tax. All people with the same income would have to spend identical sums on consumption. Actually different people with the same income spend widely varying amounts for consumption depending upon age, size of family, location, and a host of other factors. Hence, if the government wishes to tax people systematically in relation to their incomes, it cannot do so by a spendings tax.

Nevertheless, it is possible to devise a spendings tax that is progressive in the sense that the average rate of tax increases as the size of the base (spendings) increases and also progressive on the average with respect to income. Statistically, as is well known, consumption and income are positively correlated. As income rises, the amount of consumption expenditures per spending unit also rises. This correlation may be explained directly by the theory that the amount spent upon consumption depends upon income—the Keynesian approach. Or it may be explained by the theory that how much people spend on consumption depends upon their asset position and that income is positively correlated with the size of holdings or wealth. Regardless of the explanation, however, a spendings tax could be made highly progressive with respect to both spendings and income. The rate schedule in Table 8–1 illustrates such a spendings tax.

This schedule is drawn up by permitting the taxpayer to divide total spendings or consumption by the number of persons in the family, and allowing each person an exemption of $500. For a married couple with two children and total spendings of $5,000 during the taxable year, spendings per person are $1,250 and taxable spendings per person are $750. Thus the tax on the family would be 25 per cent of $750 multiplied by four, or $750. The effective rate of tax with

TABLE 8–1

A Highly Progressive High Rate Spendings Tax
(Exemption: $500 Per Person)

Taxable Spendings Class Per Person	Tax
Under $1,000	25% of amount
$ 1,000 – $ 2,000	$250 plus 40% of excess of $1,000
2,000 – 3,000	$650 plus 75% of excess of $2,000
3,000 – 4,000	$1,600 plus 100% of excess of $3,000
4,000 – 6,000	$2,600 plus 150% of excess of $4,000
6,000 – 10,000	$5,600 plus 200% of excess of $6,000
10,000 – 25,000	$13,600 plus 300% of excess of $10,000
25,000 – 50,000	$58,600 plus 500% of excess of $25,000
Over 50,000	$213,600 plus 1000% of excess of $50,000

respect to spendings is, therefore, 15 per cent. If this family had an income during the year of $6,000, the effective rate of the spendings tax with respect to income would be 12½ per cent.

A very wealthy person who has, say, an income of $1 million per year and who spends $202,000 on consumption would, according to the rate schedule suggested, pay a spendings tax of $654,000, if there are four persons in the family. The effective rate of an income tax designed to remove the same amount of money from the family would need to be 65.4 per cent. Obviously rates could be designed for a spendings tax so that if the family spent the indicated sum, their income after tax would be negative. The effective rate of a spendings tax would need to be about 500 per cent to accomplish this result. A family in such a position would find itself having to deplete its assets in order to pay the tax liability as well as to finance the total consumption expenditures made during the year. This result could be avoided, of course, by cutting down on the rather elaborate scale of living assumed in this case.

Because a spendings tax can be designed so as to put upon people in given income classes about the same tax liabilities as does a progressive income tax, objections to a spendings tax as insufficiently progressive with respect to income must fail. Within any income class, such a spendings tax would force people who spend more than the average for their income class to pay larger taxes. Those with smaller than average spendings would pay less. Objections to this result are objections to the use of spendings as a measure of taxable capacity or ability to pay.

Effects on Investment

A spendings tax excludes from the tax base expenditures for investment. Accordingly, a corporation or a person considering the acquisition of machine tools, buildings, inventories, and other things used in production, has no occasion to consider tax consequences. Thus a spendings tax may be looked upon as neutral in its direct effects upon investment.

Our earlier analysis indicated, however, that a spendings tax as opposed to an income tax induces people to spend less money on consumption and also to decide in favor of more conservative asset holdings. These two results will have effects upon both the scale of investment and upon the types of real assets demanded by investors.

To the extent that a spendings tax leads to economizing on consumption, there exists more room in the economy for investment. If this added investment is financed at the expense of consumption, no price inflation would be required to maintain full utilization of resources. Resources would be shifted away from the production of consumption items and toward the production of investment items. Prices of investment items would increase relatively to the prices of consumption items, and this would induce the indicated shift in outputs.

The desire of people to hold a more conservative combination of assets would call for some increase in the supply of money at the time the shift to a spendings tax was made. This adjustment would need to be made only once, when the spendings tax was introduced, to accommodate the desire to hold money to cover the greater cost of meeting contingencies under a spendings tax as compared with other tax devices.

Actually, none of these effects are likely to be of quantitative importance. The possible indirect encouragement of investment, in particular, is likely to be small. There is little reason to suppose that people are especially sensitive to the over-all cost of consumption, as long as their total spending power is left unchanged. These incentive effects are not nearly so important as the yield aspects. Devices that remove dollars from people are much more powerful than those that make some expenditures appear to be more expensive.

Built-in Flexibility of the Spendings Tax

The spendings tax would appear to be distinctly inferior to an income tax with respect to its built-in flexibility. A spendings tax would come out much better on this score than a sales tax or a property tax, although quantitative estimates in this regard are impossible in the absence of experience.

The built-in flexibility of a tax depends upon (1) the built-in flexibility of the tax base and (2) the marginal rate of tax. Thus if the tax base is total private income (100 per cent built-in flexibility), which it never is in fact, and the marginal rate of tax is 25 per cent, the built-in flexibility of the tax would be 25 per cent. But if the built-in flexibility of the tax base is, say, 50 per cent and the marginal rate is 25 per cent, the built-in flexibility of the tax itself becomes only 12½ per cent.

In the case of a spendings tax, the built-in flexibility of the tax base is likely to be comparatively small. For example, in the 1957-58 recession, Personal Consumption Expenditures, as estimated by the Department of Commerce, declined on a seasonally adjusted basis from a high annual rate of $283.6 billion for the third quarter of 1957 to $281.0 billion for the first quarter of 1958. For the same two quarters, Gross National Product declined from $440 billion to $424 billion. The built-in flexibility of consumption expenditures with respect to GNP was therefore about 16 per cent. If a spendings tax were as inclusive in its base as Personal Consumption Expenditures, a highly unlikely prospect even in a tightly designed spendings tax, and if the marginal tax rate were as high as 40 per cent—a very high rate indeed—the built-in flexibility of the spendings tax would be in the neighborhood of 6.5 per cent. According to Pechman's estimates for 1948-53, the built-in flexibility of the federal individual income tax is about 16 per cent.[14] Therefore a spendings tax cannot get a high rating on the score of built-in flexibility. This feature makes it distinctly less attractive as a mass tax at the federal level than an individual income tax.

This very feature, however, may make it more attractive for the financing of state and local governments. The latter need revenue devices which do not decline during periods of business recession and which provide increasing revenues during periods of business expansion. A spendings tax fits these requirements very well.

Practicality of a Spendings Tax

Whether a spendings tax could be made workable remains a speculative question, although when the Indian and Ceylonese experiments can be studied, some of the questions may be answered by experience.

[14] See Joseph A. Pechman, "Yield of an Individual Income Tax During a Recession," *National Tax Journal,* VII (March, 1954), p. 11.

As already pointed out, spendings may be ascertained indirectly in the manner suggested by Fisher. In some respects, the information required is greater than that involved in income tax administration and in some respects less. Enthusiasts for a spendings tax are somewhat inclined to play down the expected administrative difficulties of their favorite and to play up the already known ones of income taxation. Only a few of what appear to be the major problems will be discussed.

A spendings tax designed according to "funds-to-be-accounted-for" and the "accounting-for" approach requires that the taxpayer report among other facts the amount of money on hand at the beginning of each taxable year. In the past, surveys of personal finances have been able to uncover reasonably good information about individual ownership of bank accounts, but there has been no successful survey revealing the amount of currency owned by the individuals questioned. People are either reluctant to reveal or do not know how much currency they have on hand. Would a tax law that required a person to divulge his total cash position be successful?

If a person could tuck away $10,000 and not report it in his cash holdings at the beginning of the year, he could finance a large portion of his consumption for a period of time without being subject to heavy taxation. He would of course have to be consistent from year to year, or otherwise his books would not balance, inviting a friendly visit from a member of the Internal Revenue Service. If he happens to be successful in the concealment, there remains the possibility that his observed scale of living may not jibe with his reported expenditures for consumption, but this would invite a visit from the revenue people only if someone observed and reported the discrepancy. Once the revenue people became suspicious of a person, they could estimate his expenditures, as they often now do in investigations of evasion of the income tax. As compared to the enforcement of the income tax, the task of the revenue people under a spendings tax would be in some ways simpler. What is now done is to reconstruct the person's income by obtaining his net worth at some starting date, comparing it with his net worth at the end of the period, and estimating his consumption during the period. The defense of the accused confronted by such a reconstruction is to maintain either that he obtained assets from some non-taxable source, such as gifts, or that he has been living off assets previously accumulated. Using this defense, a Chicago member of the now defunct Capone organization claimed that he had been financing his lavish scale of living from a cache of $300,000 in his attic. The jury did not believe him. Under a spendings tax, in order to establish tax evasion the revenue service would only need to estimate a person's expenditures in a manner that would satisfy a court as being reasonable.

Besides providing an incentive to conceal assets, a spendings tax makes it advantageous to disguise personal expenses as business costs. In this respect it creates incentives to evade, as does an income tax, and perhaps even more so. If the rates of the spendings tax are very high, say 300 per cent, the incentive to stretch the legal boundaries defining what are and what are not business expenses may outweigh the incentive to go to bed at night with a clear conscience. Thus American lawyers may decide to hold their annual convention in London, instead of, say, Kansas City, because they feel the need of getting closer to the source of the Common Law.[15] Those lawyers' wives who always wanted to see the Crown Jewels may accompany their husbands. If the trip costs a lawyer and wife $3,000 and he treats the entire sum as a business expense, when according to the rules of either an income tax or a spendings tax he should have reported only $2,000 as a business expense, would he gain more taxwise under an income tax than under a spendings tax?

A spendings tax rate of t is equivalent to an income tax rate of t_y according to the formula $t = \dfrac{t_y}{1 - t_y}$. Thus if the income tax rate is 50 per cent, the equivalent spendings tax rate is $\dfrac{.50}{1 - .50}$ or 100 per cent. An income tax rate of 90 per cent is equivalent to a rate of 900 per cent under a spendings tax. "Equivalent" means a set of tax rates such that a person would be subject to the same tax liability provided that he spends on consumption an amount equal to his after-tax income. Actually, since the base of the spendings tax is smaller than the base of the income tax, the rate structure of the spendings tax must be higher than that given by the above formula.

If the marginal rate of income tax to the taxpayer in question were 50 per cent, he could save $500 in tax liability by overreporting his business expense by $1,000. Under an equivalent spendings tax rate of 100 per cent, he would save $1,000 by underreporting his con-

---

[15] The practice of holding professional and business conventions abroad is not of course confined to the legal profession; many associations do likewise. If the persons concerned are subject to high marginal rates of income tax, such as 60 per cent, the Treasury loses sixty cents in revenue for every dollar spent as business expense. The subject of what should be allowable business deductions is a difficult one, involving niceties of interpretation and delicate ethical questions. There is no basis for estimating the amount of understatement of taxable income arising from even clear violation of the law's intent, except that the amount is generally believed to be "large." But, see Joseph A. Pechman's paper, "What Would a Comprehensive Individual Income Tax Yield," *Tax Revision Compendium,* Vol. I, p. 275. (See annotation below in Suggested Readings for Part II, p. 349.)

sumption expenditures. The incentive to evade tax appears greater under a spendings tax than under an income tax of equivalent rates.

It has been argued by Vickrey,[16] however, that this manner of comparison is misleading. When the person who has successfully disguised consumption as a business expense comes to spend the $1,000, he will have only $500 to spend on commodities; the other $500 will have to be paid in spendings tax. Of course, if he saves the money, he would not pay any additional tax. But this to Vickrey is an extreme and unlikely case. Properly compared, then, the greater incentive to evade a spendings tax is illusory.

This argument assumes that the taxpayer would eventually have to account for the funds he did not pay in taxes. If he is at all astute, however, he could readily satisfy the formal requirements of the law by including the entire $3,000 as "accounted-for" under the category of business expense. There is never any further $1,000 to account for again. Consumption to the amount of $1,000 has already been enjoyed; there is no undoing this fact. A spendings tax of equivalent rates creates therefore a greater incentive to evade the tax by disguising consumption as business expense than does an income tax. Perhaps, however, the incentive is so large under income taxation that a shift to the spendings base would matter little in this respect.

Applications

The previous analysis has not revealed that a spendings tax has marked superiorities over an income tax as a mass revenue device. Some advocates of a spendings tax, such as Kaldor, wish to confine it to wealthy groups. He has proposed that the surtax rates, those in excess of the standard rate of income tax in British law, be abolished and those taxpayers be required, instead, to pay a spendings tax. An alternative proposal he considers calls for tightening of the definition of taxable income by bringing capital gains and losses, gambling gains and losses, and even gifts and bequests into the definition of taxable income, but for several reasons Kaldor despairs of such a solution. If the social problem of what is often called plutocracy (high concentration of wealth in the hands of a small group) is really believed to be of such seriousness as to call for drastic measures, net worth taxation, as we shall see in the following chapter, is a direct and effective way of eroding great fortunes. Both a spendings tax and an income tax are less efficient devices to accomplish such an objective.

The reader must decide for himself whether he regards a spendings tax as better or worse than an income tax. Even if some should con-

---

[16] See Vickrey, *op. cit.,* p. 346. See also Kaldor, *op. cit.,* pp. 234-37.

clude that an income tax is better, they may be reminded that according to practically any canons of taxation that have ever been suggested, a spendings tax compares favorably with the cumbersome set of excise, sales, and commodity and business taxes found at the federal, state, and local levels of government in the United States.

The administration of a spendings tax by state governments may be feasible. It would be a rather difficult tax for any smaller unit of government to employ because of the amount of information required and the ease of escaping the tax by moving elsewhere. If the tax were imposed at the state level, the rates would need to be moderate to avoid the political and economic consequences of losing wealthy residents to other states. A rate schedule possible for a state government is given in Table 8–2.

TABLE 8–2

A MODERATELY PROGRESSIVE LOW RATE SPENDINGS TAX
(Exemption: $500 Per Person)

Taxable Spendings Class Per Person	Tax
0 – $1,000	1% of amount
$1,000 – 2,000	$10 plus 2% of excess of $1,000
$2,000 – 3,000	$30 plus 4% of excess of $2,000
$3,000 – 4,000	$70 plus 5% of excess of $3,000
$4,000 – 5,000	$120 plus 6% of excess of $4,000
$5,000 – 6,000	$180 plus 7% of excess of $5,000
$6,000 – 7,000	$250 plus 8% of excess of $6,000
$7,000 – 8,000	$330 plus 9% of excess of $7,000
$8,000 – 9,000	$420 plus 10% of excess of $8,000

Such a spendings tax might be employed in lieu of state sales taxes, cigarette taxes, and various other special excise taxes now in effect. The schedule of rates is intended to be illustrative; any actual schedule would need to be tailored to the desired level of revenue. It is important, however, if such an experiment were made, that high rates be avoided. In turn, exemptions cannot be high if large revenues are to be obtained. In trying out a new tax device calling for the reporting of detailed information heretofore not required of taxpayers, a government would be foolhardy to provide the taxpayer with great temptation to evade the tax. After experience has been gained and the many bugs certain to be found in any new tax law have been removed, it may be feasible to increase the rates in the higher brackets, subject to the restriction that the rates not be so high as to induce large-scale migration of wealthy residents to other states.

As the federal individual income tax law is presently written, a state spendings tax would presumably be deductible from adjusted gross income under the federal tax. Thus the progressiveness of the tax at the rates suggested would be smaller than appears on the surface. Nevertheless, if a spendings tax were used instead of sales, commodity, and business taxation by state governments in this country, the entire tax structure would become more progressive and hence would reduce the present after-tax inequalities of income.

The political appeal of a spendings tax at the federal level will remain a question mark until the device becomes more widely understood. Groups who favor systematic progressive taxation may support the tax on much the same grounds as lead them to favor a progressive income tax. Conservative groups who oppose progressive taxation in principle cannot be expected to support a progressive spendings tax.

Some General Observations

The spendings tax is most likely to be an important revenue device in some underdeveloped countries. As already observed, India and Ceylon have installed it as one feature of a more comprehensive progressive tax structure. If the administrative problems turn out to be surmountable and if the tax meets with popular approval, other developing countries may become interested in employing the tax as well. The tax seems to be especially in accord with what is, in underdeveloped countries, an immediate major objective—greater investment, both public and private.

We have seen that a spendings tax does not directly stimulate private or total saving. The amount of saving is governed by the amount of investment, and not the other way around. However, this conclusion serves only to clarify. The more interesting question is how the tax affects private investment expenditures. We found that a spendings tax as compared to an income tax reduces consumption expenditures and thereby permits larger investment expenditures. However, this conclusion must be quickly qualified because the effects in question are likely to be small. If the motivation to install a spendings tax is only to obtain its disincentive effects upon consumption spending, the results are not likely to be worth the costs.

There remain what might be called the theoretical objections. A spendings tax "distorts" people's total expenditures by placing a penalty upon their consumption expenditures. The tax law must define what goods, especially consumer durables, classify as consumption and what as investment. If, then, the rates are high, those items that fall just over the line become highly attractive. In one country, they may be gold and gold ornaments, as in India; in another they may be automobiles or cycles. Because lines must be drawn, the cost of those goods that can qualify as investments is reduced relatively to those that cannot. Attempts by governments to solve these problems are likely to prescribe what personal investments are acceptable. What are to a person genuine investments may, as in the case of gold ornaments, be looked upon as economically objectionable investments. The tax is then likely to develop into a system of more or less arbitrary penalties, penalizing not only consumption expenditures but any expenditure deemed unacceptable to the government. A heavy burden is placed upon the tax administration to avoid arbitrary and complex rules. The main justification of a spendings tax—systematic taxation of people according to an index of tax-paying ability—may be lost from sight, leaving an expensive tax device perhaps a little superior to a set of heavy commodity taxes on items in great demand.

9

Net Worth Taxation

Along with personal income taxation and spendings or consumption taxation, a comprehensive net worth tax may be employed by governments to tailor tax liabilities to personal ability to pay. In general, the net worth of a person or a family is the money value of all assets possessed by the person or family minus the money value of all claims held by others against the assets in question. Income and spendings are flows and can only be conceived of in terms of a time dimension. Net worth is a stock concept and can only be conceived of in terms of a date in time. Net worth is a balance-sheet statement of the wealth of the reporting unit. To arrive at the net worth position of a person, an inventory of everything in his possession is taken, and a price per unit for each type of possession is established. From these quantities and prices, the total value of the person's possessions is computed— his gross wealth—and from this total his debts are then deducted. A main problem in the administration of a net worth tax is the non-arbitrary pricing of possessions and debts.

Sweden, Norway, and Denmark have employed net worth taxation as a standard feature of their revenue systems for over a half-century. The tax is used along with income taxation to raise revenue and to reduce the inequalities computed after tax in the distribution of individual income. Except for its use by these and a few other European countries, net worth taxation has, until recent years, been associated with radical measures designed to cope with the legacy of war finances under the label "capital levies." In the aftermath of World War I, several of the Continental countries, such as Austria and Czechoslovakia, experimented with capital levies in the form of taxes upon wealth holdings for the purposes of reducing public debts and of eliminating the inflation potential involved in large private holdings of money. The United States Treasury had plans drawn for a wealth tax during the first World War because of fears that sufficient funds could not be raised by other taxes and by borrowing. The war ended before it was deemed advisable to ask the Congress to adopt such a measure.

World War II did not give rise to the intense interest in capital levies which occurred during and after World War I. Many governments, confronted with excessive inflation potentials, solved the problem simply by experiencing inflation. This solution was adopted by France, Italy, and by almost all South American countries. In some countries, such as Denmark, Norway, the Netherlands, and the United Kingdom, direct controls over prices and production, coupled with nonprice systems of rationing, kept the inflationary potential more or less suppressed, but none avoided inflation. The emphasis upon drastic monetary medicine found after the first war shifted to direct controls after the second. This shift may be explained by the general concern in the leading industrial nations of the world with the possibility of large-scale underemployment, and more importantly by a radical change in financial mores, particularly in regard to what was believed to be the tolerable size of a national debt, during the intervening years.

The Equity Issue

Net worth taxation may be regarded as superior to either spendings or income taxation on the grounds that the size of a man's wealth provides a superior or even the ideal measure of his taxpaying ability. Consider A with assets of $1 million and an income of $100,000, and B with the same amount of wealth and an income of only $20,000. Under a net worth tax, both would be called upon to make the same contribution to the government, whereas under a highly progressive income tax, A would be required to pay a tax bill many times larger than would B. The large difference assumed in the incomes may be fortuitous in the sense that B happened to incur large losses on some of his investments during the particular period chosen. Over a longer period of time, they may have the same income and, provided effective income averaging is employed, pay about the same tax. However, people with equivalent amounts of wealth may and do obtain very different incomes even over long periods, reflecting merely good fortune in investment decisions or, more often, better judgment in the selection of assets. Widows are often so timid and conservative in their investment decisions, so fearful of making a mistake, that they succeed often only in obtaining a small income from a large fortune. A net worth tax treats the lucky and the unlucky, the astute and the less astute, in the same fashion as long as they have the same net worth.

The proposition that net worth provides a superior measure of taxpaying capacity rests upon the quite literal fact that different people with identical net worths have identical command over the use of resources. Both A and B can, having the same amount of wealth, spend the same amounts on consumption and upon investment; both have equal "voting power" in the economy. The fact that A happens to be more fortunate or more competent in making investment decisions than B and thus in experiencing a larger income may of course be reflected in his net worth position in the future and hence in his future tax liabilities. For the time being, both pay the same tax because both have equal power to command the use of resources.

The above argument has omitted any reference to differences in the earning power of the two people themselves. Suppose that A is a doctor, a very successful one, whereas B occupies himself or pretends to occupy himself by dabbling about in his real estate business that barely pays its expenses. The larger income of A arises from his earnings as a doctor, not from any greater rate of return on his investments. B is simply incapable of earning any important sum by self-employment or by working for others. What is fair tax treatment of the two people in question?

Digression on the Valuation of Human Beings

Computing net worth by reference to possessions and debts alone fails to take into account the different earning capacities of people, looked upon as resources. The apparent remedy is simple. To obtain a complete statement of a person's net worth, one should include the capital value of the person himself. The doctor should include the capital value of himself viewed as a source of valuable services. A horse is valuable because his future services are valuable, and so is the doctor. A net worth tax, if it is to be completely general, must therefore provide for the valuation of human beings looked upon as sources of valuable services.

Human beings are not customarily bought and sold. There are, however, exceptions. Slavery as such has largely disappeared from this globe except in some Middle Eastern areas. In sections of the Orient, marriageable girls are sometimes sold by their parents to the highest bidding prospective bridegroom. A black market exists in babies in the United States. Childless couples are prepared to pay money for a child, and as is to be expected, some entrepreneurs stand ready to satisfy the demand. Professional baseball players are bought and sold by various clubs. But in general human beings are not explicitly priced as such; they fall in the category of entailed assets like certain hereditary estates in England. One freedom is universally denied "free" people: they may not sell themselves to others. Shall we conclude, then, that a comprehensive net worth tax must fail for lack of any measure of the capital value of personal earning power?

There are many items that are valuable to people which are not bought and sold. Of the millions of varieties of physical assets existing in the United States at any moment, only a small fraction of a few varieties will change hands during the coming years. Many types of physical assets, once having been born, perform for one owner throughout their useful lives. Many types of debt contracts are held until their expiration date by the creditor who first lends the money. For all practical purposes, many assets are entailed, and yet in one manner or another, money values are placed upon them. The fact that particular classes of assets are not in fact exchanged does not mean that valuation of them is impossible.

The principles involved in placing a money value upon human earning power may be studied by first considering how to value an entailed asset. Let us suppose a person is presented on his twenty-first birthday with an income for life of $5,000 per year. He has no power to dispose of the source; it is a trust fund. When he dies, the income dies with him. What is the money value of the right to receive this series of money sums?

One approach calls for asking how large a sum of money he could borrow on the basis of the right to receive the income. If there is no doubt at all that the indicated amounts will be forthcoming, the maximum amount he could borrow would be a sum calling for payment to the creditor of $5,000 per year for life, minus the premium on a life insurance policy just large enough to repay the creditor the amount due in case of premature death. The total amount to be borrowed would then amount to the present value of $5,000 for the life expectancy of the person minus the insurance premiums. If the best bargain the person could make reflects a rate of interest of 5 per cent, the present value of an annuity for a person, assuming a life expectancy of 50 years, would be $91,290 (ignoring the cost of insurance). Actually no commercial lender would lend such a sum to a person so circumstanced even though there were no doubt in his mind that the $5,000 payment would be made to the person each year, and even though the insurance aspect were fully covered. The borrower might dissipate the sum borrowed through unwise investments or by living on an elaborate scale, and thus the lender might fear that at some future date the borrower would fail to honor the contract. Furthermore, the lender would be fearful that he also would have an entailed asset because there would be no feasible market in which he could at some future date sell the debt contract. This loss of "liquidity" would make the prospective contract unattractive. Our life-income person who has no other income might find that he could borrow no more than $50,000 on the basis of his life income. Hence the maximum present value of the terminable income as measured by the maximum amount that a person could borrow might be and probably would be much smaller than the "present value" as arrived at by discounting the future money payments at the prevailing rate of interest. Yet one conclusion is permissible. The money value to be placed upon the life-income prospect cannot be less than the amount which could be raised by borrowing against it. A lower limit is thus established.

This lower limit is relevant, however, only if the person in question has, so to speak, an overwhelming desire to lay his hands on all the cash he can obtain. This is desperation decision making rather than ordinary day-to-day choice. Our man may find that he would like to borrow, say, $15,000 because he plans to be married and needs money to buy the latest gadgets for household management. If he can borrow at 5 per cent, he is announcing that a dollar payable a year hence is worth approximately 95 cents now, which in turn implies that he values marginally his life-income prospect at about 5 per cent.

To use an example in order to clarify the point, suppose a farmer owns a thousand similar head of cattle. If he finds he can sell one for $500 and chooses to sell, say, five, he has announced that his cattle are worth $500,000. The money value of a lot of items of any given kind is what any one is worth, that is, the price, times the number in question. In economics, things are normally priced marginally. Our farmer does not need to sell all of his cattle to ascertain the value of them.

No further qualification would be necessary if the price at which a person can sell something is identical with the price at which he can buy the same thing. But if there are costs of selling, and practically speaking there always are, which price should be used—the buying price or the selling price?

If the farmer found that the cost of buying cattle was $525 per head and he wished to buy, then the value of his holdings should be placed at $525,000 because by his act he announced that a head was worth $525. The general principle, then, of valuing a stock of things owned by a person is simple. The value is the buying price times the number of units he owns if he wishes to buy, or the selling price times the number of units he owns if he wishes to sell. If he wishes neither to buy nor sell, the value of that stock of things is indeterminate within the range of the value computed for the buying price and for the selling price. This range reduces to zero if buying and selling prices are identical.

Returning to the person with the life income, the present value of his prospective income is to be computed at the relevant rate of interest to him, the rate at which he borrows if he borrows, or the rate at which he lends if he lends. If there is a spread of rates, the present value of his prospect is indeterminate within the range established by the rates of interest in question.

The valuation of human earning power involves greater difficulties than those associated with a life income from a source beyond the control of the income recipient. Like physical resources in general, the gain that a person may obtain from his efforts is an outcome in part of forces beyond his control and cannot be predicted in detail. One cannot be sure how much one will earn one year hence or even, in many cases, one month hence. Unlike the life-income example, the earnings of a human being during the period of productive activity cannot be assumed to be known in advance. The difficulty is serious; it need not be altogether fatal.

Any formula for arriving at the capital value of a human being must at best be thought of as an approximation; a theoretically "correct" formula does not exist. Limits may nevertheless be suggested. At the lower limit, the capital value of a person cannot be less than the maximum sum he could raise by agreeing to mortgage his future earning power to creditors. In free societies, there are legal restrictions upon the enforceability of contracts alienating all of one's personal earning power to others. Yet, given these restrictions, the capital value of personal earning power cannot be less than the amount that others are willing to pay. Actually few people ever put their ability to borrow to such a supreme test, and bankruptcy proceedings are available to those who try.

The present value of personal earning power cannot exceed the amount the beneficiaries would agree to accept on the condition that they forfeit the entire income of the person in question. Thus if a man does the work, and he and his wife are the only beneficiaries from the income he obtains from work, his earning capacity cannot be greater than the sum of money they would accept on condition that he continued to work but that every dollar earned had to be paid to an outsider. This may be called the compensation rule. The compensation may be hypothetical or actual. For example, a university professor finds himself divorced and has been required by court order to pay alimony to his former wife. To protect herself in the event of his death, she takes out an insurance policy on his life with herself as the beneficiary. She thereby values her share of her former husband's earning capacity by the size of the policy acquired. If that share is 50 per cent, the present value of the man's earning power may be considered to be twice the size of the policy.

In the practical administration of a net worth tax, various expedients could be employed to obtain an approximation to the capital value of human earning power. The income of the person from work could be averaged over the preceding several years, say five, and a formula applied which would take into account the work-expectancy period of that person, the trend of money income in his occupation over the preceding five years, and an interest rate. Suppose, for example, the person is a lawyer and his average annual earnings over the five-year period amounted to $25,000. Furthermore, the trend of lawyers' earnings in general reveals an average increase of, say, 4 per cent per year. The lawyer in question is forty years old, and the average work-expectancy for lawyers of that age is, say, twenty-five years. The tax administration could provide a table based upon a compound interest formula giving the present value of the earnings projected from the average of past income and the trend of earnings of the occupation in which the person finds himself. Even simpler devices might be employed; the current year's income may be projected for the period of work expectancy of a person and discounted. All such formulas would be open to the charge of being arbitrary with respect to particular taxpayers. Yet it would be much more arbitrary to impose a net worth tax with low exemptions without taking into account personal earning power at all, since in effect such treatment presupposes that personal earning power is distributed equally among persons.

The Equity Question Once More

If we may assume that the problem of assessing personal earning power for tax purposes can be satisfactorily solved, how does a general net worth tax compare with other means-test tax devices from the point of view of interpersonal equity?

From a distributional aspect, one would expect that an income tax and a net worth tax would give substantially similar results since the size of income and the size of net worth may be expected to be positively correlated. Yet examination of tax data for Norway shows a remarkably small correlation even when allowance is made for the exclusion of the capital value of human earning power from the tax base. Approximately two-thirds of those reporting taxable income reported no taxable capital, and 2.3 per cent of those reporting no taxable income reported taxable capital.[1] Although the information available is inadequate, a net worth tax appears to have the effect, as compared with an income tax, of hitting those groups in the population who prefer to hold low-yielding assets. Clearly a person who holds his assets in the form of savings accounts or government bonds would be taxed more heavily under a progressive net worth tax than would a person of the same wealth who invests more dangerously and more successfully.

The tax treatment of people of different earning capacities should be approximately the same under a net worth tax that includes human earning power because income would need to be used in any formula devised to estimate the value of future earnings. Yet differences there would be. In general, people whose only important assets are themselves would be taxed less heavily as they grew older beyond some critical point. In the years immediately prior to retirement, the tax liability would become small. There would be some tendency for the growth in external assets owned to offset the decline in the value of personal earning capacity.

No logical argument can settle the choice between income, spendings, or net worth as the appropriate measure of personal ability to pay. One must decide for oneself which, if any, is superior.

Effect on Consumption and Investment Choice

Of the progressive tax devices known, a net worth tax is probably as neutral a tax device as can be devised. It is not likely to have significant effects upon the work-leisure choice, upon the choice among types of assets to own, or upon the choice between holding assets and consuming. If the tax is severe, it may have large effects arising merely from the size of the sum of money removed from a person. But neutrality in taxation is to be viewed apart from this factor, as Professor Pigou has emphasized.[2] Any tax that has a yield subtracts

---

[1] Janet A. Fisher, "Taxation of Personal Incomes and Net Worth in Norway," *National Tax Journal*, XI (March, 1958), pp. 88-89 and Table VI.

[2] Pigou defines neutrality to mean zero announcement effect, which in turn is defined as follows: "When I rule out the announcement aspects of taxation, I assume that this £2,000 man, mulcted of £500, acts in the same way, not as he would have acted if he had not been mulcted, but as he would act if the £500 was taken from him in a lump-sum levy not alterable in amount by anything that he chooses to do." *A Study in Public Finance* (London: Macmillan & Co., Ltd., 1947), pp. 55-56.

money from some people, and they must behave differently on this account. The more interesting and pertinent question is whether the tax formula designed to extract money from them affects their choice because of the character of the formula. A lump-sum tax has by definition a zero announcement effect (strict neutrality) because the taxpayer is confronted by a formula giving him no room to alter his tax liability by behaving differently.

A person is affected by a net worth tax, apart from the subtraction of money from his bank account, because a change in his net worth induces a change in his tax liability. A person could avoid paying as large a tax by reducing his net worth.

A person can legally reduce his net worth under a net worth tax by (*a*) giving away assets, (*b*) living on a more elaborate scale, and (*c*) managing himself and his assets so as to yield a smaller income. The incentive to give away assets under a net worth tax depends upon the rate structure and upon whether the "gift" can be made so that it permits the "donor" to retain the control of the assets while alienating them for tax purposes. A progressive rate structure when the taxpayer is defined individually permits the reduction of the tax liability of the family by donating assets to younger children. This incentive can be partly blocked if the taxpaying unit is made the family, defined to include minor children. It also can be blocked by a tight legal definition of a gift: a donor may not tie any string to the gift at all if it is to be excluded from his net worth. The problem nevertheless remains. This difficulty holds for all varieties of progressive means-test taxation; an incentive exists to have the base of the tax show up in the hands of other members of the family with smaller incomes, spendings, or net worth. This result is not necessarily an objection since it does serve to reduce the inequality of wealth and income, if only within families. On the other hand, since one of the favorite devices to alienate assets is the trust fund, and these funds are by tradition managed conservatively and often at a much greater cost than would be the case if they were not established, a serious objection remains to splitting assets within the family. Trust funds may be the delight of finance officers charged with selling government bonds, but they are not a delight to those seeking money to finance business ventures.

The incentive to increase consumption in the present in order to escape a net worth tax is likely to be insignificant. If a person were to dissipate his assets currently in elaborate living, he would be obliged to live on a more modest scale in the future. Generally, people prefer to move up in their scale of living as they become older, not up and then down. Formally, a dollar spent on consumption reduces net worth by one dollar minus the marginal rate of the net worth tax.

Hence consumption is made relatively less expensive—a factor which will induce a person to consume more. On the other hand, the effective or average rate of tax reduces a person's wealth—a factor which will induce a person to restore his lost wealth. The net effect will depend upon the comparative weight of these two factors.

As concerns investment decisions, net worth taxation is similar to income taxation with full loss offsets. In one case choosing between making a safe investment, say acquiring short-term government bonds that would yield a certain return of 3 per cent, and making a risky investment that if successful would in the judgment of the investor yield 50 per cent but that might also involve a loss of the entire sum invested, a net worth tax would, given any level of consumption expenditures, appropriate a portion of the gain in either case. The gain to be obtained would increase the person's net worth or prevent it from declining. If a loss is experienced, the investor can anticipate that his tax liability will decline, since the loss subtracts from his net worth. Thus if an investor is contemplating spending $100,000 for government bonds or the same sum for a risky asset, and the marginal rate of tax is 5 per cent, the amount risked is reduced to $95,000. The odds facing him remain unchanged by the tax. The consideration that his future gains will be taxed and future losses subsidized (by reducing his tax liabilities) will, if it matters at all, induce people to select riskier asset combinations.[3]

Shifting Possibilities

A net worth tax may be expected to remain upon the people upon whom the tax is imposed; it is not shifted to others. The reason is simple. The tax cuts down upon personal financial power as does a flat-sum levy, viewed with respect to any particular taxpayer, and does not, by its formula, give him any power to increase his own pretax income at the expense of others. If the person is in business for himself, he could not, because of the tax, charge higher prices for his wares or reduce the prices he pays his suppliers. Conceivably a wealthy person who has been rather casual about the costs of running his business in the absence of a net worth tax might become more careful under the financial pressure resulting from the tax. But apart from the fact that there is no evidence to suggest that businesses managed by wealthy persons are operated less efficiently than those managed by people of moderate means, this pressure simply reflects the economy one is forced to make by the reduction in his posttax income

---

[3] For a more complete discussion of this subject, see R. A. Musgrave, *The Theory of Public Finance* (New York: McGraw-Hill Book Co., 1959), pp. 312-35.

and wealth. Since by definition a flat-sum tax is not shiftable, a net worth tax is not either. Such a tax gives no power to increase one's income computed before tax. A person is left to pay the tax liability *in toto.*[4]

Plutocracy as a Problem

Great fortunes are one of the by-products of a money-price system of economic organization when resources are privately owned and managed. Even if, somehow, everyone could start with the same talents and the same amount of wealth, large differences would soon arise in income and wealth distribution for no other reason than chance differences in making investment decisions. A man who happens to buy cattle land and later strikes a large oil pool located entirely beneath his property becomes inordinately wealthy, while another buying better land and better cattle may be wiped out by a prolonged drought. If investment results were determined altogether independently of the judgment of the investors as, for example, in a game of roulette, a thousand players each with the same beginning stake would end up, after a prolonged period of play, with some broke and some wealthy. Some large American fortunes have no other explanation than the circumstances that almost chance investments paid off in a big way.

Pursuit of economic gain may also be looked upon as analogous to a track meet. There are various prizes for performance. The winner in any event obtains the maximum award and those who fail to place obtain nothing. But unlike runners at a track meet, competitors for economic gain do not all begin at the same starting line. Two people may have about the same ability but have different amounts of initial wealth, so that they begin at different starting points, and the one with the smaller amount of initial wealth must run a longer distance to obtain the same award. A great athlete may nevertheless occasionally overcome this handicap and obtain the prize. The idea of equal opportunity in economic affairs suggests that each competitor must start at the same point and run the same distance. In fact, the economic game involves rules that are foreign to a track meet.

There is the further consideration that people differ widely in their interest and ability to acquire wealth. The intense study of philosophy is not apt to make one rich. Motivations other than gain have always played an important role in the selection of occupations. If that were not so, the professions might never have arisen, universities would

---

[4] For a view that a net worth tax may be partly shifted, see John F. Due, *Government Finance* (rev. ed.; Homewood, Ill.: Richard D. Irwin, Inc., 1959), pp. 379-80.

have died in infancy, and housewives who keep house full-time would be an anachronism. On the score of ability to make money, some seem to have it and some do not. The study of the financially successful reveals no peculiar characteristic of those who accumulate a fortune other than a drive to do so.[5] Business schools are populated by the hopeful young imbued with the faith that somehow this knack can be taught.

Despite the popular impression to the contrary, the very wealthy are not a disappearing group from the American scene. A diligent *Fortune* investigator was able to identify 155 persons each of whom owned assets in excess of $50 million and guessed that he had missed another 100.[6] This evidence suggests that this group owns assets totalling about $40 billion—a sum large enough, if so applied, to reduce the outstanding net debt of the federal government by about 20 per cent. This group of the very wealthy includes those whose present large fortunes are based on inheritance and some who have built fortunes beginning with only relatively modest means. The fortunes of the new rich have come mainly from petroleum—an industry especially prone to producing sizable fortunes.[7] The idea that the day is gone when people can accumulate large fortunes within one lifetime, an idea that seemed plausible during the thirties, is denied by the evidence.

The concentration of wealth in the hands of a few may or may not be regarded as a serious social problem. The egalitarian philosophy, as noted in Chapter 5, is a criticism of great concentration of wealth, and the endorsement of this philosophy logically calls for the support of measures to erode great fortunes. The criticism may appeal to the unloveliness of great inequality *per se* or be based upon the alleged bad consequences of great inequality. There was a time when there was little doubt that unless the power of wealthy men could be effectively curbed, their power would be a real danger to the political and economic system. During the decade prior to World War I, J. P. Morgan brooked no opposition in high finance and used his great power to reduce or eliminate competition in a number of important

---

[5] See Frank W. Taussig's interesting study, *Inventors and Money-Makers* (New York: The Macmillan Co., 1915).

[6] Richard Austin Smith, "The Fifty-Million-Dollar-Man," *Fortune,* Nov., 1957, p. 176.

[7] Petroleum gives rise to the potentiality of large fortunes because of the nature of the gamble in drilling for oil. The discovery of one sizable oil pool is commonly sufficient to make a person rich. The tax laws have also favored people who so invest because of the permission to write off intangible drilling and development expenses as they are incurred instead of having to capitalize these expenses and write them off over the period of oil recovery, and because of the special depletion allowances. For a further discussion of this topic, see chap. 10.

industries.[8] Untrammeled use of the power of great wealth in the economic sphere has considerably diminished as a result of government regulation, of corporate managements themselves having grown in effective power, and of the changes in sentiment of the wealthy themselves. A main danger of great wealth concentration lies in the political sphere. Although the day is gone when the men who controlled the Southern Pacific railroad could also control the state of California, there remain some legislatures that can be, and occasionally are, bought for a price. Of greater importance is the differential advantage of those candidates for public office who obtain the support of wealthy people. Political campaigns above the local level have become highly expensive, largely eliminating potential candidates who cannot command, in some way or other, substantial financial backing. Wealthy groups are considerably overrepresented in legislative bodies because of the financial support they are prepared to give to candidates sympathetic with their views.

If it is social policy to undermine plutocracy, net worth taxation is easily the most effective tax device now known to achieve this goal.[9] Estate taxation, for various reasons, has rather marked deficiencies for this purpose.[10] A system of rates designed to have this effect is set forth in Table 9–1.

Such a rate schedule would of course not affect people with moderate-sized fortunes, defined as less than $5 million, and would be moderate on those even up to $10 million—2.9 per cent. However, this rate structure would seriously erode very large fortunes. A wealthy Texan recently died leaving forty-one Cadillacs and enough silver dollars in his house to require eight armored cars to cart them away. He would have been required to pay annually about $12 million on his reported assets of over $100 million, in addition to the income tax for which he was liable, if a net worth tax of the type here suggested had been in effect. Before many years had passed, his assets would

---

[8] For a brief account of the period, see Shultz and Caine, *Financial Development of the United States* (New York: Prentice-Hall, Inc., 1937), pp. 459-63.

[9] See also chap. 12, p. 260.

[10] The definition of a "large" fortune is arbitrary because in fact the size of fortunes varies from zero to some large unknown figure, perhaps about $1 billion. If $50 million is used as the cutoff point, those with fortunes in excess of this figure are some tiny fraction of 1 per cent of the population. If income is employed as a measure of economic position, the top 1 per cent of income recipients were those who received $5,600 per capita or more in 1946, according to Simon Kuznets' findings. (See his *Shares of Upper Income Groups in Income and Savings* [New York: National Bureau of Economic Research, Inc., 1953], p. xxxvi.) This placed a family of three people with an income of $16,800 or more in the top 1 per cent. Kuznets' data do not, however, include all gains, such as unrealized capital gains, a factor that tends to understate high incomes.

TABLE 9–1

A SUGGESTED HIGH RATE NET WORTH TAX

(Exempted Net Worth: $5 Million)

Net Worth Class Over Exemption (in millions of dollars)	Tax
0 – 1	5% of amount
1 – 5	$50,000 plus 6% of excess of $1 million
5 – 10	$290,000 plus 7% of excess of $5 million
10 – 20	$1,190,000 plus 8% of excess of $10 million
20 – 30	$1,990,000 plus 9% of excess of $20 million
30 – 50	$2,890,000 plus 10% of excess of $30 million
50 – 100	$4,890,000 plus 15% of excess of $50 million
100 – 200	$12,390,000 plus 20% of excess of $100 million
200 – 500	$72,390,000 plus 25% of excess of $200 million
500 and over	$147,390,000 plus 30% of excess of $500 million

of course have been greatly diminished since his income after all taxes would almost certainly have been negative.

The yield of a net worth tax with such a large exemption would be substantial, although any precise figure is no more than a guess. The total asset holdings of people each of whom has assets valued at more than $5 million cannot be much less than $100 billion; this, if correct, would mean that an average rate of even 5 per cent would give a yield of $5 billion a year. This additional revenue would permit exemptions under the income tax to be raised by about $200. Such a combination of tax changes would serve to reduce the inequality of wealth presently found in this country.

The chief economic argument ordinarily heard in favor of large fortunes is that the rich save a large portion of their after-tax income and thereby promote economic growth. A net worth tax of the type suggested would guarantee that the saving of the very wealthy, say those with fortunes in excess of $50 million, would be negative. Hence, the reasoning goes, the rate of growth of the economy would be slowed down. But as shown elsewhere, this argument has little merit.[11] Private saving is equal to private investment if the government's budget is balanced. No amount of saving by the rich or by the poor can upset this equality. What matters is the effect of the tax upon consumption. A net worth tax would have the effect of forcing wealthy people to be more economical in general and to be more circumspect about their consumption expenditures. Thus there would be if anything more room for investment in the society. There are

[11] See chap. 8, pp. 182.

many ways of financing any given level of investment other than from funds provided by the very rich—by, for example, the simultaneous overbalancing of the budget and the reduction of government debt, an easier monetary policy, and by the reduction of other taxes, such as the corporate net income tax. From an economic point of view, a society that happened to escape the great concentration of wealth in the hands of a few would have no good economic reason to arrange reforms designed to encourage concentration; instead it may count its blessings.

Net Worth Taxation and Underdeveloped Countries

A common, but by no means universal, pattern of economic status in underdeveloped countries consists of two classes—a small group of very wealthy people and the mass of poor people. The wealthy commonly own a large portion of the cultivable land, which is farmed by tenants. This pattern dominated European society until recent times. Land reform has been the main goal of the peasant for centuries, and land reform means to him that he own the plot he farms. Political movements and agitation for social change have often been the consequence of the conflict arising between the landowning groups and peasants.

If and when political power passes into the hands of groups sympathetic with the peasant, measures designed to change relative economic status may become feasible. Frequently, the method used calls for outright confiscation of land, with nominal compensation to the owners. This method can be called a tax, but it is not a systematic one, and its use may lead to conflict. The question becomes, then, whether other and better measures may be effectively employed.

Any kind of systematic means-test tax, whether it is of the income, spendings, or net worth variety, is inherently complicated and requires informed and conscientious administration for its effective operation. Income taxation has not operated to erode great wealth in the United States or, even, in Great Britain. A spendings tax has its limitations on this score as well. Net worth taxation suggests itself as a more effective government tool for this purpose.

In countries in which wealth consists mainly of land, the land must be valued to assess the tax liability correctly. Some nonarbitrary measure of its value needs to be found—a problem that has not been satisfactorily solved yet by property tax assessors in the United States. Self-assessment may be used coupled with a "self-enforcing" device. The law could entitle the government to buy any piece of property at the value placed upon it by the taxpayer. Self-assessment at less than market value would permit the government to buy the land and resell it at a profit. Fear of this action might, according to this theory, prevent underassessment. The objection may be raised that this method resembles rather too closely a piece of cleverness and that it is beneath the dignity of a government.

Where land is not commonly bought and sold, values can be obtained by the government offering to buy land of various types and thereby obtaining a definite figure to use in assessing land of each type. By creating a market situation, an approximation can be reached to the type of objective pricing found in markets for securities. If the chief form of wealth consists of land, the practice suggested may have merit whether a net worth or some type of land tax is employed. Either type of tax would tend to break up large holdings. A heavy tax would force some owners to sell land to raise enough money to pay the tax. In addition, many could not afford to hold land only for personal enjoyment.

The practical feasibility of any tax must be determined with regard to the relevant economic and social conditions of the country in which it is to be used. Radical departures from previous modes of taxation usually occasion difficulties because of the lack of administrative skill and knowledge and their novelty to taxpayers. Yet even a clumsy net worth tax suggests itself as superior to outright confiscation of the property of wealthy groups and the social disturbance which may result.

10

Corporation Income Tax

Few economic phenomena have been as impressive or as significant as the rise of the modern corporation. Now the dominant form of American business organization, accounting for two-thirds of total private business employment and income and controlling all or most of the output of many industries, the corporation has given rise to a number of important and difficult fiscal problems.

In the first place, there is probably less agreement about who really pays the corporate income tax than there is about any other tax. To some the burden of the tax appears to rest primarily upon corporate stockholders; others argue that the tax is largely passed on to consumers through higher prices; and still others feel that the tax lowers wage rates and hence is paid, to an important extent, by workers. Secondly, the equity of the tax has been seriously questioned. To some it represents a discriminatory double taxation of stockholders, a fiscal sin which should be eliminated by means of some rational integration of the personal and corporate income taxes, while to others it is simply a hidden sales tax, burdening the already overtaxed consumer. To many the corporate income tax represents an effective way to collect money from the rich, but others stress the prevalence of widows and orphans among corporate stockholders. A third set of problems has to do with the economic effects of the corporate income tax. Is private investment curtailed so much by the tax that the economic growth of the country is slowed down to an undesirable extent? Does the tax stimulate wasteful business expenditures because the government is sharing not only in profits but also in all deductible expenses? Do depletion allowances granted under the tax result in a desirable allocation of resources among their various possible economic uses? Can accelerated depreciation stimulate corporate investment more effectively than the alternative fiscal devices of lowering tax or interest rates in general?

These and other questions will be considered in the present chapter. The importance of the discussion is underscored by the fact that the corporation income tax is the second most important source of revenue to the federal government, yielding more than 17 billion dollars in fiscal 1959.

Effects on Money Incomes and Prices

The effects (on money incomes and prices) of an increase in corporate tax rates will depend upon whether or not personal income tax rates are raised at the same time. If they are, we have a situation approximating an increase in a perfectly general income tax and, on the basis of the discussion in Chapter 7, we should expect very little shifting to take place. The burden of increased corporation income taxes alone, however, should be shifted in large measure to the noncorporate sector of the economy in the same way that the burden of a special tax on certain individual incomes will be shifted to recipients of nontaxed incomes. Let us see to what extent these expectations are borne out.

AN INCREASE IN BOTH CORPORATE AND PERSONAL INCOME TAX RATES. Consider first an increase in both corporate and personal income tax rates. This change will have no effect on the output and price policies of any corporation that was maximizing profits before taxes were raised. To maximize profits a corporation, like any other business, will expand its output and sales as long as the additional receipts from the expansion exceed the additional costs thereby incurred, and it will stop at the point at which costs first begin to exceed revenues. Since an income tax is levied only on the difference between revenues and costs, the production and sale of any output that was profitable before the tax increase remains profitable, although less so, afterwards. The corporation, therefore, will have no reason because of higher taxes on its income to restrict output or raise its selling prices. Such a reaction would simply reduce its profits net of tax. The same business policies which maximize profits before the tax increase will, in short, continue to achieve the same goal when taxes are higher.

It may be, however, that some corporations, for one reason or another, have set their prices significantly below maximum-profit levels. Under these conditions it is conceivable that a tax increase will induce management to introduce a price rise which they otherwise would not have considered. The corporation is then able, through its price policy, to offset some of the increased monetary burden of the tax and to shift it onto other income recipients. How likely a contingency is this?

A policy of less-than-maximum-profit pricing may be followed by a corporation for a number of reasons. Corporate managers may simply not know what the most profitable price level for their output really is, or they may feel that a price resulting in maximum profits now would attract new firms into the industry, lowering profits in the future. Forbearance now may forestall entry and maintain long-run profits at a higher level than otherwise would be possible. Similarly, a corporation may keep profits low for fear that higher rewards would excite public indignation and perhaps precipitate unfavorable legislative action. Finally, in the large, widely-owned corporation that has become a very important part of the American business scene managers may prefer to forego maximum profits in order to increase the size of the corporation more than otherwise would be possible. Their own rewards as managers, in the form of salaries and power and prestige, all of which are likely to vary in close relation to the size of the corporation, may, in other words, be more important than the monetary income they receive as stockholders. In such corporations the shareholders are treated much like the bondholders—entitled to a regular, fair return on their capital investment and to a graceful exit, through the stock market, should they become dissatisfied with this.[1]

Corporate behavior of the kinds just described may indeed be fairly widespread in the modern world. The crucial question, however, concerns not the prevalence of these conditions but rather, given their existence, whether or not increased corporate taxes will lead corporate managements to decide that higher prices represent a desirable business policy. Take, for example, a low-price policy designed to forestall entry into an industry dominated by a few large firms. Since entry is a function not of absolute profit levels but of the profit differential between the protected industry and others, a general income tax, by leaving that differential unaffected, does not increase the price-raising powers of the protected companies. Suppose, however, that the low-price policy was set up to avoid adverse public and political reactions. With higher taxes corporate profits will appear less gigantic, and man-

---

[1] For a more complete discussion of the separation of interest between managers and stockholders in the modern, large corporation, see Richard Goode, *The Corporation Income Tax* (New York: John Wiley & Sons, 1951), chap. ii.

agement may feel that they could safely be increased somewhat. In this day of public preoccupation with the upward-creeping propensities of the consumers' price index and the dangers of widespread inflation, however, the price increases necessary to move profits toward their pretax level may prove to be distinctly unpopular. In situations of this sort personal judgment replaces mechanical calculations based upon costs and revenues, and prediction of the outcome is consequently extremely difficult. Nevertheless, we note again that it is by no means certain that a tax increase will precipitate a price rise.

Other instances of less-than-maximum-profit pricing provide little additional support for the argument that many modern corporations will be induced to shift onto others the monetary burdens of increased corporate income taxes. Managers who placed corporate size ahead of maximum profits as a desirable goal before taxes were raised are likely to continue to do so after the fiscal change has been made. Lack of knowledge may result in prices that are too low, and increased taxes may provide the occasion for a successful experiment in price raising; but ignorance may also lead to prices above the most profitable levels, and under those circumstances a tax-induced price increase would prove a most unrewarding experience. Where ignorance is the sole reason for unduly low prices, furthermore, any number of occurrences may set off a profitable upward price move. In order to establish the presence of tax shifting we must demonstrate that the price increase in question would not have occurred had taxes not been increased.

Except for these exceptional instances, then, we may conclude that the monetary burdens imposed by a general increase in both individual and corporate income taxes will remain on the legal taxpayers. Opportunities for tax shifting are too restricted to provide any significant relief for these unfortunate individuals.

INCREASE IN CORPORATE TAX RATES ALONE. The foregoing conclusion does not apply, however, when taxes on corporate income are raised while personal tax rates are left unchanged. The initial effect, of course, is still to lower disposable corporate income, and, on the average, this will mean both lower dividends to stockholders and lower retained profits. Lower retained profits, in turn, will restrict corporate growth and thus reduce the prospects for capital gains on the outstanding stock. On the double count of lower dividends and impaired prospects for capital gains in the future, investment in corporate stock becomes less attractive, and investors will shift funds into those areas where monetary rewards have not been lowered by increased taxation. Depending upon the relative size of the corporate sector in the economic system, this process will either capitalize the tax burden or diffuse it over all financial investments or both.

Tax Capitalization. Consider, first of all, a country in which corporations carry on only a very small part of total business activity. As investors shift their funds from corporate stock, its price on the market will fall. Although the demand for noncorporate securities rises, the stimulus is spread over a wide area, and hence prices there will rise only slightly. Most of the adjustment, then, affects the prices of corporate stock, and it will continue until rates of return on corporate stock are raised enough to bring them back into equality with comparable rates elsewhere. It is this process that is known as tax capitalization.

Consider, for example, a share of common stock yielding $5.00 a year and selling for $100. A 20 per cent tax on corporate income now reduces the annual yield to $4.00. Rates of return on other investments of comparable risk remain at 5 per cent, however, and investors will consequently begin to shift their funds out of common stock. If the noncorporate investment sector is very large in relation to the corporate one, this shift will have no perceptible influence on rates of return on nontaxed investments. It will continue, therefore, until the price of our share of common stock has fallen to $80, thereby restoring the pretax rate of return of 5 per cent and removing all incentive for any further shift into noncorporate securities.

This is an illustration of complete tax capitalization. After the process of adjustment has ended, new investors in common stock will bear none of the money burden of the corporate income tax. Although the tax has lowered dividends and capital gains *per share* of common stock, these rewards *per dollar invested* are as high as they ever were. Before the tax was imposed the investor with $100 could buy one share of stock and earn $5.00 a year on it. Under the higher tax rates he can now buy with this sum one and one-quarter shares of stock, and his income from the investment will still be $5.00 each year.

If the new investor bears none of the money burden of the tax, the original holders of common stock must bear all of it. This is easily seen in the case of those who continue to hold their shares, since their annual income per share will be $4.00 rather than the pretax $5.00. Those who sell shares, on the other hand, realize, as a direct result of the tax increase, a capital loss of $20 per share, and this represents the capitalized value of a perpetual income of $1.00 per year computed at a 5 per cent rate of interest ($1.00 per year being the size of all future tax burdens).

Tax Diffusion. The distinguishing characteristic of the case of complete tax capitalization is that the new tax does not lower the average rate of return on investment. If the corporate sector of the economy is very large, however, the tax-induced shift of funds out of common stock may drive up prices of securities elsewhere so rapidly that a 4 per cent rate of return is quickly established on investments of comparable risk. Common stock prices will then not fall at all, tax capitalization will be completely absent, and no longer can new investors in common stock escape the monetary burden of corporate taxes collected during the period of their ownership of the stock. There has been no shifting of the corporate tax because the full money burden is borne by common stockholders.

It is, however, not only rates of return on common stock that have been reduced by the corporate tax. Other securities now have higher market prices as a result of the tax-induced flow of funds out of common stock, and owners of such securities enjoy capital gains at the expense of new investors who, because of the new tax, find themselves able to earn less per dollar invested in financial assets. In this sense the money burden of the tax has been diffused or spread over the entire investment market.[2]

From the nature of the two cases just discussed it will be clear to the reader that each represents an extreme situation, unlikely to occur in practice. In most economically advanced countries the corporate sector is an important but by no means overwhelmingly predominant part of the business system. Furthermore, the effect of the tax change on rates of return depends on the extent to which it alters people's desires to hold money balances rather than income-yielding assets. As indicated in Chapter 7, the less generous the allowances for loss offsets under a proportional tax are, the more chance there is that an increase in the tax rate will strengthen investor preferences for money holdings. If this does happen, the tax-induced fall in investment yields will be less than it otherwise would have been. Fuller

---

[2] The analogy may be drawn of a large swimming pool connected by a canal to a small wading pond. Imposing a given tax on a very small corporate sector is similar to lowering the level of the water in the wading pond by one inch. Water from the pool will then flow into the pond, raising the level there by almost one inch and lowering it in the pool by an imperceptible amount. The tax, as we have just seen, first lowers the rate of return on common stock and then, via the capitalization process, restores it almost to its pretax level, rates of return elsewhere being virtually unaffected. A new tax on a very large corporate sector, however, is similar to lowering the level of the water in the swimming pool by one inch. Just as the flow of water from the wading pond will lower the water level there by almost one inch and raise it very little in the swimming pool, the tax-induced shift of investment funds from common stock to other securities will lower noncorporate rates of return significantly, thus keeping corporate rates close to the low levels reached immediately after the new tax was imposed.

loss offsets, on the other hand, will intensify the downward pressure on rates of return.

Tax Shifting. While these developments are taking place in the financial sector of the economy, various reallocations of real resources (land, labor, and business capital assets) will be occurring as a direct result of the tax increase. In the process, money incomes, prices, and rates of return will be altered still further.

For reasons to be given below, the main immediate effect of higher corporate tax rates will be lower corporate demands for new plant and equipment, although some fall in private consumption expenditures is also likely. In a general inflationary environment only prices will be affected, both output and employment continuing to behave as they would have in the absence of the tax change. By moderating or stopping the inflation the tax increase will also change individual real incomes, helping those who typically lose from rising prices and burdening those who ordinarily gain.

Suppose, however, that increased corporate taxes actually reduce the physical volume of corporate investment. This creates some slack in the capital goods industries which may or may not be filled by increased demand for their output by unincorporated businesses. If it is not, resources will be released from capital goods production, and if full employment is to be maintained these must be re-employed in the consumer goods industries.[3] The further effects of these developments need only be touched upon briefly. To the extent that noncorporate replaces corporate investment there will undoubtedly be a change in the types of capital goods involved, and owners of resources whose services are specialized to the production of the one kind rather than the other will find themselves enjoying money gains or suffering money losses. The corporate sector will grow less rapidly, and the noncorporate sector more rapidly, than otherwise would have been the case. Since demand for the products of these two sectors is not likely to adjust itself perfectly to these changes, the prices of corporate output will soon become higher, and those of noncorporate output lower, than they would have been without the tax. These changes push corporate profits up at the expense of the profits of sole proprietorships and partnerships and institute thereby a partial shifting of the money burden of the corporation tax. Consumers find themselves faced with a different array of goods and services, and according to their tastes they are either pleased or displeased. To a man, however, they will be

---

[3] The reader is reminded that the effects of taxation on the level of output and employment are to be discussed in Part IV below. At the moment we are concerned only with the effects of different kinds of taxes on the composition of a given level of gross national product.

unable to trace the changes to the imposition of higher corporation income taxes. Nor will women, who do most of the buying of consumer items in the modern world but who are even less attracted than men by courses in public finance, be any more knowledgeable.

The other possibility is that the tax-induced reduction in corporate investment is not fully offset by higher noncorporate investment. This is likely to precipitate a somewhat painful reallocation of resources from the capital goods to the consumer goods industries. Resource incomes fall as their owners try to place them in employment somewhere; consumer goods are offered at lower prices, and consumers find themselves buying more things than they would have bought without the tax on corporate income. Since investment as a whole has fallen, the level of output of consumer goods and services will rise less rapidly in the future than it otherwise would have, and in essence consumers have, under the subtle prodding of the corporate income tax, treated themselves to a higher level of living now at the expense of a lower one in the future. A lower rate of investment also tends to bolster rates of return earned on real assets, a development which raises the yields of financial assets and hence tends to offset some of the tax diffusion effects noted previously.

These brief comments by no means exhaust the list of possible effects flowing from the imposition of higher taxes on corporate income. Changes in the allocation of resources alter relative money incomes accruing to the resource owners; this in turn alters the pattern of consumer demand; more resources are then reallocated; relative incomes are changed, and so on. We have, however, covered the most important direct effects of the tax. According to the definitional proclivities of the individual writing about them, some, most, or perhaps even all of these effects may be included under the heading of "tax shifting." We mention this merely to warn the reader who may stray onto other books on public finance. It is the *effects* that are important, not the question of whether they constitute tax shifting or not.

Even when adjustments are made for the different definitions of tax incidence used by different writers, however, considerable disagreement still remains as to how much of the burden of the corporate income tax is shifted by corporations and their stockholders to others. The lack of unanimity in the current literature on this subject is well illustrated in a recent empirical study of tax burdens in which it was deemed advisable to use three different assumptions as to the incidence of the corporate tax: (1) that the tax rests entirely on corporations and their shareholders, (2) that the tax is entirely shifted forward to consumers, and (3) (the one regarded by the authors of the study as the most realistic) that one-third of the tax is shifted forward to consumers, one-eighth is shifted backward to wage earners, and the remainder is borne by corporations and their stockholders.[4] Economic theorists, unfortunately, have not as yet developed a generally accepted theory of the price-setting policies of large corporations and large labor unions. It may be that the corporate income tax induces some corporations, especially those operating in highly concentrated industries, to set prices higher than they otherwise would have, or that the tax makes it more difficult for labor unions to obtain wage increases. As yet we know too little about the probable extent of such influences. This being the state of current theory, it is natural to turn hopefully to empirical studies of tax incidence. Unfortunately the difficulties here are equally formidable. In order to establish the presence of tax shifting, it is not sufficient simply to show that corporate profits are maintained at previous levels after an increase in the corporate income tax; we must also demonstrate that they would not have risen had the tax not been imposed. Let us see to what extent it has been possible to measure the incidence of the corporate income tax in a meaningful way.

Empirical Studies of Tax Shifting. Evidence on the incidence of the corporate income tax is by no means a scarce commodity. The difficulty, however, is that in all cases it is *presumptive* evidence only —it does indicate the effects of the tax on money incomes and prices *if* other factors have behaved in certain prescribed ways. Unfortunately, because of the lack of systematic studies of the effects of these other factors, we cannot be certain that the qualifying assumptions are always realistic.

Three postwar studies illustrate these problems very well:

1. In 1948 Lewis H. Kimmel sent questionnaires to 1,000 manufacturing corporations asking, among other things, whether the corporate income tax had conspicuously influenced their pricing policies. Of approximately 200 answers to this question 60 per cent were affirmative.[5] The significance of this evidence is seriously impaired not only by the low rate of response obtained in the sample but also by the fact that while taxation is only one among several factors influencing price policies, no attempt was made to determine its relative importance in the whole picture.[6]

[4] R. A. Musgrave, et al., "Distribution of Tax Payments by Income Groups: a Case Study for 1948," *National Tax Journal*, IV (March, 1951), 14-16.

[5] Lewis H. Kimmel, *Taxes and Economic Incentives* (Washington, D.C.: Brookings Institution, 1950), p. 28.

[6] Two earlier surveys of business opinion showed that approximately 25 per cent of the corporate executives reached believed that income taxation induced them to

2. Lerner and Hendriksen have computed the rate of return after taxes on investment for all profitable corporations in nine specific industries (and in manufacturing as a whole) for the 1927-52 period and have compared tax changes from year to year with changes in these rates of return.[7] Opposite movements in the two variables (e.g., a tax increase followed by a fall in the after-tax rate of return on investment) are taken by the authors to be inconsistent with the hypothesis that the tax is completely shifted in the short run. Similarly, a constant or rising rate of return during a period of increasing taxes is regarded as consistent with the hypothesis.

In addition, the effects of other factors on rates of return are taken into account descriptively. Both tax rates and the after-tax rate of return in total manufacturing rose between 1940 and 1941, for example, but because aggregate demand rose as well the existence of tax shifting cannot be firmly established on this evidence. Between 1950 and 1951 when tax rates rose by nearly 12 points, on the other hand, rates of return after taxes fell in all nine industries in spite of the fact that aggregate demand and total production were both rising and that prices had gone up faster than wage rates between the two years. Here, then, is a case which is definitely inconsistent with the hypothesis that the corporate tax is completely shifted in the short run. As a result of their 25-year study the authors conclude that both tax increases and tax cuts tend not to be completely shifted in the short run. Their method, however, does not permit establishment or denial of partial shifting.

3. In an analysis of the long-run incidence of the corporate tax M. A. Adelman computed the proportion which corporate profits before taxes constituted of total income originating in the corporate sector of the economy. He then showed that this proportion was approximately 23 per cent both in the prosperous but low-tax years from 1922 to 1929 and in the equally prosperous, high-tax 1946-1955 period, and concluded that the corporate tax has not been shifted to any substantial extent over the long period.[8] This conclusion rests on the assumption that between the two periods compared there was no tendency for nontax factors to decrease the relative importance of profits in the corporate sector. For if such a tendency could be estab-

---

set higher prices. National Industrial Conference Board, *The Shifting and Effects of the Federal Corporation Income Tax* (New York, 1928), Vol. I, pp. 153-54, and *Effects of Taxes Upon Corporate Policy* (New York, 1943), pp. 57-58.

[7] Eugene M. Lerner and Eldon S. Hendriksen, "Federal Taxes on Corporate Income and the Rate of Return on Investment in Manufacturing, 1927 to 1952," *National Tax Journal,* IX (Sept., 1956), 193-202.

[8] M. A. Adelman, "The Corporate Income Tax in the Long Run," *Journal of Political Economy,* LXV (April, 1957), 151-57.

lished, a diminishing proportionate role for corporate profits before taxes would be consistent with the absence of tax shifting, with the result that a stable 23 per cent figure would imply the presence of some shifting.

Effects on Income Distribution

Since dividends and net capital gains are more highly concentrated in the upper income groups than any other major kind of income, the corporation income tax, except when it is shifted to consumers or workers, is a highly progressive governmental levy. In 1952, for example, the 9 per cent of all nonfarm families of two or more persons that reported before-tax incomes of $10,000 or more received 20 per cent of total wages and salaries, 35 per cent of interest and rental income, 57 per cent of business and professional income, but 75 per cent of dividends and income from estates and trusts.[9] Less is known about net capital gains, but Seltzer's data show them to be more unequally distributed than dividends in 1943.[10]

Disagreement about the incidence of the corporation income tax and lack of data about the distribution of capital gains and losses preclude any definitive measure of the income-equalizing powers of corporate profits taxation. That these powers have been significantly greater in recent years than previously, however, is strongly suggested by the following figures showing the relative income shares of the top 5 per cent of consumer units in this country before and after deduction of corporate income taxes.

	1929	1939	1950-55
Share of total income before taxes	32%	28%	26%
Share of total income after deduction of corporate income taxes	31%	27%	22%[11]

Although only one point separated the before- and after-tax percentages in both 1929 and 1939, by the early fifties the gap had widened to four points.

[9] Selma F. Goldsmith, "Income Distribution in the United States, 1952-55," *Survey of Current Business* (June, 1956), pp. 9-16. See also Simon S. Kuznets, *Shares of Upper Income Groups in Income and Savings* (New York: National Bureau of Economic Research, 1953), especially pp. 66-67, 646-49.

[10] Lawrence H. Seltzer, *The Nature and Tax Treatment of Capital Gains and Losses* (New York: National Bureau of Economic Research, 1951), p. 377.

[11] The figures, which are based on an income concept that includes undistributed corporate profits in family income, are from Selma F. Goldsmith, "Changes in the Size Distribution of Income," *American Economic Review: Papers and Proceedings,* XLVII (May, 1957), 517.

Because of the interrelationship between the yields of the personal and corporate income taxes, the income-redistributing powers of either depend upon the extent to which the other is used. An increase in the progressiveness of the personal tax, for example, will decrease the extent to which the corporate tax transfers money from the high income groups to the government. Consider a taxpayer who receives $8 million in dividends and $2 million in various other kinds of income. A 50 per cent corporate tax which cuts dividends in half will, if there is no personal income tax at all, reduce this person's disposable income by 40 per cent. Suppose, however, that there is a personal income tax and that the marginal tax rate on all taxable income over $1 million is 90 per cent. The taxpayer's net loss from the corporate tax is now considerably less than it was in the first instance. Although he still takes a cut of some $4 million in his dividend receipts, this cut also reduces his personal tax bill by $.9 \times \$4,000,000 = \$3,600,000$. His net loss (and this is also the amount which the government obtains from him as a result of the new corporate tax), therefore, is only $400,000, or some 4 per cent of his pretax gross income.

Effects on Consumption

The extent to which an increase in corporate tax rates lowers demand for consumer goods and services will depend upon three main considerations: (1) the effect of the tax on the level of dividends distributed to stockholders; (2) the structure of personal income tax rates (the higher these are, the less will a tax-induced reduction in dividends lower the disposable incomes of stockholders); and (3) the amount by which upper income groups, since these are the people who receive most of the dividends, will, on the average, reduce consumption expenditures in response to a given reduction in their disposable incomes. A fourth factor—namely, the effects of the tax on both accrued and realized net capital gains and the further influence of these changes on the consumption expenditures of the stock owners—should be mentioned, but unfortunately the lack of empirical evidence precludes further analysis of these effects.

We do, however, know a good deal about the dividend policies of American corporations. Many companies set a certain ratio between dividends and current earnings as an ideal, or target, pay-out policy, but when earnings change, they ordinarily act so as to approach that target only gradually. On the basis of an intensive study of corporate behavior, John Lintner has estimated that on the average aggregate dividends paid out in any given year will equal a certain minimum amount plus 15 per cent of current profits plus 75 per cent of the dividends paid in the preceding year.[12] A new corporate tax which yields $100 million a year will, therefore, lower dividends by only $15 million in the first year; but in the second year dividends will be $27 million less than they would have been without the tax, and this figure will rise each year by smaller and smaller amounts, approaching a final tax-induced reduction of dividends of $60 million.[13]

Given these predictions of the effects of the corporate tax on dividends, one could then allocate the dividend reductions to the appropriate stockholder income groups, compute the offsetting fall in personal income taxes owed by the stockholders, and then use the findings of empirical studies of consumer behavior to determine what effects, on the average, the net reduction in disposable income will have on the consumption expenditures of each income group.[14] Suppose, for example, that all dividends go to an income group whose marginal personal income tax rate is 50 per cent and who, on the average, reduce consumption by 60 per cent of any decline in income. In the first year the $100 million corporate income tax will reduce consumption by only $4.5 million, but after the tax has been in force for a number of years this impact will be increased to approximately $18 million.[15]

These figures are, of course, illustrative only. Nevertheless, it is clear that the corporate income tax is not likely to have, in relation to its gross yield, an important effect on the demand for consumer goods and services. In a study of the corporate tax Goode concluded that at 1948 tax rates expenditures for consumption, gifts, and contributions would fall $14 to $19 for every $100 collected by the government.[16] Even if we take the net yield of the tax—i.e., the gross amount collected less the induced reduction in the yield of the personal income

[12] John Lintner, "Distribution of Incomes of Corporations Among Dividends, Retained Earnings, and Taxes," *American Economic Review: Papers and Proceedings,* XLVI (May, 1956), 97-113.

[13] Similar results are given by Paul G. Darling, "The Influence of Expectations and Liquidity on Dividend Policy," *Journal of Political Economy,* LXV (June, 1957), 209-24. Incorporating more variables in his explanation of dividend fluctuations than Lintner, Darling places the short-run sensitivity of dividends to changes in disposable profits in the neighborhood of 13-30 per cent and the long-run sensitivity between 40 and 50 per cent.

[14] For an example of such an analysis see Goode, *op. cit.,* chap. vi and Appendix A.

[15] In the first year a tax-induced dividend reduction of $15 million reduces stockholder disposable income by $7.5 million (because of the equally large offsetting reduction of personal income taxes due), and this in turn leads these people to lower their consumption expenditures by 60 per cent of $7.5 million, or by some $4.5 million. In later years when the tax-induced reduction in dividends approaches $60 million a year, the fall in consumption will approximate .6 × .5 × 60 = $18 million.

[16] Goode, *op. cit.,* p. 108.

tax—the facts that the full burden of the tax does not fall on dividends, that the influence of capital gains and losses on consumption may be very slight, and that most dividends go to the upper income groups, all point to a strictly limited impact on consumption. Increased personal income taxes on families receiving less than $5,000 a year may be expected to reduce consumption demand by virtually the amount of the tax yield; reduced dividends flowing to those earning over $7,500, however, are likely, on the average, to lower consumption expenditures by only 60 per cent of the total reduction in income.[17]

Corporate income taxation may also affect the level of consumption from the supply side of the market. The process starts with a tax-induced reduction in the corporate demand for capital goods. Resources are then released from those industries, and, in the process of competing for employment, some of them are re-employed in the consumer goods industries but at lower money returns than they, or other similar resources, formerly received. These lower rewards for resource owners reduce costs in the consumer goods sector, selling prices there fall, and consumers are induced to take more output than they otherwise would have purchased. At the same time, of course, the level of money demand for consumer goods and services has been reduced. On both counts—i.e., a lowered money demand and an increased supply of goods and services—the corporate tax helps to dampen inflationary pressures in the consumption sector. In a stable economy some shift of existing resources, painful as this process usually is, would probably be entailed. In a growing system, however, the effect of the corporate tax may simply be that new resources, including young workers, enter the consumer sector rather than the capital goods industries.

[17] The proportion of any additional income that is typically devoted to consumption in different income groups has been computed from Federal Reserve data for 1950 by M. Bronfenbrenner, Taro Yamane, and C. H. Lee, "A Study in Redistribution and Consumption," *Review of Economics and Statistics*, XXXVII (May, 1955), 153. The figures are as follows:

Income Class	Percentage of Additional Income Spent on Consumer Goods and Services
0 – $1,000	90
$1,001 – 2,000	84
2,001 – 3,000	98
3,001 – 4,000	82
4,001 – 5,000	85
5,001 – 7,500	79
over 7,500	60

Effects on Corporate Investment

INCENTIVES TO INVEST. As noted in Chapter 7, the extent to which income taxation impairs investment incentives increases with the progressiveness of the tax rate structure and with the degree to which the offset of losses is restricted. Both the personal and corporate income taxes have the same provisions for loss offsets—namely, a three-year carryback and a five-year carryforward. The corporation tax, however, has a proportional rate structure, except for those corporations with taxable incomes in the vicinity of $25,000, where the tax rate increases from 30 to 52 per cent. In this respect, then, it is more favorable to investment incentives than is the individual income tax. Both taxes, by reducing the level of private disposable incomes, increase the need to acquire income-earning assets, but at the same time both reduce the net reward to be obtained by increased risk-taking. Theoretically, the net effect of either tax on investment incentives is indeterminate, and empirical evidence on incentives alone is extremely difficult to obtain.

ABILITY TO INVEST. The principal impact of the corporate income tax on investment, however, undoubtedly comes from the significant reduction which it brings about in the ability of corporations to finance their purchases of capital assets. The money needed to acquire new plant and equipment or additional inventories may come from three sources: (1) deductions from gross receipts to cover current depreciation and depletion allowances, (2) retained corporate profits, and (3) the sale of securities (bonds, preferred or common stock) to outside financial investors. Corporate taxation does not, of course, affect the first source of funds, and in recent years it has provided slightly more than the other two sources combined. On this basis alone corporate investment could have varied between $12 billion and $19 billion a year from 1952 to 1956 regardless of the level of corporate tax rates.[18]

Corporate taxation does, however, reduce retained profits substantially. As noted above, Lintner's study indicates that the impact on undistributed profits will start out at the very high level of 85 per

[18] In 1956, for example, depreciation deductions alone provided corporations other than banks and insurance companies with almost $17 billion; retained profits and depletion allowances together provided $8 billion, depletion making up $2 billion or more of this total, and new issues of stocks and bonds brought in another $8 billion. In that year nonfinancial corporations spent nearly $30 billion on new plant and equipment and added nearly $8 billion to their inventories. See Loughlin F. McHugh, "Financing the Expansion of Business," *Survey of Current Business* (Sept., 1957), pp. 6-9.

cent of the tax yield in the first year and then gradually fall in each succeeding year until a stable level of approximately 40 per cent of the current tax yield is reached. Given the corporate tax that has been yielding close to $20 billion in each of the past few years, we may estimate that retained corporate profits have been reduced by that tax at least $8 billion a year. A sum of this size would have made possible more than a one-third expansion in corporate expenditures on new plant and equipment in those years.

Higher tax rates on corporate income also affect the terms on which outside capital may be obtained through the issue of common or preferred stock. New stock issue is attractive if the assets which can be purchased with the proceeds are sufficiently productive of income. Given the productivity of these assets, the incentive to buy them by selling new shares of stock on the open market varies directly with the level of stock prices. We have already seen, however, that corporate income taxation tends to lower the level of stock prices. In this way corporate managements may be discouraged from resorting to the money markets in order to expand capital expenditures.[19]

In summary, then, the corporate income tax impairs investment incentives somewhat, reduces the level of retained corporate profits substantially, and lowers corporate abilities to acquire capital assets through the sale of new shares of stock. All three work toward a lowering of the demand for capital equipment, and it is here, rather than in the consumer goods sector, that the corporate tax is likely to exert its main anti-inflationary effect, particularly in the years immediately after the tax has been imposed. In those years it is retained profits rather than dividends that bear the main brunt of the tax; and even later, when this relation is exactly reversed, reduced dividends may lead many shareholders to lower their purchases of financial assets rather than of consumer goods and services. And, as we have just seen, a fall in the prices of financial assets is indirectly discouraging to corporate investment.

To some observers, indeed, this impact on corporate investment appears to be distinctly excessive. Important opportunities for economic growth are, according to these people, being irretrievably lost every year that both personal and corporate income taxes are continued at their present high levels. Their contentions represent, of course, value judgments which it is impossible either to refute or to substantiate. There is no level of investment which is economically preferable to any other level. In any case, it is interesting to note that

[19] For a more detailed discussion of these matters see Dan Throop Smith, "Corporate Taxation and Common Stock Financing," *National Tax Journal,* VI (Sept., 1953), 209-25.

gross private domestic investment has been as high a proportion of gross national product during the prosperous, high-tax fifties as it was during the prosperous, low-tax twenties.[20]

ACCELERATED DEPRECIATION. The postwar period has heard considerable discussion of the adequacy of depreciation allowances, particularly under the corporation income tax. During World War II extensive use was made of five-year straight-line depreciation for capital assets certified as essential to the national defense regardless of the actual expected useful life of those assets, and accelerated amortization of this type was reintroduced during the Korean War. The purpose of these allowances was to stimulate private investment in plant and equipment that was deemed to be highly important to the war effort but whose economic value after the end of the emergency was open to serious question. Since the assets' physical durability was frequently much greater than five years, straight-line depreciation spread for tax purposes over the assets' entire lifetimes would have discouraged investment in those assets. Continued interest in the use of depreciation regulations to stimulate private capital formation resulted in the adoption, in the Internal Revenue Code of 1954, of two amortization methods which allow more depreciation over the early years of an asset's life than does the traditional straight-line method.[21] It is significant that these changes were advocated not on equity grounds—i.e., that straight-line amortization typically failed to reduce book values as fast as market values actually fell—but solely because of their stimulus to "employment, plant expansion, and modernization."[22] We have already noted that straight-line depreciation may well be more decelerated than it should be,[23] but in keeping with the aim of the 1954 changes in depreciation policy we shall concentrate in this section on their effects on investment.

Because of its limited allowances for loss offsets, the present corporation income tax may discourage investment in risky assets to some extent. When making such investments businessmen frequently allow for risk by insisting that a new asset be purchased only if it will "pay

[20] In each case the ratio is close to 15 per cent. For the twenties see Goode, *op. cit.*, p. 147, and data for the fifties may be obtained from the *Survey of Current Business.*

[21] The two methods are the sum-of-the-years-digits method and the declining balance method. For a detailed discussion of them see E. Cary Brown, "The New Depreciation Policy Under the Income Tax: an Economic Analysis," and William J. Edmonds, "The Effect on Business Decisions of Changes in Tax Depreciation Policy," *National Tax Journal,* VIII (March, 1955), pp. 81-98, 99-113.

[22] See the opening statement of the Secretary of the Treasury to the Senate Committee on Finance, 83rd Congress, 2d sess. Hearings before the Committee on Finance on H. R. 8300, *The Internal Revenue Code of 1954* (Part 1), pp. 97-98.

[23] Chapter 6.

for itself" over a time period shorter than its normal physical or economic life. Consider, for example, an investment of 100 expected under normal conditions to yield 20 in gross receipts each year over a normal lifetime of 10 years. If uncertainty as to the level of receipts during the second half of the period leads the purchaser to set a five-year pay-off period, it is clear that, apart from tax considerations, this asset is squarely on the borderline between acceptance and rejection. If expectations are borne out, gross receipts during the first five years will just exactly cover initial cost. As long as tax regulations permit accelerated depreciation on a straight-line pattern over five years or less the attractiveness of the investment will not be reduced by the existence of a tax on corporate income, for regardless of the tax rate full capital recovery will be possible by the end of the fifth year. Such would not be the case under any tax requiring that depreciation allowances be spread over six years or more. For any businessman who adhered rigidly to a five-year pay-off period ordinary straight-line depreciation, for example, would make the asset totally unacceptable.

The use of short pay-off periods is simply a convenient, though arbitrary, method of allowing for uncertainties as to future gains and losses. Regardless of the way in which business managers deal with this problem, accelerated depreciation is likely to stimulate investment in any one of three ways:

1. Under ordinary depreciation the recovery of capital on an investment asset whose actual useful life turns out to be less than is ordinarily expected must come either from income which the taxpayer has from other sources or from tax allowances for loss carrybacks and carryforwards. By reducing the extent to which these methods of capital maintenance, which when the time comes may well turn out not to be available at all, must be relied upon, accelerated depreciation can increase the attractiveness of risky assets.

2. Even if the investor is as certain of full capital recovery under ordinary, as under accelerated, depreciation, the latter will still give him the advantage of getting his money back sooner. Or, to put it another way, he pays his taxes later under accelerated depreciation, and in the meantime he may be able to use the funds involved to his own profit. The higher the tax rate and the larger the rate of return that may be earned on invested funds, the greater these timing advantages are.[24]

[24] An idea of the magnitudes involved may be obtained from the following example. With a tax rate of 50 per cent the reduction in tax payments resulting from depreciation allowances on an asset costing $200 will eventually equal $100. If the rate of return on invested funds is 6 per cent, the present value of the tax saving is $84 if the depreciation deductions are spread equally over five years, $73 if they must be taken over ten years, $57 if over twenty years, and only $37 if over forty years. A lower tax rate would, of course, lower these figures proportionately. Higher interest rates would also lower them, and the advantages of the five-year

3. Quite apart from its effects on incentives, accelerated depreciation makes additional funds available to the firm as long as it continues to grow, and this in turn may encourage it to increase its purchases of capital assets. This is especially likely when the owners are reluctant to seek outside funds no matter how attractive the available investment opportunities are. Other things being equal, the more accelerated the depreciation pattern the larger is the proportion of investment outlays that a growing firm can cover from internal funds.[25] Accelerated depreciation can also increase the availability of outside funds to the corporation. Since lenders frequently require that a loan which finances the acquisition of capital equipment be paid back over a period shorter than the expected useful life of the equipment, rapid depreciation write-offs decrease the danger that income taxation will interfere with the repayment of the loan.[26]

For these reasons, then, accelerated depreciation for tax purposes is likely to stimulate corporate investment[27] But so would a straight reduction in corporate tax rates. What can be said concerning the relative merits of these two fiscal policies?

1. On equity grounds a general tax rate reduction is distinctly preferable. Whenever depreciation allowances are more accelerated than actual declines in asset market values, investors in depreciable assets are being subsidized at the expense of other taxpayers. Large firms will also be favored relative to small ones, since the latter, with their limited gross margins, will be less able to take full advantage of accelerated depreciation.

2. Accelerated depreciation is likely to lessen the countercyclical sensitivity of the corporate income tax by stimulating investment in boom times when profits and tax rates are high and discouraging it in depression when tax rates are low and gross profits may be too small to absorb depreciation allowances. Depreciation regulations may, of course, be changed over the business cycle, but this must be done so as not to complicate either corporate planning or tax accounting. Particularly promising from

---

pattern over the others would increase as the interest rate rose, though only up to a maximum, after which the differentials would begin to decline. On this last point see E. Cary Brown, *op. cit.,* p. 93.

[25] A firm that is increasing its gross investment each year at a 5 per cent rate and whose capital assets have an average lifetime of 30 years, for example, could eventually finance approximately 50 per cent of its gross investment from depreciation charges based on a straight-line, 30-year pattern. Accelerated depreciation over five years, however, would raise this figure to almost 90 per cent. See Evsey D. Domar, "The Case for Accelerated Depreciation," *Quarterly Journal of Economics,* LXVII (Nov., 1953), especially pp. 496-97.

[26] Although accelerated depreciation will ordinarily stimulate investment, exactly the opposite result will occur if the firm is forced to take large depreciation deductions in years when it has insufficient gross receipts to offset against them (i.e., its net income is negative) and if loss carryovers are not sufficiently generous to permit offset of these losses against income in other years.

[27] For a fuller discussion of these effects, see Richard Goode, "Accelerated Depreciation Allowances as a Stimulus to Investment," *Quarterly Journal of Economics,* LXIX (May, 1955), 191-220.

this point of view is the British system of initial allowances, under which a specified portion (say 20 per cent) of the original cost of a depreciable asset is written off in the year of purchase and the remainder is amortized over the asset's total lifetime according to some standard depreciation pattern. When inflation threatens, initial allowances may be reduced or removed completely, and when recession sets in, they may be liberalized without requiring businesses to alter their customary depreciation procedures.

3. As a means of stimulating private investment, accelerated depreciation is a sharper instrument than general rate reductions. Whereas rate reductions help all firms with taxable income, liberalized depreciation allowances confine their favors to purchasers of new capital assets. Moreover, a system of initial allowances may be manipulated so as to stimulate certain kinds of investment and to discourage others. In any case, more can be accomplished for a given loss of revenue by accelerating depreciation, and such a policy will therefore appeal to those who prefer large budget surpluses and distrust large deficits.

Although most discussions have centered on accelerated depreciation, the opposite kind of tax policy can be used for price stabilization purposes. Convinced in 1951 that corporations, even after higher taxes, would have sufficient funds to finance investment expenditures of a highly inflationary nature, the Canadian government decreed that, except for certain capital assets deemed to be essential to the development and defense of the country, depreciation deductions on all other assets purchased after a given date were to be deferred for four years. A firm purchasing a nonessential capital asset in 1951, for example, would, under this law, be able to take its first depreciation deductions for tax purposes in 1955.[28] By these means business firms were encouraged to reconsider their plans for expansion unless these called for the purchase of tax-favored types of assets. Some indication of the results is given by Canadian statistics on new investment for 1951 and 1952. Between the two years total investment increased by 9 per cent, but investment eligible for immediate capital-cost allowances rose by 34 per cent while investment eligible only for deferred depreciation fell by 17 per cent.[29]

Effects on Corporate Capital Structure

Under the present corporate income tax, interest payments to bondholders are deductible but dividends are not. With a 50 per cent tax rate, then, a corporation must earn $2 before taxes in order to pay dividends of $1, but it need only earn $1 before taxes to pay $1

[28] H. D. McGurran, "Some Recent Developments in Canadian Taxation: Deferred Depreciation," *National Tax Journal,* IV (Dec., 1951), 299-303.
[29] Mitchell W. Sharp, "Deferred Depreciation—A Canadian Anti-Inflationary Measure," *Journal of Finance,* VII (May, 1952).

in interest charges. The tax, in other words, favors the substitution of bond issues for stock flotations. Moreover, one would expect the substitution to be mainly at the expense of preferred stock, which is intermediate in its characteristics between bonds and common stock. Critics of the tax have argued that increased reliance on bond financing will lift corporate fixed charges to a level that would be difficult to bear in a period of depression. Corporate stress on liquidity in order to meet these high payments would then intensify the depression. On the other hand, it may be that the relative advantages of equity financing are sufficiently strong to overbalance its tax disadvantage. A rough check of this possibility can be made on the basis of aggregate financial statistics. Whereas corporate security issues made in order to obtain new money during the 1924-27 period (when the corporate tax rate averaged less than 14 per cent) constituted 70 per cent of all new financing, debt sales from 1946 to 1949 (when the tax rate was 38 per cent) made up 76 per cent of all funds obtained.[30] Some shift to debt financing is indicated, but it must be remembered that 1946-49 was a period when interest rates were very low and the stock market was relatively unfavorable to new stock issues. In D. T. Smith's judgment these factors alone are sufficient to account for the observed increase in debt financing.[31] In more recent years when corporate tax rates have been still higher, the stock market more favorable, and high interest rates conducive to discouraging bond flotations, new stock issues have assumed a greater relative importance than they possessed during the early 1920's.[32] It does not appear, in other words, that corporate income taxation has significantly affected the choice between stocks and bonds as new capital issues.

Effects of Percentage Depletion

In Chapter 6 the need, under any logical and equitable income tax, for depletion allowances based upon the original money investment in a mineral enterprise was noted. Allowance is thus made for capi-

---

[30] Dan Throop Smith, *Effects of Taxation: Corporate Financial Policy* (Boston: Harvard Univ. Graduate School of Business Administration, 1952), pp. 285-89. Our expectations with respect to preferred stock are borne out by Professor Smith's data. In 1924-27 preferred and common stock issues each made up 15 per cent of new corporate money issues, but in 1946-49 preferred stock had fallen to 11 per cent and common stock to only 13 per cent. These differences, however, are far from spectacular.

[31] *Ibid.*, p. 288.

[32] From 1952 to 1955, for example, bonds constituted only 64 per cent of net new security issues, and stocks made up 36 per cent (Loughlin F. McHugh, "Financing Corporate Expansion in 1956," *Survey of Current Business* [Oct., 1956], pp. 11-16), and from 1956 through 1958 debt sales were 70 per cent of corporate external long-term sources of funds. (B. Kenadjian and G. F. Derrickson, "Business Financing in 1959," *Survey of Current Business* [Oct., 1959], p. 12).

tal maintenance, a basic requirement of all income computations. Percentage depletion, first adopted in this country in 1926, however, is well designed to allow the taxpayer deductions far in excess of original cost depletion. Hellmuth, for example, estimates this excess depletion to be $500 million under the personal income tax in 1955 and as much as $2.3 billion under the corporate tax.[33] The effects of a tax favor of this magnitude cannot be lightly dismissed. In this section we shall consider both the effects and the arguments which have been used to support continued reliance on percentage, rather than original cost, depletion.

The obvious and immediate effect of percentage depletion is to reduce the effective tax rate on mining firms significantly below the levels prevailing in other industries. Most depletion deductions, for example, are claimed by oil and gas companies, and in 1954, although the effective tax rate for all corporations was 48 per cent, the rate was only 22.6 per cent for 24 large petroleum companies as a group. For individual companies it was as low as 9 per cent.[34]

These advantages provide a powerful stimulus to exploration for new mineral deposits and to investment in the subsidized industries. Harberger has estimated that because of percentage depletion explorers will be willing to spend as much as $2 million to find $1 million worth of oil reserves; in nonsubsidized industries, on the other hand, a $2 million expenditure would be worthwhile only if it produced assets worth $2 million.[35] Not only will exploration for new deposits be stimulated in most cases,[36] but in addition mineral enterprises of all kinds will be under a strong incentive to hire additional resources and to expand output. At the same time, investors will shift funds to mining stocks, bidding up their prices until rates of return are equalized on all investments of comparable risk. The effects of these developments on money incomes are readily traced:

1. Percentage depletion will increase the disposable profits of business firms operating in the subsidized industries; since most of these firms are incorporated, existing stockholders are likely to receive larger dividends in the future, and in the meantime tax-favored capital gains will accrue on their holdings.

[33] William F. Hellmuth, Jr., "Erosion of the Federal Corporation Income Tax Base," *Federal Tax Policy for Economic Growth and Stability,* p. 914. (See annotation below in Suggested Readings for Part II, p. 348.)

[34] *Ibid.,* pp. 898, 902.

[35] Arnold C. Harberger, "The Taxation of Mineral Industries," *Federal Tax Policy for Economic Growth and Stability,* pp. 447-49. Lovers of mystery stories will find intriguing exercise for their brains here since several of the formulas contain typographical errors.

[36] Coal, the known reserves of which are already sufficient to last hundreds of years, provides an important exception.

2. As the companies begin bidding for the services of additional resources they will, in a full employment economy, increase the money incomes received by the owners of these resources, as well as resources which compete with them.

3. Since the shift of resources into the mining industry means not only more output there but also less output elsewhere, consumers will find themselves facing a somewhat different offering of final goods and services. Oil, gasoline, and all products using large amounts of metal will tend to be cheaper than they otherwise would have been, and other products will be more expensive. In response to these relative price changes consumers will reallocate their spending to some extent. Some additional money gains may be generated by these reallocations. With the price of gasoline relatively lower, for example, drivers will wear out their tires more rapidly, and increased demand for these will bid up incomes in that part of the economic system.

Although some of the effects will spread into rather remote parts of the economy, the main part of the money gain resulting from percentage depletion may be expected to accrue to the advantage of owners of mineral enterprises and of resources employed by them. We must now ask on what grounds such a money transfer from the general taxpayer may be supported. Two main, somewhat interrelated, reasons are ordinarily given: (1) that percentage depletion makes an essential contribution to the national security and (2) that mining operations involve abnormally high risks (and that this fact alone is sufficient to warrant special tax favors). Let us examine each of these in turn.

The relation of percentage depletion to national security varies considerably from one mineral to the next:

1. If production can be easily expanded from known reserves and if imports are either insignificant or from nearby, friendly countries which would continue to be feasible sources in a war, there is no need for percentage depletion for national security reasons. Coal, sand, and gravel are all excellent examples here.

2. Petroleum reserves, on the other hand, are not so large in relation to current production as are known coal deposits, and imports come from areas like the Middle East which could be cut off in case of war. Percentage depletion in this case induces high-level output now, accompanied by extensive exploration for new oil fields. The domestic industry is therefore in a strong position to meet an immediate emergency, but the longer the emergency is delayed the greater is the risk that percentage depletion will result in a faster exhaustion of limited domestic resources than otherwise would have taken place. Ideally, new oil fields should be discovered and kept out of production as an underground stockpile for a future war. In addition, higher prices for petroleum products, brought about by severance or excise taxes on the industry, would slow down the rate at which known

reserves are exploited. Although percentage depletion does encourage exploration, it also provides a powerful incentive to higher output at lower prices. Alternative measures, such as more efficient gasoline-using engines and greater recovery from existing oil fields by means of integrated and rationalized exploitation, are much more attractive as national security policies.

3. In the case of durable metals, percentage depletion involves less risk of premature exhaustion of limited resources since recovery may still be possible from scrap. On the other hand, stockpiling of metals in forms which can be quickly adapted to national defense requirements is both a feasible and an attractive alternative. The difficulty with percentage depletion in this case as well as for petroleum is that the subsidy is not closely tied to any resource-conserving action by the beneficiary. Indeed, it strongly induces him to accelerate both the discovery and the use of the minerals involved, thereby bringing into existence a vicious circle of expanded use, hence greater need for new discoveries, hence increased arguments for percentage depletion as a means of stimulating exploration; and liberalized percentage depletion, if granted, will stimulate more use and start the whole process over again.

4. In the case of sulphur, which since 1932 has received the second highest depletion rate (23 per cent), depletion allowances in 1946 and 1947 were in the neighborhood of $12 million per year, although total exploration expenses were only $7 million for the entire 1930-1948 period (an annual average of well under half a million).[37] Percentage depletion, in short, is a very inefficient means of stimulating exploration for new sulphur reserves and should be replaced by allowances tied closely to actual exploration expenditures.

In summary, the national security argument for percentage depletion is not a strong one. The special tax allowance is not closely related to the goals which it is desired to attain, and it carries with it considerable risk of achieving precisely the opposite result. Much more precise and less dangerous measures than percentage depletion are readily available.

The high-risk argument is typically applied to the crude petroleum industry and when considered in isolation is highly impressive. It is undeniable that many dry wells may be drilled before a gusher is produced. At the same time contractual arrangements, such as the purchase and sale of fractional interests in new wells, have been worked out to permit a widespread sharing of the risks involved among different companies. Furthermore, at the industry level it is by no means clear that petroleum involves more risks than the production of other products. State output controls, for example, lower the risk of rapidly

---

[37] James R. Nelson, "Percentage Depletion and National Security," *Federal Tax Policy for Economic Growth and Stability,* pp. 463-74, gives these figures as well as a comprehensive discussion of the national security problem.

falling sales prices, and, unlike many other businessmen, producers of crude petroleum have no style problem and no need to advertise in order to create consumer demand.[38] Scattered bits of empirical evidence are available to support these arguments. In the first place, a recent study of rates of return on net worth, comparing 24 oil companies with a large number of other manufacturing corporations, showed oil returns to be lower in every single year from 1934 to 1948.[39] These statistics indicate either lower-than-normal risk or an abnormal willingness on the part of investors to bear risks in this one industry. Secondly, throughout the postwar period the ratio of earnings per share to the price of the common stock has consistently been lower for companies producing large surpluses of crude oil than for those which have to buy crude from other companies. Evidently investors regard crude production as being less risky than the refining and distribution of petroleum products.[40] Thirdly, bankruptcies have not been widespread among small or medium-sized petroleum companies.

In any case, even if risks were on the high side among mineral enterprises, this alone would not support the use of percentage depletion. Limited allowances for loss offsets do discriminate against industries in which the risks are higher than average, but the appropriate solution is simply to liberalize loss carryovers. As long as every taxpayer has been given an opportunity to offset all, or at least the great majority, of his losses, no special tax favors, with the accompanying danger of interpersonal inequities, are needed. Proponents of percentage depletion frequently tie the high-risk and the national-security arguments together, pointing up the danger that high risks will preclude the amount of exploration that is desirable as a protection against future emergencies; but we have already noted that percentage depletion is not well adapted to achieving the conservation goals necessary to national security.

The case for percentage depletion, then, is far from being a cogent one. It would appear that a measure originally designed to achieve a modest stimulus in a special area over a limited period of time has grown into a "lucrative, generalized, and largely functionless subsidy"[41] which, because of powerful vested interests, will be difficult if not impossible to eradicate.

[38] Cf. Nelson, *op. cit.*, pp. 470-71.
[39] *Ibid.*
[40] *Ibid.*
[41] Horace M. Gray, "Percentage Depletion, Conservation, and Economic Structure," *Federal Tax Policy for Economic Growth and Stability*, p. 438.

Integration of the Corporate and Personal Income Taxes

In 1954 the treatment of dividends under the personal income tax was liberalized by the introduction of a special $50 per capita exemption and a 4 per cent tax credit. Defended by some as a desirable first step in the elimination of excessively high taxation of corporate income, this change was vigorously criticized by others as an unwarranted subsidy of wealthy stockholders. The point at issue is the extent to which separate income taxes on individuals and on corporations, such as existed in this country between 1936 and 1954,[42] either overtax or undertax income received through corporations, as compared with other types of income.

The answer to this question is far from simple. In the first place, if most of the corporation income tax is shifted to consumers, as many believe, corporate income is taxed only when it is distributed to stockholders in the form of dividends. The policy consistent with this view would be to devise a means of taxing undistributed corporate profits, and no special treatment of dividends under the individual tax, such as that inaugurated in 1954, would be needed. Suppose, however, that none of the corporate tax is shifted. With a 50 per cent proportional corporate rate, $100 of corporate income which is to be distributed to stockholders will first be assessed with $50 taxes at the corporate level, and then the remaining $50 of dividends will be taxed at the individual level according to the marginal tax rates of the different stockholders. If rates under the personal tax range from 20 per cent to 90 per cent, the total tax rate on distributed corporate income will be no lower than 60 per cent and will go as high as 95 per cent. In any case, it is always higher than the rates payable on other types of income, and we may conclude that separate corporate and individual income taxes discriminate against distributed corporate income. It will be noted that this inequitable double taxation is especially burdensome for the lowest income groups.[43]

---

[42] In the early years of the federal income tax, the so-called normal tax rate under the individual tax was made equal to the corporate rate, and dividends were exempted from the individual normal tax. In this way considerable integration was achieved. Subsequently, however, the corporate tax rate rose well above the normal tax rate, and in 1936 the exemption of dividends under the personal tax was completely eliminated.

[43] If the corporation tax rate is C and the relevant marginal rate under the personal income tax is P, the total tax rate on distributed corporate income is $C + P(1-C)$. Since the rate applicable to other types of personal income is P, the excess tax rate on distributed corporate income is $C(1-P)$. Given the corporate rate, therefore, the amount of excess taxation varies inversely with the personal tax rate, being highest at the very bottom of the income scale (where $P = 0$) and decreasing steadily as we move to stockholders with greater and greater incomes.

Although wealthy stockholders are also excessively taxed on distributed corporate income, they may be under-taxed on income which the corporation retains for its own use. All those whose marginal rate under the personal income tax is greater than the corporate rate will have an incentive to make long-term investments in corporations which retain most or all of their incomes. In our example, an individual in the 90 per cent personal tax bracket could keep his prospective tax rate as low as 50 per cent by this procedure. If he earns an additional $1,000 in taxable bond interest, he will retain only $100; if his shares in a "growth" company earn $1,000, the corporation will retain and use $500. Successful employment of these funds will increase the market value of the stockholder's shares by at least $500, but these accrued capital gains are not immediately taxable, and if the stock is held until the taxpayer's death, they will not be taxable at all. If we use the highest tax rate now payable on realized, long-term capital gains (25 per cent), the maximum prospective tax rate on undistributed corporate earnings in our example would be 62½ per cent.[44] For investors above the 62½ per cent personal tax rate bracket the tax advantage of undistributed corporate profits would be unambiguous. Those facing marginal rates between 50 per cent and 62½ per cent would have to balance an immediate tax rate of, say, 55 per cent on other types of income against an immediate tax rate of 50 per cent on corporate income to be followed at some later date by an additional 12½ per cent. Needless to say, this choice would depend both on the yields anticipated on the investment of after-tax income and on the length of time expected to elapse before the additional 12½ per cent becomes payable.

Two unintegrated taxes on corporate and personal income, then, generate a complex mixture of excess and deficient taxation. Although precise measures of these discrepancies are impossible, it may be noted that the undertaxation of corporation income is greater (1) the larger the amounts by which the top personal tax rates exceed the corporate rate, (2) the more stockholdings are concentrated in the hands of the wealthy, and (3) the larger the portion of the corporate income tax shifted to other groups. On the other hand, if none of the corporate tax is shifted and if personal tax rates do not exceed the corporate rate, all income flowing through the corporate sector is overtaxed in relation to other kinds of income.

In any case, some integration of the personal and corporate taxes is needed if interpersonal inequities are to be avoided. In the re-

---

[44] That is, $C + G(1-C)$ where G is the maximum rate on long-term capital gains and C is the corporate rate.

mainder of this section the standard proposals for this purpose will be briefly discussed.

1954 DIVIDEND EXCLUSION AND TAX CREDIT. The 4 per cent dividend tax credit enacted in the 1954 Revenue Code reduces, but does not eliminate, the excess taxation of distributed corporate income, and it accomplishes more in this respect for the wealthy stockholder than for those in the lower income groups. With a 50 per cent corporate rate, for example, a 4 per cent tax credit would reduce the total tax rate on distributed corporate income by 2 per cent[45] for all stockholders able to take full advantage of it. Those with no taxable personal income, of course, would derive no benefit from the provision. Taxpayers in the 20 per cent personal tax bracket would find the excess tax rate on distributed corporate income reduced from 40 per cent to 38 per cent, while taxpayers in the 90 per cent bracket would have the excess rate lowered from 5 per cent to 3 per cent. The relative improvement is clearly considerably greater at the top of the income scale. Indeed, a higher tax credit could actually introduce undertaxation of distributed corporate earnings in some cases. A 15 per cent credit, which was originally voted by the House Ways and Means Committee in 1954, would make the total tax rate on distributed corporate income only 87½ per cent for a stockholder in the 90 per cent tax bracket.[46]

The $50 dividend exclusion has its greatest effect when the taxpayer's total income from corporate enterprises equals precisely $50. Extra taxation is exactly eliminated for all such shareholders if their marginal rate under the personal income tax is equal to the corporation tax rate (50 per cent in our example); it is less than eliminated for all lower-income shareholders and more than removed (i.e., replaced by deficient taxation) for higher-income stockholders. On the other hand, when the amount of dividends received is much larger than $50, the proportionate effect of the exclusion provision recedes into insignificance. Low-income taxpayers, who typically receive only small amounts of dividends, receive, therefore, greater relief in relation to their original excess taxation than do high-income taxpayers.

The 1954 dividend exclusion and tax credit fall far short of integrating the taxation of personal and corporate income. In the first place, neither device is capable of removing the extra or deficient taxa-

---

[45] That is, $r(1-C)$ where r is the rate of the tax credit and C is the corporate tax rate.

[46] Without the tax credit the stockholder pays half of the income in corporate taxes and then 90 per cent of the other half in personal taxes. With the tax credit the personal rate is reduced to 75 per cent, and the effective rate on the total income is therefore $.5 + .75 \times .5$, or 87½ per cent.

tion which exists on undistributed corporate profits. Nor are share-holders who are not subject to the personal income tax granted any measure of relief. Secondly, although the extra taxation which does exist on all distributed corporate income is reduced, these reductions increase in proportion to the income status of the shareholder (i.e., the higher his income the greater the reduction in extra taxation), and if the tax credit is raised above 4 per cent or the corporate tax rate reduced below the present 50 per cent, deficient taxation could be introduced for the more wealthy taxpayers.[47] These weaknesses are so important in the eyes of some writers that the dividends-received credit is regarded not as a method of integrating the corporate and personal income taxes at all, but rather as a way of treating dividends under the personal tax more favorably than ordinary income.[48]

PARTNERSHIP METHOD. If corporations were treated like partner-ships, there would be no tax at the corporate level, and both dividends and each stockholder's proportionate share of undistributed profits would be taxed at the personal level in the same way as other types of income. Although this procedure would be straightforward and equitable for closely held corporations which are actively managed by their owners (since these are essentially partnerships anyway), both administrative and theoretical difficulties would be encountered in its application to large public corporations. With millions of stockhold-ers, many of whom held stock over only a portion of any given year, the allocation of undistributed profits would require the use of ad-vanced computing and sorting machines, an additional task which no corporate manager would welcome. Moreover, it is by no means clear that agreement could be reached as to how the most complex capital structures should be broken down for this purpose.[49]

From the equity point of view, the most troublesome feature of the partnership approach to integration is the taxation of stockholders on income over the use of which they have little or no control. Most owners of large public corporations exert no influence over the dis-position of retained profits, and inclusion of these in their taxable incomes implicitly assumes that, had they received them as dividends, they would immediately have reinvested them in the corporation. Needless to say, this is an assumption of rather monumental propor-tions. If the proper meaning of income is gain which, if not actually *realized* by the taxpayer, is at least clearly *realizable* by him, profits

[47] For a more extended treatment of the dividend tax credit and exclusion see Carl S. Shoup, "The Dividend Exclusion and Credit in the Revenue Code of 1954," *National Tax Journal*, VIII (March, 1955), 136-47.
[48] Cf. Richard Goode, *The Corporation Income Tax*, p. 194.
[49] *Ibid.*, p. 185.

retained by public corporations should not be included in the taxable incomes of their stockholders.

REJUVENATION OF THE TAXATION OF CAPITAL GAINS. Given the complexity of the problem to be dealt with, it is surprising to encounter a solution, such as that proposed by Henry Simons,[50] which might well greatly simplify income tax law. Eliminate the corporation income tax completely, apply the full scope of the personal income tax to capital gains and losses whenever assets are sold, exchanged, or transferred to others by gift or bequest, Simons argued, and both corporate and other types of income will be treated fairly. Such a change would immediately make obsolete the very intricate rules, contained in the Revenue Code and in a large number of court decisions, which are designed to distinguish capital gains and losses from other types of income.

There are three main criticisms of the Simons proposal:

1. The most damaging from a practical point of view is that by itself the change would entail a huge loss of revenue. Unless it is incorporated in a comprehensive reform of the tax structure, its implementation must await a large-scale cutback in federal activities for which there are few prospects at the moment.

2. A more fundamental objection is that the plan would fail to integrate corporate and personal income taxation unless undistributed corporate profits are fully reflected in increased values for corporate stock, either immediately or at some future date. If, for example, a corporation retains profits of $100 million but the market value of its stock rises by only $70 million, it is argued that $30 million would escape taxation under the Simons plan. From the long run point of view, however, the escape is completely illusory. Taxation of the $100 million when earned would increase the tax basis of the corporation's stock by the same amount, and hence as the shares were subsequently sold or transferred, an aggregate capital loss of $30 million would be realized by the shareholders. Over the entire period the correct addition to the tax base is simply the $70 million actual appreciation in stock values.

3. Even full taxation of capital gains and losses on a realization basis (including transfers at death) would postpone, sometimes for extended periods, the bringing of accrued income under the tax base. On the other hand, considerable averaging of taxable income would be achieved in this way, and large scale postponements would be discouraged by the effects of progressive tax rates on gain realizations concentrated in a short period of time. For those who wish to move closer to taxation on an accrual basis than this, a separate tax on undistributed corporate profits is a possible solution.

[50] Henry C. Simons, *Personal Income Taxation* (Chicago: Univ. of Chicago Press, 1938), chaps. vii and ix.

UNDISTRIBUTED PROFITS TAX. Conversion of the present corporation income tax law into a levy on retained earnings only may be advocated on several grounds:

1. In effect an undistributed profits tax assumes an immediate increase in stock values equal to the amount of retained earnings, and hence it eliminates much of the tax postponement inherent in the application of the realization test to taxable capital gains and losses.

2. The tax would presumably stimulate the distribution of corporate income.[51] As a result more corporate decisions to expand would be subjected to the test of the investment market, rather than simply to the scrutiny of corporate managers whose prestige frequently grows along with the size of their firm.

3. A retained earnings tax at progressive rates might form a valuable part of a general program aimed at inhibiting the growth of monopoly power. Its capabilities in this respect, however, should not be overestimated. Large corporations could avoid much of the burden of the tax by increasing their dividend payments and still finance substantial expansion both by the use of depreciation allowances and by resorting to the money market. With their much more limited ability to borrow or issue stock on reasonable terms, small corporations must base their growth mainly on undistributed profits. To many of them a slower and more gradual degree of rate progression under the present corporation income tax would be as helpful as the conversion of that tax into one on retained earnings.

4. An undistributed profits tax is less likely to be shifted than a tax on corporate income, and most, if not all, of the burden would remain where it was intended to be.

The administrative difficulties involved in taxing undistributed corporate profits depend entirely upon which of its two roles the tax is supposed to play. If it is mainly an instrument of economic control (points *2* and *3* above), there should be little trouble. Carryover allowances for excess dividends (i.e., payments greater than the corporation's current income) would be needed so that only retained earnings would be taxed in the long run, but these should be no more difficult to administer than existing regulations covering loss offsets. If the tax is viewed as a means of updating the payment by stockholders of taxes on capital gains (point *1*), however, its entire yield would have to be allocated to stockholders so that they might take credit for the prepayments when computing their own tax liabilities on realized capital gains. The problems here are no less than those

---

[51] Lent, for example, has estimated that the 1936-1937 undistributed profits tax increased dividends by approximately $1 billion a year, a rise at that time of some 33⅓ per cent. George E. Lent, *The Impact of the Undistributed Profits Tax, 1936-1937* (New York: Columbia Univ. Press, 1948), pp. 33-34.

involved in treating public corporations as partnerships for tax purposes, and it might well be simpler to attempt a shift of capital gains taxation to an accrual basis.

Summary

The federal corporation income tax has been highly successful in the most conspicuous way that a tax can be successful—namely, in raising government revenue. Like the political party that has been in power through a period of continuous high-level prosperity, it is unlikely to be quickly turned out of office by the voters. Nevertheless, it is true that the incidence of the tax is open to serious question, and that insofar as the tax is not shifted it fails to fit neatly with the personal income tax into a logical system of income taxation. Much can be said for applying the partnership method of integration to closely held corporations, for taxing capital gains and losses in the same way as other types of income, and for imposing an undistributed profits tax on public corporations. Full taxation of capital gains and losses alone would justify the elimination of both the present corporation income tax and the 1954 code's dividend exclusion and tax credit provisions. Even if these changes were combined with the withholding of income taxes on dividends and interest payments, which would greatly strengthen the administration of the personal income tax, a substantial loss of revenue would probably result. To many writers, who regard the corporation tax, imperfect as it is in some respects, as superior to the available alternative taxes, this is a sufficient reason to postpone the reform until that happy day when general tax reduction becomes desirable on economic and fiscal grounds.[52]

---

[52] Goode, *op. cit.*, p. 217.

11

Excess Profits and Excess Income Taxation

During each of the major wars of this century, the federal government has imposed an excess profits tax. Whenever the threat of serious conflict has developed, some senator has risen to announce that what the country needs, and quickly, is a tax which will take the profits out of war. Such a request has commanded a strong political following; only during the Korean War was there any formidable opposition to an excess profits tax. Yet as soon as the war ends, the demand for removal of the tax becomes strong and vigorous. The excess profits tax enjoys the distinction of being a tax deemed suitable only during wartime. Why should a tax be appropriate only as a war measure?

Excess profits taxation first became an important tax device during World War I when over twenty governments installed it into their revenue systems. Even more general use was made of the tax during World War II. The democratic countries have been especially partial to the tax. The Russian government did not, for obvious reasons, resort to this tax. The Nazi government abandoned its rather peculiar excess profits tax in the autumn of 1940.[1]

Excess Profits Tax as a Partial Excess Income Tax

To understand the basic principles of excess profits taxation, it is instructive to examine first the characteristics of a general excess income tax. No government has to date actually employed this tax,

[1] See J. R. Hicks, U. K. Hicks, and L. Rostas, *The Taxation of War Wealth* (2d ed.; Oxford: Clarendon Press, 1942), p. 146.

although in Germany a close approximation to it was tried. President Roosevelt strongly urged the adoption of such a tax early in World War II but without success. J. R. Hicks argued for the principle of excess income taxation for Great Britain during wartime.[2]

A general excess income tax means a tax whose base is the amount by which current income is greater than what we shall call "base income." This means that the tax law must set forth definitions of base income and of current income. An excess income tax, unlike an ordinary income tax, refers to the difference between the income of the taxpayer in one period and some "normal" or earlier year. The rate schedule under an excess income tax must always be higher than that under an ordinary income tax to obtain the same amount of revenue, because the size of an excess income tax base is always smaller than that of an ordinary income tax.

An excess profits tax may be defined as an excess income tax limited to incomes called profits in the tax law. In American legislation the term "profits" in this context has an even more restricted meaning because only the earnings of corporations have been made subject to tax.[3] A more accurate description of the American excess profits tax would be corporate excess profits tax. Actually, because of exemptions, many corporations were not subject to the tax during the last two occasions on which it has been used.

The Equity Issue

Both a general excess income tax and a partial one, such as a corporate excess profits tax, subject a person or a corporation to tax liability only if there is a positive change in income as compared with base income. Is it fair to tax people on the increase in their incomes? The issue may be crystallized by examining a hypothetical case, as follows:

	Base Income	Current Income	Excess Income
Family A	$10,000	$10,000	0
Family B	$ 2,000	$10,000	$ 8,000
Family C	$50,000	$35,000	−$15,000

The three families are assumed to be similar in all relevant respects except in size of income. Base income is defined as the average income of a number of prewar years, say four. Current income refers to income during a war year. Income is defined in accord with the full gain concept for all periods.

[2] *Ibid.,* pp. 29-35, 65-71.
[3] An attempt in World War I to impose the tax on partnerships was soon abandoned.

Under an ordinary income tax, A and B would pay the same tax, given the same number of dependents, in the current year, whereas C would pay a larger tax. Under an excess income tax, only B would be called upon to contribute to the war effort because B has experienced an increase in income as compared to his base income. Theoretically C should, according to the logic of an excess income tax, be subsidized because his income has fallen; his excess income is a negative $15,000. No one, to our knowledge, has advocated extending the principle to subsidizing those with negative excess incomes.

What is the justification for taxing B more than A and also more, apart from the ordinary income tax, than C? One justification is immediately evident. Suppose it could be established that the base incomes of people are just what they should be; the income received by each family in the prewar period is ethically right, the exact amount to which each is entitled. Then an excess income tax becomes a device to preserve the status quo. Upstarts are punished for moving out of line. If the tax rate is very high, they could be kept close to their original position. Logically, again, C should be subsidized to place him closer to the ideal income distribution assumed to exist in the base period.

Clearly a defense of a tax based on status as determined by some prewar experience has little to recommend it in a democratic society. It might be appropriate to a class society, such as that found in eighteenth-century England, as a method to preserve the "integrity" of the upper classes. If this argument were used, a general excess income tax would be politically difficult if not impossible to impose in the United States.

The status argument has not been used by those advocating either excess income or excess profits taxation. Instead, reliance is placed upon the argument that people who make income out of war should be heavily taxed; when a country conscripts its young men to fight, why should anyone who stays at home be permitted to profiteer? The main justification for both excess income and excess profits taxation has been that those who profit from war should be heavily taxed. It was this conviction that led President Roosevelt to request a 100 per cent excess profits tax in his 1942 Budget Message.[4] The Hicks argument referred to above also proceeds from the view that excess income taxation in general and excess profits taxation in particular are essen-

---

[4] The Duponts reportedly made over $200,000,000 on their gunpowder operations during World War I; it is such cases that give special appeal to a severe tax on profits made during wartime.

tial and efficient devices to appropriate for government a portion of what is called "war wealth."[5]

Even if the premise be granted that gains from war should be subject to special taxation, no one has yet discovered a clear technique of distinguishing war gains from other gains. War gains might be thought of as income arising out of government contracts. However, such a test is really impossible. Shall a worker in a war plant be deemed to be obtaining war gains whereas another who has stayed at his job in the local bakery be deemed to be obtaining peace gains? Shall a textile company which supplies uniforms to the Army be looked upon as obtaining war gains whereas another which moves into the civilian market, absorbing a part of the first company's business, be regarded as making peace gains? Clearly there is no sense in proceeding in this manner. If the war effort is total and properly organized, there are no gains to be described as peace gains. All profits and all other incomes experienced during wartime are war gains.

"Taking the profit out of war" was one of those slogans which passed during the 1930's for serious thinking about the proper conduct of the government finances during a war period. The doctrine was widely pronounced, and widely believed, that somehow "profiteers" were responsible for war and that if, therefore, they were told in advance that they would not make profit out of war, they would have no incentive to start wars.[6] The prevalence of this belief may have encouraged the dreams of dictators determined to impose their will on their neighbors; it enfeebled those democratic nations that might have provided effective opposition in time to prevent serious damage.

From the standpoint of tax concepts, the "war gain" justification for excess income or excess profits taxation retreats to a source concept of income coupled with the idea that some sources are contaminated as compared to others. A full gain concept of income, as already pointed out in Chapter 6, refers to the total experience of an income recipient with respect to gain regardless of the source. Contaminated gains lead to no different tax treatment of the recipient than do legitimate gains. In fact, any possible justification of differences in tax treatment along these lines fails for lack of clear distinction between war and nonwar gains.

---

[5] *Ibid.,* pp. 29-30. No explicit definition of "war wealth" is provided.

[6] The famous Nye Committee—The Special Committee on the Investigation of the Munitions Industry—is one of several responsible for spreading this pernicious doctrine. It had the unfortunate effect of curtailing the willingness of many companies to make any investment in preparation for producing war goods.

Excess Profits Taxation in the United States

During the First World War, the federal government, after some experimentation, imposed an excess profits tax with alternative formulas. One tax, called the War Profits Tax, defined base profits as an average of prewar annual corporate incomes. This feature of the tax was designed to appropriate "war gains" on the theory that the increase in a corporation's earnings over a peacetime average measured the amount it had profited from the war. A second feature of the tax, called the Excess Profits Tax, defined the base income as 8 per cent of invested capital. This feature was designed to recapture for the government a portion of those profits which were too high or excessive, regardless of whether or not the corporation was making larger profits than it had during peacetime. A political battle developed between those who believed strongly in subjecting "war profits" to tax and those who believed just as strongly in subjecting "high profits" to tax. The law required the taxpayer to compute his possible tax under both tax formulas and to select the one resulting in the higher tax, except that he was allowed in the war profits tax to use as his base an amount equal to 10 per cent of invested capital if he so chose. By this latter provision, a corporation experiencing a large increase in profits over the base period might be able to limit its tax liability to a moderate amount. In all other cases, however, a corporation was required to use the method resulting in the greater tax liability.

The rate structure of the excess profits tax used during World War I deliberately discriminated against those making what was called war profits. The rate under the War Profits Tax was 80 per cent, whereas the rates under the Excess Profits Tax ranged from 20 to 40 per cent. This principle accords with the rationale suggested by Professor Hicks.

The World War II excess profits tax is by far the most important use of this type of tax in American history. The tax was first imposed by the Revenue Act of 1940 and applied to taxable years beginning after December 31, 1939. It was in effect throughout the war, being repealed after much debate in the Congress for the corporate tax years beginning after the end of 1945. An excess profits tax was reintroduced during the Korean War by the Truman Administration, although without any great enthusiasm in the Treasury. It was in effect for the period 1950-1953 and rates were low (30 per cent). However, the corporate income tax continued and its rates were high. Since 1953, American corporations have been free of an excess profits tax but not, of course, of the corporate income taxes.

The World War II excess profits legislation was exceedingly complicated. Almost any simple statement purporting to describe the law would be incorrect. In its major features, the law defined Excess Profits Net Income, using as the starting point net income as defined for corporate tax purposes. There were certain qualifications which in general had the effect of making excess profits net income smaller, in many cases much smaller, than corporate net income. From Excess Profits Net Income, three deductions were permitted: (1) a $10,000 specific exemption, (2) an excess profits credit, and (3) an unused excess profits credit adjustment (a carryback or carryforward of unused excess profits credit from other years). The figure obtained after these adjustments carried the label "Adjusted Excess Profits Net Income." This was the tax base to which the rates were to be applied to give the excess profits tax liability of the corporation in the current year.

Of the three deductions, item (2), the excess profits credit, is the only one that makes the measure an excess profits tax. The excess profits tax credit corresponds to what we have earlier called base income. The corporation was given the option of using either of two methods, the Income Credit Method or the Invested Capital Method, to ascertain its profits tax credit, whichever resulted in the lower tax. Both of these methods involve many complications. Furthermore, Excess Profits Net Income (corresponding roughly to the current year net income) was itself differently computed, depending upon whether the taxpayer chose the Income Credit Method or the Invested Capital Method.

The Income Credit Method of arriving at base income called for averaging corporate net income for the four taxable years 1936-1939. Alternative averaging devices were permitted to take care of such cases as losses during some of these years. The Excess Profits Credit was 95 per cent of this average figure. The basic purpose of this credit was to tax corporations heavily if their profits became much greater during the war years than they had been in peacetime, provided that their profits had not been low during peacetime. The Income Credit Method gave rise to serious administrative problems. The Congress provided in the legislation for a hardship clause so that a corporation could claim, if it wished, that its prewar profits experience was unusual or peculiar. A large part of the time of the people administering the excess profits tax was taken by this and other vaguely written provisions for special treatment of hardship cases.

The Invested Capital Method defined base income or, in the technical language of the act, the Excess Profits Credit, by applying various rates to invested capital of the corporation. These rates (as well as many other features of the law) were altered in various revisions of the legislation. A summary is given in Table 11–1.

In all the years except 1940, the Congress by these provisions penalized large corporations relative to smaller ones. This procedure reflected the general philosophy of favoring "small" business.[7]

TABLE 11–1

RATES OF RETURN FOR COMPUTING EXCESS PROFITS CREDIT FOR
VARIOUS TAXABLE YEARS

| Year | $5 million or less | Amounts of Invested Capital | | |
		Over $5 million to $10 million	Over $10 million to $200 million	Over $200 million
1940	8%	8%	8%	8%
1941	8	7	7	7
1942	8	7	6	5
1943	8	7	6	5
1944	8	6	5	5
1945	8	6	5	5

Invested capital was defined, subject to many qualifications, as the equity of the stockholders in the corporation plus 50 per cent of any borrowed funds. Some assets, such as stock in other corporations and certain government obligations, were designated as inadmissible and were excluded from the total to which the rates were to be applied.

The Invested Capital Method of arriving at base profits was the important one. The prewar years 1936-1939 were depression years for business in the United States; many corporations made small profits and many made losses during this period. It paid most of them to employ the statutory rate of return on invested capital because this method resulted in higher Excess Profits Credit, a smaller Adjusted Excess Profits Net Income, and hence a smaller tax liability. Because this method was available, corporations in highly depressed industries were able to recover financially during the war without paying important amounts of tax. Had the World War I requirement been in effect requiring the taxpayer to choose the method resulting in the larger tax, the "bite" of excess profits taxation would have been much greater.

RATE STRUCTURE. The excess profits rate for 1944 and 1945 was 95 per cent, a rate that would seem sufficiently high to satisfy even the most ardent advocate of taking the profit out of war. However,

---

[7] The definition of small business is based on the size of the legal business unit. If a man effectively owns and controls ten corporations, each of which is small, is he a "small" businessman?

this rate is grossly misleading as an indication of how heavily corporations were taxed. A maximum rate limitation of tax to 80 per cent of corporate net income applied to the combined excess profits tax and the ordinary corporate net income tax. Even a large corporation that experienced profits during wartime of twenty times its peacetime earnings was required to pay no more than 80 per cent in tax. But this is an overstatement too. Corporations were permitted a 10 per cent postwar credit against the tentative excess profits tax, making the maximum effective rate 73.1 per cent.

More importantly, the income subject to excess profits taxation after 1942 was fully deductible from net income subject to the ordinary corporate income taxation. If no excess profits tax had been imposed at all and if the ordinary corporate tax rate had remained at 40 per cent, the government would have collected at least 40 per cent (actually more) of the amount collected under the excess profits tax. An example, shown in Table 11–2, may make this point clear.

TABLE 11–2

Excess Profits and Corporate Net Income Tax Computations for a
Hypothetical Corporation

1.	Corporate Net Income	$100.00
2.	Special deductions	10.00
3.	Excess Profits Net Income	90.00
4.	Excess Profits Credit (Income or Invested Capital Method)	30.00
5.	Adjusted Excess Profits Net Income	60.00
6.	Excess Profits Tax (85.5%)	51.30
7.	Corporate Tax Base [(1) minus (5)]	40.00
8.	Corporate Income Tax (40%)	16.00
9.	Total Tax [(6) plus (8)]	67.30
10.	Tax, if no excess profits tax	40.00
11.	Extra tax imposed by excess profits tax	27.30

The computations in the example are made for the rates in effect during 1944 and 1945. In any actual case, the computations leading to the figures given for items (1) through (9) would take several pages of forms and the assistance of several lawyers and accountants in the case of a large corporation. The excess profits tax was not simply an additional tax on a corporation, because it permitted the deduction of Adjusted Excess Profits Net Income from corporate net income in the computation of the corporate tax. Therefore data on the yield of the excess profits tax may not be interpreted to mean that the yield specified for that tax was an additional revenue to the government; much of it was in lieu of corporate net income tax, as the example shows.

Is an Excess Profits Tax a Desirable Feature of Wartime Finance?

As already remarked, there exists little enthusiasm for the peace-time use of excess profits taxation. If it is not a proper feature of peacetime finance—though some people would not grant this—does it play a useful role under conditions of war finance?

A major argument employed at the political level for excess profits taxation rests upon the belief that unless the government has such a tax, other groups in the society, particularly labor groups, will oppose controls upon their activities, such as restrictions on raising wage rates or on reducing the length of the work week. People generally must be persuaded that war profits are being heavily taxed in order to make them submit to wartime restrictions. By various technical provisions, the effective rate of tax on profits can be kept at moderate levels. If this view is the correct diagnosis of the political motivation, and there is a disturbing amount of evidence to support it, excess profits taxation is not likely to survive the spread of economic literacy. In any event, the argument is a political, not an economic one, and we are concerned primarily with its economic implications.

War finance as exhibited in the last great war became a highly complicated system. It is the first war in history in which the main belligerents attempted to wage total war. Much had been learned in the period since 1920 about the great power governments have and how that power may be effectively used to organize a society for war-fare. Sheer survival as a nation forced the British after Dunkirk to direct all their efforts to meeting the German onslaught. The United States, being in a position of fighting two well-prepared enemies at once, and starting from a position of great military weakness, was forced to aim at seemingly impossible goals of military output. It was essential to shift resources devoted to ordinary peacetime ends to war production. Investment projects, too, had to be shifted from those germane to peace conditions to those that would quickly result in more ships, guns, tanks, bombs, and planes. Government expenditures for roads, school buildings, and construction generally had to be vastly curtailed, and the production of consumer durables such as automobiles, washing machines, radios, and thousands of other things had to be almost entirely abandoned. Of great importance was the employment of large numbers of unemployed workers and large amounts of physical facilities standing partially idle at the outset of the war. Furthermore, the job of equipping the nation to fight effectively could not bow to any dogmas of "sound finance." Rather, finance had to be organized to assist in the goal of maximizing effective power to overcome the enemy.

Any kind of special corporate tax has a restricted role under wartime conditions. Insofar as a corporate tax of any kind can assist, it should encourage managements to be as efficient as possible and to keep their attention on the job of war production without occasionally glancing over their shoulders at their likely postwar competitive position. A further role of wartime taxation is to reduce the spending power of private groups. Theoretically a system of price control and rationing by methods other than price, such as coupons, could if effectively enforced make it unnecessary to tax people to reduce their spending power. They would be effectively "taxed" by the rationing system itself—by the substitution of a second kind of money for the usual kind. But such a neat system of coupon rationing is not feasible. In any event, failure to tax heavily during wartime merely postpones the evil day when either explosive inflation breaks out or some system of extremely heavy taxation, such as a capital levy, must be imposed to prevent inflation. The goal of reducing private spending power remains an important one under war conditions.

Nevertheless, any type of tax levied upon corporations can do little to restrict the spending power of the public. By holding down the increase in corporate profits, some increase in dividends may be prevented and some increase in security prices may also be prevented. Heavy corporate taxation can serve only in a rather minor way to hold down the increase in the public's spending power.

Tax devices to induce corporation managements to be as efficient as possible would be radically different from any that have actually been used. One possible technique would call for the government to impose a wealth tax equal to, say, 60 per cent of the present value of corporate assets at the beginning of the war. The corporation may "pay" the tax by giving the government debt claims bearing a high interest rate of, say, 10 per cent. Corporations are then invited to work themselves free of debt as rapidly as they can. The incentive to restore title to the corporate assets, that is, to have a zero debt owed to the government before the end of the war, would induce them to make as large profits as possible during the war. Granted that ordinary peacetime pursuits are barred by price controls and consumer and materials rationing, those corporations that worked hardest, so to speak, at the job of producing war equipment and other essential goods and that were able to organize labor, materials, and equipment most efficiently, would be rewarded by getting free of debt rapidly. Such a tax would also have a marked negative effect on the payment of dividends; managements do not like to pay large dividends when they have a huge debt to pay off.

Under such a plan, no great harm would be done by setting the initial rate too high. The government could always reverse itself after the period of war finance came to a close by forgiving some percentage of the initial tax. During the war, the government would actually receive a large percentage of corporate profits in the form of payment of the debt imposed upon corporations. The objections to such a tax could be expected on grounds of fairness since, by singling out corporations for a special tax, people owning corporate securities could claim that they were being discriminated against as compared with other owners of wealth. This objection is valid, but the same type of objection applies to any special tax on corporations as such.

There is no way of singling out corporations for special taxation without violating the principle of assigning the same tax liabilities to persons with equal wealth or equal income. Yet as long as it is public policy to tax corporations as such, the scheme suggested has the important advantage of providing the right incentives to managements.

Excess profits taxation, in contrast, leads to waste and inefficiency. Because the tax base is necessarily smaller than total corporate profits, and because a showing must be made of taking the profits out of war, marginal tax rates must be very high. Managements of corporations to which the tax is applicable therefore have little incentive to be careful of costs and a strong incentive to disguise investment expenditures, such as institutional advertising and research directed at improvement of peacetime products, as current business expense. The vast mountain of war material produced during the period 1942-1945 in the United States was accomplished in spite of, not because of, the excess profits tax.

If the choice must be made between a corporate net income tax and a combination of such a tax and an excess profits tax, a corporate net income tax alone is clearly superior. During the 1942-45 period, the combination of the two taxes took approximately one half of reported corporate profits. A corporate income tax of no more than 60 per cent would have raised more revenue and avoided the costly administrative problems of an excess profits tax. Likewise the extra waste resulting from a marginal rate of over 80 per cent in the combination excess profits and net income tax could also have been avoided. Furthermore, the pressure for special treatment of the extractive industries and special rapid write-offs of buildings and equipment would have been less persuasive if only a corporate net income tax had been used.

As concerns the distribution effects, the combination of corporate income and excess profits taxes took a larger proportion of the profits of those corporations that had experienced high profits judged on a rate-of-return test and much larger profits during the war than during peacetime. By comparison a corporate net income tax alone, providing about the same yield to the government, would have taxed more heavily those corporations whose earnings, judged by the test of a rate of return on invested profits, were on the low side but were substantially higher than prewar earnings as well as those whose profits were large during the war and had been large during peacetime. Whether one distribution would have been better or worse than the other is impossible to say, because standards of fairness as applied to the taxation of a corporation as such are inherently nebulous.

Incidence of an Excess Profits Tax

A tax can be shifted, it may be recalled, only if the tax formula induces reactions that have the effect of increasing the taxpayer's gains computed before tax. Shifting is complete if the taxpayer's gains computed before tax increase by the amount of the tax liability. A necessary but not sufficient condition for any shifting is a tax formula that creates an incentive on the part of the legal taxpayer to behave differently than he would have in its absence. Recall that a flat-sum tax, for example, simply removes a sum of money from the taxpayer and by definition such a tax cannot be shifted. The incidence of a tax can theoretically be located by the test of the amount of money which would need to be given to those people and organizations so as to place them in the same position as they would have been in the absence of the tax, subject to the restriction that the amount to be paid just equals the tax revenue.

The shifting possibilities of an excess profits tax are similar to those already discussed in connection with the corporation net income tax.[8] These possibilities are limited by the presence of other types of taxes, such as an individual income tax. The corporation is one of several legal devices that may be employed for business managements. To avoid heavy taxation of the corporation, one apparently simple remedy is at hand—dissolve the corporation and organize as a partnership. If such a step were always easy to take, heavy taxation of corporations might be a failure; the government would find that it had destroyed the tax base by imposing the tax. But as long as individual income is heavily taxed, there exists a positive incentive to retain the corporate form because the total tax to be paid would be

[8] See chap. 10.

even greater under the partnership form. For example, the Dupont interests had title in 1959 to about 23 per cent of the common stock of General Motors Corporation as well as shares in the several Dupont enterprises. If there were no special corporate taxation and if the share of the Dupont family in the earnings of these corporations were required to be reported as income under the individual income tax, the effective rate of tax would be very high indeed, certainly well above 80 per cent. Purely from the point of view of tax considerations, wealthy people in such a position save more in taxes by having assets in the form of shares of stock than by being partners with others in enterprise. Hence special taxation of corporations does not give rise in such cases (of which there are many in fact) to incentives to reorganize business units into noncorporate types.

Where corporations are owned by people having incomes of modest size, they could gain by dissolving the corporation and becoming a partnership because they pay more tax under the individual income tax and special corporate taxes than they would if all corporate earnings were treated as a part of individual income. Actually this option is not a relevant one because it is practically impossible to organize a large business as a partnership when the partners must be thousands of people. Consequently those who have the power to avoid the corporate form for the management and ownership of wealth have a tax incentive to continue using the corporate form, whereas those who have a tax incentive to use other forms do not have the power to do so. This condition permits governments to impose heavy special taxation upon corporations without having to worry seriously about undermining the tax base by business reorganization into other forms.[9]

Any possible shifting of an excess profits tax via abandoning the corporate form may be eliminated as irrelevant in industrialized economies. There remain other possibilities. Such a tax may set in motion developments which increase pretax corporate profits by increasing the market value of the commodities produced, by reducing costs of production, or by some combination of the two.

Under the special conditions of war finance, corporations engaged in production for government purposes may be successful in inducing procurement officers to include in the price a factor reflecting excess profits taxation. During World War II, there were numerous instances where this practice appeared to occur. Procurement officers are likely to be, and in fact are, rather casual about the financial ex-

[9] In some countries, various special taxes are imposed upon corporations as such with only nominal or no taxation of individual income. In such cases, corporations other than foreign ones may be kept from coming into being by special corporate taxes.

pense of obtaining the material desired by the military departments. Success or failure is judged by reference to speed of delivery and quality and amount of product rather than in terms of price. The money cost becomes of little importance. The government in fact recovered a portion of such overpayments by the use of contract renegotiation, a practice which may be alternatively described as a partial 100 per cent tax on the profits arising out of government contracts. A further portion was recovered by excess profits and corporate income taxation. It is impossible to estimate how much larger government expenditures actually turned out to have been and how much larger corporate profits before tax would have been because of the practices of procurement officers who included an excess profits tax allowance in government contracts. To some unknown extent, the government paid, so to speak, its own tax.

Shifting of the tax via some path resulting in higher prices to the civilian population was not a real possibility. By controls, prices were established at levels reflecting in the main the recent historical price structure of each industry with modifications to bring it into line with conditions of shortage. The large increase in profits during the war arose mainly out of the more effective utilization of plant and equipment as war expenditures pulled the economy out of the depression and by various forced economies arising out of shortages of manpower and materials.

The shifting of an excess profits tax by developments that reduce costs of production is not a real possibility under the actual conditions of war finance. Apart from any question of how such a tax might give an incentive to cut costs, the presence of various controls make cost reductions taking the form of lower prices paid to suppliers or of lower wage rates out of the question. These controls prevent prices and wage rates from adjusting in such a fashion. Actually, there exists a tax-induced incentive to pay higher prices to suppliers and higher wage rates. With corporations subject to high marginal rates of tax, the incentive of the management to be efficient and to hold down costs is seriously weakened. Had it not been for the fact during World War II that managements realized that if they allowed loose and careless practices to creep into the business during the war period they would have difficulty in eradicating such inefficiency during peacetime, the excess profits tax might have caused serious damage. Those companies that took the attitude that costs did not matter because the government would pay them anyhow often found their postwar competitive position weakened. This consideration did not apply to special enterprises established only for the war period, and in many of these highly wasteful practices were common. It is this effect of a high-rate excess profits tax that makes it especially objectionable on economic grounds under any conditions and especially during wartime.

Excess profits taxation has earned the opprobrium of tax administrators, many public finance scholars, a large section of the business community, and many legislators. From now on, those urging such a tax in times of emergency may no longer be able to place others on the defensive by the sheer appeal of taxing "excessive" profits. An excess profits tax cannot be defended as fair, as an efficient device to raise revenue, or as an inducement to economic efficiency. No doubt it will remain a favorite of those to whom the word "profits" remains a synonym for illicit gain.[10]

---

[10] M. H. Gobal urges the peacetime use of a "high profits" tax, i.e., a tax on profits exceeding some defined normal profit. He has proposed such a tax for India. See his work, *The Theory of Excess Profits Taxation* (Mysore City, India: Mysore Printing and Publishing House, 1947).

12

Death Taxation

The occasion of death might not seem the ideal time for a government to collect a toll. It is not customary for governments to levy a tax upon the occasion of a birth (though this oversight may eventually be corrected). From very early times and in societies of varying types of organization, governments have insisted on sharing in the estate of a decedent. It is customary to wait for this share until after the funeral.

Death taxation is a general term to describe a family of tax devices. The two most common types are the estate tax and the inheritance tax. Each of these may be further subclassified.

In general, the base of an estate tax is the net estate of a decedent, defined as the value of the assets minus the value of any debts. Funeral expenses and the costs of settling the estate are ordinarily deductible. Technically, an estate tax classifies as a type of net worth tax taking effect at death.[1]

The base of an inheritance tax is the value of assets distributed to a beneficiary or successor. The amount of the tax liability depends upon the size of the wealth obtained by successors rather than upon the size of the net estate. The two types of taxes come to the same thing when there is only one successor. In all other cases, they are different because the tax liability under an estate tax depends upon the size of the net estate, whereas under an inheritance tax it depends upon the size of each successor's share. An inheritance tax can be tailored more or less finely to the economic position of the beneficiary. An estate tax has much greater limitations on this score.

[1] See chap. 9.

Gift taxes are also usually classified as death taxes even though taxes of this type do not necessarily make death the occasion for extracting revenue. Gift taxes have been looked upon as complementary to ordinary death taxes. They are a device to prevent avoidance of death taxes by giving wealth away prior to death. Actually gift taxes might be imposed on their merits and apart from any avoidance implications. The United States federal government imposes a gift tax as do some of the state governments. The British manage to get along without such a tax.[2]

Inheritance tax devices may be subclassified in various ways. One is the accessions tax; it has as its base the sums received by any one beneficiary from the estates of decedents, cumulated over the entire lifetime of the beneficiary. Thus a person who received $100,000 at age 35 from his grandparents' estate and $400,000 at age 55 from a parent's estate would be required to pay a tax on $500,000. A tax of this type to be consistent with its rationale should be progressive in its rate features so that a person who obtained large amounts of wealth in this manner would be subject to high effective rates.[3] An accessions tax can also be looked upon as a partial cumulative income tax; it is partial because some gains are segregated for tax purposes.

Although it has not been customary to do so, the inclusion of all gains to a person in the form of gifts, bequests, or inheritances in a personal income tax can be looked upon as a form of inheritance taxation. In this approach, however, no special treatment of gains of this type is made. They are simply added to all other gains, such as wages, interest, and rents that a person may experience. Henry Simons has forcibly argued for this type of provision.[4] Its adoption would substantially increase the tax revenue if income-tax rates and exemptions were left unchanged.

United States Death Taxes

The federal government levies an estate and a gift tax. The estate tax applies to all estates of net amounts exceeding $60,000. In computing the taxable estate, funeral expenses and costs of administering the estate are deductible. Grants made to religious, charitable, and

---

[2] Mr. G. S. A. Wheatcroft, an authority on the British inheritance law, has suggested that a gift tax might be a desirable addition to British legislation. See his article, "The Anti-Avoidance Provisions of the Law of Estate Duty in the United Kingdom," *National Tax Journal,* X (March, 1957), 46-56.

[3] For a discussion of this type of tax, see the article by Harry J. Rudick, "A Proposal for an Accessions Tax," *Tax Law Review,* Vol. XXV (Oct.-Nov., 1945).

[4] Henry Simons, *Personal Income Taxation* (Chicago: Univ. of Chicago Press, 1938), pp. 125 ff.

educational organizations are also fully deductible. In community property states, such as the state of California, one half of the wealth accumulated during a marriage is looked upon as belonging to each spouse. There is no transfer under the law of one half of the community property at the death of one spouse. In non-community property states federal law permits one half of the property of one spouse to be left to the other free of tax. The rates of tax begin at 3 per cent for taxable estates from zero to $5,000, and range to a maximum incremental rate of 77 per cent. A taxable estate of $1 million carries a tax liability of $325,700, an effective rate of 32.57 per cent. A taxable estate of $10 million carries a tax liability of $6,088,200, an effective rate of about 60 per cent. The maximum rate of 77 per cent applies to that portion of a taxable estate in excess of $10 million.

The federal law also provides for a tax credit for state death taxes. The maximum credit ranges from .8 per cent of the amount by which the taxable estate exceeds $40,000, for a taxable estate between zero and $90,000, to 16 per cent for the portion of a taxable estate exceeding $10,040,000. For a taxable estate of $1 million, the maximum credit for state death taxes is $36,560. Thus if a state levies a death tax of $20,000 on such an estate, the actual credit is $20,000. If it levies a tax of $50,000 on such an estate, the credit allowed is $36,560 against the federal tax liability.[5]

The federal gift tax is levied on the donor. The tax base is cumulative over the lifetime of the donor—the only tax with this feature in the federal revenue system. In computing the tax base, the donor is permitted to exclude the first $3,000 per year given to any one recipient. In addition, an exemption of $30,000 is allowed. This exemption is computed by adding the amounts in excess of the $3,000 annual exclusion. When the donor is married, one half of any gift is assumed under the law to be made by each spouse, effectively doubling the exemptions and exclusions in such cases. The rates of the gift tax are set at three-fourths of the rates under the estate tax. They actually are even lower because the base of the gift tax is the sum (after exclusions and exemptions) given to the recipient rather than the total amount of wealth changing hands, i.e., the gift plus the tax on it.

Gifts made in contemplation of death are treated as a part of the estate and are subject to the estate tax. Gifts made within three years of death may be so construed, but need not be. According to the law, the issue is to be decided on the basis of fact, whether the donor did or did not make the gift in contemplation of dying. This rule means that the intention of the decedent must be discovered—a difficult procedure.

[5] For the entire schedule of rates, see Sec. 2011 of the *Internal Revenue Code.*

Gift tax yields are trivial. Since they are designed to complement the estate tax, a small yield is no objection. The tax does assure that the alienation of large sums of money by wealthy people will entail taxation. How much it deters such transfers must be a speculation.

State death taxes, as might be expected, vary widely among the states. The exemptions are much lower than under the federal law and the rates are moderate. Thirty-three of the states levy an inheritance type of tax and a differential estate tax designed to absorb the full federal tax credit. Seven levy an estate tax designed to absorb the full federal tax credit. South Dakota and West Virginia levy an inheritance tax only, failing to take full advantage of the federal credit. There are other variations, including the case of Nevada, which levies no death tax at all.[6]

States entered the field of death taxation before the federal government did, but neither they nor the federal government have succeeded, if they can be said to have tried, in making this type of tax yield substantial revenues. The states operate under the competitive constraint that if any one should attempt to tax large estates heavily, wealthy residents would move to more congenial tax climates. The federal credit originated as a device to reduce state residence competition for wealthy citizens by light death taxes. Although it has reduced tax competition among the states, the fear of losing wealthy residents as a result of high state death taxes has by no means disappeared. The rather messy situation still existing suggests the desirability of the federal government pre-empting this field of taxation, with provisions for sharing the revenue with the states. Yet messiness is a part of the price we pay for a federal system of government. Some esthetics may perhaps be sacrificed in the interests of preserving the system.

Revenue Implications of Death Taxes

Viewed simply as a way of raising money, death taxes do not rate very high in any country in which they are found. The federal estate and gift taxes yielded $1,486 million in 1958 out of a total of net budget receipts of $72 billion, or approximately 2 per cent. The yield of state death taxes is similarly small, about $112 million in 1957 as compared with total revenues of about $24 billion. In state death taxation, a yield equal to 3 per cent of total revenue is unusually high. If for some reason death taxation had to be abandoned, the revenue loss would be embarrassing for a time, but scarcely serious in the

[6] See the article by William H. Sager, "Practicability of Uniform Death and Gift Tax Laws," *National Tax Journal*, X (Dec. 1957), 361-69.

long run. A small increase in the rates of income taxes or of sales taxes could easily be made to compensate for the revenue loss.

In Britain, death taxation is a more significant revenue device than in the United States. The yield of their death tax amounts to about 4 per cent of ordinary revenue. This yield is greater than that of the surtax—the portion of the British income tax (often looked upon as a separate tax) assessed at rates above the standard rate. They obtain this greater comparative yield by permitting smaller exemptions and by imposing higher rates on modest estates, and also perhaps by more successful tax administration.

In the United States, according to one estimate, the total amount of wealth passing at death was about $20 billion in 1953. The yield of all death taxes amounted to about 5 per cent of this sum.[7] If this information is approximately reliable, people who gain financially from the demise of others are taxed much more lightly on these gains than they are on other gains such as wages or profits. The revenue from death taxes could be substantially increased by any of several methods, all within the realm of technical feasibility.

Some Philosophical Issues

Death taxation has stimulated more philosophical discussions among lawyers and economists than any other type. Transfers occasioned by death involve difficult questions of interpretation, especially interpretations about the financial burden of taxes on them.

One famous thinker and legal reformer, Jeremy Bentham, held that if the state were to take all wealth left at death—a tax of 100 per cent effective rate—no one would be hurt; such a policy would be a tax without a burden. The reasoning is simple. If the state announces in advance that it has title to all wealth left at death, private beneficiaries are eliminated. Since they expect nothing, they lose nothing. Applied to the United States, this reasoning means that the government could obtain about $20 billion in revenue a year without imposing a tax pain on anyone.

The crucial feature of reasoning of this sort is the premise that property passing at death does not inherently belong to anyone. The former owner is no longer of this world. Whatever adventures his soul may experience, these adventures are not conducted with worldly goods. If the state announces that it is the owner of such wealth, and its power to do so is not seriously disputed, what would have been

---

[7] These data are estimates of John C. Bowen, "Some Yield Estimates for Transfer Taxes," *National Tax Journal*, XII (March, 1959), 54-68. This study is one of the few to provide quantitative information relevant to death taxes.

the wealth of some private persons becomes the state's. Bentham reasoned that if such persons could not expect to own this wealth, they are not hurt. The argument, however, proves too much. If a person cannot expect to own himself, the wages his services earn go to his master, not to him, and since he cannot expect to receive wages, their acquisition by another does not hurt him. Taxation is a device to extract valuable things from people and unless these things would be owned by private individuals or organizations, there is no taxation. In a pure socialist system of the type where all wealth, including human earning power, is owned by the state, there can be no taxation. Any income obtained by private groups is a gratuitous transfer from the state to them. In a society such as our own, it is taken for granted that people can and do own things and hence it is meaningful for a government to take what would otherwise be theirs. A person who pays $1,000 in settlement of an income tax liability is only too vividly aware that if the government did not request this money, it would be his.

Nevertheless, ambiguities do exist in connection with the ownership of wealth passing at death, and as a result some ambiguities are associated with the meaning of imposing a tax upon some person or persons in this connection. To clarify this issue, some cases may be considered.

Let us consider first the simple case of a predecessor who feels morally bound to leave all of his wealth to one person, for example a man who wishes to leave all of his wealth to his wife. If he dies and if the government insists upon taxing the estate or the wife's inheritance, she and she alone is the one from whom the tax money is collected. If the wealth is $500,000 and the government collects $50,000, she received $450,000 instead of $500,000. By the supposition that she is to be the sole beneficiary in any event, she is the one who would own the entire estate, and hence any sums taken in tax are taken from her. In this case, a death tax is imposed upon her just as clearly as is an income tax imposed upon the person who obtains income.

Consider a man who dies without kin and who has made no will. The estate escheats to the state. Who has lost? No person who can be identified has lost anything because no person would have owned the wealth if the state had not taken it. One might say that his neighbors or friends are the ones who lost because in the absence of the 100 per cent tax—if the government's taking of the wealth is to be viewed as a tax—they could have acquired the wealth by simple removal of it to their own possession. This reasoning assumes that they would have title to the wealth, an assumption that does not hold. In this case, it is correct to hold that what the government gets is not at the expense of any actual person.

Let us come now to more difficult cases. An eccentric old man has made a will which provides that of the wealth remaining after payment of all taxes, the executor shall present to each of the first *n* young ladies he meets on the street between the ages of 18 and 25 a check for $100,000 until the entire estate is dissipated. If the net estate amounted to $10 million and the tax amounted to $6 million, the executor is able to pay out $100,000 to each of 40 qualified young ladies. Granted that the same formula would have been employed if there were no tax, some 60 young ladies of unknown identity would have each received $100,000, but did not do so because of the tax. In this illustration, the identity of those who would have obtained the wealth is unknown, although the fact that, whoever they are, they failed to receive what the government took in tax is clear and definite. The government took what would have been theirs. That no tears may be shed about their loss is beside the point.

More generally, to ascertain what particular individuals do without the assets which the government receives from death taxation, we must know what the ownership of the decedent's wealth would have been in the absence of the tax and how that ownership has been altered by the operation of the tax. If the law provides, as it does in some countries, that the wealth of the parents must pass to the elder son, any tax levied upon the estate or upon his inheritance is a tax upon him. The law establishes the wealth as his. Where the predecessor has a choice as to how the estate is to be divided, there can be ambiguity because the choice of successors and the amount each is to receive in the absence of the tax may be unknown and, indeed, even unknowable. It is unknowable if the decedent had no definite plans as to how the estate was to be divided in the absence of the tax. Many colleges may be losing large sums of money because of the federal estate tax. The fact that donations made to colleges are exempt from estate taxes is relevant but not conclusive evidence in this connection. A person with an estate of $400,000 may leave all of what remains of it after tax to his offspring. If the government were to take less in tax, he might have decided to leave a modest sum to his Alma Mater. The smaller the after-tax estate of a person is, the more likely he is to take care of what he regards as the financial needs of close relatives first.

No empirical study has yet been made of the question posed by the above remarks. We do not know what people or organizations fail to receive the assets now taken by tax from estates. There is a strong presumption that in the overwhelming number of instances, the family

of the decedent pays the tax. Normally wealth is passed from generation to generation within the family unit. What we really wish to
know is the answer to the marginal question: if the federal estate tax
were smaller, who would gain? No definitive answer to this question
is possible at the present state of knowledge.

Although the issue is controversial among students of this topic,
it seems reasonably clear that an estate or inheritance tax cannot rest
upon the decedent.[8] Those who bear the tax are those who would,
but for the intervention of the government's tax claims, obtain title to
the wealth previously owned by the decedent. This interpretation involves no shifting considerations. The contemplation of a future tax
liability can and does affect the behavior of a person with a taxable
estate, including for example the hiring of a legal expert to hold down
the size of the government's claim to be imposed at death. Yet to
hold that a dead body pays taxes is a contradiction. The living pay
what taxes are imposed.

Economic Effects of Death Taxes

The economic effects of death taxes, whether the tax takes the
form of an estate or an inheritance tax, operate through the decisions
of the predecessor in contemplation of the tax and upon the successors
through the brute fact of the size of the tax liability.

From the point of view of a predecessor, a tax payable upon his
death may affect his decisions during his lifetime in a number of ways.
He may take steps to protect the assets from the eroding effects of
taxation. Many foundations owe their origins to wealthy people who
wished to avoid the substantial tax liabilities that would otherwise
fall upon their estates. Foundations have become a current fad of
wealthy people in the United States. A rich man without one is becoming as rare as a rich man without a Cadillac. The opportunities
to safeguard assets from death taxation are many and complicated.
This is the province of legal experts and will not be pursued here.

In the class of economic effects are those that influence decisions
to work or not to work, the amounts spent for consumption, and the
form of the assets held. Each of these will be considered in turn.

THE WORK-LEISURE CHOICE. A death tax may affect a person's
decision to stay on the job or to retire in much the same way as may
an income tax. The higher is the average rate of tax to be imposed
upon the estate, the smaller of course will be the estate to be dis-

_____

[8] For another view, see the article by James K. Hall, "Incidence of Death
Duties," *American Economic Review*, XXX (March, 1940), 46-59.

tributed. If a person has a strong motivation to leave wealth to survivors, for example a wife and children who are dependent, he will be more inclined to work in order to increase his estate. Something he wants—wealth for survivors—is reduced by the tax. The utility of a dollar of after-tax estate has increased because the after-tax estate is made smaller, and hence it becomes relatively more important to him than vacations without pay. If a person does not care about building up an estate, any tax effect is ruled out. Such people are, however, rare.

On the other hand, the contemplation of the marginal rate of tax upon the estate, taken by itself, would induce a person to work less hard to build up his estate. If he works another year when he might retire instead, he can increase or prevent a decrease in the size of his estate. But for every dollar that he adds to his estate in this way, he commits the executor to pay, perhaps, seventy cents to the government. The price of loafing as opposed to working is, then, thirty cents for every dollar he adds to the estate. The price of leisure in terms of after-tax net estate is reduced by the amount of the marginal rate of tax upon the estate. Since leisure has become a less expensive commodity, he may wish to "buy" more of it by not working as much.

These two effects, operating in opposite directions, suggest an indeterminate outcome on theoretical grounds alone. A person either may work more or he may work less because of future taxes upon his estate. Actually it is highly unlikely that the work habits of people are affected in a quantitatively significant fashion by any death taxes currently in use. Contemplation of death taxes is likely to affect only the older group of the population. Of this group, a substantial fraction will have no choice about the date of retirement. Of those who do have a choice, some are professional people who typically enjoy their work and who retire only when poor health or other circumstances beyond their control dictate the decision. Few people like to announce to themselves and to the world that they have become economically useless, even when in fact they have. Retirement for many people promotes the disease of boredom, a disease with often fatal consequences. The possibility of estate taxes seriously affecting the working habits of people capable of working can be dismissed as a theoretical possibility of little quantitative significance.

CONSUMPTION CHOICE. The size of an estate and hence the amount of tax liability can be increased or reduced by spending less or more money for personal expenses. Wealthy people can thwart the tax collector by dissipating assets while alive, taking round-the-world tours, becoming a candidate for public office, or buying an honorary degree from a university. If people have no interest in the welfare of survivors, presumably they will dissipate their wealth even apart from tax considerations. According to time-preference theory, consumption is all that matters to a person and hence he should dissipate his wealth prior to death. That people do not behave in this fashion is a serious criticism of the theory.

Granted a concern for survivors, a person can assume that the tax will reduce the wealth of successors. As in the work-leisure choice, the taking away of something a person likes, namely wealth from successors, should induce him to prefer a course of action that increases the quantity of what he likes. The effective-rate effect then should induce a person to be somewhat more circumspect in his consumption expenditures. Even though the government gets more tax revenue as a result, survivors get more too.

Here again, the marginal-rate effect works in the opposite direction. A person sees that when his estate is increased one dollar, the government will take seventy cents. The cost of a dollar of consumption viewed in terms of its estate consequences is thus only thirty cents. Concentration on this consideration may induce a person to take that round-the-world cruise because it costs his survivors so little.

The effects of these considerations upon the actual consumption expenditures of people are likely to be unimportant. By the time people have reached the age when estate considerations weigh heavily, they have also reached the age when radical departures from previous modes of living are generally unwelcome. If somehow reliable empirical information could be obtained, it would be likely to show that few people allow death-tax considerations to affect their living expenses. Such an empirical study has not, however, been made.

CHOICE OF ASSET COMPOSITION. Estate tax considerations are probably more important in influencing the types of assets held than in decisions affecting the size of the estate itself. Two types of considerations enter: the effect of the contemplation of death taxes upon asset holdings classified by degree of risk and the liquidity problem posed by the need of raising the money to pay the tax.

Death taxes, like general net worth taxes and general income taxes, may be expected to induce people to take more risk. The tax automatically provides for complete loss offsets. If a person invests, for example, $200,000 in a particular venture with the prospect of the asset being worth $300,000 at his death, a death tax at a marginal rate of 60 per cent will reduce the net gain from $100,000 to $40,000; but if the asset should turn out unhappily to be worth only $100,000, a 60 per cent tax rate reduces the $100,000 gross loss to a $40,000 net loss. On a probability basis, a net worth type of death tax leaves the relative chances of gain and loss unaffected. As explained elsewhere, a tax with full loss offsets can be expected on theoretical grounds to induce investors to take more total risk.[9]

A similar conclusion holds for other types of death taxes, provided that the relevant marginal rates of tax are about the same. For an inheritance tax, the present estate owner, contemplating the amounts to be left to his chosen successors, knows that successful investments will increase the amount to be provided them as well as the amount of tax to be paid. Unsuccessful investments have opposite effects, and the conclusion given above follows.

Of much greater importance is the liquidation problem occasioned by the transfer of property at death. Even without a tax, a liquidation problem exists if the estate is to be divided among several successors. It is not ordinarily feasible to divide and distribute an estate by type of asset, although it is done. The older a wealthy person becomes, the more concerned he is likely to be about leaving an estate in a form that can be easily distributed. Death taxes, especially heavy ones, increase this concern. Governments insist upon being paid in cash.

If an estate consists of assets with a wide market, little difficulty is apt to be encountered. Assets such as securities traded on organized markets can be readily sold. Cash is of course ideal and many large estates include a substantial amount of the assets in this form. The liquidation problem arises for items with a thin market. An operating business, whether incorporated or not, is an illustration. Piecemeal sale of the assets may destroy the business. Sale as a going concern may be difficult; buyers are few and usually tough bargainers. Much concern has been expressed in congressional circles about the effects of death taxes upon small business, partly on grounds of the hardship to survivors if the assets must be sold on highly unfavorable terms to raise the cash to pay the tax and partly on grounds that an ideal setting is created for larger companies to acquire a competing business, thereby possibly reducing competition. To mitigate possible hardship cases, an executor is permitted under federal law the option of delaying the payment of the tax for as long as ten years if such a period is necessary to permit favorable liquidation.

An owner of an estate, realizing that a liquidation problem may arise, will often take steps to meet it by selling nonliquid assets as the opportunity to do so arises and acquiring readily marketable assets in their place. Insurance is a simple, but often expensive, way of meeting the problem since the insurance company supplies cash on the occasion of death. A general bias is created by heavy death taxes toward holding highly marketable securities as opposed to real estate, works of art, libraries, or the securities of small corporations.

[9] See chaps. 7, 9.

EFFECTS ON SUCCESSORS. Those incentive considerations having to do with marginal rates of tax have little effect on successors. By the time the wealth comes into their hands, the crucial decisions have been made. Transfers to a successor at death may be influenced by persuasion and kindness, but not typically by economic means.

The main fact about a death tax is the seemingly simple one that what the government takes, the successors do not obtain. The tax thus makes the gain of a successor smaller than it would have been in the absence of the tax, or, looked at another way, it makes his total asset position smaller than it would have been in the absence of the tax.

It follows that the amount of consumption and investment expenditures that a successor can finance in the future is diminished by the amount of the tax imposed upon him. His spending power is reduced because his net worth is reduced. Absolutely of course, the successor owns more wealth than he did before. But his net worth is reduced by the tax because the tax makes the amount transferred to him less large. From the point of view of a successor, an estate tax is like a lump-sum levy because nothing he can do affects the size of the tax.

Any tax that has a yield will reduce people's consumption expenditures, their investment expenditures, or both. As observed in other connections, whether a tax cuts mainly into consumption or investment expenditures of a person depends upon his tastes and total net worth position.[10] If taxable estates are left mainly to poor people, unlikely as that may be, the effect of heavy death taxation would be primarily to hold down their future consumption expenditures because the poor spend their money mainly for this purpose. By the same token, if estates are left mainly to the rich, and this appears to be the case, the effects are likely to be felt primarily in holding down investment expenditures. Recall, however, that apart from the well established fact that wealth normally is retained within the family group, we have little firm information about the characteristics of the "marginal" people and organizations cut out of wills. Hence circumspection is indicated in attempting to generalize about the spending effects of death taxes.

Equity Considerations

Ideally a tax of any type should be fair in the sense that people in the same position should be treated in the same way. It also should be equitable in the sense that the amount of money removed from

---

[10] See Part IV.

people accords with some defensible index of relative taxpaying ability. How do death taxes score on these counts?

Granted that, in the main, wealth remains within the family, a death tax such as the federal estate tax will typically impose heavier burdens on wealthy successors than on the less wealthy for the reasons already mentioned. In any statistical study of tax burdens, no great inaccuracy occurs if the yield of these taxes is assigned to the high income or large wealth groups. Reliable detailed evidence about the relation of the size of the tax to the size of the income or wealth of successors does not, however, exist.

Successors are not treated equally under this type of law if they are otherwise equal in all relevant respects. Two people of identical economic positions who obtain identical bequests from separate decedents will not ordinarily be treated equally by death taxes. They will only be treated equally in the event that the estate tax happens to reduce their final shares by the same amount. Since the size of the tax depends upon the size of the net estate, such a result is fortuitous.

All types of death taxes currently in vogue share the defect of failing to take into account the relation of the amount of a bequest, gift, or inheritance to some defensible index of the recipient's taxable capacity. If a grown son with an annual income of $100,000 is provided with $50,000 from the estate of his father and a spinster daughter with an annual income of $3,000 is provided with the same amount, both are taxed under an estate or an inheritance tax by the same amount. Yet the son obviously has a much greater ability to pay than does the daughter. Reflection upon considerations of this type suggest redesigning death taxes so that any sums obtained by successors are required to be counted as income under the individual income tax and taxed accordingly.

A death tax may work great injustice when the husband dies prematurely leaving a dependent wife and children. If the husband was a doctor with a flourishing practice, he may have earned perhaps $30,000 per year. His premature death ends this earning power, resulting in a large capital loss to his wife and children. This loss may be compensated by insurance, but only rarely is in full. If the estate of the decedent amounts to $300,000 and is subject to tax, the wife may be bitter about a tax law that further erodes her position. Her objections are well-taken; she has lost financially, not gained, as a result of her husband's death and so of course have the children. Attention to hardship cases helps explain the lack of enthusiasm in the Congress for a revision of the federal estate tax law in the direction of lower exemptions and higher yields.

One solution to this type of difficulty is exemption of transfers from one spouse to another at death, with provisions to prevent circumventing the intent of the law by marriages designed to reduce tax liabilities.[11] Measures of this type designed to eliminate hardship cases are justified in themselves, and in addition they remove one obstacle to increased taxation in this area.

A similar provision might be made in the event amounts transferred at death are treated as income for tax purposes. Such a reform would largely eliminate the present erratic tax treatment under estate and inheritance taxes.

Alternatives to Existing Death Taxes

Advocates of estate types of death taxes are concerned about the presence of loopholes in current laws. The loopholes are numerous and large. The gift of wealth prior to death is a simple method, a method that is only partially blocked by the gift tax. A common solution proposed is an integrated death and gift tax, aimed at the outcome of an approximate equal tax liability.[12] Proposals of this type can be defended only on the assumption that estates of equal size should be taxed equally. The weakness of this assumption has already been stressed. The assumption is that the tax must fall upon the decedent.

Vickrey has advocated death taxation based upon a bequeathing power formula. The aim is to provide the same tax liability regardless of the method of devolution of the estate. To accomplish this end, the size of the tax is made to depend upon the age differences between decedents and beneficiaries and on a number of highly complicated provisions.[13]

The decision as to what type of tax, if any, should be employed in connection with transfers at death depends upon the objective in view. Lack of agreement about objectives explains in large measure the persisting differences among economists and lawyers as to the best form of death tax to be employed. If the objective is the erosion of

[11] Full exemption might be provided under an estate tax of the amount left to the surviving spouse in all cases where any of the following conditions are met: the marriage results in offspring, the age of each spouse at marriage is less than 60 years, the age-difference does not exceed fifteen years, or the marriage lasts ten years or more. If none of these conditions are met, the surviving spouse would be entitled only to some normal exemption, say $60,000. The purpose of such a provision would be to discourage young people from marrying old people at the expense of the revenue.

[12] Numerous writers have proposed reforms along these lines. See U. S. Treasury Department, *Federal Estate and Gift Taxes* (Washington, D.C.: Government Printing Office, 1947).

[13] See William Vickrey, *Agenda for Progressive Taxation* (New York: The Ronald Press Co., 1947), chaps. viii, ix.

plutocracy, death taxation of the estate tax type is not especially efficient. Granted the value judgment that great wealth in the hands of a person is objectionable *per se,* there is no reason to wait until a person dies to begin undermining his wealth. An annual graduated net worth tax with a large exemption would be much more effective than any death tax. The details of how such a tax might be designed are set forth in Chapter 9.

If a society is dedicated to individual income taxation there is little rationale for exempting gains from some sources and taxing gains from others. Equal treatment calls for imposing equal tax liabilities upon people in similar circumstances. A man who obtains a salary of $50,000 need not have more taxpaying power than another man who receives $10,000 in salary and $40,000 as an inheritance. Both have gained $50,000 during the year. Emphasis upon this consideration suggests that transfers at death and gifts should be required to be reported as individual income and taxed as such. Such a treatment would substantially increase the yield of the individual income tax at current rates. One estimate suggests that approximately $20 billion of wealth was transferred in 1953,[14] an amount that can be expected to grow if no serious depression occurs, and almost all of this sum would become taxable at the first bracket rate of 20 per cent at least because such transfers would be added to other yearly income. In addition, because the children of wealthy people typically have large ordinary incomes, the additional reportable income resulting from the inclusion of gifts, bequests, or inheritances would be taxed at high rates. Instead of obtaining about 5 per cent of the total potential tax base, as appears to be the case under present death taxes, the government could expect to obtain at least 30 per cent and probably more by income tax treatment of these transfers. This added yield would permit the reduction of other taxes or the increase of exemptions and the lowering of rates in the individual income tax itself.

Such a reform would call for an effective averaging device to prevent people with small steady incomes from being pushed up into high brackets in one year as a result of an inheritance or bequest. The case for averaging, strong in any event, becomes even more compelling if the suggested tax treatment of transfers at death is adopted. The reform would also need to exempt small gifts from the tax base to avoid spoiling Christmas by having to estimate what a pair of socks and a necktie are worth. An exemption of gifts from living people up to some total, such as $500 per person per year, might be provided. No exemption would be necessary for transfers at death.

---

[14] The figure is Bowen's estimate, *op. cit.,* p. 56, Table I.

13

Sales Taxation

Sales taxes, which existed in ancient Athens and Rome long before an income tax was even dreamed of, have had a tumultuous history. Roundly condemned as regressive and ruinous burdens on the poor and on honest sellers of merchandise, they have even, on a few unfortunate occasions, been factors in bitter rebellions against governments. From this unlikely background, they have now grown to respectable and influential old age. This is not to say, however, that the sales tax family is now without its critics or is likely to pass on quietly to an early grave. Indeed, quite the contrary appears to be the case. In spite of vigorous opposition in many quarters, sales taxes are currently the third most important type of tax in the United States, bringing in one-sixth of federal, state, and local governmental revenues and ranking close behind the personal and corporate income taxes. In other countries sales taxation typically plays an even more important role.

The federal government has never made use of a general sales tax —although one was strongly urged upon it during the War Between the States, in the early 1920's, and during both the Great Depression and World War II—but it has imposed excises on a long list of goods and services which together bring in over 10 per cent of federal budget receipts. By far the most productive of these levies are the ones on alcoholic beverages, cigarettes, motor vehicles, and gasoline. Table 13–1 contrasts the rates and relative importance of these four excises in the fiscal years 1939 and 1959.

Other excises range from those on the transportation of persons and property and on telephone and telegraph services, which together

TABLE 13–1

RATES AND RELATIVE IMPORTANCE OF FEDERAL EXCISES ON ALCOHOLIC BEVERAGES, CIGARETTES, AUTOMOBILES, AND GASOLINE, 1939 AND 1959

Product	Tax Rate		Yield as a Percentage of Total Federal Excise Taxes	
	1939	1959	1939	1959
Alcoholic beverages per proof gallon	$2.25	$10.50 ⎫	33	28
Malt liquors per barrel	$5.00	$ 9.00 ⎭		
Cigarettes per thousand	$3.00	$ 4.00	29	16
Automobile sales price	3%	10%	2	16
Gasoline per gallon	1¢	3¢*	12	10
Total federal excise tax collections (millions of dollars)			1,768	10,760

* Increased to 4¢ on Oct. 1, 1959.

yielded $1 billion in 1959, to those on fishing rods, safe deposit box rentals, mechanical pencils and pens, which bring in only a few million dollars a year.

Retail sales taxation at the state level first became widespread during the Great Depression. No less than twenty-five states adopted such a tax during the 1933-35 period. A second flurry occurred between 1947 and 1951, when eight states and the District of Columbia enacted retail sales tax laws. Not all of these states have retained the sales tax up to the present time. Nevertheless, in 1958 some thirty-four states had general sales taxes which brought in 14 per cent of their total tax receipts. It will be noted from Table 13–2 that the great majority of these states obtained from 20 to 40 per cent of their revenues from this source. Rates in almost all cases were either 2 or 3 per cent.

Standing close to the general sales tax in importance at the state level is the gasoline tax. In 1958, for example, it was imposed in all states and yielded $2.9 billion, as compared with general sales tax receipts of $3.6 billion. Rates ranged from 3¢ to 7¢ a gallon, with 6¢ the most common. Excises on tobacco and alcoholic beverages ranked next, each producing more than half a billion dollars in tax receipts. Other commodity taxes touched insurance companies, public utilities, and parti-mutuel betting. Altogether, sales taxes of all kinds produced $8.9 billion, or 59 per cent of all state tax collections in 1958. At this level of government it was far and away the most important type of taxation.

TABLE 13–2

STATES IMPOSING RETAIL SALES TAXES GROUPED ACCORDING TO THE
RELATIVE IMPORTANCE OF THAT TAX IN THEIR FISCAL SYSTEMS, 1958

Retail Sales Taxes as a Percentage of Total Tax Collections

More than 40%	From 20% to 40%		Less than 20%
Alabama	Arizona	Missouri	Maryland
Illinois	Arkansas	Nevada	North Carolina
Indiana	California	New Mexico	
Washington	Colorado	North Dakota	
West Virginia	Connecticut	Ohio	
	Florida	Oklahoma	
	Georgia	Pennsylvania	
	Iowa	Rhode Island	
	Kansas	South Carolina	
	Louisiana	South Dakota	
	Maine	Tennessee	
	Michigan	Utah	
	Mississippi	Wyoming	

Source: Tax Foundation, *Facts and Figures on Government Finance,* 10th ed., 1958-
1959.

Sales taxation at the local level of government has been a fiscal development of relatively recent origin, yielding in 1958, 7 per cent of total tax collections. Even so, commodity taxation has a long way to go to challenge the dominant position of the property tax. One deterrent has been the potential loss of business to tax-free areas. In large closely knit urban areas individual cities are usually reluctant to adopt a sales tax unless their neighbors agree to do so. A second disadvantage of local sales taxes is found in the compliance costs put upon large-scale retailers who have to deal with different rules and regulations in each city. Finally, the administrative costs resulting from one state sales tax and several hundred different and independently managed municipal levies are likely to be high indeed. All of these problems can be solved by the simple device of transforming city and county sales taxes into a uniform levy collected by the state and then returned to the local government units. In this way administrative costs are minimized, retailers' compliance simplified, and if the levy is extended to all areas, tax burdens within the state equalized. By 1956 four states—California, Illinois, Mississippi, and New Mexico—had adopted state collection of local sales taxes.[1]

[1]See John F. Due, "The Role of Sales and Excise Taxation in the Overall Tax Structure," *Journal of Finance,* XI (May, 1956), 217-20.

Types of Sales Taxes

Sales taxes are all alike in being imposed upon the sale of commodities or services. They differ among themselves, however, according to the generality of the tax levy, the stage in the production process at which they are imposed, and the manner in which the tax burden is computed.

GENERALITY. The sales tax with the greatest possible scope is one levied on all sales of goods and services at all stages of production. Known as a turnover tax, this kind reaches not only sales by retailers to consumers but also sales by farmers and manufacturers to wholesalers, and by wholesalers to retailers. Any transfer of output from one firm or person to another, in short, is taxed. Since through this process any particular item is likely to be counted several times, the base of the tax will be considerably greater than the total gross national product of the country.[2]

No sales tax can employ a base that is, except by accident, exactly equal to gross national product. The closest approach to this would be a tax levied on all final sales of goods and services within the country. Like gross national product, the base of such a tax would encompass all consumer goods and services (including houses), together with business purchases of capital equipment. The tax base would differ from GNP, however, through (1) including imports, (2) excluding exports, and (3) excluding the change in the level of business inventories.[3] No such commodity tax exists at the present time. Retail sales taxes are typically much less general in scope.

The least general sales tax is a single excise on a specific commodity, such as gasoline or cigarettes. Most countries employ an extensive set of individual excises that, in operation, may be difficult to distinguish from a retail sales tax that exempts certain commodities entirely and imposes special low or high rates on others.

LOCATION IN THE PRODUCTION PROCESS. A turnover tax, as we have just seen, is levied at every stage of production. In this sense it it a multiple-stage sales tax. Single-stage taxes, on the other hand, are confined to one point in the movement of goods from the primary producer to the consumer. The most common kinds are manufacturers,' wholesalers,' and retail sales taxes.

[2] For an illustration of such multiple counting, see below, p. 280.
[3] Elimination of these differences would move the base of the levy away from total sales and make it coincident with total output, which in turn is equal to the base of a gross income tax without deductions or personal exemptions.

MANNER OF COMPUTING THE TAX. Sales tax rates may be based either on the physical unit of sale or on the dollar volume involved in the transaction. The former are known as *specific* sales taxes and are illustrated by the federal levies on gasoline (based on the gallon) or cigarettes (based on the number). *Ad valorem* taxes, such as the federal excise on automobiles and all state general retail sales taxes, on the other hand, impose a money burden that is a fixed percentage of the sales price.

The essential difference between the two types of sales taxes may be seen by considering an inexpensive bourbon selling for $4.00 a bottle and a quality brand selling for $8.00, each subject to a 50 per cent excise. In this case the tax liability is $2.00 on the first brand and $4.00 on the second.[4] Suppose now that the government, wishing to shift to a specific excise with the same yield, makes the tax $3.00 a bottle. If prices remain unchanged, the tax burden is now 75 per cent of the sales price of the standard bourbon and only 37.5 per cent of the price of the quality brand. This change will induce the retailer to push sales of the better brand by reducing the price spread between the two. If, for example, he reacts to the tax shift by keeping his after-tax gross profit per bottle constant, he will sell the two brands for $5.00 and $7.00. Since consumers will thereby be induced to buy more of the select brand and less of the standard type, producers of the latter will not find the tax change to their liking.

In general, then, *ad valorem* sales taxes place the same proportionate burden on all products whereas specific excises make the relative tax liability vary inversely with the price of the article.

Prominent Members of the Sales Tax Family and Their Idiosyncrasies

THE CANADIAN MANUFACTURERS' SALES TAX. This tax, which has been in existence for over thirty years at rates varying between 1 and 10 per cent and which yields an important part of Dominion tax revenues, is of more than casual interest to Americans. A number of organizations in this country, such as the National Association of Manufacturers, argue that the present set of United States federal

---

[4] It will be noted that the tax liability has been computed by applying the *ad valorem* rate to the actual sales price. An alternative procedure, common in this country, is to base the tax on the sales price minus the tax liability. In the present instance this would require a 100 per cent excise, and retailers might well state the "sales price" as $2.00 plus a tax of $2.00 for the inexpensive bourbon and $4.00 plus an equal amount of tax for the select brand. Such practices, however, do not alter the fact that the tax liability is 50 per cent of the price at which the sale is actually made.

excises, apart from those on tobacco and alcoholic beverages, should be replaced by a general manufacturers' sales tax, and interest in this type of tax would certainly be stimulated by any future need for increased federal tax revenues.[5]

The Canadian tax is based upon the sales of all finished products by manufacturers, but numerous exemptions are allowed. These are designed to accomplish four purposes: (1) to ensure that the tax is a true single-stage levy by exempting items which will subsequently become embodied in taxable finished products, (2) to free from tax some of the most essential consumer goods, (3) to place both imports and exports in the same tax positions as the products with which they must compete (by taxing imports and exempting exports), and (4) to confine the tax to the consumption sector of the economy. The last goal is only partially attained, however, since a number of important investment goods, such as trucks, railroad rolling stock, and office equipment, are taxed.[6]

The main advantage of a single-stage, manufacturers' sales tax is that ordinarily the government must deal with a much smaller number of firms than are involved in either a wholesale or a retail tax. This makes tax evasion more difficult and keeps down administrative costs. John Due, for example, estimates that the cost of the Canadian tax is less than 1 per cent of the yield.[7] This advantage is particularly important in countries in which much retail trade is in the hands of small businessmen who keep only rudimentary accounting records.

The tax does, however, present a number of difficult problems. Arbitrary lines are virtually inevitable in delineating the manufacturing sector, with the result that some businessmen will feel discriminated against. In Canada, for example, peanut-salters are classified as manufacturers while peanut-roasters are not.[8] Secondly, a tax confined to manufactured consumer goods must in principle base exemptions upon the intended use of the commodity. A typewriter sold to a grocery story, for example, would not be taxable whereas a typewriter sold to an individual (other than a professional writer) would be. In practice, however, detailed tracing of the final use of all manufactured products would seriously complicate the administration of

[5] See *A Tax Program for Economic Growth* (New York: National Association of Manufacturers, 1955), pp. 35-44. The Chamber of Commerce, although it does not mention a manufacturers' tax specifically, advocates replacement of selective excises by a general excise tax at a low uniform rate. Cf. *Policy Declarations on Finance,* adopted by members of the Chamber of Commerce of the United States, 1957, p. 9.

[6] For a detailed treatment of the Canadian tax, see John F. Due, *The General Manufacturers' Sales Tax in Canada* (Toronto: Canadian Tax Foundation, 1951).

[7] John F. Due, "Canada's Experience with the Manufacturers' Sales Tax," *Journal of Business of the University of Chicago,* XXVII (July, 1954), 243-53.

[8] *Ibid.,* p. 244.

the tax, and lines must in most cases be drawn on a product by product basis according to the majority use to which each is put. Portable typewriters, for example, could be made taxable even though some are used for business purposes, while standard models were exempt even though some are bought by consumers. It should at the same time be noted that distinctions of this sort become more and more unworkable as the rate of the tax increases. A 50 per cent tax confined to portable typewriters, for example, might drive them completely out of circulation.

At first glance the definition of the taxable sale price may appear to be a far simpler problem than it is. Consider a manufacturing firm which does its own distributing and sells directly to consumers. To tax the actual sale price in this case is to extend the scope of the levy beyond the manufacturing stage and in the process to discriminate against integrated firms. Canada attempts to solve this problem by allowing manufacturers who sell directly either to retailers or consumers to reduce the actual sales price by a standard percentage for tax purposes. In other cases, where some sales are made to wholesalers, the price on these transactions may be applied for tax purposes to all sales. The complexity of distribution channels is such, unfortunately, that any of these solutions must be regarded as approximate only.

A standard difficulty with any sales tax levied on the early stages of production is the strong possibility that some pyramiding of the money burden of the tax will take place. This process, whereby the final price to the consumer rises by more than the yield of the tax, may be illustrated as follows. Consider a manufactured product sold for $100 to a wholesaling firm whose standard markup over cost is 20 per cent, and then to a retailer who ordinarily adds on 50 per cent in setting his sales price to consumers. The final price is then $180 (the wholesaler, in other words, sells the item for $120 and the retailer increases this sum by $60). Suppose, now, that a 10 per cent manufacturers' tax is imposed on the sales price (exclusive of tax) and that the manufacturer increases his selling price by the full amount of the tax. The tax yield, therefore, is $10 and the product is sold to the wholesaler for $110. If subsequent markups remain at their pretax levels, the wholesaler will transfer the item to the retailer for $132, and the latter will offer it for sale for $198. The price to the consumer, it will be noted, has risen by $18, or by 10 per cent of its pretax level. The relative increase, to be sure, is equal to the tax rate, but the absolute rise is $8 greater than the yield of the tax. This excess is the amount of pyramiding that has taken place. Its fiscal significance lies in the fact that a shift from a 10 per cent manufacturers' levy to a 10 per cent retail sales tax could increase tax yields by $8 on this particular product without disturbing the level of consumer prices. As an anti-inflationary device, then, the retail sales tax is preferable to either a wholesale or a manufacturing sales tax as long as any pyramiding at all takes place. For a given rise in the price level the retail tax channels more money to the government where it may be kept out of further circulation and prevented from contributing to further price rises.

Pyramiding will not, of course, take place if competition among wholesalers and retailers and price resistance on the part of consumers cause pretax markup percentages to shrink. Empirical evidence on these reactions is difficult to obtain, but Due cites some indications of pyramiding in the case of the Canadian manufacturing tax.[9]

GERMAN TURNOVER TAX. This tax, which has existed in virtually unchanged form for forty years, is one of the world's most broadly based sales taxes. It includes within its purview all sales of goods at all stages of production and distribution, all imports, and most services rendered to consumers, including those of the professions. Among the few exclusions from the tax base are exports, education, the rental of real property, and most public utility services. Although the rate is low (4 per cent in 1957), the tax is the most important single source of revenue in West Germany. This ability to accomplish much by means of a very light touch is the chief attraction of a turnover tax.

The tax, however, is considerably less neutral than the wide application of a single tax rate would indicate at first glance. The burden it imposes on a given industry or product depends to a considerable extent on how many stages the raw materials and processed items pass through before they become finished products. One empirical study showed a rate of 3.2 per cent on electricity in comparison with a rate of 12.5 per cent on linen bedcovers.[10] The result, of course, is a significant incentive for the integration of several productive stages within a single business enterprise. While some welcome this tendency on the grounds that efficiency is thereby promoted, others challenge the generalization that integration and efficiency necessarily go together and point to the dangers and inequalities arising from increased monopoly power and lessened competition. German tax law, which contains some rather complex provisions which lessen but do not eliminate the discrimination of the turnover tax against nonintegrated businesses, straddles the issue neatly. Finally, since domestic products

[9] John F. Due, "American and Canadian Experience with the Sales Tax," *Journal of Finance,* VII (Sept., 1952), 468-69.
[10] Cited by John F. Due, "Sales Taxation in Western Europe, Part II," *National Tax Journal,* VIII (Sept., 1955), 301.

bear different effective rates of tax according to the structure of production, it is difficult to set a rate on imports which will place the two
types of output on an equal competitive basis. Businessmen have
frequently criticized the German tax for treating imports too leniently
as well as for failing to remove completely the tax burden from exports.

Needless to say, if pyramiding is a problem with a manufacturers'
sales tax, it will be an even greater one with a turnover tax.

VALUE-ADDED TAX: A FISCAL INNOVATION IN MICHIGAN AND
FRANCE. A relative newcomer to the fiscal scene, introduced in
Michigan in 1953 and in France in 1954, is the so-called net value-
added tax. This levy is so new that there is still some doubt about
whether it falls in the sales, or in the income, tax family—the Bureau
of the Census, indeed, prefers to place the Michigan tax in the
anomalous category entitled "other."

Value added for a given business is defined as its gross receipts
from sales minus all expenditures for goods and services purchased
from other business firms. In this way the productive value created
by each business enterprise is measured, and these figures may then be
summed for the entire economic system to obtain a measure of total
production from which all double and triple counting is absent. Consider, for example, some raw cotton which is sold by the farmer for
$150 to a shirt manufacturer, who in turn sells the shirts to a retailer
for $350. If the shirts are bought by consumers for $400, this figure
measures the total value of output in our illustration. Of this amount,
the value added is $150 by the farmer, $200 by the manufacturer, and
$50 by the retailer.[11] Total sales on which a turnover tax would be
based, on the other hand, are $900.

If the private sector of an economy is neither investing nor disinvesting, total value added by all business enterprises, aggregate sales
of final output, and total personal and corporate incomes must all be
equal. In this special case identical bases would be employed by a
value-added tax, a general retail sales tax, and an income tax which
allowed neither nonbusiness deductions nor personal exemptions. In
a growing private sector, however, retail sales of consumer goods and
services are less than total incomes (by the amount of net investment),
and a value-added tax, according to the wishes of those legislating it,
may be based upon either aggregate. On the one hand, if each business is permitted to include capital equipment in its deductions of
purchases from other firms, the base of the value-added tax will equal
total retail sales. If, on the other hand, investment expenditures are

---

[11] These figures ignore, for simplicity, the fact that the manufacture and sale of
the shirts would require purchases from other business enterprises not included in
the illustration.

not deductible but depreciation allowances are, and if the net change in the level of inventories is included in the tax base, total value added and total incomes will be identical. The value-added levy, then, is a versatile one, being able by a suitable change of costume to seek entrance into either the income or the retail sales tax household.[12]

The income variant, however, differs in one important respect from other income taxes. A flat-rate general income tax collected at the source will be automatically deducted by business firms from their payments of wages, salaries, interest, and rents. Its initial incidence, in other words, is upon all income receivers in proportion to the amounts of income received. A value-added tax, on the other hand, must be paid by each business without benefit of reductions in contractual income payments to employees, landlords, and bondholders. Its initial incidence is entirely upon profits, and in this respect it is similar to any sales tax. Ultimately, by means of business adjustments to be discussed in detail below, the incidence will be spread to other income receivers in a typical sales-tax pattern. Regardless of whether it employs total sales or total income as its base, then, a value-added tax belongs in the sales tax family.

The French and Michigan value-added taxes, although not conceptually pure, fall basically in the consumption and income variants respectively. The French levy, which employs a relatively high rate (20 per cent) and raises a significant portion of total tax revenues, does not apply to all stages of production, exempts a number of products completely, and permits the deduction by taxable firms of some, but not all, capital equipment acquired from other businesses. The Michigan tax, on the other hand, allows depreciation to be deducted but not purchases of assets with a useful lifetime greater than one year. With a basic rate of less than ¾ per cent, the Michigan value-added tax raised 8 per cent of state tax receipts in fiscal 1956. Taxpayer compliance costs are reportedly low, and at less than 1 per cent of receipts state administrative expenses are slightly lower than those for a general sales tax.[13] Finally, a value-added tax, unlike a turnover tax, does not favor integrated businesses.

BRITISH PURCHASE TAX. This levy, a single-stage, wholesale tax on luxury and semiluxury products, eschews one trait which is said

---

[12] Cf. Carl S. Shoup, "Theory and Background of the Value-Added Tax," *Proceedings of the 1955 National Tax Association Conference*, pp. 6-19. In the above discussion we have assumed either a closed economy or one in which exports of goods and services exactly equal imports and that none of the taxes discussed is imposed on either government output or the incomes generated by governmental activities.

[13] See C. W. Lock, D. J. Rau, and H. D. Hamilton, "The Michigan Value-Added Tax," *National Tax Journal*, VIII (Dec., 1955), 357-71.

to endear sales taxes to politicians if not to consumers and producers. Unlike most of its brothers and sisters the purchase tax is conspicuously exposed to the glare of public attention. Even when initiated in 1940 it featured rates of 16⅔ and 33⅓ per cent which, although not unknown elsewhere in the sales taxation field, are well within the select, upper rate brackets. By 1943, however, the top rate had reached 100 per cent, and in the early postwar period when Britain was facing what Keynes called "a financial Dunkirk" the tax employed rates, graduated upward according to the dispensable or luxurious qualities of the goods taxed, that began at 33⅓ per cent and ended at 125 per cent. This represented its zenith, a position from which it has since retreated, although by no means precipitously. In spite of several reductions its rates still went as high as 60 per cent in 1959. Because of the limited scope of its field of application, however, the tax has never yielded as much as 10 per cent of total British tax revenues.

Any set of excises designed to reach only luxury and semiluxury items faces the difficult problem of distinguishing these from necessities. A simple commodity classification will not do because although a coat of some kind, for example, is essential (certainly in England) it need not be made of high-quality tweed or of mink or sable. Tax categories, then, must cut across commodity lines. No matter how carefully this is done, however, there is no escaping the fact, arising from different personal tastes, that what appears as a luxury to one individual will be regarded as an absolute necessity to another. Arbitrary distinctions are therefore inevitable. The reader may test his own tastes against the following much abbreviated list of commodity classifications under the purchase tax in 1954:

1. Exempt from taxation were food, books, cooking appliances, toilet paper, and school satchels.
2. Taxable at 25 per cent were sewing machines, soap, spoons, knives and forks, umbrellas, clocks and watches not made of precious metals, and bicycles.
3. Taxable at 50 per cent were refrigerators, washing machines, vacuum cleaners, clocks and watches of precious metal, radios and television sets, wallets and purses, cameras, and motor cars.
4. Taxable at 75 per cent were fur skins, perfume, cosmetics, picture postcards, and pictorial calendars.

This or any other selective excise list is bound to provide ample opportunity for taxpayer complaints against "discriminatory taxation." One look at any of the excise tax hearings before Congress in this country will provide a graphic illustration of this point.

As in the case of any commodity tax imposed prior to retail sale, definition of the appropriate wholesale price to which purchase tax rates should be applied is by no means a simple matter. In the early years of the tax the prices charged by wholesalers on sales to retailers in ordinary quantities were taken as the standard to which other prices were to be adjusted. Often, of course, because of quantity discounts on large lots of goods, or because of the undertaking by the retailer of wholesaling functions, or the elimination of some distribution costs through direct sales by manufacturers to retailers, the actual sales price to the retailer was lower than the standard price, and in these cases the former was "uplifted" to obtain the taxable price. This system, although strongly supported by small retailers and wholesalers, was criticized by manufacturers and large retailers on two grounds: (1) the uplift percentages were arbitrary, and (2) they tended to offset economies of improved distribution methods by basing the tax burden on traditional procedures.[14] In response to these criticisms some changes were made in 1955, but the tax still does not completely distinguish between wholesale prices which are low because of strong buying power on the part of the retailer and prices which reflect real economies of distribution.

Two final problems, although present for any selective excise tax, are particularly troublesome because of the very high purchase tax rates. In the first place, anticipations of rate increases are bound to stimulate immediate buying by both consumers and retailers in order to avoid later price rises, while expected rate reductions will have the opposite effect. Even in England, where tax changes are announced without warning by the government, these effects have caused considerable concern.[15] Needless to say, they are likely to be much greater in this country, where any alteration in the tax laws must be preceded by prolonged Congressional hearings which give maximum publicity to the projected changes and allow buyers much time in which to act on their expectations.

The second problem arose, paradoxically, from the fact that the purchase tax was in some cases too successful in shifting domestic demand away from the taxed products. This result occurred when, because of the existence of relatively close substitutes which were free of tax, demand for the taxed goods was highly sensitive to price increases. The tax then induced a sharp fall in domestic sales and tended to push the products into the export trade as the government wished. The trouble was, however, that in some cases home consump-

[14] Cf. John F. Due, "The British Purchase Tax," *Canadian Tax Journal,* III (March-April, 1955), 97-104.

[15] *Ibid.,* pp. 104-8.

tion fell by more than exports could be expanded, and the industry was forced to contract to a less efficient level of production which threatened its ability to compete successfully abroad. In 1952 this problem was met by making higher priced products taxable not on their full sales price but only on the amount by which it exceeded a given deduction, or D-level. In this way sudden large increases in tax liability were avoided. A D-level of $100 together with a 50 per cent tax rate, for example, would make the tax $10 on a commodity selling for $120 as compared to $60 when the full wholesale price is taxable. In either case a slightly less luxurious item worth $90 would be tax-free. Since D-levels were generally set below pre-1952 exemption levels, effective tax rates on necessities were raised at the same time that rates on luxuries and semiluxuries were lowered. Both changes tended to strengthen domestic demand for higher-priced products.

RETAIL SALES TAXATION IN THE UNITED STATES. Retail sales taxes in this country are neither so broad nor so restricted as their name would suggest. In the first place, considerable difficulty has been encountered in confining the tax base to sales to final consumers. Although all states exempt the sale of products which are to be resold, some, like California and Illinois, exclude in addition only producer goods which become ingredients in or component parts of other products, thereby making taxable all sales of machinery and equipment by retailers to other businessmen. Other states, such as Michigan and Ohio, exempt assets used directly in further production but not those used by the administrative or sales departments of manufacturing firms. The result is that a significant part of the sales tax base is typically made up of business equipment and supplies. On the other hand, state sales taxes do not begin to cover all sales to final consumers. The list of exemptions and exclusions is a long one, and only the most important items will be noted here.[16]

The tax base is ordinarily confined to the sale of tangible personal property. All professional services and all rentals of houses and apartments are exempt. Many transactions, of course, such as the installation or repairs of consumer durables, involve both services and tangible property. A common practice is to exempt the services if the amounts collected for them are stated separately in the bill to the consumer.

As a matter of administrative convenience casual and isolated sales are frequently not taxable. These may involve sales by a retailer of property not related to his regular business or occasional sales by

[16] For a more extensive treatment see Clinton V. Oster, *State Retail Sales Taxation* (Columbus: Ohio State Univ. Bureau of Business Research, 1957), chaps. v and vi.

people not ordinarily in the selling business. The dividing lines will necessarily be arbitrary.

Nine states exempt food although this one item may constitute 25 per cent or more of the potential tax base,[17] and its exclusion increases administrative and compliance problems for grocery stores selling nonfood items. Not only is it considerably simpler for a businessman to apply the tax to his total gross receipts rather than to keep the detailed records of different transactions necessitated by a partial tax, but opportunities for tax evasion are also opened up whenever exemptions are allowed, and these must be carefully checked by the tax authorities. Nevertheless, the food exemption is likely to have wide popular support since its main purpose is to reduce the burden of the tax on the lowest income groups and on large families. A number of empirical studies of sales tax burdens, for example, indicate that, although a general retail tax tends to be regressive over a wide income range, a levy which exempts food is roughly proportional except in the lowest and highest income groups.[18] As we shall see below, however, the incidence assumptions upon which these studies are based are open to rather serious question.

Because of the constitutional doctrine of federal immunity from taxation,[19] no state sales tax that is legally imposed upon the purchaser can be collected on sales to the federal government. Designation of the levy as a "privilege tax" on the retailer, however, is sufficient to remove this prohibition even though nominal alterations of this sort are not likely to change the incidence and effects of the tax. Nor does the Supreme Court's interpretation of the immunity doctrine seek to go beyond direct sales to the federal government. In 1941, for example, an Alabama sales tax levied on sales to a government contractor was upheld even though the contractor was working on a cost-plus-a-fixed-fee basis and the tax law required the seller to collect the tax from the purchaser by increasing his sales price.[20] State governments may, of course, as is done in California and Illinois, tax sales to themselves and to their political subdivisions. For those who believe that the burden of a sales tax is borne by the purchasers, such a policy appears to involve a wasteful transfer of money from one pocket to another. The cost to the government of doing this, however, is likely to be insignificant as compared to the administrative and compliance costs of an additional exemption in the tax law. Furthermore, if a significant part of the burden of the tax falls on groups

[17] *Ibid.,* p. 124.
[18] For a convenient summary of these see Oster, *op. cit.,* pp. 36-40.
[19] See the discussion of government bond interest in chap. 6.
[20] *Alabama* v. *King and Boozer,* 314 U.S. 1.

other than consumers, there is no case for exemption of sales to any level of government.

Charitable, religious, and educational institutions are frequently exempted from sales taxes as a matter of public policy. In Ohio, for example, sales to such organizations are tax-free, but sales made by them are taxable unless such transactions are casual or isolated. This policy, of course, rests squarely on the assumption that consumers pay the sales tax. If, instead, the burden rests upon the factors of production in the taxed industry, the policy should be exactly reversed in order to achieve the desired results. In addition, either type of exemption may be criticized on the ground that it constitutes a hidden subsidy not subject to periodic review by the legislature as to its desirability relative to other budget alternatives.

Finally, the existence of interstate sales gives rise to a number of gaps in the retail sales tax structure. In general, exports have not been taxed but imports have been subject to varying degrees of taxability as the United States Supreme Court has changed its interpretation of the commerce clause in the Constitution. There is no question that a separate import duty on goods coming from other states is unconstitutional.[21] A more difficult problem, however, concerns the extent to which such transactions may be subjected to the same tax burdens as intrastate sales. At one time the Supreme Court held that a state could not tax the first sale of an imported product in its original package,[22] but this rule has gradually been broadened over time to permit nondiscriminatory taxation of imported commodities if the seller, by means of offices or agents within the taxing state, comes under its jurisdiction and if the transfer of goods to the purchaser occurs within the state.[23] In the meantime a number of sales tax states enacted use taxes, levied at the same rate and on the same commodities as the sales tax but based on use of the item within the state rather than on its sale. Since commodities which had already been subject to the sales tax were exempt from the use tax, the two levies together provided a theoretically perfect coverage of both interstate and intrastate sales. Purchases made outside the state and brought into it by the buyer or orders of goods by mail from companies not maintaining offices or agents in the taxing state, for example, would escape the sales tax but be subject to the use tax. In practice, of course, many transactions of this sort escape both taxes because the consumers do

[21] *Constitution of the United States of America,* Art. I, Sec. 10, and *Ward* v. *Maryland,* 12 Wall. 418.

[22] *Brown* v. *Maryland,* 12 Wheat 419 (1827), *Standard Oil* v. *Graves,* 249 U.S. 389 (1919), and *Phipps* v. *Cleveland Refining Co.,* 261 U.S. 449 (1923).

[23] Oster, *op. cit.,* pp. 119-21.

not report them, and there is no easy way for the state to check up on them. Products for which legal registration is required, such as automobiles, however, may readily be assessed with a use tax.

A potential drawback of any retail sales tax is a high level of administrative costs because of the large number of businesses with which the taxing authority must deal. A 1955 study by the Research Division of the Ohio Department of Taxation showed an average cost for twelve states equal to 1.5 per cent of sales tax revenues, with individual states ranging from less than 1 per cent to 2 per cent.[24] These costs do not appear to be excessive. It was also noted in the survey that states with higher cost ratios tended to have greater numbers of field examiners and auditors in relation to the total amount of revenue collected. The addition of administrative personnel is a profitable operation so long as the increased revenues obtained thereby exceed the amount of salaries paid even though the cost ratio rises as a result. A low cost ratio, in other words, does not necessarily indicate a highly efficient administrative structure, nor does a high ratio imply a waste of resources.

Considerably less evidence exists as to the level of taxpayer compliance costs, but what there is places them between 2 and 6 per cent of taxes paid, with great variability among individual taxpayers.[25] To compensate for these expenses and also to encourage prompt payment of tax bills a number of states allow retailers discounts on the total amount due ranging from 2 to 5 per cent.

Effects on Prices and Money Incomes

The doctrine that the burden of sales taxation rests upon the consumer has lived a long and vigorous life. To the layman its plausibility is greatly enhanced by the common practice among sellers of quoting a price and then adding on the tax in order to obtain the final sales price. In addition, many legislatures place the legal incidence of the tax on the consumer and impose fines on any retailer who advertizes that he absorbs the tax burden himself.[26] Yet it must be clear that the wording of the law cannot by itself control the economic effects of the tax, nor does a separate listing of the tax imply that the sales price is higher than it otherwise would have been by that amount.

The consumer-burden doctrine does not, of course, rest upon foundations as nebulous as these. A thorough discussion of it would

[24] James H. Maloon and Clinton V. Oster, "State Sales Tax Administration Costs," *National Tax Journal,* X (Sept., 1957), 228-35.

[25] *Ibid.,* p. 234.

[26] Cf. Oster, *op. cit.,* pp. 95-97.

take us through the full range of economic value and price theory, but we need not attempt so ambitious a program here. Instead we shall first outline the main features of the traditional analysis of a single-commodity excise tax on a competitive industry, consider the modern criticisms of this theory, and then finish with a discussion of markets dominated by a few large buyers or sellers.

SELECTIVE EXCISE TAX ON A COMPETITIVE INDUSTRY. In an industry consisting of many small sellers handling a single, homogeneous product—in other words, where there are no brand names and the items sold by any one business are indistinguishable from those of any other—each firm will accept the market price as a given factor over which it has no control and adjust its scale of operations to it. No firm is large enough to raise the level of that price by withholding part of its own output, and each is well aware that it cannot simply set a higher price itself without losing most or all of its business since consumers have no reason to prefer its output to that of any other firm. Under these circumstances all sellers must accept the reduction in profits brought about by a new tax on their product as a loss that cannot, because of strong competition from their rivals, be recouped by marking up selling prices. On the other hand, they can and will adjust their level of operations to the new situation. To some extent each will find it profitable to cut back output, and some firms, attracted by the relatively higher profits now prevailing in other industries, may leave the taxed field entirely. On both counts, then, sales of the taxed product fall back in volume and, demand conditions remaining the same, its market price will rise. What no firm acting by itself could do the entire industry, each member firm acting simultaneously but independently, is able to accomplish.

This whole process will take a certain amount of time—longer if firms have to contract in size or leave the industry before profits there are restored to a level competitive with other industries; shorter if the adjustment process, as it will be in a growing industry, is simply a matter of fewer new firms entering and less rapid expansion by existing firms. The amount of time involved in all this, however, is less important for our present purposes than the extent to which the price of the taxed product finally increases. Although it appears to be widely believed that the price will rise by the exact amount of the tax, such a result would occur only if business costs remained constant as output in the taxed industry was contracted. If, as appears more likely, the tax reduces costs, or if the industry dispenses with its least efficient resources as it reduces output, the price will rise by less than the full amount of the tax, the extent of the increase depending upon how strongly consumers are attached to the taxed product.[27]

We note, then, that a selective excise tax on a competitive industry will lead to some increase in the market price of the product sold and that this result is brought about by a movement of resources out of the taxed field into other industries. Traditional incidence theorists concluded from this that the burden of the tax rested entirely on the consumer of the taxed product whenever its price rose by the full amount of the tax; when it rose by less, on the other hand, part of the burden was imposed on the owners of resources specialized to the taxed industry. This last result rested on the following arguments:

1. Although the reduction in output within the taxed industry implies a lower demand for the services of all resources located there, the non-specialized ones could avoid a fall in their money incomes by moving to other industries. In their case the tax-induced fall in the demand for their services would be matched by a reduction in supply sufficient to maintain incomes at their pretax levels.

2. Specialized resources, on the other hand, being unable to earn nearly as much in other industries (and in some cases being unable to earn anything at all), would have to accept lower money incomes or withdraw their services entirely from productive activity. The induced withdrawal, however, could not be large enough to prevent a fall in money incomes. In the first place, workers would find leisure more attractive only as their money incomes fell, and the increased taking of leisure, therefore, could only cushion the tax-induced fall in money incomes. Furthermore, some, and perhaps even most, workers would try to work harder as their incomes fell. In the short run, then, there might well be no reduction in the supply of specialized labor services to offset the income-lowering effects of the tax-induced fall in demand for those services. Over the longer period, however, incomes would gradually recover as fewer people trained themselves for positions in the taxed area. Similar adjustments would occur in the money incomes of owners of specialized assets the production of which may be contracted. Land, however, is not such an asset since its supply is fixed.

Critics of traditional incidence theory have concentrated upon two aspects of the above line of reasoning: (*a*) the assumption of competitive pricing throughout the taxed industry, a restriction which has become increasingly unrealistic with the growth of labor unions and giant corporations; and (*b*) the neglect of the effects on the rest of the economic system of the shift of resources out of the taxed industry.

[27] The stronger their attachment—i.e., the more inelastic the demand—the more will the price rise and the closer, therefore, will it come to increasing by the full amount of the tax.

The first criticism, which accepts the validity of traditional theory as far as it goes but argues that it applies to only a very small part of the real world, will be examined in a later section. The second, however, is even more serious since it argues that traditional theory is incomplete even for an economic system in which all markets are perfectly competitive. Let us look at this contention in more detail.

The nature of the second criticism may be seen most clearly in the case of an excise tax on a constant-cost industry which, as a result, will lose resources and reduce output until the price of its product rises by the full amount of the tax. How realistic is it to say that the incidence of the tax rests entirely upon the consumer? As the tax-induced shift of resources takes place, factor prices will be lowered on the hiring markets toward which the different resources are redirected. In these areas increased competition for employment results, and business firms operating there will be induced to hire more resource services, expand their own output, and offer it to consumers at lower prices. If, in addition, demand for the taxed product is inelastic —that is, if consumers react to the tax-induced price rise by increasing the amount of money they spend on that product—then consumers are very likely to reduce their expenditures on a number of nontaxed items. In these industries prices, outputs, and the money incomes of factors employed all fall, and to some extent resources will shift to other areas and, by increased competition for jobs there, bring about lower money incomes to resource owners, together with lower market prices and increased real output.

The effects on incomes and prices of a single-commodity excise tax imposed in a competitive economic system may be summarized as follows:

1. The price of the taxed product rises and the prices of some, but not necessarily all, other products fall.

2. The money incomes of three groups of resource owners are reduced, the total reduction being equal to the yield of the tax. The three groups are owners of resources employed in the taxed industry, owners of resources producing goods and services on which consumers economize in order to offset increased money expenditures for the taxed product, and owners of resources which, because of the nature of their productive services, are competitive with either of the first two groups.[28] Accompanying these financial changes, of course, is an alteration in the composition of final output, consumers obtaining less of the taxed product but more of a number of other goods and services. Consumers who are strongly attached to the taxed product will suffer an important reduction in their real stand-

---

[28] For a fuller discussion of these developments see Earl R. Rolph, *The Theory of Fiscal Economics* (Berkeley: Univ. of California Press, 1954), pp. 132-42

ard of living; other consumers, however, will be benefited by the increased supply of certain nontaxed products. Nevertheless, since economists are generally agreed that the composition of output is ideal from an economic point of view in a perfectly competitive world, the excise tax must impose a net burden on consumers as a group. To this extent traditional theory, although incomplete in its scope, did contain an element of truth. On the other hand, it overlooked completely the fact that the tax would reduce money incomes of a much wider group of resource owners than those specialized to the taxed industry and that these income losses would occur regardless of the extent to which the tax pushed up the price of the taxed product. These effects form an important part of the incidence of any excise tax.

BROADLY BASED SALES TAXES IN A COMPETITIVE WORLD. The preceding analysis may readily be generalized from single- to multi-commodity excise taxes. As the size of the taxed area increases, the tax-induced shift of resources is channeled toward a more and more restricted set of industries. As this happens the reductions in product prices become deeper and more concentrated while the price increases on taxed output become smaller and more spread out. In the extreme case of a perfectly general sales tax, no resource shift at all occurs since there is no tax-free area to which it may be directed. Under these circumstances prices do not rise at all and consumers bear no real burden. Output remains unchanged both in total amount and in composition, and the incidence of the tax consists entirely of a proportionate reduction in the money incomes of owners of resources that are actively employed in production.[29]

As we have already noted, sales taxes in practice do not begin to attain the scope of a perfectly general tax. One less broadly based levy that is of considerable economic interest is a tax on the sale of all consumer goods and services. Since newly produced capital goods are excluded from its base, such a tax will induce a shift of resources from consumption to investment, and the rate of economic growth will be accelerated.[30] Money incomes received by workers and by the owners of capital assets will fall because of increased competition for employment resulting from the release of resources by the taxed industries, and the prices of capital assets will fall as consumer goods and services become more expensive. Since both the prices and earnings of investment goods fall, rates of return tend to be maintained and the tax is capitalized to some extent.[31] Consumers are burdened in the short run

[29] *Ibid.,* pp. 126-32.

[30] The reader is reminded that in a competitive economic system the unemployment caused by the imposition of the sales tax will be of only short duration.

[31] For a fuller discussion of these effects see J. A. Stockfisch, "The Capitalization and Investment Aspects of Excise Taxes Under Competition," *American Economic Review,* XLIV (June, 1954), 287-300.

because of the reduced availability of consumer goods and services, but in the more distant future they may look forward to a more productive economy capable of a greater consumption output than would have been attainable in the absence of the sales tax.

SALES TAXES IN NONCOMPETITIVE MARKETS. We turn now to an economic system in which product markets are frequently dominated by a few large sellers and various kinds of productive resources are sold either by large business firms or by powerful labor unions, with varying powers to control entry by other firms or other workers in order to maintain their own incomes at a high level. Such a world differs from the competitive one we have just been considering in two important respects: (*a*) in noncompetitive markets business firms do not regard selling prices as beyond their control but set them according to their own assessment of the state of consumer demand and the reactions which their main rivals may be expected to have to any price change, and (*b*) a noncompetitive pricing system does not adjust automatically so as to maintain full employment. Since incidence analysis is concerned only with the effects of a tax at a given level of employment, we must be careful to avoid the analysis of fiscal changes which, like the imposition of a new tax in an environment of price stability, threaten to lower the existing level of employment.

Let us suppose, for simplicity, that a general sales tax is to replace a set of flat-sum poll taxes in such a way that government revenues are not changed by the tax shift. Removal of the poll taxes will increase every person's income by the same amount, and the question before us concerns the effects of the new sales tax on both money incomes and prices. In order to sharpen the contrast with a perfectly competitive economic system let us assume that all sellers, as soon as the tax change is announced, increase prices by the full amount of the new sales tax.[32] At this point consumers find themselves facing both a higher price level and the prospect of lower poll tax payments in the future. Furthermore, this future tax relief will increase their buying power by the same amount that the higher price level has reduced it. The difficulty, however, is that the higher prices are here now but the tax relief is not.[33] Under these circumstances consumers may wait

[32] In reality, of course, some, and perhaps many, markets will be sufficiently competitive to preclude price increases of this size. The possibility of diverse behavior, however, does not alter the conclusions to be reached in the text.

[33] Both sales and poll taxes may, for example, be collected monthly. The tax shift will then be made at the beginning of the month, and at the end of it the government will collect sales taxes from businessmen rather than poll taxes from consumers. The increment in consumer buying power, therefore, occurs at the end of the month, but prices rise at the beginning of it.

until the additional income is actually received before they increase their money spending, or they may increase it immediately in anticipation of the future tax relief, or they may adopt some intermediate course.

Suppose, first, that consumers react to the tax shift by immediately increasing their money expenditures, and further that the increase is sufficient to buy, at the new higher price level, the same amount of output as was purchased when the poll tax was in existence. Under the sales tax, then, national product and national income are higher in money terms but unchanged in real terms. The sole effect of the tax shift, apparently, has been to raise prices, and it is tempting to conclude that the incidence of the sales tax rests upon consumers.

The straightforward conclusion that it is the sales tax that causes the higher price level, however, oversimplifies considerably a rather complex situation. In order to increase their expenditures immediately consumers will either have to reduce the level of their money balances, sell assets, or borrow money from others. Their actions, of course, are based on the expectation of higher disposable incomes in the future as a result of lower poll taxes. These anticipations, however, provide no immediate funds to finance higher current expenditures, and even when the tax relief is actually received it will be needed to maintain living standards in the following period and will not be available either to replenish money balances or to pay back loans. In other words, a monetary expansion in the form of either an expanded money supply or more rapid use of the existing supply must occur and continue in existence as long as the sales tax is in effect. We are dealing, then, with a situation in which consumers hold excess money balances and unused borrowing power which they are quite prepared to use should prices begin to rise. In this explosive monetary environment any number of developments may set off a price inflation. The igniting factor may be a widespread wage increase obtained by organized labor, or a desire on the part of the leading firms of a strategically placed industry for more profits to finance large-scale capital expenditures, or simply a belief on the part of consumers that prices are likely to rise in the future. Under these conditions, then, the sales tax is not a necessary condition for the occurrence of a price increase.

Suppose now, to take the opposite case, that when the sales tax is imposed and all sellers increase prices by the full amount of the tax, consumers refuse to increase their money spending at all. They are not, in other words, willing to reduce their money holdings or go into debt in order to maintain the same real standard of living as they enjoyed before the price rise. The effect of this behavior, of course, will be a fall in both output and employment. The continued existence of a significant amount of unemployment, however, can scarcely be regarded as a stable situation in the modern world. On the one hand, to counteract it the government may step into the breach by easing monetary controls, lowering taxes, or increasing expenditures. In this case the higher price level which followed the imposition of the sales tax is likely to continue in existence, and here again we find monetary expansion as a very necessary element in the whole picture. On the other hand, in the absence of monetary expansion on the part of either the government or private groups, it is highly probable that gradually over time the increased competition for jobs will so lower factor incomes—inducing employers to rehire workers, put idle equipment back to work, and offer their products at lower prices—that the pre-sales-tax price and output levels will, on the average, be restored. In such an eventuality we have basically the same incidence pattern as for a perfectly competitive world. In the place of a proportionate reduction in all factor incomes, however, we are likely to find some resource owners who, because of their protected positions and control over competition, are able to escape any loss of income and others, less fortunate, who suffer more than proportionate reductions. In the aggregate, however, the income reductions induced by the tax will be the same as in the perfectly competitive economy. It is interesting to note that this result can occur regardless of how noncompetitive product markets happen to be.

Although the imposition of a selective excise or general sales tax may well be followed by an increase in the general price level, the tax itself is neither a necessary nor a sufficient condition for the price rise. The willingness and ability of the economic system to initiate and support a monetary expansion, on the other hand, is a necessary condition and hence should be regarded as the primary causal factor. Commodity taxation, in other words, does not burden consumers by pushing up the average price level. It may, of course, alter the price structure and the composition of final output, but since in the real world that composition is not likely to be ideal in the economic sense, selective sales taxes may actually improve consumer welfare.[34] Under these circumstances the traditional consumer-burden doctrine cannot be accepted as an adequate description of the incidence of sales taxes. Like any other tax, sales taxes reduce personal money incomes by the full amount of their yield to the government. The individuals who suffer these burdens are primarily those owning resources employed in the taxed industries, or resources which compete for employment with those resources. In addition, if consumers are induced to spend

[34] See the discussion below, pp. 298-300.

more for the taxed commodities than they did before the taxes were imposed, they will necessarily spend less on certain other items, and producers of these will consequently suffer losses of income. The one difference between a competitive and a noncompetitive world lies in the resource reallocating effects of selective excises. In a perfectly competitive economy the result must be a net burden on consumers as a group; under other economic conditions, however, resource allocation may actually be improved.

The reader may well wonder what practical value all this rather esoteric argument about incidence can possibly have. He will have noted that we have stressed not the actual sequence of events following the enactment of a new sales tax—i.e., whether it is more likely that higher prices will be supported by a monetary expansion or that a downward adjustment in factor incomes will permit prices to fall back to their pretax levels—but rather the proper interpretation of that sequence, whatever it may be. Is it not sufficient for the practical man of affairs to know something about the sequence (which will be discussed in more detail below in the chapters on fiscal policy) and to leave the intricate peregrinations of incidence theory to the specialist? Before he slips into this comfortable attitude, however, let him reflect on the implications which a rejection of the traditional consumer-burden doctrine carries with it:

1. The case for allowing the consumer to deduct sales taxes in computing his taxable income under the personal income tax collapses completely.

2. Similarly bereft of its basic rationale is the widespread support, to be discussed in the next chapter, of the gasoline tax as a "special benefits" levy imposed in order to collect money for highways from the groups who benefit from highway services.

3. Special treatment of sales to governmental agencies and to charitable and educational institutions need no longer clutter up the sales tax law.

4. The case for eliminating food from the sales tax base in order to lessen the regressiveness of the tax is seriously weakened, especially if owners of resources employed in the food industry are more strongly concentrated in the lower income groups than are those in other industries.

In addition, such effects on the supply of labor and on aggregate consumption and investment as are attributed to sales and excise taxes —and these are all important considerations whenever there is a question of raising or lowering taxes or of changing the tax structure— will depend to a considerable extent on the incidence theories held by the observer. Let us now turn to a brief consideration of these matters.

Effects on Incentives to Work

That sales taxation inhibits work incentives less than income taxation is a widely accepted fiscal generalization. Two lines of argument, both based on the traditional theory that the incidence of commodity taxation rests upon the consumer, support this conclusion. In the first place, it is pointed out that the consumer may avoid a sales tax, but not an income tax, by saving part of his income. Under the sales tax, therefore, he may continue to work in order to save, whereas an income tax, by increasing the amount of effort that he has to put forth in order either to spend or to save, may induce him to take more leisure time. The second argument is that, although a 10 per cent increase in prices reduces a person's real income to exactly the same extent as a 10 per cent reduction in his money income, many people may be less aware of price changes than they are of direct reductions in their incomes as a result of the increased withholding of income taxes. In a 1954 study of consumer reactions to excise tax reductions, for example, Robert Ferber concluded that individual awareness of tax or price changes was quite limited.[35]

The strength of these two arguments should not be overrated. In the first place, the advantages, as far as work incentives are concerned, of a tax that raises prices over one that lowers incomes are unequivocal only when higher taxation is widely believed to be temporary. Given this belief, the consumer may well wish to shift some of his consumption from the present, when the cost (in terms of the amount of effort required to obtain it) is relatively high, to the future, when the cost is expected to be lower. Under an income tax this shift can be accomplished only by working less hard now and harder in the future; under the sales tax, however, the consumer may simply save now and spend later while keeping his working hours unchanged. For each consumer who acts in this way the sales tax has no effect on work incentives, while the income tax exerts a disincentive influence. If each tax is expected to be long-lived, however, the inducement to reduce consumption now in order to increase it later is significantly weakened and for many people may be completely eliminated.

If we turn from traditional incidence doctrine to the alternative theory that sales taxation imposes its burdens by making individual money incomes lower than they otherwise would be, we find even less difference between the two taxes as far as their effects on the supply of labor are concerned. Each tax exerts both an incentive and a disincen-

---

[35] Robert Ferber, "How Aware are Consumers of Excise Tax Changes?" *National Tax Journal,* VII (Dec., 1954), 358.

tive influence—the former by reducing the taxpayer's disposable income and the latter by making less attractive the terms on which he can add to that income by working harder—and whatever differential effects on the supply of labor these influences have must stem from the fact that they reach different groups of people. An income tax, for example, can be imposed upon the income received by retired people in the form of pensions and annuities; a sales tax, on the other hand, is powerless to lower contractual incomes of this sort. Similarly, a selective excise and a given increase in the bottom bracket rate of the personal income tax could not be expected to affect each person's money income in exactly the same way. Differences of this kind may in turn lead to differential effects on work incentives. There is, however, no presumption that sales taxation will either favor or impair work incentives as compared with income taxation; only empirical evidence, derived specifically for the two taxes being considered, can resolve the issue.

We see, then, that a settling of the incidence problem is an important first step in determining the effects of sales taxation on incentives to work. On the basis of the classical, consumer-burden theory, commodity taxes may be judged more favorable to incentives than income taxes, particularly if they are to be employed only on a temporary basis. According to the factor-burden theory of incidence, on the other hand, the two types of taxation affect incentives in exactly the same way, and hence there are no theoretical grounds for choosing between them.

Effects on Consumption and Investment

Traditional theory, by placing the incidence of a sales tax on the consumer, implied, of course, that the direct effects of the tax were confined to consumption. Fewer consumer goods and services would be bought as a result of the tax, and if private investment were affected at all, it would be through the indirect path of a lowered consumption demand. Income taxation, on the other hand, unless confined entirely to the very lowest income groups would be expected to reduce both consumption and investment directly (and investment indirectly as well, as a result of reduced sales of consumer goods and services). Of two taxes imposing the same deflationary effect on private spending, then, the one belonging to the income family would be less favorable to investment than the one belonging to the sales family.

Once again we find that the factor-burden theory minimizes the differences between commodity and income taxation. With sales-tax incidence taking the form of reduced money incomes, private spending for either consumer or investment goods may be lowered by such a levy. Whether investment will be curtailed less than it would be by an income tax will be a matter entirely of whose incomes are lowered by the two taxes. According to this view there is no presumption that commodity taxation will curtail private capital formation less than will income taxation. As in the case of work incentives the issue must be settled for each specific pair of taxes on the basis of empirical evidence.

Effects on Economic Welfare

Until quite recent times selective sales taxes have been under a long-standing indictment that they impose upon consumers an "excess burden" from which both poll and income taxes are free. The discussion of this issue has been carried out in highly technical and abstract terms, but the basic ideas around which it has revolved are relatively straightforward and will be presented here without the theoretical refinements necessary to satisfy the specialist. We shall consider first the classical excess burden doctrine itself and then turn to modern extensions and criticisms of it.

One of the basic problems in economics is the allocation of scarce resources among a number of alternative uses. In order to simplify the argument, let us concentrate upon two consumer goods which can be produced with the same resources. We assume, in other words, that more of commodity X can be obtained only by giving up some units of commodity Y. The problem now is to determine the optimum allocation of resources between the production of X and that of Y. Economists have long been agreed that this ideal economic state occurs when the rate at which X and Y may be substituted in production, as determined by the nature of the resources and productive techniques available to the society, is equal to the rate at which consumers may substitute X for Y in the market place, as determined by the conditions under which final sales take place. Let us see what this means in more specific terms.

Suppose that a certain group of productive assets, composed of land, labor, buildings, machinery, and other capital equipment, can be used to produce either 1,000 gallons of wine or 2,000 gallons of beer. In other words, the total costs involved in producing a given amount of wine, including wages to all suppliers of labor services, rent to landlords, interest to bondholders, and profits and dividends to resource owners, are exactly twice those required to turn out an equal amount of beer. In production, then, two units of beer may be substituted for one unit of wine. Suppose that in the market place, however, a gallon of wine, instead of being twice as expensive as a gallon

of beer, is four times as costly solely because of the presence of an excise tax on wine. Consumers, then, can obtain an additional unit of wine only by giving up four units of beer, and each, according to his individual tastes, will have adjusted his purchases of the two products to this situation.

In order to visualize this process of choice, consider a seller of beer who is exchanging it at the going market rate for wine for his own consumption. At first, let us assume, he is more than happy to trade four units of beer for one unit of wine. Having much beer and little wine, his own subjective evaluation of the two products places wine considerably higher relative to beer—say fifty of beer to one of wine—than does the market place where the ratio is four to one. Initially, then, he obtains large gains in satisfaction by trading beer for wine. As he continues to do so, however, the attractions of more wine begin to diminish at the same time that those of beer rise. His subjective evaluation ratio, in other words, moves in the direction of the market ratio. As soon as the two coincide it will no longer be worth his while to trade beer for wine, and he will have adjusted his holdings of the two products both to their relative market prices and to his own tastes. At this point he will be willing to give up slightly less than four units of beer in order to obtain yet another unit of wine. In production, however, an additional unit of wine can be obtained by giving up only two units of beer, and if such a substitution were offered to the consumer, he would gladly take it. In other words, it is technically possible for consumers to increase their satisfaction by buying more wine and less beer, but they are prevented from doing so by the relatively high price of wine brought about by the excise tax. With the tax in existence the allocation of resources between the production of wine and that of beer is not ideal. As the tax rate is lowered, wine will be substituted for beer, and consumers will increase the total satisfaction obtained from the two products. This process continue until the rates of substitution between wine and beer are same in production and in consumption—an equality which will, in the present instance, occur when the excise tax on wine has been completely removed. It is this kind of misallocation of resources that constitutes the classical excess burden of excise taxes.[36] In essence it arises because a selective excise opens up a gap between the rates, in consumption and in production, at which taxed output may be substituted for nontaxed output. No such gap was thought to occur if either income or poll taxes were imposed.

[36] For a more detailed treatment of the classical case see M. F. W. Joseph, "The Excess Burden of Indirect Taxation," *Review of Economic Studies,* VI (June, 1939), 226-31.

Two main criticisms have been made of the classical indictment of commodity taxation. The first simply expanded the classical argument by demonstrating that both income taxes and sales taxes distort the choice between work and leisure. Either kind of taxation, it was concluded, reduces economic welfare, and which is to be preferred to the other will depend upon the specific circumstances under which it is to be levied.[37] The second criticism goes farther by attacking the general validity of all excess burden theories and relegating them to the position of one special case among many possibilities. The traditional argument, it is pointed out, implicitly assumes that the rates of substitution between two commodities in consumption and in production are equal before an excise tax is levied on one of them, since only under these conditions must the commodity tax move the rate of substitution in consumption away from the rate of substitution in production (thereby reducing economic welfare). When the equality assumption is dropped, it is readily shown that an excise tax may move the two rates of substitution either closer together or farther apart. The tax, in other words, may just as well impose an "excess benefit" as an "excess burden."[38]

Suppose, to return to our example, that before any commodity tax is levied two units of beer can be substituted for one unit of wine in production but that, because of strong monopoly powers on the part of brewers, beer is sold to consumers at the same price per unit as wine. Under these conditions an excise tax on beer would, by increasing the price of beer relative to wine, move the rate of substitution between the two products in consumption still farther away from the rate of substitution in production. Economic welfare would consequently be reduced. An excise tax on wine, however, would move the prices of the two commodities more into line with the natural production ratio (two units of beer equal one of wine), and economic welfare would be improved. Since, in the real world, distortio individual choices among different commodities and between wor leisure are widespread, no general indictment of income or commod taxation on welfare grounds is valid. Either type of tax may lessen economic well-being, but either may also do exactly the reverse.

[37] H. P. Wald, "The Classical Indictment of Indirect Taxation," *Quarterly Journal of Economics,* LIX (Aug., 1945), 577-96; A. Henderson, "The Case for Indirect Taxation," *Economic Journal,* LVIII (Dec., 1948), 538-53; and I. M. D. Little, "Direct *versus* Indirect Taxes," *Economic Journal,* LXI (Sept., 1951), 577-84.

[38] E. R. Rolph and G. F. Break, "The Welfare Aspects of Excise Taxes," *Journal of Political Economy,* LVII (Feb., 1949), 46-54, reprinted in the American Economic Association's *Readings in the Economics of Taxation* (Homewood, Ill.: Richard D. Irwin, 1959). See also Milton Friedman, "The 'Welfare' Effects of an Income Tax and an Excise Tax," *Journal of Political Economy,* LX (Feb., 1952), 25-34.

14

Special Types of Commodity Taxes

Sales taxes, whether designed to include a wide list of commodities or only a few, were discussed in the last chapter. In general, the conclusions reached were that an excise tax has the following effects: (1) raises the price of the taxed commodity, (2) restricts the production of the taxed commodity, (3) lowers the prices of nontaxed or of lightly taxed commodities, (4) lowers the money incomes of people whose resources are used in the taxed industry and of similar resources in other industries. These results were found for the comparatively simple conditions of perfectly competitive pricing throughout the economy. They were also shown to hold, with modifications in detail, for other types of pricing arrangements.

A number of interpretative implications were noted in connection with these results. From the point of view of consumers, excise taxes may leave the composition of output unchanged in the special case of uniform taxes upon all products. In all other cases, the composition is altered more or less. As a result, some people gain and some lose. The yield of the tax to the government has as its counterpart a reduction in the money earnings of the factors of production. The distribution of the financial burden depends upon the relative changes in the prices paid for the services of the many kinds of manpower, equipment, buildings, land, and so on,

In this chapter, we continue to examine excise taxes, giving attention to some which are especially important features of actual revenue systems found in many countries. We have chosen taxes upon gasoline, tobacco, distilled spirits, and the set of taxes known as import duties.

Taxation of Tobacco, Liquor, and Gasoline

Tobacco, liquor, and gasoline illustrate commodities which can support heavy taxation. Cornflakes could not, both because the dollar value sold is small and because heavy taxation would largely eliminate that food from the breakfast table. People could and would eat other foods instead.

Tobacco and liquor, but not gasoline, are attractive from the point of view of governments because they are widely believed to cater to "sinful" habits. The taxation of sin appeals to the politician. Pressure groups composed of the sinful to counteract taxation are difficult to organize. The field has been left largely open, politically speaking, making the delicate task of separating people from their money relatively easy. No political movement exists to reduce, let alone repeal, the United States federal tax of $10.50 per proof gallon of distilled spirits or the $4.00 per 1000 federal excise tax on cigarettes. Morality may give the political excuse for heavy taxation of liquor and tobacco, but this does not explain why these taxes can be used to yield a revenue of $4.6 billion in 1958 for the federal government alone. Yields of such magnitudes are possible because both commodities are highly popular and because high prices do not reduce their consumption to an important degree.

The taxation of gasoline has developed for different reasons than those noted for liquor and tobacco. Popularly, gas taxes are looked upon as benefit taxes, as a kind of indirect charge for the use of highways and streets. So widespread and persuasive is this belief that all states impose a gasoline tax, typically about six cents per gallon, and earmark substantial portions of the revenue obtained, approximately $2.5 billion, to highway departments. This same philosophy has been adopted by the federal government; the federal tax of four cents per gallon provided an estimated $2.6 billion in revenue in 1960 and was earmarked to the Highway Trust Fund to finance highway construction and improvement.

The earmarking practice has enabled highway departments to engage in elaborate and expensive programs almost without regard to the claims upon a state's finances for other purposes. Thus during the fiscal year 1958-1959, the California Highway Department had over $600 million to spend (about half of this amount coming from federal sources) while the entire state budget stood at a substantial deficit. From the point of view of prudent public administration, this practice falls short of the ideal. Responsible officials cannot transfer public funds from highway construction to other public programs, even if a strong case can be made that such a pattern of expenditure would more effectively promote the public interest.

Motor vehicle taxation rests mainly upon the benefit theory. This theory suggests that, in some meaningful sense, the trucker and the motorist "pay" the tax. This position, as an explanation, seems reasonable enough on the surface, but as we look below the surface at its foundations, some deficiencies become apparent.

DEMAND CHARACTERISTICS. From an economic point of view, the three groups of commodities, distilled liquor, tobacco, and gasoline, have one very important characteristic in common. They are commodities that people are prepared to buy almost regardless of price. In technical terms, the demand schedules for these commodities are highly inelastic. Within the relevant range of price experience, the quantities bought do not vary substantially. The empirical information available is too scanty to establish this observation beyond question. Yet anyone knows that smokers are notorious in refusing to give up the habit because of price. The demand for liquor appears to be inelastic also. The Alcohol Unit of the Treasury has even maintained that the quantity sold has nothing to do with the price. In the case of gasoline, an increase in cost can be offset by using a smaller car and many have already taken this step. Highway departments are already concerned about the resulting implied loss of revenue.

If we may assume that the demands for these three classes of commodities are highly inelastic, what then are the effects of the heavy taxes imposed upon their sale?

SHIFTING. To get at essentials, let us initially think of gasoline, cigarettes, and liquor as a composite commodity and of all other commodities that people like as another composite commodity. The term "composite" means that a unit consists of a perfect sample of the actual quantities of the various separate commodities produced and sold. This procedure has the danger of obscuring certain important differences in the demand or supply circumstances surrounding any one commodity. Some of these will be taken into account presently.

DD' in Figure 14–1 is a representation of the demand schedule for our composite commodity—gasoline, cigarettes, and liquor—labelled commodity *X*. Within the range of relevance, *DD'* is to be viewed as highly inelastic, but not as having a zero elasticity. The line *TT'* shows the quantities of *X* that can be sold to the public at various *net* prices to the sellers. The line is constructed so that the vertical distance between *DD'* and *TT'* is the amount of tax per physical unit of the commodity. We have shown *TT'* as parallel to *DD'* to reflect the fact that the taxes upon gasoline, cigarettes, and liquor are specific

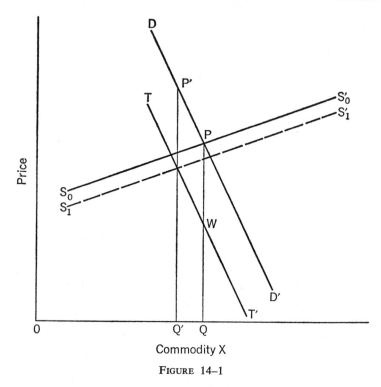

FIGURE 14–1

rather than *ad valorem*.[1] The supply schedule for the commodity is shown by the line S_0S_0'. Its meaning will be made clear in the course of the discussion.

In Figure 14–2, a demand schedule, D_0D_0', for all commodities other than the three under consideration is shown; this composite commodity is labelled Y. It is constructed on the condition that the price of our taxed commodity is PQ (Figure 14–1). The two demand schedules are interdependent; it is necessary to prescribe a definite price for the one commodity in order to have a unique schedule for the other.

Without any tax, the price of the taxed commodity is PQ and the quantity produced and sold is OQ (Figure 14–1). The price of all remaining commodities is RV (Figure 14–2) and the quantity produced and sold is OV. Furthermore, when these quantities of the two composite commodities are produced and sold, the economy has no underemployed resources, whether human or nonhuman. In other

---

[1] If an *ad valorem* tax were being considered, the lines TT' and DD' would converge to a point on the horizontal axis, because as the market price falls a tax of a given percentage of the price becomes smaller absolutely and is zero when the price is zero.

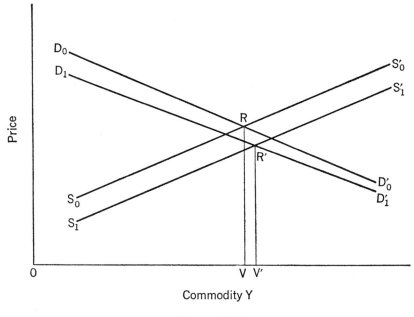

FIGURE 14–2

words, the economy is operating at its highest possible efficiency in the sense that it is not possible to increase the output of one commodity without reducing the output of the other.

Now suppose a large tax, say approximately 40 per cent of the price (see Figure 14–1) is imposed upon our composite commodity, X. Then the net price of X falls to WQ if the same quantities are to be produced. But such an outcome would be wholly disastrous in its effects upon those engaged in producing the taxed commodity. They react by reducing output, and as they do so, the market price of the taxed composite commodity rises. Let us think of these adjustments as a process.

Fixing our attention now on the nontaxed commodity, we find that as the price of the taxed item rises, *the whole schedule for the non-taxed item falls.* In other words, the schedule D_0D_0' (Figure 14–2) shifts to the left, shown as D_1D_1'. The reason for this shift arises from two circumstances. As the prices of cigarettes, spirits, and gasoline rise, people react by spending more money for them. Because each family has limited funds, it must economize by spending less on other things. These two circumstances are incorporated into Figure 14–2 by showing the demand schedule as shifting to the left, to D_1D_1'. Putting the observation in another way, people are demonstrating that cigarettes, liquor, and gasoline are important commodities to them; they refuse to curtail significantly the quantities they buy as the price rises against them. Some of them may take shorter vacations. Some postpone buying some piece of household equipment. Some fail to see a doctor for an annual check-up. Many economize by buying less of a variety of commodities. All these adjustments are represented by allowing the demand schedule for the other composite commodity to fall as the prices of the taxed commodities rise.

As a result of the tax, there is a decline in the output of the taxed commodity to OQ' and a rise in market price to $P'Q'$ (Figure 14–1). There is a rise in the output of the nontaxed commodity (all remaining commodities) from OV to OV' and a fall in its market price from RV to $R'V'$ (Figure 14–2). The downward shift shown for the two supply schedules reflects the change in the *money* costs of production arising from the tax on X. Stated in another way, there is a tax-induced shift of resources to the production of the nontaxed commodity. This process continues until no one can gain by shifting his resources away from the taxed field. This reshuffling of resources will be small. Only a relatively small reduction in the output of the taxed industries is necessary to relieve the financial squeeze placed upon them. Hence there is likewise only a small increase in output of other things. A system of excise taxes placed upon commodities whose demands are highly inelastic operates almost like a general system of sales taxes on the allocation of resources. The product mix or menu offered the public by industry is not altered at all by a system of general sales taxes; it is not altered much by a system of selective excise taxes, provided that the demands for the commodities are highly inelastic.

The outcomes of OQ' for the output of X and $P'Q'$ for the price of X, and of OV' for the output of Y and $R'V'$ for the price of Y (Figures 14–1, 14–2), are equilibrium outcomes in the sense that they are consistent with people's demands and with the condition that resources of the same kind earn the same return in all fields.

These conclusions have some importance for tax administration. If a government must rely heavily upon commodity taxes to obtain sufficient revenue because, for example, primitive business practices and the absence of bookkeeping habits preclude mass income taxation, a system of selective excise taxes, if the commodities in question have highly inelastic demands, will not greatly disturb the composition of output to which the public has become accustomed. Such a system has the advantage of being cheaper and often easier to administer than a general system of sales taxes.

The effect of selective excise taxes on the size and distribution of money incomes is similar to that found in the last chapter for a general system of sales taxes. If Figures 14–1 and 14–2 are again examined, one may readily appreciate that the taxed industries recoup their fortunes in part by restricting output and through this process obtain higher market prices for their wares. Producers of other things must, however, experience lower money incomes. This result comes about in part from the decline in the demand for other goods as the price of the taxed commodities rises. The value added by these industries must fall, and with it, the amount of income generated in production.

It is a mistake to assume that the tax on gasoline, for example, is simply an addition to the price charged motorists and truckers. Likewise the theory that the revenue should be used only or mainly to finance highway construction turns out to have a shaky foundation. Motorists, being people, buy other things besides gasoline. They do pay more for their gasoline as a result of the heavy taxes levied by the states and the federal government upon this commodity, but they get other commodities at lower prices. They are worse off on some counts and better off on others; individually some will on balance be better off and some worse. In addition, the groups in society who are required to provide the dollars the governments obtain from a tax of this type are in large part people who make their incomes producing things not taxed at all. Farmers growing corn as well as workers in factories producing furniture may be hit financially by taxes upon gasoline, not because they must pay higher prices on balance but because they must accept smaller money incomes. Such excise taxes affect them in much the same way as would a collection-at-the-source income tax without any deductions or exemptions, with the difference that they will not ordinarily know how much has been taken from them. There is accordingly no more reason to use money collected from taxes upon motor vehicle fuel to finance public construction of highways than there is to use money collected from taxes upon cigarettes to finance public construction of firehouses.

SUPPLY CHARACTERISTICS. Our results have ignored the peculiarities of the industries providing tobacco, liquor, and gasoline. Each of these is highly complex and to explore them in detail would lead us far afield. A few general remarks may be helpful.

The petroleum industry obtains its main raw material from oil sands in the earth. The price of crude petroleum depends upon its potential uses, including gasoline. The quantity flowing or pumped to the surface depends immediately upon wells already sunk and the costs of getting the oil above ground. Over a longer view, the quantity available depends upon the amount of drilling and the successes or failures to tap new pools by drilling.

Heavy taxation of gasoline, a main product from crude petroleum, tends to reduce the demand for crude, and this factor in turn tends to reduce the price of crude. Owners of existing wells obtain a smaller gross income. The supply schedule of crude oil from existing wells appears to be of the normal type; at a lower price of crude, less is produced because more wells become marginal or submarginal. Of greater quantitative importance is the operation of restriction controls. "Allowables" are established by state agencies, of which the Texas Railroad Commission is the most important, establishing the number of days per month that any well may be permitted to flow. At lower prices of crude, allowables are reduced to assure that the amount of crude oil produced during the period approximately equals the estimated withdrawals from inventories during the month. This cartel arrangement polices the price structure by preventing excess supplies from coming into being and driving down the price.

The drilling of new wells is motivated by the large gains to be achieved if a large pool is discovered. There is no significant relationship between the amount of exploratory work and the current price of crude. Of greater importance is the special tax concession given investors in oil in the form of percentage depletion and 100 per cent accelerated depreciation of the intangible drilling and development costs.[2] Over a long period, the combined effects of heavy taxation of gasoline and of the liberal concessions made under the tax laws to oil investors may together increase or decrease the known supply of tapped oil reserves. It is not unlikely that the combined effect has been to increase the supply. If so, it is doubtful that tax measures, including the high taxes upon gasoline, have resulted in much, if any, higher market prices on the average than would have been the case without these taxes and without the special tax treatment of petroleum gains under the federal corporate and individual income taxes.

The supply situation with regard to alcoholic beverages and cigarettes has few unusual features. Some types of hard liquor must be aged to obtain an acceptable flavor, requiring a heavy investment in inventories as a normal feature of the industry's operations. This factor in turn makes production somewhat less sensitive to current demand and to price than is the case, for example, for automobiles. The process of production itself has few noteworthy peculiarities. The complications arise in the distribution branches of the industry. The liquor industry has successfully surrounded itself with many devices to prevent competition. Retailing in particular is commonly protected by fair-trade laws in many states, enforcing abnormally high

2 See pp. 230-43.

markups. The public's willingness to vote for regulation of the liquor traffic has created a favorable political climate for types of regulation favorable to the income position of the industry. To some unknown extent, the prevalence of monopolistic practices may have made the task of shifting heavy liquor taxes somewhat easier. Sellers can generally assume that when taxes are increased, prices will be increased by something like the same amount. They cannot, however, prevent introductions of low-priced brands, and the use of various types of aggressive selling tactics which result from the tax-induced high prices.

Cigarettes are a simple commodity to produce. The market structure is dominated by the requirement that volume sales require volume advertising. Were it not for this fact, the industry would probably be close to a perfectly competitive one. Customer loyalty to particular brands precludes easy entry of new companies on a substantial scale. The threat of entry does, however, serve as a brake upon pricing according to simple monopoly principles, even if the large manufacturers were able to act together as a unit. As far as tax shifting is concerned, the results are probably little different from what they would be if the industry were perfectly competitive.

Appraisal of Excises on Liquor, Tobacco, and Gasoline

An appraisal of these taxes must take into account the administrative problems involved. Tax rates of 10 per cent do not give rise to as many problems as do tax rates of 60 per cent of the market price.

At the federal level, the tobacco taxes occasion little difficulty. Manufacturers report quantities sold and pay taxes monthly. State cigarette taxes occasion some difficulties. In relation to their bulk cigarettes are high in value, making concealed shipment easy.[3] In view of this special problem, a case can be made for federal collection of state-imposed taxes on tobacco products.

Liquor tax enforcement has been the topic of many a melodramatic tale of battles between moonshiners and "revenuers." The Southern mountain people in particular believe they have an inalienable right to produce and consume corn liquor free of tax. The Alcohol Unit of the Treasury has fought the battle of enforcement in this area for decades, taking and inflicting casualties in this peculiar war. Their success has been limited; large amounts of hard liquor, which can be only roughly estimated, are produced illicitly, and no end to this practice is in sight.

[3] For an account of the problems of administration, see Warren A. Law, "Evasion of State Tobacco Taxes," *National Tax Journal,* VII (June, 1954), 164-76.

This unhappy state of affairs might be remedied by a substantial reduction in federal taxes on distilled spirits, leaving to the individual states the decision of how severely they wish to tax this commodity. Such a policy would permit each state legislature to decide in the light of the mores of its citizens and the cost of enforcement how high to make its tax. It is unfortunate that large groups of people concentrated in a region of this country should be induced into criminal behavior by a tax law. To be sure, the choice is theirs to obey or violate the law. Legislation could, however, be designed to make life simpler and safer all around. If the federal government would be willing to forego a substantial part of its present revenues from liquor taxation, state-imposed taxation could take its place, except in those states where heavy taxation results in large-scale evasion.

The administration of motor vehicle fuel taxes has worked smoothly. Since all state governments tax gasoline, cooperation among them to police interstate shipments has been feasible. The chief administrative problems arise, at the state level, from exempting sales to special groups, such as farmers, for use in off-the-road vehicles. Little except the farmer's conscience prevents him from using tax-exempt gasoline in the family car, and the practice is common. To eliminate this violation of the law would require expensive policing and create much ill will. A simple solution is available. The states might tax gasoline however and wherever used. As we have already seen, the justification of the tax as a user-charge for highways is anemic at best. Consequently, the justification of exemption for nonhighway uses is equally unsupported.

Apart from administrative issues, heavy taxation of mass-consumed commodities, such as tobacco, liquor, and gasoline, has the basic defect shared by all types of sales and excise taxes of placing financial burdens on people in an erratic manner. Some people are hit severely and others little or not at all. On distributional grounds no good substitute has been discovered for systematic income or wealth taxation. Commodity taxation must be low on any list of tax devices defensible on grounds of equity.

Import and Export Duties

Among the oldest of revenue devices used by governments are charges imposed when goods leave or enter a country. Originally, these charges were designed to enrich the pockets of the local ruler. As national states developed, the charges were imposed on the occasion of goods passing over national boundaries. A tax imposed on goods leaving a country is called an export tax or duty and one imposed upon goods arriving in a country is called an import tax or duty. Import taxes are quantitatively much more important than export taxes. Many countries still continue the latter type. Costa Rica and Honduras tax the export of coffee; Ecuador taxes the export of rice; Peru taxes the export of hides, cotton, sugar, flax, and a number of other commodities. The United States government does not impose export taxes—the Constitution prohibits their use. Industrial countries, such as Great Britain, France, and Germany, usually try to encourage exports rather than to block them by taxation.

Explanation of the Effects of Duties

A number of explanations have been developed about how import taxes alter the economic scene. A businessman bothered by foreign competition may request duties upon imports to protect his business. He wants import duties to handicap his foreign competitors, leaving the home market to home producers. Ultraconservative political groups in the United States, Canada, Great Britain, and France as well as in other countries cling fiercely to this doctrine even though it does not have much justification. Business groups have been more or less aided and abetted by some labor union groups. According to this view, economic paradise is a world in which everyone has a monopoly.

PARTIAL EQUILIBRIUM APPROACH TO DUTIES. Of the various approaches to explain this complicated subject, one calls for the same procedure often used to analyze a tax upon a domestically produced and consumed commodity. The British import duty on tea, for example, makes tea more expensive to a British tea drinker. To be sure, the tea producers in India may be adversely affected because the quantity of tea consumed in Britain falls as a result of the higher price. In graphical representation, this combination of effects is pictured in Figure 14–3.

The line DD' shows the demand schedule for tea in Great Britain. The line SS' shows the supply schedule for producing tea in India. Under competitive pricing, the price in pounds is PR. Let an *ad valorem* import duty be imposed equal to 25 per cent of the price. The line TT', then, represents the net price in pounds—the market price minus tax—for each quantity sold. The new market price then moves to VW. Hence the price rises but by less than the tax, the quantity of tea produced in India falls, and the net price in Indian rupees falls.

This analysis can be extended to take account of the demands of tea-lovers in other countries. One may think of another demand

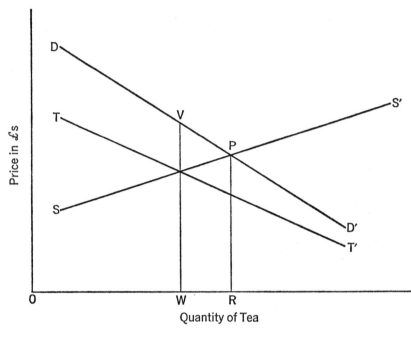

FIGURE 14–3

schedule for tea, that of American tea consumers, added to that of
the British. The Indian supply schedule remains the same. Then
from the starting position of no tax on tea in Great Britain, there is a
price for tea in the United States and Great Britain which just divides
the quantity exported from India. A British import duty on tea has
the following effects: (1) increases the pound price of tea in Great
Britain; (2) lowers the rupee price of tea in India; (3) lowers the
dollar price of tea in the United States; (4) reduces the Indian production of tea; (5) reduces the British consumption of tea; (6) increases the American consumption of tea.[4]

The analysis, step by step, may be expanded to include the demand
conditions in each country for tea and the supply conditions not only
in India but also in Ceylon and elsewhere. Import duties may be
placed upon tea in many countries, and their effects in each country
upon price, quantity imported, and quantity produced may be ascertained. In general, the more countries there are taxing the import
of tea, the less will be produced in the countries of origin. The results do not differ importantly from those often believed relevant for

---

[4] These effects can be shown graphically. One may test his facility with simple
graphical analysis by demonstrating the above results.

an excise tax levied within a country. As in that case, the producers find themselves forced to take a lower net price for their product. Hence, import duties may partially "tax the foreigner." The consumer "pays" part of the tax in a higher price at home. In other words, the tax burden is divided between the producer and the consumer, depending upon the elasticity of demand at home and the elasticity of supply abroad. Because the consumers in one country are only one outlet for the commodity, an import tax will divert some of the supply to consumers in other countries as well as reduce production in the countries of origin.

GENERAL EQUILIBRIUM APPROACH TO DUTIES. There are, however, rather serious limitations to the type of analysis just suggested. It ignores the peculiarities of international trade by assuming among other things that currencies, such as pounds, dollars, and rupees, stand in a fixed relation to one another and that import duties do not affect the rates of exchange, such as the dollar price of rupees. Economists early realized that exchange rates among the monies of different countries may be affected by import taxes. The kind of analysis we have just presented would have been treated scornfully, for example, by John Stuart Mill, who lived a century ago. He discovered a better approach that has held up in its main features to this day and deserves the same acclaim as many of the great nineteenth-century discoveries in the physical sciences. His discovery nowadays is often called the *offer curve* approach.[5]

Let us think of two countries, say the United States and Great Britain, trading with each other. Each produces commodities of which some are sold in the home market and some are shipped to be sold in the other country. Merely for simplicity, let us think of the British exports as consisting of small cars and the American exports as consisting of wheat. There are two initial questions to answer: (1) What determines how much British producers of small cars will sell of this commodity in the United States market? (2) What determines how much American producers of wheat will sell in the British market?

Select any arbitrary amount of small cars to be shipped per month to the United States, as indicated by *OM* in Figure 14–4. That quantity would sell at the price per unit *PM* (say $2,000) which, if *OM* is 1,000 per month, would result in British car agents in this country obtaining $2 million. Now British sellers want pounds, their national money; they offer to sell the $2 million for pounds in the market for foreign exchange in New York. How many pounds they finally get

---

[5] For references, see the Suggested Readings for Part II, p. 352.

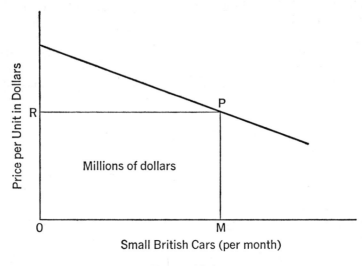

FIGURE 14–4

depends upon the exchange rate—the dollar price of pounds. If that rate is $2.00 = £1, then they obtain £1 million, and if it is $3 = £1, they get £666,666. Thus to know what they would get in pounds we must know the exchange rate.

Let them experimentally sell the $2 million and see how much they get in pounds. The amount they get will be whatever amount their counterparts—American sellers of wheat—earn by selling wheat in Great Britain. American sellers of wheat will, under our experiment, end up with $2 million because when they sell in the foreign exchange market whatever amount of pounds they earn, they receive the dollars offered in the market by the British car agents. American wheat dealers find that it pays them to ship, say, just one million bushels of wheat per month under these circumstances, because by so doing they obtain $2 per bushel for wheat ($2 million/1 million bushels). Two dollars is the "right" price because it equals the price that can be obtained for wheat at home and because wheat producers, when they get $2.00 a bushel, are content to produce that particular quantity of wheat instead of, for example, producing more barley or leaving the farm to work in the city.

All this can be summarized as shown in Figure 14–5. We measure small cars along the vertical axis and wheat along the horizontal axis. We start with *OM* British cars imported. Then we ask how much United States wheat will be exported. It is the amount *ON*, giving the point *R*. This point is an "equilibrium point" with respect to the United States (but not Great Britain); American exporters find it

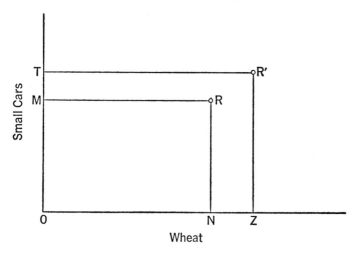

Figure 14–5

just pays to ship *ON* amount of wheat if 1,000 small British cars (*OM*) are landed each month at United States' ports.

To get a second point on the schedule, we repeat the experiment by selecting a different number of British cars imported. Suppose the number is 1,100 cars. To sell this larger number, the dollar price will have to be lower, say $1,985 per car. Then the British agents will obtain $2,183,500 from the sale of cars. Again we repeat the experiment of their placing these dollars on the counter of the foreign exchange market in New York. On the other side of the counter are American wheat agents with some number of pounds from selling wheat shipped to Liverpool. They now find that they obtain more dollars. Hence, they are prepared to ship more wheat abroad because the export price has risen from $2.00 ($2 million/1 million bushels) per bushel to $2.18 per bushel ($2,183,500/1,000,000 bushels). More wheat is shipped until the price of wheat at home and abroad is again the same, e.g., $2.10 per bushel. At that price, a somewhat greater quantity of wheat will be produced (more wheat and less barley, corn, and rye on the farms in Missouri and Kansas) because farmers shift their crop schedules and fewer farm boys and girls are lured away to work in the city. Thus we may plot a second point *R'* on Figure 14–5, which means that when *OT* small cars are imported, wheat agents ship *OZ* bushels of wheat to Liverpool.

The experiment may be continued, by permitting a different number of small cars to be imported. The outcome of each experiment is the amount of wheat to be shipped to Liverpool. In technical language, imports of cars are the independent variable and American wheat exports are the dependent variable. What will the function be like?

In general it will be like *OA* in Figure 14–6. As more and more small cars are imported, American wheat exports will also get larger and larger (positively sloped relation). But this relation will not hold indefinitely. As more and more British cars are placed in the hands of dealers in this country, the price in dollars will decline. For some quantity, perhaps a very large amount, the dollar value of cars

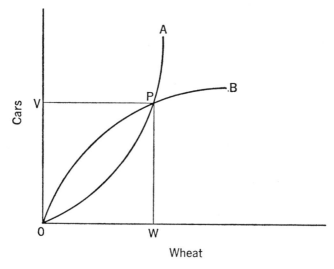

FIGURE 14–6

sold (price times quantity) will fall instead of rise. At this point, American wheat agents, when they appear at the counter in New York to exchange their pounds for dollars, find that they get the same amount of dollars, and hence ship the same amount of wheat to Liverpool. At this point, *OA* becomes vertical to the horizontal axis.

The function *OA* is called the *United States offer curve*. It shows the quantity of exports (wheat) that will be offered abroad for each amount of imports (small cars).

The same experiment must now be repeated to derive the British offer curve. To do this, American wheat becomes the independent variable and British small cars exported, the dependent variable. We shall not do this because it would be mainly a repetition of the previous analysis.[6]

---

[6] The student reader should, however, derive points on *OB*, the British offer curve, as an exercise to make sure he understands the relation involved.

Both offer curves are shown on Figure 14–6, the curve *OA* showing the various amounts of exports of the United States that would be exported for each possible amount of imports, and the curve *OB* showing the corresponding quantity for Great Britain. The point *P* is the equilibrium point of exports and imports for both countries; it is the only such point. Hence it indicates how much the exporters in each country will ship to the other country.

An exchange rate between pounds and dollars will also exist for this amount of trade—*OW* exports of wheat and *OV* imports of small cars. The exchange rate will equal the ratio of the dollars earned by British exports in the United States market to the pounds earned by sale of American exports in Great Britain. Thus if *OV* equals 2500 cars per month and these sell for $1200 apiece, the British exporters earn $3 million; and if *OW* equals 1 million bushels of wheat per month selling for £1 per bushel in England, American exporters earn £1 million. The trade in the foreign exchange market of $3 million and £1 million results in an exchange rate of $3.00 = £1.

The foregoing merely sets the stage for finding out the effects of import duties.

Suppose that the United States Congress, having listened to the doleful prophecies of financial ruin from Detroit, decides to place duties upon small British cars. The aim of some congressmen may be merely to obtain revenue for the government; others wish to protect American industry from foreign competition. What in fact may be expected to happen?

Strangely, or perhaps not so strangely, what in fact happens is that American producers of wheat are taxed. Detroit is favored at the expense of Kansas City!

Let us assume that a tax amounting to 33⅓% of the value of imported cars—and this rate is now a low one as import duties go—is levied. The United States Treasury will appropriate one-third of the $3 million that the British had been earning by selling small cars to Americans. But note, only $2 million is then left to go into the foreign exchange market. When the $2 million is offered for sale across the foreign exchange counter in New York, those on the other side, the American wheat dealers, end up with only $2 million instead of $3 million. But the British car dealers have not been hurt at all, at least not yet. Producers of wheat are the ones who are financially hit by the duty on imported cars. Notice that they obtain $2 million instead of $3 million for the pounds they obtain by sales of wheat.

The principle being illustrated here is a fundamental one in international trade. The local money value of the exports of a country depends upon and is equal to the value of its imports. How well a nation's export industries fare abroad depends upon that nation's demand for imports. In effect, the size of the pot of money the exporters of a country obtain from sales abroad is given by the money value of the country's imports.

Thus, in the first instance, the import duties are borne by the country's exporters, by wheat producers in our illustration. We may immediately observe that the import duty has the same financial effects as an export duty. Import duties are financially symmetrical to export duties.

American producers of wheat will not ordinarily be willing to take this large cut in the dollar value of their wheat sold in Great Britain. Instead, they ship less wheat abroad and sell more at home, they produce less wheat and more barley, and farm boys leave the farm in greater numbers for city jobs. This adjustment may be shown in Figure 14–7 by moving the offer curve for the United States from *OA* to *OA'*. The duty removed $1 million from American exporters.

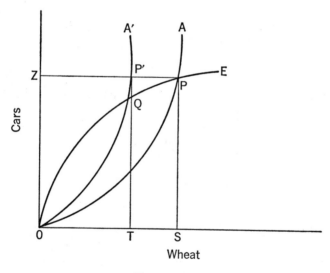

FIGURE 14–7

Thus when *OZ* cars are being imported and subject to a tax of one-third their dollar price, American wheat producers will not ship as much as *OS* wheat to Liverpool; they will ship only the amount *OT*. The entire curve moves over, as shown by *OA'*, as a result of the import tax.

Taxing imports reduces exports and imports. Trade shrinks both ways. The tax on imports has made selling abroad less attractive to exporters in both countries.[7] The formal solution is shown by point Q.

We are now ready to introduce more complications. Countries do not sell only one commodity to one another; they commonly trade in thousands of commodities. Yet this complication gives no trouble, provided exports and imports remain unchanged in composition, just like the weekly menu of a college dormitory dining room. Exports and imports can be treated as a composite commodity—Alfred Marshall labelled this concept a "bale"—and what was earlier stated for the case of one import holds with only minor qualifications for all imports and all exports.

Selective Import Duties

Governments do, however, place duties of varying severity upon imports. In the United States, coffee is imported free of duty, whereas many manufactured articles, textiles, glassware, furniture, and thousands of others are subject to high duties. To crystallize the effects of nonuniform duties, we shall suppose that the United States imports two commodities from Great Britain, say motor cars and whiskey. Exports will continue to be illustrated by wheat. The import duty is confined, let us suppose, to imports of Scotch whiskey. Motor cars enter duty-free.

The tax on Scotch will, as before, remove dollars from Scotch exporters and, as before, when these dollars are offered in exchange for pounds, American exporters of wheat will end up with fewer dollars. They therefore have an incentive to export less wheat to Great Britain. In this respect, selective import duties have the same type of effects as do uniform duties or as does the import tax on one import when there is only one. American exporters find that the financial rewards from exporting are smaller. Thus they sell more wheat at home and also produce less. Again, the people in the Great Plains region are hit financially.

There are, however, effects upon the composition of United States imports. The dollars spent to pay the United States tax on Scotch leave fewer dollars in the hands of our Scottish friends. The bundle

---

[7] The exposition in the text presupposes that the demand schedule in Great Britain has an elasticity of more than unity throughout the relevant range. If the schedule becomes inelastic within the relevant range, American duties on small cars would result in more cars being imported and hence a lower price for cars in dollars. This inelastic schedule case illustrates the paradox that a tax upon a commodity may *reduce* its price.

of dollars in the hands of English producers of small cars has so far been left unchanged. Thus, if we think of the Scots and the English as competing for pounds with the dollars they obtain from selling products in the American market, the Scots get the short end of the stick. If they grossed $3 million from the sale of Scotch and the English motor companies grossed $3 million also from the sale of cars, a tax of $1 million on Scotch means that when dollars are offered for sale in the foreign exchange market, the Scots will obtain one-third instead of one-half of the pounds sold by American exporters of wheat, amounting to, say, £2 million. They obtain £666,666 instead of £1 million. But the English car manufacturers get two-thirds instead of one-half, or £1,333,333.

Therefore the Scots will ship less Scotch to the United States market and the dollar price of Scotch will rise, much to the chagrin of lovers of Scotch whiskey. The English, however, will ship *more* cars to the United States and the dollar price of English cars will fall. Selective import duties do not simply restrict the imports of those commodities which are heavily taxed; they also stimulate the imports of commodities that are not taxed at all.

Financial Burden of Import Duties

Import duties are a roundabout way of taxing exports because these taxes, to the extent that they yield a revenue to the government imposing them, subtract from the value exporters obtain from sales abroad. This financial burden will not remain solely upon the corporations and workers in export trades; some of the financial burden will be spread to other groups. If the main exports of a country are agricultural commodities, the tax will be partly shifted to growers of crops for the domestic market. For example, during the nineteenth century in the United States when cotton was king, the federal taxes imposed upon imports reduced the dollar price of cotton. The South had to accept lower prices for cotton and, to the extent that the cotton not grown was replaced by the production of other crops, lower prices for these too. Countries with one main export, such as petroleum from Venezuela, coffee from Brazil, or cotton from Egypt, may be so rigidly geared to the production of the one commodity as to preclude transferring production to other commodities. In this event, the export industries are unable to shift the tax significantly, and the owners of land, equipment, and manpower devoted to the production of the single exportable commodity are doomed to pay the tax upon imports through a smaller money return from exports.

Place of Taxes upon Internationally Traded Goods in Revenue Systems

As observed earlier, import duties are one of the most important classes of taxes found in countries' revenue systems. As actually levied, they are selective; some imports are taxed heavily, some lightly, and some, such as foreign travel, often not at all. This selectivity gives rise to arbitrary distinctions and difficult administration, and it "distorts" the pattern of imports as well as restricts exports.

A simpler solution consistent with the revenue requirements of governments would be a tax imposed directly upon exports as they leave the country. Such taxes should for simplicity in administration be at a uniform percentage of the domestic price of all exports. This system has the merit not only of administrative simplicity; it would also be much easier for laymen to understand and hence to approve or disapprove. In the United States, because export taxes are prohibited by the Constitution, this solution cannot be used. The yield of import taxes is, however, trivial in this country; these taxes could be eliminated without embarrassment to the Treasury.

The replacement of selective import duties by export taxes would of course be greeted with alarm by protectionists who believe that duties protect domestic industry. As already seen, import duties hurt export industries; it is not possible to protect all industries of a country by import duties. Yet so strongly is this doctrine held that many governments surround their economy with high duties at the insistence of special-interest groups. Various devious efforts are made to stimulate exports and thus to offset the restrictive effects of import duties. While one hand restricts exports by imposing import duties, the other hand pushes exports by subsidies and special concessions to the export trade.[8]

If general export duties are rejected, a next best solution calls for uniform duties on all imports, assessed at a given percentage of their value. This procedure minimizes the "distortion" of the pattern of imports and avoids allowing industries that require cheap raw materials, made cheap by heavy taxes on other imports, to expand. There is always the danger that such industries will be unable to weather temporary economic adversities and will become a public charge by requiring a subsidy for their survival.

Another solution is the imposition of import duties upon commodities of mass consumption at home whose home demand is highly in-

[8] See J. Wemelsfelder, "A Rehabilitation of Export Subsidies," *American Economic Review*, XLVI (Dec., 1956), 880-93.

elastic, illustrated by tea in some countries, tobacco, or petroleum products. Such duties will not change the pattern of imports very much because their highly inelastic demand tends to hold up their volume in the face of heavy taxation, and the same facts tend to minimize the stimulation of other imports. The depressing effect upon export industries remains, but this result is unavoidable. Taxing imports is, as we have seen, an indirect way of taxing exports.

A country which cannot obtain its revenue requirements by reliance upon means-test taxes, such as income, net worth, or spendings taxes, and which finds that taxes upon imports are indispensable for its revenue needs, can avoid subjecting its citizens to a highly arbitrary menu of goods if it levies taxes only upon those imports having highly inelastic demands, as explained above. In addition, it should then tax goods entering into domestic trade. This latter action would serve to keep resources locked into the export industries by making the opportunities for obtaining income in domestic trade less attractive. For any set of import duties, there exists a set of taxes upon domestic trade that will prevent any decline in exports.

Governments are still acting upon highly primitive economic thinking in international economic relations. They commonly assume that imports are bad and exports are good—a set of value judgments which can be justified only on the theory that they wish to be good samaritans, thus giving away the potential output of their own economies to foreigners. Of course, they do not really wish to do this; what they want or seem to want is to build for their citizens the ownership of assets or claims to assets in other countries. Actually no sensible value judgments can be found to justify a policy of maximizing the difference between the value of exports and of imports, which is apparently the goal of government policy in many countries. Perhaps they regard as ideal the arrangement forced on the Finnish people for several years after World War II to export substantial amounts of their products to the U.S.S.R. in return for nothing at all.

15

Property Taxation

Property taxation in one form or another has been in existence for many centuries, and in most countries there have been long periods of time during which it provided the main part of the public revenues. Even in the most primitive early societies land was an obvious and natural base for taxation. Later, when economic growth had brought into prominence a great variety of different kinds of wealth, the tax was gradually extended to them as well. Such general property taxes gave the appearance of treating each taxpayer equally, although, as we shall see, this was not really true either in theory or in practice. In any case, not long after the tax had achieved a broad and impressive scope of operation in a given country a slow but steady shrinking process typically set in. Some types of property began to be taxed at especially favorable rates and others were excluded from the tax base entirely. The result is that in many areas today the tax is primarily or exclusively a levy on real estate and has returned, therefore, almost full circle to its starting point as a tax on land.

Rise and Decline of the General Property Tax in the United States

As was the case elsewhere, property taxation appeared first in the American colonies as a tax on land, sometimes levied according to area as in Vermont, sometimes according to fertility or the way in which the land was cultivated as in Connecticut and Ohio, and later universally according to the money value of the land. By the early eighteenth century other types of property had been added to the tax base in New England and neighboring areas, and a truly general tax began to appear by the end of that century. Thereafter the general property tax spread steadily both southward and westward and reached its zenith in this country during the latter half of the nineteenth century, when it was by a considerable margin the single most important tax in existence. Since that time, however, a steady decline has taken place, and the 1950's have seen the property tax firmly relegated to the fourth rung of the American tax ladder, well below the individual income tax, the corporate income tax, and sales and excise taxes. This decline poses the question of whether it may be expected to continue into the future, or whether the property tax can, or should, be renovated so as to assure its place as an important part of the fiscal structure. Before turning to the various aspects of this complex issue, however, we shall first glance briefly at the statistics of the decline in order to see how precipitous it has actually been.

The present century began with the property tax providing over 50 per cent of total state tax receipts and some 90 per cent of local tax collections. For the first two and a half decades the tax accounted for over 80 per cent of combined state and local tax receipts, but thereafter it fell off steadily, reaching 45 per cent during World War II and remaining at or slightly below that level during the postwar years. Among state tax receipts its fall from power has been almost complete—in 1958 property taxes made up only 4 per cent of that important family. At the local level the decline has been much more moderate, starting from a high of over 95 per cent of tax collections in the late 1920's and early thirties and receding to 87 per cent by 1958. We must not forget, however, that local tax collections have been increasingly supplemented with financial aid from the federal and state governments, and hence account for an ever smaller share of total local revenues. While such grants-in-aid made up only 7 per cent of all local government revenues in 1902, they had increased to 26 per cent in 1958. The result is that the once dominant property tax now contributes less than half of the total revenues of local governments.[1]

In the fiscal world, then, the decline of the property tax has been a significant and impressive modern development. It is also of interest, however, to consider the changes in its role in the economic system as a whole. What, for example, has happened during the present century to the relation between property taxes and net national product, and have property tax rates been rising or falling?

[1] For a detailed analysis of the fall of American property taxes during the first half of the twentieth century see Mabel Newcomer, "The Decline of the General Property Tax," *National Tax Journal,* VI (March, 1953), 38-51.

Table 15–1 presents the relationship between property taxes collected by state and local governments and net national product. It will be noted that in the fifties property taxes were a smaller percentage of net national product than they were in 1902, 1912, and 1922—so in this respect, too, property taxes have lost some ground. The other striking feature of the table is the sharp rise in the relative importance of the tax from 5 per cent of net national product in 1929 to nearly 9 per cent in 1933 at the bottom of the Great Depression. This illustrates a well-established trait of property taxes—their relative burdens typically increase as national income and employment fall and decrease when prosperous times return.

TABLE 15–1

THE RELATION OF PROPERTY TAXES TO NET NATIONAL PRODUCT,
SELECTED YEARS, 1902-1958

Year (1)	Property Tax Revenue of State and Local Governments (billions of $) (2)	Net National Product (billions of $) (3)	Ratio of Property Taxes to Net National Product (%) (4)
1902	0.7	19.1	3.7
1912	1.4	32.8	4.3
1922	3.3	66.7	4.9
1929	5.0	95.8	5.2
1933	4.3	48.8	8.8
1939	4.3	83.3	5.2
1948	6.1	244.0	2.5
1950	7.1	265.5	2.7
1956	11.7	384.5	3.0
1958	14.0	406.1	3.4

Sources: For col. (2), 1956-58, U. S. Bureau of the Census, *Summaries of Governmental Finances;* 1902-50, Mabel Newcomer, *op. cit.,* p. 40. For col. (3), 1902-1922, Raymond W. Goldsmith, Dorothy S. Brady, and Horst Mendershausen, *A Study of Saving in the United States,* Vol. III (Princeton: Princeton Univ. Press, 1956), p. 427; 1929-1958, Department of Commerce national income data from the *Survey of Current Business.*

It is no easy task to determine the change in effective property tax rates (i.e., the ratio between total taxes paid and the true market value of all the property contained in the tax base) over any given period of time. Nominal rates, which give the relationship between property taxes due and the assessed valuation of the property on which they are levied, are, of course, readily available from official sources. The ratio between these two figures, however, gives the true tax rate only if the assessed valuation of the property is equal to its

market value. Since state and local governments typically assess
property for tax purposes considerably below market value, nominal
rates ordinarily exceed effective rates. A piece of real estate recently
purchased for $20,000, for example, may be assessed at $4,000 for
tax purposes, and its owner may be called upon to pay a property tax
of $400. In this case the nominal tax rate is 10 per cent, but the
true rate is only 2 per cent. Table 15–2 shows the variation in assessment ratios for nonfarm residential property in this country in 1956.

TABLE 15–2

DISTRIBUTION OF STATES BY THE AVERAGE RATIO OF ASSESSED VALUE TO SALES PRICE
FOR TRANSFERRED NONFARM RESIDENTIAL PROPERTIES IN 1956

Average Ratio of Assessed Value to Sales Price (%)	Number of States
Less than 10*	3
10 – 14.9	3
15 – 19.9	7
20 – 24.9	10
25 – 29.9	8
30 – 34.9	5
35 – 39.9	4
40 – 49.9	5
50 and over*	3

* The smallest average ratio was 6% in South Carolina and the largest was 60% in
Rhode Island.

Source: Bureau of the Census, *Assessed Values and Sales Prices of Transferred Real
Property,* 1957 Census of Governments, Advance Release No. 7 (May,
1958), p. 6.

In no tax jurisdiction do assessed valuations bear a given and invariant relationship to market values over time. As a result nominal
tax rates cannot be used to show the change in effective rates from
one year to the next. One study of property taxes in a sample of
several hundred cities, for example, found that the average taxes due
per $1,000 of assessed valuation had increased from $39 in 1945 to
$51 in 1954.[2] When adjustments were made for the ratios between
assessed and market values reported by each city, however, it was
discovered that estimated effective tax rates had actually declined
slightly from 2.7 to 2.1 per cent. These figures can only be taken as
first approximations since they are based not on systematic studies of
assessed and market values but on the personal judgment of assessors
and other government officials. Nevertheless, a more comprehensive

[2] Citizens Research Council of Michigan, "Tax Rates of U. S. Cities," *National
Municipal Review,* XLIV (Jan., 1955), p. 16.

study of both rural and urban property in this country led the author of the study to conclude that effective property tax rates were not higher in 1949 than they were in the 1920's.[3] Within that period he found that they tended to move countercyclically, rising when the level of general business activity was falling and declining when output and employment were rising.

Tax Base as a Measure of Ability to Pay

A truly general property tax would impose a single tax rate on the current, assessed money value of all types of property; and, furthermore, assessed valuations would bear the same relation to actual market values on all taxable properties. The base of such a tax may be subdivided into the following three main categories:

1. Real property, consisting of land and all buildings and structures attached to it (ordinarily called "improvements" by tax administrators), as well as minerals and timber.
2. Tangible personal property, consisting of all the more mobile types of material wealth from business inventories and office furniture to automobiles, wrist watches, clothes, and other personal effects.[4]
3. Intangible personal property, consisting of claims of various kinds such as corporate stocks and bonds, mortgages, money, and deposits in savings banks and building and loan associations.

Of the three basic measures of individual abilities to pay taxes which we have noted in previous chapters—namely, income, spendings, and net worth—it is clear that the last named bears the closest resemblance to the base of the general property tax. Yet between the two there are sharp and important differences. These may be illustrated by considering two farms, each worth $30,000 on the rural real estate market. Suppose that individual A owns the first farm outright but that B, the owner of the second, has a $15,000 mortgage on it. Restricting ourselves entirely to these facts, we see that A has a net wealth of $30,000, B owns $15,000 more assets than he has liabilities, and C, the holder of the mortgage, also has a net worth of $15,000. A general property tax, however, because it is levied on the property rather than on the person according to his total property,

---

[3] Colin D. Campbell, "Are Property Tax Rates Increasing?" *Journal of Political Economy,* LIX (Oct., 1951), 434-42.

[4] Since there is no sharp line between movable and immovable types of wealth, it is not surprising to find that some states classify business machinery and building fixtures as real property while others treat them as personal property. A similar problem, which is likely to become increasingly important in states which exempt personal property from taxation, occurs in the case of built-in dishwashers, china cabinets, book shelves, hi-fi sets, and other consumer durables.

or wealth, would assess A and B equally (at $30,000 if assessment levels are 100 per cent of market values) and C at half that figure. Such a procedure would greatly overestimate B's ability to pay taxes as compared to those of A and C. Interpersonal inequities of this sort are an inherent and important part of any general property tax, and can be eliminated only by transforming the levy into a tax on each person's net wealth.

The situation just described is frequently identified as a case of double taxation which can be eliminated in more than one way. It is pointed out that although the total wealth in the illustration is only $60,000—a figure which may be obtained either by considering only the material items of wealth present (i.e., the two farms) or by adding up the net worths of the three individuals—the property tax base is equal to $75,000. Double counting exists under the property tax because B's farm has been allocated entirely to him in spite of the fact that C has a 50 per cent claim to it which is also part of the tax base. One solution would be to exempt all intangible personal property from taxation. This, however, would underestimate C's ability to pay as compared to those of A and B and overestimate B's ability in relation to A's. Only a net wealth tax is capable of using property as a measure of taxpaying ability in such a way as to avoid interpersonal inequities.

A property tax, then, no matter how general its application inherently discriminates against certain taxpayers and favors others. As we have seen, property owners who are greatly in debt to others are relatively heavily taxed in relation to their true net worths as compared with owners with large equities in their property holdings. Even more important is the omission from the property tax base of the capitalized earning powers of human beings, all of which would be included in a perfectly general net worth tax. Nor are these the only inequities which have come to plague existing property taxes. The others, which we shall discuss in the following two sections, are not inherent in the structure of the tax but have resulted, in many areas, from political and administrative considerations.

Erosion of the Property Tax Base by Exemptions

Exemptions from property taxation, although there is considerable variation in trends from one state to another, have long been on the increase in this country. The evidence on this score is not as precise as we would like because figures on the value of exempted property are not ordinarily collected along with other fiscal statistics, but what information we do have points toward a significant and continued erosion of the general property tax base. The nature and extent of this erosion is the subject matter of the present section.

INTANGIBLE PERSONAL PROPERTY. Although at the beginning of this century all but three states included intangibles in the general property tax base, in 1956 the number doing so was only thirteen.[5] Sixteen other states taxed intangibles at lower rates than were applied to other kinds of property, and nineteen states exempted them completely.[6] Even in states which do treat them on a par with other property intangibles constitute only a very small proportion of the tax base. In the six states which listed them separately in 1956, for example, this proportion was 3 per cent or less in five states and 17.5 per cent in the other (West Virginia).[7]

The reason for this is not that intangibles are in fact a relatively unimportant type of property—at the end of 1949 the kinds that are ordinarily included in the tax base were over half as important as all tangible property in the country[8] —but that very few of them are reported to the tax assessor. Rather than tightening up on administration by having the assessor ask more closely after the elusive intangible, a procedure which many taxpayers might regard as an unjustifiable invasion of their privacy (especially those with large holdings of investment assets of one kind and another), many states have preferred to give up the struggle entirely and make honest men of the tax evaders by exempting intangibles altogether. Other states attempt to lure intangibles into the tax base by means of very low tax rates (typically ½ per cent and less). An added encouragement to these developments has been the argument, noted above, that to tax both the material wealth and the intangible claims to its earnings is to count the same property twice. The equitable solution, of course, is not to exempt intangibles but to include them, together with all other kinds of property, in a net wealth tax.

[5] One of the thirteen was Georgia, which taxes bank shares as general property but other intangibles at special, low rates.
[6] For further details see U. S. Bureau of the Census, *Property Tax Assessments in the United States,* 1957 Census of Governments, Advance Release No. 5 (Washington, D.C.: Bureau of the Census, 1957), especially pp. 5, 37-40.
[7] *Ibid.,* p. 13.
[8] See Raymond W. Goldsmith, Dorothy S. Brady, and Horst Mendershausen, *A Study of Saving in the United States,* Vol. III (Princeton: Princeton Univ. Press, 1956), p. 56, where the total value at the end of 1949 of currency, deposits in commercial banks and other financial institutions, mortgages, and corporate stocks and bonds is estimated to be nearly $500 billion as compared with slightly over $850 billion for all tangible assets other than the monetary metals which are not subject to property taxation. On this basis intangibles should constitute approximately one-third of the total property tax base.

TANGIBLE PERSONAL PROPERTY. The treatment of this important category ranges all the way from complete coverage in Illinois to complete exemption in Delaware, New York, and Pennsylvania. Among the items most frequently favored with exemptions or preferential tax rates are mechanics' tools; manufacturers' inventories, machinery, and fixtures; farm tools, machinery, and livestock; growing crops (these may be exempted either specifically in the tax law or by the more subtle method of setting the assessment date at a time of year when crops are at a minimum); and household goods (by 1956 thirteen states had abandoned all attempts to tax these).[9] The reasons for these favors may be to keep down administrative costs, to attract new business by holding business taxation below the levels prevailing in other states, or to secure the support of powerful political groups. In the case of household goods another factor is undoubtedly the feeling of irritation which many taxpayers have when the assessor makes a summary entrance into their homes and attempts to appraise the value of their personal belongings.

HOMESTEAD EXEMPTIONS. In 1956 five states allowed taxpayers to exclude from the local property tax base a stated amount of the assessed value of any residential real property owned and occupied by them. This policy permits owners of small homes to be completely freed from real property taxes and other home owners to be more lightly taxed than owners of other types of real estate. Consider, for example, a state which assesses property at 25 per cent of its true market value and allows a $2,500 homestead exemption. If A owns a home worth $10,000, B one worth twice as much, and C business real property valued at $20,000, their assessed valuations will be $2,500, $5,000, and $5,000 respectively. With the homestead exemption in operation, however, A will pay no property taxes, and B will pay only half as much as C.

Local homestead exemptions, which covered $4.2 billion of assessed valuations in 1956, amounted in that year to some 33⅓ per cent of the gross assessed valuation in Florida, slightly over 20 per cent in Georgia, Mississippi, and Louisiana, and 15 per cent in Oklahoma.[10] It will be noted that in all these states the exemptions constitute an important part of the potential property tax base. Mabel Newcomer has estimated, for example, that in 1950 the Florida home-

[9] Cf. Mabel Newcomer, "The Growth of Property Tax Exemptions," *National Tax Journal*, VI (June, 1953), 118-19.

[10] U. S. Bureau of the Census, *Property Tax Assessments in the United States*, pp. 6, 12. Gross assessed valuation means the total valuation placed upon property before deduction of the homestead exemption.

stead exemption increased taxes on non-homestead property by as much as 30 per cent.[11]

Other states grant tax favors of varying kinds to homesteads. These include exemptions allowable against state property taxes only, special tax credits, and lower assessment-to-value ratios than are applied to other types of property. One state sets a lower tax rate limit on homesteads, but this kind of provision does not help the home-owner unless local tax rates are higher than the limit.

VETERANS' EXEMPTIONS. In 1956 the fourteen states which allowed partial exemptions (i.e., up to a fixed amount of assessed valuation, usually $1,000 or $2,000) to all or most of their veterans reduced, by this means, their total assessed valuation subject to tax by some $2 billion. Although California alone accounted for almost one-half of this total and New York and Connecticut came next with aggregate exemptions of $400 and $200 million respectively, the two states in which veterans' exemptions constituted the highest percentage of gross assessed valuations were Nevada and New Mexico. Table 15–3 ranks the states according to the relative importance of

TABLE 15–3

RELATIVE IMPORTANCE OF VETERANS' EXEMPTIONS IN 1956

Veterans' Exemptions as a Percentage of Gross Assessed Valuation	States
5 to 6	Nevada, New Mexico
4 to 5	——
3 to 4	California, New Hampshire, Connecticut, Rhode Island, Arizona
2 to 3	Iowa, Wyoming, New Jersey
1 to 2	Maine, New York
Less than 1	Oregon
Not available	Indiana

Source: Computed from the figures given by the Census Bureau in *Property Tax Assessments in the United States.*

their veterans' exemptions. It should be noted that meaningful interstate comparisons can be based upon percentages of this sort but not upon absolute dollar amounts. A $1,000 veterans' (or homestead) exemption in a state which, on the average, assesses property at 25 per cent of full value, for example, is equivalent to a $2,000 exemp-

[11] Mabel Newcomer, "The Growth of Property Tax Exemptions," *op. cit.,* p. 124.

tion in a state where assessments are typically 50 per cent of true market value. In either case the exemption is worth $4,000 in market values.

REAL PROPERTY. The exemption of federal- or state-owned real estate from local property taxes poses an important problem only in areas where government property constitutes a significant proportion of the potential tax base. These may be state capital cities, towns in which a state university is located, or counties (such as some in Oregon) in which extensive national forests or parks are located. From an equity point of view these exemptions are indefensible. If the basic purpose of a local tax system is to allocate fiscal burdens according to a fair and reasonable pattern, local governments should either be allowed to tax property belonging to other governmental units at the same rate as privately owned property, or be paid a compensatory grant by the higher echelon of government to make up for the taxes which would have been levied upon the property had it been privately owned.

It may, of course, be argued that the location of a given state or federal enterprise in a certain town will, by attracting home owners and businesses to the area, increase the property tax base more than the shift of the real estate from private to public hands will decrease it. This very real possibility, which is more frequently cited as support for the exemption of new businesses from property taxation, will appeal to those who see no objection in allowing one local government to benefit its citizens to the detriment of others elsewhere; many, however, will feel that the location of productive activity within the country should depend upon natural economic resources and not upon fiscal policies. In any case, as we have already noted in Chapter 7, an impressive number of empirical studies indicate that tax differentials play a very minor role, if indeed any at all, in business decisions to locate plants in one area rather than another. Nevertheless a number of states, particularly in the South, do grant to new businesses five- or ten-year temporary exemptions from real property taxes. In 1950 such exemptions amounted to nearly 20 per cent of the total assessed value of property subject to tax in Louisiana, and in some areas within the state exempt assessments were 50 to 100 per cent of taxable assessments.[12]

Property taxes on forest and mineral lands have frequently been criticized for speeding up the use of the resources in question to the detriment of conservation policies. A tax on realized income, for example, would place no burden on the owner of forest lands while the

[12] *Ibid.*, p. 121.

trees were growing but would concentrate its exactions in the years in which the trees were cut and sold to the lumbering companies. A property tax, on the other hand, would be payable during each of the years of growth and might, therefore, induce an earlier cutting than would the income tax. In the interests of conservation of natural resources a number of states have replaced property taxes on forest and mineral lands with severance taxes payable only when the resources are separated from the land as part of the production process. In 1958 twenty-seven states collected $370 million by this means, a sum which was 2.5 per cent of total state tax receipts in that year.

EVALUATION. It is clear that tax exemptions have eroded the property tax base to a significant extent in a number of states. A necessary effect of such exemptions is that the property tax is a less general, and hence less equitable, tax than it otherwise would be. In addition, although it is conceivable that widespread exemptions will not decrease total property tax collections (in which case they merely shift the burden onto owners of nonexempt property), it is highly probable that property tax receipts are less than they would be under a more general tax. This loss, of course, must be made up either from other taxes or from other revenue sources such as increased state aid to local governments, or it must be matched by a lower level of local governmental expenditures. Some interesting evidence on this issue is contained in Mabel Newcomer's study of tax exemptions. She shows that in 1950 property taxes were 3.0 per cent of individual income payments in those states which allowed a homestead exemption, 3.2 per cent in the three states exempting tangible personal property, and 3.5 per cent in all other states. In addition, property taxes per capita increased by only 5 per cent from 1930 to 1950 in the homestead exemption states, by 9 per cent in the personal property exemption states, and by almost 20 per cent in the remaining states.[13] It seems clear that one effect of the exemptions has been to decrease the fiscal importance of the property tax.

Assessment Process and Its Problems

The most intractable step in the assessment of property for tax purposes, a process which begins with the making of a complete inventory of all taxable property within the taxing jurisdiction and ends with the drawing up of an assessment roll setting forth the total tax base and the parts of it belonging to each taxpayer, is the assignment of a fair market value to each item of property. The simplest case

[13] *Ibid.,* p. 127.

to deal with is one in which the sale of an identical or closely similar asset has taken place in the recent past. The assessor then need only obtain the sales price in question and make certain that the transaction was carried out, as the saying goes, "at arm's length"—i.e., that it was not a friendly exchange between two members of the same family or of the same business partnership and consequently unlikely to yield the same price as a sale carried out between strangers. Placing a market value on a share of Ford Motor Company or American Airlines common stock, on a house in a large tract development, or on an automobile, for example, should ordinarily be a straightforward matter. Other cases, unfortunately, are not likely to be nearly so simple. A painting by Picasso which had been held by one owner for a large number of years would require the judgment of an art expert, and even this would be an opinion with which other dealers might well disagree. Tangible business property is ordinarily carried in a company's accounting records at original cost less depreciation charges already taken, a value which may depart significantly from that for which the assets in question could be sold on the open market. An apartment house in a city where no sales of similar properties have taken place for years offers a still different problem. On the one hand, the cost might be estimated in terms of current construction prices for similar apartment buildings, but such a value could be regarded only as a ceiling beyond which a prospective buyer would not be likely to go in bidding for the existing property. Alternatively, a forecast could be made of the future net income to be earned by renting the apartments, with the income then discounted to the date of assessment at an appropriate rate of interest. If, for example, a net return of $30,000 a year, after full allowance for maintenance and replacement costs, property taxes, losses from fire, average vacancy rates, and the like, were expected indefinitely, the building would be worth $1,000,000 at a 3 per cent rate of profit. This figure, of course, is no better than the forecasts upon which it is based, and even if it were, by some miracle, the true current value of the property, the owner might well not be able to sell it at that figure to buyers whose knowledge of the future is notoriously imperfect.

These, then, are some of the dimensions of the property tax assessor's formidable task. It is clearly one requiring highly trained, conscientious personnel of unquestioned integrity. Yet it is difficult to imagine an environment less likely to attract such people than that prevailing in many local governments in this country. The position of county or city assessor is frequently a poorly paid job unlikely to appeal to those with notable ability and training. In the smaller communities the position typically offers only part-time employment, and even under the best of circumstances an assessor, no matter how able, is frequently so hampered by lack of funds that he has to get along with wholly inadequate staff and equipment. Finally, the fact that assessors are frequently elected by the voters at large rather than appointed by competent officials on the basis of merit exposes the position to pressures from those who are willing and able to pay for especially favorable tax assessments.

Given these facts, one would expect to be able to find numerous instances of incorrect and inequitable assessments, and this indeed has been the experience of many empirical investigators. To see some of the magnitudes involved, consider the results of a 1953-54 analysis and appraisal of the property tax in Kansas.[14] Although the law required tangible property to be assessed at 100 per cent of true value, no county was found to have achieved, or even approached, that goal. The average county assessment within the state was approximately 23 per cent of true value, with individual counties ranging from a low of 12 per cent to a high of 49 per cent. Nor were assessment discrepancies any less pronounced within the counties themselves, even where all valuations were made by the same assessor's office. In one county, which was by no means atypical, a $10,000 farm might easily be assessed at any figure from $640 to $2,560, the larger value producing exactly four times as high a tax bill as the lower one. Interpersonal inequities of this magnitude speak for themselves. In addition, it was found that property of low value, both rural and urban, tended to be assessed at a higher percentage of its true worth than did more expensive assets. This tendency does not necessarily reflect either conscious or unconscious favoring of the wealthy and powerful on the part of the assessor, since high-priced assets more frequently than cheap ones have unique features which complicate the valuation process by offering no basis for comparison in the estimate of sales figures.

The Kansas property tax, then, appeared in 1954 to be both capricious in its incidence and regressive in relation to the true value of individual property holdings. In addition to these facts, the study turned up considerable evidence of widespread tax evasion in personal and intangible property. In a state which is presumably no less time-conscious than the rest of the country, only 3.5 per cent of the taxpayers reported ownership of watches, and the average personal property assessment in a sample of nearly 2,000 returns in 1953 was

[14] John D. Garwood, "The Kansas Citizens Examine their Property Tax," *National Tax Journal,* IX (Sept., 1956), 258-67; and Lawrence A. Leonard, "Property Taxation in Kansas: an Historical Analysis," *National Tax Journal,* XI (Sept., 1958), 230-40.

less than $141. In 1950 the assessed value of stocks and bonds was $39 million although two years later a Brookings study estimated stocks and bonds owned by Kansas residents to be worth $690 million.[15]

ASSESSMENT DIFFERENTIALS WITHIN A SINGLE TAXING DISTRICT. There is no need to emphasize the obvious inequities which result whenever a tax assessor fails to value all properties in his district at the same ratio to true market value. Varying ratios simply mean that people with the same property holdings will pay different tax bills, and people with significantly different holdings will have similar tax liabilities, a situation which exactly reverses the basic canon of tax equity.[16]

The elimination of unwarranted assessment differentials is not a simple task. What is required is not only a reform of assessment practices but also provision for adequate judicial review of all seemingly unfair assessments. In the first place, the assessor should be a person with ability and training, rewarded with an adequately paid position and freed, through appointment on the basis of merit, from the pressures likely to accompany the need periodically to seek elective office. In the second place, he should be provided with a sufficiently large and competent staff and encouraged to discuss his problems with other assessors. In the small counties and districts particularly, the assessor should feel free to draw upon, wherever feasible, the superior resources possessed by state and large city assessment boards. Finally, no matter how carefully these problems are attended to, provision must still be made for individual taxpayers to protest and have reviewed by competent authorities what they consider to be unfair assessments. The initial review is ordinarily done by a local agency such as a city council or a county board of supervisors, and appeals may then be taken to a state board of equalization or state tax commission.

It is not enough, however, simply to set up such a process of equalization and review. A 1946-1955 study in the state of Washington provides a useful illustration of what can go wrong. Stimulated by the discovery of wide variations in assessment ratios,[17] the survey yielded several surprising and significant results:[18]

1. Although a widespread lack of uniformity in assessment-to-true-value ratios did in fact exist, relatively few taxpayers appealed to the county boards of equalization which in Washington constitute the first line of de-

[15] Garwood, *op. cit.*, p. 261.

[16] See chap. 5.

[17] James K. Hall, "Sales-Assessment Ratio Survey in Washington," *National Tax Journal*, IX (June, 1956), 177-92.

[18] James K. Hall, "Assessment Equalization in Washington," *National Tax Journal*, IX (Dec., 1956), 302-25.

fense against inequitable assessments. In 1955, for example, only seven of the thirty-nine counties had ten appeals or more, and over the entire ten-year period only twelve counties averaged more than ten appeals a year.

2. The counties with the fewest appeals typically had less uniform property assessments than counties with the most appeals. In no less than four counties the boards had completely abdicated their equalization functions—in one county there were no taxpayer appeals during the ten years, and in the other three the few appeals made were all rejected—yet three of these counties were among the five with the least uniform assessment-sales ratios. Where the need was greatest, in short, the relief provided by review and equalization was least.

3. Only 40 per cent of the appeals made were granted by the county boards, and the result of these was a reduction in assessed values of less than 4 per cent. The effects of these changes on the total property tax base were infinitesimal—it was lowered by approximately $3 in every $10,000.

4. Less than 5 per cent of the petitions acted upon by the county boards were appealed to the State Tax Commission (either by the taxpayer or the assessor) and only 35 per cent of these were granted by the commission.

It is clear from these findings that the review and equalization process in Washington failed completely to remove the very great inequalities which existed in individual property tax assessments. It is no wonder that the 1955 legislature concluded that the situation constituted "a grave emergency adversely affecting state and local government and the welfare of all the people."[19]

The fact that typically there are relatively few taxpayer appeals may be attributed to a number of factors:

1. Lack of knowledge on the part of the taxpayer about the average ratio between assessed and true market values in his county makes an appeal difficult, particularly when his property is assessed at a lower ratio than that required by state law. Under these circumstances the taxpayer may simply assume that his assessment is, if anything, on the low side even though, in reality, other property may be underassessed to a still greater degree. Even if he does feel that his property is overassessed in relation to that of his neighbors, the taxpayer still may not appeal for fear that the only result will be an increase in all assessments cited in the petition to the legally required level. He may prefer, in other words, to let well enough alone.

2. The money, time, and effort involved in preparing and presenting a well-documented appeal may discourage many taxpayers. Readily available, reliable information on average county assessment ratios, however, will simplify this task to a considerable extent.

[19] *Ibid.*, p. 325.

3. In some instances fear of reprisals by the assessor or lack of confidence in the ability or integrity of members of the county boards of assessment may be important deterrents to the taxpayer in deciding whether to appeal.[20]

ASSESSMENT DIFFERENTIALS AMONG COUNTIES. Assessment of property at a lower ratio to fair market value in one county than in another does not necessarily constitute an inequitable fiscal practice. If each county is a completely separate and self-contained taxing district within which all property is assessed by the local assessor's office, and if no state fiscal laws relate in any way to assessed valuations, each county may be left entirely free to determine its own assessment level. The fact that one county assesses under these circumstances at, say, 80 per cent of fair market value while another uses a 40 per cent figure does not mean that property owners in the former are more heavily taxed (since the two county tax rates may vary inversely to the assessment ratios), and even if it does, the result is no more inequitable than the fact that residents of the state of New York pay an individual income tax while residents of Illinois do not.

Nevertheless, the circumstances under which intercounty equalization of property tax assessments is unnecessary have become increasingly rare in the United States. In 1952 all but five states needed intercounty equalization for one or more of the following reasons:[21]

1. *State Participation in the General Property Tax.* In some cases a state property tax is levied and based upon local assessments. By underassessing in such circumstances a local government may reduce the amount of the state tax paid by its own residents, and consequently the burden of the tax will vary inversely (and inequitably) with the degree of underassessment in each county. Still more frequently large holdings of property which overlap a number of county boundaries, such as those owned by railways and other public utilities, are assessed by state authorities and then returned to the local tax rolls. Under these circumstances it is conceivable that the state and the various counties will each assess property at a different ratio to true value. Interpersonal equity can then be achieved either by adjusting assessments in each of the counties upward or downward to the level used by the state (known as the uniform-ratio method) or by changing the state assessment ratio on the property added to the tax roll of a given county to correspond with the average ratio prevailing in that county (the variable-ratio method). Unless one of these adjustments

[20] *Ibid.,* p. 306.
[21] Eugene C. Lee, "State Equalization of Local Assessments," *National Tax Journal,* VI (June, 1953), 176-87.

is made the owners of locally assessed property will be over- or under-assessed in relation to the owners of state-assessed property.

2. *State Grants-in-Aid Based upon Assessed Valuations.* In states such as California where aid to school districts, in an attempt to guarantee a minimum education program throughout the state, is based in part on need as measured by assessed valuations, there is strong incentive for assessors to value property at a relatively low ratio to true value in order to qualify the district for more state aid. Similarly, where state aid to the needy aged, blind, orphans, and other groups is given only to those owning property valued for tax purposes below a certain maximum figure, a given person might qualify for that aid if he lived in one county but not in another. As in the first case, equity among recipients of state aid requires the use of either the variable- or the uniform-ratio methods of intercounty assessment equalization except in that rare utopia where all assessors value property at the same ratio to true worth.[22]

3. *State-Imposed Tax Rate and Debt Limitations.* Many states attempt to control the spending propensities of their local authorities by setting maximum property tax rates and placing a ceiling on the ratio which local debt may bear to total local assessed valuations. Such restrictions may, of course, be nullified by widespread over-valuation of property, and, in any case, intercounty assessment differentials prevent them from operating in a uniform manner.

In spite of the widespread need for it, effective intercounty assessment equalization is likely to encounter a number of difficulties. In addition to the purely selfish opposition of assessors who have not adhered to legally required assessment ratios or of taxpayers who suspect that they are underassessed in relation to others, there may be widespread fears in counties whose assessments are to be raised by the equalization process that the changes will result in increased tax burdens. Instead of reducing tax rates, in other words, hard-pressed local governments may simply use the occasion to implement what they regard as a long-overdue increase in service levels.[23] Needless

---

[22] A special kind of state aid is the use of standard property tax exemptions throughout the state. In California, for example, veterans are granted an exemption of up to $1,000 of assessed valuation if they own property valued at less than $5,000. It is clear that the uniform application of this subsidy depends upon successful equalization of the different county assessment ratios.

[23] An increase in county assessments in California, ordered by the State Board of Equalization in 1955, evidently led a number of school districts to raise both expenditures and revenues. See Ronald B. Welch, "Intercounty Equalization in California, Part II: Action and Reaction," *National Tax Journal,* X (June, 1957), pp. 152-54.

to say, not all taxpayers will oppose such fiscal developments, but those who do may be more vocal and have more political influence.

More fundamental objections may be raised concerning the validity of the sample surveys on the basis of which intercounty equalizations are to be carried out. There are difficulties here, but none with which careful, scientific procedures cannot cope. One approach is to determine assessment ratios from a statistically designed probability sample of all taxable properties in the state. The chief attraction of this procedure is that sampling errors may be brought under strict control, but since few properties chosen for the sample will have been sold during the year in question, true values will have to be determined to a large extent by qualified property appraisers. Alternatively, one may rely on the actual market values reported in recent sales transactions but only at the cost of abandoning a random sample for one whose sampling errors cannot be controlled or computed. There is no escape, in short, from both appraisal and sampling errors at the same time. Nevertheless, experience indicates that either type of error can be held within reasonable bounds, especially when the two procedures are used as checks on each other.

Property Tax Payments and Nonpayments

Once the assessment process has been completed, the remaining steps in the administration of the property tax are relatively straightforward. The tax rate is ordinarily set in relation to expected expenditures and expected revenues from other sources so as to yield enough from property tax collections to fill the gap. Tax bills are then payable in one or two instalments, although many residential mortgage contracts transform these lump-sum liabilities into monthly charges collected from the home owner along with the interest and principal repayments on his mortgage. In such cases the lender undertakes the task of setting aside regular sums of money so that sufficient funds will be available when the due-date for property taxes comes around. Other taxpayers might well find a similar arrangement, shifting property tax payments from a lump sum to an instalment basis, a most welcome one.

Tax delinquencies, although inevitable, are not necessarily a serious problem in ordinary times. In many cases the person owing back taxes will, given a reasonable opportunity, be able to overcome his own difficulties; in others, however, a foreclosure will be necessary, with the government taking over the property in question and then selling it in an attempt to collect both the taxes due and the costs, by no means negligible, involved in the whole procedure. Vigorous pursuit of all delinquencies is an essential task of any tax administration. In its absence taxpayer morale will suffer, and eventually the tax will degenerate into a set of haphazard levies paid by the more honest or timid property owners.

It is during a severe or prolonged depression, however, that delinquencies are likely to become so widespread as to prove both embarrassing to the government and provocative of much sharp criticism of the property tax on the part of the people. A tax on property, unlike the individual income tax, does not disappear whenever the wage earner loses his job and is forced to subsist either on unemployment insurance or on outright public relief. Although his income has fallen sharply, the person in question is likely to hold on to most of his material possessions, for a time at least, and these, of course, form the base of the property tax. It is true that the market values of many of these items are likely to fall substantially, but property tax assessments may be counted on to show a perverse resistance to this trend. This may result from a practice of not reassessing every item of property on the tax roll each year or from a belief on the part of the assessor that assessed valuations should reflect "normal" values, which are necessarily above market prices during a depression. Since tax rates can always be lowered, however, it is not these assessment practices alone which make the property tax insensitive to declines in national income. That characteristic of the tax, which showed up very clearly during the Great Depression when state and local property tax receipts rose from 5 per cent of net national income in 1929 to 9 per cent in 1933, is attributable to the fact that state and local governments, who typically find their expenditures relatively stable or even rising during a recession, do not have the powers of the federal government to issue debt or create money in order to finance a deficit. Nevertheless, increased federal aid and more diversified state and local tax systems should lighten the pressure which any future major depression is likely to place on the general property tax.

Tax Limits and Their Effects

It has long been a custom in this country to attempt to hold in check the spending propensities of state and local governments by means of both statutory and constitutional tax limits. These vary from specific ceilings on property tax rates set forth in city charters to state-wide limits on the taxes that may be levied on given kinds of property regardless of how many different taxing jurisdictions those properties may lie within. During the Great Depression there was a flurry of interest in these matters, and as a result old limits were made more restrictive and new ones were introduced. Since that time, however, few additional changes have been made.

We need not concern ourselves here with the myriad variations which property tax limits may take. Regardless of its idiosyncrasies each type is likely to have approximately the same effects. Although these are by no means easy to untangle, there is some evidence that tax limits do tend to inhibit the growth of the property tax. Between 1930 and 1950, for example, property taxes in twelve states with comprehensive tax limits increased by only 16 per cent whereas the increase in the remaining states and the District of Columbia was 42 per cent. Over the same period property levies per capita in the twelve tax-limit states decreased slightly (from $38 to $37) while they were rising elsewhere from $43 to $50.[24] The further effects of this shrinkage in the role of the property tax cannot readily be identified. It may be that where tax limits are effective state and local expenditures are less than they otherwise would be, but it seems more likely that the use of alternative sources of revenue, including grants from higher levels of government, has been stimulated instead.

Effects of Property Taxation on Incomes and Prices

The changes which a property tax may be expected to bring about in the prices paid by consumers and investors and in the money incomes received by different individuals depend to a large extent on the types of property that are included in the tax base. Since the nature of the relevant analysis has already been indicated in detail, we shall deal here only with three kinds of property with features of special interest: (1) land, which constitutes for many people the ideal base for taxation, (2) residential property which permits a comparison of the effects of taxes on consumer and on investment goods, and (3) tangible business property, the taxation of which has important effects on risk-taking and on the rate of economic growth. The reader should have no difficulty in applying the same kind of analysis to other kinds of property.

TAX ON THE SITE VALUE OF LAND. When economists speak of a tax on land, they are ordinarily thinking of land in a somewhat more restricted sense than would occur to most laymen. For reasons that will become clear as we go along, it is convenient to separate the value of improvements to land, such as drainage and fertilization (which require the efforts of human beings), from the value of land itself as

[24] Mabel Newcomer, "The Decline of the General Property Tax, *op. cit.,* p. 44.

determined by its location and natural endowments. It is the latter, or site, value which forms the base of the tax to be discussed in this section. The distinguishing feature of this levy is that it rests upon a type of property which is fixed in supply and cannot be altered by the efforts of human beings.

The immediate effect of the tax, of course, is to lower the net incomes received by all landowners and to provide an incentive for them (and others) to invest in assets other than land. This shift of funds will continue, forcing down the price of land in the process, until the rate of return on investment in land is raised to the point at which it is once more equal to profit rates on assets of comparable risk. Rates of return in general are not likely to be lowered by a tax on the site value of land, for it is in the markets for newly produced income-earning assets—an area to which our tax does not apply— that these rates are determined.[25] We have, then, a case of complete tax capitalization in which the owners of land at the time the tax is announced bear the full burden of it. New investors are able to acquire land at a price sufficiently low to yield them the same income per dollar invested, after deduction of the new land tax, as could have been obtained before the tax was imposed.[26] If the supply of land were not fixed, the lower selling prices on it would induce a contraction in that supply which, in the face of an unchanged demand for the goods produced with the help of land, would push land values back up again. These developments, however, do not take place in the present instance, and we may conclude that the incidence of a tax on the site value of land rests on present and past landowners.

Single Tax. There are features about a tax on land which in the past so appealed to a number of articulate observers of the economic scene that they elevated it above all other taxes and argued that it alone should form the fiscal base of government. In this country a journalist by the name of Henry George, who moved to San Francisco in 1858 and later published an economic best-seller entitled *Progress and Poverty,* did most to popularize the idea of a single tax on land values. In the years between his arrival in California and the appearance of his book in 1879 George had ample opportunity to observe the fortunes that could be made from land ownership in an economy

[25] It is true that if the tax on land were to induce such a large shift of funds into these markets that output could not be expanded sufficiently to keep prices from rising, rates of return in general would fall as the prices of newly produced assets rose. It is quite unlikely, however, that a tax on the site value of land would induce such a large shift.

[26] For a fuller discussion of tax capitalization see chap. 10.

with a rapidly growing population. Since these capital gains were created not by the efforts of specific individuals but by society as a whole, it seemed eminently fair to him that they should be returned to society in the form of taxes. All of the gains should be taken, he argued, and the need for any other type of tax would then be completely eliminated.

The single tax doctrine is open to criticism on two main grounds. The less important of these is that we have, fortunately or unfortunately, long since passed the time when a confiscation of all increases in land site values would provide adequate public revenues. Between 1945 and 1955, for example, when total federal, state, and local tax collections rose from over $50 billion a year to nearly $100 billion, land values increased by only $7-8 billion a year, and these figures are not pure site values but include the effects of an unknown amount of man-made improvements.[27] A much more serious criticism is that increases in site values are not the only type of income that is due far more to good luck than to hard work and sacrifice on the part of the recipient. Furthermore, the more one pursues the problem of classifying gains into those which are ethically justifiable (i.e., defended as "truly earned") and those which are not, the more one realizes that this is an impossible task. In what sense, to cite only one example, is the income earned by a beautiful young movie star, whose acting talents are not among her best-developed features, more deserved than the capital gains of a dowager who bought land in Los Angeles in 1939 and, for lack of anything better to do, held it through the postwar population boom? In neither case is the income derived so much from persevering effort on the part of the recipient as from a happy combination of circumstances of which she was the beneficiary.

It is undeniable that there are, scattered throughout the economic system in any given period of time, many windfall gains which on either ethical or practical grounds constitute ideal tax bases—i.e., they are not "merited" in the sense of being earned by the efforts of the recipient; and, furthermore, since the recipient did no work to get them, his work incentives are not going to be impaired by having them taxed. The problem is to isolate these ideally taxable gains. The likelihood is that in the process of separation more inequities would be created than eliminated.

TAX ON RESIDENTIAL PROPERTY. We turn now to the incidence of a tax on residential dwellings. These are consumer goods when

---

[27] Computed from the national wealth estimates of Raymond Goldsmith reported in *The Statistical Abstract of the United States* (Washington, D.C.: Government Printing Office, 1957), p. 319.

occupied by their owners and investment goods when rented out to tenants, and it will be convenient to treat the two types separately.

The principal effects of a tax on rental properties are as follows:

1. The incomes received by landlords are lowered, and as a result funds begin to be shifted into other types of investment.

2. In the short run these developments bring about a fall in the prices of existing homes and apartment houses.

3. As contrasted with the case of land, fewer new dwelling units will now be built, and the supply of the taxed property will gradually become less than it otherwise would have been.

4. The restriction in supply raises rents and moves both landlord incomes and home prices back toward their pretax levels.

5. Whether or not they return exactly to pretax levels depends upon whether or not rates of return on other types of investment assets are lowered by the tax on residential property. Since an important type of reproducible investment asset has had its yield lowered by a tax, it is very likely that profit rates everywhere will be somewhat lowered. In this way the tax on landlords is diffused to investors in general,[28] rental property prices do not return to their pretax levels, and the tax is partially capitalized.

6. The decline in residential construction lowers the money incomes of factors of production in that industry, and their shift elsewhere in search of better prospects both reduces the incomes of competing resources and expands production, thereby lowering the prices of other goods and services. Once again the familiar reaction to a partial tax has taken place: the composition of the national output is changed, less of the taxed product being matched by more of certain other things.

7. Most writers interpret the tax-induced increase in residential rentals as a complete, or nearly complete, forward shifting of the tax to consumers. This conclusion, as we have argued in greater detail above in connection with sales taxes,[29] neglects on the one hand the consumer gains that flow from the increased production of nontaxed output, and on the other the reductions in money income suffered not only by the owners of resources originally located in the construction industry but also by owners of resources that compete with them for jobs.

The effects of a tax on owner-occupied dwelling units are similar to, but not identical with, the foregoing:

1. The annual cost of owning a home of given quality is increased by the tax, and hence the imputed net income received by owner-occupants is reduced. Potential buyers of new homes are induced either to spend less on the building itself or not to buy one at all.

2. In the short run the prices of homes fall.

[28] See the more complete discussion of this phenomenon in chap. 10.
[29] See chap. 13.

3. Fewer or less expensive houses are built and the supply of dwelling units gradually becomes less than it would have been without the residential property tax.

4. The reduction in supply raises both the prices of, and the imputed net rentals on, owner-occupied houses, but whatever the owner gains as a landlord he loses as an occupant.

5. The funds which potential home-buyers no longer spend on houses are likely to be spent on other consumer goods and services although they may, of course, be saved and invested in various kinds of financial assets.

6. Spending on other consumer goods, then, may be expected to increase, but the resources available to turn out these products have also been increased by the contraction in the residential construction industry. It is conceivable, although unlikely, that these released resources will shift precisely to those areas toward which the increased spending is directed, thus minimizing the price adjustments that must take place. In that case potential home-buyers have simply altered the composition of their consumption in response to the property tax, and other consumers are not affected at all. In the more complex situation in which the resource and spending shifts do not match, some consumer prices will rise and others will fall, and many more consumers will be affected, some adversely and some favorably, by these changes.

7. There is wide agreement that a tax on owner-occupied dwelling units is not shifted but is borne in each case by the owner of the house.

TAX ON TANGIBLE BUSINESS PROPERTY. This type of property tax is of especially great interest today because it includes within its base durable capital assets which, together with human abilities and talents, form the foundation for rapid economic growth and development. The initial impact of the tax is to reduce the level of money income to be earned by owning tangible business assets. Investors in these assets will then find three alternative uses for their funds relatively more attractive than they were before the tax was imposed. To some extent businessmen may find it possible to substitute labor for capital assets in the operation of their firms, and by this means they will then be able to reduce their tax liabilities without impairing unduly the quality of their output. Secondly, although common stock earnings will reflect the lower after-tax incomes received by corporations, fixed-income securities such as government and corporate bonds will not and thereby will become relatively more attractive investments. Thirdly, some investors may be induced by the tax on their assets to shift to consumption, say by buying a more elaborate house for themselves, or by going on a more extended vacation trip. In addition, since the use of varying proportions of property and labor in different businesses will make for different tax burdens in relation to income, labor-intensive industries with their relatively low taxes will become more attractive to investors than those capital-intensive industries which use large amounts of taxable property.

What, then, will be the major effects of these various inducements that are brought into existence by the tax on tangible business property? In the first place, it is clear that the demand for new capital assets will be reduced by the tax and that as a consequence fewer of them will be produced. This will make available more resources for consumption purposes in the short run, but it will also reduce the rate of economic growth and hence the level of potential consumption in future years. What consumers gain at one time, in other words, they lose at another. Secondly, the tax reduces the amount of risk-taking in the economy because it is a tax confined to the riskiest types of investment assets. In addition, it may be noted that the tax is similar to an income levy without loss offsets since it reduces the net returns from successful ventures but not the losses from unsuccessful ones. This necessarily makes risk-taking a less attractive undertaking. Finally, a number of groups of people who may not even know that a tax has been imposed on tangible business property are likely, nevertheless, to experience income increases or decreases as a direct result of that tax. Workers with special talents for the production of capital assets will suffer cuts in their wage rates when the capital goods are dispensed with by businessmen, but other workers are likely to be hired at higher incomes to take the place of the machines and equipment.[30] Nor will people as far removed from the active world of production as corporate and government bondholders escape the tax web. Those holding bonds during the period immediately following the first announcement of the property tax will enjoy unforeseen capital gains, but new investors will find that they cannot earn so high a rate of return on their funds as they could have received had the tax never been imposed.

Property Taxation in Underdeveloped Countries

Although property taxation has many inequities, some inherent and others attributable primarily to the limitations of human beings, it may still constitute a relatively attractive source of revenue for underdeveloped countries. If the major part of a country's wealth is held by a small group of people, a property tax is easy to administer, and if the holders are addicted to a lavish scale of living, heavy taxes

---

[30] A business, for example, in turning out its workload of letters and reports, may choose a staff of stenographers or the purchase of a number of tape-recording machines together with the hiring of a small number of typists. A tax on tangible business property would be one factor favoring the first alternative.

on dwellings and other consumer goods may induce a shift of funds into the acquisition of those types of business plant and equipment which are so badly needed for economic development. Since population is typically growing rapidly in these countries, increases in the site value of land are likely to be important; and these form, as we have seen, an attractive base for taxation. In addition, land taxes may force the previously unutilized holdings of large landowners into productive activity.

As the financial and monetary structure of a country develops, to be sure, a property tax becomes more difficult to administer and more inequitable in its incidence. At the same time, fortunately, the operation of an income tax, as well as spendings and net worth taxes, becomes increasingly feasible and desirable.

Part II

SUGGESTED READINGS

General:

AMERICAN ECONOMIC ASSOCIATION. *Readings in the Economics of Taxation.* Homewood, Ill.: Richard D. Irwin, Inc., 1959.
A very useful selection of writings (published before 1953) on the economic theory of taxation. Note especially F. Y. Edgeworth's "The Pure Theory of Taxation," Harry Gunnison Brown's "The Incidence of a General Output or a General Sales Tax," and the classic Domar-Musgrave study of "Proportional Income Taxation and Risk-Taking."

MUSGRAVE, RICHARD A. *The Theory of Public Finance.* New York: The McGraw-Hill Book Co., 1959.
A theoretical analysis with extensive references to the literature. See especially chaps. vii, viii, and Part III.

MUSGRAVE, R. A.; J. J. CARROLL; L. D. COOK; and L. FRANE. "Distribution of Tax Payments by Income Groups: a Case Study for 1948," *National Tax Journal,* IV (March, 1951).
A detailed quantitative analysis of the income distribution of tax burdens in the United States. The study elicited considerable discussion and criticism. See the comments of Rufus S. Tucker, Gerhard Colm, Haskell P. Wald, and the original authors in *National Tax Journal,* Sept., 1951, and March, 1952, as well as A. R. Prest, "Statistical Calculations of Tax Burdens," *Economica,* Aug., 1955.

NATIONAL TAX ASSOCIATION. Both the *National Tax Journal,* which is published quarterly, and the *Proceedings* of the Association's annual conferences contain papers dealing with various aspects of taxation.

PIGOU, A. C. *A Study in Public Finance,* 3rd ed. London: Macmillan & Co., Ltd., 1947.
The finest exposition of public-finance theory in the neo-classical tradition.

ROLPH, EARL R. *The Theory of Fiscal Economics.* Berkeley: Univ. of California Press, 1954.
Chaps. vi-xii contain an economic analysis of sales and excise taxes, import duties, and the effects of taxation on incentives to work and to invest.

U.S. CONGRESS, JOINT COMMITTEE ON THE ECONOMIC REPORT (now the Joint Economic Committee). *Federal Tax Policy for Economic Growth and Stability.* Papers Submitted by Panelists Appearing before the Subcommittee on Tax

Policy, November 9, 1955. Washington, D.C.: Government Printing Office, 1956.
Covers a wide range of topics including the effects of federal taxation on consumption, investment, and work incentives; various structural problems under the individual and corporate income taxes; federal-state-local fiscal relations and the effects of federal estate and gift taxation.
U.S. CONGRESS, COMMITTEE ON WAYS AND MEANS. *Tax Revision Compendium.* 3 vols. Compendium of Papers on Broadening the Tax Base. Washington, D.C.: Government Printing Office, 1959.
A comprehensive set of papers dealing with six major topics:
1) Major objectives and guides for tax reform;
2) Statistical analysis of the individual and corporate tax bases;
3) Specific elements in the computation of taxable income;
4) The appropriate taxable entity;
5) Special problems in corporate taxation;
6) The structure of tax rates.

The following are works in a series of empirical studies published by the Harvard University Graduate School of Business Administration:

BUTTERS, J. KEITH and JOHN LINTNER. *Effect of Federal Taxes on Growing Enterprises.* 1945.
BUTTERS, J. KEITH. *Effects of Taxation on Inventory Accounting and Policies.* 1949.
BUTTERS, J. KEITH; JOHN LINTNER; and WILLIAM L. CARY. *Effects of Taxation on Corporate Mergers.* 1951.
SANDERS, THOMAS H. *Effects of Taxation on Executives.* 1951.
HALL, CHALLIS A., JR. *Effects of Taxation on Executive Compensation and Retirement Plans.* 1951.
BROWN, E. CARY. *Effects of Taxation on Depreciation Adjustments for Price Changes.* 1952.
SMITH, DAN THROOP. *Effects of Taxation on Corporate Financial Policy.* 1952.
BUTTERS, J. KEITH; LAWRENCE E. THOMPSON; and LYNN L. BOLLINGER. *Effects of Taxation: Investments by Individuals.* 1953.

Income Taxation:

GOODE, RICHARD. *The Corporation Income Tax.* New York: John Wiley & Sons, Inc., 1951.
A comprehensive analytical and statistical treatment of this important tax.
HOLLAND, DANIEL M. *The Income-Tax Burden on Stockholders.* (A National Bureau of Economic Research Study.) Princeton: Princeton Univ. Press, 1958.
A quantitative analysis of the extent to which stockholders in this country paid higher or lower taxes than other income receivers between 1940 and 1952.
PECHMAN, JOSEPH A. "Erosion of the Individual Income Tax," *National Tax Journal,* X (March, 1957).
A path-breaking study of the quantitative effect of leakages on the base and yield of the federal individual income tax in 1956. Similar estimates for 1957 are given in Pechman's paper in Vol. I of the *Tax Revision Compendium,* cited above. In the same volume William F. Hellmuth, Jr. computed the potential yield of a broad-based corporate income tax in 1959.
SELTZER, LAWRENCE H. *The Nature and Tax Treatment of Capital Gains and Losses.* New York: National Bureau of Economic Research, 1951.
Contains a wealth of statistical data covering the 1917-1946 period, together with a survey of the development, economic nature, and controversial aspects of capital gains and losses.
SIMONS, HENRY C. *Personal Income Taxation.* Chicago: Univ. of Chicago Press, 1938.
A stimulating and provocative analysis of the definition of income as a problem of fiscal policy. A classic in the field.

VICKREY, WILLIAM. *Agenda for Progressive Taxation.* New York: The Ronald
  Press Co., 1947.
  A detailed and rigorous theoretical analysis of income, spendings, and succession
  taxes.
U.S. TREASURY DEPARTMENT, DIVISION OF TAX RESEARCH. *The Postwar Corporation
  Tax Structure.* Washington, D.C.: Government Printing Office, 1948.
  Prepared by Richard Goode. Contains a detailed analysis of different methods
  of integrating the personal and corporate income taxes.

The Spendings Tax:

FISHER, IRVING and H. W. FISHER. *Constructive Income Taxation.* New York:
  Harper & Bros., 1942. A plea for a spendings tax and the first proposal to make
  such a tax administratively feasible.
KALDOR, NICHOLAS. *An Expenditure Tax.* London: George Allen & Unwin, 1955.
  A proposal for a spendings tax for Great Britain.
PIGOU, A. C. *A Study in Public Finance.*
  See chap. x for an argument favoring spendings over income taxation on
  theoretical grounds.
PREST, A. R. *Public Finance in Theory and Practice.* Chicago: Quadrangle Books,
  Inc., 1960. Pp. 79-84.
  Compares income and spendings taxation with regard to effects on saving.

Net Worth Taxation:

CHOU, SHUN-HSIN. *The Capital Levy.* New York: King's Crown Press, 1945.
  Reviews capital levies and examines certain mathematical features of tax laws.
DUE, JOHN F. *Government Finance,* rev. ed. Homewood, Ill.: Richard D. Irwin,
  Inc., 1959. Pp. 376-84.
  Argues that a net worth tax may be shifted.
KUZNETS, SIMON. *Shares of Upper Income Groups in Income and Savings.* New
  York: National Bureau of Economic Research, Inc., 1953.
  A comprehensive statistical study of high income groups in the United States.
MUSGRAVE, RICHARD A. *The Theory of Public Finance.* Pp. 312-35.
  Sets forth an important theory of investment choice.
PREST, A. R. *Public Finance.* Chicago: Quadrangle Books, Inc., 1960. Pp. 49-50.
  A brief comment on net worth taxation.
SHULTZ, W. J. and M. R. CAINE. *Financial Development of the United States.*
  New York: Prentice-Hall, Inc., 1937.
  An excellent reference work on U.S. financial history.
TAUSSIG, FRANK W. *Inventors and Money-Makers.* New York: The Macmillan Co.,
  1915.
  An examination of why some people are financially successful and others, such
  as inventors, commonly are not.
VICKREY, WILLIAM. *Agenda for Progressive Taxation.* Pp. 352-54, 362-66.
  Sets out a plan for net worth taxation aimed at eroding great fortunes.

Excess Profits and Excess Income Taxation:

BLOUGH, ROY. *The Federal Taxing Process.* New York: Prentice-Hall, Inc., 1952.
  The tax history of World War II is discussed, pp. 224-49.
HICKS, J. R.; U. K. HICKS; and L. ROSTAS. *The Taxation of War Wealth,* 2d ed.
  Oxford: Clarendon Press, 1942.
  A wartime study of excess income and profits taxation in many countries.
KEITH, E. GORDON. "The Excess Profits Tax of 1950," *National Tax Journal,* Vol.
  IV (Sept. 1951), 193-207.
  A revealing account of the most recent excess profits tax used in the United
  States.

PRENTICE-HALL, INC. *Federal Excess Profits Tax.* New York: Prentice-Hall, Inc., 1954. The tax law, administrative rulings, and court decisions of the Korean War Excess Profits Tax. Supplement on World War II tax.

Death Taxation:

PIGOU, A. C. *A Study in Public Finance.* Pp. 138-146.
Analyzes the Rignano plan.

SHULTZ, WILLIAM J. and C. LOWELL HARRISS. *American Public Finance.* New York: Prentice-Hall, Inc., 1954. Pp. 431-54.
An analytical and descriptive study of death taxation.

SIMONS, HENRY. *Personal Income Taxation.* Chicago: Univ. of Chicago Press, 1938. Chap. vi.
Argues for the inclusion of gifts, legacies, and inheritances as taxable income to the recipient.

U.S. TREASURY DEPARTMENT, ADVISORY COMMITTEE. *Federal Estate and Gift Taxation.* Washington, D.C.: Government Printing Office, 1947.
Examines estate and gift taxation from the point of view of their possible integration.

VICKREY, WILLIAM. *Agenda for Progressive Taxation.* Chaps. vii, viii, and ix.
A systematic examination of succession taxation and a proposal called a "Bequeathing Power Succession Tax."

Sales Taxation:

DUE, JOHN F. *Sales Taxation.* Urbana: Univ. of Illinois Press, 1957.
A re-examination of the appropriate role of sales taxes in the light of the experience of various countries with them. Detailed attention is given to Canada, Australia, and New Zealand and to numerous European countries, as well as to municipal and state taxes in this country.

ROLPH, EARL R. *The Theory of Fiscal Economics.*
Chaps. vi and vii present a detailed criticism of traditional theories of sales tax incidence. For other, frequently conflicting, views on this subject, see Due's "Toward a General Theory of Sales Tax Incidence," *Quarterly Journal of Economics,* LXVII (May, 1953); Musgrave's *The Theory of Public Finance,* pp. 379-82; and J. A. Stockfisch, "The Capitalization and Investment Aspects of Excise Taxes Under Competition," *American Economic Review,* XLIV (June, 1954).

Import and Export Duties:

EDGEWORTH, F. Y. *Papers Relating to Political Economy.* London: Macmillan & Co., Ltd., 1925.
Vol. II expounds and elaborates the Mill approach, expresses doubt about symmetry of import and export taxes.

GRAHAM, FRANK. *The Theory of International Values.* Princeton: Princeton Univ. Press, 1948.
An exposition of international trade that is critical of the Mill tradition and especially of the theory of import-export taxation set forth by Rolph.

LERNER, A. P. "The Symmetry between Import and Export Taxes," *Economica,* N.S. III (1936). Pp. 306-13.
A clear exposition, using graphical techniques, of the "symmetry" doctrine.

MARSHALL, ALFRED. *Money, Credit and Commerce.* London: Macmillan & Co., Ltd., 1923.
Book III, chaps. ix and x and Appendix J give a further elaboration of the Mill approach.

MILL, JOHN S. *Essays on Some Unsettled Questions of Political Economy,* Essay I, largely reproduced in *Principles of Political Economy,* Vol. II, Book III, chap. xviii and Book V, chap. iv, paragraph 6.
The classic exposition of the reciprocal demand theory of international trade.

ROLPH, EARL R. *Theory of Fiscal Economics.* Pp. 172-226.
Provides a theory of the incidence of import and export taxes for fluctuating and fixed exchange rates.

VINER, JACOB. *Studies in the Theory of International Trade.* New York: Harper & Bros., 1937.
An elaboration of international trade theory.

Property Taxation:

BUEHLER, ALFRED G. "The Capitalization of Taxes," *National Tax Journal,* III (Dec., 1950).
A summary article.

DAVENPORT, H. J. "Theoretical Issues in the Single Tax," *American Economic Review,* VII (March, 1917).
Contains a concise statement of the theory of tax capitalization in a footnote (pp. 26-28).

MORTON, WALTER A. *Housing Taxation.* Madison: Univ. of Wisconsin Press, 1955.
An analysis of the burden of property taxes on home owners at different income levels. Empirical data are mainly for the state of Wisconsin.

Part III

SPECIAL PROBLEMS IN GOVERNMENT FINANCE

Introduction

In this part attention is turned to four fiscal problems which require the analysis of both government receipts and government expenditures. Public enterprises, for example, ordinarily sell goods and services to consumers and businessmen at a price, thereby providing the government with revenues to offset at least part of its costs. The appropriate scope of such operations, the levels at which their prices should be set, and the criteria by which their investment plans should be judged are all discussed in Chapter 16.

Although government programs to protect individuals against loss of income from old age, sickness, and unemployment need not be tied to specific government revenues, such has been the case in this country since the passage of the Social Security Act of 1935. In Chapter 17, accordingly, we discuss the economic effects of both old-age and unemployment insurance payments and the payroll taxes by which the transfers are financed. Related programs, such as general assistance, which are supported from general government revenues are also included in the analysis.

Fiscal relations between different levels of government have in recent decades become increasingly important and complex on both sides of the budget. In this country the federal government makes grants and loans both to other sovereign governments under its well-known foreign aid programs and to state and local governments in connection with a wide variety of domestic undertakings. Chapter 18 deals with the effects of these federal expenditures as well as with the problems involved in developing an equitable and workable integration of the taxes levied by different levels of government. Such integration is needed both to minimize waste in the collection of taxes and to rationalize the treatment of tax bases which overlap several governmental jurisdictions. In addition, integration can be used to bring the superior fiscal powers of national governments to the aid of hard-pressed state and local treasuries.

The economic and fiscal problems of metropolitan governments are now sufficiently important to warrant separate treatment. Housing slums, traffic congestion, and air pollution are all problems that are likely to occupy local officials for some time to come. Chapter 19, accordingly, discusses the contributions which governmental expenditure and revenue policies can make to the development of economically efficient and esthetically pleasant urban areas.

16

Government Enterprise

Governments engage in practically every known enterprise from roasting nuts to operating steamship lines. The conservative businessman may shudder with horror to observe the TVA producing and selling fertilizers in competition with privately organized business. The same businessman, if he lives in Los Angeles, may insist that the government should provide cheap water and may contribute heavily to the campaigns of candidates for office who are committed to government provision of this commodity. Steel producers would no doubt be troubled if the federal government produced steel for sale on a large scale, but the same producers would strongly object if the government refused to sell them steel scrap. Socialists rejoice at the contemplation of government operation of public power projects or of almost anything else, because their solution for the world's social ills calls for government operation of everything, or rather almost everything. Even some of them have qualms about exclusive government operation of newspapers, and scarcely any contemplate that the government should take over the business of preparing meals in the home.

In this chapter, attention will be directed to three main topics. The first is the question of what types of enterprise, if any, governments are peculiarly suited to operate. The second is the principle of pricing the products produced by government. Any principles of pricing applicable to government will also be applicable to government regulation of the prices charged by private business. The third is government investment. What types of investments should be undertaken by governments, and once the new resources have been produced, what shall be done with them? All three topics are closely interrelated. If it is appropriate for governments to operate water works, it is necessary to arrive at prices to be charged for water, and decisions must be made about the construction of new facilities to augment existing supplies of water, especially in growing regions. Although attention will be directed primarily to government enterprise in the United States, the general principles to be discussed should be equally applicable to Great Britain, France, or India.

Scope of Government Enterprise

The belief is widely held that a thinking person must take a stand on the side of socialism or capitalism; he must favor either government operation or private operation of enterprise. The choice is like that among religions—one must be a Protestant, a Catholic, a Jew, or a Mohammedan. The lines are drawn. Some are "converted" to socialism or "converted" to capitalism, with the converts of each camp proselyting the young and the uncommitted as well as one another. Yet in practice, the question of the scope for government enterprise rarely appears in these terms. Actual issues are typically issues of more or less, not of all or none. Shall the Post Office Department provide the service of delivering parcels of any size, or should it limit its service to those under a given weight and cubic dimension? Shall Marines get their hair cut at the post or at the town's local barber shop? Shall a prospective dam site be committed to government or to private production of electricity? Apart from primitive societies, pure socialism is an invention of the mind and so is pure capitalism. All actual complex systems, including the Russian one, are mixtures of private and public enterprise. The real questions are those of more or less.

The slogans employed by those on the "right" and "left" are almost useless in determining the extent to which governments should engage in enterprise. Consider the slogan, "Government should not compete with business." It was the principle, insofar as there was any principle, which guided the elaborate inquiries of the Hoover Commission into the operations of the federal government. If taken seriously, this principle would condemn the operation of the George Washington Bridge over the Hudson—the bridge put some ferries out of business. Airmail service competes with long-distance telephone service. The Treasury by selling savings bonds competes with savings banks for funds. State universities compete with private universities and colleges for students and, more importantly, for mathematicians, chemists, and instructors in English. The slogan reduces to foolishness. Anyone who proclaims it could not possibly mean what he says.

Consider the slogan of the socialists, "Production for use and not for profit." This slogan suggests that there is something tainted about producing things where the motivation of those concerned is to make a profit. It implies that the production of milk shakes at the corner drug store is not "for use" because the proprietor aims at making a profit out of such business.[1] Yet the young lady pulling on the end of a straw enjoys the milk shake. Somehow we are supposed to believe that if the milk shake were produced by a government organization, all would be different and better. Maybe there would be no milk shakes, or maybe only those who could supply a medical prescription to prove that milk shakes were a dietetic necessity would be permitted to get them. The slogan may have an attractive ring, but it is useless in solving any actual problem.

Is there, then, any principle capable of providing a rational test for the selection of activities to be conducted by public or by private organizations? The test here suggested is the one of *comparative efficiency*. In general, it means that government should expand, contract, or maintain its enterprise activities if its costs are less than, greater than, or equal to the costs of privately organized production of similar things. The test is a severe one. It could imply that the federal government should turn over the postal service to private organizations. On the other hand, it could also imply that cities should go into the business of delivering milk. Conservatives should welcome the test because if private enterprise is inherently more efficient than government as they claim, there should be little scope for government enterprise. Socialists should likewise welcome it because if government is more efficient than private organizations, government enterprise would have much room to expand. The principle has the advantage of reducing the issue to questions of fact. The qualification should immediately be made that the relevant facts are often difficult to ascertain.

The comparative-efficiency test implies that both private and public organizations should be "free" to enter any business activity. "Free enterprise" presumably implies freedom to compete for the public's dollars by any and all forms of enterprise. Governments, however, are prone to exclude private endeavor from a field selected by them. Thus the mail service is an exclusive prerogative of the post office. The British Broadcasting Company is legally protected from private competition in radio broadcasting (except from foreign stations). In states with state-operated liquor outlets, private competition is dis-

[1] Much to his sorrow, he often finds that teenagers have managed to persuade him to provide a subsidized club.

allowed. The potential revenue of newly constructed bridges is some-times protected by prohibiting the operation of privately operated ferries. The jealous concern of government agencies engaged in an enterprise function to exclude private competition would, if duplicated by a private organization, be roundly condemned as monopolistic exploitation. Subject to certain qualifications to be noted, the practice of excluding competition has no more justification when carried out by a government than by a private organization.

ENTERPRISES OF SPECIAL GOVERNMENT CONCERN. There are several classes of enterprise in which government has a special inter-est over and above its obligation to provide rules applicable to eco-nomic activity in general. These are (1) services or goods which for technical reasons cannot be subject to pricing, (2) services and goods which if priced would be "spoiled," (3) the distribution of goods and services where there are substantial economies in a unified system of delivery to a given group of customers, (4) goods or services which, as a matter of public policy, should be provided below cost.

1. There are some types of products which cannot be priced at all, such as lighthouse services, as was once pointed out by Adam Smith. There are others, such as highway service, which although not impossible to price (e.g., tollroads) would be extremely costly both to the agency collecting the charge and to the motorist, in terms of delay and exasperation. It should be noted that the activities in question do provide services which can be taken in various amounts by individual users. They are not similar to the functions of a military establishment, a tax-collecting agency, or a foreign consulate, none of which provide services that can be taken, let alone priced, by indi-viduals. When the community wishes to have services that cannot be priced at all or are difficult and expensive to price, the government or some private philanthropy must enter the picture. It can either perform the function itself, as is done in the case of highways, or contract with a private organization to provide the service. In all such cases, the potentiality of overuse occurs since private users have no incentive to economize on the service. As illustrated by highways, the consequence of zero pricing is drastic congestion in critical areas, leading to the political demand for more and more facilities to relieve the overuse. Granted that an effective price system is ruled out— the device of taxing motor fuel is a poor substitute for direct pricing— the government is faced with a hard choice. The cost of providing such "free" services, i.e., free to users although not to the government, needs to be weighed against alternative ways of relieving congestion, such as subsidies to alternative forms of transportation.

Rarely does such a choice present itself in a relevant political context. Highway department engineers dream of bigger and more elaborate highways, in the hopeless aim of getting permanently ahead of the demand for highway services. Railroad officials, having been nurtured in the role of heavy-handed monopolists, scarcely know how to compete, and sit wistfully by watching alternative modes of transport rob them of customers when railroads are by far the most economical system for moving freight. Obsolete pricing of rail service by increasing the demand for highway use gives rise to a large part of the substantial expenses of federal and state governments for highway construction and maintenance.

2. Some types of services or goods cannot be priced without spoiling them for the recipients. One does not ordinarily invite guests to dinner and charge them for the number of mouthfuls of meat taken or the number of martinis consumed. A host who did this would scarcely be viewed as having arrived socially. Similarly there are community services which must be kept free of any suggestion of commercialism to be worth taking. Playgrounds for children should not be rationed by price; a child should feel entitled to use the facilities when he pleases. In such cases, some community organization is needed to provide the facilities. Governments have taken responsibility for local parks so that their enjoyment is ordinarily feasible without charge.

The extent to which facilities are made unattractive by a pricing system depends upon the tastes of those concerned. People accustomed to "free" television, which ought to be described as expensive television insofar as expense takes the form of watching the commercials, might be upset by having to insert coins in a slot to see their favorite programs, even though the amount to be paid is of trivial concern. Custom plays a large role in these cases. People in many regions have long been accustomed to treating the street as a garage, as if such space were a free good. The claim that a service is spoiled by the very fact of pricing may be no more than a reflection of outmoded practice.

3. By far the most important cases of industries in which government has a special interest are those usually called "public utilities." We do not, however, intend to refer to just these cases; for example, we do not include railroads. There are a number of services which for technical reasons are much more economically provided by a single supplier than by more than one supplier. Electricity, gas, water, and telephone services are illustrations. In each case of this kind, several suppliers for the same group of customers would needlessly duplicate facilities. For similar reasons, services taking the form of regular

delivery to a large set of customers in a given area, such as mail delivery, garbage collection, and milk delivery can be performed with less expense to a society if provided by one supplier than by two or more.

The single supplier provides a less costly service because the amount of the service demanded in any one household is small relative to the feasible capacity of a delivery system, and the amount of resources needed to supply any group of customers diminishes as the regional concentration of the group increases. Two mail-delivery companies serving a thousand customers located within a square mile would each have to travel about the same distance as would one alone. The cost of delivery depends in part upon the distance to be travelled between stops. The greater is the concentration of stops, the less is the amount of distance to be covered. In the case of electricity, the length of wire to be strung or placed underground becomes the "distance" factor. Although the diseconomies of having multiple distributors of water, gas, electricity, and telephone service are generally appreciated, multiple delivery systems for milk continue to be tolerated even though the wastes involved are conspicuous and avoidable. A city milk distribution service, or alternatively a private organization with an exclusive contract, could provide the service at a substantial saving in resources and, incidentally, could reduce congestion on city streets.

4. Governments become committed for a variety of reasons to the responsibility of providing a service or good taken by the public at prices deliberately set to assure losses. In the United States, but not in Great Britain, the postal services entail substantial deficits. Political groups who support continuing deficits justify their position by appealing to the alleged social advantages of cheap communication.

In the United States, the most expensive type of service provided by governments to persons, as measured by the expense to governments, is public education. For reasons of public policy, the American people are committed to free schooling to at least the college level. A pricing system, even one of nominal charges, is inconsistent with the public objective of educational opportunity for every child; any pricing scheme would exclude some children from the classroom. It is also inconsistent with the legal requirement that children attend some school, whether public or private. It does not follow, to be sure, that because this service is to be free it must be provided directly under government auspices. Conceivably, parents might be paid a flat sum per child, subject to the condition that that sum or more be spent for the child's education at any approved privately-managed school. The comparative advantages and disadvantages of such a system are discussed elsewhere.[2]

Many other types of services are sponsored by governments at unremunerative prices. In Great Britain, medical care is provided free of charge except for nominal payments in connection with some prescriptions. However, there is the expense in the form of waiting to enter hospitals for some types of ailments. Housing is provided on a limited scale in the United States through public housing projects. Prices are charged for the service, but they are distinctly lower than the prices would be under competition. Consequently, other methods of selecting tenants must be used. The most common technique is an income means test; families with incomes above some defined amount are declared ineligible, and those already located in such housing projects are asked to move, assuming that the officials in charge discover the amount of the offending family's income.

In none of these cases is it absolutely essential that the service in question be provided by some government organization. Services or goods that cannot be priced, either for technical reasons or because they would be spoiled by pricing, could be supplied by making suitable arrangements with private organizations. The same observation applies to public utilities of the type mentioned and to goods and services which are for reasons of public policy to be supplied well below cost. In principle, the test of comparative efficiency would dictate that governments operate some of these activities themselves and allow private companies to supply some, depending upon which method results in lower costs to society. Well-run cities might therefore engage in a large number of the types of enterprise mentioned. Some cities should perhaps stick to the bare essentials of government. Milwaukee could be expected to engage in more enterprise successfully than perhaps could Chicago.

For enterprises which have been described as those in which government has a special interest, the choice between government enterprise and competitive private enterprise does not present itself. The choice is between private enterprise subject to control of its charges and service by a government agency or public enterprise. In assessing the comparative efficiency of government and private management, weight must be given to the extra costs involved in public regulation. If a city government contracts with a private firm to remove the garbage, specifications must be laid down by the city about the kind of garbage removal service to be provided and the charges to be made. Complaints about the service may then require that the

2 See chap. 5.

householder deal with two agencies, the garbage company and the city. A setting for buck-passing is thus created. The objection applies to public utilities where there is a single supplier. If government management and private management are about equal in operating efficiency, a presumption exists for government operation because the responsibility for the charges and the service provided is more firmly assigned and the chances of conflict are reduced.

Principles of Pricing

If a price system is to operate efficiently, the prices charged must adhere to a rather definite pattern. Just any set of prices will not do. Many of the deficiencies of contemporary economic societies are the result of improper pricing practices. Virtually all groups sin more or less on this score. Labor unions have the belief that wage rates must always rise through time, almost regardless of the economic facts. Steel corporation managements abhor competitive pricing of basic steel products. Small businessmen in many fields bring pressure for price "umbrellas" in the form of so-called fair trade laws. Yet of all sinners, governments are among the most flagrant. The state of California sets prices of milk for human consumption well above what sellers could obtain in a free market. A tax on milk which would give equivalent price results would be regarded as intolerable. The British Overseas Airline Corporation, a government concern, insists upon fares which exceed competitive levels by a wide margin. The railroads in the United States, aided and abetted by the Interstate Commerce Commission, engage in an elaborate system of price discrimination designed, it would almost seem, to increase the business of competing modes of transport. Governments set prices for electric power and irrigation water based on past construction costs of dams and power plants—an almost completely irrelevant consideration. The price for passage over the Richmond-San Rafael Bridge in San Francisco Bay is set at three times the level of the toll on another bridge in the area which has at least twenty times the amount of traffic. The costly new bridge is largely being wasted by unfortunate pricing policies. The New York Subway System by adopting a flat-fare scheme promotes the well-known rush-hour cramming together of people which if done to cattle would be condemned as outrageous by humanitarian societies throughout the country. More scientific pricing of government enterprise and of government-regulated enterprise would not solve all our economic problems, but it would help.

Economic analysis has resulted in the formulation of rules to achieve efficient pricing. However, there is by no means general agreement about what these rules should be.[3]

As a preliminary to a discussion of efficient or rational or sensible pricing, objectives must be laid down as to what may be expected to be achieved or not achieved by one pricing system as opposed to another. Only if some ends or objectives can be laid down as worth achieving can there be any rational method of selecting among pricing systems. The following postulates are suggested as appropriate to democratic societies:

1. *People shall have the freedom to choose what they take from the economic system unless there is an explicit and definite showing that the exercise of such freedom in some items would be detrimental to the general interests of society.* This proposition means that a person shall be permitted to buy and consume commodities in the amounts he pleases even though other people may be thoroughly convinced that such commodities are not "good for" anyone. Thus meat-eaters are to be allowed to eat meat even if the remaining 99 per cent of the population should be convinced that meat-eating is a dreadful sin. On the other hand, the use of some drugs may be prohibited or narrowly restricted on the grounds that their use results in irresponsible and dangerous behavior and tends to make the addicts a public charge. The rule is not categorical; it is intended to establish a strong presumption in favor of freedom of choice. This presumption follows easily enough in a democracy. If people are to be allowed to vote and select their own government officers, presumably they are to be allowed to exercise freedom in smaller things.

2. *Policies that result in more things that people want are better on that account.* This postulate means that if, by some rearrangement of the productive system, more of some things can be produced without producing less of others, the new arrangement is better than the old. If there are ten million people unemployed, the use of their labor power to produce golf courses would be better than not using them at all, if by producing golf courses there need be no reduction in the production of other things. This rule holds regardless of whether those people who are put to work receive more or less pay than they would as unemployed; it holds even if they would obtain the same money income in either event.

[3] A readable account of recent thinking on welfare economics is provided in a paper by K. E. Boulding, "Welfare Economics," in *A Survey of Contemporary Economics,* ed. B. F. Haley (Homewood, Ill.: Richard D. Irwin, Inc., 1952). The comments by M. W. Reder and Paul A. Samuelson will be found illuminating.

3. *Considerations of who gets what income and in what amounts shall be deemed irrelevant in the appraisal of alternative pricing schemes.* This is a radical doctrine and requires some special defense.

Suppose, for the moment, that people like opera and beer, and these are the only two commodities produced in the society in question. Opera singers are paid $1,000 per month and beer producers are paid $100 per month. But this state of affairs is made possible only because some wealthy philanthropists with a high regard for opera have been heavily subsidizing opera. In the new situation, the wealthy patrons have run out of extra funds; it is no longer feasible to pay opera singers such high wages. A readjustment occurs, taking the form of reducing the wages of singers, increasing the price of opera, decreasing the price of beer, and converting some of the less able singers into beer producers, with the net result that the public enjoys less but better opera and more beer.

The principle set forth means that the new situation is to be judged as better or worse than the old one on the basis of the change in the product menu confronting the public (more beer and less opera) and not at all on account of the change in the money incomes of people in the two occupations. Some singers may have to do their singing while taking a shower rather than for pay. Alternatively, this principle can be dubbed the "no-vested-interest principle." No one is entitled to a particular amount of money income because he happens to have some particular skill or even because he has gone to college.

This principle follows from the fact that an economic system is an organization designed to deliver goods. Given whatever menu of goods may be produced under some set of prices, there will be a "fall-out" of incomes and of their distribution from that set of prices. If this menu is compared with another possible menu, we may be able to say which is the superior menu provided that we are allowed to ignore the change in income distribution. If we are not, the task becomes a hopeless tangle involving questions of whether the losers can or cannot compensate the gainers and whether they do.[4] As an example, druggists selling under the protection of fair-trade laws may frankly defend their protected position on the grounds that they need the extra gains to send their children to college. Conceivably the abolition of the fair-trade umbrella may rob the world of an educated genius. If we are entitled to neglect such considerations, fair-trade

[4] In the history of welfare economics, the refusal by some writers to adopt the rule of income-irrelevance gave rise to what may be called the "vested-interest principle." From any starting position, a change accompanied by the reduction in income of some group had at least to be compensated in principle, if not in fact, by the gainers. Logically this leads to an ultra-conservative position favoring a do-nothing policy.

laws can be shown to be objectionable. They result in waste by increasing the number of outlets and by reducing the volume of any one
outlet. Hence such laws reduce the potential output of other good
things.

OPTIMUM PRICING: A SIMPLE CASE. The simplest case of enterprise is a facility or set of facilities with a definite maximum output
and with a demand which does not vary through time. In Figure 16–1,

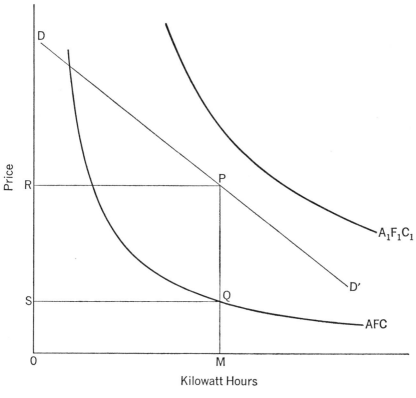

FIGURE 16–1

DD′ represents the demand schedule for electricity and *OM* represents
the potential maximum output of a hydro-electric plant and its distribution system for a given group of customers. The plant, the water,
and the distribution system can be used for nothing else and the equipment is worth less than nothing as scrap. There are no costs involved
other than the costs of billing customers, which for the moment we assume to be trivial. What is the correct price?

The correct price is *PM,* the price at which the amount of electricity demanded equals the amount that is available to be supplied.

At any price higher than *PM,* some potential power goes to waste. Some users take less electricity without any others taking more. At any price lower than *PM,* some rationing system in addition to price must be used. In that event, those who for some reason get all they want at the low price have an incentive to resell to those who get less than they want. The price *PM* may also be described as the competitive price. If there were a thousand persons each owning 1/1,000 of the potential output of power, competition among them in selling electricity to one another would result in the price *PM.* If the price were higher, some sellers could not sell all of their share, and thus would bid down the price. If the price were lower, some buyers would be going without and would bid up the price.

Some important conclusions follow even in this simple case. At the price *PM* and with zero costs, the enterprise would earn the profit *ORPM.* Some citizens may object to this result, holding that a government enterprise should not "exploit" the people by making profits at their expense. Their objection is groundless. The profit realized is a by-product of the correct price. To operate the facility on a break-even basis would call for giving the electricity away, and this in turn would lead either to some getting much less than they want or alternatively to the need for an extra-price device whereby those who get more than they can use sell to those not so favored. Price is a device to limit the amount of the commodity demanded. Any profits made are an incidental by-product.

The costs of constructing the plant in the first instance and the method of financing these construction costs are totally irrelevant to the setting of the correct price. The project cost, let us suppose, $8 million to construct; the government unit in question sold $8 million of bonds at a yield of 4 per cent per year, calling for interest payments of $320,000 per year plus amortization charges if any. In Figure 16–1, assume that the amount of this annual charge is the (constant) area under the rectangular hyperbola labelled *AFC.* Then the profits after the interest charge would be the area *SRPQ* at the price *PM.*

The interest expense is irrelevant to the proper price regardless of what theory of interest one adopts. According to one approach, the interest expense is not a cost of production at all. It is the share of the earnings of the enterprise to which one group of owners, the owners of bonds, are entitled as a result of past contracts. This is the distribution or transfer theory of interest.[5] According to another ap-

---

[5] For a defense of this theory, see E. R. Rolph, *The Theory of Fiscal Economics* (Berkeley: Univ. of California Press, 1954), chap. iv. The British now use the same theory in the construction of social accounts. (*National Income Statistics,* prepared by the Central Statistical Office, H.M. Stationery Office, 1956, pp. 1-2.)

proach, the interest expense is a cost of production, but it is a fixed one—i.e., invariant with respect to the level of output. According to this view, interest charges are also irrelevant to the pricing of the service since a higher output results in no larger total cost.

If the interest expense were much greater, as represented by the line $A_1F_1C_1$, would there be any justification for charging a price higher than *PM*? The answer is again in the negative. There is no justification for wasting the electricity by charging a high price; such a practice amounts to cutting off one's nose to spite one's face. Something must be done, to be sure, to finance the interest and amortization expense. Whatever way is chosen, such as by a tax on local property, the one firm rule to be followed is that the amount to be paid should not depend at all upon the amount of electricity purchased. Perhaps the plant should never have been built in the first place, although even this conclusion does not necessarily follow. Yet, given the facts, wasting electricity in order to earn a larger profit to pay the interest must make the residents of the region worse off, since they go without the use of some electricity needlessly and must still provide the money to pay the interest expense. The cost of construction and the interest charge are important, in fact crucial, in the decision to build a plant and distribution system; they are not relevant in the decisions to use the plant, once it has been constructed.

The practice in some American communities of financing bridges by the flotation of bonds subject to the condition that a toll be set to cover the interest and other expense is almost certain to result in the wrong price structure. William Vickrey points out that the practice of charging tolls on the relatively new New York bridges, the Triborough, Midtown, and Battery crossings, in conjunction with no charges on the old bridges, results in use well below capacity on the new bridges with great congestion on the old ones.[6] To correct this bad distribution of use, tolls should be imposed on the old bridges while reducing the charges on the new ones. Bitter complaints could be expected from some users of the old bridges on the grounds that the old bridges are "paid for" and hence do not need to be financed. The prevalence of such thinking indicates how inadequately people understand the rudiments of economics. The same kind of wasteful charges are exemplified by the Mackinac Straits Bridge and by San Francisco Bay Bridges, as mentioned earlier.

[6] William Vickrey, *The Revision of the Rapid Transit Fare Structure of the City of New York* (New York: Mayor's Committee on Management Survey of the City of New York, 1952), p. 47. This is one of the best studies available on pricing of rapid transit.

To cut down on inefficient pricing of bridges, the public should insist upon a single management of competing routes with freedom to impose and vary charges on each bridge. Then if bonds must be sold to construct a new bridge, it would no longer be financially necessary to impose a high toll in its early history when traffic is commonly thin. The separate financing of each bridge under a separate "authority" practically guarantees wasteful pricing.

Bridges illustrate very well the importance of pricing in relation not only to demand but to variations in demand. In the simple power illustration, the demand schedule for power was assumed constant through time. In the case of bridges, there are large hourly variations in demand. During the night, traffic may be very thin whereas during rush hours the capacity of the bridge and its approaches is severely taxed to accommodate the traffic. Proper pricing calls for varying the price directly with the variations in demand. If the toll during the rush hours is to be 50 cents, off-peak use should be charged at a lower price, and the toll reduced possibly to zero at night. The rationale for this system of pricing is identical to that already described. During the night hours, the amount of bridge service demanded is commonly so small that the addition of another car or truck would not slow down the movement of traffic. The bridge is then not being used to the point of diminishing returns. As an additional factor, the costs of toll collectors can be saved by abolishing tolls. Zero pricing at night would also have some effect, possibly small, in moving traffic away from the period of peak loads. Trucking companies might decide, in order to save toll expense, to move their vehicles at night instead of during the day. To the extent that this type of adjustment occurs, the demand for service is reduced during the daytime hours, making feasible a somewhat lower toll and a safer and less irksome ride for those who must use the bridge during these hours. There is a gain all around.

OPTIMUM PRICING: SOME PRELIMINARY CONCEPTS. In the previous illustrations, the capacity of the facility has been taken as fixed. We proceed now to a case in which the amount of the service to be rendered is a variable. In this case, the general rule for proper pricing is the equating of the price of the commodity with the marginal or incremental cost of producing it, subject to some qualifications. The general rule, of which the equality of price to marginal cost is one instance, for optimum pricing holds that all prices shall be identical with those that would emerge under perfectly competitive conditions.

The meaning of this principle will be explained. Before the marginal cost rule is applied, we propose to see what it means and, importantly, to understand its limitations. For this purpose, we need certain concepts and relations which may or may not be familiar.[7]

The first concept is alternatively called *production-possibilities* or the *transformation relation*. If the drastic simplification is made that there are only two commodities produced, the relation can be shown graphically as in Figure 16–2.

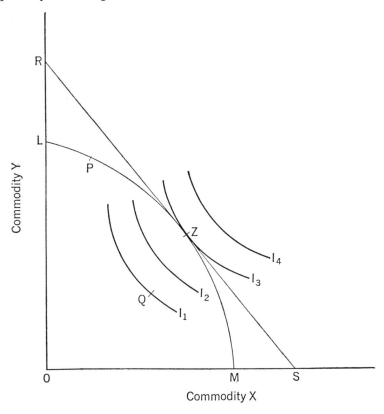

FIGURE 16–2

The line *LM* shows the combinations of two commodities, *X* and *Y*, that can be produced from the resources of the economy. The term *resources* means anything capable of being used in production; it is the environment of the society at the date in question, including human working capacity. The transformation curve *LM* is shown as concave

[7] A student who is rusty on the meaning of the technical terms used herein may find it helpful to consult either of the following texts: George J. Stigler, *The Theory of Price* (New York: The Macmillan Co., 1953), chaps. iii, iv, v, vi (especially chap. iii); Joe S. Bain, *Pricing, Distribution, and Employment* (New York: Holt, Rinehart & Winston, 1953), chaps. iv, v.

to the origin because in general the more of X produced and the less of Y, the more must relatively ill-suited resources be shifted to produce X. For example, if the two commodities were opera and beer, starting with some output of each, the production of more beer would require the shifting of opera singers who may not be very adept at the beer business, and the conversion of opera buildings into breweries. The relation might be very concave in this event. On the other hand, to use an illustration of Adam Smith's, suppose the commodities are deer and beaver, and Indians find that they can kill either two deer or one beaver in a day. Then for the Indian economy the transformation relation would be a straight line. Furthermore, as long as the Indians like to eat deer and beaver, the rate of exchange between them must be 2 deer = 1 beaver. In general, if there is only one type of resource in the society, the transformation relation must be linear (instead of concave) and it can be linear with any number of resources, provided they are used in the same proportions, which they almost never are, for producing each commodity. If resources are completely specialized to each commodity, a right angle result emerges. This case is occasionally of interest. In fact, resources are by and large highly adaptable in spite of superficial evidence to the contrary. The concave relation may be taken as representative.

The second basic concept is an *indifference map,* which is a fairly simple method, but not the only method, of rationalizing a person's tastes for commodities. A set of indifference curves, I_1, I_2, I_3, I_4, are shown in Figure 16–2 for one consumer confronted by two commodities. Any one curve shows the combinations of the two commodities which from the point of view of the consumer in question are equally desirable—hence the term "indifference." Any one relation is typically convex to the origin because, given the combination indicated by point Q on I_1, the successive reduction in the amount of Y to be consumed would call for increasingly larger amounts of X to leave a person in the same position. This is the convexity condition— sometimes called the diminishing marginal rate of substitution. This proposition cannot be proved; it seems to fit experience and, if it is basically wrong, its implications would work havoc with other seemingly established propositions, such as that the amount demanded is generally a negative function of price.[8]

"Higher" indifference curves, such as I_2, show combinations of the two commodities that are preferred to combinations represented by I_1. More of both of the commodities will be preferred to less of both. This proposition holds generally provided that both commodities are

[8] Much of the modern discussion of indifference analysis stems from the work of J. R. Hicks, *Value and Capital* (Oxford: Clarendon Press, 1939), chaps. i-iii.

desired by a person and that a person is not, within the range, satiated by either.

A transformation curve and an indifference map are together sufficient to state a maximum or an optimum for an economy consisting of one free person—the Robinson Crusoe economy. Although such a society has little interest except in literature, this ultra-simple case serves to set the stage for discussion of efficient pricing in a complex system.

Crusoe could, with his rather generous supply of tools, produce raisins and dried goat meat, in the combinations shown by the transformation curve *LM* in Figure 16–2. His tastes for these commodities —according to Defoe he was very fond of both—are represented by the indifference curves as shown. The point Z shows the maximum or optimum solution. This point has the following characteristics: (1) it lies on the transformation curve and thus is consistent with the physical facts of Crusoe's domain; (2) it lies on the highest possible indifference curve, I_3; any higher curve is one he cannot reach and any lower curve is less preferred; (3) it defines the relative price of raisins and goat meat; this price is the slope of the line RS, $\dfrac{OR}{OS}$, or, say, two pounds of goat meat equal one pound of raisins. This price is the theoretically optimum one, because, if this price were chosen at random, he would find that it suited him better than any other. It is the "best" price when "best" means getting as large a desired result as possible from given means.

OPTIMUM PRICING IN A MONEY ECONOMY. In a complex system, prices are set in terms of money, and millions of people instead of just one enjoy the output of the economic system. An optimum system of money pricing calls for the fulfillment of the following main conditions: (1) the output combination must be a maximum in the sense that more of one thing cannot be produced without producing less of some other. In the two-commodity case, this condition means that any outcome lies on the transformation curve. (2) For any output combination, buyers must be able to buy all they wish to buy or, in other words, there is no rationing by methods other than price, and no amount of any kind of output may remain unsold. (3) Resources of the same type earn the same net money return in the production of each kind of commodity.[9]

---

[9] These conditions hold for a single economy without international trade. Parallel conditions could be stated for a world of many economies engaging in trade. Compare the discussion in chap. 3, pp. 37-38, where optimum pricing in the absence of money is discussed.

To give these conditions meaning and content, attention will be focused on a two-commodity world with two buyers. The results can be generalized to any number of buyers and commodities. Let us assume two commodities, X and Y, and two buyers, A and B.

Select some output combination, say P in Figure 16–2, of the two commodities X and Y so that condition (1) is satisfied. To satisfy condition (2) for two buyers, we may use a box diagram, shown in Figure 16–3. The commodity X is measured along the horizontal

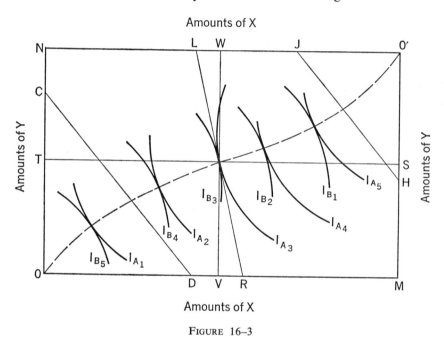

Amounts of X

FIGURE 16–3

boundaries when the amount produced is *OM*. Commodity Y is measured along the vertical boundaries when the amount produced is *ON*. The problem is to find a set of money prices satisfying condition (2). From the origin O, construct an indifference map for A so that we have the indifference curves I_{A1}, I_{A2}, I_{A3}, I_{A4}, I_{A5}. Turn the diagram upside down and starting from the origin O', do the same thing for B, giving the indifference curves I_{B1}, I_{B2}, I_{B3}, I_{B4}, I_{B5}. Construct now a budget line for A and another for B. To do this, we must know how much money each has to spend. Suppose A has $100 and B has $200 to spend. Assume any set of positive money prices for the two commodities. Budget lines for A and B are constructed according to the formula

$$E = xP_x + y P_y$$

where E stands for potential expenditures, P for price, x and y for the amounts of the commodities, and the subscripts identify the commodities. Using O for the origin in the case of A and O' in the case of B, and assuming a price for X and a price for Y, we obtain two lines shown as CD in the case of A and JH in the case of B. Now let the money prices adjust, keeping their relation unchanged until the two lines coincide. Then at any point on such a line (not shown), the two buyers could buy exactly the output of the two commodities being produced. But, except by accident, one commodity will be demanded in amounts larger than its supply and the other in amounts smaller than its supply. Now we raise the money price of the commodity whose supply is less than the amount the two buyers want to buy, and lower the price of the one whose supply is greater than the amount they want to buy, until both commodity markets are exactly cleared. The outcome is the price line LR. At this set of prices, each person is on his highest indifference curve when each is spending all of the money he set out to spend. Thus A obtains OV of X and OT of Y, whereas B obtains $O'W$ of X and $O'S$ of Y. The solution must lie along the curve OO' because only points on this curve are consistent with the condition that each consumer is simultaneously on his highest indifference curve when they divide the total output of the two commodities between them.[10]

The line OO' describes all possible sharing arrangements between the two buyers resulting from all possible combinations of spending power of the two when each maximizes his own position and the outputs of X and Y are given.

With condition (2) satisfied, we now turn to condition (3)—the same resources must earn the same net return in the production of each commodity.[11] To satisfy condition (3), take a line of the same slope as the price line LR of Figure 16–3, and, using the same scale, apply it to Figure 16–2, which shows the transformation curve—the technical possibilities of production between the commodities. Such a line may or may not be tangent to the transformation curve. If it is tangent, as is the line RS in Figure 16–2, condition (3) is satisfied. If, however, the prices of X and Y result in a price-line passing through the transformation curve at some other point, condition (3) is violated. Economically, this means that a worker employed in producing

---

[10] Note that the solution depends very much on the relative amounts of money we initially assumed each has to spend. For example, if A is given $10 more and B $10 less (by a tax-subsidy transfer), a new solution would emerge along the curve OO' in the direction of O' resulting in A getting more and B less of the two commodities.

[11] Complications arising from the concept of "net" in the above statement will be ignored in this discussion.

X obtains a different wage than does a worker of identical skill employed in producing Y and that a piece of equipment, such as a fork-lift, employed in producing X earns a different amount of dollars than does an identical fork-lift employed in producing Y. Condition (3) means that workers of the same skill and equipment of the same type earn the same dollar amount per unit of time in both industries.

To satisfy condition (3), we may proceed by the process of closer and closer approximation. If the dollar earnings of manpower and equipment are greater in the production of X than in Y, we let more of X be produced and less of Y. Then we can, by using a new box diagram, satisfy condition (2) once again. Then the price of X will be lower and the price of Y will be higher. We continue this process until all of our conditions are satisfied at once.[12]

In other words, the "correct," "best," or "most efficient" system of pricing the two commodities is that set of prices simultaneously satisfying the conditions that buyers buy the amounts being produced without any leftovers and that producers (owners of resources) get the same money gain per unit for the same type of resources used to produce both commodities. If that set of prices is \$2.00 per unit of X and \$5.00 per unit of Y, then the cost of producing a unit of X is \$2 and the cost of producing a unit of Y is \$5. Stated otherwise, if someone considered producing another unit of one of the commodities, say X, he would have to use resources valued at \$2. With a greater amount of the commodity offered for sale, its price would be less than \$2, and likewise with a smaller amount of the other commodity, Y, offered for sale, its price would be greater than \$5. Prices would thus deviate from those prescribed by condition (3).

The pricing rule just given refers to present resources to be used this way or that way. Nothing in the above discussion refers to the cost of the facilities constructed for the purpose of producing the one commodity or the other or both. Given whatever these facilities may be, correct pricing calls for an outcome that maximizes the possible output combinations of the two commodities as well as producing a product menu that the public prefers, as measured by their willingness to spend money on each of the commodities. Efficient pricing has nothing to do with the question of the proper division of spending power between the buyers; there is a most efficient system of pricing for any such division. The proper division of spending power is unavoidably an ethical question to be settled by appeal to the same ideas

---

[12] Students with mathematical training may prefer to use equations to solve for the consistent outcome.

already discussed in connection with the distribution effects of alternative tax schemes.[13]

There are a number of qualifications to be made to the principle of competitive pricing as the most efficient system of pricing, some of which have already been touched upon. The principle is not applicable if the commodity or service is, for reasons of public policy, to be provided at a zero price, for example elementary and secondary education. It is modified to the extent that there are substantial costs involved in the pricing process, illustrated by streets and roads.

A further theoretical qualification concerns by-product effects, made famous by A. C. Pigou.[14] The point may be stated by reference to the transformation curve LM shown in Figure 16–2. That relation must imply that the technical possibilities of producing various combinations reflect the actual facts confronting those employing resources to produce the commodities. Suppose that the production of X involves liquid wastes which are dumped into a river, and this same water is used in the production of Y which requires, for best results, clean water. Then the larger the amounts of X produced, the greater are the costs of producing Y. To get the theoretically correct result, producers of X should be required to pay for the damage they do. Otherwise, in the absence of government charges, private costs are too high for Y and too low for X, and too much of X and too little of Y will be produced. To have the transformation relation reflect the correct facts, the government could levy a charge for the use of the river as a disposal system.

More generally, private costs fail to reflect the social costs whenever someone uses a limited resource which is also used by others but which for one reason or another has no charge for its use. Piecemeal ownership of land above an oil pool—a limited resource—gives each owner an incentive to tap the pool by sinking wells. In the absence of regulation, too many wells are sunk, judged from the point of view of what would be best for a single owner of the land. The same applies to underground water when it is scarce, as it is in many regions of California and Arizona. The correction for this refusal to economize

[13] The reader should be warned that some economists deny the propriety of separating efficient pricing as defined from the question of the distribution of spending power. A judicious discussion of this point among others is provided by Nancy Ruggles in two articles: "The Welfare Basis of the Marginal Cost Pricing Principle," *Review of Economic Studies* XVII (1) (1949-50), pp. 29-46 and "Recent Developments in the Theory of Marginal Cost Pricing," in the same volume (2), pp. 107-126. Both are worth careful study.

[14] Pigou's views are developed in his work, *Economics of Welfare* (London: Macmillan & Co., Ltd., 1932).

on a limited resource is metering the water pumped and charging a fee to assure approximate long-run maintenance of a given flow of water. Farmers would of course object to a charge. Perhaps their opposition could be partly placated by a provision that the funds earned be returned to the locality to support its functions, such as public education. In any event, it is foolish to pretend that underground water is a free good when it is not.

REORGANIZATION DESIGNED TO PROMOTE BETTER GOVERNMENT PRICING. Optimum pricing is an ideal system. Regardless of the kind of economic organization found, such a system can never be expected to be duplicated in fact. However, the more those who produce and sell commodities behave competitively, the more likely it is that the public will enjoy a product mix of the ideal type. It behooves a government, therefore, to arrange its pricing policies to achieve results as close to the ideal as is practical. Are there practical ways of achieving this outcome?

At the federal level of government, some change in organization as well as in ideas is indicated if rational pricing results are to be achieved. In the history of federal regulation of prices charged by public utilities, special agencies have been established to lay down rules, such as the Interstate Commerce Commission. In the areas of government enterprise, no firm rule exists to determine the prices to be charged. Congress attempts to set in detail the prices for the varieties of postal services. Electric power from federal projects is priced according to the costs of construction, operating expenses, and interest. The crucial facts of the characteristics of the demand for power are given little attention. The main objection, however, is simply the absence of any understanding of the simple but fundamental principles of what a pricing system needs to accomplish. As long as legalistic approaches continue to dominate decision making in this area, the hope of genuine improvement is small.

One possible remedy would be the establishment of one agency exclusively charged with the responsibility of setting prices of government-produced goods and services and of regulating, insofar as needed, the prices charged by public utilities. Such an agency might also be given the responsibility for making studies of the operating practices of government enterprise with the purpose of increasing efficiency, recommending the use of private management instead of public where private enterprise is superior, and setting maximum prices in public-regulated private enterprise. At the same time, the existing regulatory agencies might be consolidated and their pricing responsibilities removed from them. The ICC, for example, may have been appropriate and necessary in 1910, but its usefulness in this epoch of economic organization is more than doubtful.

As an illustration of what might be accomplished, consider the sad state of the railroads. Each year, railroads lose business to trucks even in the long-haul fields in which railroads have great advantages. Financially, many lines are operating in the red. Railroad managements push for higher rates and for economies by reducing the frequency of service, resulting in a loss of yet more business. The remedy for the loss of business is to reduce prices and to improve the service; yet both moves appear to occasion only greater losses. If the charges reflected actual marginal costs, there would be little occasion for concern; it would simply be evidence that competing forms of transportation provide a more economical service. In fact, this is not the case. The incremental or marginal costs of moving goods between distant cities is much lower by rail than by truck. Between such centers as Los Angeles and Chicago, railroads could probably haul the truck and its contents piggyback, provide the driver with a lower berth, and still experience a lower incremental expense than that entailed merely by the operating costs of the truck for the distance by highway.

For long hauls, the costs of rail transport may be something like that illustrated by Figure 16–4. The costs are divided into three classes, average fixed, average variable, and marginal. Average fixed costs, shown by the line AFC, are made up in large part of the costs of maintaining the right-of-way, the shops, and the stations. Average variable costs, shown by the line AVC, are by definition those that depend upon output, such as the wages of engineers and trainmen, fuel for engines, and maintenance of equipment that wears out with use. Marginal costs, shown by the line MC, are the differences between the total cost of a given number of ton-miles and that of a slightly greater (or smaller) number. The price is set, let us suppose, at PN, and at this price the line obtains the business, measured in ton-miles, of ON. The total revenue, the area $OSPN$, is less than the total costs, the area $ORTN$, resulting in a loss of $SRTP$. As represented, the price is much higher than marginal cost. In the situation pictured, there is no pricing scheme other than one of discrimination which would permit the railroad to break even.

From the point of view of the rail officials, a higher price may have some appeal since it might reduce the loss. Socially what is required is to reduce the price to VW. Financially such a policy would be ruinous to the line because losses would become very high indeed. A private agency cannot be expected to take large losses indefinitely

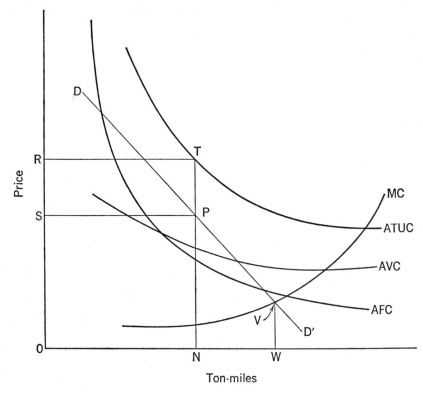

FIGURE 16–4

because a particular pricing scheme used would be in the public interest.

One remedy is to relieve the line of some of its costs. Mechanically, a simple way of doing this would be for the government to assume the loss by paying a subsidy. But such a scheme would give the line no incentive to keep down its costs, and the rail unions might be tempted to appropriate Treasury funds for themselves in the form of much higher money wages and fringe benefits.

Another and perhaps superior solution would call for the federal government to buy the right-of-way of the railroads and take over the financial responsibility for their maintenance. This solution would relieve the railroad companies of a large part of their fixed expense in maintenance. Each railroad could then be permitted to run its trains over any line instead of being restricted, as now with unimportant exceptions, to owned rights-of-way. Individual railroads could then compete for traffic with one another and with alternative modes of transport. With the high costs of right-of-way maintenance eliminated, prices could be set much lower than at present. Low prices in turn would have the effect of driving much truck traffic, and possibly bus traffic as well, off the highways between distant centers. The trucks would continue to dominate the short-haul business and that long-haul traffic of a kind requiring especially careful handling.

This solution would probably call for the abandonment of many existing lines originally laid out merely to assure the existence of a railroad. The several routes now existing between Chicago and the West Coast might be reduced to no more than three. Unless and until the train traffic became so heavy as to entail congestion on any given line, and this result could be expected to occur on occasion, the government should make only a nominal charge for use of right-of-way on the same principle that no charge should be made for automobiles using a bridge during the thinly travelled night hours.

At all levels of government, aggressive application of the principle of charging prices according to the incremental value of the resources used—the marginal-cost pricing principle—would call for the elimination of many agencies whose sole or main function consists of using government power to augment the incomes of special groups by monopolistic and discriminatory pricing decrees. Milk marketing boards are thus nominated for oblivion. Fair-trade enforcement agencies, designed to protect a given markup, special laws protecting undertakers, building-trades unions, retailers of liquor, and thousands of others found in various states contribute negatively to efficient pricing and in addition waste the resources directly involved. They also distract the attention of officials and legislatures from dealing effectively with the many serious problems that only governments can solve.

No simple solution is to be found for wasteful pricing rules laid down by government regulatory bodies of privately supplied goods and services; the one hope is the spread of economic enlightenment.

Investment Criteria for Governments

Huge sums are spent each year by local, state, and federal governments on what are, essentially, public investment projects. The dividing line to be made between government operations and government investment is more or less arbitrary. The state department exists largely to provide the country with policies which will pay off in the future in the form, one hopes, of a peaceful, harmonious world. In an important sense, the costs of its activities are an investment. We shall here restrict attention to investment projects that result in the production of things that can be described in physical terms, such as dams, highways, school buildings, veterans' hospitals, parks, public housing, power plants, and many others.

Investing may take the form of acquiring some already existing physical assets, claims, or newly produced goods. Investing in old assets results in zero net investment in a closed system because while the buyer invests $1,000 to acquire the asset, the seller disinvests to acquire the $1,000. Investing in newly produced things is commonly called "real investment," and the amount spent for this purpose means that resources are being devoted to the production of the new things. The purchase of new things does not imply disinvestment by others; those who help to produce the new things thereby obtain money income. It should be emphasized that investment, like consumption, refers to demands for things rather than to costs of producing things. Failure to be clear on this point has spoiled many theoretical and empirical studies in this area.

The output of a society during a period of time consists of consumption items, investment items, and those government items not included in the first two classes. Given the resources available to a society, the more of any one class of output produced, the less of the other two classes that can be produced. For example, consumption might be reduced to the level where people who work obtain only the amounts of those things necessary to keep them working and those who cannot work are allowed to scramble for crumbs. In this extreme case, investment could be very large indeed in a country like the United States. At the other extreme, consumption along with a minimum of government services could be pushed to a level that uses all the resources. A society that persisted in this policy would soon collapse as resources deteriorated from lack of maintenance and replacement. These extremes suggest that there is some optimum or best combination of government investment and consumption output. Perhaps there is, but if there is, it has yet to be defined. At a minimum, more investment must not be assumed to be better than less, when more investment implies less consumption or less government "consumption" activities. The worship of investment *per se* has become almost an obsession both in advanced and in less developed economies.

The issue of the scope of government real investment can be pursued some distance without attempting to solve the larger question of the proper amount of investment for the society as a whole. Given the fact that government engages in a variety of activities, tests are needed to ascertain what new physical assets the government is to acquire and in what quantity. In principle, the same type of question confronts the newly married couple in setting up housekeeping, subject to qualifications for differences in scale.

The general principle for selection among physical assets and quantities for any investor, including a government, is to maximize the "gains" from any given outlay. Thus if the state of California has $100 million to spend for state-financed investment projects, it should get the "most" for its outlay. The tricky and crucial feature of this principle is the precise meaning of "most" and of "gains." It is obvious enough that one should get the largest gain one can for a given cost, provided and only provided that "gain" is a meaningful concept.

"Gains" from different investments are readily comparable if the different investments are alternative methods to achieve the same result. For example, suppose a given watershed is subject to floods. Engineering studies reveal that the damage from floods can be reduced equally well by one large dam or hundreds of beaver-like dams scattered in the headwaters region. If these are the only two methods of controlling floods, and if a system of small dams would cost only two-thirds as much as that of the single large one, clearly the small dam project is to be preferred.

This illustration, however, concentrates attention on a single variable—investment costs of alternative methods of accomplishing the same result. There are many other variables that need to be taken into account. The single large dam may be subject to silting; according to the best estimates, let us say, it will be a large mud-flat with a stream running through it eighty years hence. Small dams will be undermined by severe storms, and some, say one in a hundred, will need to be replaced each season. Information about the costs of installing the two systems in the first instance is no longer sufficient to make a rational judgment. Account must be taken of the difference in the deterioration of the two systems. The small-dam system will call for a maintenance expense of approximately $150,000 per year indefinitely. The large dam calls for no expense of this type for approximately seventy years, but at that time, a new dam costing several hundred million dollars may need to be constructed, because the old one will be almost useless to control floods. The two sums cannot simply be compared directly because a dollar spent in 1960 is not the same as a dollar spent in 1961, let alone in 2030. Somehow dollars spent in different years must be reduced to a common denominator before a comparison is possible. The procedure for doing this is "discounting," about which more will be said presently.

There are yet other variables. Study of the history of storms in the region reveals that minor flooding can be expected, on the average, every ten years and that extremely heavy flooding can be expected only once every 100 years. To contain the extremely heavy flood would cost five times the investment outlay of containing the more frequent but moderate floods. Shall the government go to the expense of containing the heavy flood? The political answer is often in the affirmative if a disastrous flood has only recently been experienced. Yet a system of dams designed to control such a heavy flood may entail an annual cost several times as large as the average annual expected damage.

In the case of floods, the gain to be achieved by flood control devices is in principle measurable. Information about precipitation is available from past records, and the assumption may be reasonably made that future experience will be similar to past experience. The value of the property exposed to damage can be ascertained, and the amount of the expected damage in the absence of flood control devices can be estimated. The "gain" thus becomes the value of the property protected from destruction. From the annual estimated gain should be deducted the annual estimated expense of the control system in question, thereby giving the annual net gain (which may be negative). Let us suppose that this annual net gain from a given project turns out to be as follows:

Year	1962	1963	1964	1965	1966
Net Gain (in millions of dollars)	10.50	15.37	13.89	12.16	12.76

For simplicity, we assume the project is worn out in five years. If an investment of $57 million is required for the construction of the project, annual gains of the indicated amounts show a rate of return of approximately 5 per cent. The present or discounted value of the $10.5 million gain delayed one year hence, plus the discounted value of $15.37 million delayed two years hence, and so on, adds to $57 million at a discount rate of 5 per cent.[15] Does this fact justify the project?

No easy answer may be given to this question. The state government may have other projects available that would yield a rate of return on investment of 10 per cent. In general, if a government has a definite sum of money to devote to investment projects, it should pursue each eligible project to the point at which another dollar of investment would yield identical marginal rates of return with each other project. For example, the dam project costing $57 million

---

[15] The student interested in the mathematics of interest rates, present values, and related topics may consult any text on the mathematics of finance, such as Roger Osborn, *The Mathematics of Investment* (New York: Harper & Bros., 1957).

yields 5 per cent; but another project, say the widening of a highway costing $100 million, yields only 2 per cent. The highway investment should be reduced and the dam project expanded until the rates of return on each are the same. For many projects, each should be pursued to the scale such that the marginal rate of gain per dollar of investment is equal.

If the over-all rate of return is "high," say 20 per cent, should the amount of money spent annually on government investment be augmented; or, if it is low, say 2 per cent, should the amount be curtailed? This question might be decided by reference to the average or typical rates of return to be expected from private investment. It might also be decided by reference to some average rate of interest on private debts or on private and public debts taken together. It might be decided purely by reference to the rate at which the governmental body in question could borrow in the market. Perhaps there is no guide other than the wishes of the electorate.

RATIOS OF BENEFITS TO COSTS AS CRITERIA FOR GOVERNMENT INVESTMENT. The federal government has been engaged in water projects entailing substantial investment over a long period of time. The main agencies responsible are the Army Engineers, the Bureau of Reclamation, and, to a lesser extent, the Department of Agriculture. To select and justify irrigation, flood control, and hydro-electric power, these agencies have developed a test described as the ratio of benefits to costs. Although the exclusive reliance on this test is explicitly repudiated, nevertheless the actual use of it has, naturally enough, been treated by the members of Congress and others as the crucial if not the only test. In practice, different agencies use the test differently, mainly because of different definitions given to benefits and costs. The Bureau of Reclamation, for example, includes so-called indirect benefits (discussed below) whereas the Army Engineers do not.

For any given project, the benefits are assessed and reduced to an average annual money value. Costs are likewise converted to an average annual figure. Then the ratio of annual benefits to annual costs is computed. Thus in a simple case, the facts may be as follows:

(dollars in millions)

Initial investment		$10
Annual benefits		$ 5
Annual costs		
Operation	$2	
Depreciation	$1	
Total		$ 3

Ratio of Benefits to Costs 5/3 or 1.66

In this case, the initial investment is written off, on a straight-line basis, in ten years, the assumed life of the project. That expense is shown by the annual depreciation figure of $1 million. Since, in this case, the ratio is greater than one, the project becomes tentatively eligible for consideration. Ratios of less than one are viewed as excluding the proposal from consideration.

The ratio of benefits to costs is a somewhat curious test, and its justification is by no means self-evident. Suppose, for example, a student obtains a hot-dog concession at a stadium during the football season. He must pay, say, $100 a season for the concession. His sales are, let us suppose, $800, and his operating costs excluding his own labor amount to $500, so that his total costs for the season are $600. The benefits are $800 and the costs $600; the equivalent ratio of benefits to costs is 800/600 or 1.33. Why should this ratio be of any interest to him or to anyone else? He finds that he will make $200 on the arrangement, and it is this sum, the profit, which is either adequate or not from his point of view for his time and his initial investment.

The equivalent test applied to a business would suggest that a business involving large operating expense in relation to sales (e.g., a grocery store) is inferior to a business involving low operating expense (e.g., a barber shop). Yet, of course, on the basis of profitability, a grocery store with a low markup and hence a large expense per dollar of sales may be extraordinarily profitable whereas a haircutting business may be a failure. The test is not an appropriate one.

A major mystery is why these government agencies have seized upon a test that has so little justification. Very elaborate, expensive engineering studies are made of water projects and their results presented to the Bureau of the Budget and to the Congress. Because it is difficult for anyone to find his way through the various figures in such studies, he is inclined to grasp, for lack of anything better, the ratio figure. Although the use of an incorrect test does not imply that the projects undertaken are necessarily badly chosen or carried out on the wrong scale, it does create the suspicion that a bad test is leading to poor decisions.[16]

INDIRECT BENEFITS. The use of the marginal rate of return to select projects and to determine their scale implies that government

[16] Those interested in pursuing this topic further should consult the excellent work by Roland N. McKean, *Efficiency in Government Through Systems Analysis* (New York: John Wiley & Sons, 1958), especially Parts III and IV. A more detailed study covering more projects is presented by Otto Eckstein, *Water-Resource Development: The Economics of Project Evaluation* (Cambridge: Harvard Univ. Press, 1958). Eckstein defends the benefit-cost ratio test whereas McKean views it as fallacious.

investment should be governed by the same type of consideration relevant to intelligent private investment. Yet many have insisted that government investments should take into account different factors than those ordinarily of concern to the private investor. In a private investment decision, the investor takes into account the possible gains and losses to him. He ordinarily ignores gains and losses that his investment may occasion others. When a person decides to have a new house built, he does not take into account that owners of similar houses in the area may now sell their houses only at a somewhat lower price. Nor does a department store company by a decision to build new quarters in a less busy section of a downtown area take into account the added business that will accrue to those having sites near the new building. Should a government, being above mere matters of financial gain or loss, take into account all the repercussions of its investment policies or only some of them, and if so, which ones?

The general rule may be laid down that government investment should count as benefits only the value of the physical results to be provided by the new facility and ignore purely monetary gains which are often called "indirect benefits." More accurately, the benefits to be assessed are the total incremental benefits of the project, with strong stress on the term "incremental." Two illustrations may be used to provide substance to this rule.

A metropolitan region has a smog problem and a public transportation system using motor buses. Engineering studies establish a functional relation between the outpouring of fumes from motor vehicles, including buses, and the density and duration of smog. Expansion of the transit system to cover growing suburban areas would call for more buses, which would produce yet more smog. In the weighing of alternative devices, such as electric buses, should the comparative effects in smog-production be included? The answer is definitely in the affirmative. A motor bus produces both transportation and smog. It would be completely arbitrary to ignore the negative product, smog, in reaching decisions about transportation techniques. The additional transportation services and the additional smog are both incremental products of an expanded transportation system by motor bus.

Consider, as another illustration, the construction of a large dam in a desert region, the obvious direct products of the dam being electricity and irrigation water. The water can and will be used largely to produce agricultural crops. Proponents visualize the growth of towns where only lizards now dwell and are anxious to count, somehow, the total benefits of converting a barren desert into a blooming and flourishing agricultural community. On the basis of an estimate of direct benefits and costs, the project is not justified; the rate of return would be only 1 per cent. The Bureau of Reclamation, however, may hold that the project is justified because of the large indirect benefits, based on the following reasoning:[17]

Indirect irrigation benefits are project effects which comprise the increase in:

A. Profits of local wholesalers and retailers from handling the increase in sales of farm products consumed locally from the project without processing.

B. Profits of all other enterprises between the farm and the final consumer, from handling, processing, and marketing the increase in sales of farm products locally and elsewhere.

C. Profits of all enterprises from supplying goods and services for the increase in farm purchases for family living and production expenses.

D. Land value of local residential property.

This reasoning has little to recommend it. The profits described under points *A, B,* and *C* are not indirect benefits; they are not even benefits. The output of agricultural products will be increased as a result of the project, and these products will involve processing as well as handling by wholesalers and retailers. But such activities entail costs—the use of manpower, equipment, buildings, and so forth. Additional profits experienced by handlers reflect the value of some of the resources used for processing and handling. The indirect "benefits" are not benefits; they are a part of the costs to society of processing and handling the additional agricultural output.

Should account be taken of the problem of surplus agricultural production in the establishment of irrigation projects? The practice has been to ignore this consideration. If, as is the case, the federal government is committed to a price-support program for many agricultural commodities, additional output leads to their adding to the amounts acquired by the federal government. A price-support program implies an official policy asserting that more of these products are not valuable to the public; marginally they are a waste. Any additional resources devoted to the production of such items are also a waste. There is, of course, a good reason why federal agencies devoted to water projects wish to ignore this consideration. If it were taken into account few federally financed irrigation construction programs could be justified.

Summary

Government enterprise is neither better nor worse than private enterprise *per se*. Government enterprise is to be preferred to private when the evidence suggests that government can do the job, what-

[17] Quotation from the *Bureau of Reclamation Manual* reproduced in McKean, *op. cit.,* p. 155.

ever it may be, better than can private agencies. Cases where, for reasons of efficiency, there must be only one agency supplying the product to a given group of customers are especially qualified for government operation. In other cases, private and public enterprise may exist side by side in competition. Only occasionally and in very special cases is there any justification for a government to usurp the field. The nationalization of the entire coal production in Great Britain may have been such a case because of the traditional and deeply rooted hostility between the workers and mine owners in that industry. The solution chosen, however, has not proved to be an especially happy one.

A much more important issue than government versus private management concerns the pricing rules to be employed by government in its own enterprises and in the regulation, where required, of the prices of private enterprise. The rule advocated here is to make the price of a commodity equal to the incremental value of resources used to produce it whenever the amount of output can be varied. Objections can be made to this rule, but any rational system of pricing would be certain to result in a drastic overhaul of present pricing practices. The waste arising from poor pricing practices has been suggested as a major weakness of contemporary industrial societies.

Government investment, like government enterprise, involves the question of whether or not it is better to leave the decisions to private or to public agencies. With several layers of government in a federal system, a systematic test administered by one agency must be ruled out as inconsistent with the political system. Some suggestions have been made as to what should and what should not be included in government-sponsored investment programs. Economists have only recently, however, begun to devote the attention to this topic that its importance deserves. Yet more study may eventually reveal the need for a basic overhaul of the manner by which government decisions are reached in this field and perhaps provide yet more efficient and practical tests for selecting investment projects and determining their scale.

17

Social Security Systems

One of the most important and lasting effects of the Great Depression has been a heightened awareness of the human distress caused by economic insecurity and of the need for public programs to alleviate it. Modern social security systems, with their protections against such hazards to income-maintenance as old age, unemployment, sickness and disability, and the broken family, are a far cry from the harsh and degrading provisions of the old poor laws, and presumably few people would wish to see a return to those "good old days." Yet social security is not without its difficult problems, and this chapter considers those which are economic in nature. Although the discussion will be concentrated on the existing American social security system, other methods of dealing with the problem of economic poverty will be dealt with as well.

Social Security in the United States

In the early years of the country the existence of free land fostered the belief that anyone, no matter how poor his start, could provide an adequate living for himself and his family, and although paupers were given food and clothing or cared for in the workhouse, they were generally regarded as a lazy and worthless lot. However, with the separation of the great majority of people from the security of farm life as a result of the rapid growth of cities and towns, the increased longevity that accompanied improvements in medical science, and the decreased numbers of internally self-sufficient families that came with the fall in the birth rate, the need of certain groups of people for public assistance became increasingly clear. The strong and developing interest in social insurance in Europe during the early part of the present century also helped, but it was the economic collapse of the 1930's that jolted the American people from their complacent dream of an ever-growing economy and prosperity for all. At first the unemployed were helped from state and local funds, supplemented to a limited extent by federal loans, grants, and emergency relief programs. Then in June, 1934, President Roosevelt sent to the Congress a message urging the drafting of social insurance legislation, and after extended study and public hearings the Social Security Act of 1935 was signed.

Thus began the first national program of social insurance in this country. Numerous changes in and additions to that basic system have since been made,[1] and by 1958 about 90 per cent of the people in paid employment were earning credits toward old-age, survivors, and disability insurance, while over three-quarters of wage and salary earners were covered by the federal-state system of unemployment insurance. In that same year expenditures for social security totaled between 4 and 5 per cent of gross national product, depending upon how many of the programs to be noted below are included in the computation.

FEDERAL OLD-AGE, SURVIVORS, AND DISABILITY INSURANCE. In spite of the varied list of programs included under the 1935 Act, social security to most people probably means the contributor-financed payments made to retired workers and their families from the Federal Old-Age and Survivors Insurance Trust Fund (OASI). With the exception of a few groups such as federal employees and railroad workers (who have their own retirement systems), self-employed medical doctors, and employees of state and local governments and nonprofit organizations (who may enter the system under special arrangements), all workers are now automatically covered by OASI and make regular payments to the federal government for this purpose. Beginning in 1960 the contribution rates were set at $4\frac{1}{2}$ per cent of self-employment earnings and 6 per cent of covered wages and salaries, up to an annual maximum of $4,800 per worker (in the latter case 3 per cent being paid by the employee, 3 per cent by the employer). After increases in 1963, 1966, and 1969, these rates are to reach a stable level of 9 per cent for wage earners and $6\frac{3}{4}$ per cent for the self-employed.

---

[1] For a convenient chronologial summary of significant events in this country in social security and related fields see United States Department of Health, Education, and Welfare, *Social Security in the United States* (Washington, D.C.: Government Printing Office, 1959), pp. 41-51.

To be eligible for benefits a worker must have been in covered employment for a certain number of calendar quarters. Special arrangements were made for those old enough to retire by 1970, but a younger worker becomes fully insured only after he has accumulated forty quarters of covered employment. If an insured worker dies, benefits are paid to his family. Otherwise benefits for him and his family begin when he retires (minimum ages: 65 for men, 62 for women), but only on condition that he really does, for all serious purposes, leave the labor force; if he earns in wages more than $1,200 a year his social security benefits are cut, one dollar of benefits being lost for each two dollars of earnings up to $1,500 a year, and thereafter the benefit loss exactly equals the worker's additional income.[2] A family benefit of $180 a month ($2,160 a year), therefore, would not be completely lost until earnings reached $3,510.[3] It should be noted that these restrictions apply only to earned income; the receipt of dividends, interest, pensions, or annuities does not affect individual qualifications for social security. However, after age 72 full benefits are paid regardless of the amount of earnings.

Benefit amounts increase both with the number of dependents which the retired worker has and with the average level of his earnings in covered employment. Both maximum and minimum amounts have been established, and payment formulas have been set up to favor the lower-paid worker. In 1960, for example, basic retirement benefits were 59 per cent of average monthly earnings of $100, but only 32 per cent of earnings of $400 a month. At the bottom of the scale a monthly benefit minimum of $33 was paid regardless of the level of covered earnings.

The 1956 and 1958 amendments to the social security law added disability insurance for workers between the ages of 50 and 65 and for children who become disabled before age 18. This program, which is administered through the Federal Disability Insurance Trust Fund, provides only money grants to those who are judged, by competent medical authorities, to be incapable of substantial gainful work, but the names of all applicants are referred to state vocational rehabilitation agencies in the hope that their services may be able to prepare the individual for some kind of employment.

FEDERAL-STATE UNEMPLOYMENT INSURANCE. In order to stimulate the development of unemployment insurance at the state level, the 1935 Social Security Act imposed a 3 per cent federal payroll tax

---

[2] This rule was first put into effect in 1961.

[3] Regardless of the amount of annual earnings, benefits are paid in any month in which wages received do not exceed $100 and substantial services are not rendered in self-employment.

on employers but allowed any sums paid under an approved state unemployment insurance law to offset as much as 90 per cent of the federal tax. By mid-1937 all states and the District of Columbia had set up acceptable unemployment insurance programs under which workers with specified minimum amounts of pay in covered employ-ment[4] could receive benefits for limited periods of time (ranging from 6 to 39 weeks in 1960). In general, benefits are intended to be one-half of the worker's previous wage, but statutory maximum pay-ments have, in the postwar period of rising wage rates, held most actual benefits well below the 50 per cent level. A worker may be disqualified from assistance (for varying periods of time) if he has quit his job voluntarily without "good cause" or was discharged for misconduct, if he refuses an offer of "suitable work" or is not avail-able for employment, or if he is unemployed because of a work stop-page resulting from a labor dispute. It will be noted that considerable room is left for administrative discretion in the operation of the dif-ferent unemployment insurance programs.

Although unemployment taxes are set at 3 per cent of covered payrolls up to a maximum $3,000 per worker per year, all states except Alaska reduce rates on employers with good employment records, and in 1958 the average state tax was only 1.4 per cent.[5] The purpose of these so-called "experience-rating" systems is to in-duce employers to reduce unemployment by stabilizing their own operations, but their efficacy has been challenged by many on the grounds that for the most part employment fluctuations are at-tributable to factors beyond the control of the individual employer.

The federal share of unemployment taxes (0.3 per cent of covered payrolls) is deposited in the Treasury general fund, and the adminis-trative expenses of state unemployment insurance programs are paid by federal grants. In 1954 Congress provided that any excess federal revenues from this arrangement be used to build up and maintain a $200 million reserve, available for interest-free loans to support bene-fit payments by states with low reserves of their own, and that any remaining excess be distributed among the states in proportion to their taxable payrolls.

Since each state sets its own qualification requirements and bene-fit amounts and durations, considerable variety exists in unemploy-ment insurance programs in this country. In general, however, it is

---

[4] "Covered employment" now means firms employing four or more workers in as many as twenty weeks of the year.

[5] The federal offset applies also to state taxes from which the employer has been excused because of his favorable employment record. Since state rates may fall to zero, the minimum unemployment tax is the 0.3 per cent federal levy on covered payrolls.

clear that they are far from comprehensive in their coverage and that they are not adapted to deal with long-period unemployment. In March, 1958, for example, it was estimated that 37 per cent of the 5.2 million workers then unemployed were not protected by unemployment insurance, and even the short recession which lasted from August, 1957, to April, 1958, stimulated federal legislation to extend benefit payments on a temporary basis.[6] The limited nature of unemployment insurance has led to many proposals for a broadening of the program on the basis of federal minimum standards, but these changes have so far been successfully opposed by those who argue that the states are capable of handling the problem and should be left to do so in their own ways.

FEDERAL-STATE PUBLIC ASSISTANCE. The Social Security Act of 1935 as amended authorizes federal grants to states to be used toward the assistance of needy individuals who are either aged 65 or over, blind, totally and permanently disabled, or supporting children deprived of care by a parent's death, disability, or absence from the home. These grants not only cover part of the total benefit payments made by the states but also meet half of all administrative expenses. Federal participation in benefits varies with both the size of the payment and state per capita incomes so as to give maximum aid to low-income states making relatively small payments. In 1958 the federal share of all Public Assistance benefit payments was 57 per cent.

The general aim of public assistance is to supplement individual resources sufficiently to provide low-income families with the money needed to maintain a minimum standard of living, but benefit ceilings or a simple lack of funds frequently means that less is given. As with unemployment insurance, regulations differ from state to state, covering such things as the minimum period of residence required for qualification, maximum property holdings permitted, and the extent to which relatives are expected to contribute.

Since public assistance requires a means test, many people do not apply, either because they object to having their financial and personal affairs investigated by strangers or because they are unwilling to publicize the extent of their poverty. As the OASI program expands, however, the numbers of needy aged, and hence the volume of public assistance, should gradually shrink. In 1951 the number of OASI recipients exceeded public assistance beneficiaries for the first time, and by mid-1958 the OASI group outnumbered the other by more than 3.5 to 1.

---

[6] See Maurice C. Benewitz, "The 1958 Temporary Unemployment-Compensation Act," *National Tax Journal,* XI (Dec., 1958), 335-46.

STATE-LOCAL GENERAL ASSISTANCE. Since public assistance is restricted to the special groups noted and unemployment insurance is far from comprehensive, many low-income families must rely on relief and general assistance supplied by states and localities under their own laws and from their own funds. Needless to say, the amount and kinds of help available under these programs vary greatly from one place to another, depending upon the locality's resources and the generosity of its taxpayers.

FEDERAL-STATE PROMOTION OF MATERNAL AND CHILD HEALTH AND WELFARE. The Social Security Act also authorizes federal grants to state health and welfare agencies to help support services rendered to mothers and children. All of the grants require matching state funds, and apart from a flat amount paid for each program, the grants are based upon such factors as birth rates, the number of children living in rural areas, and state per capita income. In this way prenatal clinics are financed, crippled children are assisted, and the difficulties of problem-children are dealt with.

OTHER PROGRAMS. Among the remaining government programs in this country which relate to social security, three should be mentioned briefly:

1. Workmen's compensation laws, designed to provide a worker injured in connection with his job with prompt medical attention and cash benefits, are in force in all states.
2. Temporary disability benefits to cushion the loss of wages caused by nonoccupational illness or injury are available in California, New Jersey, New York, and Rhode Island.
3. Benefits of various kinds are paid to special groups; these include medical services, pensions and unemployment insurance for veterans, especially generous social insurance for railroad workers, and retirement programs for federal, state, and local employees.

Social Insurance and Private Insurance

Social insurance covering death and retirement is distinguished from private insurance for the same purposes by the looseness of the relationship between social insurance contributions and benefits. Under private insurance contracts, premiums bear a close actuarial relation to benefits, varying not only with the age at which a person takes out a policy but also with the amount of the benefits to be received and the conditions under which they are to be paid. Federal old-age and survivors insurance differs from that sort of arrangement in the following ways:

1. Contributions are compulsory upon employment in covered areas and may entitle the contributor to no benefits at all.
2. Low-income contributors receive relatively larger benefit payments than high-income contributors.
3. Additional benefits are paid for dependents at no extra cost to the contributor.
4. Benefit payments to those aged 65 to 72 are contingent on at least partial retirement from the labor force.
5. Older workers coming under the system have been paid substantial benefits even though their contributions were frequently very small in amount.
6. Congress has on several occasions increased benefit levels both for current contributors and for those already retired to reflect changes in the cost of living.

Two basic aims of social insurance, then, are (1) to assist workers unable to protect their families privately against income losses resulting from death or retirement, and (2) to provide protection against risks, such as unemployment, which are ordinarily not covered in private insurance contracts. In either case, considerable redistribution of income, both among income levels and among families at the same level, ordinarily takes place. Still another aim of social insurance may be to increase individual saving for old age and other contingencies on the part of those who are able to finance their own protection but would otherwise fail to do so. If this were its sole purpose, social insurance would not be applicable to the lowest income groups, and apart from its compulsory nature, it would be identical with private insurance arrangements. The strong redistributive elements in modern social insurance systems, however, give them an important distinctive nature. This being the case, it appears more realistic to treat payments into the system as taxes levied upon specific groups in the society than to classify them with premiums paid to private insurance companies and contributions made under individual company retirement plans.

Financing Problems

Given the multiple aims of social security, it is not surprising to find disagreement as to the proper methods of financing the system. On the one side are those who advocate taxation according to "benefits received," or more accurately "benefits to be received," an arrangement which necessitates the accumulation of a reserve from which future benefit payments will be made. It is on this principle that both federal old-age, survivors, and disability insurance and federal-state unemployment insurance are based. On the other side of the issue are those who support financing on the basis of "ability to pay." Programs such as public and general assistance, which draw their monies from the general fund, conform with the second principle. In this section the merits and effects of each system of financing will be discussed.

TAXATION OF BENEFICIARIES AND THE USE OF RESERVE FUNDS. Strict adherence to the "benefits-received" principle would confine social insurance to a forced saving program for those with sufficient lifetime incomes to provide for their own security and that of their families. Addition of "unearned benefits" both for the low-income groups and for those already in the labor force when the system is inaugurated creates a presumption in favor of general fund financing, since there is no reason why the redistribution of income involved should be solely at the expense of social security beneficiaries. On the other hand, taxation of beneficiaries has been advocated as a defense, curiously enough, against both excessive liberalization of benefits and undesirable curtailments of them. Critics of social security, for example, have argued that general fund financing would induce beneficiaries to raise their own incomes higher and higher at the expense of the general taxpayer, while many supporters of the program have felt that a contributory system is a powerful bulwark against cuts in benefit levels by economy-minded legislators.[7] Both of these arguments, it may be noted, become weaker as the scope of social security is extended. With nearly universal coverage beneficiaries have much less scope to improve their own positions at the expense of someone else, and legislators will be well aware both of the advantages of higher benefit payments and of the disadvantages of higher tax rates. With comprehensive social security, in other words, the question is not so much "who shall pay for it?" as it is "how should the required taxes be allocated among the general population?"

Before considering this question, however, we must look briefly at the monetary and economic effects of the building up of a reserve fund during the early years of operation of a contributory social insurance system. By mid-1957 the OASI Trust Fund had accumulated assets of over $23 billion, mostly from yearly surpluses of tax receipts over benefit payments. These excess revenues have been invested in Treasury securities, and in this way the money in question was re-

---

[7] The earmarking of tax revenues for specific expenditures is a widely used device to protect specific programs against budget cuts. See chaps. 4 and 14.

turned to the Treasury general fund and interest income has been earned for the benefit of OASI contributors.[8] What difference would it have made if the system had been placed on a "pay-as-you-go" basis from the beginning, with payroll and wage-and-salary taxes held down each year to the level of current benefit payments?

The immediate effect of the absence of excess social security revenues would have been to reduce the flow of funds into the hands of the Treasury. If expenditures exceeded other tax receipts, the reduced flow would have necessitated either more taxation, debt sales to outside investors, or the creation of new money.[9] Which of these alternatives would have been followed cannot be determined, but they would have had different economic effects.

Substitution of other taxes for excess social security revenues would not have affected the balance of the consolidated cash budget,[10] but it would have altered the nature of the tax structure and therefore, to some extent, the economic effects of the federal government. Unless the new taxes differed sharply from social security taxes in their effects on private spending propensities, however, aggregate price, employment, and output levels would not have been appreciably changed. At the other extreme, reliance on money creation would have both increased the cash deficit and stimulated private spending. If this is thought to be the most realistic of the three alternatives, in other words, social security programs may be blamed for some of the unemployment and loss of output suffered during the thirties but praised for their anti-inflationary effects during the immediate postwar period. Offsetting the lost social security taxes by the sale of additional debt to outside investors represents an intermediate policy in the sense that although fewer tax revenues would have stimulated private spending, these effects would have been partially eliminated by open market sales of federal securities.[11] In general, then, the accumulation of social insurance reserves is a deflationary fiscal policy

[8] As long as OASI taxes exceed current benefit expenditures, the "payment" of interest to the OASI Trust Fund is simply a bookkeeping transaction between it and the Treasury. When benefits rise above OASI taxes, the excess, looked at from the point of view of the OASI Trust Fund, can at first be financed from current interest earnings and then subsequently by the liquidation of Trust Fund assets (i.e., Treasury securities). From the point of view of the federal government as a whole, however, the excess, like any other expenditure, must be financed either by taxation, by the sale of debt, or by the creation of new money.

[9] The case where expenditures are equal to or less than other tax receipts is left for the reader to work out.

[10] Since the OASI Trust Fund is not included in the administrative budget, the substitution would have reduced the deficit or increased the surplus shown by that budget. See chap. 4.

[11] For a fuller discussion of these effects see chap. 3 and Part IV.

unless the excess social security levies simply replace taxes which otherwise would have been levied.

It has sometimes been argued that the building up of a reserve fund lightens the burden of social security benefit payments on future generations. Although this *may* be the result of such a fiscal policy, it need not, and frequently will not, be. Accumulating a reserve fund always increases the society's total monetary assets, but since these assets are exactly offset by an equal amount of monetary liabilities, no increase in net wealth occurs by this process. The important question concerns the effects, if any, which the policy has on economic activity. Suppose, on the one hand, that the collection of excess social security taxes affects neither consumption nor investment levels—as would occur, for example, if the additional social security taxes replaced other taxes with similar effects on private spending propensities. If this is the case, the growth in national output over time is not altered by social security taxes, and when benefit payments begin to exceed current tax collections the society will be no better off than if no reserve fund had been accumulated at all. If, on the other hand, the collection of excess social security taxes reduces private consumption and increases either private or public investment—as could happen, for example, if the taxes were concentrated on the middle- and low-income groups and if the induced reduction in the amount of federal debt held by outside investors brought about a fall in interest rates and an increase in the availability of loans—the growth of national output over time is likely to be increased, and future generations will then be better able to support the aged and the retired at a given standard of living.

SOCIAL SECURITY TAXES AND THE PRINCIPLE OF ABILITY TO PAY. If, as we have argued, "benefits-received" financing becomes increasingly less appropriate as both the scope of social insurance is expanded and its income redistributing powers strengthened, the financing of modern social security programs should be judged primarily on the basis of the ability-to-pay principles discussed above in Chapter 5. How well do the payroll taxes and worker contributions used by the American old-age and unemployment insurance systems reflect individual differences in ability to pay?

The most difficult part of the answer to this question is to determine the groups in the society on whom the burden of payroll taxes rests. Since problems of this sort have been discussed in detail in Part II above, only a brief outline of the relevant arguments will be given at this point. Under competitive market conditions a general payroll tax would reduce the demand for labor on the part of all firms, and wage rates would therefore fall until it was once again profitable for business to hire as much labor as before the imposition of the tax. In this case, the burden of the tax is shifted by employers to employees, and the result is the same as if the latter had been taxed in the first place.

Suppose, however, that in an economy whose market structure departs significantly from the competitive model, employers react to the new payroll taxes by raising the selling prices of their products sufficiently to cover their increased contributions to the government. If output and employment are to be maintained, buyers must now increase their spending rates in relation to current incomes. If they refuse to do this, unemployment will develop, and unless the government steps in with expansionary measures, underemployment will persist until wage rates have fallen to the point at which the pretax level of prices can be restored. Once again the burden will have been shifted backward to employees. But suppose that the price increases induced by the payroll taxes bring forth sufficient additional private spending to maintain both employment and the higher price level. Interpretations of this situation differ. To some it represents a forward shifting of tax burdens to consumers who must pay higher prices for the things they buy. To others the higher consumer prices appear to be more attributable to the monetary conditions that permit the increase in spending than to the payroll tax itself, and certainly it is clear that in such an environment higher payroll taxes are a far from necessary condition for price inflation. On the other hand, it cannot be rigorously demonstrated that prices would have risen in the absence of the payroll taxes (although any number of factors could have set off such a reaction), and one is left with a complex problem in causation and probability analysis.

It is not surprising, therefore, that opinions differ as to the incidence of payroll taxes. Those who attach high probabilities to the higher-tax-higher-price-higher-spending sequence, and discount the chances of other factors setting in motion the same sequence, think of payroll taxes as primarily borne by consumers. At the opposite extreme are those who conclude that the burdens are shifted backward to workers.[12] If the first possibility is assumed, payroll taxes cannot

[12] Few, in any case, feel that the incidence remains on the employer. In his empirical studies Musgrave adopted a middle position, assuming in his 1948 study that one-third of the incidence was on wage earners and two-thirds on consumers, and in his 1954 study that these two groups bore the tax burden equally. See "Distribution of Tax Payments by Income Groups: a Case Study for 1948," *National Tax Journal*, IV (March, 1951), 23-25, and "The Incidence of the Tax Structure and Its Effects on Consumption," in the Joint Economic Committee's *Federal Tax Policy for Economic Growth and Stability*, Papers Submitted by Panelists Appearing Before the Subcommittee on Tax Policy (Washington, D.C.: Government Printing Office, 1956), pp. 101-2.

be regarded as a method of making beneficiaries pay for social security, and their rate structure is probably regressive through most of the income range. If, on the other hand, backward shifting is accepted, payroll taxes are equivalent in their economic effects to direct wage and salary taxes, and it appears that their rate structure will be mildly progressive over the lower ranges and regressive thereafter.[13]

In any case, it will be noted that payroll taxes depart from ability-to-pay principles by being regressive over at least part of the income range. In addition, like wage, salary, and self-employment levies, they take no account of differences in family sizes and hence in the amounts of surplus income possessed by different taxpayers. Worker contributions of the type used in this country also tend to be regressive in relation to total income, partly because of the ceiling on taxed earnings and partly because of the omission from the tax base of such highly concentrated kinds of income as interest and dividends.

In the United States, then, social security taxes add some regressive elements to the total tax structure. This does not mean, of course, that old-age and survivors insurance is regressive as a whole, since benefit payments may favor low-income groups relatively more than payroll and wage taxes disfavor them.[14] Financial arrangements in other countries show considerable variation. In Great Britain, for example, contribution rates depend upon sex and upon employment status but not upon the amount of the worker's income, and funds are obtained not only from employees and employers but also from the general taxpayer. Some governments, such as those in New Zealand and Sweden, are committed to make up any differences between actual social security expenditures and the yield of specifically earmarked taxes, and Canadian old-age pensions (granted without a means or retirement test) are financed by 2 per cent levies on sales and on both personal and corporate incomes.

Incentive Problems

Social security benefit payments have two main effects on the incentives of the recipient to work. First, any subsidy (negative tax) lightens the pressure to work by increasing the family's disposable

[13] Musgrave's 1948 study (*op. cit.,* p. 44) showed a steady decline in effective payroll tax rates from 4.6 per cent on the lowest income group to 1.2 per cent on the highest if the incidence is taken to be entirely on consumers. With the burdens assumed to be on wage earners, however, effective tax rates rose from 2.2 per cent on the lowest income group to 4.4 per cent on the $2,000-$3,000 group and then declined to only 0.1 per cent on the highest income class.

[14] See, for example, Eugene R. Schlesinger, "The Statistical Allocation of Taxes and Expenditures in 1938/39 and 1946/47, in Kenyon E. Poole (ed.), *Fiscal Policies and the American Economy* (New York: Prentice-Hall, Inc., 1951), pp. 410-21.

income. Secondly, the benefit formula may alter the attractiveness of an additional hour of work by changing the effective wage rate to be obtained from it. Prior to age 72, for example, old-age benefits in this country will cut the effective wage rate in half between earnings of $1,200 and $1,500 a year and above $1,500 will reduce the wage rate to zero until all benefits are lost.

Any social security system that makes old-age benefits conditional on partial retirement from the labor force will have some disincentive effects. Even pensions based only on age, which will leave effective wage rates unchanged, will discourage some recipients from working by bringing their disposable incomes up to satisfactory levels. How seriously these effects on the labor supply are regarded by a society will depend upon how wealthy it is, how many people there are in the working ages to support both the young and the old, and upon how much unemployment there happens to be when the system is set up.[15]

Possible disincentive effects are also an inherent problem in any program providing unemployment benefits. Among the devices used to maintain incentives are:

1. Setting benefit rates significantly below the normal wage rate of the recipient.
2. Restricting benefits to a relatively short period of time.
3. Conditioning benefits on the recipient's availability for and willingness to accept suitable employment.
4. Paying benefits only to those with previous employment records in an attempt to exclude chronic malingerers.

Although helpful from the point of view of incentives, each of these measures has disadvantages from other points of view. Unless minimum wage rates are high, setting unemployment benefits significantly below them will impose extreme hardships on many families, and the payment of benefits for limited periods only is likely to deny help when it is most needed to workers who are unemployed through no fault of their own.[16] Many difficulties beset administrative determinations of what constitutes "suitable employment," refusal of which disqualifies the worker from the receipt of further unemployment benefits;[17] and finally, the basing of benefits on previous earnings favors workers in higher-paying jobs.

[15] The conditioning of federal old-age benefits on retirement from the labor force was strongly influenced by the high level of unemployment existing in the mid-1930's when the social security program was planned.

[16] During the relatively high-employment years of the late forties and early fifties approximately one-fifth of all beneficiaries exhausted their benefit rights.

[17] See Eveline M. Burns, *Social Security and Public Policy* (New York: McGraw-Hill Book Co., 1956), pp. 70-79.

To a considerable extent the disincentive problem is solved automatically by the strong dislike which most people have for idleness. Explicit administrative controls are undoubtedly needed in unemployment insurance programs, but no matter how elaborate, they are unlikely to be fully effective, and their incentive gains should always be carefully balanced against both costs of operation and effects on worker living levels. Finally, it may be noted that only careful administration of the law can minimize misuses of the system by groups who have no strong, continuing attachment to the labor force. Students, married women, and old people, for example, must be discouraged from accepting unemployment benefits when they have little or no desire for work, and chronic job losers should be encouraged to seek more basic solutions for their problems, such as occupational retraining or even psychiatric care.

Stability Problems

Unemployment benefit payments have, for obvious reasons, a strong, automatic, countercyclical sensitivity to business fluctuations. It has been estimated, for example, that during the 1949 and 1953 recessions unemployment payments expanded by 17-35 per cent of the fall in national income and that in the 1957-58 recession unemployment insurance was the only automatic stabilizer that reacted quickly and sharply.[18] Even OASI benefits tend to expand during depression and contract during prosperity, since old people find it much easier to locate and hold jobs in boom periods. Being based upon need, public assistance contributes additional offsets to fluctuations in private incomes arising from the business cycle.

On the expenditure side, therefore, social security is an important addition to the government arsenal of automatic stabilizers. Its performance on the revenue side, however, is much more doubtful. In the first place, OASI taxes are based largely on wages and salaries, which are a relatively stable part of total personal income, and the ceiling on taxable earnings means that for some workers OASI tax payments will not decline at all as their wages fall, while for others taxes will fall relatively less than wages. Secondly, the basing of unemployment insurance on accumulated reserve funds may mean an increase in tax rates as reserves become depleted during a recession or if the decision is made to extend benefit periods beyond statutory

[18] M. O. Clement, "The Quantitative Impact of Automatic Stabilizers," *Review of Economics and Statistics,* XLII (Feb., 1960), pp. 56-61, and Ernest Bloch, "Automatic Fiscal Stabilizers in the 1957-1958 Business Contraction," *Review of Economics and Statistics,* XLI (Aug., 1959), pp. 312-16.

SPECIAL PROBLEMS IN GOVERNMENT FINANCE

maxima in a severe depression. State experience-rating schemes have also been criticized for reducing employer assessments during years of high employment and increasing them when unemployment develops. Lags in the operation of these changes, however, may lessen or even reverse such effects during relatively short cycles of around three years in duration.[19]

Finally, although "benefits-received" financing does not preclude the application of countercyclical fiscal policies to social security taxes, it may in practice remove them from consideration for that purpose. Furthermore, if contribution rates were lowered in recession and increased in prosperity (as is provided for by legislation in Great Britain), it might be difficult to maintain reserves at satisfactory levels in the long run in the absence of a relatively balanced mixture of boom and depressed periods.

Extensions and Modifications of Social Security

Probably the most widely discussed proposal for adding to social security in this country in recent years has been some sort of public medical insurance plan. Various groups, such as armed service personnel and veterans, workers with employment-connected disabilities, and needy families, are already assisted in this respect, and there have been strong pressures for an extension of social protection against medical risks. Solutions to this problem might range all the way from public subsidies to reduce the cost of voluntary, private medical insurance to a comprehensive system of free medical treatment like the National Health Service in Great Britain.

This is not the place for a full discussion of this complex area of public policy, but three of the most important issues may be noted briefly.

1. The strongest arguments for medical subsidies are that catastrophic illnesses can impose very severe financial burdens on even well-to-do families and that proper health care is sufficiently important to the good society that it ought not to be denied to anyone because of cost considerations. If the position is adopted that assistance need not be given to families with sufficient income to afford both the normal amount of medical and dental services and the costs of private insurance against major illnesses, public medical programs can be confined to families with incomes below these levels. Opinions will, of course, differ as to exactly what minimum living costs are for families of different size. Still more controversial, however, is the question

---

[19] W. A. Andrews and T. A. Miller, "Unemployment Benefits, Experience Rating, and Employment Stability," *National Tax Journal,* VII (Sept., 1954), pp. 193-209.

of whether families who can afford adequate medical services can be relied upon to purchase them. Those who feel that they cannot will tend to support relatively comprehensive subsidization of medical costs.

2. As the price of medical services is reduced, demands for them can be expected to increase, and if drastic reductions are made in a short period of time (as happened when the British National Health Service was begun), existing facilities and personnel are likely to be overwhelmed with patients. A decline in quality is then inevitable, at least in the short run, and the long-run position can be improved only if additional hospitals are built and more doctors and nurses trained. There may well be a fundamental clash between the public's desire for high-quality, free medical service and its willingness to devote a sufficiently large portion of national output to that purpose. In addition, free or nominally priced services encourage their use by people who do not really need them, and the whole arrangement may become highly inefficient. The pricing system, in short, has as important a role to play here as it has elsewhere, and its abandonment may mean that the allocation of resources is seriously distorted.

3. As soon as the government becomes widely involved in medical assistance, the question of appropriate pay scales for doctors is bound to come up. In Great Britain, for example, this issue elicited both heated discussion and extended statistical and economic analyses. The more successful the medical profession has been in raising its income to a high level by restrictions on entry, the more vehemently will it oppose any changes in the status quo. Even an expansion in medical school facilities may be opposed because of its potentially depressing effects on earnings, although the reason usually given is that expansion will lower the quality of medical services.

A second extension of social security that is widely used in other countries but has aroused only limited interest in this country is the payment of subsidies to large families. In Canada family allowances are paid for each child under sixteen regardless of family need, and in Great Britain they are paid for each child after the first. When no means test is used, children's allowances can be a costly program, particularly if the payments are made large enough to take care of the largest families at the lowest income levels. In France it is said that a man need only work hard enough at increasing the size of his family—if that is the word for it—to be able to retire to a life of ease financed by his family allowances. Whatever the truth of this allegation, baby bonuses are frequently paid to the mother, on the argument that she is more likely than the father to use the money for the benefit of the children. Effects of such programs on the birth rate are debatable, but children's allowances are not likely to be popular with policy makers in countries where there is serious concern over the effects of a rapidly rising population.

Since federal social security is restricted to specific groups, such as the needy aged or the unemployed, there is no nation-wide program of assistance to all low-income groups. Although opinions will differ as to the desirability of initiating one, it is useful to keep the main features of a federal general assistance program in mind in evaluating future proposed extensions to social security. Perhaps the most direct approach would be to define, for families of different sizes, a critical income level at which they would neither pay income taxes nor receive income subsidies. Above that level taxes would be paid (as is now the case), and below it money subsidies, computed as a percentage of the amount by which actual family income fell short of the critical level, would be received. The percentages used could increase as the amount of deficient income rose, thereby simply extending the present progressive federal income tax in the opposite direction.

The notable features of such an arrangement are its comprehensiveness, its automatic tendency to offset fluctuations in income from private sources, and the anonymity with which it could presumably be administered. Careful checks on the underreporting of income would of course be needed but even a significant intensification of the current efforts of the Internal Revenue Service should leave the receipt of income subsidies free of many of the unpleasant features (investigations of family finances by caseworkers, etc.) associated with receiving aid through existing state-local general assistance and relief programs.

The effects of the program on national output are difficult to judge. On the one hand, a uniform shoring up of low incomes can be expected to improve worker efficiencies and capabilities not only in the short run but, by permitting more schooling for the children of low-income families, in the long run as well. Income subsidies will, however, increase family disposable incomes and lower effective wage rates,[20] and both of these changes give rise to work disincentives.[21] In some cases, such as divorced or deserted mothers with young children, these effects may be regarded as socially desirable. In others, where the potential subsidy recipient is in the normal working ages and not required for family duties, administrative controls similar to

[20] Effective wage rates are lowered because an additional dollar of earnings will, by reducing the amount of deficient income, decrease the amount of income subsidy received.

[21] The financing of the subsidy payments may also give rise to disincentive reactions on the part of taxpayers, especially if the taxes are concentrated on the highest income groups. See the discussion in chap. 7.

those now employed in the unemployment insurance program would probably be required.

The relief of poverty is a world-wide problem of great complexity requiring the combined attention of economists, psychologists, social workers, and many others. The fiscal transfers and subsidies discussed in this chapter can make an important, though limited, contribution to the required solution. Along with social security systems will be needed such developments as a continued accumulation of inventions and of new capital equipment, an expansion of educational opportunities so that inadequate training and knowledge cease to be a major cause of substandard incomes, and an improvement in psychiatric and other social welfare services. Only a comprehensive and well-integrated attack of this sort can hope to raise the minimum living standards prevailing in a rapidly growing population.

18

Intergovernmental Fiscal Relations

Without doubt the most spectacular example of intergovernmental fiscal relations in our time has been the foreign aid programs of the United States under which, during the twelve-year period following the end of World War II, more than $60 billion were transferred to various foreign countries. These grants and loans have been the subject of widespread controversy almost from their very inception; to some they have represented ill-conceived "giveaways," designed to win friends but producing instead only ungrateful critics of American foreign policy; to others they have been an essential, though undersized, contribution to the struggle against Communist political and economic expansion. In the first section of this chapter we shall describe the main features of these programs and discuss their principal economic effects.

While loans and grants-in-aid from one sovereign government to another have been occupying the center court of public attention, a number of equally important side matches have been taking place in the smaller arenas of government finance. How to allocate specific functions among the federal, state, and local levels of government has been a question of great concern in this country from the very beginning and has been discussed and rediscussed by commissions and committees, both public and private. Those who believe that an increasingly large number of important government services can only be carried out satisfactorily by the federal government, or at least must be based on the superior fiscal resources of that body, are vehemently opposed by those who are fearful of overcentralization and loss of local autonomy. This long-standing controversy has greatly stimulated the search for compromise solutions whereby both the financial resources of the federal government and the virtues of decentralized administration can be enjoyed together. The strengths and weaknesses of these different proposals are taken up in the second section of this chapter.

Finally, the modern revolution in methods of transportation has, by greatly increasing the movement of both goods and people from one governmental jurisdiction to another, given rise to a number of difficult and important tax problems. When income is earned in one country or state but received by a resident of another, for example, both governments may tax it, with the result that the total tax rate is higher than it would have been had the income been earned and received within a single tax jurisdiction. Adjusting the competing fiscal claims of different governments so as to achieve both intergovernmental and interpersonal equity is no small task. In the third section of this chapter, the nature of the various possible solutions will be discussed.

Foreign Aid for Economic Development and Mutual Security

Grants and loans to foreign countries, which have run between $4.5 and $6 billion in each year since the end of World War II, have been extended by this country for a complex mixture of reasons. In general these may be classified as either humanitarian, economic, or political. Humanitarian considerations have shown up most clearly in the many spontaneous gifts to the victims of floods and famine and on a still larger scale in the assistance given countries in both Europe and Asia to speed their recovery from the ravages of World War II and the Korean War. In addition, a feeling of sympathy for the less fortunate, for the underdog in the economic game, has undoubtedly been one of the motives supporting the various aid programs which are not specifically related to some natural or man-made disaster. On the economic score, foreign aid has, as we shall see, conferred important benefits on a number of industries in this country, and insofar as it raises levels of material living abroad it creates better markets both for the sale of American products and for the purchase of goods and services desired by American consumers. Important as these reasons are, however, they are far overshadowed by the political ones. The postwar grants which helped Western Europe attain by 1950 its prewar level of industrial production were designed in large part to weaken the power and appeal of communism. Still more obviously aimed in the same direction have been the substantial amounts given in recent years to help our allies maintain or expand their military forces. Our long-run foreign policy is designed to encourage the growth of democratic political institutions in as many countries as possible, and democracy flourishes best among people who are sufficiently well fed to appreciate it and sufficiently well educated to make it work.[1]

ECONOMIC EFFECTS OF FOREIGN AID IN THE UNITED STATES. Like any other government spending program foreign aid involves both economic benefits and costs. As we have already noted in Chapter 3, the economic costs of a specific program can be determined by measuring what is given up by society in order to devote resources to that program—that is, the value of the alternative benefits which could be gained if those same resources were put to some other use. For the most part the foreign aid programs use resources by increasing the shipment of American goods abroad. In the absence of these exports, more output would be available for domestic use. In addition, foreign assistance requires a relatively small amount of manpower, supplies, and equipment to administer the different programs.

The domestic benefits of foreign aid are diverse in nature and difficult to evaluate, being both general and specific, tangible and intangible. If international tensions are reduced, it may be possible to cut U. S. defense expenditures and release resources for the expansion of private output. It is conceivable, in other words, that foreign assistance may actually reduce, rather than increase, federal expenditures.[2] Among the intangible benefits are the personal satisfactions which U. S. citizens may receive from the generosity of their own government. On occasion, there may be more material individual rewards in the form of increased hospitality shown to American tour-

[1] For a more extended discussion of these matters see Howard S. Ellis, "A Perspective on Foreign Aid," in *Federal Expenditure Policy for Economic Growth and Stability*, Papers Submitted by Panelists Appearing Before the Subcommittee on Fiscal Policy of the Joint Economic Committee, (Washington, D.C.: Government Printing Office, 1957), pp. 613-19.

[2] In this connection it has been pointed out that while it costs about $3,500 to maintain a soldier in this country (including his pay, subsistence, housing, and clothing), the comparable figures for Greece, Turkey, Thailand, or South Korea range only from $240 to $425. See *The Foreign Aid Programs and the United States Economy, 1948-1957* (Washington, D.C.: National Planning Association, 1958), p. 15. Foreign soldiers, even in the friendliest of countries, do not contribute as much to U. S. national defense as American soldiers, but they do contribute something, and the budgetary gains from the substitution are impressive. The economic gains, however, are something else again. By paying, say, $400 to a foreign soldier we give his country that much additional claim to U. S. output. Against this loss we have the additional output which the released U. S. soldier can produce in private employment. Since the value of this extra output may be considerably greater or less than the $3,500 maintenance cost for one soldier, the net economic gain from foreign military assistance may exceed or fall short of the budgetary gain of $3,100.

ists in the recipient countries. Finally we may note the differential effects of foreign aid on specific U. S. industries and businesses. Exporters, shippers, and the manufacturers of a wide variety of products have all been given increased business. In 1949, for example, shipments of foreign-aid products were 46 per cent of total U. S. exports of goods, and such products as aluminum, machine tools, motor vehicles, aircraft engines and parts, cotton, and tobacco have all been shipped abroad in some years more for foreign assistance than for all other purposes.[3] Offsetting these individual gains, however, are the losses which other producers suffer because foreign aid uses certain goods rather than others. Foreign grants and loans, in other words, alter the structure of demand for U. S. output, and this change will be to the advantage of some resource owners and to the disadvantage of others.

Of all the domestic industries aided by foreign aid agriculture has been one of the most consistent beneficiaries. In the early postwar years large amounts of food were shipped to Europe to tide countries there over until their own economic systems could be revived sufficiently to permit the necessary food either to be grown at home or imported through regular channels from abroad. That point was reached in the early 1950's, and it is no mere coincidence that those years also saw the accumulation, under our domestic agricultural price support programs, of substantial surpluses of food in the hands of the federal government. This in turn induced Congress, by means of the Mutual Security Act of 1953 and the Agricultural Trade Development and Assistance Act of 1954, to arrange a marriage between the foreign aid and agricultural surplus disposal programs.

Three principal linkages were thereby provided between agricultural surpluses and foreign aid. The most important has been the sale of surplus food for foreign currencies under an agreement whereby these monies, instead of being converted into dollars and used elsewhere, are loaned within the country in question to help finance specific developmental projects. By this procedure assistance has been given, for example, for electric power works in Japan and Israel, for reforestation and watershed control in Spain, and for highways in Chile. The second linkage consists of the donation of surplus foods (over $300 million in fiscal 1956) to various private welfare agencies for distribution to an estimated forty million needy persons in 84 foreign countries. Finally, agricultural surpluses have also been used from time to time to make emergency grants in kind to countries suffering from such natural disasters as drought, floods, hurricanes, and

[3] *Ibid.*, pp. 67-68.

earthquakes.[4] These programs have materially reduced federally owned inventories of agricultural commodities, and since these might well have become acutely embarrassing to the government had they been allowed to accumulate, the whole procedure has undoubtedly been of considerable indirect value to American farmers.

ECONOMIC EFFECTS OF FOREIGN AID ON THE RECEIVING COUNTRIES. To a poor country striving to expand investment rapidly without unduly curtailing domestic consumption, grants or loans of foreign exchange have an obvious appeal. By using the funds to purchase capital equipment from other countries or to hire foreign experts to impart technical and professional skills to its own citizens, the recipient draws upon the resources of others in order to increase its own economic growth. In the case of grants, the benefits from these transactions accrue entirely to the underdeveloped country. Loans, on the other hand, must be repaid, and to do this the debtor must increase its exports by the amount of the loan charges. In this way resources are returned to the lending country, but the borrower will still be left with a net gain from the whole transaction as long as the loans have been invested by it in sufficiently productive projects. Given successful use of the funds, then, loans share the gains between the two countries involved, whereas grants channel all of the benefits to the underdeveloped nation. Loans may nevertheless be preferred by the recipients. This may result in part from the greater satisfaction of paying one's own way and in part from the tendency of grants to carry more strings than loans. In any case, both devices can provide very helpful stimulants to economic growth.

Intergovernmental support for economic development need not take the form of loans and grants for specific investment projects. Gifts of food or other consumer items, for example, may be used by the recipient not to increase aggregate consumption but to shift resources from domestic consumer-goods industries to the investment sector of the economy. Defense support grants are designed to enable an ally to maintain military forces which it otherwise would not have, but in the process of accomplishing this purpose, highways and other transportation facilities with both civilian and military uses are frequently constructed for the underdeveloped country. The economic importance of all foreign assistance lies in the addition which it makes to the resources of the receiving country. With its economic abilities

---

[4] For a more detailed treatment of these programs see the National Planning Association's "Agricultural Surplus Disposal and Foreign Aid," in *Foreign Aid Program,* Compilation of Studies and Surveys prepared under the direction of the Special Committee to Study the Foreign Aid Program, U. S. Senate (Washington, D.C.: Government Printing Office, 1957), pp. 372-81.

increased in this way, the underdeveloped nation may then expand its investment and hope thereby to improve the welfare of its people.

SUMMARY. Although foreign grants and loans have consistently been less than 3 per cent of the gross national product of this country, they have had important economic effects here as well as abroad. On the "plus" side at home are the contributions made to our own national security and the monetary gains enjoyed by specific producer groups. On the "minus" side are the monetary losses suffered by other producer groups and the lower level of domestically enjoyed output resulting from the use of resources for foreign aid. Abroad, however, a chance has been given to various underdeveloped countries to break out of the rut of chronic poverty and to begin the long, slow climb toward a higher standard of living for their people.

Federal-State-Local Fiscal Relations

THE PROBLEM. There has long been a spirited debate in this country about the need for changes in the extent to which public services are performed by the three different levels of government. Those who favor an increased role for state and local governments have used three main arguments in support of their position:

1. The opportunities for citizen participation in government—both direct, through personal public service, and indirect, through close association and discussion of public problems with government officials—are much greater at the state and local level, and this sort of activity is the essence of democracy.
2. New fiscal devices of various kinds can be experimented with at the local level without the risks and expense involved in doing the same thing at the federal level.
3. The federal government is already too large, and with increasing size have come the usual inefficiencies and "red tape" of large-scale organizations.

These are impressive and widely understood arguments. There are on the other side of the debate, however, a number of equally impressive points which are perhaps less well appreciated by the average voter. In the first place, the trend in this country as well as elsewhere is toward increasing integration and interdependence. Widespread internal travel and migration and the growth of large-scale interstate businesses mean, for example, that it is no longer a matter of indifference to the citizens of the state of Washington what kinds and qualities of educational and health services are provided to people in Maine or in Florida. The need for a uniform national minimum level of public services of various kinds, in other words, is increasing daily. The chief impediment to its achievement lies in the unequal distribution of incomes among the different states. In 1958, for example, per capita personal incomes ranged from a high of over $2,800 in Connecticut to a low of just over $1,000 in Mississippi.[5] Low service levels typically occurred in areas that were hampered in their efforts by the small size of their potential tax bases. In other instances public indifference or a determined opposition to increased government spending of any kind have brought about the same result.

The major obstacle which any large-scale expansion of state and local governments would have to overcome lies in the inherent weaknesses of their revenue-raising powers as compared with those possessed by the federal government. For one thing, the complex problems involved in dealing equitably with interstate transactions and in preventing tax evasion and avoidance make state and local taxes more costly to administer than federal taxes. Secondly, interstate competition for business and for wealthy residents exerts a powerful depressing influence on state and local tax rates. It is true, as we have already noted,[6] that no empirical evidence has so far been produced to show that taxes exert an important influence on industrial location, but legislatures nevertheless appear to be strongly influenced by such possibilities, and the advertising of so-called "favorable tax climates" is a favorite pastime of state and local boosters. Because of these fiscal weaknesses, then, state and local government expenditures are not likely to be expanded rapidly without considerable federal help. Indeed, many people who ostensibly favor decentralization as a fiscal principle really regard it as a means toward a general lowering in the level of governmental activities.

A third argument against any increase in the relative powers of state and local governments cites both their political faults and the regressiveness of their revenue structures. In many cases, for example, recently developed centers of population are seriously underrepresented in one or even both state legislative bodies, and only infrequently have reform efforts been successful. Nor have many state and local governments, for whatever reasons, been in the vanguard of those seeking solutions to some of our important modern problems. It is the federal government, for example, that has played the major role in stimulating the urban renewal and public housing developments

---

[5] Robert E. Graham, Jr., "Regional Markets in 1958," *Survey of Current Business* (Aug., 1959), p. 15. The fourteen states which in 1958 had per capita incomes greater than the national average of $2,057 were all concentrated in the Northeast, East-Central, Great Lakes, and Western parts of the country.

[6] Chap. 7, p. 172.

which seek to remove some of the ugliest features of our city life. In addition to these shortcomings, many students of public finance would cite the regressiveness of state and local tax systems as a strong argument against increased reliance on those sources of revenue. On the basis of his 1954 study Musgrave, for example, concluded that state and local tax rates were 9.8 per cent on those with annual incomes below $2,000 but only 7.4 per cent on those receiving more than $10,000 a year.[7]

In the field of federal-state-local fiscal relations, then, there are two major problems to which our attention in this section must be directed:

1. By what means, if any, may the superior revenue-raising powers of the federal government be brought to the aid of state and local governments without sacrificing unduly their zealously guarded independence.

2. To what extent and by what means should specific state and local spending programs be stimulated by the federal government.

Solutions to these problems may be sought either on the revenue or on the expenditure side of the public budget. Let us look first at some of the tax devices which can be used to strengthen state and local finances.

REVENUE COORDINATION. *Separation of Tax Sources.* To a limited extent both federal and state tax structures could be strengthened by taking taxes now being collected by both levels of government and allocating them exclusively to the one or to the other level. In the first place, since it frequently costs less to collect additional revenue from an established tax than to set up a new law and raise the money from it, tax separation can reduce administrative expenses and increase the efficiency of the economic system. If both levels of government levy taxes X and Y, for example, money and resources may be saved by having one government give up X and expand its collections from Y while the other gives up Y and increases its reliance on X. In addition, taxpayer compliance costs will be reduced by the resulting simplification of the tax system. The gains to be realized by such changes, however, will for the most part be relatively small.

A second aim of tax separation is to allocate to each level of government those taxes which it can administer most efficiently. The difficulty here, however, is that most of the productive taxes are best

---

[7] R. A. Musgrave, "The Incidence of the Tax Structure and Its Effects on Consumption," in *Federal Tax Policy for Economic Growth and Stability,* Papers Submitted by Panelists Appearing Before the Subcommittee on Tax Policy of the Joint Committee on the Economic Report (Washington, D.C.: Government Printing Office 1956) p. 98.

administered by the federal government. Although such levies as excises on theater admissions or on local telephone service have been strongly recommended for state rather than federal use, sales, income, and death taxes can all be collected with less expense at the national level. Separation of tax sources in the interest of economic efficiency, therefore, would be likely to leave the states with much more inadequate revenue systems than they now possess. Needless to say, little enthusiasm for such a fiscal policy will be found among state officials.

Tax Sharing. Whenever a tax can be collected at relatively lower cost over a larger area than over a smaller one—the costs of administration rising less than proportionately with revenues as the collection area is expanded—it may be more efficient for the central government to collect the entire tax and then to share a portion of it with state and local governments. By this means a set of fifty widely different state taxes which pose for each legislature the difficult problem of reaching interstate transactions in a fair and equitable manner could be transformed into a uniform nation-wide tax that would eliminate all incentives for taxpayers to move their businesses or residences from one state to another and would greatly reduce opportunities for tax evasion and avoidance.

The major disadvantage of tax sharing from the point of view of the state governments is their loss of budgetary control over the tax in question. No longer can revenues from that source be raised or lowered by any one of them in isolation. Instead, changes in tax rates or in the proportion of the total tax going to the states have to be initiated by the federal government in response to substantial agreement among the different states.

The sharing formula may be based upon the actual amount of revenue collected in each state, or it may be set so as to return relatively greater amounts to the poorer states. In Canada, for example, a set of tax-rental agreements which are renegotiated periodically with each of the ten provinces grant the federal government exclusive use of income and death taxes in return for annual payments to the provinces made primarily on a per capita basis. In this way the revenues going to the provinces with relatively low per capita incomes are increased.[8] Tax sharing is widely used in this country between state and local governments, and, as we shall see, the federal government has come close to achieving the same results by granting tax credits in connection with certain state levies.

[8] Cf. John F. Due, "Some Observations on Intergovernmental Fiscal Relations in Canada," *Proceedings* of the Forty-Eighth (1955) Annual Conference on Taxation (Sacramento, California: National Tax Association, 1956), pp. 538-49.

Tax Credits. During the interwar period the federal government adopted two kinds of tax credits: a limited credit for state death taxes against federal estate-tax liabilities, and a 90 per cent credit against federal payroll levies for similar payments into state unemployment compensation plans.[9] More recently a 40 per cent credit against the federal excise on local telephone service has been proposed as part of a law designed to return the vocational education program and the construction of waste treatment facilities to full state financial control.[10]

A federal tax credit, it will be recalled, allows the taxpayer to deduct from his federal tax liability part or all of any similar tax payments which he makes to a state government. In this way a virtually irresistible incentive is provided to state governments to adopt the tax in question since they can do so without imposing any additional burdens on their own taxpayers. Consider, for example, the granting of a 40 per cent credit against the existing 10 per cent federal excise on local telephone service. If each state then adopts a 4 per cent tax on local telephone service, the sole effect will be to divert 40 per cent of the money which the telephone companies formerly paid to the federal government into the hands of the state governments. No additional taxes are imposed on the telephone companies, and if the tax credit law requires the state taxes to be identical with the federal levy, no additional compliance costs are involved either.

A tax credit differs from tax sharing in two main ways: first, the collection and administration of the tax is left in the hands of the state governments; and second, the state governments are free to increase tax rates on their own if they wish to do so. In other words, the state governments have greater fiscal powers under the tax credit system, but these are gained at the expense of any reduction in administrative costs which might result from centralized federal collection of the tax. If no state goes beyond the maximum federal credit allowed, taxpayers will be given no incentive to shift their businesses or residences in order to reduce their tax liabilities, but any state which wishes to expand its tax further must consider the possibility of such reactions.

Tax Supplements. Widely used in the Scandinavian countries, tax supplements involve the application by local governments of their own exemptions and rates to a tax base defined by the central government. Income and net wealth taxes, for example, are entirely collected and

[9] These credits are discussed more fully above, in chaps. 12 and 17.

[10] See the *First Strengthening of State Governments Act* (H.R. 12524, 85th Congress, 2d Session, 1958). This law included some of the recommendations of the Joint Federal-State Action Committee which was set up by President Eisenhower to explore the possibilities of increasing both the relative amount of public services performed by state governments and their revenue-raising powers.

administered by the central government, but part of the total revenue is then returned to the local governments in accordance with the supplementary exemptions and tax rates which they have chosen to enact. Tax supplements are also beginning to be used in this country. The Alaskan income tax, as we have already noted, is set at a given percentage of the taxpayer's federal income-tax liability, and a number of states have adopted (with minor adjustments) the federal income-tax base for their own purposes.[11] At the state-local level Mississippi has authorized its cities to levy a tax equal to one-fourth of the state sales tax, and these municipal supplements are collected along with the state tax on a single return.

Tax supplements strengthen state fiscal powers by eliminating the excessive compliance and administrative costs frequently associated with completely independent state taxes. They do not, however, eliminate the possibility of continued interstate competition for businesses and wealthy residents. As long as this competition is active, state taxing powers will be significantly weakened. Against this disadvantage may be set the relatively high degree of fiscal freedom which tax supplements allow the state and local governments.

Summary. Tax coordinating devices of several kinds may be effectively used by different levels of government both to improve tax administration and to minimize revenue-eroding intergovernmental competition for profitable businesses and wealthy residents. Balanced against these gains, however, must be the losses of local fiscal independence which some of the devices involve. While tax sharing, with its high degree of centralization, is likely to be an attractive arrangement between a state government and its dependent cities and counties, the greater freedom available to the user of tax supplements will be more appealing to the states in their fiscal relations with the federal government.

EXPENDITURE INTEGRATION. *Types of Intergovernmental Expenditure.* From the point of view of the recipient the most attractive kind of monetary grant that can be made to it by another level of government is one that is completely unrestricted as to purpose. Such gifts, which may be spent in whatever way the receiver thinks best, are in that respect similar to shared taxes. Unlike shared taxes, however, grants do not depend upon the yield of any specific tax, nor need they bear any fixed relationship to the total tax collections of the granting government. During an economic recession, for example, unrestricted grants to state and local governments might be increased

[11] Chap. 7, pp. 171-72.

while state and local receipts from taxes shared with the federal government were declining.

Unrestricted grants may be made in equal amounts to each recipient, or they may be based upon population or some more complex equalizing formula. A system of grants from state to local governments similar to British block grants, for example, would function in the following way. The value of taxable property per capita in each local government in the state would be estimated and its average level for the entire state determined. Each below-average local government would then have the amount of its deficiency in per capita taxable wealth entered on its tax rolls in the name of the state government. Local tax rates would be set in the ordinary way, and the state would contribute according to the amount of property that had been assigned to it.[12] In this way state grants-in-aid could be made to vary inversely with per capita taxable wealth (up to the state average only, since above-average localities would receive no grants) and directly with the fiscal effort made by the local government as reflected in the level of its property tax rates. A similar system of federal grants to the states could be based on per capita state income payments or retail sales.

When the purpose of a grant is to stimulate specific kinds of governmental activity, use of the funds involved will be restricted to the programs in question. Varying degrees of supervision may be exercised by the granting government, and in addition, it may require that the recipients contribute funds of their own to the same programs. In effect, matching grants reduce the price at which the recipient can purchase specific goods, and hence can normally be expected to stimulate the demand for these goods. A 50-50 grant for public hospitals, for example, would reduce the local price of a $1 million building to $500,000. The grantee, however, need not react to the price cut by keeping its expenditures on the aided programs constant. It may either spend less than it would have in the absence of the grants, thereby releasing funds for other purposes, or it may spend more, thereby putting pressure on other programs or requiring additional revenues.

Instead of grants, loans may be used, the degree of assistance then depending upon the interest rates and terms to maturity at which the

---

[12] Suppose, for simplicity, that there are only three local governments: X, with taxable property per capita of $1,000; Y, with $3,000; and Z, with $5,000. The average amount of taxable property per capita for the group is then $3,000, and X is the only below-average local unit. X's tax rolls would consequently be increased by its per capita deficiency ($2,000) times the size of its population, and the state would pay the property taxes due on this dollar amount according to the tax rate which X chooses to set for all property owners.

money is extended. Finally, the federal government may agree to stand behind the credit of state and local governments when they borrow on the open market for specified purposes. As long as guarantied loans of this sort are repaid on schedule, no federal expenditures will be required, but should the state or local governments get into financial difficulties, the loan charges will be paid by the U. S. Treasury. Given such assurances, private investors will regard guarantied state and local securities as relatively riskless investments and will consequently purchase them on terms more favorable to the borrowing governments than otherwise would be available.

Principal Present-Day Federal Grants and Loans. Our present system of restricted federal grants and loans to state and local governments was set up under permanent legislation in 1879, and since that time it has grown into a multi-billion dollar program. Assistance is provided for a wide variety of purposes, the most important of which will be reviewed in this section.

1. *Public Assistance.* Cash payments to the needy aged, blind, and dependent children deprived of parental support were begun as a joint federal-state venture by the Social Security Act of 1935, and in 1950 aid to needy persons who are permanently and totally disabled was added. In fiscal 1958 $1.8 billion was granted to the states under these programs for distribution to more than five and a half million needy individuals. In addition the states contributed funds of their own, partly in order to qualify for the federal grants in the first place and partly to raise the level of the total aid given.[13] Monthly federal payments for the aged blind and disabled, for example, were 80 per cent of the first $30 paid to each recipient plus one-half of the next $30. In order to qualify for the maximum federal aid, then, the states had to pay $21 a month from their own funds for each $39 received from the federal government. Beyond an aid level of $60 a month for each recipient the states were entirely on their own.[14] All federally aided public assistance programs are administered by the states, but the federal government contributes to the expenses so incurred as long as certain minimum standards set by the Social Security Administration are met.

2. *Federal-Aid Highways.* The foundations for this program, which has grown into the largest public-works undertaking in the country, were established by the Federal-aid Road Act of 1916. Since

---

[13] Altogether, state and local expenditures under the four federally supported public assistance programs constituted 45 per cent of the total aid distributed in 1958.

[14] A similar formula governed the allocation of federal funds for needy dependent children. For a fuller discussion of these programs see chap. 17 above.

that time annual grants to the states for highway construction have been apportioned on the threefold basis of relative area, population, and rural mail-route mileage, and these funds have in turn been matched by equal state expenditures. Each receiving state was required to have a highway department capable of administering the joint program (in many cases no such agency existed prior to 1916), and the responsibility for selecting new projects was assigned to those departments.

An important postwar addition to these regular programs is the construction of the National System of Interstate and Defense Highways, a project which during the dozen or so years required for its completion will dwarf all other highway programs. Conceived in 1944 and begun in a modest way ten years later, the Interstate System as defined by the Federal-aid Highway Act of 1956 envisaged 41,000 miles of high-speed roads, mostly freeways, linking together 90 per cent of the cities in the country having populations of 50,000 or more. During the height of its construction in the 1960's expenditures on the system are expected to run well over two billion dollars a year. The federal government is to provide 90 per cent of the funds required and has established engineering standards designed to meet anticipated traffic volume over the next twenty years.

In addition to accelerating construction of the Interstate Highway System, the 1956 act altered the administration of highway grants by setting up the Highway Trust Fund. Into this fund are channeled specified taxes on gasoline, tires, trucks, and other products closely connected with highway transportation, and from it are paid all grants for federally aided highways. In any given year these are restricted to the current tax receipts of the fund plus any surpluses accumulated from previous years.

3. *Distribution of Surplus Agricultural Commodities.* Whenever the level of federal inventories of price-supported agricultural crops is unduly high, donations of these foods are made to needy persons through state distributing agencies and to the school lunch program (described more fully below). These gifts in kind need not be matched by state or local grants, but all expenses of storage and distribution after the goods are first received in each state must be met locally.

4. *The National School Lunch Program,* which in 1955 provided meals for nearly one-third of the country's 35 million school children, was set up in 1946 by the first law to spell out in detail an equalization formula for federal grants. The federal payments, which go to meet part of the cost of the food served in each meal, vary directly with the number of school-age children in each state but inversely with the

amount of per capita state income. In fiscal 1955 federal grants of
$80 million were matched by state and local expenditures which ex-
ceeded $450 million.[15] In other words, the annual cost of the meals
was approximately $55 for each child served.

5. *Unemployment Insurance and the U. S. Employment Service.*
As noted above in Chapter 17, the federal government pays the administrative costs of the unemployment insurance program and to this
extent makes to the states money grants which do not have to be
matched. The United States Employment Service also makes grants
to cover the administrative costs of state-operated public employment
offices. These agencies run a comprehensive placement service without
charge to either employer or employee. Workers are helped to evaluate their own abilities by employment counseling and assisted in
finding jobs to suit their skills and knowledge. Employers in turn are
helped in their unremitting search for qualified personnel.

6. *School Construction and Operation in Federally Affected
Areas.* Any local school district which finds that, as a result of a high
level of federal governmental activity in its vicinity, enrollments have
been increased beyond its capacity to deal with them may apply for
fiscal help under this program. If the case is a reasonable one the
federal government will then make grants to cover the construction
costs of the needed school facilities. In addition, maintenance and
operation payments are made to replace local school revenues lost as
a result of tax-exempt federally owned property. In 1955 districts
aided in this way educated about one-fifth of the children in the
country.

7. *Hospital and Medical Facilities Survey and Construction Program.* Authorized in 1946, this program initiated the first comprehensive survey of existing health facilities in the history of this country. In addition to financial assistance for these surveys, federal
grants are made to the states, on the basis of both need and ability to
pay, for the construction of public and other nonprofit hospitals and
medical facilities. The federal share of construction costs may vary
from a minimum of one-third to a maximum of two-thirds in the
lower-income states.

8. *Construction of College Housing and Other Educational Facilities.* Unlike the preceding programs the federal assistance in this

---

15 U. S. Congress, H.R. Intergovernmental Relations Subcommittee of the Committee on Government Operations, *Staff Report on Replies from Federal Agencies
to Questionnaire on Intergovernmental Relations* (Washington, D.C.: Government
Printing Office, 1956), p. 115. This document gives a very useful, comprehensive
description of the federal grant programs as they existed in early 1956.

case takes the form of low-interest-rate loans granted to both private and public institutions of higher learning for the development of housing and other educational facilities. Since the aid is entirely in the form of loans, state governments must eventually finance their own educational construction projects, but they do receive the advantage of lower interest rates than they otherwise would have to pay on borrowed funds.

Several effects of this program are worth noting. If colleges spend the same amount of money on housing as they would have in the absence of the low-rate federal loans, they simply acquire additional housing facilities. If, on the other hand, their housing needs are given and constant, the lower charges on federal loans provide them with additional funds which may be used for other purposes. The college housing program, in short, may fail in its ostensible objective but instead enable universities to have more sport facilities or higher salaries for their faculties. Effects on the bond market will depend upon how the federal loans are financed. If federal securities are sold, they in effect replace the securities which colleges would otherwise have offered to private investors, and the character of security offerings is thus shifted in the direction of fewer risks for bond purchasers. If, on the other hand, additional taxes are used to finance federal college housing loans, the private bond market will find the demand for funds less (because of the withdrawal of colleges as borrowers), and unless the supply of funds falls correspondingly (because of the new taxes), interest rates will fall.

9. *Low-Rent Public Housing Program.* Under the authority of the United States Housing Act of 1937, as amended, local housing authorities had planned and built by the end of 1958 some 420,000 housing units for low-income families unable to afford the full cost of decent, safe, and sanitary housing facilities. While the federal aids for this purpose include technical advice, direct loans and assistance in obtaining low-cost private credit,[16] the principal ones take the form of annual contributions designed to make up the difference between the costs to the local governments of constructing and operating the housing projects and the rents which the tenants can afford to pay. State and local governments also assist the projects by exempting them from property taxes.

---

[16] This assistance includes not only the exemption of the interest on the local housing authority bonds from federal income taxation but also an effective guaranty by the Public Housing Administration of the borrowers' ability to pay. Both of these provisions lower the interest rate at which the housing authorities are able to obtain funds from private lenders.

10. *Slum Clearance and Urban Renewal.* In order to stimulate both the elimination and the prevention of urban slum areas the federal government, under the authority of the Housing Act of 1949, provides professional advice, loans, and grants to any community with a workable plan for local improvement. The capital grants may cover as much as two-thirds of the net cost of the different projects, the remaining one-third being contributed by local governments in the form of cash, donations of land, or the improvement of project facilities.

11. *Other Grant and Loan Programs.* In addition to these ten programs, which in fiscal 1958 accounted for nearly 90 per cent of all federal grants and loans (Table 18–1), are a large number of less important programs ranging from assistance for agricultural research and airport construction to grants for vocational education and the

TABLE 18–1

PRINCIPAL FEDERAL GRANTS- AND LOANS-IN-AID IN FISCAL 1958

Program	Amount (millions of dollars)
A. *Grants-in-Aid:*	
Public assistance	1,795
Federal-aid highways	1,493
Unemployment compensation and employment service administration	291
Contributions of surplus agricultural commodities	174
National school lunch and special milk programs	165
School construction and operation in federally affected areas	109
Hospital construction	105
Low-rent housing program	95
Slum clearance and urban renewal	35
Other programs	563
Total grants-in-aid	4,831
B. *Net Loans and Repayable Advances:*	
College housing	99
Slum clearance and urban renewal	20
Low-rent housing	—3
Other programs	24
Total net loans	140
Total grants- and loans-in-aid	4,971

Source: *The Budget of the United States Government for the Fiscal Year Ending June 30, 1960* (Washington, D.C.: Government Printing Office, 1959), Special Analysis G, pp. 982-88.

construction of waste treatment facilities.[17] Since the features of these grants and loans are similar to those noted above, no further details need be given here.

Summary and Evaluation. From a relatively modest level of $0.1 billion in the mid-1920's, federal grants-in-aid expanded rapidly during the next decade, and following a brief retrogression during World War II, they have continued to expand during the postwar period (Table 18–2). In fiscal 1959 this form of intergovernmental aid

TABLE 18–2

FEDERAL GRANTS-IN-AID TO STATE AND LOCAL GOVERNMENTS,
SELECTED FISCAL YEARS, 1925-1959

Fiscal Year	Amount (millions)
1925	124
1930	114
1932	228
1934	1,848
1936	2,318
1938	2,180
1940	2,401
1942	1,826
1944	1,009
1946	901
1948	1,629
1950	2,226
1952	2,393
1954	2,986
1955	3,126
1956	3,642
1957	3,943
1958	4,831
1959	6,355

Sources: For 1925-57, Committee on Government Operations, *Federal-State-Local Relations: Federal Grants-in-Aid* (Washington, D.C.: Government Printing Office, 1958), p. 79; 1958-59, U. S. Budgets.

exceeded $6 billion for the first time, and further expansion appears likely during the nineteen sixties. The net volume of federal loans to state and local governments, on the other hand, has fluctuated erratically around an average annual level of only $37 million between mid-1948 and mid-1960 (Table 18–3).

[17] For a convenient short summary of federal grant programs as they existed in 1957 see U. S. Congress, Committee on Government Operations, *Federal-State-Local Relations: Federal Grants-in-Aid,* House Report No. 2533, 85th Congress, 2d Session (Aug. 8, 1958), pp. 7-19.

TABLE 18–3

NET VOLUME* OF FEDERAL LOANS GRANTED TO STATE AND LOCAL GOVERNMENTS, BY FISCAL YEAR, 1949-1959

Fiscal Year	Amount (millions)
1949	−73
1950	15
1951	147
1952	173
1953	25
1954	−395
1955	−80
1956	29
1957	72
1958	140
1959	357
Total	410

* Net volume equals gross loans made minus repayments of loan principal.
Source: United States Budgets.

By stimulating state and local governmental services of national importance, restricted federal grants- and loans-in-aid can contribute materially to the achievement of national minimum levels of public services without placing heavy burdens on taxpayers in the poorest areas. In fiscal 1952, for example, the 29 states with below-average per capita incomes received 51 per cent of all federal grants even though their share of national income payments was only 32 per cent and their residents paid only 28 per cent of federal tax revenues.[18] In 1957 the eight states with the lowest per capita incomes all received an above-average proportion of their general revenue in the form of federal aid, whereas of the eight highest-income states only one received proportionately as much federal assistance.[19] On the other hand, the largest per capita grants have not typically gone to the lowest-income states, a fact which may be attributable to the inability of those states to meet the matching requirements upon which most federal grants are based. Although this type of aid, therefore, has been relatively more important to the low-income states, only a modest amount of service-level equalization has been achieved.

Not only may matching grants fail to bring public services of national importance up to the desired minimum level in each state, but

[18] Selma Mushkin, "Federal Grants and Federal Expenditures," *National Tax Journal*, X (Sept., 1957), pp. 205-6.
[19] L. Laszlo Ecker-Racz, "A Foreign Scholar Ponders the 1957 Census of Governments," *National Tax Journal*, XII (June, 1959), p. 109.

they may also divert state and local funds from other, more important activities. Such dangers are also present when loans-in-aid are used, since these must be repaid by the recipient governments, but are absent when grants are made without matching requirements. Nonmatching grants, however, may to a considerable extent simply replace local funds which otherwise would have been used for the same purpose. In such cases the primary effect of the grants would be to substitute federal for state and local taxes and hence to make the entire fiscal system more progressive.[20] Even this seemingly ineffective use of federal grants would, in other words, have some income-equalizing effects.

The ideal grant-in-aid program must possess the balancing qualities of a highly skilled politician. The assistance given should neither be too generous nor too niggardly. The allocation principles should be specific enough to indicate clearly the intentions of the legislature but not so detailed and rigid that as economic conditions change they soon become out-of-date and fail to accomplish their original purpose. Much can be done through federal assistance to coordinate and improve the administration of the aided public services, but excessive zeal in this respect can result in the creation of an overcentralized, inefficient bureaucracy. Programs should be firmly established for long enough periods of time to permit effective operation, but regular budgetary reviews of the desirability of expansion or contraction of service levels are essential. It will be seen that the planning and operation of an effective set of grant-in-aid programs is no easy task. Federal activities in this area have not only been criticized on most of the grounds noted above, but their failure to cover all state and local services with a strong national interest has been stressed by numerous writers.[21] Public assistance grants, for example, help to support certain groups of needy individuals but not others, and in the health field some programs receive more attention and aid than other equally important ones.

Overlapping Tax Bases

One result of the increase in large-scale business and in the mobility of people during the twentieth century has been a vast complication of the state and local tax picture. The operation of businesses in more than one tax jurisdiction is part of the problem; another is the tendency

[20] Cf. Howard G. Schaller, "Federal Grants-in-Aid and Differences in State Per Capita Incomes, 1929, 1939, and 1949," *National Tax Journal*, VIII (Sept., 1955), 287-99.
[21] See, for example, Paul Studenski, "Federal Grants-in-Aid," *National Tax Journal*, II (Sept., 1949), 193-214.

of people to live in one city or state and to work in another—a more and more common situation as the trek to the suburbs continues. The multiple tax claims resulting from this picture frequently mean that overlapping tax bases are treated differently from bases confined entirely to one tax jurisdiction. These problems are discussed in the first section below and then illustrated, in the second section, with reference to the United States tax treatment of income originating abroad.

THE PROBLEM. When income originates in two different tax jurisdictions and flows to a resident of a third, the income receiver in question enjoys the services of three separate governments. Although these benefits give each of the tax agencies a claim on the income flow, they do not, unfortunately, enable the relative sizes of the three claims to be computed with precision. The benefits of most government services, as we have seen in Chapter 5, cannot be allocated to specific individuals or groups and hence do not provide a unique solution to the tax problems posed by overlapping tax bases.

From the point of view of the government, the important goal is some reasonable adjustment of the competing claims of jurisdictions of origin and jurisdictions of residence. In part this can be accomplished by the types of taxes selected for use by each government. Taxes on real property (land and buildings) or on the net value added by productive activity reach income originating in a given area regardless of the residence of its recipients, and such personal levies as income, net wealth, and spendings taxes can be designed to rest on the entire income of residents regardless of its source. Alternatively, the adjustment may be made by negotiation between the jurisdictions having a claim to the tax base in question. Property taxes on such items as railroad rolling stock or airplanes, for example, might, in the absence of intergovernmental agreements, be levied several times on the same tax base, imposing thereby discriminatory burdens on the transportation companies in question. Negotiations in such a case would need to settle both the rights of the various states of origin (on the basis, presumably, of some measure of the proportion of total economic activity taking place within each state) and the claims of the state of residence.

From the point of view of the taxpayer, equity requires the elimination of discrimination against overlapping tax bases. The problems involved here may be illustrated with reference to two state income taxes which include in their bases not only the total income of residents but also any income originating in the tax jurisdiction but accruing to residents of the other. As noted in Chapter 7, two types of tax credit may be used to eliminate the discriminatory double taxation of interstate income which would otherwise exist in such a fiscal system.

Suppose, first, that each state allows residents to deduct out-of-state income taxes from the in-state taxes due on that same income. Such a credit system gives priority to the claims of the state of origin. As its rates are raised, additional revenues are first obtained at the expense of the state of residence and later, when rates in the state of origin exceed those in the home state, at the expense of the taxpayer. A firm residing in a state with a 20 per cent income tax and drawing its income equally from that state and from another with a 10 per cent tax, for example, would pay 5 per cent of its taxable income to the other state and 15 per cent to the home state. As the other state increased its tax rate first to 20 per cent and then to 30 per cent, the firm would find its total taxes unaffected by the first step (10 per cent of its taxable income going to each state, the home state losing the revenue gained by the other state), but its taxes would be increased by the second since it would then owe 15 per cent of its taxable income to the outside state and 10 per cent at home. It may be noted that under this arrangement interstate firms will bear tax burdens greater than those imposed on firms residing and operating entirely within the low-tax state but less than or equal to those imposed on firms confined to the high-tax state. Discriminatory double taxation has been eliminated, but tax effects on economic location have not, since firms may still reduce their taxes by shifting residence to the low-tax state and then by shifting income-earning activities out of the high-tax state.

The second, and opposite, kind of tax credit is one allowed to non-residents for taxes paid on interstate income to their home state. In this case all income tax revenue goes to the state of residence until tax rates elsewhere reach higher levels. In the example of the preceding paragraph the firm would pay 20 per cent of its taxable income to its home state, regardless of whether the other state had a tax of 5, 10 or 20 per cent. With rates at 30 per cent, however, an additional 5 per cent of its taxable income would be due to the outside state, making for a total effective tax rate of 25 per cent.[22] As in the previous case interstate firms bear tax burdens greater than those of local firms in the low-tax state but lower than or equal to those of local firms in the high-tax state, and there is some incentive for taxpayers to

---

[22] Note that this is the same total tax rate as would be imposed under similar circumstances by the first kind of tax credit, but the interstate distribution of the revenue is different, being 15 per cent to 10 per cent in favor of the outside state under the first kind of credit and 20 per cent to 5 per cent in favor of the home state under the second.

shift residence, as well as income-earning activity, to the low-tax state.

Still a third solution to the double taxation problem would be for taxation to be used only on the income of residents, citizens, and domestic corporations. If all jurisdictions adhered to this rule, income taxation would be neutral as far as sources of income were concerned (residents being assessed equally on income from home or abroad), but if tax rates differed sharply, inducements to shift residence would be present. Needless to say, other factors would also enter into these decisions, tax-induced shifts from one country to another being less frequent than changes within a given country.

If tax rates were proportional rather than progressive, income taxation could be based solely on the origin of the tax base.[23] In this case the residence of the taxpayer would be immaterial, but tax gains could be reaped by shifting activity to the low-tax areas. A firm with half of its business in a 20 per cent state and half in a 10 per cent state would, for example, be subject to a 15 per cent effective rate but could reduce this by moving its operations more and more to the 10 per cent area. Such a move might, of course, reduce its total earnings as well as its tax rate and hence prove unprofitable on balance.

ILLUSTRATION: THE U. S. TAX TREATMENT OF INCOME FROM ABROAD. Citizens, domestic corporations, and resident aliens are all subject to U. S. tax on their entire income, but foreign income taxes may either be deducted from gross income in the computation of taxable income or be credited in full against U. S. taxes due on foreign income.[24] As noted in the preceding section, this type of tax credit grants foreign countries considerable freedom to tax American incomes originating within their jurisdictions at the expense of the U. S. Treasury rather than the recipient of the income. By the same token, however, foreign countries cannot, as long as their income tax rates do not exceed U. S. rates, count on attracting American business to their shores by means of special reductions in income tax rates, since in many cases these tax remissions will accrue to the benefit of the U. S. Treasury but not the taxpayer. This will always be true if the foreign activity is carried on by a branch of an American cor-

---

[23] As already noted in chap. 7, the use of this principle with progressive rates would impose substantially lower burdens on interstate income, since that income would be split into a number of parts for tax purposes and assessed only at the lowest tax rates, whereas an equal amount of intrastate income would be aggregated and thus subjected to higher marginal rates.

[24] U.S. citizens who are out of the country for 17 out of 18 consecutive months, however, may exclude all of their earned income, up to a maximum of $20,000, from taxation in the United States.

poration. If, on the other hand, a foreign subsidiary corporation is organized, U. S. income taxes on foreign earnings can be deferred until these earnings are transferred to the United States in the form of dividends, and hence the parent corporation may enjoy foreign tax concessions as long as it reinvests foreign income abroad.

Both the tax credit arrangement and the opportunities for the deferral of U. S. taxes on foreign income have been the subject of considerable discussion in recent years. A 1957 tax treaty with Pakistan incorporated for the first time a so-called "tax sparing credit" under which American corporations, in computing U. S. income taxes, could take credit for certain Pakistan taxes from which the government of that country had exempted them for a limited period of time. Welcomed by some as a promising means of stimulating foreign investment, this innovation was criticized by others for setting up the potentially dangerous precedent of giving credit for taxes *not* paid and thereby favoring certain U. S. investors in relation to others,[25] and in the final consideration of the treaty the provision was eliminated by the Senate.

An alternative means of stimulating foreign investment would be to allow all American corporations to defer U. S. income taxes due on foreign income until that income is transferred home in the form of dividends. A bill to permit such deferrals on income earned in the underdeveloped nations of the free world passed the House in 1960 but was rejected by the Senate Finance Committee. Interest in the stimulation of private foreign investment was strong on the part of the Eisenhower Administration because of its desire, whenever possible, to substitute private for public economic activity. Regardless of what form foreign investment takes, of course, its benefits should be weighed against those obtainable from alternative uses of the resources in question, and neither tax subsidies nor federal foreign aid should be granted unless a clear net gain results from the policy.

Other more specialized features of the U. S. tax treatment of foreign income cannot be gone into here. In late 1959 the United States had income tax treaties with twenty-one countries[26] designed to integrate the treatment of international income flows by eliminating double taxation. Their provisions, however, tend to be of only tech-

[25] See the discussion of the Pakistan Tax Treaty by Joseph P. Crockett and Stanley S. Surrey in the *National Tax Journal,* XI (June, 1958), 146-67.

[26] Raphael Sherfy, "Special Problems in Corporate Taxation Foreign Income," in the Committee on Ways and Means, *Tax Revision Compendium: Compendium of Papers on Broadening the Tax Base,* Vol. III (Washington, D.C.: Government Printing Office, 1959), p. 2161. The first part of this paper gives a useful summary of the legislative history of this part of U. S. tax policy.

nical interest and need not be considered here. Finally, it may be noted that since 1942 specially favorable tax rates (38 per cent in 1960 as compared with 52 per cent for other corporations) have been granted Western Hemisphere trade corporations which do most of their business outside of the United States in North, Central, or South America, the West Indies, or Newfoundland.

19

Economics of Metropolitan Living

A conspicuous feature of contemporary societies is the concentration of people in contiguous regions. In Western societies, the large city, large in relation to the total population, has been a dominant economic unit for decades and in some countries for centuries. Urban areas have grown in relative importance as well. During the decade 1950-1960 in the United States, about 80 per cent of the 26.4 million increase in population occurred in metropolitan areas. Year after year, young people and many of their parents as well forsake the smell of new-mown hay to sniff automobile exhaust fumes in and about such centers as New York, Los Angeles, and Chicago. Urban concentration, already large in the United States, becomes more so as each day passes. The American people are becoming, or perhaps one should say have become, a city people. There remain the hermits, the prospectors, the lumbermen, and the tillers of the soil, but as a group they are vastly outnumbered by people making a living in some metropolitan area.

The metropolitan region is testimony to the wonders of Adam Smith's "invisible hand." If the hand is not occasionally located and guided by deliberate intelligence, some rather serious consequences emerge. Our booming metropolitan areas do permit large numbers of people to work and live together and, apart from occasional backward steps in the trend of economic growth, permit them to do so at higher levels of living as the years pass. Yet there are problems; there always are problems, arising from these large-scale experiments in "togetherness." In this chapter, we shall touch on some of these and raise the question as to what, if anything, can be done to improve urban living.

Economic Basis of Urban Concentration

Urban living is rooted in fundamental and persistent characteristics of social organization. Throughout the history of mankind, since man escaped from the stone age, concentration of people in cities has paid substantial dividends. Cities are as old as civilization itself, and they have stood on their own economic feet. People found that they could produce more of the things they like, and in greater variety as well, by living in close proximity to one another. It was no accident that cities quickly came into being in the settlement of the North American continent. Even when the main products of an area are grown on the land, cities are needed to permit trading of crops, to provide financing facilities, to produce the many goods that farmers need in order to produce crops, as well as to satisfy their other demands. Were it not for the fact that people must eat to live, it is likely that the urban type of regional unit would have been the only important type to emerge even in early times.

On the North American continent, both cities and rural living grew together; there was a vast empty area to settle. In examining the dramatic migration of people from Europe and the Eastern seaboard to the Mississippi basin and to the West Coast during the nineteenth century, one may easily forget that New York, Philadelphia, and Boston were growing too, and fast. Since about the 1880's, in fact, the urban population in the United States has been increasing relatively to the rural.

The economic power of the city rests in the gains to be achieved by economic specialization. Were it possible, somehow, for every family to produce anything it liked to have, and to do so on any scale without loss of efficiency, urban concentration would arise only because people like to be together. Actually, of course, the talent for doing anything and everything is not generally found. Apart from this fact, specialization pays off merely because of scale considerations. Even what are ordinarily regarded as small-scale business operations are much larger than those feasible for home industry. In addition, economic activity by one organization requires for its effective functioning the presence of other business organizations. Retailing requires supplies as well as customers and clerks; a machine shop must have access to materials and parts for its equipment. Specialization of function becomes more feasible and efficient in a setting in which operations are carried on in close proximity to one another, where supplies can be ordered by telephone and deliveries made within a short period of time.

The advantages of close proximity of various types of business depend upon the nature of the operations, the types of commodities provided, and the relative costs of operations associated with the degree of urban concentration. The concentration of large financial transactions in New York City, in fact their concentration in tall office buildings on Wall and Broad streets on Manhattan Island, continues because of the interdependence of banks, stock markets, dealers in government securities, bond houses, and the literally thousands of highly specialized services available to such agencies. If some catastrophe were to demolish lower Manhattan Island, such operations could be located in another city, such as Chicago or San Francisco, provided all those complementary agencies moved together. There is no special characteristic of Manhattan Island that makes it peculiarly suitable to the concentration of wholesale financial activities. Once begun, however, whatever the historical reasons may have been, this type of highly localized specialization tends to persist. It would be a hardy individualist who would undertake to establish a firm specializing in the marketing of government securities with an office only in Los Angeles. His chances for economic survival would be poor.

The growth of particular urban regions is subject to economic limitations as well. New York never was the only city in the country. Against the advantages of locating where complementary facilities already exist are the increasing costs associated with high concentration. These take the form, in large part, of the increasing value of mere space. An office in downtown Manhattan, even a small one, is costly. To cover the rent, the services must be highly valuable, and the amount of space needed for effective operations must be small. Manufacturing industries ordinarily require large amounts of space, and a gradual decrease in their numbers on Manhattan Island has resulted. The land is more valuable when used for apartment houses, office buildings, hospitals, and night clubs. The disadvantages arising from density can be ascribed to diminishing returns from land. The growth of any metropolitan region is governed by the opposing forces of the gains from concentration against diminishing returns from land use.

Another and important factor contributing to the relative growth of cities is the natural restriction of agricultural industries to a narrow range of products and the special characteristics of people's tastes for these products. One might expect that as a society grows, it would grow in all dimensions. Not only would more steel pipe be produced but more eggs and barley also. In fact in some periods of history, a more or less balanced growth of goods produced in rural and in urban areas may be observed. However as people become more affluent, as a result of improvements in techniques and growth of resources, they buy more of the type of goods and services produced in cities, and absolutely more, but relatively less, of the things (mainly food items) provided by rural industry. The human stomach, as Adam Smith observed, has a narrowly restricted capacity; the application of food to that organ is quickly subject to diminishing returns. People prefer to take their higher level of living in the form of more medical care, education, automobiles, personal services, and mechanical gadgets—products of urban industry—rather than to stuff themselves with more bread, meat, and beans.

In advanced countries, farming is generally a declining industry. It is not doomed to extinction by any means—people must eat—but it is doomed to increasingly smaller importance in economic organization. In the United States, various government measures designed to alleviate the economic distress of farmers have slowed down the industry's decline. Otherwise large sections of the Great Plains region and of the Deep South might well long since have become virtually depopulated. In almost any sizable area presently dominated by agriculture, urban centers within it must grow if the region is not to decline in population.

The growth of urban concentration, then, is the product of the substantial gains to be achieved by specialization of function and the increasing preference of people for urban as opposed to rural products. Unless there is a radical revision of these fundamental influences, and there are no straws in the wind to suggest such a change, urban areas will continue to expand relatively to rural areas in the United States as well as in France, Great Britain, and the U.S.S.R.

Pattern of Growth in Urban Areas

The historical pattern of growth in large metropolitan regions has varied in detail. The local topography dictates where growth can and cannot occur. In the few cities built in flat open country, such as London, expansion is feasible in all directions. In such cases, the historical pattern of growth can be roughly described by a simple parabolic curve of concentration, with the high point of maximum density at the center dwindling off to small density per acre at the fringe. One would not expect, for example, that the density per acre would be uniform and then abruptly drop to that dictated by agricultural use of land or that it would vary in a nonsystematic fashion over the entire metropolitan region. Purely economic considerations, apart from any government rules with respect to zoning, lead to a maximum density point, called the center, and a tapering off in density in all directions from this point. There are, as already observed, gains to be achieved from concentration; activities providing the maximum gains from close association concentrate at the center. In turn, this fact makes land in such areas have the highest use value, serving to exclude those uses which for efficient operation require a relatively smaller degree of concentration. Enterprises such as large manufacturing establishments, as well as homes of people who like gardens and yards, are pushed to the periphery because use values are smaller than those in more centrally located areas. On the other hand, the periphery does not extend into the countryside indefinitely. There are costs of transportation to the center, serving to set limits on the spread. The growth of a city, then, is similar to the growth of a pile of sand as more sand is added at the top. In turn, land values reflect the concentration, being greatest at the center and gradually diminishing, but not becoming zero, at the fringe.

This pretty pattern is of course spoiled by rivers, oceans, mountains, and swamps. Topography excludes some areas altogether and selects the use of others. Steep hillsides are often treated as especially desirable residential areas and are unsuited for manufacturing. Sites along navigable rivers are especially suited to industries using large quantities of bulk merchandise shipped by water. Sites along busy streets are especially suited for stores. Topography, plus the density factor discussed above, gives rise to what is sometimes called "natural zoning." The term may be misleading in suggesting that the mere facts of local geography dictate the location of particular types of activities. Geography matters, but so does the underlying fact that land use values depend upon the economic gains from concentration plus the diminishing returns from high density. Even if geography is uniform, land use is not.

The actual pattern of growth of metropolitan regions has been strongly influenced by the local modes of transportation. Before the days of mechanical vehicles, human legs were the main means of getting from home to work and back again. For movement of things, a city depended upon horses and wagons and human-pushed-or-pulled vehicles, as was the case in Roman times. The resulting congestion in the late nineteenth century was something fearful in large cities such as New York, London, and Chicago. A horse and wagon requires more space than does a Cadillac. Congestion is nothing new in cities; it has simply taken a different form.

With human beings and horses as the chief agencies for local transportation, cities tended to grow less rapidly at the fringe and more rapidly at the center. Locating one's residence at a point requiring two hours walk per day to and from work was attractive to only a few.

Furthermore, such people had trouble getting the groceries home and the coal delivered.

The first major advance in local transport in urban areas was the street car, first drawn by horses and later propelled by electricity. This device greatly widened the area of feasible location by reducing the cost of transportation to areas distant from the center. Street cars have managed to survive here and there; they may still be seen in Washington or San Francisco. Of much greater importance, certainly in large metropolitan regions, was the local train with its own right-of-way either underground or elevated or both. This device had two important effects upon the pattern of urban growth. Like the street car, only more so, it greatly extended the fringe by lowering the cost of transport to the center, and it made for heavy concentration in the vicinity of the right-of-way.

In more recent times, dating from about the close of World War I, the dominating factor in the growth of urban areas has been the product of Detroit—the automobile and truck. As more and more people found themselves able to afford a car, a range of choice opened that had not existed a few years earlier. People began spreading out from the center. As a result, the fringe has grown much more rapidly than the central district. According to the 1960 census, of the five largest cities—New York, Chicago, Los Angeles, Philadelphia, and Detroit—all except Los Angeles lost population, whereas in each case the suburbs of the city grew. The smallest increase was 32.7 per cent for the Philadelphia region, and the highest was 82.5 per cent for the Los Angeles-Long Beach region. When a metropolitan region has grown slowly, as illustrated by the 6.3 per cent for the Boston metropolitan area, the central city has shrunk substantially (15.4 per cent). On balance, the suburbs become the dwelling places of newcomers to a metropolitan region and of many former residents of the central cities as well. Few large cities in the United States have grown significantly in population during the past twenty-five years; the exceptions are mainly those that have extended their boundaries or had large areas of undeveloped land. Every census becomes an occasion of alarm for the city fathers. They find themselves governing a region that is often dwindling in population while the bedroom communities and outlying industrial areas are growing rapidly. The long faces to be seen at almost any meeting of a downtown merchants' association, whether it is in Chicago, Illinois, or Berkeley, California, reflect the fact that the central areas are losing their economic *raison d'être*. The business is going to the new shopping centers located in places which a few years ago were nothing but crossroads, if that.

The new pattern of metropolitan growth, a pattern clearly established in the 1920's but having its strong impact since World War II, is what some students call "metropolitan sprawl." Tracts of houses are built in what appears to be the middle of nowhere and sell for a profit. Companies locate plants out in the country, several miles from the city, surrounded by magnificent parking lots. In terms of speed of commuting, people can get more quickly from home to work by driving to plants so located than they can by going one-third the distance in heavily settled areas.

The prospect laid before us is a more or less continuous metropolitan area extending roughly from Boston to Washington on the East Coast and, according to some more imaginative predictors, from Seattle to San Diego on the West Coast. Whatever the long-run prospects, the immediate indications are for continued metropolitan sprawl. While on the one hand people are gathering together in increasing numbers in metropolitan regions, these regions themselves are spreading out over the countryside.

Meanwhile, this pattern of growth is creating problems of its own as well as magnifying difficulties as old as cities. Attempts to treat these problems are subject to the severe handicap that there is no agency clearly in charge. Metropolitan government, insofar as there is any such government, consists mainly of committees representing various municipalities. Their proposals are often similar to treaties drawn up by suspicious diplomats representing not-too-friendly countries.

Transportation

The development of a high concentration of people within a region, along with the rapid growth in the size of the area itself, has been made possible by fast and relatively low-cost transportation. The personal automobile or truck, as already mentioned, has been the dominant agency determining the pattern of metropolitan growth in recent decades. In many areas, this mode of transport has undermined or eliminated its competitors, initially the street car and the interurban line. Local bus transport has survived; it has become something less than a flourishing industry. The commuter train has been in trouble for years, and the main source of trouble is the loss of traffic to the automobile. Local rail lines are reduced to commuter business, hauling people to work and back, and little more. With two peak loads for five days per week, giving about twenty hours of business weekly, the local rail lines commonly find themselves operating at a loss. The maladies of the rail passenger business have been discussed for years. Unimaginative management and short-sighted labor union policies have played some role in the undermining of this mode of transport in and about metropolitan regions. Yet the basic difficulty is a simple economic one; there is too little demand for the available service. Were people to be found waiting in line at commuter stations throughout the day, railroad companies would be only too happy to provide the service and show a profit to their stockholders. Providing service only twenty hours per week or thereabouts means that highly expensive equipment must stand almost idle the remainder of the time. Labor, too, cannot be hired simply to handle the morning and evening peak loads at rates of pay comparable to those paid for an eight-hour continuous day. The average costs of operating commuter trains as a result of the loss of off-peak traffic have led to higher fares for all traffic, placing this mode of transport at a further disadvantage with its main competitor, the automobile.

Yet, greatly to the surprise of some and the dismay of many, the automobile as a device for mass transport is proving itself to be increasingly impractical. For the first time since before World War I, we are witnessing a comeback of the rail-wheel device. In Boston, New York, Philadelphia, Cleveland, Los Angeles, and San Francisco, serious moves are being made to develop an efficient system of mass rail transport. Only rarely in economic history has a device eliminated by "progress" had the opportunity for a reincarnation. These moves to re-establish rail transport do not merely result from the pressures of city planners; they are rooted in some simple but unpleasant facts. The personal automobile as a mass transport device is proving unsatisfactory. Furthermore, its prospects, from a long-run point of view, are not good. The movement of people by rail seems to many to be the only promise for rescuing urban regions from throttling congestion.

The automobile has no serious competitor for door-to-door transportation if two conditions are satisfied: cheap parking and uncongested routes. On a cost basis, when the costs of driving are restricted to the operating expense, one can drive the round trip distance of twenty miles from home to factory for less than a dollar, and if an economical car is used, for no more than fifty cents. If two ride, the cost per person is cut in half. It is much cheaper in many areas to commute in car pools than to use public transportation. Granted the two conditions stated, the automobile has no effective competitor.

These conditions have never been satisfied in some areas of heavy concentration, such as New York City, for the great mass of people. The critical factor is sometimes parking, sometimes great congestion on the route, and commonly both. As a result, the automobile in

New York has been the regular commuting device of only some of the more affluent citizens who can afford the parking charge and whose offices and residences are located outside the worst areas of congestion. In areas of relatively light concentration, such as cities of less than 200,000 people, the two conditions are commonly satisfied for large numbers of people even of modest means. But in our large metropolitan regions, the automobile is being confronted by the obstacles of increasing congestion, reduced speeds, and increased costs of parking. As time goes on, these conditions are virtually certain to become aggravated. Hence, there is a demand for alternative forms of transport to escape these difficulties.

Highways are subject to diminishing returns with the addition of vehicles. As more cars are added, after a certain point, the average speed per car, even in the absence of legal restrictions, decreases and for some number of vehicles approaches zero—the traffic snarl. The remedy for this condition seems simple: increase the number and size of highways. To further increase the average speed, the highways should be of the limited-access type, illustrated by the freeway or expressway.

The construction of highways in areas of dense concentration has been extraordinarily expensive and will become more so. To make room for the elevated expressway, the bulldozer and the wrecking ball must cut a path through the city. If the structures in the way are commercial and residential slums, perhaps few tears are to be shed. In practice, the path for the expressway often requires the invasion of fine residential areas as well as prosperous mercantile and business sections. Although owners of the property in the right-of-way are compensated they are rarely delighted to be forced to move their residences or their business establishments. Others close to the routes are not ordinarily compensated; they are asked to enjoy the noise and fumes from cars moving on the expressway and to get what esthetic comfort they may from contemplating a wall of concrete. Much to the dismay of the highway engineer, he finds himself a thoroughly unpopular fellow at public meetings called to discuss routes for a new expressway. Yet if he is allowed to have his way, cities will more and more take on the character of Los Angeles and not be cities at all, but various communities, each with its shopping center, separated from others by a maze of freeways. In this maze, the center of the city tends to disappear, and the special advantages of urban living are dissipated. Actually, even this prospect understates the difficulties of continued construction of the urban expressway as a means of transport. As more of them are built, the interchanges become increasingly complicated and expensive, encroaching increasingly on alternative uses of land, and thereby driving people further out along the fringe. This spread in turn increases the demand for transportation facilities —yet more freeways—and even the highway engineer begins to have doubts about his ability to meet the demands.

The movement to develop rapid mass transit by rail rests mainly upon the fact that a person takes up much less space than a car and that furthermore, when he gets to where he wants to go—to the office, the factory, or the store—he has only himself to park. One double-tracked rail line can carry as many people as ten four-lane express-ways. Since in fact automobiles must get off the expressway and onto streets, even this comparison overstates the carrying capacity of high-ways. Given the present street structure of large cities, a 20 per cent increase in automobiles results in impossible congestion.

Mass rail transport would entail no great economic difficulties if it could clearly be made to pay. Actually, there are few systems in the United States that do fully pay their own way, and plans under way for the installation of rapid mass transit must somehow over-come the problem that they may not be self-supporting. The San Francisco transit plan, an ambitious one, will probably require a sub-stantial subsidy for some years after its installation. Even if these projections turn out to be unduly pessimistic, any added burden on the local taxpayer will generate serious voter opposition. People who do not plan to use rapid transit are likely to oppose any financial proposal requiring that they contribute to subsidizing the system. If rapid transit would clearly pay its own way, the problem of sub-stituting mass transit for personal transit would be relatively simple to solve.

A subsidy to an industry providing a service to particular groups can be justified on economic grounds if the actual benefits bestowed, in addition to the service for which it makes a charge, are sufficiently large; if the costs involved are, for some special reason, overstated; if there are valuable by-products to the community at large; or if some combination of these factors exists. Ordinarily, there is a presump-tion that public or private industry should not become a public charge. In certain cases, such as the mails, the Congress has deliberately ruled that the service provides sufficient indirect benefits that it should be subsidized. If the usual presumption is to stand, should rapid mass transit in metropolitan regions be encouraged and supported?

Rapid mass transit would pay, and pay for itself easily, if the demand for service existing during the two peak-load periods con-tinued throughout the day. Given any schedule for frequency of service, the noncommuter traffic demand is too small to fill the seats. Attempts to cut costs by cutting service also reduce the demand further because people dislike the added delay in travelling between any two points.

One remedy, an important one, is to charge more for travel during the peak loads than at other times. This very ordinary economic pricing device meets with strong resistance in the case of transit service. Although this technique is to be recommended on economic grounds, there is little evidence to suggest that any such change in pricing tactics would of itself be sufficient to make transit a profitable enterprise.

Another attack on the question is therefore indicated. Such an attack calls for another look at the chief competitor of rail transit—the private automobile. If it is true that this mode of transit is now subsidized, a case can be made for removing the subsidy and thereby pushing the business to rail mass transit systems.

If we concentrate attention on the streets in the central areas of New York, Cleveland, Detroit, Chicago, or San Francisco, the typical condition found during weekdays is heavy congestion by automobiles, taxis, trucks, buses, and pedestrians. This heavy congestion slows down the movement of any vehicle and thereby increases the costs of each. For taxis, buses, and delivery trucks, the manpower requirements per vehicle-mile increase as the congestion increases. If some practical administrative devices can be found, a system of tolls would result in more efficient use of the streets. A car using Manhattan streets, for example, might be charged twenty-five cents per mile travelled during daylight hours on weekdays. At such a charge, the amount of street congestion would diminish. The costs of operating the remaining vehicles would of course fall as the diminished congestion permitted more rapid movement of those left. Ideally, the charge would be set at a level equal to the difference between the total operating cost for a given number of vehicles and that for a slightly greater or smaller number. Or, in other words, price should equal marginal cost.

Actually, such a charge if it amounted to, say, 25 cents per mile, might be too low. Other costs occasioned by traffic on city streets have not been included. As street traffic increases, it becomes difficult for pedestrians to cross a street; and as the hazard to both pedestrians and drivers increases, insurance costs become higher, more traffic policemen must be used, the expense to the city in court cases arising from accidents increases, shopping becomes less pleasant in the vicinity, as does strolling and apartment house living. When all these costs are added together, even forgetting the pollution caused by exhaust fumes, the proper charge might be another five or ten cents per mile in heavily concentrated areas.

What do these considerations imply? They imply that automobile travel in heavily concentrated areas is (1) highly inefficient and (2) heavily subsidized.

A pricing system applied to the use of streets is confronted by the technical difficulty of collecting a charge. With the advance in technology, however, this problem may be solved. One technique[1] calls for the installation of TV cameras on heavily congested streets, photographing the license plate of each car, and then by high-speed automatic equipment, computing the amount due and sending a bill once per month to each car owner. When those who use the city streets heavily find themselves being called upon to pay $20 or so per month, many will leave their cars in the garage and avoid travel in heavily congested areas. Other methods could be devised if talented engineers were given the assignment and if the city fathers could be convinced that some such system would greatly improve the tone of the city. As long as automobile travel is heavily subsidized, competing modes of transport are at a serious disadvantage. With the removal of this subsidy in the larger metropolitan regions, the demand for mass transit service would become much greater and the likelihood of its having to be subsidized would substantially decrease.

In fact, the policy with regard to automobile traffic in our larger cities has been misguided in several ways. Many cities have undertaken the installation of public garages. These are regarded as paying their own way as long as they cover operating costs plus interest on the initial investment. Actually, the decision to build in the first instance should take into account the amount of property removed from the tax rolls and the increased congestion and hence higher costs to all traffic in the vicinity of the public garage. The receipts from parking meters are sometimes earmarked for the construction of additional parking facilities—a curious practice. What city officials have not yet generally realized is that the private automobile spells death to central cities. These areas exist and survive because of the advantages of high concentration of people. The private automobile is a large space-user, when it is moving and when it is not. Reliance upon it as a mode of general transport of persons takes away valuable space for other purposes. Let the New York Port Authority determine traffic policy in New York, or let the California Highway Department determine where to build freeways in San Francisco, and the decay of these central areas, a decay that has been evident now for at least two decades, will continue.

[1] Suggested by William Vickrey.

With this decay comes the loss of many of the advantages of urban living. The central city must provide the facilities for specialized cultural activities, such as plays, concerts, museums, and for a great variety of specialized business activities, if these are to be provided at all. The unattractiveness of the downtown areas of many cities is a direct consequence of the reliance upon the automobile as the main transit device. In some cities almost the only central facilities left for after-work activities are hotels, and these are used by travellers who have little choice. Central districts are becoming merely dull for leisure activities and costly for business activities.

The reversal of this trend calls for efficient, cheap, and pleasant mass transit in and about metropolitan areas, accompanied by charges for the street and highway use by the private automobile. Street parking might be altogether prohibited in highly congested areas because such space is more valuable for other uses. Overnight parking in streets might also be subject to a charge to cover the increased costs of cleaning the streets, the difficulties of moving emergency vehicles, such as fire-fighting equipment, and the costs of policing because such a valuable piece of property as an automobile invites the attention of the thief. Some observers, impressed with the great social costs of the private automobile, are recommending its complete prohibition in heavily congested areas of large cities.

If automobile travel is to continue to be heavily subsidized, there may be no alternative except to subsidize rapid transit as well. The day will more quickly arrive when rapid mass transit will pay its own way if the efforts of the various authorities and state highway departments to build highways into cities are more firmly resisted and if the cities themselves take more steps to make owners of vehicles pay more of the costs which their presence entails. The impossible congestion that has emerged in central areas, and which can only get worse, may then be reversed.

Recreation

One class of commodities which people like, wherever they may live, is recreation. In rural areas, there is the Saturday night dance, the beer tavern, the movie house, and the great outdoors. In metropolitan areas, there exists a great variety of recreational facilities, most of which are operated ordinarily under private enterprise rules. There are some types of recreational facilities which may require governmental action and support if they are to be provided on a sufficient scale, and it is these to which our attention is now directed.

The traditional type of recreational facility provided by local government is the park, which may be little more than a small open space with "keep-off-the-grass" signs or may be an elaborate layout equipped with facilities for various games, swimming, outdoor eating, and the like. In the metropolitan boom of the last several decades, park-like facilities have failed to keep pace with the population growth. The sprawl tendency, already noted, carries with it a lack of concern for open space because new communities are built in what had been rural regions. At the time, open space is apparently plentiful. As new subdivisions develop, open space disappears and the contiguous urban area emerges. To the real estate promoter, provisions for parks rarely pay off in terms of the value of the sites sold. Open space continuously recedes from the center, relieved only by the old parks of the central cities and by undeveloped locations out toward the fringe. As the population increases, open areas become increasingly inaccessible.

From the point of view of a hypothetical government unit encompassing the entire metropolitan region, park-like facilities may be economically an asset, even though no explicit charges are made for their use. Looking at parks as a source of financial gains may seem strange; yet in fact they can be and are sources of gains to a government unit. The presence of parks tends to increase the value of residential sites close to them because people prefer to look at trees or grass rather than to contemplate the walls of a building or a street from their living-room windows. In addition, proximity to parks provides opportunities for strolling, especially if one has a dog, and even for communing with nature. If the government unit were in a position to appropriate the increase in land values as a result of parks, the financial gain to be achieved would be vivid and substantial. Indirectly the government unit may in any event gain. Judicious scattering of parks through an area increases private land values and hence increases the potential yield of the property tax.

Another source of gain to the government arises from keeping land out of private ownership. In areas of expensive land values, the normal economic tendency calls for intensive use. Hence the higher the land values, the greater is the amount of floor space per acre. This economic tendency can be prevented from fully operating by zoning restrictions. The pressure, however, to push for more intensive land use reduces open space in the form of yards and gardens. Parks may be looked upon as common open space, available to people in the vicinity, reducing the intensity of land use on the average, and therefore tending to reduce the government costs associated with more, as opposed to less, concentration. Savings take the form of reduced costs of education, reduced requirements for fire protection and sewage disposal, and to the extent that playgrounds do reduce juvenile delinquency, somewhat reduced police, court, and jail costs. On the other side of the ledger are the specific expenses of maintaining the park.

For metropolitan areas, the traditional park has an important role. Some greater emphasis might be given to the large open-area type of park. A major defect of many large metropolitan regions in the United States, and Europe as well, are miles and miles of unrelieved buildings and streets. Those in search of open space must travel long distances, and unless public facilities are provided toward the fringe, people are restricted to merely sight-seeing.

Large open areas within metropolitan regions, scattered so as to permit easy access to all groups within the region, and large enough to give the impression of a "natural area," would be a desirable partial solution to the human desire for a respite from urbanized living. Such areas could be used to define communities by providing genuine dividing boundaries. Various types of facilities could be provided, depending upon the local climate and the dominant desires of the residents, and many could be made to pay their own way, apart from the costs implied in the value of land use. Thus golf courses, which give a large expanse of pleasant terrain, could be installed with a charge sufficient to cover operating expenses, with the land use to be looked upon as yielding gains, in the form of pleasant scenery and relief from the monotony of streets and structures, to others who may merely play chess.

As in other matters, there are costs involved in establishing such areas. Here the crucial requirement is acquisition prior to the development of an area by the real estate promoter. Once streets, public utilities, and a few dwellings have been built, acquisition costs mount to a multiple of the undeveloped value. A major defect of present government organization is again the absence of any agency empowered to take aggressive steps to save open areas for regional parks before they are partially developed for homes and industrial sites.

There is no inherent reason for governments to be restricted in the provision of almost any recreational facility. However, governments are not ordinarily very good at operating night clubs or taverns—these facilities seem to be adequate in numbers, in any event. Provision of open space and of outdoor facilities requires, in large metropolitan areas, government action if they are to be available on the required scale. Failure to take these steps has the effect of making urban living less pleasant and contributes to the large-scale exodus from the city on sunny week ends when many could enjoy themselves more by remaining close to home.

Urban Blight and Slums

Large cities have been characterized by large slum districts for decades, and it is only in recent years that much attention has been given to remedying this feature of urban living. Residential slums arise from the presence of large numbers of impoverished people. Characteristically they are found in the older sections of cities, where the structures have often been converted from what had in the past been expensive residential dwellings and commercial structures, such as warehouses.

Slum use of the buildings may be temporary in the sense that their owners are simply waiting until the land values rise sufficiently to sell out or convert the land to another use. Often, however, the income obtained from slum use may justify indefinite use of the land for this purpose. The structures are grossly undermaintained, and the landlords are habitually in trouble with the law on the score of providing substandard facilities. Were the operators of the slum structures of New York, Chicago, Baltimore, or Los Angeles given a choice between fixing the electrical wiring, plumbing, stairways, fire escapes, and various other features to the standards required by local law and closing down, the number of such structures would shrink rapidly. An important aspect of the financial success of slum structures comes from lack of maintainence and absence of proper facilities.

Residential slums are synonymous with intense crowding. To make the building pay, the operators must insist upon crowding many people into a room, collecting a "low" rent per family or person. Rents are low in the sense that a family may pay less than twenty dollars per month for quarters on Manhattan Island.[2] What they get for their money is, perhaps, a room, access to a toilet, makeshift kitchen facilities, and plentiful and noisy neighbors.

Correction of this form of urban blight requires diagnosis and remedial measures appropriate to the diagnosis. Consideration of

[2] According to 1950 census data, 132,386 rental units, or 7.4 per cent, rented for $29 per month or less, and 1.3 per cent rented for less than $20. In a city where space is highly valuable and where almost ten per cent of the families were reported to have incomes of less than $1,000 (1950 census data for 1949 incomes), crowding to economize on space is to be expected. For example, in New York in 1950, 226,800 families consisting of four persons (about 11 per cent of all families) were found to be living in dwelling units with one bedroom. See *Report of Subcommittee on Special Problems* (New York: Mayor's Committee for Better Housing of the City of New York, June, 1955), mimeographed.

several common misapprehensions about the causes of slums may help to get at the relevant issues.

People who live in slums do not do so because they prefer crowded quarters and filthy conditions. When the opportunity presents itself, most people choose to move out to better neighborhoods. From an economic point of view, slum quarters are an inferior commodity. As a person's spending power increases, he takes less of that commodity —he moves. People who live in slums do so because the quarters are cheap and because they would rather live there than on the street, as do some very poor people in Bombay.

The observation is often made that slums are the product of "slummy" people. In one sense this has some truth in it. People who have never known clean and commodious living quarters may, when given the opportunity, convert new quarters into slums also. However, the possible implication that slums are inevitable because the people living in them are too lazy or unconcerned to keep quarters livable by ordinary standards misses the main point. Bad housekeeping can be found among people of all walks of life. However much the squalor may offend relatives and friends, it is a more or less private affair. Slums by contrast are the product of large numbers of people attempting to share space in dilapidated structures. Attempts at good housekeeping are found even under such conditions, although the attempt must be cruelly frustrating.

The basic reason for slums is large-scale poverty. Many people cannot afford to pay more than twenty dollars per month for space and still eat, if they do eat regularly. Conversion of run-down structures into crowded living quarters reflects the high value of space and the low financial ability of the tenants. Crowding reduces the amount of space taken by one person and permits what appear to be low rents. In fact, for the total amount of space and the condition of the building, slum use does pay. It pays because the total rental is large for the building. In addition, old, worn-out buildings are used because it would not pay to make the investment in a new building to rent it to people who are poverty-stricken. Unless such old buildings were left unoccupied, they would ordinarily require maintenance, and hence the return that could be earned would be reduced.

Any serious attack upon the problems of slums must start with the factors that make large numbers of urban dwellers poor. For the period of large-scale immigration to this country prior to World War I, no special explanation is necessary. People arrived poor, and many were destined to stay poor for some time. With the advance of technical knowledge and efficiency during recent decades, why do there remain these large groups of slum dwellers? A person regularly employed in a job calling for modest skills can and does earn enough to finance adequate housing, a car, and the usual but expensive household gadgets. Why has the vaunted American standard of living not made slums disappear merely by creating a shortage of poor people?

In the Northern section of the United States, poverty is concentrated among certain minority groups. In the South, average income is much lower, and poverty more general. Part of the poverty found in the North is the direct result of migration from the South. People moving out of areas such as Oklahoma and Arkansas, for example, to the Northern cities, when they do so in large numbers, often become slum dwellers. In fact, one of the few white, Protestant slum areas in any large Northern city is found in Chicago, inhabited by migrants from border states. This type of poverty is similar in its basic cause to the poverty of Polish people in Chicago in 1910. They arrived poor and for a time had serious difficulty in finding good jobs. Whenever people emigrate from a poor region, they will be found to continue to be poor when they live in the city, regardless of ethnic characteristics. Thus the poverty observed in city slums is, in one sense, simply an illustration of a concentration of poverty that has been with us all the time. Movement of poor people from country areas is for them a change of a rural slum for a city slum. They may have a greater chance for economic advancement in the city; if they do succeed in getting regular jobs, they can expect to break the dismal self-perpetuating hold of poverty over their lives and over the lives of their children. Remaining in the rural area greatly reduces their chances of significant economic advancement.

One means of reducing city slums is to improve economic opportunities in the regions from which the poor emigrate. In the United States, the main regions are found in the South, including the so-called border states, and in Puerto Rico. Radical economic rehabilitation of these sections would reduce the exodus of local inhabitants to large cities. However expensive programs designed to develop these regions might be, and they would be expensive, there is the offsetting consideration that cities are very expensive environments for attempting to eradicate the basis of poverty. In cities, these people occasion substantial costs for education, policing, and welfare measures. Some similar services would need to be provided in the areas from which they have come. Schools of given quality could be provided at less expense in the South than in Manhattan. In addition, a large influx of children from low-income, poorly educated families causes a deterioration in the quality of public schools and results in a kind of segregation whereby wealthier groups either send their children to private schools or move to suburbs where the equivalent is provided.

The central city schools are then left to specialize in the education of the children of poor parents. The same expenditures for education of children in poor regions would permit at least as good, if not better, educational service for them, and also would prevent the quality deterioration found in the public schools in central cities.

City slums can be reduced by measures which accelerate the upward movement of poverty groups or which restrict the influx of poor people to the city. On a national scale, the termination of unrestricted immigration illustrates the latter device. However discriminatory and unjust, this policy does reduce the incidence of poverty. The large-scale migration to Northern cities from the South dates from about the First World War. The twin conditions of good employment opportunities in the North and the curtailment of immigration from abroad made this internal migration relatively more attractive. If, somehow, cities could be given a respite, they might be able to get two or three steps ahead and even begin to make serious inroads upon the incidence of urban poverty. As matters presently stand, the costs of reducing the incidence of poverty fall heavily upon city residents. To escape these costs and also to get the kind of government services they like, people have been moving in large numbers to the suburbs. The decentralization of the metropolitan region previously mentioned is further increased and, in extreme cases, the central city becomes a vast slum.

One possible national solution for poverty is a systematic redistribution of income through subsidies to people whose incomes fall below some critical level.[3] Thus far the American people have not indicated a willingness to tax themselves sufficiently to make such large-scale redistribution feasible. One may hazard the guess that if such a proposal were put to the test of a nation-wide popular vote, it would fail overwhelmingly. To finance such a proposal would require a first-bracket rate on the income tax perhaps as high as 40 per cent, even if present loopholes were largely eliminated. The American people may appear to European and some native observers to be super-affluent, but there are at least 20 per cent who live under wretched conditions, including inadequate nourishment, little or no professional medical or dental care, and meagre educational opportunities.

The obvious solution to city slums is their literal removal from the scene. Observing a block of low-grade structures teeming with people, one may easily believe that the apparent choice is to fix them or tear them down and erect new, neat ones. Repair often turns out to

---

[3] See p. 519 for a discussion of one such proposal.

be much too expensive because the buildings are in fact beyond repair. The solution again is the wrecking ball. In their place may be erected public housing facilities, restricted to families with incomes below some defined level. Public housing programs designed to remove slums and provide people with attractive living quarters have been a main government device aimed at solving the slum problem in this country.

How good is a solution that relocates people in specially constructed buildings restricted to low-income families?

The experience with this device is not easy to appraise. With the continued migration of the rural poor to the large city, the task of reconstruction appears unending. Those who do succeed in obtaining living quarters continue in poverty. Even free quarters are only small help to a family with a few hundred dollars per year of money income. Although rules set down may prevent crowding, a public housing structure surrounded by grass may become another slum. To keep costs from skyrocketing, the buildings are constructed in a plain, utilitarian fashion. In their architectural features, some have more in common with prisons than with dwellings in which to live decently and to bring up children. Although conditions vary, depending upon the quality of the local officials and the degree of crowding, there is a basis for debate as to whether the new slums are less bad than the old. Tearing down a block of structures in which people have been living over a long period invites trouble. Uprooting people disturbs the social customs of the neighborhood that give stability and hold down violence. Along with the destruction of the buildings and their replacement by public housing goes the local merchant with the corner delicatessen, the small-time lawyer with connections at city hall, the elderly philosopher to whom families could turn to settle quarrels, and the familiar policeman who grew up only two blocks away. The settling influences of such people are removed because they cannot ordinarily qualify for subsidized housing. The accepted balance of national and racial groups is upset. The new quarters may be occupied by an alien group—alien to the old neighborhood—and an environment is immediately created for hostile juvenile gangs.

Furthermore, the design of public housing has failed to fit the needs of the tenants. Observing crowded, decrepit structures, located close together, architects and planners designed the new buildings so as to have large areas of grass and to be set back from the streets. To economize on space, structures had to be several stories tall. A tall building requires elevators. Children promptly convert the elevators into public toilets. Those with delicate nostrils must climb the stairs. The costs of maintaining such buildings have risen well beyond original estimates, because facilities are damaged and repairs are made by expensive labor. And what the dwellers have for this expense would not be regarded by people of even modest means as livable quarters. If we solve the problem of poverty in the United States, some of the piles called public housing will have to be torn down or radically redesigned to make them usable as apartments of the type that people of ordinary means would care to rent.

Public housing as practiced in the large cities of this country has provided an engineering solution to a social problem and, as usual, an engineering solution does not work. The one large gain of public housing is appearance; from the outside the passer-by may obtain the impression that the new buildings and grounds have eliminated slum living conditions. Even this impression is dangerous; it may induce the belief that the basic problem has been solved when it has not been solved. When large numbers of poor people must group together, slum-like conditions are bound to occur, however pretty may be the public structures housing them. As each year passes, the proportion of the land in Manhattan, for example, given over to slums increases and a real danger exists that the area will eventually become one vast slum.

Any practical solution must reduce the incidence of poverty of people in urban areas. What measures are available to accomplish this result?

One set of measures has already been discussed. The city poor were the rural poor. To the extent that measures can be taken to relieve the economic condition of these people where they originate, their incentive to emigrate to the city is reduced. In part, the problem could be solved by making Puerto Rico a separate country and applying immigration restrictions. For New York City, such a move would be of great benefit. Such a solution may seem ungracious; yet unless one is prepared to hold that immigration should be completely unrestricted, the case exists for restricting entry of these people. Poor people from foreign rural areas, and especially those whose traditions and outlook are radically different from those in this country, are almost certain to create slums in the large cities of this country if they are permitted to enter. The reply that the country has absorbed various national groups in the past, although a potent one, presupposes that the proper immigration policy should be unrestricted entry. Such a policy would be disastrous for large cities in this country, and it would postpone the day when native poverty can be effectively remedied.

The erosion of poverty occurs naturally in the sense that some members of the group will rise economically by obtaining regular employment. As the output of the economy rises, the level of living of poor groups will tend to rise also. If the number escaping from poverty conditions exceeds the recruits, slums tend to decline. Hence measures which accelerate the upward movement of people living in slum conditions help to eliminate this form of social blight.

The standard method of achieving this result is education. Given good educational opportunities, children may then break out of the vicious self-perpetuating hold of poverty, leaving the slums behind. This solution has worked, and worked on a large scale, with regard to the children of foreign-born parents who settled initially in large cities. Although the pace may appear to be dismally slow in relation to the size of the problem, education continues to work. Education as a solution works less quickly for groups who are subject to various forms of social and economic discrimination. In the United States, the large group in this class is of course the Negroes. When members of a group are subject to discrimination, those who do succeed in educating themselves may nevertheless be held in poverty by being denied the opportunity of obtaining well-paid employment.

The occupations from which Negroes are effectively excluded are many. The reasons stem partly from plain prejudice and are partly by-products of restrictive tactics. Many labor unions, especially those organized along craft lines, bar Negroes altogether from the occupation. Where no such rule has been laid down, they bar them by controlling apprenticeship. The number of Negro plumbers, carpenters, electricians, painters, and airplane pilots found in Northern cities is small relative to the proportion the Negro population bears to the white population, and this cannot be attributed to some inherent lack of the ability to obtain the necessary skills. The shortage of employment opportunities plus the social discrimination which tends to confine Negroes to given localities makes them the dominant inhabitants of slums in large Northern cities. Aggressive moves to break restrictions upon entry into the better-paying occupations, as well as the standard remedy of education of children, are needed if these slums are to be eradicated from the scene.

In addition to slums, cities and their satellites exhibit a number of features which detract from the potentiality of pleasant, challenging living and working arrangements. Some of these could be corrected by relatively simple measures. Others are deeply rooted in the very fact of heavy population concentration.

American cities, like elementary textbooks in economics, tend to exhibit a depressing sameness. During the period when cities were growing rapidly—roughly the period between the Civil War and the First World War—taste had already become corrupted. The deterioration of architectural taste may be easily observed by comparing structures built in the eighteenth century with those built in the nineteenth century after the Civil War. This corruption, attributed by some observers to the process of industrialization itself, made for a sameness in design, as well as ugliness. To improve the appearance of cities, many of these old structures must simply be replaced. The recognition of the desirability of radical urban renewal has been growing, and steps are being taken to replace eyesores with attractive buildings. Yet old buildings, like old friends, obtain a certain attractiveness by virtue of age. The British recognize this fact to the extreme of preserving and using buildings of little or no architectural distinction years after they have become obsolete. American sentiment tends to err in the opposite direction, preferring the new merely because it is new. As a result, some fine old structures are too often demolished to make way for undistinguished new ones.

Esthetic considerations have been seriously underrated in urban regions. In many cities and bedroom communities, poles and wires continue to spoil the scenery even though it has been practical for years to place wires underground. Only public indifference can explain the tolerance of such crude devices to deliver electricity in an affluent society. Steps are being taken to reduce the pollution of streams, lakes, and ocean waters in and about metropolitan regions although the time has yet to arrive when the measures are sufficiently stringent to permit unrestricted use of many of them for swimming. Pollution of the air has become a major problem in a number of metropolitan areas, calling for aggressive measures to stop the use of the atmosphere as a garbage dump. Heavy concentration of people inevitably creates pollution problems, the human race being particularly prone to create a mess, and the more affluent the society becomes, the larger is the amount of debris of one kind or another produced, calling for government action to prevent intolerable living conditions. Open sewers have been eliminated in Western cities for over a century. Their contemporary counterparts are the paper-littered street, the foul water front, smog, the landscape dominated by poles and wires and garish signboards, and the streets filled with automobiles and the automobiles filled with ill-tempered people fighting one another for space, scattering pedestrians in their path.

Governmental Organizations in Metropolitan Regions

Solution of these and many other urban problems calls for organizations to diagnose the specific problem and to apply the means appropriate to it. In American metropolitan areas, various types of organizations have emerged to deal with some of these. The type of political agency or agencies to handle these problems is another of the more controversial questions found in almost all large metropolitan regions in the country.

The traditional type of government unit in urban areas is the municipality. Traditionally, growth was accompanied by gradual extension of the boundaries of the city. Insofar as public problems were solved, they were solved by the city officials. As urban regions continued to grow, and especially after the large-scale use of the automobile, municipalities began in various areas to grow into one another, and the continuous urban area emerged. Meanwhile, the new urban areas outside of municipalities tended to insist upon their own separate identity by becoming incorporated areas or by setting up some combination of service districts to provide themselves with government services. The resulting pattern is a jig-saw puzzle of municipalities of various sizes, villages, and various political districts providing local government services for people living in metropolitan regions.

One solution is again the traditional one, calling for one government unit to be in charge of the entire metropolitan region. At one stage, New York City approximated this type of arrangement, but with the growth in surrounding communities, it no longer does so. The difficulties with this solution are several. The one big city, governing the entire region, requires that the political identity of the existing municipalities be submerged or eliminated. Public officials have a natural disinclination to vote themselves out of their jobs. People living in the smaller municipalities within the region have resisted annexation to larger centers for various and sundry reasons or for no reason at all. Insofar as such attitudes are rational, they are based upon a preference for the kind of government arrangement they have over that which appears likely to be obtained if complete consolidation were to occur. There are simple but fundamental financial reasons as well. Those living in areas in which taxes are lower or government services better see higher taxes and less service—scarcely an inviting prospect. One factor of importance to many people retreating to the suburbs is to obtain the kind of government service they like. A group of high-income people living together in a bedroom community can provide better school facilities for their children than they could expect in the city. The choice between living in New York City or in Westchester County is for many people the choice between good schools and mediocre ones. One effective way to object to the kind of government service provided is to move elsewhere. This desire for particular types of government service tends to undermine the central cities, to augment the satellite settlements, and to prevent the large city from encroaching by annexation upon the satellites.

If the "one big city" solution is to be adopted, it will not emerge naturally. The state government will have to impose such a solution. For interstate metropolitan regions, this solution is ruled out. Even for intra-state regions, the political obstacles to such action are sufficiently powerful to eliminate the device of an all-embracing unit of government from the realm of feasibility. Even if it were feasible, there are many objections on other grounds.

Another type of agency to provide metropolitan government is the authority, such as the New York Port Authority. Authorities are established to provide and manage designated facilities, such as bridges, ports, airports, subways and, outside of metropolitan regions, toll turnpikes. Authorities have the advantage of workability. They do provide certain types of government service. If the definition of their responsibilities is sufficiently broad, they can operate over a region of expanding population. In fact, what metropolitan government exists today in the United States is largely the government provided by authorities of one kind or another.

Authorities have serious limitations. The officials in charge are not ordinarily elected and hence do not need to look to popular support for their programs. They must have some support to be sure, otherwise the public outcry would sooner or later remove them from their positions. In practice, they cater for support to the interests they serve. The New York Port Authority, for example, obtains the bulk of its revenues from motorists using the bridges and tunnels into and about New York. They aim to please, and those to be pleased are the motorists. If, to please this group, whole sections of New York must be demolished, then whole sections will be demolished. The people in charge come to view themselves as having been specially ordained to promote progress. Their parallel is the captain of industry of fifty years ago, exhibiting much the same arrogance and much the same disdain for representative government. The existence of such organizations, even if run by able and sensitive people, limits the ability of city officials to solve problems which overlap the jurisdiction of the authorities, and in any event, the vigor of local government is undermined by having important issues removed from the political arena. Occasionally, those in charge come to look upon the facilities which the authority has been established to manage as a personal empire, using public funds to oppose measures which might undermine their comfortable positions. They are inclined to oppose comprehensive proposals to deal with metropolitan problems, fearing, perhaps correctly, that their positions would be abolished in the process.

A further government device is the special district established to provide specified services. These districts may be defined to include the metropolitan area in question, with provisions for expansion. In the San Francisco Bay area, for example, a district has been established to lay down and enforce rules to reduce smog. Transit districts have also been established, one to provide rapid transit and another to provide local service. Districts, like authorities, may be established piecemeal for specific functions. Unlike authorities, their officials are ordinarily selected by a political process. Their limitation to specific functions, such as smog control, slurs over the question of the division of governmental powers within the area. Questions of conflict with city governments are thereby largely bypassed. But as in the case of authorities, important political issues are removed from the control of municipal governments, a change that makes such political organizations less important and may tend to undermine their vigor.

Various federal-local government combinations have been suggested, and some have been tried. The crucial feature of these plans is the continuing identity of the old cities in the region but with a metropolitan government being placed over them with provisions for settlement of disputes arising among them. Such government organizations are inherently clumsy but may be better than the alternative, which is no type of comprehensive government responsibility for the important questions that concern the entire region.

Financing Metropolitan Government

If some type of metropolitan government is established, how is it to be financed? A number of the topics already discussed indicate that solutions will cost sizable sums of money. What options are available for providing these sums?

The financial tasks of a metropolitan government will depend upon the responsibilities assigned to it. For present purposes, we shall assume that these responsibilities consist of regional planning, provision and maintenance of regional (large) parks, all rapid transit facilities including bridges, freeways or turnpikes, water services, pollution controls such as those concerned with the air, local streams, bays, lakes, etc. This list is not intended to be exhaustive nor is there any presumption that any area called metropolitan by the Census definition would require a metropolitan government of some kind. In all of the large metropolitan regions of the United States, the list of functions mentioned would seem to be close to the minimum if the special problems of large metropolitan regions are to be solved.

Of these functions, planning, parks, and controls cannot be expected to pay their own way and hence must be financed either by taxation or by the income from government enterprise. The question is whether the enterprise functions may be expected to stand on their own feet financially.

For reasons already discussed, rapid rail transit is not likely to be profitable and may in many regions entail losses if provided on a scale and of a design in accord with the functions it is to perform. For this reason, if for no other, control of rail and of highways within a metropolitan region needs to be centralized in one agency. Charges for highway use can be employed to meet deficits of rail transit. The subsidy element arising from virtually free use of highways becomes a source of revenue if tolls are more generally employed. Highways and streets may then be made less congested and hence provide better service for those who prefer to drive. The otherwise insatiable demand for more and more highways will be curtailed, thus saving on capital costs. If these monies could be placed in the hands of a metropolitan government, no further current financing might be necessary. Strong objections to such a proposal are to be expected from highway departments, authorities, gasoline companies, automobile associations, and automobile manufacturers.

Integration of other facilities, such as water works, and in addition, a practice of charging for the use of their products in a manner more in accord with normal competitive pricing tactics would in some areas provide a substantial revenue. Integration would permit some economy in operations and reduce the amount of premature investment. The water organization serving one area may engage upon extensive construction projects to augment supplies when another organization supplying an adjacent city has excess capacity. The principle of making charges commensurate with costs would call for the end of the practice of charging industrial users nominal prices and making up the deficit by the use of the taxing power. The booster-club mentality has called for cheap water for industrial purposes as a carrot to attract and hold industry. A well-managed public water system should be able to show a profit on its operations without making excessive charges.

If the profits from enterprise activities, including charges for the use of bridges (old ones as well as new) and highways, are not sufficient to finance those activities of a metropolitan government which cannot ration their services by price, tax devices are required. The standard such device is the property tax. Its merits and demerits as a local tax have already been discussed in Chapter 15, and they apply as well to the financing of metropolitan functions.

Because of the inherently vague boundaries of a metropolitan region and the lack of a single all-embracing government unit to deal with metropolitan problems, any tax measure should ideally be imposed by a larger government unit, normally by the state government, and the proceeds turned over to the agency in charge. Where metropolitan areas cross state lines, some help may be required from the federal government to obtain a workable solution. If more of the money presently collected from urban groups by state governments, such as taxes imposed in connection with the use of automobiles, were returned to the metropolitan government, there might be no need for additional tax sources. In any event, many tax devices are available to provide revenue for financing metropolitan government. Of greater importance is the requirement that the tax or taxes yield sufficient revenue to permit a metropolitan government to provide adequate facilities so that large urban regions may be tolerably livable and attractive.

Part III

SUGGESTED READINGS

Economic Welfare and Optimum Pricing:

BAIN, JOE S. *Pricing, Distribution, and Employment.* New York: Holt, Rinehart & Winston, 1953. Pp. 235-66.
Discusses allocation under conditions of general monopoly.

BOULDING, KENNETH E. "Welfare Economics," in *A Survey of Contemporary Economics,* ed. B. F. Haley. Homewood, Ill.: Richard D. Irwin, Inc., 1952.
A summary statement of the main issues in welfare economics.

BREAK, GEORGE F. "Excise Tax Burdens and Benefits," *American Economic Review,* XLIV (Sept., 1954), 577-94.
Discusses allocation problems under noncompetitive conditions.

ECKSTEIN, OTTO. *Water-Resource Development: The Economics of Project Evaluation.* Cambridge: Harvard Univ. Press, 1958.
Develops tests for water projects, setting out in some detail problems of specific projects.

HOTELLING, HAROLD H. "The General Welfare in Relation to Problems of Taxation and of Railway and Utility Rates," *Econometrica,* VI (July, 1938), 242-69.
The pioneering article on the marginal-cost pricing principle. See also the comments by Ragnar Frisch and Hotelling in the April, 1939, issue of the same journal.

KNIGHT, FRANK H. "Fallacies in the Interpretation of Social Cost," in *Ethics of Competition and Other Essays.* New York: Harper & Bros., 1935.
A criticism of Pigou's argument that industries experiencing increasing costs produce too much, judged from the point of view of a social optimum.

LERNER, ABBA P. *The Economics of Control.* New York: The Macmillan Co., 1944.
A systematic presentation of the conditions necessary for a social optimum allocation of resources; employs a utility approach.

MARSHALL, ALFRED. *Principles of Economics,* 8th ed. London: Macmillan & Co., Ltd., 1930. P. 467.
Expounds the famous doctrine of consumers' surplus.

MCKEAN, ROLAND N. *Efficiency in Government Through Systems Analysis.* New York: John Wiley & Sons, 1958.
Analyses efficiency tests for government programs with applications to water projects.

PIGOU, A. C. *Economics of Welfare.* London: Macmillan & Co., Ltd., 1932.
The pioneering study of the welfare implications of a competitive system.

ROLPH, EARL R. *The Theory of Fiscal Economics.* Berkeley: Univ. of California Press, 1954.
Chap. iii states the author's view of the concept of cost in a money-price system, with special emphasis upon the costs of government programs.

ROLPH, EARL R. and GEORGE F. BREAK. "The Welfare Aspects of Excise Taxes," *Journal of Political Economy,* LVII (Feb., 1949), 46-54.
Develops the view that excise taxes may improve as well as worsen resource allocation. States the conditions for optimum pricing under several welfare approaches.

VICKREY, WILLIAM. *The Revision of the Rapid Transit Fare Structure of the City of New York.* New York: Mayor's Committee on Management Survey of the City of New York, 1952.
An analysis of a rational pricing system for local transport, with practical suggestions relevant to the New York subway system.

Social Security:

BROWN, HARRY GUNNISON. "The Incidence of Compulsory Insurance of Workmen," *Journal of Political Economy,* XXX (1922), 67-77.
The original analysis of the incidence of a payroll tax.

BOND, FLOYD A., et al. *Our Needy Aged: A California Study of a National Problem.* New York: Holt, Rinehart and Winston, 1954.
A comprehensive study of Old Age Assistance in California, containing original statistical data, comparisons of the California law with those in other states, a summary of individual opinions on the operation of the program, and recommendations for improvement.

BURNS, EVELINE M. *The American Social Security System.* Boston: Houghton Mifflin Co., 1951.
A detailed description of the system as it existed in 1950.

——. *Social Security and Public Policy.* New York: McGraw-Hill Book Co., 1956.
An excellent, comprehensive discussion of problems and issues.

PEACOCK, ALAN T. *The Economics of National Insurance.* London: William Hodge & Co., Ltd., 1952.
An analysis of British National Insurance, concentrating on the effects of the system on consumption, investment, and the distribution of income.

STEINER, PETER O., and ROBERT DORFMAN. *The Economic Status of the Aged.* Berkeley: Univ. of California Press, 1957.
A detailed analysis based on a nationwide 1952 statistical study made by the U.S. Census Bureau.

U.S. CONGRESS, JOINT ECONOMIC COMMITTEE. *Characteristics of the Low-Income Population and Related Federal Programs.* Washington, D.C.: Government Printing Office, 1955.
A very useful source of statistical data.

——. *Federal Expenditure Policy for Economic Growth and Stability.* Washington, D.C.: Government Printing Office, 1957.
Pp. 861-1046 deal with federal health, education and social security programs.

U.S. DEPARTMENT OF HEALTH, EDUCATION AND WELFARE. *Social Security in the United States.* Washington, D.C.: Government Printing Office, 1959.

Numerous up-to-date descriptive pamphlets are available from the Social Security Administration, an agency of this department.

Intergovernmental Fiscal Relations:

BUCHANAN, JAMES M. "Federalism and Fiscal Equity," *American Economic Review,* XL (Sept., 1950), 583-99.
An analysis of the need for intergovernmental transfers to achieve an equitable distribution of income.
———. "Federal Grants and Resource Allocation," *Journal of Political Economy,* LX (June, 1952), 208-17.
A criticism of the argument that interregional income transfers distort resource allocation.
MAXWELL, JAMES A. *The Fiscal Impact of Federalism in the United States.* Cambridge: Harvard Univ. Press, 1946.
Discusses both federal-state grants-in-aid and the problems raised by overlapping tax jurisdictions.
———. *Federal Grants and the Business Cycle.* New York: National Bureau of Economic Research, 1952.
A compact description of the development, cyclical behavior, and defects of federal grants, together with a proposal for a grant program with automatic sensitivity to business cycles.
MUSHKIN, SELMA. "Federal Grants and Federal Expenditures," *National Tax Journal,* X (Sept., 1957), 193-213.
An analysis of the distribution, by states, of per capita federal expenditures and grants in fiscal 1952.
NATIONAL PLANNING ASSOCIATION. *The Foreign Aid Programs and the United States Economy, 1948-1957.* Washington, D.C.: National Planning Association, 1958.
Discusses the effects of the foreign aid programs in this country.
SCHALLER, H. G. "Federal Grants-in-Aid and Differences in State Per Capita Incomes, 1929, 1939, and 1949," *National Tax Journal,* VIII (Sept., 1955), 287-99.
Estimates quantitatively the effects of federal grants-in-aid on the relative dispersion of state per capita incomes.
U.S. BUREAU OF THE BUDGET. "Special Analysis of Federal Aid to State and Local Governments."
A statistical summary included each year in the *United States Budget.*
U.S. CONGRESS, JOINT ECONOMIC COMMITTEE. *Federal Tax Policy for Economic Growth and Stability.* Washington, D.C.: Government Printing Office, 1956.
Part XIV discusses the taxation of income derived abroad, and Part XVI treats federal-state-local fiscal relations.
———. *Federal Expenditure Policy for Economic Growth and Stability.* Washington, D.C.: Government Printing Office, 1957.
Part IX deals with federal expenditures for foreign aid.
U.S. CONGRESS, COMMITTEE ON GOVERNMENT OPERATIONS. *Federal-State-Local Relations: Federal Grants-in-Aid.* Washington, D.C.: Government Printing Office, 1958.
Contains a short description of federal grant-in-aid programs (in 1957), an historical summary, an evaluation of the programs and an analysis of reform proposals.

Metropolitan Problems:

FISHER, ROBERT M. (ed.). *The Metropolis in Modern Life.* Garden City, N.Y.: Doubleday & Co., 1955.
A collection of papers on various aspects of metropolitan life.
MUMFORD, LEWIS. *The Culture of Cities.* New York: Harcourt, Brace & Co., 1938.
An early and important discussion of cities, their difficulties and advantages. Suggests a number of reforms.

SALISBURY, HARRISON E. " 'Shook' Youngsters Spring from the Housing Jungles," *New York Times,* March 26, 1958, pp. 1, 32.
One of a series of articles on large-city housing, juvenile behavior, and related subjects.

WENDT, PAUL F. and R. J. MONSEN (eds.). *Readings in Urban Land Economics.* Berkeley: Univ. of California Bureau of Business & Economic Research, 1957. Selected articles setting forth information and explanations of urban development, location, transportation, and related topics.

WENDT, PAUL F. *The Influence of Transportation Changes upon Urban Land Use and Values: A Paper Presented at the Annual Meeting of the Highway Research Board.* Washington, D.C., 1960.

————. "The Theory of Urban Land Values," *Land Economics* (Aug., 1957), 228-240.
Develops an explanation of land values in urban areas.

Part IV

FISCAL THEORY AND FISCAL POLICY

Introduction

Fiscal theory and policy, the subject-matter of Part IV, constitutes the portion of public finance usually looked upon among economists as glamorous and of special importance. Economists who have little knowledge or interest in such technical questions as the size of the brackets of a personal income tax or the comparative merits of carry-backs versus carryforwards under a corporate income tax have often studied carefully and written extensively about how a government may use budget operations and debt management to achieve economic stabilization. The interest in fiscal policy reflects the importance attached to the avoidance of widespread unemployment and of substantial price inflations.

Fiscal theory, as opposed to policy, is the explanation of how various actions of a government, especially a central government, can influence private and total expenditures for goods and services. This topic is closely akin to monetary theory; in fact, it may be looked upon as simply the application of some monetary theory or theories. In the chapters to follow, especially Chapter 22, the effects of fiscal policies are examined with reference to a number of monetary approaches. This emphasis calls attention to the crucial importance of money, and of explanations of the role of money in economic life, for the understanding of government fiscal operations.

Debt management as a topic in public finance has become of special importance only since about 1945, when governments have had to cope with huge debts as a result of war finance and fears have arisen that improper management of a large debt might have severe or even disastrous results upon the economy. For a number of years in the United States, the policy of supporting the prices of government debt instruments was followed—a policy that assured results incompatible with flexible and adaptable monetary management. Gradually increasing criticism of the policy of supporting the prices of government securities brought a change in practice—illustrating once again how economic research and writing affects practical affairs. Monetary policy is now generally employed as a weapon for economic stabilization in Western countries and in a number of the underdeveloped countries as well.

In the fields of fiscal and monetary management, the goals to be achieved are several and are occasionally conflicting. If the goal of full employment is pursued with great vigor, for example, there is the danger, if not the certainty, that the goal of stability of the general level of prices will be sacrificed. Political conflict has arisen between those people who believe that full employment should be given priority over price stabilization and those who believe the priority should be the reverse. We have set forth in Chapter 21 the conditions believed necessary to achieve both goals—to have one's cake and eat it too—in a progressive economy. This apparently happy result carries with it some rather disturbing implications. Many features of government regulation of business and agriculture and some practices of business and labor organizations may need to be altered, in some instances rather drastically, if full employment and price stability are both to be achieved more or less continuously in the United States.

As in the earlier parts of the book, there is provided at the end an annotated list of selected readings for the student wishing more information and analysis of the various topics in fiscal theory and policy.

20

Principles of Compensatory Finance

Compensatory finance, as the name implies, refers to those financial activities of government which compensate for variations in private expenditures. If private expenditures threaten to decline through time, compensatory finance calls for steps to prevent the decline. One important function of government is to offset undesired variations in private expenditures for goods and services. In a society in which total expenditures are always just right, compensation has no place. No such money-using society has ever been found.

Compensatory finance as an explicit principle of government finance has developed within the lifetimes of living people. A student studying economics in 1928 would not have heard about how a government may act as a financial balancing agent. Such a function might have been discussed, if it were discussed at all, in connection with central banks. Central banks were regarded as the agency, almost the exclusive agency, to regulate over-all expenditures. The change in point of view developed out of the Great Depression on the one hand and the preachings of advanced economic thinkers on the other. Without the Great Depression, bankers, leading industrialists, political officials, economists, and other purveyors of "practical wisdom" would have dismissed, and in fact often did dismiss, suggestions of using government finance as a compensatory device as visionary. Such ideas were often labelled "crackpot" or by even more disapproving terms.

The depression, however, eroded the hold of tenets of financial wisdom on people's minds by providing a pointed demonstration of their unworkability.[1] Radical ideas, radical in the sense of being highly different from prevailing financial thought, finally obtained a hearing. The idea of using government as a compensating agency had floated about in economic literature for years; almost every idea of a compensatory governmental function can be found in the writings of some nineteenth-century economist. The Great Depression, however, stimulated economists capable of flexible thought to develop patterns of ideas specifically designed to show how a government might manage its finances to end or to prevent depressions in economic activity. These ideas emerged mainly between 1930 and 1940 and continue to be developed at the present time.

How can a government act as a balancing agency? The immediate and obvious answer calls for a government to vary its own expenditures in a compensating manner. If private expenditures are falling, the government could increase its expenditures; if private expenditures are rising too rapidly, it could decrease its expenditures. If, and this is a big "if," government expenditures are capable of being changed in the same magnitudes as private expenditures depart from their "proper" trend, full compensation may be achieved. It is not surprising that many early suggestions for using government as a balancing agency concentrated on its expenditures, especially on public works. The Socialist Party and the Hearst newspapers were both agreed early in the 1930's that what the country needed and needed badly was a large public works program. Even those with only a meager understanding of economics could see that if total expenditures are too small, they can be increased by increasing government expenditures. This point of view has not gone out of style, although it no longer commands the support it once did. Yet even in 1958, many Congressmen voted for programs to increase federal expenditures as a device to get the economy out of the recession experienced in that year.

A government is not limited, however, to variations in its own expenditures upon currently produced goods and services. It can influence private expenditures also. The devices available are several: (1) taxes, (2) transfers to private groups, sometimes called negative taxes, (3) purchases and sales of "old" things, i.e., land, buildings, war surplus, (4) lending programs to private groups, such as loans to veterans for house financing, (5) government debt operations. In addition to these, central bank policy, if included as a government operation, may be employed to stimulate or depress private expenditures. In some countries, especially small ones, private expenditures can be influenced by a government-announced policy of altering the foreign exchange rate. Attention will be directed at this time to the

[1] As pointed out in chap. 1.

manner by which total and private expenditures are influenced by government expenditures and by positive and negative taxes.

The assessment of how a government may influence private expenditures depends upon the theory one adopts of the determinants of private expenditures. Unfortunately for the novice, there happen to be several points of view. We shall discuss four of them: The Simple Keynesian System, the Full Keynesian System, the Simple Quantity Theory, and the Asset Theory. The results of the latter three systems are similar in their directional effects. The Simple Keynesian System, however, gives results different in important ways from the others. In recent years, this theory has dominated theoretical discussion of fiscal affairs. Each of these four systems of the determination of private expenditures will be discussed by examining the results they give for various patterns of government expenditures, taxes, and transfers.

Simple Keynesian System

This system of thought begins from a national income equation. The product side of the social accounts is divided into consumption (C), investment (I), and government expenditures upon goods and services (G). Ignoring international activities which can be taken into account separately, we have then the identity

$$C + I + G = GNP$$

when *GNP* stands for gross national product.

The income side of the social accounts is handled variously by economists and statisticians. A fairly simple way consists of segregating all private incomes, including not only the incomes of persons but also of impersonal organizations such as foundations, that are generated by production, adding to these the payments by government to private groups, such as subsidies, and subtracting the transfers, mainly taxes, made by private groups to government. Then, if Y is the total of net incomes arising from production, R is the total of government transfers, and T is the total of tax liabilities to government, Y plus R is the total of private incomes before tax, and Y plus R minus T is the total of private incomes after tax.

On the product side of the social accounts, the value of resources *used up* in production, sometimes called *depreciation* and sometimes *capital consumption,* is deducted from gross investment (I) to obtain net investment (I_n). Hence,

$$C + I_n + G = NNP,$$

where NNP stands for Net National Product.

Combining the product side with the income side, we then have

$$C + I_n + G = Y = (Y - T_n) + T_n,$$

where T_n is government net revenue or $(T - R)$.

Net national product equals by definition the sum of private incomes arising from production. The equality does not necessarily hold for one country having economic relations with other countries. It would not hold, except accidentally, for New York State either. The equality holds for an entire country for any period, provided international transactions are treated as zero or if certain rather special conditions are satisfied.

All terms relate to the same period of time, whether the period be two minutes, a week, a month, or a year. Also all terms are *flows,* that is amounts per period, stated in money terms. Nothing is assumed about prices except that all products are priced.

The issue to be discussed is the determination of the total net national product (NNP). The question can be broken down into the determinants of three factors: consumption (C), net investment (I_n), and government expenditures upon goods and services (G).

The Simple Keynesian System offers the following explanation. Net investment is left unexplained; it is treated as autonomous. Although net investment might be explained somehow or other, it is to be taken as a given fact.

Government expenditures upon goods and services are also treated as autonomous. The size of these expenditures is considered to be determined by political decisions. They cannot be explained on purely economic grounds without considerable strain.

Consumption expenditures are to be explained. In this system, the amount spent upon consumption per period depends upon the size of private after-tax incomes during the same period. The larger are peoples' incomes computed after deducting taxes, the larger is the amount spent on consumption. The justification of this proposition is of course crucial, and it may be and has been disputed. We are not, for the time being, concerned with this fundamental issue. The functional relation must be positive; the larger is net income, the larger is consumption. The only further restriction upon the function is that its first derivative must be less than one. This restriction can easily be shown by reference to Figure 20–1.

Along the vertical axis is measured C and I and $G,$ and along the horizontal axis is measured income, all in money terms.[2] The line labelled C is the functional relation postulated in this system of thought

[2] To simplify the notation, the symbol I will henceforth stand for net investment unless otherwise specified.

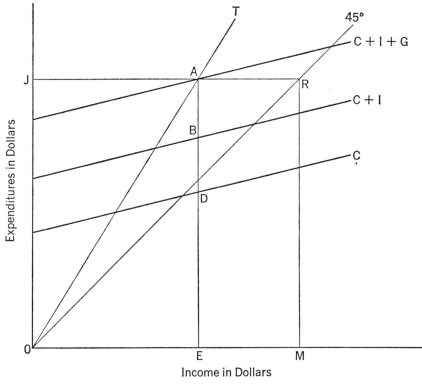

FIGURE 20–1

between consumption expenditures and income, called the *consumption function*. The restriction is that the slope of the C line must be less than one (not parallel to a line drawn at 45° through the origin or not steeper than such a line). The reason for this is not based upon any appeal to facts; it is a logical necessity. If, for example, that relation were one for one, the system would be impossible. It would assert that people are prepared to spend an amount equal to their income and also assert that by definition their income would always exceed the amount they spent upon consumption by the amount of net investment. These statements are inconsistent.

The solution of the system depends upon the position and the characteristics of the consumption-function (also called the propensity-to-consume), upon the amount of net taxes (which in turn depends upon the size of incomes before tax), upon the assumed size of government expenditures on currently produced things, and upon the assumed size of net investment. The solution or outcome is shown in Figure 20–1.

Draw a 45° line through the origin O. It is the graphical equivalent of the definitional proposition

$$C + I + G = Y,$$

where Y is income. Any actual solution must fall on this line.

Draw the line OT so that the horizontal distance between it and the 45° line measures net tax yields. If the tax system is proportional to income, OT is a straight line as shown. If it is progressive OT is a curve bending away from the 45° line, because as income rises, taxes rise more than proportionally. Similarly, an OT line that curves toward the 45° line depicts a regressive tax structure. OT would be parallel to the 45° line in the special case where all taxes (and transfers) were fixed sums, like poll taxes.

The line C, shown as a straight line, is the consumption-function. Whether it is a line or a curve is immaterial for present purposes. To the C line, add the fixed amount of investment, giving the line labelled $C + I$. To this line, add the fixed amount of government expenditures, giving the line $C + I + G$.

The solution, the outcome, is given by the intersection of the $C + I + G$ line with the OT line, point A, giving also point R on the 45° line. This outcome means that government expenditures equal AB (assumed), net investment equals BD (assumed), and what is important, consumption equals DE (not assumed). Since we are trying to discover the amount spent on consumption, the crucial issue is why consumption turns out to be DE.

The proof is easy. Consumption of the amount DE is the only amount consistent with the premises and the definitions. By definition $C + I + G$ must equal Y (income before taxes and transfers). This condition is satisfied since, by construction, $OJ = OM$. Likewise income minus taxes plus taxes must equal total income. It does because $OE + EM = OM$. In addition, by the Keynesian theory of consumption that consumption depends upon income computed after taxes, the amount of consumption must be consistent with the consumption-function, which it is; D is a point on the line C. The further conditions that I and G are given are automatically satisfied. Thus consumption is determined and so is net national product ($C + I + G = NNP$).

A definite solution emerges regardless of the comparative sizes of tax yields and of government expenditures. If the government has a deficit, then AB is larger than AR and the solution holds. A lower level of consumption will emerge if there is a government surplus. A solution can be obtained for any amount of government expenditures and any amount of net taxes, including zero taxes or even net negative taxes.[3]

BALANCED BUDGET THEOREM. This system of thought has led to the famous or, depending upon one's point of view, infamous *balanced budget theorem*. This theorem asserts that a change in government expenditures upon goods and services of a given amount plus a change in tax yields of the same amount result in a change in net expenditures (net national product) equal to the change in government expenditures. This theorem has been discussed by so many writers in so many places that one may readily get the impression that fiscal policy theory is the balanced budget theorem.[4]

To prove this theorem, we shall use the graph shown in Figure 20–2. Let there be an increase in government expenditures on goods and services of some definite amount, such as $1 billion per year. This increase may be represented graphically by constructing a line parallel to the $C + I + G$ line, raised vertically by $1 billion or $\triangle G$. The theorem asserts that the new solution must be an increase in total expenditures equal to the increase in government expenditures, or in terms of the graph the outcome must be *OH*. Hence our solution must be at the point *K* (*JH = KA* by construction). Keeping in mind that tax yields are measured horizontally to the left of the 45° line, let us increase tax yields by *VR*, equal to *VS*. This step is the condition of the problem; the change in government expenditures, $\triangle G$, must equal the change in tax yields, *VR*. Since *VR = VS*, the triangle *SVR* is an isosceles triangle, with a hypotenuse of a slope of one, and hence *AS* (the previous tax yield) equals *KV*, or *KR* (the new tax yield) exceeds

---

[3] To become familiar with the implications of this system of thought for public finance, the student may drill himself by demonstrating the outcomes for several alternative fiscal circumstances. Graphical representation is adequate and simple to employ. Identical results can be obtained by simple algebra or, for that matter, by the use of plain words.

[4] A good exposition of the theorem and of other implications of the Simple Keynesian System is provided by John G. Gurley, "Fiscal Policies for Full Employment: A Diagrammatic Analysis," *Journal of Political Economy*, LX (Dec., 1952), 525-533. The above graphical analysis relies heavily upon his work. Those who prefer algebra may find Paul Samuelson's article, "Simple Mathematics of Income Determination," in *Income, Employment and Public Policy, Essays in Honor of Alvin H. Hansen* (New York: W. W. Norton & Co., 1948), clear and to the point. Good criticisms of the theorem are rare. A critical note by W. J. Baumol and M. H. Peston, "More on the Multiplier Effects of a Balanced Budget," *American Economic Review*, XLV (March, 1955), 140-148, concerns minor issues that had been taken into account by earlier writings. Any effective criticism of the theorem must challenge the monetary theory on which it is based. Professor Haberler is one of the few to have done this, although his remarks are highly condensed. See his paper "Multiplier Effects of a Balanced Budget: Some Monetary Implications of Mr. Haavelmo's Paper," *Econometrica*, XIV (April, 1946), 148 f.

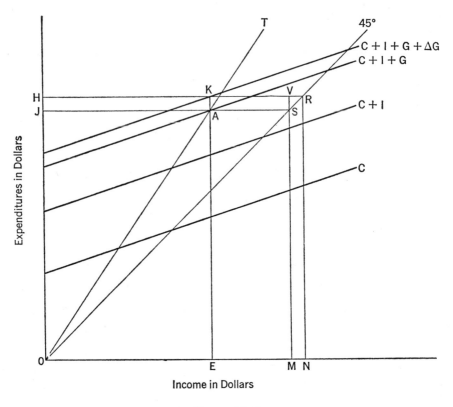

FIGURE 20–2

AS by *VR*. We have then the result that point *K* must lie on a vertical line projected from point *A*, giving the result asserted by the theorem, that is, *OH* exceeds *OJ* by *JH*. Thus if a new *OT* line were constructed, it would pass through point *K*.

The economic reason for this outcome is readily seen. The increase of government expenditures would, if nothing else changed, increase private incomes by $1 billion. People would, on this account, wish to spend more upon consumption. But the increase in government expenditures is to be accompanied by an equal increase in tax yields. Thus private after-tax incomes are not to be increased at all by the increase in government expenditures. By the theory of the consumption-function, consumption is uniquely determined by after-tax income. Since income computed after tax remains unchanged, it follows from the consumption-function that consumption remains unchanged. *I* is also unchanged by assumption. Thus the increase in government expenditures is the only change in total expenditures, and this conclusion is what the theorem asserts.

The objection may be raised that the distribution of income may change, as indeed it may, and hence the increased consumption of those whose incomes increase may or may not equal the decrease in the consumption of those whose incomes (after tax) fall. The objection is met by proponents of the doctrine on three different grounds.

1. It may be asserted that the distribution of income *is* to be assumed unchanged. This answer avoids the objection, but it limits the application of the doctrine.

2. It may be asserted that the distribution of income *must* be assumed unchanged. This point is subtle, having to do with the meaning of an aggregate consumption-function and may be further explored.

Such a relation is not unique unless specifications are given about the distribution of income. Let us suppose, for example, that a person wishes to add together the individual propensities-to-consume of a group of his friends. He observes how much each spends for consumption during a month. He also finds out, accurately somehow, the size of each of his friends' incomes. He adds the consumption figures and adds the income figures, obtaining, say, $900 of consumption expenditures and $1000 of income. The following month he again ascertains the consumption expenditures and incomes of the same group of friends. He finds that their total income is $1,000 but that their consumption expenditures have fallen to $800. Now he might conclude that their tastes had changed somewhat and indeed they may have. But such a result would also be entirely consistent with no change in tastes. Closer investigation discloses that one friend had a much larger income in the second month than in the first, but only a slightly larger amount of consumption. Another friend had his allowance or earnings from side jobs reduced and cut his consumption expenditures by a very large amount. For total consumption to be a unique function of total income, its distribution must be specified; otherwise there are several, instead of one, consumption-expenditure figures that may accompany the same amount of income. Nevertheless, this method of meeting the objection has the difficulty of the first one: it does not meet it.

3. It may be assumed that each person's individual consumption-function is linear and that each one has the same slope. This method, often preferred by the mathematically inclined, avoids having to specify the distribution of income, since consumption will be the same for

any distribution. But the cost is serious. The probability of this assumption holding for any large group of people is close to zero.

Thus there is no happy solution of this difficulty in the balanced budget theorem.

Other objections may be raised, usually along the lines that some of the income generated in the society does not become personal income, as for example, undivided corporate profits. This is a minor objection. Undivided profits as well as any taxes paid at the expense of such profits perform the same function in the Simple Keynesian System as do personal taxes. The theorem then asserts that a change in government expenditures and an equal change in taxes plus undivided profits results in a change in net national product equal to the change in government expenditures. It is a peculiarity of this system of thought that undivided profits play the same economic role as do actual taxes. This view would no doubt come as a shock to many corporation executives.

Fundamentally, any attack upon the balanced budget theorem must be based upon a demonstration of weaknesses of the underlying system of thought—what we have called the Simple Keynesian System. It may be attacked on the grounds that it is *static* theory, implying or at least permitting the implication that it is inadequate to discuss change over time. It may be attacked as incorrectly explaining consumption. This position implies an attack on the theory of the consumption-function. It may be attacked as merely inadequate—as too simple. Simplicity is not, however, a valid objection to a theory. Many theories, such as Newton's first law of motion, are simple. The objection may be rephrased: the theory is inadequate. Keynes himself, for example, did not assert the balanced budget theorem. His views were more complicated. We turn next to a statement of his position.

Full Keynesian System

This system of thought differs from the Simple Keynesian System by including within it an explanation of the scale of investment. This difference is an important one. Government expenditure policies, tax and transfer policies, government deficits or surpluses, and debt operations are found to have effects on private expenditures in this system of thought differing from those found for the abbreviated theory.

The explanation of investment provided by Keynes involves two fundamental theories: a theory of the relation between the scale of investment in a society and the rate of interest, and a theory of the relation between the rate of interest and a certain portion of the quantity of money. Investment, it may be emphasized, refers to the purchase of new physical assets, including in the word "purchase" the acquisition of new assets by persons or organizations actively engaged in their production. A company that produces to add to its inventory of goods which it eventually plans to sell is investing.[5]

INVESTMENT SCHEDULE. The scale of investment in a society in a period of time is treated as depending upon the rate of interest. For each rate of interest, there is some money amount of investment. The lower is the rate of interest, the higher is the scale of investment. Keynes called this relationship "the marginal efficiency of capital." The wording is unfortunate because it may suggest incorrectly that the concept is closely allied with the productivity of tractors, stamping machines, coke dispensers, or dams. A. P. Lerner, a strong Keynesian sympathizer, has suggested the name "marginal efficiency of investment."[6] If such a relation is graphed, it has a negative slope as shown in Figure 20–3, when the rate of interest is measured along the vertical axis and investment in dollars is measured along the horizontal axis.

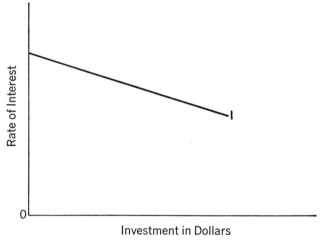

FIGURE 20–3

[5] The term "investment" may be generally defined as the purchase of any asset. For existing assets, each act of investment is accompanied by an equal negative counterpart; the buyer invests and the seller disinvests, yielding zero net investment. Investment for a group can be positive then only if some invest without others disinvesting an equal amount. For a closed system, such a condition means that some investment takes the form of the acquisition of new physical things, including improvements in old things, because the other side of the coin is not negative investment, but the generation of income to the owners of the resources used to produce the new things. This approach is the one adopted by Keynes.

[6] See Lerner's article, "On the Marginal Product of Capital and the Marginal Efficiency of Investment," *Journal of Political Economy,* LXI (Feb., 1953), 1-14. This excellent piece of clarification is recommended for close study.

The line labelled *I* is an investment schedule. It is negatively sloped and continuous. Its features in other respects are not specified.

The economic justification for this schedule appeals to three factors.

1. Any one prospective investor, say a corporation, is viewed as having various alternative ways of investing, for example buying new machines of one kind or another, constructing new buildings, increasing its inventories of parts, and literally thousands of other ways. If the management lays down the rule that only those things are to be acquired which will yield, say, a 10 per cent rate of return per year or more, some of these prospective investments would qualify and some would not. This introduces one variable making for a negative relation, because at a cutoff rate of return of 8 per cent, for example, more things would qualify.

2. The usefulness of any one type of thing diminishes as the company acquires more of that thing. A thousand kegs of bolts may be necessary to keep production lines going smoothly, but if the number of kegs were increased to five thousand, the subtraction of one keg might not be noticed. The same observation applies to buildings, stamping machines, and even coke dispensers. This variable means that the lower the rate of interest, the more of each type of thing a management can afford to possess even though such things are less useful.

3. Prices of the new real things vary. This factor does not apply to any one investor unless he happens to operate on such a large scale that he can consciously influence the price of machines and equipment produced by others. It applies to the economy as a whole. The lower the rate of interest becomes, the more investment individuals and corporate managements will wish to undertake. But this means that they are trying to spend a larger sum of money for these things. The larger is the sum of money they try to spend, the higher will be the prices of new equipment; hence the lower the rate of return an investor can expect to obtain. Increasing prices of instrumental goods serve to hold down what would otherwise be a larger scale of investment. Keynes strongly emphasized this factor, although it is curious that he did so.[7]

---

[7] The critical passage in Keynes' book is the following: "If there is an increased investment in any given type of capital during any period of time, the marginal efficiency of that type of capital will diminish as the investment in it is increased, partly because the prospective yield will fall as the supply of that type of capital is increased, and partly because, as a rule, pressure on the facilities for producing that type of capital will cause its supply price to increase; the second of these factors being usually the more important in producing equilibrium in the short run, but the longer the period in view the more does the first factor take its place." *The General*

Granted that there is an investment schedule for an economy, the rate of interest remains to be explained. Keynes employed two considerations, although actually another comes quietly in by the back door. These two are (1) the desires of people to hold money versus debt securities, and (2) a portion of the quantity of money. The first is called "liquidity preference." The second is called "speculative money" or "speculative balances." The question of the determination of the rate of interest can be posed by asking: Why, in a world of well-organized markets for debt instruments, should any sensible person or any sensible corporate treasurer hold money?

In part, people hold money because they must. If a corporation is to carry on its business or a family is to finance the purchase of groceries and the installment payments on the car, each must hold some money at any given date; otherwise no business or no groceries or maybe even no car. Such money may be called "transactions money." In addition, people and businesses hold money for what is called "precautionary purposes." The breadwinner may become ill and receive only sick-pay. A business may experience a series of expensive reverses; if it is short on cash it may find itself in the hands of receivers. Money is a very handy item to have about when the going gets a little rough. But not all money held, says Keynes, consists of these two types. People, especially wealthy people, and businesses hold some money, or rather may hold some money, because they are afraid that if they hold government bonds instead they will get a negative return. How can this be?

It is possible to lose money by buying bonds. Suppose a $1,000 bond with a coupon return of 3 per cent and a twenty-year maturity is selling in the market in New York at $1,250. Such a bond will pay its holder $30 per year for each of twenty years, and then at retirement pay $1,030 in the twentieth year after the date of issue. Obviously one cannot lose money if he holds the bond for the entire twenty years. But an investor may not know when he will need to sell the bond; or even if he does know, he fears that the market price of the bond may be lower then than it is today. Suppose this worrier thinks that the price a year from date will be $1,100, in which case he would gain the interest, $30, but lose in capital value $150, making a net loss of $120. Clearly if these are the correct facts, investing in such a

---

Theory of Employment, Interest and Money (New York: Harcourt, Brace & Co., 1936), p. 136. Note the statement after the semicolon. This view is curious because the increase in the price of equipment would not be operative in a situation with large-scale unemployment and underutilization of resources, a situation presupposed as crucial in other connections in his book. The justification of a negatively sloped investment schedule remains a sticky problem even today.

bond is no way to get ahead. Our worrier then holds cash, speculat-
ing that the price of the bond will fall; hence the term "speculative
money." Different investors, however, have different views about what
will happen to the price of bonds. Some will not believe that the price
will fall by more than $10 in a year, and hence the bond will earn a
net sum of $20. Some will believe that the price will remain un-
changed. Some are so optimistic as to believe that the price may even
rise. People of the latter view will hold bonds and no speculative
money.

Keynes held that people do entertain different views about the
future of the price of bonds. At any given price, some will believe that
they can obtain a positive rate of return by holding bonds when account is taken of the possible fall in the price of bonds; the more
pessimistic will hold money and no bonds. The higher the price of
bonds, and hence the lower the yield on the bonds to maturity, the
fewer dollars will be spent on bonds for two reasons: the range left
for the price of bonds to fall has increased, and it takes a smaller
percentage decline in the price to wipe out the coupon return.

The resulting schedule is viewed as negatively sloped as shown in
Figure 20–4. The vertical axis depicts rates of interest or yields on
bonds to maturity. The horizontal axis shows the quantity of speculative money. The curve *L* is the functional relation between the
quantity of speculative money and the yield. Point *H,* for example,
means that at the rate of interest *OR,* people will hold the amount *OM*
of speculative money.

The lower is the rate of interest, the more of such money people
will hold. If the curve becomes flat, and Keynes suggested strongly

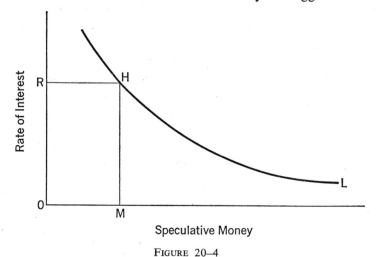

FIGURE 20–4

that it might, an attempt by the central bank to purchase bonds would result in no increase in the price of bonds at all. These pessimistic investors treat bonds and money as perfect substitutes, both yielding, in their judgment, a zero rate of interest—zero because they expect the price of bonds to fall during a period by an amount just equal to the cash value of the coupons. This range is called the "liquidity trap."

The theory has its difficulties, in fact it is full of difficulties. It does not describe the behavior of any known group of investors. Investors do not typically hold all bonds or all cash as the theory says they should. They hold a variety of asset combinations, including cash.

Keynes actually provided yet another theory. It is based upon the view that an investor may be uncertain about the price of bonds. The higher the price of a bond of given coupon characteristics, the more reluctant he is to hold it and the more inclined he is to hold safer securities, such as Treasury bills. This theory has the fatal defect that it can only explain differences in rates of interest; it cannot explain the rate of interest. The details of this point of view will not be pursued here.[8]

Granted, then, Keynes' theory of investment and theory of the rate of interest, how do various government financial practices affect private expenditures under this system of thought?

Consider initially a deficit in the government's budget when the deficit is not covered by any sale of debt. The government simply continues period after period to have a deficit. It gets the money it requires to finance the deficit from the central bank. This assumption is no mere invention. It is common practice in many countries for governments to have deficits without selling any debt to members of the public. The central bank finances the government. No change in government expenditures and no change in taxes occur. Our question is what happens to private expenditures when a persistent deficit occurs.

An uncovered deficit, that is, a deficit with no offsetting sale of government debt, increases the quantity of money in private hands in each period by the size of the deficit in that period. There is, then, an increase in the total quantity of money. Nothing happens merely on this account. It does not *mean*, for example, that incomes are increasing; not at all. It means that people together have a combined surplus in each period equal to the government's deficit. An increase in the quantity of money can influence private expenditures only by

---

[8] See *The General Theory*, chap. xiii, and pp. 200-202. These passages are worth careful study.

influencing the rate of interest. In turn, this happens because people find they have more money than they need to hold. Hence they buy bonds, thus increasing the price of bonds, a change which *means* a reduction in interest rates. At a lower level of interest rates, investment increases. This is the first crucial development. The increase in investment induces an equal increase in income, and then, because consumption is a function of income, induces a further increase in consumption. Both consumption and investment are increased by a government deficit.

These steps can be readily understood by looking at our graphs. In Figure 20–4, let the quantity of speculative money increase from some starting point, OM. Now move to Figure 20–3, and observe the amount of investment at this lower rate of interest. Using, then, the same diagram employed to work out the implications of the Simple Keynesian System (Figure 20–1), add the additional amount of investment to the $C + I$ curve and hence to the $C + I + G$ curve. Now read off the rise in net national product from the intersection of the OT line with the new $C + I + G$ curve.

A persistent deficit, if not offset by debt operations, increases private expenditures and does so period after period indefinitely as long as the deficit persists. However, the deficit itself will decline through time, provided government expenditures do not rise and provided tax yields increase as national income increases. But, if price rises accompany the increase in aggregate expenditures, government expenditures must increase merely to maintain the same old programs. As supplies, labor, and other things purchased by government increase in price, it takes more money to buy the same quantities. In this event, there is no guarantee that the mere passage of time will wipe out the deficit and hence end the persistent rise in private expenditures.

The balanced budget theorem may or may not hold for the Full Keynesian System. If the added government expenditures are financed in the first instance by new money, or, what amounts to the same thing, by simply spending out of an existing cash balance, we have, as in the Simple Keynesian System, a rise in total expenditures. But private expenditures will remain unchanged, as happened in the Simple Keynesian System, if and only if the rate of interest remains unchanged. It will remain unchanged if the quantity of speculative money remains unaffected and if all the schedules of the system do likewise. From a theoretical point of view, the touchy question is what happens to the quantity of speculative money. No firm answer can be provided without making several assumptions of a questionable sort. However, the presumption is that the increase in government expenditures will not be offset by a decrease in private expenditures and may be accompanied by an increase in private expenditures.

A government surplus, if not covered, tends to force down private expenditures. The argument is the reverse of the one given for a deficit. Again, this deflationary influence tends to wear itself out through time because tax yields will decline as national income falls. The process may be nevertheless exceedingly painful.

We may summarize the differences in their implications for public finance of the two systems of thought thus far considered. For a persistent deficit, the Simple Keynesian System implies that private expenditures will not rise, and the same conclusion holds for a persistent surplus. In the Full Keynesian System, deficits are stimulating and surpluses are depressing with respect to private expenditures. The balanced budget theorem holds for the simple version, but it may or may not hold for the more complete system.

Quantity Theory of Money

We are concerned, at this stage, only with what the Quantity Theory of Money has to say about public finances as they affect private expenditures. The theory is commonly identified as a theory of the general level of prices. This identification is not objectionable, but it serves our purpose better to concentrate on what it has to say about the determinants of private expenditures. In this way, this point of view may be kept on the same level and compared directly with the first two systems of thought discussed.

The quantity-of-money theory, stated in its most general terms, asserts that the level of private expenditures during a short period depends upon the quantity of money owned by people at the opening of the period. The larger the quantity of money owned by people, the larger on that account are their expenditures. This relation may or may not be linear.[9]

The economic justification of the quantity-of-money explanation of private expenditures upon current output will be discussed for a single individual or business concern and then for the society as a whole.

---

[9] The quantity-of-money theory of expenditures is one of the oldest ideas in economic thought. It dominated monetary thinking during the nineteenth and early twentieth centuries among economists, although not among laymen. Such distinguished economists as David Ricardo, J. S. Mill, Alfred Marshall, A. C. Pigou, Allyn Young, Knut Wicksell, J. M. Keynes (at one stage in his life), and Irving Fisher embraced this point of view. Fisher's book, *The Purchasing Power of Money* (2d ed.; New York: The Macmillan Co., 1920), is one of the best works and certainly one of the most readable. There has been a tendency in recent thought to deprecate this point of view. One who wishes to understand the theory is well advised to read an original work such as Fisher's rather than to rely on some secondhand account.

If all the facts about a person's circumstances are kept unchanged except the quantity of money he owns, a larger as opposed to a smaller stock of money will induce him to spend more. Some of his additional expenditures will be for other assets; for example, he may acquire some shares of stock. But part of the additional expenditures will be for other things he likes, for consumption items and durable equipment for his home, office, or farm. With a larger as compared to a smaller sum of money and with given prices, a person will be likely to hold more money as a cash reserve also. People enjoy the feeling of security obtained from holding a cash balance and they can more easily afford this pleasure with a larger as opposed to a smaller amount of money at any given date. Hence the larger the sum of money a person owns, the larger, other things being equal, will be his expenditures and his cash reserves.

There are, however, complications to be considered. One complication arises from the particular system of due dates for paying bills in force in the society, the system of dates for paying employees of companies, the practice of using credit cards and charge accounts, the dates when these bills are to be settled, and the dates when the government insists that people pay their taxes. These institutional practices require a person or a business to hold some money at any given date which has, so to speak, already been spent. The money has not really been spent, of course, but commitments have been made in the past calling for payment today, tomorrow, or next week. Let us call this portion of one's bank account or currency holdings "committed money." The remainder of a person's or company's money may be called "free money."

Of the free money a person owns (for some not very careful souls it may be zero) a choice is made between holding it or spending it. The spending choice does not necessarily mean rushing out to part with money. The more relevant choice takes the form of decisions that will result in bills coming in to be paid at later dates. Of the free money owned by a person or a business at a given date, more or less of it may be committed during a period of time by acquiring services, goods, or various types of securities. In modern societies, this commitment procedure is the important way to acquire what a family or business wants. A new machine is ordered; the bill comes later. The liquor store sends up a case of Bourbon and sends a bill on the first of the next month. A government imposes a property tax and calls for payment in semi-annual installments. Employees work for a company which pays them by check a week or two later.

The payment dates affect the speed that money moves from bank account to bank account in the system. At one limit is what may be called a *simultaneous payment system*. In such a system, payment for services would be made in money simultaneously with the performance of the service and the acquisition of the goods. Bank accounts would have to be geared, perhaps by some electronic device, to the light meter, the gas meter, or to the operator of a drill press. Inability to pay would mean immediately shutting off one's heat or, in the case of a business, immediately terminating the work being performed by employees. Such a system would permit the speed of money to be very high indeed. Once a dollar was placed into the system, it would move from bank account to bank account at perhaps the speed of light.

But, observe that the speed of money movement could no more be infinite than could the rate at which anything moves in the physical world. In actual money systems, the discontinuities—the big bills to be paid on some dates, the entire system of due dates—make for a lazy movement of money. It moves, rests awhile in someone's bank account, abruptly moves to another, rests again, and so on. Few can be precisely sure just how much money they need to keep on hand, because the bills coming in to be paid, although predictable more or less, are difficult to predict in detail. The prudent hold enough money to cover these contingencies. Those with simple financial affairs, such as farm workers, may be found holding no money at all on the day prior to payday.

For a society as a whole, these payment customs are relevant to the influence of money upon the amount of private expenditures. They set the speed, called velocity, at which money moves from hand to hand. This speed will not, however, be a constant. Even if all people and all organizations were always trying to spend money just as fast as they could and if the quantity of money were constant, the velocity would vary from day to day and from season to season, depending upon how money is redistributed among people with long intervals between dates of payment and among those with short intervals. There are large geographical differences too. Money moves faster, for example, in New York than it does in San Francisco.

The choice, however, between keeping one's money committed or not remains crucial. The large variations in private expenditures one observes during a period of the so-called business cycle cannot be explained simply by observing what happens to the quantity of money and by variations arising from money being shifted among groups with long payment intervals and those with short ones. These variations are largely, but not wholly, to be explained in terms of changes in attitudes toward holding money as opposed to holding other things. Corporations, for example, may greatly reduce their purchases of new real assets because for one reason or another they believe that the new real assets will not pay off. They may hold more cash or alternatively spend the money on government securities, inducing others to hold the cash instead.

The quantity-of-money theory of private expenditures is simple to apply to government finance. We shall again consider three circumstances, an uncovered government deficit, an uncovered government surplus, and an equal increase in government expenditures and in taxes.

An uncovered government deficit during a period will, other things being equal, induce an increase in private expenditures during the *following* period. The reason is simple. People will find that their money holdings are increased during the period by the amount of the government's deficit. They therefore will spend more money in following periods. One must say "following periods" because the deficit of the federal government during a period of one month shows up as an increase in private money holdings during the month and, according to the quantity-of-money theory, people's cash position must first increase before they spend more money. The postulate could be made, of course, that people anticipate the increase in their cash positions and immediately take steps to spend more as a result of the government's deficit. But this reasoning presupposes an amount of detailed knowledge which would be exceedingly difficult, if not impossible, for anyone to obtain.

With the kind of monetary system in effect in the United States, the stimulating effect of a government deficit, if not covered, is much greater than the above reasoning would lead one to suppose. The government's deficit not only increases the money holdings of individuals and business organizations, it also increases the reserves of commercial banks. Banks find themselves with growing bank reserves, and to take advantage of such developments, they will buy securities and lend more money to their customers. They are given a strong inducement to do both if the government deficit is large, say $1 billion per month. In turn, their greater willingness to buy certain securities drives up the prices of those securities, thereby inducing others to sell in order to buy yet other securities. Individuals and companies wishing to sell securities in order to finance the acquisition of new assets are enabled to do so on more advantageous terms. The increased willingness of banks to lend will drive down rates of interest on loans and mortgages, making it easier as well as cheaper for people to buy new cars, houses, boats, and remodeled kitchens.

Turning now to an uncovered government surplus, the reverse holds and for the same reasons, in reverse of course. A large uncovered government surplus would be devastating in its effects upon private expenditures in any normal period, or even in a period of high prosperity. Such a measure, keeping in mind that we are discussing a surplus not covered by purchase of debt, would be beneficial medicine for an economy already in the throes of an inflationary spiral. Not surprisingly, some governments have employed this measure to cope with such situations.[10]

A marginally balanced increase in government expenditures and tax revenues will induce an increase in total expenditures according to the quantity theory, provided that the increased government expenditures are financed by the government creating, or having created for it, the additional money to be spent. However, the timing of the expenditures and the timing of the tax receipts become of crucial importance. If the government increases its expenditures, this, taken by itself, automatically results in an increase in total expenditures. Now private expenditures will change if and only if people find themselves with more or less money. To keep private money supplies constant through time, it is necessary for the government to collect tax money, and not merely to assess tax liabilities, at precisely the same rate as it disperses money. Then, if similar assumptions are made as above for the balanced budget theorem, that theorem will hold. For in such an event, the new money created and spent by the government comes back to it through additional taxes at precisely the same moment that it is spent. Private groups are left with an unchanging quantity of money, and hence private expenditures remain constant. Since, however, government expenditures have increased and other expenditures have not changed, the balanced budget theorem holds.

The conclusion is, however, farfetched in the extreme because it would not actually be possible for the government to arrange to add to its expenditures and to add to its tax receipts in the precise way required. If an extended period of time, say a year, is allowed, it would be feasible to increase government expenditures and to increase tax yields by approximately the same amount. But if the expenditures are made first, even if higher tax rates are imposed at the same time, there must be a delay in time before the new tax liabilities become due and payable to the government. In the meantime, total expenditures have increased because government expenditures have risen and, more likely than not, so have private expenditures. The latter tend to rise because people find themselves with more money and thus spend more, generating, to be sure, additional tax liabilities. These do not cut into private expenditures until the legal taxpayers

[10] The postwar Japanese inflation was brought under control largely by this technique.

must commit their bank accounts to this purpose. Thus the answer to our problem depends on whether the taxes are due in a few weeks or in several months after the assumed increase in government expenditures.

There is a yet more important point. If a government is determined to increase its expenditures and is also determined not to permit any increase in total expenditures, it must first collect new tax receipts equal to the increased government expenditures. Private expenditures are to fall dollar for dollar as public expenditures rise. To achieve this neutral policy, neutral in the sense that government policy is to be neither stimulating nor depressing on total expenditures, additional taxes equal to the new government expenditures will have to be imposed *before* the government increases its expenditures.

Asset Theory

The asset theory is more similar to the quantity-of-money approach than to either of the Keynesian types of theory discussed. It is also the least well-known of the theories being considered.[11] Like the others, the asset approach is an attempt to explain the size and variations in private expenditures on goods and services and to show how various government financial policies affect private expenditures. Private consumption and investment expenditures of a person are, in this theory, determined by the amount of the net worth of that person. Aggregate private expenditures are treated as determined by aggregate net worths.

The amount a person spends for new physical things depends, according to this point of view, upon the money value of his wealth minus the value of the claims of other people against this wealth. Net wealth, or what is more commonly called net worth, has the same meaning as discussed in connection with net worth taxation.[12] At any particular date in a person's history, he finds himself with various possessions, such as a house, furnishings, a car, shares of stock, a savings account, a checking account, and currency. Very commonly he also finds himself encumbered with debts—a mortgage on his house, amounts due to the dentist, to the finance company for his automobile, and to a petroleum company for gas and oil. These possessions and debts are to be taken as given; they are what they are. To explain why a particular person is found with a particular

---

[11] Accounts of a pure asset approach to the explanation of private expenditures are few. See Earl R. Rolph, *The Theory of Fiscal Economics* (Berkeley: Univ. of California Press, 1954), chap. v.

[12] See chap. 9, p. 194.

asset-debt combination involves in principle an indefinite retreat in time, theoretically to the "beginning" of society.

A business organization likewise finds itself with possessions and with claims against these possessions. An operating business possesses things used within the business for production. Some of its possessions may be claims against its customers (accounts due) or against the government (public debt). Some assets consist of money in the bank—a checking account.

The particular combination of possessions and claims a person or a business inherited from the past may or may not be the combination the person or the management of the business prefers. A holder of wealth may be said to be content with his asset-debt position if the combination he inherits from the past is just right from his point of view. If it is not just right, he may sell some assets, buy some assets, retire some debt, incur new debt, or engage in some combination of these possibilities. Discontent with inherited asset-debt structures is essential for the operation of markets in shares of stock, such as the New York Stock Exchange, for markets in government securities—in fact for all markets for claims and for old real assets. It is also discontent that leads to the acquisition of new real things, in other words, to new investment.

Putting to one side, for the moment, the fact that people like to consume—find it indispensable, in fact—let us concentrate attention on the factors relevant to decisions leading to investment. There are markets in which old physical things and claims of various kinds may be priced. One holder of wealth may, in view of the prices of the things he owns, be discontented with some of them; these he will wish to sell. If other people have similar attitudes, the price of such items must fall until enough people are willing to hold all of the existing items of that class of wealth. Likewise, at some set of prices, some types of wealth are bargains. People will want to hold more of this class, and its price will be corrected to a higher figure.

Prices may not only be out of line relative to one another; they may be in general too high or too low. Prices of assets are too high in general if at those prices people prefer to hold more money. The attempt to hold more money cannot actually succeed in everyone holding more money. It means that people are willing to part with their possessions, and this choice lowers the money prices of them. Similarly, people may find that they wish to hold less money. This attitude takes the form of their attempting to buy more possessions, thus bidding up prices. This adjustment process results in a money price for each class of physical wealth and for each type of claim.

Investment—the purchase of new things—requires that the new things be produced. The types of new wealth to be produced depend upon whether it pays to produce them. It does not ordinarily pay to produce some types of wealth, such as land, because the costs are ordinarily prohibitive. Yet Swiss peasants did produce land in their mountain country in a sense; they carried soil from areas where it would not be missed to suitable spots in high mountain country to make gardens and even sizable fields. Millions of things are easy to produce, however, and will be produced if the price at which they can be sold makes it profitable to do so. Some of the new things are much like old ones, such as dwellings, and some new things are really new in the sense that nothing similar exists. The opportunity to produce new physical things along with the desire to own wealth of various types makes investment feasible.

The amount spent in any period upon new real wealth depends objectively upon the valuation placed upon old wealth and subjectively upon the estimates of possible gains and losses associated with the ownership of new wealth. In general, new assets will look more attractive to acquire if assets of that sort are already providing their owners with income. Thus in prosperous periods, when companies are generally doing well, new assets are attractive. In depressed periods, however, only those new assets that are different from old ones are likely to be much in demand. They must not only be different, but better. In the competition between new things and old things, a competition that goes on indefinitely, new things have some advantage by merely being new, but to achieve high sales they must be superior to old things. When plant capacity is already redundant, a new machine cannot make a place for itself by being just like an old one that stands idle. If a new one promises to pay for itself even in competition with idle machines, it has a chance of being accepted. In any case, however, a company, like a person, cannot acquire a new machine unless somehow the money can be found to pay for it. This objective constraint applies on a different scale but with the same force to John Jones, the truck driver, and to the Coca-Cola Corporation.

As concerns consumption expenditures, an asset approach makes net worth, and not income, the objective determinant. The objective limit to the amount a person can spend in any period is the net value of his assets. No sane person would, however, test out this limit except under circumstances of dire emergency—for example, when the life of a member of his family is at stake. Among individuals of differing financial circumstances, those with more wealth will generally consume more. For an entire group of people, consumption expenditures in money terms grow if the money value of their wealth grows. Thus if people have saved last month and have larger wealth positions on the first day of this month, they will, on this account, spend more upon consumption (and investment) this month than they spent last month.

Unlike either of the two Keynesian positions discussed, current income is treated as irrelevant in determining current expenditures. Current income, being a flow, does not impose any limit, one way or the other, upon how much a person does spend during the same period; it can influence conduct only in anticipation.

The asset theory becomes identical in its results with the quantity-of-money theory in the special case when the money value of the wealth of a community is a constant multiple of the quantity of money. Under certain rather rigid conditions, such a constant relation would prevail. In fact, however, the quantity of money may increase while the money value of wealth decreases and vice versa. In a general sense, the one theory does not reduce to the other.

With this abbreviated sketch of the asset approach in mind, let us again examine the implications of three situations of the public finances—a large persistent deficit, a large persistent surplus, and a marginally balanced increase in government expenditures and in tax revenues.

If the government experiences a large deficit, which again is not covered by sale of debt, the effect is to stimulate both private consumption and private investment expenditures. The stimulation is now greater under this theory for any given-sized deficit than it is under the Full Keynesian or even the quantity-of-money approach. The existence of a government deficit during a period means an equal increase in the quantity of money in private hands in that period. Those people who find their cash positions rising will wish to spend more on currently produced things because they have become wealthier in money terms. But they will also wish to acquire old physical things and securities. This desire will tend to increase the net worth positions of other groups measured in money terms. As one aspect of this development, rates of interest will also tend to fall because the prices of bonds tend to rise. Those who wish to borrow, that is, to sell new debt instruments, can now do so on more attractive terms, and this fact in turn stimulates their expenditures. Thus, according to this point of view, the increase in the quantity of money induces a further increase in the money value of wealth, and the two together induce an increase in private expenditures. A government deficit, then, is definitely stimulating.

An uncovered surplus in an over-all government budget has the opposite effect. The surplus wipes up money previously owned by private groups. Some, finding themselves with less money than they wish to hold, sell some of their wealth. The prices of these things fall, spreading the deflationary impact to other groups. The general deflation in wealth holdings results in a general decline in both consumption and investment expenditures.

A marginally balanced increase of government expenditures and of tax revenues will, according to the asset-theory approach, lead to an increase in total expenditures equal to the increase in government expenditures. The balanced budget theorem holds for this system of thought as it does for the Simple Keynesian system, in spite of the fact that they are radically different ways of viewing the economic scene.

The increase in government expenditures results in an increase in total expenditures provided private expenditures do not change. Likewise, the increase in government expenditures results in an increase in current money incomes (before tax) under the same conditions. Since, however, tax revenues are to be increased also, private money incomes after-tax are left unchanged. The government neither increases nor decreases the wealth position of private groups by its marginally balanced change. There being no induced change in the net worth position of private groups, private expenditures should remain unaffected. This conclusion requires that wealth distribution remain unchanged, corresponding to the condition in the Simple Keynesian system that income distribution remain unchanged; and it also requires that tastes remain unchanged.

These results are also farfetched as earlier pointed out in connection with the quantity-of-money theory of expenditures. For a government to arrange an increase in its expenditures and an equal simultaneous increase in tax liabilities calls for a precision in forecasting unavailable to mere humans in economic affairs. The important point to keep firmly in mind is the implications of the asset approach for the cases of government deficits and surpluses, because these rather than the case of a balanced change reveal the significant differences between this approach and other points of view.

Conclusions

Four points of view explaining the effects of government budget actions have been discussed. Economic writings will commonly contain elements of all four of these theories, depending upon the subject being discussed and the emphasis of the particular thinker. The temptation is strong to resolve their conflicting features to obtain some judicious compromise. Yet eclectic compromises should be made with great caution. One runs the danger of ending up with an inconsistent pattern of ideas that will fall apart under the least strain. Selection among economic theories cannot be made on the same principles as those used to arrive at a compromise at a meeting to discuss the parking problem on a campus. What is, in the current mode of thought, an "extreme" view may err in not being extreme enough. If some hold that the earth is flat like a board and some hold that it is round, it does not follow that the correct view is that the earth is shaped like a salad bowl. Correctness of ideas cannot be discovered by a process of compromise.

Of these four points of view discussed, the results found for the Simple Keynesian system are by far the most pleasing in their financial implications. Only in that system of thought is a persistent deficit viewed as inducing no change in private expenditures. If this theory is accepted as the correct one, consider what a boon it is. All taxes can be abolished! There will be a period of readjustment in which private expenditures will rise, and presumably so will prices. Then the economic world will settle down again. Persistent large deficits will go on and on without any further increase in private expenditures. Courses in public finance could be abolished; there would be so little to talk about. The headaches associated with taxation would disappear, tax enforcement agencies could be abolished, many members of the legal profession would find themselves without work, and the much-talked-about taxpayer would cease to exist. Financial paradise is thereby achieved.

The remaining three points of view promise no financial paradise. In all of them, taxation remains indispensable to the conduct of an orderly society. Without taxation private expenditures would grow far too rapidly. The basic common ingredient in these three points of view dictating the social requirement of taxation is the change in the quantity of money induced by uncovered government deficits and surpluses. These theories are dismal only by comparison to the popular but rather precarious simplified Keynesian theory. They do promise that orderly economic affairs can be achieved in part by careful design of automatic fiscal stabilizers, and by intelligent financial-monetary management—topics to be investigated in the following chapters.

21

Objectives of Compensatory Fiscal Finance

The principle of compensation applied to government finance calls for the achievement of the desired level of private and government expenditures on currently produced goods and services. In a growing society, such expenditures must increase. Each year should establish an all-time record of expenditures and of production. If total expenditures merely cease to grow, a recession begins; there is no standing still. Each year there are more people entering than leaving the work force, and more machines installed than discarded. If total expenditures do not grow, some of the potential increase in the output of goods and services does not appear, with the result of economic waste and underemployment of both human and nonhuman resources.

The goal of smoothly increasing money expenditures upon current output does not command our support in and of itself. It is a means to ends that are closer to the fundamental aspirations of mankind. Various points of view have crystallized as to what these goals of a country's global fiscal and monetary policies ought to be. Some disputes over policy in this area concern differences of opinion as to what the economy should achieve; some disputes are traceable to differences of opinion about what is regarded as practical to expect the economy to achieve. Evidences of these differences of opinion are recorded almost every day in the newspapers. Business spokesmen, for example, may emphasize the importance of protecting the "value of the dollar," meaning presumably that prices in general should either not rise or should perhaps even fall. Congressmen, especially if they are from industrial centers, are more inclined to emphasize the importance of full employment.

There are in fact many, many goals for the economy to achieve. Economic organization should, for example, provide people with the goods and services they want. The production of things people do not want seems foolish as well as wasteful. Yet of course things are produced every day that no one wants. Wheat is produced in great quantity, far beyond the amounts that will be eaten. The economy produces smog, polluted rivers and beaches, and some polluted people, all of which we would be pleased to get along without. The growth in the complexity of society may produce new liberties; it also produces new restrictions upon our liberties. The new liberties arise in part from the material gains. A worker in a factory in Indiana may take his family on a vacation in Florida. Even twenty years ago, such a freedom for a factory worker was almost unknown; he could not have afforded the expense. New restrictions upon our liberties arise in many ways. The freedom of action and of speech is closely associated with the size of the organization in which a person spends his working hours; he becomes a cog in a machine, and a cog has little freedom. Contemporary society is dominated by large organizations, especially by business corporations and governments, and they grow larger year by year. Modern industrial societies are risking the hazard of becoming revised feudal systems.

The establishment of norms or goals for the functioning of an economic system would be a comparatively simple matter if there were general agreement about what goals are to be pursued, and, it should be emphasized, if these various goals did not conflict. The troublesome issues arise mainly because of the conflict of goals. It would be easy enough to eliminate smog over our cities; simply ban the use of internal combustion engines. As our metropolitan areas are presently organized, such a step would result in chaos. Similarly, it would be within the competence of a society to guarantee continuous full employment. The measures necessary to achieve this goal might entail as much detailed government regulation of economic life as occurred during World War II. In such an event, the large goal of full employment conflicts with many small but important goals, such as being able to walk into a store and walk out with the article one wishes to acquire. The establishment of some particular goal entails costs in the form of sacrificing other goals. The phrase *the end justifies the means* illustrates the cynical doctrine that one goal is to be pursued regardless of its cost in terms of other goals. In fiscal and monetary policies, as well as in policy decisions in other government areas, single-minded pursuit of one goal regardless of the consequences courts disaster.

Goals of Full Employment and Stable Prices

Two main goals for over-all fiscal and monetary policy are *full employment* and *stable prices*. Both of these are, ideally, to be achieved without having to sacrifice other ends, at least by not "too much." In this discussion the other ends must be left vague and in the background, but they are not to be forgotten. For example, in striving for the goal of stable prices, the methods employed should not require government regulation of every price. Yet it may be that additional government regulation is essential to achieve the goal. The intelligent citizen must decide whether the gain in the form of price stability is worth the cost of the various restrictions upon behavior presupposed in the government regulations. The danger is always that the many small goals sacrificed fail to excite attention merely because they are small and numerous.

The ideal of full employment requires no special defense. A person who has something to contribute to society should be permitted to do so. He thereby adds to the total of goods and services available, and he enjoys the money gains from doing so. Involuntary unemployment indicates a malfunctioning of the economy, and if it persists on a large scale, serious questions arise about the justification of that particular economic system. Not surprisingly, the socialist type of reformer finds a more sympathetic audience during periods of mass underemployment than during prosperous times. The unemployed have a grievance by being excluded from paid work; the employed have a grievance too, because they live under the spectre of being forced to join the idle.

The ideal of stable prices does need a special defense. Why should there be any particular attractiveness about living in a society in which the price level is stable as opposed to one in which the price level is rising by, for example, 5 per cent per year, or one in which the price level is falling by the same percentage? It should be kept in mind that none of the options being considered imply that individual prices are stable. Prices of individual commodities may fluctuate over wide ranges while prices of some large sample of commodities remain the same month after month. Why then should there be any special merit in having prices of a large sample of commodities remain approximately constant? Furthermore, few industrial countries have in fact experienced price stability over extended periods. The price level has only rarely been stable for periods as long as five years during the past century in any Western country.

In economic literature, the discussion of this topic has produced valid reasons for price-level stability as a goal, although rarely because price-level stability is believed to be worthwhile in itself. The reasons for supporting price-level stability usually rest upon an appeal to side-effects—to the by-products, so to speak, of price-level instability. A fluctuating price level is deemed to be bad because the effects it carries with it are bad. These effects are variously emphasized in lay and in economic circles.

1. Rising prices are sometimes viewed as bad because they make people feel they are being cheated. A person earns $100 after tax during one week and at one set of prices. When he exercises his choice of spending the money the following week, he finds that prices have risen and he may feel put-upon. This argument logically implies that falling prices are good because when a person gets around to spending the money he earns in one period, he finds that he can buy more goods than he expected; he is pleasantly surprised.

2. Rising prices are deemed to be bad because they promote inefficiency in production. A businessman can become very casual about his operations and yet make profits because he finds he can obtain higher prices for his wares merely by holding on to his stocks of goods. Likewise, this argument implies that falling prices are good because only the most efficient businesses can survive in such a setting.

3. Rising prices may be condemned because they change the pattern of money income distribution by making it more unequal. This view requires a demonstration that price-level increases do make income distributions more unequal and the acceptance of the value judgment that less inequality is better than more. The economic argument that rising prices do make for greater inequality suffers from the defect that there is little evidence to support it.

4. Rising prices are said to undermine the established institutions of society, such as those of borrowing and lending. People become more reluctant to lend because the real value (money value divided by a price index) of their wealth is expected to fall through time. This argument is symmetrical because with falling prices, people who might otherwise borrow become reluctant to do so because the real value of what they owe increases through time.

5. Radically changing prices, such as those exhibited in hyperinflations, are intolerable; they interrupt the normal routine of society, force drastic changes in institutions, and generally create a confused social situation.

The choice among possible price-level trends depends upon subtleties that permit no clear-cut answer. Perhaps, if an accurate poll could be taken, most people in the United States would be found to prefer approximately stable prices. No such poll has been taken to the authors' knowledge. Perhaps many people would prefer gradual and persistent declines in the prices of commodities. Perhaps most people would prefer to see the prices of the things they buy decline while the prices of the services and goods they sell increase.

Price-level goals and employment goals may be appraised in the light of what an economy can reasonably be expected to achieve. Price stability in the sense of variations in some appropriate index by less than 1 per cent per year would be almost impossible to achieve as long as individual prices were permitted to fluctuate. Full employment in the sense that 99 per cent of the workers have the kind of job appropriate to their skills, with each working full time, would be a little too much to expect. Only approximations to these goals can be achieved. There can be reasonable differences in views about what level of performance is a good enough approximation.

Goal of Economic Development

The goals of full employment and price-level stability are commonly believed to be appropriate objectives of Western societies. In the various countries described as "underdeveloped," the main goal has become economic development. In India, China, and Indonesia, to name a few, this aim dominates the policies of governments. Price stability and full employment would certainly command some following in such countries, but not as much as the goal of rapid economic development. If the cost of progress is price inflation, and in almost all of these countries there has been in recent years substantial price inflation, the cost is accepted.

The full employment ideal, so dear to the hearts of British, Scandinavian, and American peoples, takes on a different aspect in the heavily overpopulated countries of Asia. These people earn their livelihood mainly from the land, and often there are far too many workers for the available land. It is reported conservatively that one-quarter of the working population in the rural areas of India could be removed from agriculture without decreasing output at all.[1] Economically, this fact means that rural labor service is a free commodity like air, and its theoretically correct price is zero. Under these conditions, removing people from agriculture and setting them to work

[1] Norman S. Buchanan and Howard S. Ellis, *Approaches to Economic Development* (New York: Twentieth Century Fund, 1955), pp. 44-45.

doing anything at all that is useful would be a net gain to society. It is little wonder that the people in such areas stress development. Only by a radical shift of the working population from agriculture into other pursuits can their services become useful to society.[2]

Conditions Necessary for Stable Prices and Full Employment

Economists have often asserted that the goals of full employment and product-price-level stability are conflicting. The conflict arises because some prices are pushed up by various economic power blocs in the society; labor unions in particular come in for strong criticism in this connection. Unless total expenditures upon output increase at a certain rate, some potential output remains unborn because of sagging sales. An increase in aggregate expenditures pulls up other prices, resulting in a general rise in prices. Governments have the unhappy choice of allowing unemployment to develop or of permitting the price level to rise. It is this conflict that accounts for many of the hesitations and confusions of official monetary and fiscal policies in the United States, Canada, Great Britain, and many other countries.

Product-price-level stability and full employment in a growing society are not necessarily conflicting. If the conditions that must be satisfied can be discovered, we may learn what specific practices of private groups and of the government are leading to the conflict and may judge whether it is feasible or even desirable to attempt to correct the practices in question.

GROWTH THROUGH EXPANSION OF ALL RESOURCES. We consider first the case in which a society grows with no significant improvement in techniques and with a uniform growth in all resources. This case requires that the labor force grows year in and year out without any

---

[2] Free labor service seems strange and unreal to Westerners. It is ordinarily taken for granted that people's services are potentially valuable, and if for any large group this is not the case, there must be something very wrong with the society and with its economic organization. Yet we consider an inexpensive supply of water, electricity, or transportation as a blessing. To hold that free water is good whereas free labor is bad for a society is not as paradoxical as it sounds. For water to be free, the supply need only be so large as to take care of all our needs for water, meaning that another acre-foot would be of no use at all. The supply of particular kinds of labor service can be free in the same sense. However, human beings are adaptable and can supply services that command a high price. In India, for example, competent teachers, engineers, doctors, mechanics, and thousands of other types of professional and skilled workers are extremely scarce. The existence of redundant labor in some pursuits becomes a great social waste if these people could be trained to useful occupations.

significant change in the distribution of skills, that new machines, buildings, and equipment generally are produced which are copies of old ones and in relative quantities of various kinds that sample the existing resources.

The pertinent facts are represented graphically in Figure 21–1. Imagine an industry consisting of many individual companies when the industry is defined by the type of output produced. This type of output has the special feature that it is a perfect sample of all kinds of commodities produced. By observing this industry, we observe in miniature the entire economy.

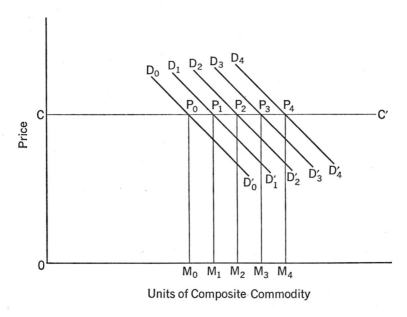

Units of Composite Commodity

FIGURE 21–1

In the base period, the output is OM_o, the price P_oM_o—which is now the price level because the commodity is a sample of all output. Full employment is assumed. Resources are to grow so that in the following period potential output has increased by M_oM_1 and so on. The condition of price-level stability is simply that the price of this composite commodity must remain unchanged as indicated by moving to the right along the line CC'. For this condition to be satisfied, the money demands on the part of the government and the general public for the composite commodity must grow as indicated on the graph. The demand schedule in period one must pass through the point P_1 and in period two through point P_2. One can see that if the demand schedules shift by more than these amounts, the price of the composite commodity will rise and the condition of price stability will be violated.

The second condition is that the money costs of producing the commodity must remain constant, or as the graph shows, unit money costs of output must always be a point on the CC' line. This condition is severe. It means that prices of services used to produce output must remain unchanged through time. If, as a result of power tactics, labor unions push up wage-rates, the costs of producing the total potential output of OM_1 in period one would rise above P_1M_1. Thus in such a case, price stability would require that demand increase by less than that indicated by $D_1D'_1$, in which case some potential output would be wasted in underemployment; or alternatively full employment would require that demand increase by more than the amount indicated by $D_1D'_1$, in which case some price inflation would result. If there is to be no conflict between the two goals, the prices of services used to produce output must remain unchanged over time and the money demand for output must increase by just the amount necessary to buy the increased potential output at no change in price.

There is a third, concealed condition. It is that companies producing and selling this commodity remain in about the same competitive status vis-à-vis one another through time; otherwise product prices would rise even with unchanging costs.

GROWTH THROUGH EXPANSION OF ALL RESOURCES PLUS IMPROVEMENT IN TECHNIQUE. New techniques permit more output to be produced from the same batch of resources. This is the same result as if more resources had been added to the society.

A society which merely grows by adding to all its resources can have full employment and price stability provided the prices of services which are costs of production remain constant in a setting of proportionately growing demands for output. New techniques call, on the average, for an increase in the money prices of services that are costs. To take a simple illustration, suppose the new techniques introduced in our typical industry are such that the productivity of every kind of resource increases uniformly by 12½ per cent per year—a very large increase. It is as if a worker could accomplish in approximately 35 hours per week this year what took him 40 hours per week to accomplish last year. The same observation applies to buildings, machines, and everything else used to produce output. Then, a worker *must* receive, not *should* receive, the same total pay for working approximately 35 hours this year as he received for working 40 hours last year. Stated in terms of hourly rates of pay, if he had been paid at the rate of $2.00 per hour last year, his pay is to be $2.25 per hour this year. Thus the money income of the typical worker will rise if the work week is kept stable and so will the income of the typical owner of property. On the average, business profits will grow absolutely in our typical industry year after year because the amount of equipment is growing and because its productivity is growing. The total wage-bill of the typical industry will also grow in the same manner.

On the demand side, total expenditures should grow as indicated in Figure 21–1, but in this case at a higher rate. If it would have required an increase of $10 billion per year to maintain full employment with no improvements, it may now require an increase of perhaps $15 billion per year, the exact amount depending upon the rate of technological improvement.

Technical improvement will not in fact simply increase the productivity of all types of resources. A new technique may result in making some existing machines obsolete because they can no longer be used at all. Sadly enough, the same effects may make some kinds of labor service obsolete. A man who formerly earned $25 per day by hand-striping automobile bodies in 1928 found his skill made obsolete by a simple device that permitted young ladies paid forty cents per hour to do the job instead. Given these facts, full employment with stable prices of products requires changes in particular prices. People whose skills are more in demand because aggregate expenditures are rising and because their skills remain at least as useful as before can happily tend to their knitting. Those in occupations where the demand for their skills remains steady over time, even as aggregate expenditures are increasing, may have trouble. As long as their numbers remain unchanged, those initially employed can remain so, provided they are willing to work at the same money wage-rate while they see the wages of their fellow workers in other occupations rising. Young people looking for work who try to break into such occupations (and the trade may be very attractive because the wage-rate is high) will find that room can be made for them only by a reduction in the money wage-rate.

Some groups will find themselves in even worse circumstances. Improvements in techniques may greatly reduce the demand for their services. People with such skills must take a reduction in their wage-rates, and, depending upon the severity of the reduction in the usefulness of their skills, perhaps retrain themselves for other occupations. Those entering the labor force will shun such occupations because of the difficulty of finding a position. They will direct their talents to jobs of the type whose demands are increasing. This type of adjustment process means that the upward movement of wage-rates will be accompanied by a smaller dispersion in the change of wage-rates.

Instead of skills of the type whose demands are rapidly increasing, leading to much higher wage-rates, and those whose demands are falling, leading to much lower wage-rates, the adjustment in the numbers of those entering particular occupations holds the wage-rate changes within a narrower range.

GROWTH THROUGH EXPANSION OF ALL RESOURCES, IMPROVEMENT IN TECHNIQUE, PLUS IMPROVED RESOURCES. Growing resources and improved technique accompanied by new and improved resources give results generally similar to those just observed. New equipment makes for more radical changes, and thus for the need of greater adjustments in the mobility of other resources and of their prices, than do changes in techniques alone. New equipment displaces large groups of workers and makes what formerly had been highly expensive equipment obsolete. Even whole industries may be forced into serious trouble by new types of equipment, illustrated by the long-distance passenger service of the railroads being undermined by airliners. In such a rather unusual case, the price of passenger land transportation must fall. For this to happen, wage-rates of workers in such an industry may also have to fall because even if no new workers try to break into the industry, those already there must either continue to work in the industry at lower wage-rates or face becoming unemployed.

Yet, the grim side should not be overemphasized. New types of resources will permit an increase in average wage-rates just as do improved techniques and for the same reason. The demands for many kinds of labor services will be increasing. In such a setting, there are possibilities of adjustment by the more adaptable existing workers and by those entering the work force. Pockets of hard-core unemployment may exist, and indeed are likely in regions where the demands for many of the principal products produced there have fallen. Attempts to cure such difficulties by increasing over-all total expenditures lead to a conflict between full employment and price stability.

Institutional Deterrents to Full Employment and Price Stability

The foregoing analysis of the conditions for realizing both full employment and price stability point to the importance of careful social engineering. Policies must succeed in (1) increasing aggregate demands for products by just the "right" amount and (2) adjusting the prices of products and of services used in production by the "right" degree. Fiscal and monetary devices are aimed at accomplishing objective (1); they are of only incidental importance in accomplishing objective (2). The latter objective requires that the economy do its own adjusting somehow or other. If the economy cannot adjust, there are defects in its institutions that require diagnosis and may need to be remedied.

Of the many defects of our economy, one of the more important is the practice of many labor unions of adhering to the wage philosophy of "push 'em up." Whatever social good organizations of this type accomplish by way of curtailing arbitrary management practices, assisting workers with hardship problems, acting as counterpropaganda agencies against the advocates of social plutocracy and of monopolistic practices in business, they have become something of an economic nuisance from the point of view of achieving both full employment and price stability. Successful efforts to increase money wage-rates practically assure some unemployment. Even in a rapidly progressing society, some industries and some occupations are certain to suffer persistent declines in demand. If wage-rates are advanced even in the face of unemployment, and this practice has become regrettably common, employment opportunities in such industries can only be worsened.

Furthermore, the belief held by labor union leaders that wage-rates should be increased to reflect the increase in productivity in an industry, meaning an increase in output per hour of work, also serves to thwart the goals of price stability and full employment. Industries experiencing large increases in output per man-hour, typically the mass-production industries and agriculture in the United States, will with unchanging wage-rates find their unit costs of production falling more than those in industry in general. If, as a result of powerful labor unions, the cost-reducing effect of improvements is fully offset by rising money wages, the increase in employment in these industries is narrowly restricted to the share they obtain of the growing aggregate expenditures upon output. Other industries without these advantages must, if there is to be full employment, absorb a larger share of the growing work force. But they cannot do this unless the prices of their products decline, a development feasible only with a reduction in costs. Hence wage-rate differentials in various industries may become increasingly out of line with economic reality. Workers already entrenched in industries with large scope for the introduction of improved facilities and techniques become a special class of highly paid workmen whose skills do not justify their pay on economic grounds.

In the professions, increased productivity through the introduction of new techniques and equipment ordinarily plays a minor role. The reward of labor effort on the basis of increases in productivity calls for little or no change in professional money incomes, and hence little or no change in real income (money income divided by price index). Yet ideally, the prices of products that become relatively easier to produce should fall whereas the prices of other things should rise in a regime of a generally stable price level and of full employment. Likewise, as we have seen, wage-rates on the average should rise also. Yet wage-rates must not rise any faster in industries in which the productivity gains from better equipment and better techniques happen to be especially large than in those, like the professions, where productivity gains are small or zero.

Another major institutional obstacle to the accomplishment of stable prices and full employment consists of certain types of business price policies. The philosophy of "push 'em up" found in labor organizations has its counterpart in business management. Companies may push up prices on any auspicious occasion, including occasions when wage-rates rise. For years, the price of anthracite coal either rose or remained stable even though the demand for coal fluctuated widely from year to year. Only rarely do the railroads request lower prices from the Interstate Commerce Commission. Basic steel prices move only in one direction—up. The steel workers union can be blamed only partly for this trend. The advance of the prices of products almost regardless of demand is possible only because of the absence of effective price competition among steel companies. If labor unions behave responsibly when "responsibly" means that their policies are to be consistent with the twin goals, equally responsible behavior on the part of management calls for exercising no greater monopoly power in the future than it has in the past. Thus if, in the steel industry, it is policy for the management to charge a price per ton twice as high as its marginal costs per ton, stable costs result in stable prices. But in view of the peculiar system of throttling effective competition in that industry, stable costs do not by any means guarantee stable prices.

Managements, however, normally pay more attention to the effect of price on volume of business than do labor unions. Experimental increases of prices may meet with buyer resistance and result in declining sales, pointing to the need of a downward revision of prices. Unions by contrast will not, with occasional exceptions, permit such revisions when definite overpricing of particular kinds of labor service has occurred. The battle for prestige in the labor movement alone, when prestige is measured largely by the size of the money gains for the workers who remain employed, usually rules out such concessions even in cases where they are clearly in the interests of the workers concerned.[3]

There are many institutional practices standing in the way of the adjustments needed in the economy to give full employment without price inflation. No piece of legislation will assure the required flexibility. The general need, however, is plain. The troubles in the pricing of labor services and of products arise because of monopolistic practices. It is wrong to hold that monopoly tactics and price stability with full employment are necessarily incompatible. Actually only for a few periods in recent history has the United States had price stability with approximately full employment; never has there been perfect competition throughout the society. But once monopoly price power exists, it can be used and often is used to increase money costs and prices when from an economic point of view they should be falling.

Possible Remedial Measures

The twin goals of full employment and price-level stability are being thwarted in the United States and in many other countries by poor management of fiscal and monetary affairs and by perverse price and wage policies of some business organizations and labor unions—policies sometimes supported by government action. The following chapters will discuss methods by which more sensible fiscal and monetary policies may be achieved. The question of how special-interest groups are to be kept from sabotaging the twin goals goes far beyond the ordinary province of public finance. No simple panacea is feasible, but a few possible remedial measures may be mentioned.

A partial solution for perverse pricing tactics both by business organizations and labor unions calls for curtailment of their power to control prices. Much could be accomplished by simply removing the umbrella devices supplied by governments to protect special-interest groups. Various agencies have grown up within the federal and state governments to promote the interests of particular industries by stifling competition. The Department of Interior looks after the interests of the mining industries. Under the guise of conservation, the Texas Railroad Commission, a state regulatory agency, restricts the output of crude petroleum to keep up its price. The liquor industry

[3] The Textile Workers Union of America (TWUA) permitted a 6.5 per cent wage reduction in 1952 on the representations of the New England employers that their competitive position had been made untenable by a wage-rate structure higher than that prevailing in the nonunion Southern mills. The union's power in this case was contained by lack of control of wage-rates in a large section of the industry. See Lloyd G. Reynolds and Cynthia H. Taft, *The Evolution of Wage Structure* (New Haven: Yale Univ. Press, 1956), pp. 87-88.

is protected by government-enforced resale price maintenance. The list could be extended almost indefinitely.

Greater price competition could be obtained by reducing present government obstacles to effective foreign competition. The elimination of quotas, such as those for oil imports, and the reduction of high tariffs on imports would induce managements in many industries to hesitate to increase prices and also induce them to resist the more extravagant demands of labor unions.

Fairly radical measures may be needed to contain the power of labor unions. A ceiling might be imposed by law upon the amount of yearly increases in wage-rates negotiated in collective-bargaining agreements—for example, a 3 per cent increase per year. Any increases in highly paid occupations by collective action might be prohibited. If wage-rates including fringe benefits exceed, for example, $5 per hour, collective bargaining to raise wage-rates might even be prohibited. Sooner or later, the power presently being exercised by strong labor unions may have to be brought under control if the public goals of full employment and price-level stability are to be achieved. Labor unions have important social functions other than wage-rate negotiation, and many of these need to be preserved. Yet the use of naked force exercised by special-interest groups seems a curious way to conduct a complicated industrial society.

22

Implementing Fiscal Policies

Successful achievement of the goals of price-level stability and full employment requires that there be a continuing growth in aggregate expenditures. If the government in its policies could somehow be neutral, private spending might increase from month to month and from year to year in just the right amount. There is, however, no assurance that privately determined expenditures left alone will give this happy result. An unguided economy may experience small or large short-term fluctuations and exhibit trends either upwards or downwards in aggregate private expenditures. More than a century's sad experience with radical variations in private expenditures has led to the now spreading conviction that governments have some responsibility to bring system and order into the change in aggregate expenditures upon current output. Successful execution of this responsibility is by no means simple. A cynic can point to much experience to support the belief that little can be accomplished and that the wise should resign themselves to living with booms and busts, with periodic large-scale unemployment, price-level instability, and large-scale waste.

A government can influence aggregate expenditures by deliberate acts designed for this purpose or it can do so by relying on devices that once installed will act automatically. The first method is described as *discretionary* and the second as *automatic*.

Automatic Devices

An automatic device means one that tends to keep private expenditures closer to their proper trend than would occur in its absence. In the fiscal field, the main such automatic devices are taxes and government transfer-payment programs. In the monetary field, there are the reserve requirements of banks, federal deposit insurance, gold and foreign exchange movements, and currency flows into and out of banks. In a larger sense, all self-correcting features of an economy exhibit automatism. An economy without any ability to heal its own wounds is dead.

Taxes are said to have built-in flexibility—to be automatic—when tax *yields* tend to increase with increased private expenditures and to decrease with decreased private expenditures. Formally, the built-in flexibility of any tax or any set of taxes may be defined as $\triangle T/\triangle Y$ where T is tax yield, Y is national income computed before tax, and $\triangle$ is the change in the respective items. If, for a change in national income, Y, tax yields do not change at all, the built-in flexibility of the tax system is zero. If, for a change in national income, Y, tax yields change by the same amount, the built-in flexibility of the tax system is 100 per cent. The expression, $\triangle T/\triangle Y$, would be zero only in the event that the tax legislation called for payment of fixed sums such as poll taxes. Actually, a tax law is a formula, as has been emphasized, and the yield depends upon the size of the tax base and the rate structure. Since in fact the changes in the size of the tax base are positively correlated with changes in national income, practically all taxes exhibit some degree, though sometimes a very small degree, of built-in flexibility.

Similar observations apply to many of the transfer-payment programs of government. When private expenditures decline and national income thereby declines, the amount to be paid under these programs commonly increases. The unemployment insurance program provides a good illustration. As national income declines or fails to increase, the number of people unemployed increases and so does the duration of unemployment of particular workers. Their incomes drop as a result of being laid off or dismissed. The government unemployment payments prevent the decline from being as large as it would otherwise be; the partial protection of the unemployed helps to keep up aggregate expenditures.

The amount of reliance one is prepared to place on automatic devices to keep the economy operating at its proper level depends in part upon the theory held as to the effect of such devices and in part upon the severity of the departure of private and aggregate expenditures from their proper level. In the literature on this subject, many economists place little or no faith in the efficacy of the built-in features of tax and transfer devices; they advocate the use of sheer intelligence in public policy designed to provide the proper medicine as needed.[1]

---

[1] Professor Alvin Hansen is one who takes this view. See *Monetary Theory and Fiscal Policy* (New York: McGraw-Hill Book Co., 1949), p. 182.

Others, like the Committee for Economic Development, place large, but not exclusive, faith in automatic devices. The issue may seem artificial. How can anyone rationally oppose vaccination, for example, against a dread disease even though with vaccination one may nevertheless be liable to get a mild case? Likewise how can anyone rationally refuse to see a doctor if he does get the disease? Tax and transfer devices that work in the right direction are *per se* desirable on that account. Opposition to installing such devices appears equivalent to a doctor's opposing vaccination of children against smallpox on the grounds that if they do contract the disease, he can always treat them.

The effectiveness of the built-in flexibility of any actual tax-transfer system depends, as already pointed out, on the quantitative value of the expression $\triangle T/\triangle Y$. It also depends upon the theory believed to be appropriate to explain private expenditures. The same four theories discussed in Chapter 20 may again be employed.

By far the most popular position holds that any built-in flexibility of a tax-transfer system can at best only *dampen* fluctuations in gross national product. For example, suppose that private investment expenditures decline for several months for some spontaneous reason. With constant government expenditures and without any initial change in consumption expenditures, some people will find their incomes falling, especially the people who become unemployed. The decline in tax yields at the same time makes it easier for these people, because their tax bills decline and some receive financial assistance from the government. But because their after-tax, after-subsidy incomes are nevertheless smaller, they must curtail their consumption expenditures. They may curtail them less than they would if their total tax bills had remained unchanged, but curtail them they will. Hence built-in flexibility of tax devices is said only to dampen the change in private expenditures; it definitely does not tend to reverse the change and push private expenditures toward their higher previous levels.

The theory behind this view is the now familiar Simple Keynesian position. In Figure 22–1, the slope of the OT line measures the built-in flexibility of the tax-transfer system. If the slope is one, built-in flexibility is zero. If it is perpendicular for a range, the built-in flexibility within that range is 100 per cent. The line as drawn here assumes that the tax-transfer system is proportional. The level of net national product is found at OJ. Investment is then assumed to drop by the amount RS. With government expenditures remaining unchanged, the new $C + I + G$ line, shown by the line labelled $C_1 + I_1 + G_1$, drops by the same amount. Thus the new outcome shown as OH results not only in less investment but in less consump-

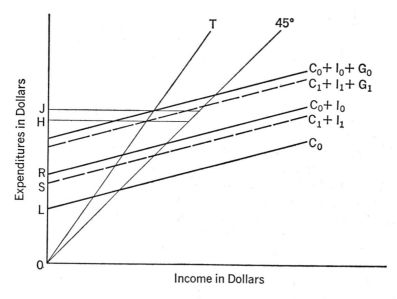

FIGURE 22–1

tion as well. One can see that if the slope of *OT* had been closer to that of the 45° line—smaller built-in flexibility—the outcome would have been a yet lower level of net national product. In other words, built-in flexibility keeps consumption expenditures from falling as much as they otherwise would, but it does not keep them from falling. Economists who hold to the Simple Keynesian point of view cannot very well place faith in built-in stabilizers. To them, such devices do not stabilize; they only dampen fluctuations.

Furthermore, the built-in flexibility of the tax system works as a handicap to the economy when underemployment already exists and recovery has begun. If the recovery comes about from a rise in investment, built-in flexibility keeps consumption expenditures from rising as rapidly as they would have if the tax-transfer system had little or no built-in flexibility. This observation can be shown graphically. Starting with some outcome, such as *OJ*, let the *C* + *I* line, and hence the *C* + *I* + *G* line, rise. It follows that the steeper is the slope of *OT* the larger must be the increase in investment to get the economy up to a given level. Again, it is easy to see why those who hold to the Simple Keynesian theory have little enthusiasm for built-in stabilizers.

The Full Keynesian point of view gives a different, a very different answer. Suppose as before that investment falls for some reason. There is immediately one adjustment; the fall in investment tends to reduce rates of interest. Out of the total money supply, less money is now needed for transaction purposes and hence more money finds its way into speculative balances. The fall in the rate of interest has the effect of cushioning the decline in investment. It falls less than it otherwise would. This adjustment occurs with or without built-in flexibility.

The reduction in net tax yields, however, results in a rising government deficit (or a decreasing surplus). If the budget had been approximately in balance before investment fell, the decline in tax yields with given government expenditures results in a deficit. The deficit, when not accompanied by an increase in the national debt, gives rise to an increase in the quantity of money. As explained in Chapter 20, such an increase leads to a yet greater fall in the rate of interest. In turn, this decline in interest rates pushes up investment along the now lower investment schedule. As investment rises, so does consumption via the consumption-function. Hence, and this is the important point, in the Full Keynesian system a recession tends to cure itself. It also cures itself more readily the greater is the built-in flexibility of the tax-transfer system. It is not true that built-in flexibility merely dampens changes in expenditures; it tends to reverse the movement of aggregate expenditures.

Under the Full Keynesian theory, in an economy already experiencing a depression and unduly low private expenditures, built-in flexibility acts as a drag on the recovery of the economy, but it does not prevent the recovery. With the government experiencing a deficit, private expenditures tend to rise. As they rise, tax yields increase too. Thus the deficit dwindles. But as long as the deficit continues, it acts as a stimulant which decreases in potency as the deficit grows smaller and smaller.

According to the quantity-of-money theory of private expenditures, built-in stabilizers of the tax-transfer type can be very effective indeed. Let us suppose again that investment tends to decline for some reason and that the government's budget is balanced before the decline begins. Now as private investment declines, tax yields also fall while government transfer payments increase. Hence a deficit comes into being, and furthermore it grows. But if the deficit is uncovered (no sale of debt to the public), the quantity of money is increased. Hence both investment and consumption expenditures tend to increase. They increase because as people find themselves with more money, they spend more. The conclusion follows that built-in flexibility is a potent type of stabilizer.

If this reasoning seems to resemble a sleight-of-hand trick or to be contrary to plain common sense, let us look at it from another point of view. If the government is having a deficit, all private people and business organizations are together experiencing an equal surplus.

The reason for this is obvious upon reflection. In a closed system, the sum of all deficits must equal the sum of all surpluses. Let us examine the position of a typical person. He is typical in two respects: he always spends upon current output a sum which is some constant fraction of all private expenditures; his income is also a constant fraction of national income. Now let us suppose his budget was in balance before the trouble began and also that the government's budget was in balance. Our typical person after the trouble starts finds that he is experiencing a surplus. The reason for this is that he among others initially curtailed his expenditures. That fact started the trouble. Now if his income were to remain constant, obviously he must experience a surplus. But it is not that easy. His income falls too, but *it always falls by less than do his expenditures.* The government now requires that he pay less tax so that his after-tax receipts, although declining, exceed his expenditures. The difference is the increase in his money holdings, which in turn reflect the government's uncovered deficit. Clearly the objective circumstances surrounding him will induce him to increase his expenditures.

The asset theory gives similar results although the steps involved are somewhat different. The details of the argument may be omitted. This theory, like the Full Keynesian and the quantity-of-money approach, implies that built-in flexibility tends to reverse and not merely to dampen downward or upward movements in private expenditures.

Shall we conclude, then, that built-in flexibility of the tax-transfer system is sufficient? The answer must be *no* on any of these theories. One need only recall that in a growing society, total expenditures upon current output must grow and at a certain rate. Part of this growth is ordinarily, but not always, taken care of by the growth in government expenditures themselves. All government expenditures, including the expenditures of state and local governments as well as the federal government, are usually larger one year than they were the previous year. In practice, private expenditures must increase as well. If the government's policies were neutral with respect to private expenditures, that is, if its policies tended neither to increase nor to decrease private expenditures from one year to the next, a sufficient increase in aggregate expenditures would occur only occasionally. For consistently correct levels of aggregate expenditures to be maintained, measures other than automatic devices are required.

Discretionary Measures

Discretionary measures refer to government acts tailored at the moment, so to speak, to compensate for undesired change in aggregate expenditures. They may take the form of altering the tax system, the transfer system, government expenditures on services and new things, government purchases and sales of old things, debt operations, and monetary policies. Attention will be confined to the first three measures mentioned.

Aggregate expenditures upon current output may rise too rapidly or not rapidly enough and on occasion may rise by just the right amount. The first step in discretionary action calls for a diagnosis. Will total expenditures rise, will they fall, or what?

This first step is especially troublesome; it calls for prediction of what will happen—i.e., it calls for a crystal ball that works. Now, sadly enough, no one has yet invented a workable crystal ball for economic affairs. Effective discretionary policies may be postponed while those in a position to initiate policies vacillate. In fact the danger is even greater. Policies may be executed based on predictions that total expenditures may rise too rapidly during the next three months when they will in fact be falling, or vice versa. In this event fiscal policies, insofar as they are effective, will tend to magnify the undesired variation in expenditures. Thus in 1948-1949 the Council of Economic Advisors proposed measures to fight inflation while in fact a recession was taking place. During the 1957-60 recession, Chairman Martin of the Federal Reserve System made speeches and testified before Congressional committees suggesting that private expenditures were too large and should be reduced. Immediately after World War II, many economists in this and other countries were predicting a large-scale depression and advocating measures to stimulate private and aggregate expenditures, when in fact aggregate expenditures increased much too rapidly. The general theme of central bank leadership in many countries has been for years that private expenditures either are increasing or are about to increase too rapidly. Occasionally, like a stopped clock, their predictions turn out to be correct. Some university economists, on the other hand, always see a recession just around the corner. There are others who always fear more inflation. The poor Congressmen who must pass legislation increasing or decreasing taxes become confused from listening to the conflicting voices of presumed experts and rely even more upon their own confused theories.

There is no easy solution for this muddle. Nor is there any occasion for despair, either. Thanks to the routine of a society, we do not wake up some morning to find the economy in a deep depression though it was in the throes of inflation when we went to sleep. An economy is not like an automobile that may be travelling at sixty miles per hour one minute and be wrapped around a telephone pole the next. The basic routine of social affairs provides the fundamental stability of economic life. Routine can change only slowly in relation to the speed by which proper compensatory actions can be introduced. In modern history, the underlying routines of society have been uprooted by wars and by revolution. Very infrequently have these routines been seriously undermined in any other manner.

This relatively comforting fact about economic societies suggests that one can project in the large what will happen from what has recently happened. Such projections will almost certainly be false in detail. But if, for example, the evidence accumulates that, over the past three months, business activity has been falling when account is taken of normal seasonal variations, it is fairly safe to conclude that it will either continue to fall or perhaps level out during the next three months. It is not safe to conclude that its level will return to what it had been three months ago of its own accord, or even worse, that it will rise of its own accord much too rapidly. Only rarely, however, have measures been introduced to compensate for declines in total expenditures as quickly as three months after a downward turning point. Indeed little has been done even after a few years have elapsed, as illustrated by the recession of 1957-1960.

In clear cases, there ought to be little question about whether stimulating or depressing measures are to be adopted. If five million people have been unemployed for many months, further vacillation based upon beliefs that private expenditures will somehow rise of their own accord seems foolhardy and even cruel. Refusal to take action can only be reasonably justified by the rejection of the goal of full employment. It would be refreshing, indeed, if those who advocate doing nothing or who favor repressive measures would state that they reject the goal of full employment. Rarely can a public official be found who is willing to announce such a stand clearly.

Likewise, clear cases of undue increases in aggregate expenditures require prompt anti-inflation medicine. Tax rates should be increased, transfer rates decreased, government purchases decreased, or all three. Politically none of these moves is likely to be popular. People object to increased taxes, for example, and it requires forceful leadership to persuade the Congress to take such action; politicians are allergic to voting for higher taxation, reflecting the widespread but mistaken theory that people are thereby injured.

In many periods in recent history, the evidence about the movement in aggregate expenditures is conflicting or, at least, ambiguous. Perhaps the level and the change in the level of private expenditures seem about right to some skilled observers but too low or too high to others. Rational fiscal policy in such circumstances requires first of all close impartial analysis of the evidence. Those capable of such analysis may or may not get a hearing. Those who have one medicine to sell are often more influential if only because they can appear definite and emphatic in their pronouncements. Thus economic spokesmen for labor organizations call for expansionary measures on almost any occasion regardless of the evidence. Economic spokesmen for conservative groups have another medicine for all circumstances— a reduction of government expenditures and of taxes, especially taxes falling on the high-income groups.

The machinery exists in the United States federal government to provide as expert an assessment of the evidence as is likely to be possible, given the state of knowledge, by fallible human beings. The Council of Economic Advisors, the Treasury, the Department of Commerce, the Federal Reserve Board and the Federal Reserve Banks, to mention some of the more important, have highly trained economic staffs to detect which way the economic wind is blowing.

The differences reported about their diagnoses may be genuine and often are traceable to differences in goals laid down as the proper ones to achieve. Central banks, for example, exhibit a strong bias against inflation. They drag their feet when stimulating measures are indicated. Their economic advisers meanwhile are more likely to see an inflation around the corner than a recession, reflecting the "line" laid down by the agency. Diagnosis becomes intermingled with value judgments, with general confusion as the product. Central banks are by no means the only sinners in this connection. Treasuries are apt to insist on high taxes even during periods of recession; deficits continue to be viewed as contrary to sound morality in many countries. This bias worked serious harm during the 1930's in the United States and in Western Europe. Since World War II, however, only occasionally has this emphasis been harmful. Political objections to heavy taxation have been a major source of trouble at all levels of government in the United States since 1945.

The manipulation of tax rates, transfer rates, and government expenditures at frequent intervals to stabilize the economy are not as yet feasible in any Western country. Suggestions will be made as to how more appropriate policies might be devised.

Appraisal of Discretionary Policies

Of the discretionary measures under consideration—namely a change in government expenditures, taxes, and transfers—government expenditures have the advantage of being direct and of definite impact. But there are two disadvantages and both are formidable.

A program calling for a reduction of government expenditures to counter an inflation is difficult to install. It means that some government programs must be given up. If the programs were justified on their merits, the cost of achieving economic stability by this device comes rather high. To cut the defense program to fight an inflation implies that the program was not very useful to the country in the first place. Or if it was useful, the country is now asked to live dangerously in order to prevent inflation. Likewise to increase government expenditures to counteract a recession suggests that the programs are presumably not justified on their merits and should be dropped when better times return. Thus one kind of waste—the waste of unemployment—can be curtailed only by adopting programs entailing another kind of waste. Such hard choices may have to be made, but obviously should not be if better alternatives are open.

The other disadvantage of using government expenditures as counter-cyclical measures concerns timing. Only rarely is it feasible to get a large government expenditures program in operation quickly. A year is about the minimum time and by the end of a year the economy may already have recovered. A policy of curtailing existing programs can be achieved somewhat faster, depending upon the type of program. In any case, apart from the issue of the justification of government programs on their merits, a stabilizing policy that relies upon the variation in government expenditures as a counter-cyclical device is crude and clumsy.

Consideration of either or both of these disadvantages has led many thinkers to stress the use of taxes and transfer programs. They have difficulties also, but these are not as formidable.

A tax reduction without any change in government expenditures is definitely stimulating for reasons similar to those discussed in connection with the reduction in tax yields as a result of built-in flexibility, but more so. A government might forgive a portion of taxes already paid and return these sums promptly to the former taxpayers. Such a measure would put money into people's hands as quickly as the government could send out the refund checks. A device which requires a longer time to take effect is a reduction of existing tax rates. Recalling the remarks in Chapter 21 about how a government deficit implies an equal private surplus, such a measure would make the private surplus larger and thus be stimulating. Its stimulating effects operate by providing people with more money to spend (or more after-tax income).

To some extent, altering taxes either up or down as a compensatory device has difficulties similar to the first one mentioned for government expenditures. A tax program is designed to achieve effects other than providing revenue. A progressive income tax, for example, changes the after-tax pattern of income distribution. To alter the exemptions and tax rates will change the amounts to be paid by various income groups. Disputes then arise about the desirability of the new pattern of after-tax income distribution.

In the case of excise taxes, the "taxpayer" is difficult to identify because the tax is partly shifted. When the tax is removed, various prices must become realigned. If the tax later is to be restored, the painful process of getting prices into their proper relation must again be undergone. Excise taxes are for this reason poor candidates for manipulation from the point of view of counter-cyclical measures.

An extreme case of a tax whose change interferes with other objectives is the death tax. To change this tax in any one year gives large gains to the heirs of people who happen to die in that year and defeats the presumed objective of the tax to erode economic plutocracy.

A reasonably good candidate for manipulation is the Federal Individual Income Tax. As this tax is administered, the amounts due are withheld at the first bracket rate. A simple measure calls for changing the first bracket rate, leaving other bracket rates alone. To stimulate private spending, the entire tax for a period of, say, three months could be forgiven. Collection at the source then ceases for the period. Then if such a stimulus is sufficient, the taxpayer is instructed to compile his final tax return with the first bracket rate at three-quarters of the regular rate.

There are some difficulties in using a parallel measure to combat inflation. Because the second bracket is only two points above the first, a rise in rates by two points would turn the first and second brackets into a single bracket. Although there is nothing inherently wrong about such a move, a two-point rise in the first bracket might not be sufficient to curtail private expenditures sufficiently. This difficulty could be overcome by raising bracket rates all along the line.

To minimize political squabbles involving rate changes among brackets, the best procedure might be to redesign the income tax on a long-run basis by providing that the first bracket should normally be, say, 20 per cent but with a provision that the first bracket may be varied up or down by five percentage points. For this plan to work, the Treasury or the President must be given the power to alter the first bracket rates within this range. However, the Congress has been highly reluctant to delegate its tax responsibilities in the past, although it has done so in a few cases, such as permitting variations in the rates of import duties. There would be strong Congressional opposition to the proposal; yet for quick and powerful results, such a plan recommends itself highly. No serious effort has yet been made to install such a tax program.[2]

Variations in transfer payments are subject to qualifications similar to those involved in taxation. To pay more to certain groups who are being subsidized merely as a kind of gesture because of their political potency has little justification. Once these groups get more money from the Treasury, they will strongly resist any future retrenchment. The public becomes saddled with the greater costs of such programs indefinitely.

An obvious choice is the unemployment program, a feature of the social security system. There is the difficulty that the program is administered by the states under state laws. Action at the federal level requires implementary legislation in the fifty states to become effective. However, if unemployment is permitted to develop, there is a strong social obligation to prevent needless poverty. In this particular case, the presumed objective of the program and the achievement of the goal of full employment are strictly compatible. The program under present law is based on an appeal to insurance principles and it is not designed to handle large-scale and persistent unemployment.[3] Fortunately this difficulty can be overcome by providing for supplementary payments to the unemployed out of general funds.

Some Suggestions for Improvement

Discretionary policies are essential for orderly economic life. Automatic measures are needed too. It is a mistake to treat this choice as a competitive one. Automatic stabilizers help the economy to correct its own mistakes. A thermostat is a useful gadget even if the best it can do is to restrict the temperature to a range of five degrees. A thermostat that can be designed to confine the temperature range to four degrees would be even better.

The federal tax and transfer system may need to be reformed to make it more effective as an automatic stabilizer. There are other goals of the tax system, such as fairness, equity, and adequacy of yield which must also be kept in mind. Happily, many changes that would achieve greater built-in flexibility would help to attain these other goals also.

---

[2] The Council of Economic Advisors has the responsibility for making recommendations to counter undesired economic fluctuations and presumably should be the federal agency to provide the leadership in proposing such a plan.

[3] For a discussion of the program, see chap. 17.

FEDERAL INCOME TAX. This tax could be made more of an automatic stabilizer by some simple and some drastic changes.

The value of the expression $\triangle T/\triangle Y$, a measure of built-in flexibility, has been shown by Joseph Pechman to depend on the built-in flexibility of the tax base and upon the rate structure.[4] He found that the built-in flexibility of the income tax base is about 65 per cent. This means that if personal income (adjusted gross income) rises by $1 billion, the portion of the increase reportable on tax returns is about $650 million. The income tax would have greater power to promote stability if personal income and reportable income were closer together. They could be moved closer together if income for tax purposes were defined more generally; if, in other words, less income escaped the tax net. Several reforms suggest themselves:

1. Reduce evasion. If people persistently underreport their taxable income, to that extent a change in personal income leads to a smaller change in reportable income. Clearly this reform is desirable on other grounds, but it is expensive and difficult to implement.

2. Install averaging of the cumulative type. This reform, also desirable on other grounds, would substantially improve the built-in flexibility of the income tax during downswings.

3. Narrow the income brackets, especially for small taxable incomes. Such a reform would induce a larger change in tax liability for a given change in personal income because the tax becomes more progressive in the range where a large percentage of reportable income is found. The proposal has some weaknesses on administrative grounds.

4. Eliminate present preferred treatment of special types of income. Among the more important of these are interest on state and local securities, unrealized capital gains and losses, implicit income from owner-occupied houses, fringe benefits, and expense-account consumption expenditures. Such reforms are also desirable on grounds of fairness and equity.

FEDERAL EXCISE TAXES. Insofar as these taxes are to be used as a permanent feature of the tax system, they could be made more sensitive by shifting them from specific to ad valorem bases. A specific tax is sensitive to changes in the quantities produced (or sold). An ad valorem tax is sensitive to both quantity and price; during the periods of excessive private spending, the government shares in any price rise as well as in any quantity increase. During periods of declining spending, the government's revenue is reduced by any price concessions as well as by quantity reductions. A general shift to ad valorem taxation of commodities is clearly desirable on grounds of

---

[4] See reference to Pechman's article in the Suggested Readings at the end of Part IV.

increasing built-in flexibility and is usually not objectionable on other grounds.

TRANSFER PROGRAMS. In general, these programs can be made more responsive to changing expenditures by the greater use of formula as opposed to fixed-sum methods of determining the size of the subsidy. A radical move calls for the elimination of all programs presently based upon either a partial means-test, for example having been unemployed two weeks, or those based upon presumed need, such as old-age and survivors insurance, in favor of a systematic progressive subsidy-tax system based upon size of income. In such a system, people whose incomes fall below the socially established minimum would be subsidized. The amount of the subsidy is to increase as income decreases. Such a system could be designed to be highly sensitive. Incipient recessions would be countered by immediately falling tax receipts as income fell and by rising subsidy payments. The program would also work in reverse as well. The appraisal of such a scheme on all counts has too many further complications to be pursued here.

The Congress and the Treasury have not as yet been persuaded to re-examine our tax-transfer devices in this country systematically from the point of view of promoting built-in flexibility. What built-in flexibility there is has arisen almost accidentally.

Fiscal measures to compensate for undesired variation in aggregate expenditures by no means exhaust the armory of weapons available to governments. The chief agency in charge of guiding the economy has historically been the central bank. Its role will be discussed in connection with the management of the debt.

23

Public Debt and Debt Management

Governments are typically in debt. The United States, Canada, the United Kingdom, Australia, and New Zealand are, on a per capita basis, among the large-debt countries of the world. The governments of poor countries ordinarily have small per capita debts. On an absolute basis, the United States federal debt exceeds the combined public debts of all national governments of the world today.

Why a government has a debt of any size can be explained only in terms of its past history. The size of the public debt at any date means that in earlier periods the government created and sold debt. In 1914, the U. S. federal debt was negligible in size. The present large federal debt arose during World War I, the Great Depression, and World War II. Much the same pattern holds true of the other English-speaking countries.[1]

The United States federal *gross* debt stood at about $64 billion in 1941 and rose to about $279 billion by December, 1945, after the end of World War II. It moved down to a low of about $257 billion in 1950, and has since that time risen to about $291 billion (December, 1959).

The federal gross debt figure is the figure talked about in the Congress and reported as the federal debt in the newspapers and in

[1] Countries with histories of dictatorship, curiously enough, usually have small national debts. Large national debts come into being during wartime. In World Wars I and II, the powerful countries governed by antidemocratic leadership, with the exception of the U.S.S.R. in World War II, were defeated. Defeat in turn undermined the determination to provide an orderly financial setting. Tax yields were inadequate, government expenditures continued high, controls over prices broke down, and inflation resulted. The debt, being fixed in money terms, became relatively smaller and sometimes disappeared.

current periodicals. Actually, it is a figure of little economic significance. The gross debt includes items owed by the government to itself. An individual who carried about IOU's he had made out to himself and who counted these notes as debt might be considered eccentric. Governments do just this. Given the many agencies of a national government, the practice is at least understandable. It remains misleading to count as debt, obligations payable by the government to itself. The significant concept is what may be called the *net debt.* We define the net debt of a government as the total of its obligations owed to others. Any national debt held by a government department or agency is called *duplicating debt,* and is to be deducted from reported gross debt data to ascertain the size of the net debt.

In Table 23–1, figures are given for the gross debt, the duplicating

TABLE 23–1

GROSS, DUPLICATING, AND NET FEDERAL DEBT
FOR SELECTED YEARS

(billions of dollars)

End of Calendar Year	Gross Debt	Duplicating Debt	Net Debt
1941	64.3	11.9	52.4
1945	278.7	51.3	227.4
1947	257.0	57.0	200.0
1951	259.5	66.1	193.4
1953	275.2	74.2	201.0
1955	280.8	76.5	204.3
1957	275.0	79.4	195.6
1958	283.0	80.7	202.3
1959	290.9	80.3	210.6

Source: U. S. Treasury Bulletin

debt, and the net debt of the U. S. federal government for selected years. The gross debt is a legal concept: it means the direct obligations of the federal treasury in the form of legal instruments. It does not include debts in the form of unpaid bills. The duplicating debt consists of items defined as that part of the gross debt held by government agencies. These agencies are mainly the Social Security Trust Fund and the Federal Reserve banks. The Trust Fund item is mainly a bookkeeping entry. The holdings of the Federal Reserve banks are actual legal instruments which they could sell if their policies called for such action.

Actually, of the approximately $26 billion of federal obligations held by the Federal Reserve banks, no more than $5 billion at the

outside would ever be needed for open-market operations. Some of
the overstatement of the federal debt could be simply corrected by
wiping out $20 billion of this "debt." To continue the esthetic fic-
tion that the balance sheet for the Federal Reserve banks must balance, the Treasury could provide a bookkeeping entry called, for
example, "Certificates due to the Federal Reserve banks—$20 bil-
lion." No doubt, many people would feel relieved to discover that
the federal debt had declined by $20 billion in this painless manner.

The inclusion of the Federal Reserve banks in the class of government agencies, and hence the classification of their federal debt
holdings as duplicating debt, may be disputed. Legally, the Federal
Reserve banks are owned by the member banks, not by the U. S.
Treasury. Actually, this ownership has little significance. The Federal Reserve banks, along with the policy-making body, the Board
of Governors of the Federal Reserve System, are assigned the responsibility of operating the banking and monetary system. They are
federal instrumentalities. Debt owned by them has no net interest
cost to the Treasury; the interest payments are in lieu of appropriations which, incidentally, are generous.

The federal net debt, it may be emphasized, is much smaller than
than the gross debt. While the gross debt stood at about $291 billion
in December, 1959, the net debt was about $211 billion; hence the
gross debt overstates the correct debt figure by about 38 per cent.

Furthermore, the gross debt and the net debt change differently
through time. As may be observed from the table, the gross debt
rose from $257 billion in December, 1947, to $291 billion in December, 1959, an increase of $34 billion. Between the same dates, the
net debt increased by $10.6 billion. All of the increase in the net
debt occurred from 1957 to 1959. The duplicating debt usually
increases year after year, reflecting mainly the surpluses in the Social
Security accounts. It is less likely that this trend will continue during
the next decade, because these "funds" now operate closer to a pay-
as-you-go accounting basis than in the past.

A similar pattern may be found in many countries. Various accounting funds have been established in the national governments and
these record "surpluses," by being assigned revenues larger than their
expenditures. The cumulative difference is recorded as government
debt holdings. In addition, it is the universal custom of central banks
to show government debt among their assets. In a few countries,
practically all of the debt is located in the central bank, and the net
debt is close to zero. This case reflects the absence of a market for
government debt among private groups; Chile is an illustration. It is
a mistake to suppose that a government can always finance itself, if

it must, by borrowing. In some countries no market may exist for government debt and any money not obtained by taxation must be created for the government by its central bank.

Kinds of Public Debt

Public debts, like ladies' hats, come in various styles. One major classification consists of the portion of debt that is marketable and the portion that is not. A marketable government bond permits an owner to sell it to anyone who wishes to buy. Nonmarketable debt permits the owner to sell or redeem it only by turning it back to the government that issued it. The familiar "E" Savings Bonds are non-marketable U. S. federal debt. They also have the characteristic that the price a holder can obtain for his bond is announced in advance on the bond itself. Such bonds are similar to, but not identical with, savings accounts. The U. S. federal government has in the past issued several varieties of nonmarketable debt instruments.

Marketable debt may have one price today and another tomorrow. Such pieces of paper are bought and sold in much the same manner as are corporate shares of stock. Usually, but not always, bonds of governments are traded in organized markets. In the United States, the market for federal debt is located in the financial district of downtown New York. In Great Britain, government debt, except for short-term instruments, is bought and sold on the London Stock Exchange.

Another feature of government debt is what is called its "maturity distribution." A 20-year bond issued yesterday has a 20-year maturity minus one day. After it has been outstanding five years, it has a 15-year maturity. Debt gets younger as it gets older! The longer a bond has been outstanding, the fewer are the number of years it has to live. Maturity-age would be like human age if we were to say that a newborn baby has seventy years to "mature," that is, to die. A child of six then has a maturity of 64 years.

The limited life of debt results in what is called *debt turnover.* When $51 billion of outstanding marketable debt is due within one year, the Treasury must find $51 billion to pay off present holders of this debt. It obtains the wherewithal by selling new debt, usually to the very same people and organizations. Actually money need not change hands. Holders of old debt that is about to mature pay for new debt with the old debt. This turnover process goes on and on, providing news stories for financial reporters and a modest profit for government-security dealers.

The average maturity of an outstanding debt depends upon the number of years each issue has yet to run, the size of each issue, and the maturity and size of new issues. To use an example, a college has, let us suppose, a population of 1,000 students, consisting of 280 freshmen, 260 sophomores, 240 juniors, and 220 seniors. The average "maturity" of the student population is 2.6 years at the beginning of the school year, when "maturity" means the number of years to graduation.[2] If the college population is kept constant by always enrolling 280 freshmen, and if the size of each class remains unchanged, the average "maturity" will remain unchanged too, if computed at the same date each year. If, however, the college administration should decide to enroll only 200 freshmen one year and to accept 80 new transfer students as juniors, the average "maturity" of the student body would shrink.

In debt management, the same observation holds. To keep the average maturity constant, debt that is "graduating"—just coming due—must be replaced by issues having as many years to live as did the maturing debt originally, when the total debt is constant. The maturity of debt has occasioned much concern in official management decisions, especially in recent years. Whether the average life expectancy of debt matters significantly will be discussed presently.

Social Issues Involved in Public Debt

The size and composition of a national debt is a fact, just as the Atlantic Ocean is a fact. There is little point in raising the question as to whether the debt is too large or too small, any more than there is a point in asking whether the Atlantic Ocean is too large or too small. The issues at stake are questions of a different type: Shall the national debt be increased? Reduced? Shall 100-year bonds be issued? Shall more Treasury bills be offered for sale? The issues that matter are those that concern what to do or what not to do. Long debates have occurred as to whether in some abstract sense large public debts are good or bad for society. Such debates have almost no relevance to any social decisions. Having decided that large public debts are bad, let us suppose, then what follows? One has yet to decide how a public debt may be reduced and whether the proposed method has good or bad effects. Shall the public debt be increased? Obviously it should not be increased if the effects of doing so are

---

[2] The average maturity, 2.6, is computed as follows:

$$\frac{280 \times 4 + 260 \times 3 + 240 \times 2 + 220 \times 1}{1000} = 2.6$$

contrary to the public interest. To ascertain whether such a policy is or is not in accord with the public interest, the economic effects of increasing the public debt must first be ascertained.

The important question is what to do and what not to do.

The Effects of Changing the Size of the Public Debt

Confining our attention to national domestic debts, what difference does it make if a national debt is increased or reduced? The answer to this question breaks down into two parts: the effects of borrowing or repaying upon the government itself and the effects upon the general public.

If a government borrows, that is, sells debt, one effect is to increase the government's checking account. If money is the sole object of government borrowing, a successful issue means that the Treasury gets the amount of money needed. Treasury officials as well as financial observers commonly stress this test. If the Treasury announces that it intends to sell $3 billion of Treasury notes during the next twelve days, and actually succeeds in selling only $2½ billion, there is gloom in the Treasury and much clucking of tongues by financial reporters of the New York Times and the Wall Street Journal. The issue is called a "failure." Success in this context means selling the goods—the Treasury notes—at the announced price.

The other effect on the issuing government of selling debt is the interest expense it thereby incurs. If another $1 billion of debt is added to the outstanding amount and the rate of interest is 3 per cent, $30 million of annual interest is added to the total interest bill. As the interest expense mounts, the government adds to its future budget problem. Either other programs must be curtailed or taxes must be increased or both, as compared with what would be necessary in the absence of the additional interest commitment.

To a government, then, the main effects of selling debt consist of the amount of money it obtains and the amount of future interest expense it incurs.

The effects of selling debt on the entire economy are more complicated. To sell pieces of paper called government debt, buyers must be found. These buyers, in the United States, consist of financial organizations (such as insurance companies, mutual savings banks, commercial banks), business corporations, foreign governments and their central banks, and individuals. The government must induce investors to buy the debt just as automobile companies must induce the motoring public to buy new cars. To induce people to buy, the government must make its pieces of paper attractive; it must price them low enough to persuade an insurance company, a bank, or a business corporation that it is good business to acquire the new debt. Otherwise insurance company executives, bank presidents, or corporation treasurers will buy other merchandise—perhaps the debts of local governments or of other business corporations, or mortgages on the homes being purchased by newly married couples.

The effect of an official offering to sell more government debt is always *depressing* with respect to private expenditures. Sometimes one reads or hears the statement that government borrowing stimulates the economy. This point of view is misleading. Government borrowing depresses private expenditures; it cannot be stimulating.

The reason is easy to understand. If a government offers to sell anything, including debt, it is absorbing money formerly held by private groups. In the process of acquiring the money, it must lower the price of debt of any given description, as illustrated in Figure 23–1. The horizontal axis shows the amounts of some kind of government debt, say a 10-year coupon bond, issued in $100,000 denominations, paying a coupon return of 3 per cent. This means that an owner of the bond will receive $3,000 per year for nine years and $103,000 in the tenth year. Price (not interest rates) is measured along the vertical axis. The demand schedule to hold debt of this kind is shown by the line DD'. If there is no new sale of government debt, the price in the market is $O'P$, which is, say, $101,000 per unit. To persuade people to buy a new debt offering of the quantity $O'Z$, the price must fall to RZ, a decline of $1,000. Now the price of this debt becomes $100,000 per unit—it happens to be sold at par. The government obtains $O'VRZ$ for the debt sold.

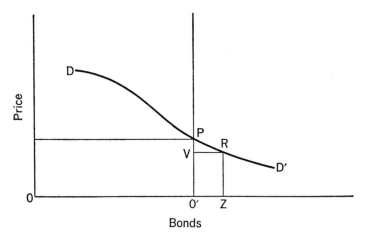

FIGURE 23–1

The depressing effect of this operation on private expenditures may be discovered by asking what the buyer, say an insurance company, would have done with its money had it not purchased the government debt. The insurance company executives were debating, perhaps, whether to push aggressively into the business of acquiring mortgages on new houses being built in the rapidly expanding regions of the country. According to their best calculations, the company could buy mortgages that would carry a rate of interest of 7 per cent. The extra costs of taking on this business are calculated to be about 2 per cent, giving a prospective net return on their money of 5 per cent. But the government 10-year bonds priced at $100,000, giving a rate of interest of 4 per cent, are regarded as equally attractive. The bonds are easy to buy and sell, and look better on the balance sheet than do mortgages. When the new issue of government bonds is announced, the insurance company buys several million dollars worth *instead* of financing the buying of new houses. Hence people who wish to buy houses have lost a potential market for their mortgages. Builders feel the pinch too, because they cannot sell as many new houses at the price of $20,000 as planned. They must construct less expensive or fewer houses and take a smaller profit on their business. The sale of government bonds on Wall Street places a financial squeeze on Main Street.

What if the new government bonds are sold to commercial banks? Some observers call such an operation inflationary because the banks may create money and hence stimulate expenditures. But this conclusion is also misleading. If banks happen to buy new government bonds, the effect on private expenditures remains depressing.

In the kind of monetary system found in advanced industrial countries in the world today, banks are the crucial institutions because the checking accounts provided by them are the main kind of money used. Bank operations create and destroy this money, as may be seen by taking a hypothetical bank located, say, in Kalamazoo, Michigan, whose balance sheet is represented by Table 23–2.

If the bank makes a loan of $50,000 to the Good Papermaking Company, item (2) on the balance sheet increases by $50,000 and item (7) increases by $50,000. The Good Papermaking Company will spend some portion or all of this money, resulting in a shift of ownership of deposits. Yet item (7) is money, and $50,000 has been *created* by the loan agreement between the bank and the company. Similarly, if the Extra-Sheer Lingerie Shoppe pays off its debt of $5,000 to the bank, item (2) declines by $5,000 and item (7) also declines by $5,000. By this transaction, $5,000 of money has been *destroyed*.

TABLE 23–2

THE SECOND NATIONAL BANK OF KALAMAZOO
(STATEMENT OF CONDITION AS OF JANUARY 1, 1960)

Assets		Liabilities	
1. Cash Items		6. Demand deposits of in-	
a) Deposit with F. R.		dividuals	$ 6,000,000
Bank	$ 5,000,000	7. Demand deposits of busi-	
b) Till Money	$ 100,000	ness corporations	$18,000,000
2. Loans	$15,000,000	8. Demand deposits of U. S.	
3. U. S. Gov't. Securities	$ 4,000,000	Treasury	0
4. Other Investments	$ 5,000,000	9. Other Demand Liabilities	0
5. Bank premises and equip-		10. Capital and surplus	
ment	$ 1,000,000	accounts	$ 6,100,000

The power of one bank to create money is limited by its actual reserves, by legal reserve requirements, and by the fact that as it increases demand deposits, it tends to lose reserves to other banks. We shall ignore the last factor because our bank is assumed to be typical of all banks. Typical means that customers by writing checks in favor of people having accounts at other banks cause our bank to lose a part of its cash—its deposit with the Chicago Federal Reserve Bank—to other banks. But our bank gets back an equal sum from the clearing of checks received by its customers written on other banks. The restriction on its power to create money is the size of its reserves, item (1*a*), and the legally required reserve ratio of, we assume, 20 per cent.[3]

Let us examine the theory that sale of federal debt to banks is stimulating or inflationary. Suppose the Kalamazoo bank subscribes to $1 million worth of ten-year 3 per cent federal bonds which the Treasury is offering for sale. It pays for them by providing the Treasury with a demand deposit of $1 million, item (8). At this stage, the bank now has smaller excess reserves by $200,000 ($1,000,000 × .20). Hence it can create less money for others as a result of buying the securities.

Not only has the bank's power to create money for private groups been curtailed, but the very fact that the bank's officers chose to buy these government securities depresses private expenditures. The bank could have bought old ten-year federal bonds; it did not have to wait for the Secretary of the Treasury to offer new ten-year bonds in order

---

[3] Actual reserve ratios may be varied, and also may differ by class of bank. To find actual required reserve ratios, consult the *Federal Reserve Bulletin*.

to acquire more federal bonds. The bank presumably bought the new bonds because they were more attractive to buy; the lower price persuaded the bank to buy the bonds. In turn, this decision means that alternatives were rejected, such as buying municipal bonds, corporate bonds, making term-loans to local businesses, or acquiring insured F.H.A. mortgages. Our bank's demands for the securities of private agencies fall because the Treasury offered the new bonds for sale at a more attractive price.

Sale of government debt to commercial banks or to any private agency is a restrictive measure; it is not and cannot be stimulating. The belief that the sale of government debt may be stimulating has developed apparently as a result of attributing to the sale of debt effects which are in fact the effects of expenditures and revenues. When the Treasury, having sold debt, finds its newly acquired money disappearing because government expenditures exceed tax collections, privately owned money increases. Thus, in the case of our Kalamazoo bank, the deposit obtained by the Treasury will decline as the deficit continues.[4] Private money holdings thereby increase. *But it is the deficit that increases private money holdings, not the sale of debt.*

A second main effect of selling debt is the added interest income provided to private groups who hold government debt. This effect is just the reverse of the effect already mentioned on the government. One kind of income, interest income, increases. This income is not a gain arising from the management of resources, such as holding down a job in a factory; it is a contractual form of transfer income. The significance of interest income arising from the national debt is discussed in Chapter 24.

From the point of view of a government, the effects of selling and buying (retiring) its own debt are, then, to obtain cash or to give up cash and to increase or reduce its future interest commitment. From the point of view of the public at large, the effects are just the reverse.

Yet this symmetry can be misleading. A national government can obtain any amount of money it needs by suitable arrangements with its central bank. A government does not need to sell its debt to

---

[4] In the United States, the U. S. Treasury holds accounts with individual commercial banks, called Treasury Tax and Loan Accounts. In selling debt, the Treasury agrees not to use the account immediately, and furthermore it gives banks advance notice when the account will be withdrawn. The Treasury ordinarily spends by writing checks payable at the Federal Reserve banks. Commercial bank deposits are used as averaging devices and to prevent abrupt changes in bank reserves. This practice is not typical; in most countries, national governments hold checking facilities only with the central bank.

obtain money. The methods of creating money for government account vary from country to country, but the fundamentals are the same. Some type of government asset is turned over to the central bank. In return the central bank provides a checking account or currency for the government. The asset may be only a statement that the government owes the central bank a sum of money; it may consist of actual debt instruments; it may also be government-created currency. The important point is that the government obtains money without reducing the amount of money owned by the public. In every major war, belligerent governments obtained substantial amounts of money by this process.[5] But this procedure is not and need not be confined to war periods.

For a national government to sell debt merely to get money makes little economic sense. With an efficient money-creating mechanism under its thumb, a national government does not need to tax or to sell debt if its sole purpose is to obtain money. Thus the justification for selling debt is to be found in the effects of such sales upon the economy. As already pointed out, sale of debt is depressing and government reduction of its debt is stimulating.

The following maxims may then be laid down:

1. *The government should increase the net debt only if it wishes to depress private expenditures.*

2. *It should reduce the net debt only if it wishes to stimulate private expenditures.*

These are fundamental principles to guide those in charge of debt management. Failure to heed these principles has been and continues to be a major deficiency of the financial policies of the United States, Canada, Australia, Great Britain, and indeed of almost all countries.

Ownership of U. S. Government Securities

In the United States, the Treasury provides detailed information, using a survey technique, of the ownership of U. S. Government securities. Similar detailed data are rarely found in other countries. In Great Britain, for example, economists and financial experts must

---

[5] During World War II, the U. S. government's huge excess of expenditures over tax receipts was accomplished by having both commercial banks and the Federal Reserve banks create money in its favor, as well as by selling debt to financial intermediaries, business corporations, and individuals. Sale of debt to commercial banks during this period had almost a zero depressing effect because banks were permitted access to unlimited reserves. They could buy government debt without having to reduce their holdings of other assets. The large inflation potential was kept from breaking out by specific controls over materials, manpower, and prices. After the war, the potential wore itself out by economic growth and by price inflation.

make guesses even about the size of what corresponds to the net debt figures shown for the United States in Table 23–3; officially prepared breakdowns by ownership class are not provided.

The data in Table 23–3 are given for year-end dates; the series is monthly and current data may be found by consulting the *Federal Reserve Bulletin* or the *Treasury Bulletin.*

TABLE 23–3

OWNERSHIP OF U. S. FEDERAL SECURITIES, DIRECT
AND FULLY GUARANTEED—SELECTED DATES

(billions of dollars)

Date	Net Debt	Com. Banks	Mut. Sav. Banks	Insur. Cos.	Other Corps.	State & Local Gov'ts.	Indi- viduals	Misc. Investors
Dec. 1951	193.4	61.6	9.8	16.5	20.7	9.6	64.6	10.6
		(31.8)	(5.1)	(8.5)	(10.7)	(5.0)	(33.4)	(5.5)
Dec. 1953	201.0	63.7	9.2	15.9	21.5	12.7	64.8	13.2
		(31.7)	(4.5)	(7.9)	(10.7)	(6.3)	(32.2)	(6.6)
Dec. 1955	204.3	62.0	8.5	14.6	23.5	15.1	65.0	15.6
		(30.3)	(4.2)	(7.1)	(11.5)	(7.4)	(31.8)	(7.6)
Dec. 1957	195.6	59.5	7.6	12.5	18.6	17.0	63.7	16.5
		(30.4)	(3.9)	(6.4)	(9.5)	(8.7)	(32.6)	(8.4)
Dec. 1959	210.7	59.8	6.9	12.3	23.5	17.5	71.9	21.8
		(28.4)	(3.3)	(5.8)	(11.2)	(8.3)	(34.1)	(10.3)

Source: U. S. Treasury Bulletin.

Figures in parentheses are percentages of the total net debt.

Several facts of interest are revealed by these data. The net debt has over the eight-year period increased by $17.3 billion or on the average of $2.16 billion per year. No trend may be projected from these data because the actual change reflects government policies, which may change with a change in the political complexion of the Congress and of the Administration. The large increases during this period have occurred during recessions, and effective measures to shorten and reduce their amplitude would reduce the occasion for debt increases of substantial amounts.

Of the details of debt ownership, attention is directed to several developments. In terms of absolute amount, commercial bank hold-ings have changed little over the eight-year period. In percentage of the net debt, commercial bank holdings have declined from 31.8 to

28.4 per cent over the period. Both in terms of dollar amounts and in percentage held, mutual savings banks and insurance companies had smaller holdings in 1959 than in 1951. The two classes of holders that in percentage terms have grown significantly are state and local governments and the catch-all class, miscellaneous. Note, however, that individuals hold a substantial fraction of the net debt, and both in dollar amounts and in percentage their holdings have increased.

The distribution of holdings of the federal debt depends upon several factors. Of major importance is the distribution found at any starting date. Unless one is prepared to retreat indefinitely into the past, some initial distribution must be taken as unexplained. Given any starting date, the distribution found at that time will tend to persist. Owners continue to own mainly what they began by owning.

The changes in ownership depend mainly upon the attractiveness of federal debt as compared with other assets. These other assets consist of money and other types of securities, in part because the financial organizations holding government debt are organizations with large funds to invest. The classes of other corporations, state and local governments, and individuals may to some extent treat real things as opposed to claims as alternatives. To push out more federal debt, the Treasury must make the securities palatable to some groups, and the kind of debt issued will automatically select the class of buyer. Short-term Treasury bills in large denominations have little appeal to individuals and 40-year bonds have little appeal to commercial banks. A policy, for example, of concentrating all of the debt in maturities of greater than 20 years might after a period of time reduce the holdings of commercial banks and business corporations to a small percentage of the debt and greatly increase the percentage held by individuals, insurance companies, and mutual savings banks. The appeal of such debt would come almost entirely from its yield because its liquidity would be even less than that of many classes of private debt. Actually such a policy would probably be drastically deflationary unless accompanied by a decrease in the net debt and an increase in the quantity of money.

Debt Composition

As already mentioned, the debt of a national government consists of a variety of instruments. Debt forms vary by maturity, marketability, denomination, tax-status, callable features, conversion rights, coupon rates, and other features. The British government has a type of savings bond outstanding that has a guaranteed redemption value but pays the interest in large amounts to a few holders chosen by lottery. The British and the French governments have outstanding *perpetuities,* which are promises to pay a given amount of money per year indefinitely. Perpetuities are not used by the U. S. federal government.

The costs of debt to a government are the interest payments and the administrative expenses, or "paper work." In general, the larger the denomination of a debt form, the less is the paper work expense per dollar of debt. A million dollar denomination costs the same to print as a thousand dollar denomination. A large denomination bond also entails less bookkeeping work per dollar than a small one. To service 1000 creditors who hold $100,000 worth of debt is likely to cost 1000 times as much as to service one creditor holding $100,000 of debt in one form and denomination.

The principles involved in this connection are duplicated in ordinary merchandising. For the same quantity of apples, it is cheaper to sell them by the carload than at a stand to passers-by. In financial affairs, a large corporation can borrow $250,000 at a lower cost than can ten small corporations each borrowing $25,000, even if there is no difference in credit standing. The lender must investigate ten companies instead of one and make ten loan agreements instead of one. In government finance, there are substantial economies of scale.

The federal government has one large retail debt program in the form of Savings Bonds. These have been issued in small denominations. The $47.6 billion (April, 1960) of these bonds outstanding consists of billions of pieces of paper. A large staff does nothing but process this paper as it is issued and redeemed. Whether this expensive method of handling debt is justified has not as yet been given serious attention in the Congress. Actually, the people who want to hold a Savings Bond type of asset can readily do so by acquiring a savings account at a commercial bank, mutual savings bank, a building and loan association, or a credit union. The social cost of providing savings accounts as compared with Savings Bonds is much smaller per dollar. Yet criticism of the Savings Bond Program is viewed as almost sacrilegious in important official and financial circles.

The interest expense of a national debt may remain constant through time even though interest rates may vary widely. If all the outstanding debt were perpetuities, like British Consols, the interest expense would remain unchanged as long as the debt outstanding remained constant. At the other extreme, the interest cost may change substantially from one day to the next. If all government debt were to consist of obligations payable in twenty-four hours, a rise in interest rates from 2 per cent on one day to 3 per cent the next would increase the interest cost by 50 per cent within twenty-four hours. In practice, as debt matures, the new debt replacing it carries a lower or higher interest expense if rates of interest have changed since the old debt was first issued. Because about 30 per cent of federal net marketable debt consists of obligations due within one year, a rise in interest rates from 2 to 3 per cent will, after a year's time, increase the total interest cost by almost $450 million.

A government with a large short-term debt outstanding is exposed to large variations in the interest expense on the debt. If interest rates have a persistent upward trend, it is cheaper to have the debt in long-term form, and the longer the term in this event, the better. The reverse also holds. If interest rates become lower, the debt that comes due can be refinanced at rates of interest lower than those at the time of issuance, providing the government with a reduction in its annual interest bill.

When a treasury must decide upon what kind of debt to sell, either because it wishes to obtain new money by increasing the outstanding debt or to replace maturing debt with new debt, it has a wide choice of options. It may sell debt of a maturity ranging from a few months, in some countries even a few weeks, to fifty years or even longer. One might expect that a treasury would make its decision simply on the basis of selecting the debt of that maturity which carries the lowest interest rate if rates happen to be different for different maturities. If, for example, the rate on one-year debt is 3 per cent and the rate on all longer maturities is 4 per cent, a treasury could save on its interest expense by selling only one-year maturity debt. Actually many other considerations are taken into account by officials in charge, including for example the probability of the issue being a failure if only one maturity is chosen instead of a variety of different maturities. From an economic point of view, the intriguing question is why in fact a treasury could gain at all by issuing one maturity instead of another or, in other words, why is it that actual interest rates on treasury securities differ from one another.

One type of explanation of different interest rates on government securities runs in terms of expectations of investors about future yields. Let us suppose, for example, that a one-year maturity is selling in the market at a price giving a yield of 2 per cent and a two-year maturity shows a yield of 3 per cent. Why do these rates differ in organized markets? The minds of investors must be investigated. An investor is said to believe that interest rates on one-year maturities a year hence will rise to approximately 4 per cent. If he buys a one-year maturity each year for $100 he will obtain $2 in the first year and, if interest rates rise to 4 per cent, he will obtain $4 (approximately) in the second year. Hence he is willing to buy a two-year maturity on the condition that he obtain the same total income ($6) for the two-year period as he would obtain by buying a one-year bond and then another one-year bond.

This type of explanation becomes a bit involved to account for all observed differences in yield. It creates no presumption that short-term issues, such as Treasury bills, should persistently carry a lower interest cost than do long-term bonds unless somehow investors can be shown to assume falsely that interest rates are forever about to rise.[6] This type of explanation also assumes that investors care only about the interest gain and the possible capital gain or loss in deciding to buy or hold one kind of government debt as opposed to another.

If this theory is adopted, the task of officials in managing the debt becomes that of outsmarting the market. If investors typically assume that interest rates will rise and officials believe that future rates of interest will remain unchanged, debt should be concentrated in short-term form. A government thereby gets the advantage of lower short-term interest rates, and if the officials are correct in their judgment about the future trend of interest rates, it does not have to pay more interest next year or the year after. On this theory, the relative interest cost of various debt forms is the only consideration of importance to a treasury in deciding on the kind of debt to issue and to leave outstanding.

Another point of view holds that the differences in interest rates reflect differences in "liquidity." Short-term debt usually has a lower interest cost than long-term because, it is argued, investors prefer short-term to long-term. This preference comes from the extra liquidity of short-term debt. "Liquidity" in this context means the characteristic of being like money. Money by definition is perfectly liquid. Savings accounts are almost perfectly liquid; Treasury bills are highly liquid but less so than are savings accounts; five-year bonds are less liquid than are one-year bonds, and so on. Liquidity in this sense refers to the absence of possible variation in the future price of the debt form. A Treasury ten-year bond may be selling at $101 in the market today. If a corporation acquired $101,000 worth of

---

[6] For an exposition of the expectation theory of differences in yields, see J. R. Hicks, *Value and Capital* (Oxford: Clarendon Press, 1939), pp. 144-52, and F. A. Lutz, "The Structure of Interest Rates," *Quarterly Journal of Economics,* LV (Nov., 1940), 36-43, reprinted in *Readings in the Theory of Income Distribution,* American Economic Association (Philadelphia: The Blakiston Co., 1946), pp. 512-20. A careful critique of this approach is provided by Joseph Conard, *Introduction to the Theory of Interest* (Berkeley: Univ. of California Press, 1959).

these bonds today and its officials should decide six months hence to sell them because the money was needed for an investment program, they might find that the price had fallen to $96, resulting in a capital loss of $5,000. If they had purchased six-month maturities instead, they would not have experienced the capital loss.

An investor may shun long-term issues because he guesses that prices of bonds will decline. Or he may shun them, even though he has no definite views about whether their prices will rise or fall, because he dislikes a dollar loss more than he likes a dollar gain. An asymmetrical attitude toward possible gains and losses is found in many walks of life. A student may be willing to bet 50 cents at even odds that Smith will beat Vassar at field hockey, but he may not be willing to bet $5. Logically, if one believes that the odds are better than even that the Smith girls will carry the day, one should stake all the money he has on Smith. For if the odds do favor Smith, what is called his *mathematical expectation* is always larger than his bet.[7] But of course, people do not behave in this "logical" but foolish way. The student thinks about the consequences of losing. A loss of 50 cents may only mean having to give up two beers whereas a loss of $100 would occasion a call home for more funds, with consequences too unpleasant to contemplate.

This lack of symmetry in attitude toward gains and losses afflicts commercial bankers and corporation treasurers as well as college students. Even insurance company officials are not immune. Hence at the same interest rate on government securities, investors will prefer the more liquid (more money-like) securities to the less liquid, and this preference will make short-term securities carry a lower rate of interest than long-term. In addition, some groups will care less about liquidity than will others. A life insurance company is less concerned about possible capital losses than is a commercial bank. The principal business of a commercial bank is making loans to business, and a banker does not like to turn away a good business loan for lack of the necessary reserves. If a banker ties up the bank's assets in long-term bonds, he may find that to accommodate his regular clients he will have to sell the bonds at a time when the market price is low. Bankers do not like losses. Actually banks which normally hold large amounts of government securities hold various maturities, using the short-term ones primarily to obtain more cash when the need arises.

Business corporations ordinarily prefer to hold short-term debt also. Their main business is producing commodities, not holding

---

[7] In tossing a coin, betting one dollar per toss, the mathematical expectation of gain is zero.

government debt. Ordinarily, they hold government debt instead of holding money. Government debt, especially short-term securities, is highly liquid, that is, free from capital losses, and provides some interest income. When business picks up and a company finds it requires more money to expand, it can sell or simply not rebuy maturing securities. Corporations also use government debt to adjust their seasonal requirements for cash, buying debt when their cash receipts exceed their cash payments and allowing their holdings to decline when big payments come due, such as installments on the corporate income tax.

According to a liquidity theory of the differences in interest rates on government debt, highly liquid securities should carry lower rates of interest than less liquid securities. A holder of Treasury bills gets two types of return, the interest and the liquidity. He "pays" for the extra liquidity by giving up some interest income. However this extra liquidity will be valued differently by different investors. Some will not care for it at all; life insurance company executives are likely to have this attitude. Some value it very much, such as some commercial banks.

The liquidity explanation does not require that short-term debt always show a lower yield than long-term debt. The relative quantities of different types of debt instruments are also relevant. If the U. S. Treasury starves the market for short-term securities, the competition to get what remains sends their yields down. If the Treasury allows the average maturity of the debt to decline, yields tend to cluster. The underlying economic considerations are similar to those governing the price relation among sizes of eggs. Large eggs are preferred to mediums, and mediums to smalls. This factor makes the price per dozen of large eggs exceed that of mediums and that of mediums exceed that of smalls. Yet this price structure may vary. If mediums, for example, come on to the market in abnormally small quantities, their price rises in relation to large and to small eggs. There have occasionally been periods, short periods, when mediums have sold at a higher price per dozen than large eggs. For short periods, the price per dozen of all sizes of eggs may even be the same. Likewise, the "normal" pattern of yields on government securities consists of a pattern of the type shown in Figure 23–2, called a *yield curve*.[8] The slope is positive, that is, short-term debt carries lower

[8] Yield curves on federal securities may be found in the *Treasury Bulletin,* a monthly publication of the U. S. Treasury. The actual yields give a series of points to which a curve is fitted by eye. These points do not fall on a smooth curve such as we have shown, and often there is room for disagreement about the line of best fit. A line has the advantage of summarizing a large number of observations, even though it distorts the facts somewhat.

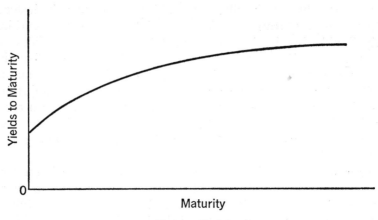

FIGURE 23–2

yields than long-term. However, by aggressively selling short-term and retiring long-term, officials can make the curve "flat"—a line parallel to the horizontal axis. In this event, the special advantages of short-term are worn out by providing so much of this quality, just as the special advantages of red apples over yellow ones can be worn out by a sufficiently large supply of red ones relatively to yellow ones.

The U. S. Treasury and the Federal Reserve have in recent years permitted the average maturity of the debt to decline. During the two-year period from June, 1955 to June, 1957, the portion of the *net* marketable debt of one year or shorter increased from 25 per cent in 1955 to 39 per cent in 1957. Treasury officials are reported to hold the belief that the average maturity should be increased rather than reduced. They have been frustrated by the difficulties encountered in attempting to market large amounts of long-term securities. The effect of their actual policies, as opposed to their announced policies, has been to narrow the yields among securities.

According to the liquidity approach, but not the expectation approach, changing the debt composition alone will stimulate or depress private expenditures. Lengthening the average maturity is depressing, whereas shortening the debt maturity is stimulating. The functional relation involved is shown in Figure 23–3.

This construction presupposes that the dispersion of maturities remains unchanged and hence the average maturity can be looked upon as the only significant variable; the net debt is to be held constant. At the practical minimum of average maturity, perhaps thirty days, private expenditures would be *OH*. As the maturity lengthens, debt can be used less and less in lieu of money because its liquidity is decreasing. If only long-term securities are left outstanding, people

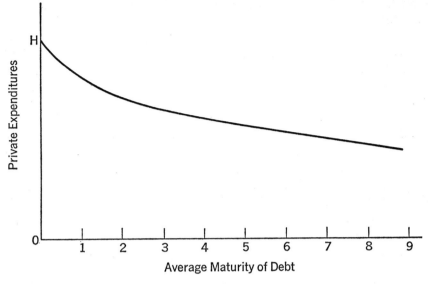

and organizations would have to take care of their liquidity needs by holding cash. Hence for any given amount of money, more of it will be tied up for contingency purposes, leaving a smaller amount available to finance consumption and investment purchases. Stated in yet another way, the velocity of money decreases as the debt maturity increases up to some point.[9]

Hence if the size of the net debt cannot be changed because of a lack of effective coordination between the treasury department and the central bank, steps that alter the average maturity could be used to stimulate or depress private expenditures. During recessions, the debt composition should be concentrated at the short-term and during booms at the long-term end of the maturity spectrum.

Reorganization for More Effective Debt-Monetary Policies

Confining our attention to the United States, what might be done to achieve more effective debt and monetary policies? As matters presently stand, both the Treasury and the Federal Reserve determine

---

[9]Some students believe that the possible change in private expenditures arising from changes in the maturity of debt is too small to be of any importance, and advocate in turn that the Treasury sell long-term debt during recessions in order to save on interest costs. See the Study Paper by Warren Smith (reference in Suggested Readings at the end of Part IV).

monetary policies. With two cooks running one kitchen, the soup may turn out to be too salty or on occasion merely curdled.

The Treasury influences monetary policy by the maturities it chooses to sell or retire and hence influences the pattern and level of interest rates. The Federal Reserve does so also by buying and selling government securities, called "open-market operations," by changing reserve requirements and discount rates, and by other less important means. When interest rates rise, the Federal Reserve officials may (and have) wash their hands of responsibility, pointing out correctly that a large sale of debt by the Treasury was the main cause of the rise in rates. The Treasury, on the other hand, absolves itself by pointing out that it is forced to get money, and lots of it, to meet the government's bills. Nobody is prepared to accept the responsibility. Yet an observer, noting that interest rates have risen, points out that the effects are holding down the recovery of the economy. If he wanders about Washington looking for the people who decided that a depressing monetary policy was in the public interest, he finds that all the officials who are paid to take such responsibilities are busily engaged in washing their hands. Some reorganization of our monetary and debt management programs might materially improve policy accomplishments.

A simple reform designed to obtain a more coordinated debt-management policy without making a radical change in existing institutions calls for placing the entire responsibility for debt management upon the Federal Reserve System. All new issues of debt would be issued by the Federal Reserve banks. The servicing of the debt would also be turned over to them. In effect, the relation between the Federal Reserve and the Treasury in regard to debt would be the same as now exists with respect to currency. The Treasury prints all currency; the technique of getting new currency into the hands of the public and the retirement of old currency operates through the Federal Reserve banks. Similarly new debt would be issued by the Federal Reserve and old debt would be retired. The Treasury would cease to have any responsibilities in this area apart from record keeping.

As a part of this plan, the Treasury would cease to hold demand deposits at commercial banks. All checks payable to the Treasury would be cleared through its checking account with the Federal Reserve. All checks written by the Treasury would be automatically honored for payment by the Federal Reserve banks.

If this plan were adopted the Federal Reserve Bank Balance Sheet would look rather different than it does at present. An abbreviated balance sheet statement, shown in Table 23–4, may assist in understanding the nature of the proposal. For simplicity, several items have been omitted, and figures have been liberally rounded. Attention should be directed to the asset item (3), and the liability items (9) and (11).

TABLE 23–4

FEDERAL RESERVE BANKS
HYPOTHETICAL STATEMENT OF CONDITION

(millions of dollars)

Assets		Liabilities	
(1) Gold Certificate account	22,000	(7) Federal Reserves notes	27,000
(2) Discounts and advances	780	Deposits:	
(3) U. S. Gov't. securities due from U. S. Treasury	224,000	(8) Member bank reserves	19,000
		(9) U. S. Treasury	5,000
(4) Uncollected cash items	5,000	(10) Deferred availability cash items	4,000
(5) Other assets	5,000	(11) U. S. Gov't. Securities outstanding	200,000
(6) Total assets	256,780	(12) Capital accounts	1,780
		(13) Total liabilities	256,780

Item (3), U. S. Government securities due from the U. S. Treasury —$224,000 million—represents the gross federal debt minus the amounts held in the trust funds (G.T.A. accounts). Item (9) is the demand deposit of the Treasury. This account will increase when tax receipts exceed government cash payments and fall in the reverse case. Item (11)—U. S. government securities outstanding—is what we have earlier defined as the *net debt*. These are the federal debt instruments in private hands.

To see how our proposed system would work, let us examine two cases: (1) a government deficit in a period of recession, and (2) a government surplus in a period of excessive private expenditures.

1. At the mechanical level, a deficit will reveal itself in a reduction of the U. S. Treasury's account, item (9). At the same time, member bank reserves, item (8), will automatically increase, because as the checks written by the Treasury are cashed, those cashing the checks add the proceeds to their bank accounts. The commercial banks that now receive the checks send them for payment to the Federal Reserve banks. Since Treasury outpayments exceed cash receipts, member bank reserves are increasing. Now comes a purely bookkeeping step. To restore the Treasury's cash balance, item (3)

is to be increased by whatever amount is necessary to keep item (9) constant.

The events of substance that have occurred, then, are the increase in member bank reserves and the increase in private cash holdings in the form of checking accounts.[10] Now a policy decision must be made by the Federal Reserve officials. Since a recession is assumed, these officials will presumably wish to see the economy stimulated. Under our plan, they may achieve such a result simply by doing nothing because doing nothing means not offsetting the increase in member bank reserves. Interest rates will be falling as they normally do early in a recession, but more so. The results of the automatic built-in flexibility of the tax system are being allowed to operate without restraint. There will be no increase in item (11)—U. S. Government securities outstanding—unless the Federal Reserve officials believe that the deficit is too stimulating.

2. During a period of excessive private expenditures when the Treasury has a cash surplus, item (9) will increase and member bank reserves will decrease. As before, the Treasury's account will be kept stable by bookkeeping entries. The important development, the decrease in member bank reserves, will force banks to raise interest rates, placing all groups who operate with borrowed funds in a financial squeeze, and will force down private expenditures. If this medicine is too strong for the economy, some outstanding debt may be retired. In this case item (11) will decline and offset some or all of the decrease in member bank reserves resulting from the government's surplus.

The reform being suggested alters the responsibility for debt management, placing it entirely in the hands of the Federal Reserve System. Some reforms in that organization may be desirable before full responsibility for monetary-debt management is placed upon it. The details of how the Federal Reserve System might be reorganized to make it more efficient is a topic more appropriate for consideration in a study of money and banking than in a discussion of public finance.

The foregoing plan is only one of many that might be suggested. The entire responsibility both for debt management and monetary policies may be centralized in the Treasury department, with the central bank operated or directed by Treasury officials. In many countries, central banks are controlled by officials who answer to the finance minister.

---

[10] This change would reveal itself on the books of member banks rather than of the Federal Reserve banks.

Reforms in organization are less important than the ideas and capabilities of the people who make the important decisions. Much improvement in monetary and financial management can be achieved in many countries by selecting conscientious officials anxious and able to learn the many intricacies of high finance.

Conclusions

The foregoing discussion has emphasized the close association between debt management by a treasury and the monetary policies of a central bank. In this area, sharp distinctions between fiscal and monetary affairs are impossible; an insistence upon a sharp distinction is likely to lead to confusion in understanding by the student and to inconsistent policies by the government. Debt management, defined as changing the size and composition of an outstanding debt, has been in many countries the joint responsibility of central banks and of a government department—the treasury. Inconsistent policies are sometimes found even though the officials of the agencies concerned cooperate readily and entertain no great differences in fundamental views. The actual outcomes are looked upon rather often as the responsibility of neither.[11] The regulation of private expenditures by changing the debt composition or the size of the outstanding national debt, by varying reserve requirements of commercial banks, and by changing the discount rate of the central bank could be much more effective in a country such as the United States than they have been in the past if the responsibilities were more definitely located. Reorganization, however, is no guarantee in itself of appropriate policies.

The above discussion has also emphasized why the net debt, also sometimes called the outstanding or the publicly held debt, is a much more significant concept than the gross debt. Americans take a special pride, it would seem, in reporting a huge federal debt. When the net debt figure is used instead, the amount of debt still seems large enough to fulfill this need.

The most important single fact about national debt management concerns the directional effects of changes in the debt with respect to private expenditures. Increases in the net debt are depressing and decreases are stimulating on private expenditures.

For any given amount of net or outstanding debt, actions by a government that lead to shortening the average maturity of the debt are stimulating and those that lead to lengthening are depressing.

[11] This observation would not apply to such well-governed small countries as the Netherlands.

Hence official policies, if they are to be properly designed, must consider a good deal more than the current yields of government debts of various maturities. If, for example, short-term securities are found to carry lower yields than long-term, it does not follow that the appropriate policy should be to concentrate more debt in the short-term form. The differences of various types of debt instruments in potency to affect private expenditures must be given consideration as well.

Our discussion has concentrated upon the effects of national debt management within the nation's economy. There are also effects upon international economic relations, including changes in ownership of the national debt of one country by persons and organizations in other countries. To explore these aspects properly would lead us rather far into the subject of international finance—a subject bristling with fascinating problems.

24

Use of Debt to Finance
Government Operations

The large debts of national governments reflect the past use of borrowing to finance expenditures. The topic now to be investigated has two main aspects: (1) the economic effects of using debt to finance governments and (2) the pros and cons of this method of financing. Both aspects will be discussed for the federal and for the state and local governments. In connection with the latter, alternative ways of managing state and local debts will be suggested.

Federal Borrowing

As pointed out in the last chapter, the U. S. Treasury ordinarily borrows money when it finds its cash balance too low. In turn, its cash balance falls during periods when it experiences a deficit—when expenditures are exceeding receipts. This borrowing may be genuine or it may be nominal. It is genuine when the sale of securities by the Treasury results in a net increase in federal debt in private (non-federal) hands. It is nominal when a government agency or the central bank acquires the new securities or old existing debt in equal amounts. Genuine borrowing implies an increase of what has already been defined as the net debt.

Increasing the net debt, looked upon by itself, tends to reduce private expenditures, as already pointed out in the last chapter. In certain rather unusual cases, borrowing by a national government may have a zero effect upon private expenditures. This extreme case is found when the sale of debt persuades people to give up the holding of money or persuades banks to create money which they would not otherwise spend or create at all. Some students of this topic have been inclined to treat this limiting case as the typical case. Actually, it holds only in unusual circumstances.

From the point of view of private groups, borrowing by a national government may seem painless. As compared to taxation, which hits some groups in the pocketbook immediately, borrowing may be looked upon as a postponing of the evil day to the future. Eventually people will be called upon, perhaps, to pay more in taxes as a result of borrowing in the present, but for the time being, life is not made more difficult by increased taxation. Borrowing is sometimes thought of as shifting the contemporary costs of governments to future taxpayers— our children and those of us who remain alive will be called upon to pay in the future. Those who die escape from this world without having to pay in tax all of the costs of government operations occurring during their lifetimes.

The view that government borrowing is painless to the present generation has its difficulties. Borrowing inflicts financial burdens upon people at the time, even though those so affected may be unaware of it. The choice between financing government by taxation and financing by borrowing is not a choice between a presently painful and a presently neutral method of finance; both are painful to some people and immediately.

Let us recall that for a national government to sell more debt in the net sense, it must persuade people to part with money. These people, if they are so persuaded, presumably decide that it is better from their point of view to hold the government debt instead of holding other assets. They are not hurt. On the contrary, they are, if anything, benefited by the new offering. A commodity they like, namely government debt, has become somewhat cheaper in price. If the government were to sell apples, for example, people addicted to eating apples would clearly gain. So it is with people who like to hold government debt. Who, if anyone, then is financially hurt by a sale of government debt?

To get at the essentials, let us for the moment concentrate attention on the people who borrow money. Let us suppose, for simplicity, that lenders have exactly $1 billion to spend for debt instruments. They will spend all of this money, and only this money, to acquire debt securities either from the government or from private individuals or both. Let us suppose also that lenders do not care whether they buy private securities or government securities; they like both types and treat them alike. Clearly, then, any dollar obtained by the government in the sale of debt will subtract one dollar from the amount available for the purchase of private debt. The dollars obtained by the government will, in this event, never reach the bank accounts of some potential private borrowers. These people must spend less on goods and services than they otherwise would. In turn, the business concerns who would have produced and sold these goods and services to them make smaller profits and their employees make smaller wage incomes as a consequence.

In Figure 24–1, some of these relations are set out. On the horizontal axis, debt instruments, either public or private, are measured.

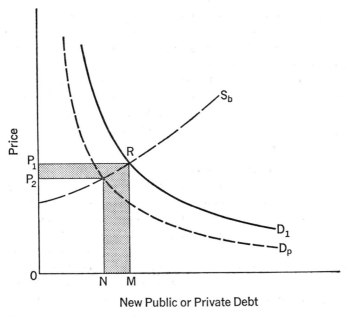

New Public or Private Debt

FIGURE 24–1

The unit may be thought of as a coupon bond paying $4.00 per year for twenty-five years with a maturity value of $100 in the twenty-fifth year. For the purpose of this representation, we may temporarily think of this type of bond as being the only debt instrument that borrowers may provide, leaving for later consideration the fact that debts come in many varieties. The vertical axis shows the price of this bond. The higher the price of the bond, the lower is the yield, or rate of interest.

D_1 is the demand schedule of lenders for new bonds, public or private. It has been drawn with an elasticity of unity, fitting the assumption that lenders have a fixed money sum to lend. S_b is the supply schedule for private debt instruments. It shows that amount of bonds private individuals and organizations would be prepared to supply at various prices of the bonds. If the government is not in the market to sell debt, the price of bonds would be OP_1 and the amount of money obtained by borrowers would be OP_1RM. Borrowers would be in a position to spend this sum of money for the various things they want, such as new houses, new factory buildings, machines of various kinds, and so on. Now let us suppose the government borrows. The government wishes a fixed sum, which is represented by the difference between D_1 and D_p. Thus D_p is the demand schedule for private securities as a result of government borrowing.

The price of bonds is now lower; it is OP_2 instead of OP_1. The shaded area shows the amount of money that private borrowers do not get, and by the same token, the amount of money obtained by the government in the sale of debt. We have then the following results in this case: (1) the price of bonds is lower (the rate of interest is higher), (2) the government gets the money it wishes to borrow, (3) private borrowers get less money by the amount the government borrows. These results may be classified into *distributional considerations* and *deflationary effects*.

DISTRIBUTIONAL CONSIDERATIONS. As a result of government borrowing, rates of interest on the debt of new borrowers are made higher. Any lender who makes a contract with a private borrower will now do better because, per dollar spent, he will obtain, or so he hopes, a larger number of dollars in the future. In acquiring the bonds, he can acquire more of them at a lower price for the same amount of money. Hence he can obtain a larger flow of future income from owning these debts. On the other hand, debtors must give up a larger flow of dollars in the future per dollar obtained now. As a result of the government debt operation, lenders will have larger future incomes and debtors will, on this account, have smaller net future incomes computed after deducting the interest expenses. This commitment to pay more interest is the aspect which is likely to trouble potential debtors. It is also a main reason why people who usually borrow are opposed to policies that result in higher rates of interest.

DEFLATIONARY EFFECTS. The deflationary effect of government borrowing arises from the fact that some or all potential borrowers obtain less money because of the government's competition for the dollars of lenders. If this were to mean only that some or all borrowers obtained less cash but continued to spend the same amount on goods and services, the government borrowing would have no deflationary effect. But people who borrow do so not merely to have larger bank accounts, but perhaps to pay family doctor bills, to buy new cars or, in the case of a public utility, to pay for a new hydro-electric installation.

If borrowers simply spend less on currently produced goods in general and their relative demands stay the same, the financial impact of the government borrowing will be to reduce or to prevent an increase in money incomes in general. All industry will be negatively affected. Yet it is unlikely that the impact will be spread over all industries evenly. Some will be hit sharply whereas others will be scarcely affected. Those hit sharply are the ones producing products of the kind that require a relatively large amount of financing to sell them. Houses, automobiles, power plants—expensive durable items —are commonly purchased jointly with the finance company or the local bank. If these lenders have less money to lend because the government has taken a portion of it by its borrowing operation, the buyers of goods cannot buy as much as they otherwise would. The deflationary effect of the sale of debt by the government is felt by industries, including their employees, producing goods of this type. In turn, because these people receive less money, they have less money to spend on other things. It is in this way that the deflationary impact of government borrowing spreads itself through the economy.

COMPLICATIONS CONSIDERED. Several additional factors need to be considered. We supposed in the previous discussion that lenders had a fixed sum to lend. Actually, the amount financial organizations will lend depends on many considerations, including the rate of interest on the new debt. At higher and higher rates of interest, money has a way of coming out of what seem to be hiding places into the hands of borrowers. When the yield on Treasury securities is about 2 per cent, a small town banker may not wish to buy Treasury bills because the interest on $10,000 he has available for ten days will barely pay the costs of telephoning in his order. If the rate rises to 4 per cent, he becomes more interested. A person may hold a larger checking account than he needs at a low rate of interest, but at a higher rate he may shift extra sums quickly to a savings account. At higher and higher rates of interest, the amount of money that people and organizations hold merely for convenience declines, and more of this money finds its way into the hands of borrowers.

The more efficient use of money arising from higher rates of interest is from a social point of view a useless economy. It does not help to increase production or to reduce any wasteful use of resources; it merely speeds up the velocity of money—the speed at which money moves—in the economy. In terms of Figure 24–1, the demand schedule of lenders shown should be thought of as having an elasticity of more than unity. Lenders will lend more money at lower prices of bonds (higher rates of interest) instead of simply lending a fixed sum.

This characteristic of lender behavior means that a part of the money the government receives is obtained at no one's expense. Lazy money is induced to become more active. The remaining part of the money is obtained at the expense of private borrowers.

There is another complication. Private debts differ among themselves and also differ from the types of debt used by governments. These differences are too many to catalogue here. An important feature of government securities in Western countries is their superiority over private instruments with respect to default risk. A person holding U.S. federal debt instruments does not need to worry, or thinks he does not need to worry, about the possibility of the government refusing to meet the terms of the contract. This feature, although important, does not upset the conclusion that what the federal government succeeds in borrowing will either be at the expense of other borrowers or that it will speed up the velocity of the circulation of money. The superiority of government securities in this regard makes it more likely that the borrowing of, say, $1 billion during a period by the federal government will do more to speed up the velocity of money than would the borrowing of the same amount by a large number of private organizations. The reason is that government debts are treated by investors as a closer substitute for money than are private debts.

The financial burden, then, of a government debt operation rests initially upon other borrowers. They succeed in borrowing less than they otherwise would. Are they, then, the people who should be looked upon as the victims? Are they chosen to bear the brunt of the borrowing operation?

A potential borrower who is either refused outright or who finds that it has become more expensive to borrow retains the same net worth position. He obtains fewer assets but he also holds down his debts by the same amount. Although he will scarcely enjoy this state of affairs, his financial position in a formal sense has been left quantitatively unchanged. This fact suggests that our borrower should not be regarded as being financially hurt by the debt operation.

Those who do get hurt in the bank account are those whose money incomes are reduced because private borrowers spend less money to buy things. If borrowers borrowed money to buy only one commodity, such as new houses, the house construction industry would bear the entire brunt of the government's sale of debt. The corporations organized to produce houses, the companies supplying plumbing, nails, lumber, and the thousands of other items that go into a house would experience a reduction in the demand for their products. The employees of construction companies and employees of suppliers would find their services less in demand. The income generated by the construction industry would thus be smaller and the size of the industry measured by the number of workers would also be smaller. Their position would be affected by a government debt operation in much the same way as it would be if the government were to place a special tax upon the production of new houses. The tax would reduce the profitability of the industry and its attractiveness to young men who can drive a nail.

Although the housing industry is a conspicuous case of one that is injured by rising costs of borrowing, it is by no means the only one. Corporations engaged in producing machines of various kinds, those producing steel, automobiles, and freight cars, as well as local medical practitioners may be adversely affected financially because their potential customers find themselves with less money to spend. In general, the industries likely to be hit most severely by a government sale of debt are those producing investment types of goods and those producing expensive durables for the home; these are the types of items in the United States that often require the buyer to find a lender to help him finance the purchase. In India, by contrast, other types of industries would be affected. In that country, borrowing is not used on any large scale to finance the purchase of automobiles or washing machines. Many borrowers are small-scale farmers who wish to spend borrowed money for seed, farming tools, and living costs. There, the depressing effect of the government's sale of debt is likely to be felt by the businesses engaged in supplying the needs of small farmers.

If the sale of government debt does act like a tax upon certain groups of people in the economy, why not, then, tax these people by an outright tax device instead of taxing them by the roundabout method of selling new government debt? The question is pertinent and important. Clearly from the point of view of the government, an outright tax device has the merit that it leaves no hangover in the form of future interest payments or repayment of the principal. On the same score, future taxpayers are relieved of one additional demand from the government for revenue, the demand to meet the interest and other expenses of the loan. One may therefore conclude that the use of debt financing by a national government cannot be given a high mark. If so, we are back with that formidable thinker of the last century, John Stuart Mill. In discussing the question of the desirability of a government's borrowing instead of taxing to finance itself, Mill reached the following conclusion:[1]

> If the government had abstained from taking this capital by loan, and had allowed it to reach the labourers, but had raised the supplies which it required by a direct tax on the labouring classes, it would have produced (in every respect but the expense and inconvenience of collecting the tax) the very same economical effects which it did produce, except that we should not now have had the debt. The course it actually took was therefore worse than the very worst mode which it could possibly have adopted of raising the supplies within the year . . .

This train of thought asserts the proposition that the government sale of debt acts like a tax on workers, the value judgment that such a tax is a very bad one, and the additional value judgment that the loan because of its aftereffects is even worse than an outright tax upon workers.

The Postponement Question

Can the present generation of people somehow postpone the cost of some government projects to the future? If they can, should they? The issue arises each time a bond authorization is voted upon to finance the construction of a new school building. Instead of those presently living in the district paying the entire cost of the building by taxes imposed to raise the large sums involved, the sale of bonds seems to spread the costs to future residents as the interest expense is met and the bonds are paid off. Thus parents of children in school ten years hence will meet a portion of the present cost of constructing the school building. Likewise, it is argued, at the national level the costs involved in a severe catastrophe such as a war could be spread over future generations by borrowing. So convinced were French officials of this position that during World War I they allowed taxes to fall, maintaining that the French people were being made to suffer enough from the German invasion without having a heavy tax load placed on their backs.

As already pointed out, the theory that somehow living people can postpone the costs of some government projects to future generations by sale of debt has the weakness that debt sales, if they are genuine, do

---

[1] *Principles of Political Economy,* Book V, chap. vii, I. Mill tempered this harsh judgment by two main qualifications: (1) If people would lend abroad instead of lending at home, the government borrowing would, to the extent it curtailed foreign lending, not reduce workers' incomes; (2) if the government could somehow borrow without raising rates of interest, the bad effects mentioned would not follow. A main issue in Mill's thought is the claim that a debt sale would be at the expense of workers only. In taking this position, he is clearly wrong.

inflict financial burdens upon some section of the population living at the moment. We pay as we go even if we try not to. However, there are further aspects of the topic deserving special attention.

A society can organize itself so that it uses a larger or smaller portion of its present resources to produce yet more resources. The Russians have for years concentrated upon building up heavy industry instead of allowing people to enjoy better housing, good restaurant meals, clothing, and household furnishings. The choice was made to produce heavy equipment and less of other things. In the United States, we too have for years devoted some of our efforts to building up more resources. This process of development of new resources has gone on for centuries and promises to go on indefinitely. Currently in the United States we are spending huge sums building missiles, highways, schools, housing, service stations, and supermarkets.

People living now can enjoy a larger amount of consumption now at the expense of new facilities whose fruits will emerge in the future. A government can, by its financial arrangements, either increase or decrease the maintenance of old facilities and the construction of new ones. Those financial arrangements that lead to more consumption now and less investment now may be looked upon as involving a postponement of present government costs or at least of some portion of them.

Suppose, then, purely for the sake of getting the issues clearly before us, we assume that the federal government wishes to postpone the costs of its present use of resources to the future. What type or types of financial policies, if any, would accomplish this objective?

What is needed are financial measures that make consumption higher and investment lower. At the same time, we should not forget that there are other goals of government policy, such as fair treatment of people and economic stability.

Stimulating an increase in consumption is comparatively simple. Taxes that remove large amounts of money from people who normally spend their money for groceries and shoes for the children and who do not spend their money to acquire corporate stocks, new buildings, or new machines must be reduced. As these people find they are receiving larger disposable incomes, they will spend more money for what they want. We know that, generally speaking, people in the lower income groups are mainly interested in consumption items, and hence we can be reasonably confident that a reduction of the taxes paid by them would result in a larger amount of consumption spending.

The stimulation of consumption by reducing taxation may, however, lead to an undue increase in aggregate expenditures, an increase which may be inconsistent with economic stability. In this event, measures would need to be adopted to cause investment expenditures to fall. If we wish to use tax devices, the parallel measure calls for greatly increasing the amounts of money taken from those people who would otherwise spend it directly to buy new machines or new buildings or who would spend it to acquire new debts or new issues of corporate shares of stock. In this event, there is the same deflationary effect we already pointed out in connection with the effects of government borrowing. The important point is that consumption can be stimulated by reducing taxes on people who spend their money for consumption, and investment can be retarded by increasing taxes on people who spend their money for investment directly or indirectly.

Similar results can be obtained by using debt operations, although they are apt to be less effective than appropriate tax measures. What is required are very high rates of interest on debt securities and very low prices of corporate shares of stock with the purpose of making those who do the investing, such as corporation managements, experience great difficulty in raising money to finance expansion. As concerns government debt, the government should therefore sell debt on a substantial scale. But because such a measure is deflationary, it must be offset, which can be done by lowering taxes. To make certain that corporations cannot sabotage official policies, they might be required to return to their stockholders in the form of dividends a large fraction of corporate earnings. Special measures might be necessary to place obstacles in the way of selling new corporate securities. As concerns the federal budget, the government would need to plan for a deficit and to sell government debt perhaps in amounts exceeding the deficit. The interest expense would continue to mount from year to year as the debt grew in size, but there is the perhaps comforting result that the public would enjoy a larger abundance of consumption.

Running a deficit, selling debt, and various other complementary measures are ways of curtailing investment and increasing consumption. Another method already mentioned calls for imposing heavier taxes on those who finance investment. No special reason has been found for looking upon the sale of debt as some peculiarly appropriate way of "postponing" costs to future generations. Furthermore it always has the defect that some hangover of interest expense is created, just as Mill emphasized. Since there is no particular justification for a government to complicate its financial problems just to make them more complicated, taxing as opposed to borrowing to achieve objectives has the merit of cleanliness. Genuine borrowing does not avoid inflicting financial burdens upon people; it just seems to do so. The case for a long-run persistent increase in government debt appears, therefore, to be a weak one.

State and Local Government Borrowing

There are in the neighborhood of 100,000 local units of government and, of course, fifty state governments in the United States. These various governments provide a variety of services, levy taxes, and on occasion borrow to finance themselves. Unlike the federal government, none of these government units has been required to finance a war. The astronomical increase of the debt of the federal government during wartimes is not duplicated by any state. Actually, during World War II the state and local governments reduced their debts.

If all state and local units are grouped together, their collective gross debt stood at about $53 billion in 1957. In gross terms, the corresponding figure five years earlier, in 1952, was about $30 billion, giving an absolute increase of $23 billion or about $4½ billion per year. This increase in state and local debts suggests rather free and fancy borrowing.

Actually, gross debt figures and the change in them over time have little significance. In state and local government finance, there exists a large measure of "cross-hauling" on debts. A unit reports its debt on a gross basis and does not cancel out the amounts of its own debt held by it. Some correction for these facts should be used to portray accurately and to interpret local and state debt.

One procedure, used by the Department of Commerce, defines state and local net debts as gross debts minus holdings of "own debt" —i.e., the obligations of the unit itself which are held by it. According to this concept, the net debts of state and local governments were as shown in Table 24–1 for the years 1952-57.

TABLE 24–1

NET DEBT OF STATE AND LOCAL GOVERNMENTS, 1952-1957

(in billions of dollars)

Year	State & Local	State	Local
1953	28.6	6.4	22.2
1954	33.4	8.3	25.1
1955	38.4	9.8	28.5
1956	42.7	10.8	31.9
1957	46.7	11.8	34.9

Source: U. S. Department of Commerce, *Survey of Current Business*

Note: For definition of net debt, see text and also *Survey of Current Business*, Sept., 1953, p. 24.

On this definition, the net debt figures are of course absolutely smaller than the gross debt figures because holdings of own debt have been deducted. Of more importance is the change in debt. State and local "net debt" rose by $18.1 billion over the five-year period, or about $3.6 billion per year.

The Department of Commerce procedure has deficiencies. If a state buys back some of its old outstanding securities and holds them in one of the innumerable "funds" that states like to employ, the reported net debt figure reflects the facts properly. If the state instead acquires an equal amount of federal government securities of a similar maturity and interest return, no deduction is shown.

To obtain a more relevant figure we have deducted from reported gross debt of state and local governments the duplicating debt consisting of the following items: (1) "own" government securities, (2) other state and local securities, (3) other securities, and (4) federal securities. The results of this computation are shown in Table 24–2.

TABLE 24–2

Gross and Net State and Local Debts, 1952-1957

(in millions of dollars)

Year[1]	Gross Debt (1)	Duplicating[2] Debt (2)	Net Debt (3)
1952	30,100	17,082	13,018
1953	33,782	19,238	14,544
1954	38,931	21,622	17,309
1955	44,267	23,935	20,332
1956	49,161	26,669	22,492
1957	52,733	28,694	24,039

Source: U. S. Bureau of the Census, *Summary of Government Finances*

[1] Figures are for June 30 of each year.
[2] For definition of duplicating debt, see text.

Attention to column (3) will show that the net debt as now defined has increased by $11 billion over the five-year period, or at an annual rate of $2.2 billion per year. Considering that these data cover all state and local governments in the United States, an increase of $2.2 billion per year appears to be a fairly modest one. State and local governments have not as a whole been engaged in the extravagant use of borrowing as a method of financing. Perhaps they would have been better advised to have reduced instead of increased their net indebtedness.

A breakdown of government units gives a more detailed picture and shows where the main increases in debt have occurred, as shown in Table 24–3.

TABLE 24–3

STATE AND LOCAL NET DEBT BY UNIT OF GOVERNMENT
1952-1957

(in millions of dollars)

Year	State (1)	County (2)	City (3)	Town-ships (4)	School Districts (5)	Special Districts (6)
1952	—3,303	1,454	7,750	543	3,112	3,465
1953	—3,785	1,809	8,157	568	3,882	3,915
1954	—3,688	2,050	8,853	696	4,860	4,535
1955	—3,408	2,283	9,584	737	6,054	5,084
1956	—3,670	2,577	9,943	874	7,459	5,308
1957	—4,113	2,261	10,059	908	7,036	4,438

Source: U. S. Bureau of the Census, *Summary of Government Finances.*

Note: Data for local governments are gathered by the U. S. Census on a sampling basis. The data are subject to a sampling error. The error is larger for units which are few in number, such as townships, than for numerous units, such as school districts.

There are two types of units of government which have been especially important borrowers—school districts and cities. School districts increased their net debt by $3.9 billion and cities by $2.3 billion over the five-year period, thereby accounting for 56 per cent of the increase in the net debt of all state and local governments. School districts have been under especially heavy pressure during recent years, a pressure which will continue for some time, to expand educational facilities. Many municipalities have been under similar pressure.

State net debt as we have defined this concept is negative (see column [1] of Table 24–3); states own securities in greater dollar amounts than they owe. This fact is sufficiently unusual to merit special attention. Net debt has been defined as gross debt minus holdings of debt, including some other types of claims, such as shares of stock in the catchall census class "other securities." By deducting these holdings, we obtain a figure that is something like the concept of net worth.[2] However, other assets such as cash holdings, which are very large for our states, are not deducted. How then is it that states are apparently so affluent?

States have various funds established to cover state liabilities for retirement of employees and other purposes. As employees retire,

[2] See chap. 9 for a discussion of this concept.

pensions are paid to them according to formulas previously arranged. State workers contribute, ordinarily through withholding, to the funds. The amounts paid into the funds typically exceed withdrawals, thereby increasing the size of the funds; the extra money is spent for securities, including the state's own securities in some cases. The trust funds of the state governments held about $9.4 billion in assets on June 30, 1957.

The conception of the net debt used above (see Table 24–3) treats these assets as "belonging" to the state by deducting them to obtain the state's net indebtedness. Should they not be looked upon as "belonging" to individuals—to state employees who have contributed to the funds and who will be entitled to pensions? In this interpretation, the state is the trustee for its employees in these funds.

The interpretation of funds of this type raises many intriguing questions. Let us suppose that a state has a pension scheme providing that retired employees shall receive on the average $300 per month. The ratio of state workers to pensioners is, say, 20 to 1. State employees are assessed on the average $15 per month for retirement. With no fund at all, those working are financing those who have retired. They pay an amount which just covers the amount received by pensioners. Clearly no fund is required; one group pays money through the state to another group.

Let us suppose that the state in question is increasing the number of its employees, as indeed has typically been the case for many years. The state does not of course hire retired employees; it ordinarily adds young people to its staff. The ratio of workers to retired employees thus increases from 20 to 1 to 25 to 1 and higher. If the state increases the number of its employees each year this ratio will continue to rise. In this event, a system of pensions based strictly on current contributions would call for a decreasing contribution per month per employee to provide the same monthly pensions to those who have retired. Alternatively, if state workers are assessed the same or increasing dollar amounts, the amounts paid into the fund will exceed the amounts paid out, and as a consequence, the fund will grow. The actual facts reflect, more or less, the latter situation; each year more money is ordinarily paid into state retirement funds than is paid out.

To whom then does the fund "belong"? As long as the number of employees grows, the fund grows, and hence if this growth continues indefinitely, there is never any need to draw upon the fund to pay pensioners even at "doomsday." The excess of retirement assessments on employees over amounts paid to pensioners means that the state accumulates assets or, what amounts to the same thing, reduces its other liabilities. Whether we say the assets of the fund "belong" to the state or to its employees does not then matter; in fact, the state gets more money into its hands than it pays out under the program, thereby permitting it to finance more expenditures, cut taxes, reduce its debt, or increase state-held assets.

Pension programs are designed to provide retired employees with the wherewithal to keep them from want during their unproductive years. To make such plans work, employees must be forced to contribute, and the claim they obtain on the state while they continue to work must not be subject to alienation by them. If a worker could realize on his claim, if a retirement fund were like a savings bank, the assets of the fund would clearly belong to contributors, and the scheme as a retirement device would not work. It would not work because people who prefer to take their chances on financing their retirement years may dissipate their claims as they work. The assets of a retirement plan cannot be fully owned by employees and still be a retirement plan. Some people, those who work only a short period for a government, may find, and often do find, that they have contributed without getting anything valuable in return. These people are paid less than the announced rate of wage.

Some Special Aspects of Local Borrowing

A local government can operate without borrowing by holding its expenditures to its tax revenues. If it borrows on balance, it must finance the future interest expense and the amortization of the bonds. For a school district, confronted with a growing school population, the usual procedure is to sell bonds to finance expensive new additions to the school plant. The debt is an obligation of the district, which in turn means that it is a claim against the revenue sources of the district. If the only source is property on the tax rolls, owners of property within the district have indirectly mortgaged their property as a result of the new bond issue. If there is property of $50 million assessed valuation in the district, and a bond issue of $1 million is successfully sold, an owner of property assessed at $100,000 has a new liability of $2,000 against his property.

The offset to this added liability is the asset—the new school facilities. Purely as an economic calculation, this asset of the district may add to the value of one's property more or less than the new bond issue subtracts. Thus a tight-fisted wealthy man with large holdings of property may favor a bond issue for a new school, not because he cares at all about proper schooling for other people's children, but because he figures that the bond issue and the school building will together increase the value of his property. He may, it should be mentioned, calculate the other way.

Good schools do enhance the value of residential property in an area. They may do little for commercial properties and perhaps nothing at all for industrial properties. Taxpayers' associations made up of businessmen often campaign against bond issues mainly because of this fact. However, such groups would not often be successful if they could not get the support of owners of residential properties, who may assume, falsely, that the bond issue will have only a negative effect on the value of their property. Cold-blooded economic calculation would often call for the passage of bond measures that now fail.

People do not always allow purely economic calculations of net money gains and losses to decide questions of whether or not to vote for a school bond issue. Beliefs in what is right and proper play a large and crucial role. Democracy as we know it in this country could not have been born or have survived without strong ethical beliefs transcending calculations of personal financial gains and losses.

An extreme case where economic considerations dominate a local government unit is found in some single-purpose districts providing a service instrumental to producers located in the district. Irrigation districts are examples of this case. A group of landowners combine to form a district, sell bonds to raise money, and spend the money on irrigation facilities. The water may be rationed on some formula basis, commonly with charges sufficient to cover current expenses and the debt service. Individual farmers get cheap water as a dividend on their investment. The advantages of such an arrangement are many. As a government unit, the local district is not subject to many taxes to which a private corporation providing the same service would be. Districts often command the support of state legislatures because of the district's government status. Such districts may be entitled to buy from other government units some items, such as publicly produced power, at favorable rates. There is the disadvantage that the irrigation district, unlike a private corporation, is precluded from paying dividends in money; owners of irrigated land can, however, realize on the gains through sale of the property.

"Profit-making" government units have the choice of selling debt or of obtaining funds by assessing members of the district. The choice to any one owner of land is simple in principle. Let us suppose that there are 100 landowners whose total acreage and quality of land are alike, and that the capital cost of more irrigation facilities would be $5 million, so the share of the capital cost to any one farmer would be $50,000. If each were called upon to finance his share, he would have to give up other assets yielding, let us suppose, 8 per cent return per year. If the district can borrow at 4 per cent, the securities being tax-exempt, the choice is easy—borrow. In practice, such districts can normally borrow at lower rates than can individual farmers.

For government units with bona fide public functions, the choice between borrowing and taxing entails greater difficulties. A small district, one that builds a new school about every ten years, could "overtax" for ten years, accumulate a fund, and then construct the building; such behavior would show the utmost financial prudence. Alternatively, the district might tax heavily during the period when the school was being constructed. In this event, the local officials would be confronted with serious technical problems in trying to raise such a large sum in a short period. By borrowing the sums needed and repaying the debt over an extended period, tax rates can be kept more steady.

Borrowing becomes a kind of averaging device for the smaller districts, permitting tax rates to be adjusted gradually to the requirements of greater revenue. The averaging consideration becomes less important as the government unit becomes larger. A city such as New York or Chicago could only occasionally justify borrowing merely on the grounds of averaging. Large capital expenditures occur every year; these can be financed from tax revenues without radical variations in tax rates.

On the whole, state and local governments, especially the states, have exhibited a modest disposition to use debt as a major financing device. Particular government units can be charged with excessive use of borrowing, and many others with hampering needed programs by excessive fear of borrowing.

State and Local Debt Management

Debt management of the type discussed for the federal government scarcely exists at the state and local levels. Typically, borrowing is accomplished by the sale of serial bonds. After the initial marketing, the local unit takes no further steps other than to comply with the terms of the contract. Occasionally a district will buy its own bonds, holding them as an asset in some fund.

The actual marketing is accomplished through private financial houses. A district may wish to finance an addition to its sewage disposal facilities. The capital costs are estimated at $10 million, and the decision is made to sell bonds. The details of financing are usually worked out by representatives of the district and a bond house specializing in this function. The bonds typically will have a number of maturities, ranging from one year to perhaps twenty years—i.e., serial bonds. This practice permits the district to pay off a portion of its debt each year.

A main difficulty in the marketing of local debt as practiced in the United States arises from the small size of many districts and the high costs of borrowing arising from the diseconomies of small-scale debt marketing. This diseconomy is often further aggravated by the lack of familiarity on the part of the district officials with the details of possible financing techniques. Any borrower, whether an individual or a business corporation or a government, operates at a disadvantage merely by being small. When a loan or a bond issue is contemplated, many of the expenses involved are much the same whether the amount involved is $10 million or $100 million. The small scale of the borrower also acts as a limit on the market for new debts. Only a few potential buyers of bonds will be acquainted with the credit rating of a school district or a local water district. Bond houses must use promotional measures to locate buyers, a procedure which involves considerable expense. The lack of knowledge of finance by local officials more or less forces them to rely upon the advice offered by bond houses, often with good but sometimes with bad results.

Yet another limitation arises from the disorderly condition of the secondary market—the market for old issues—for local securities. An investor contemplating the purchase of bonds about to be issued has no assurance that if he should at some future time wish to sell them he would be able to find a buyer except at a substantial discount. This lack of well-organized secondary markets for local bonds restricts their marketability in the first place. As a consequence, local governments must pay a higher rate of interest to overcome this handicap. A plan for reorganizing the marketing and resale of obligations of state and local governments will be considered presently.

Tax-Exemption of State and Local Government Securities

State and local government securities provide interest income to their holders, and under present law this income is completely exempt from the federal income taxes, both individual and corporate. This interest income is also exempt from the issuing state's income taxes, and from taxation by local governments within that state. The securities must, however, be included in the estate for purposes of federal estate taxation and also, normally, in the base of the death taxes imposed by state governments. Theoretically, these securities count as property for purposes of property taxation in many states, but as pointed out in the discussion of the property tax, securities of all kinds pretty much escape the property tax net.[3]

POSSIBLE GAINS TO HOLDERS. The important tax-exemption feature of state and local securities arises from tax-exemption under the two federal income taxes. As pointed out in Chapter 6, this practice is a kind of subsidy.[4] The federal government foregoes the tax revenue it would receive if this interest income were included in taxable income. Some of this revenue loss will be the gain of people who buy and hold state and local securities. If, for example, the income tax were proportional at a rate of 40 per cent on all income, any person holding taxable securities receiving $100 in interest would be required to pay $40 in tax, leaving him $60 after tax. Under the tax, if he held tax-exempt securities providing him with $100 in interest income, he would pay no tax, and the government of course would get no revenue from him. This fact may be described by saying that the government (really, all other taxpayers) contributes $40 in foregone taxes to this person. In this illustration, the entire amount of tax not collected is retained by the holder of state and local government securities. This need not be the case and generally is not the case. Suppose the holder could have obtained $100 per year by acquiring equivalent taxable securities but can obtain only $90 by acquiring tax-exempt securities. Now the government foregoes $40 in revenue as before, but the holder gains only $30 in tax-saving by holding the tax-exempt securities. The "tax-subsidy" has been partly shifted, three-quarters going to the holder and one quarter going to the government unit that issued the tax-exempt security. The $40 of tax-saving might at one extreme go entirely to holders of tax-exempt securities and at the other extreme entirely to the state and local governments. In practice, it will be divided between them.

With a highly progressive individual income tax and with a high corporate income tax rate (52 per cent) one would expect that a completely tax-exempt security would be gobbled up by wealthy people and by corporations. Data have already been cited about the concentration of tax-exempt securities in the hands of people with large incomes.[5] What may seem a little surprising is why wealthy people hold assets of any type other than tax-exempt securities. A wealthy person can, if he wishes to do so, completely avoid paying any federal income tax by investing in state and local securities.[6]

---

[3] See chap. 15, pp. 329-30.

[4] Pp. 118-21.

[5] See chap. 6, p. 120.

[6] If the state in which he resides has an income tax, he can usually also avoid this tax by investing in the securities issued by that state or its local units.

Suppose a person has assets of $10 million. He can acquire tax-exempt securities yielding 3 per cent per year. His income is, then, $300,000 per year free of federal income taxation. If he were instead to acquire federal bonds yielding, say, 4 per cent per year, his income would be $400,000 per year. Because federal securities are taxable, he would be required to pay a substantial sum to the federal government. If the rate of tax on him were 80 per cent, he would retain $80,000 as after-tax income and pay $320,000 in taxes. Clearly, he has a strong incentive to acquire tax-exempt securities; the net advantage is $220,000 income per year in our illustration.

More generally, the extra rate of gain of tax-exempt securities over taxable securities depends upon the comparative differences in market yields and upon the tax rate relevant to the investor. These factors can be combined in the formula

$$g = r_1 - (1\text{-}t)r_2,$$

where g is the differential rate of gain, r_1 is the yield on tax-exempt securities, t is the tax rate, and r_2 is the yield on taxable securities. In the above illustration

$$g = .03 - (1\text{-}.80).04 \text{ or } .022.$$

The investor gains .022 times his investment of $10 million, or $220,000, by acquiring tax-exempt instead of taxable securities.

The gain differential, given the yields on tax-exempt and taxable securities, directly varies with the tax rate. If the rate is zero because a person has only a small potential income, the gain differential is simply the difference between r_1 and r_2. In this event the investor has an incentive to pick the higher yield. As the tax rate approaches 100 per cent, the gain differential approaches the actual yield on tax-exempt securities.

OWNERSHIP CHARACTERISTICS. Considerations of this type suggest that tax-exempt securities would be concentrated in the hands of taxpayers who would be subject to high rates of tax. Empirical studies more or less bear out this expectation as pointed out in Chapter 6.[7] They do not, however, fit the theoretical expectations as closely as one would expect from the mathematical computations of the difference in gain to be achieved by holding tax-exempt versus taxable assets. As far as individuals are concerned, the failure of all tax-exempts to be more concentrated in the hands of the wealthy may be partly due to mere irrationality, but of perhaps much greater importance are other sources of tax-exempt or of lightly taxed income.

---

[7] See. pp. 118-21.

A person who chooses to hold oil property may do as well as or better than he could by holding tax-exempt securities. Likewise another source of taxfree gains is unrealized capital gains. If all possible gains were fully taxable except the interest on state and local government securities, the theoretical expectation would in all likelihood be much more closely realized.

Because many local governments are unknown to individual investors, financial organizations not only provide the marketing facilities for new issues but hold them as well. Were there no tax-exemption under the individual income tax, wealthy people would not have an incentive to search out the debts of small local governments and these securities would be even more heavily concentrated in financial corporations than they are now.

The tax-exemption under the corporate income tax makes for a rather special distribution of state and local securities among financial organizations. For example, in 1953 savings banks held only about 1.4 per cent of all privately held state and local government securities, whereas commercial banks held 38.8 per cent.[8] From the nature of the facilities operated by savings banks and by commercial banks, this distribution makes very little sense. Savings banks normally hold long-term securities of various types; they do not ordinarily make loans to businesses or individuals. Apart from various legal regulations, they could not do so on a large scale; they do not have the staffs and facilities to carry on such functions. Hence one would expect them to hold large amounts of local securities. Commercial banks, on the other hand, are equipped to make loans, both of short- and long-term types, to individuals and corporations. The larger banks maintain specialized staffs to seek out prospective borrowers, appraise the credit standing of a potential borrower, and arrange for the details of the repayment process. The acquisition of municipal bonds requires only modest office facilities and staff. Yet, instead of state and local securities being concentrated more in savings banks than in commercial banks, the facts are just the reverse. The reason is of course the tax-exemption feature. Savings banks are practically tax-exempt under the federal corporate income tax whereas commercial banks are subject to the full rates.

SUBSIDY TO STATE AND LOCAL GOVERNMENTS. Because their securities are tax-exempt, state and local governments can borrow more cheaply than they could otherwise, which explains why local units oppose moves to end this subsidy. The subsidy is the difference

[8] See George E. Lent, *The Ownership of Tax-Exempt Securities,* Occasional Paper 47 (New York: National Bureau of Economic Research), p. 129.

between the interest actually paid by debtor governments and the amount that would be paid without the tax-exemption feature. Suppose, for example, a local unit finds that it must commit itself to a 3 per cent rate of interest to borrow $50 million, but would have to commit itself to a 4 per cent rate if there were no exemption of the interest from tax. Then the subsidy is $500,000 per year ($2,000,000 — $1,500,000) in absolute amount.

The actual size of the subsidy resulting from tax-exemption can only be approximately estimated. We do not know with precision how much borrowing costs to state and local governments are lowered by the tax-exemption feature. Nor do we know the relevant rate of tax that would be effective if the interest on these securities were fully taxable.

The amount of the subsidy could in principle be discovered if various batches of securities were offered for sale differing only in that some batches were taxable and some not. To make the experiment strictly scientific, all features of the securities would need to be identical except the one whose effects are to be observed—tax-exemption. Actually no such precise, neat experiment has been carried out. Unlike federal securities, local government securities are rated by the rating services with of course varying results. The higher its credit-rating, the lower is the rate of interest on new borrowing by a locality. Memories of hard days of the Great Depression still color attitudes toward some local debt obligations, and some experts allow that experience to influence their judgment of the current quality of some government obligations.[9]

In our attempt to discover the subsidy provided by tax-exemption, the varying quality of local securities can be largely eliminated by using data on Public Housing Authority Bonds. These bonds are fully guaranteed by the U. S. Treasury and are just as safe as federal bonds. They are, furthermore, tax-exempt. The interest rates of the housing bonds may be compared with those on comparable Treasury bonds, the interest on which is fully taxable. In this way, the subsidy provided by tax-exemption may be estimated.

In Table 24–4, the average yields on Treasury and on Housing bonds are set forth. In column (3), the excess of the yield of the taxable Treasury bonds over the nontaxable housing bonds has been

---

[9] Walter H. Tyler, head of the Municipal Bond Department of Standard and Poor's Corporation, writes: "Is anyone so naive as to rule out completely a drop in income such as occurred in 1929-1933?" ("Debt Management and Municipal Credit," *Municipal Finance*, XXIX [Feb., 1957], p. 126.) Economists now typically do rule out such a catastrophe, not because drastic deflations are believed impossible, but because knowledge of how to avoid such debacles is reasonably well established, and a political party that failed to use this knowldge would commit political suicide.

computed. The excess has ranged from a high of .58 to a low of .39 until February 1958. The abrupt decline to .23 in May 1958 and the low excess since that time may have a special significance.

TABLE 24–4

AVERAGE YIELDS ON LONG-TERM TREASURY BONDS
AND THE NET AVERAGE YIELD ON NEW HOUSING AUTHORITY BONDS,
1953-1958[1]

Date of Issue of New Housing Authority Bonds	Average Yield of Long-term Treasury Bonds (1)	Net Average Yield on New Housing Authority Bonds[2] (2)	Difference between (1) and (2) (3)
May 1953	3.26	2.82	0.44
Sept. 1953	3.19	2.83	0.36
Dec. 1953	2.96	2.47	0.49
March 1954	2.73	2.34	0.39
June 1954	2.70	2.27	0.43
Sept. 1954	2.64	2.33	0.31
Jan. 1955	2.77	2.34	0.43
April 1955	2.92	2.42	0.50
July 1955	2.96	2.55	0.41
Oct. 1955	2.96	2.40	0.56
Feb. 1956	2.93	2.35	0.58
June 1956	2.98	2.49	0.49
Feb. 1957	3.26	2.77	0.49
April 1957	3.35	2.88	0.47
Feb. 1958	3.28	2.89	0.39
May 1958	3.12	2.89	0.23

Sources: For (1), *Treasury Bulletin* (yields are for bonds due or callable 20 years or after); for (2), 1953-57, *Daily Bond Buyer*, Jan. 8, 1958, p. 93; for (2), 1958, data supplied by the Public Housing Authority.

[1] Data prepared by George F. Break for a study of federal loan insurance and guarantee programs.
[2] Net refers to yield computed on the basis of terms to first sellers.

According to these data, tax-exemption has been worth, for the period 1953-1958, roughly 0.40 percentage points to local governments. If correct, this means that local governments have been able to sell their bonds at a yield of 0.4 per cent less than they would have if their obligations had been fully taxable. Stated in another way, a city selling bonds at 3.5 per cent would, without tax-exemption, have been forced to commit itself to 3.9 per cent.

The size of the excess varies from time to time as the figures in column (3) of Table 24–4 show. Since 1957 the evidence suggests that the subsidy provided to local governments has been decreasing and the portion obtained by investors has been increasing. The subsidy is becoming more and more inefficient.[10]

REFORM MEASURES. The tax-exemption feature of state and local government securities is inconsistent with a systematic progressive income tax; and it is, as emphasized, an inefficient subsidy. What, then, might be done to improve matters?

A simple measure is outright abolition of any special treatment of such interest income under the tax laws. This remedy would meet substantial opposition from existing bondholders who could argue that their contract rights would be violated. State and local governments would also strongly oppose such a step.

The remedy could be made more palatable by compensating existing holders for losses on the capital value of their holdings, for example, by allowing full loss offsets of any realized capital loss from this source against ordinary income.

A less drastic remedy calls for the repeal of the tax-exemption privilege for all new issues of state and local governments. By such a measure, old holders instead of losing would gain, because as old issues were paid off and the quantity outstanding fell, the tax-exemption feature would make what was left more attractive to highly taxed groups and push up prices. Only after an extended period had passed would the eroding effect of tax-exemption on systematic progression become negligible. The subsidy on new local borrowing would immediately disappear. Strong objections from state and local governments could be expected to this plan.

There is no compelling objection in principle to federal government subsidies to state and local governments. Many programs already involve such measures.[11] Hence a remedy which leaves the state and local governments with a subsidy but which eliminates the tax-exemption feature for private investors should meet the objections to present practices in this field.

Given these conditions to be satisfied, a simple, direct solution calls for federal purchase of tax-exempt state and local securities at interest rates below the market rates. A federal agency could be established, or the functions of a present one expanded, for the purpose of acquiring new and old state and local government securities.

---

[10] See the article by Roland I. Robinson, "Factors Accounting for the Sharply Increased Cost of State and Local Government Borrowing," *Journal of Finance,* XII (May, 1957), 126-35.

[11] See chap. 18, pp. 418-25.

This agency would be instructed to outbid any private group which might wish to buy new obligations. Old issues could be purchased from time to time as market conditions dictated.

To finance the acquisition of state and local securities, the federal government, through the Treasury, could sell federal obligations. These of course would be fully taxable. Thus federal obligations would replace state and local in the market. The potential opposition of state and local governments could be largely placated because they would get better terms on their new borrowings than under present conditions. Opposition to the plan could be expected from financial houses and the rating services; a potential source of gain from marketing new issues would be lost.

The federal government would not lose and could gain appreciably from this arrangement. The subsidy in the form of lower-than-market rates of interest on state and local securities would become a budget item. The present subsidy provided to new investors would, however, disappear, resulting in higher federal tax yields. The general taxpayer would gain because tax rates could be somewhat reduced to obtain the same yield.

Some Conclusions

Government borrowing by a central government from its own citizens as a long-run policy turns out, if the previous analysis is correct, to be inferior to the use of taxation. The reasons for this position are essentially simple. Borrowing is a disguised type of taxation and not a type of tax whose distributional effects or other features are notably superior to many actual taxes in use. In addition, the net debt carries an interest charge, and hence future taxation must be larger. These results hold to the extent that a government borrows from its own citizens; they are modified if the lenders are outsiders.

On the other hand, when a small local government borrows, it sells securities to others. By borrowing, it obtains command over resources now in return for an increase in its liabilities now. The justification for borrowing by such units, with modifications for the special nature of the government activities involved, comes in part from avoiding the disadvantage of having to make abrupt changes in tax rates. There may also be advantages strictly analogous to those relevant for private borrowing. By becoming indebted, a person comes into possession of assets, such as a house, a car, or furniture which he otherwise could not afford. If the gains obtained exceed the interest expense, he is better off by borrowing than by adopting the austere policy of buying something only when he can pay cash. A local government may gain for essentially similar reasons. Residents of that community may obtain the school, the larger sewage system, or whatever it may be, through borrowing, whereas if taxes of sufficient yield were levied instead, the individual resident might feel obliged to borrow because he would prefer to spend the usual amount for commodities he likes instead of greatly increasing his saving within a short period of time. As a member of the community he shares in the gains from the new asset, the school or sewage plant, which he pays for either directly by taxes or indirectly by first incurring a liability and then gradually amortizing it over an extended period of time.

For similar reasons, some countries, especially small and poor countries, may frequently find that the best policy will require some borrowing abroad. If the people of Afghanistan wish to irrigate their arid country to obtain more food and other crops, heavy taxation in order to finance a large project may not be feasible. Such taxes would decrease the amount of local money people have to spend, and, with given prices, would also reduce imports. As people were forced to curtail their expenditures, they would curtail those made on goods imported from abroad. But even so, the government may not as a result obtain sufficient command over foreign money to pay for the supplies needed for the irrigation project. Actually, taxation on a scale sufficient to finance a large project in such a poor country is not practical; tax devices to obtain large yields cannot be enforced. Borrowing becomes in practice the only relevant way of obtaining the wherewithal to make the project feasible. The question of the selection of the projects and the scale on which they are to be constructed involves issues of essentially the same type as already discussed in Chapter 16. If the gains to be achieved promise to yield a return after deducting the interest costs involved, such projects are profitable for the country and may permit its citizens to break out of the self-perpetuating hold of poverty.

Where, as in the United States, the interest income of the securities of some government units are exempt from important taxation, the gain provided the governments in question is less than the revenue cost to the central government. Such a method of helping local governments has little rationale, and its persistence comes from the combined shortsightedness of state and local governments in opposing full tax treatment of such income plus the political support at the federal level for placing various loopholes in the income tax laws, partly to protect those who would otherwise be more heavily taxed, and partly as a subtle technique to undermine income taxation by providing a pointed and vivid illustration of how people with large incomes can and do pay less in tax than cleaning women and unskilled workmen.

Part IV

SUGGESTED READINGS

Monetary Theory:

AMERICAN ECONOMIC ASSOCIATION. *Readings in Business Cycle Theory,* ed. Howard S. Ellis. Philadelphia: The Blakiston Co., 1944.
See especially the contributions of Frederick A. Lutz, Abba P. Lerner, Gottfried Haberler, Fritz Machlup, and D. H. Robertson. One of the best sources for an understanding of the subtleties involved in the investment-saving equality.

FELLNER, WILLIAM. *Monetary Policies and Full Employment.* Berkeley: Univ. of California Press, 1946.
A difficult but rewarding analysis of fundamental monetary and fiscal topics.

FISHER, IRVING. *The Purchasing Power of Money,* 2d. ed. New York: The Macmillan Co., 1920.
The famous study of the quantity theory of money based on the monetary system of the United States prior to the Federal Reserve System.

HANSEN, ALVIN H. *Monetary Theory and Fiscal Policy.* New York: McGraw-Hill Book Co., 1949.
The development and application of his interpretation of the Keynesian system to money and fiscal affairs.

HART, ALBERT G. *Money, Debt, and Economic Activity.* New York: Prentice-Hall, Inc., 1953.
A sophisticated textbook on money and an especially clear exposition of various monetary theories.

KEYNES, J. M. *The General Theory of Employment, Interest, and Money.* New York: Harcourt, Brace & Co., 1936.
The famous work setting out what is now generally known as the Keynesian system.

PATINKIN, DON. *Money, Interest, and Prices.* White Plains, N. Y.: Row, Peterson & Co., 1956.
A systematic treatise adopting a modified Keynesian approach to monetary affairs.

ROBERTSON, D. H. *Banking Policy and the Price Level.* London: P. S. King & Co., 1932.
A technical study of monetary theory using the "saving-investment" approach. Provides the first explicit statement of the gap in time between receipts and expenditures—the "day."

ROLPH, EARL R. *The Theory of Fiscal Economics.* Berkeley: Univ. of California Press, 1954. Chap. v.
Sets forth the asset approach to the explanation of consumption and investment expenditures and criticizes "flow" theories such as the Keynesian version.

SHAW, EDWARD S. *Money, Income, and Monetary Policy.* Chicago: Richard D. Irwin, Inc., 1950.
Especially useful for more advanced students.

Price Theory:

BAIN, JOE S. *Pricing, Distribution, and Employment.* New York: Holt, Rinehart & Winston, 1953. Chaps. v-x.
A textbook on economic theory for advanced students. Contains a sophisticated explanation of business pricing policies.

STIGLER, GEORGE. *Theory of Price.* New York: The Macmillan Co., 1952. Chaps. xii, xiii, xiv.
A tightly-written textbook on economic theory. Chapters mentioned give the author's views on noncompetitive pricing arrangements.

Compensatory Fiscal Finance:

COHEN, LEO. "An Empirical Measurement of the Built-in Flexibility of the Individual Income Tax," *American Economic Review* (May, 1959), 532-41.
Extends and significantly modifies Pechman's study listed below.

FRIEDMAN, MILTON. "A Monetary and Fiscal Framework for Economic Stability," in *Readings in Monetary Theory*, pp. 369-94. Philadelphia: The Blakiston Co., 1951.
A reform proposal emphasizing automatic controls to govern expenditures upon current output.

HALL, CHALLIS A. *Fiscal Policy for Stable Growth.* New York: Holt, Rinehart & Winston, 1960. Pp. 190-281.
Examines fiscal policy, employing a multiple-model approach.

HANSEN, BENT. *The Economic Theory of Fiscal Policy,* trans. P. E. Burke. London: Allen & Unwin, 1958.
A highly technical theoretical exposition, directly concerned with the compatibility of full employment and price stability.

PECHMAN, JOSEPH A. "Yield of the Individual Income Tax During a Recession," *National Tax Journal,* VII (March, 1954), pp. 1-16.
An important statistical study of the built-in flexibility of the Federal Individual Income Tax.

SLITOR, R. E. "The Measurement of Progressivity and Built-in Flexibility," *Quarterly Journal of Economics,* LXII (Feb., 1948), 309-14.
Provides definitions of tax progression and built-in flexibility and shows interrelations between the measures of each.

U.S. CONGRESS, COMMITTEE ON WAYS AND MEANS. *Tax Revision Compendium.* Vol. III, pp. 2331-2363. Washington, D.C.: Government Printing Office, 1959.
(Papers submitted on Flexibility of the Revenue Yield.)

Debt Management:

BUCHANAN, JAMES M. *Public Principles of Public Debt.* Homewood, Ill.: Richard D. Irwin, Inc., 1958.
A highly provocative statement of the role of government debt in a society.

CONARD, JOSEPH W. *Introduction to the Theory of Interest.* Berkeley: Univ. of California Press, 1959. Pp. 287-369.
A careful exposition of the expectation view of the differences in interest rates.

CULBERTSON, JOHN M. "The Term Structure of Interest Rates," *Quarterly Journal of Economics,* LXXI (Nov., 1957), 485-517.
A clearly written, well reasoned explanation and defense of the liquidity approach to the explanation of differences in yields.

LUTZ, F. A. "The Structure of Interest Rates," in *Readings in the Theory of Income Distribution.* American Economic Association. Philadelphia: The Blakiston Co., 1946.
One of the best expositions of the expectation approach to explain differences in yields of securities classified by maturity.

MURPHY, HENRY C. *The National Debt in War and Transition.* New York: McGraw-Hill Book Co., 1950.
An interesting account of World War II finance by an insider.

MUSGRAVE, R. A. *The Theory of Public Finance.* New York: McGraw-Hill Book Co., 1959.
A highly technical discussion for advanced students.

ROBINSON, M. A. *The National Debt Ceiling. An Experiment in Fiscal Policy.* Washington, D.C.: The Brookings Institution, 1959.
A criticism of a legal debt ceiling.

ROLPH, EARL R. "Principles of Debt Management," *American Economic Review,* XLVII (June, 1957), 302-20.
Proposes a rule for efficient management. Contains a technical mistake, noted by R. M. Friedman, in the same journal, June, 1959.

SIMONS, HENRY. "On Debt Policy," *Journal of Political Economy,* LII (Dec., 1944), 356-61.
A brief and pointed argument for the exclusive use of perpetuities. A "must" for the serious student.
SMITH, WARREN. "On the Effectiveness of Monetary Policy," *American Economic Review,* XLVI (Sept., 1956), 588-606.
A skeptical emphasis on the question of the effectiveness of monetary policy.
————. *Debt Management in the United States.* Study Paper No. 19, Study of Employment, Growth, and Price Levels. Joint Economic Committee, 86th Congress, 2d. sess. Washington, D.C.: Government Printing Office, 1960.
Brings together empirical information concerning debt management, reviews the theoretical literature as well; carefully documented.

Name Index

Subject Index